REBELS™

S.C.
N.C.
V.
M.
P.
N.J.
N.Y.
N.E.

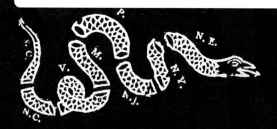

REBELS

A WELL-REGULATED MILITIA

STORY
BRIAN WOOD

ART
ANDREA MUTTI (CHAPTERS 1, 4 & 5)
MATTHEW WOODSON (CHAPTER 2)
ARIELA KRISTANTINA (CHAPTER 3)
TRISTAN JONES (CHAPTER 6)

COLORS
JORDIE BELLAIRE

LETTERING
JARED K. FLETCHER

COVER ART
TULA LOTAY

DARK HORSE BOOKS

PRESIDENT & PUBLISHER
MIKE RICHARDSON

EDITORS
SIERRA HAHN & SPENCER CUSHING

COLLECTION DESIGNER
BRENNAN THOME

DIGITAL ART TECHNICIAN
ALLYSON HALLER

PUBLISHED BY DARK HORSE BOOKS
A DIVISION OF DARK HORSE COMICS, INC.
10956 SE MAIN STREET
MILWAUKIE, OR 97222

DARKHORSE.COM

FIRST EDITION: MAY 2016
ISBN 978-1-61655-908-3

1 3 5 7 9 10 8 6 4 2

PRINTED IN CHINA

TO FIND A COMICS SHOP IN YOUR AREA, CALL THE COMIC SHOP
LOCATOR SERVICE TOLL-FREE AT (888) 266-4226.

INTERNATIONAL LICENSING: (503) 905-2377

NAMES: WOOD, BRIAN, 1972- AUTHOR, CREATOR. | MUTTI, ANDREA, 1973-
ILLUSTRATOR. | WOODSON, MATTHEW, ILLUSTRATOR. | KRISTANTINA, ARIELA,
ILLUSTRATOR. | JONES, TRISTAN, 1984- ILLUSTRATOR. | BELLAIRE, JORDIE,
ILLUSTRATOR. | FLETCHER, JARED K., ILLUSTRATOR. | LOTAY, TULA, ILLUSTRATOR.
TITLE: REBELS. VOLUME 1, A WELL-REGULATED MILITIA / STORY, BRIAN WOOD ; ART,
ANDREA MUTTI (CHAPTERS 1-6 & 9), MATTHEW WOODSON (CHAPTER 7), ARIELA
KRISTANTINA (CHAPTER 8), TRISTAN JONES (CHAPTER 10) ; COLORS, JORDIE
BELLAIRE ; LETTERING, JARED K. FLETCHER ; COVER ART, TULA LOTAY.
OTHER TITLES: WELL-REGULATED MILITIA
DESCRIPTION: FIRST EDITION. | MILWAUKIE, OR : DARK HORSE BOOKS, 2016. | "THIS
VOLUME COLLECTS THE COMIC BOOK SERIES REBELS #1-#10 FROM DARK HORSE
COMICS."
IDENTIFIERS: LCCN 2016001258 (PRINT) | LCCN 2016003018 (EBOOK) | ISBN
9781616559083 (PAPERBACK) | ISBN 9781630083489 ()
SUBJECTS: LCSH: UNITED STATES--HISTORY--REVOLUTION, 1775-1783--COMIC BOOKS,
STRIPS, ETC. | GRAPHIC NOVELS. | GSAFD: COMIC BOOKS, STRIPS, ETC.
CLASSIFICATION: LCC PN6727.W59 R43 2016 (PRINT) | LCC PN6727.W59 (EBOOK) |
DDC 741.5/973--DC23
LC RECORD AVAILABLE AT HTTP://LCCN.LOC.GOV/2016001258

NEIL HANKERSON EXECUTIVE VICE PRESIDENT TOM WEDDLE CHIEF
FINANCIAL OFFICER RANDY STRADLEY VICE PRESIDENT OF PUBLISHING
MICHAEL MARTENS VICE PRESIDENT OF BOOK TRADE SALES MATT
PARKINSON VICE PRESIDENT OF MARKETING DAVID SCROGGY VICE
PRESIDENT OF PRODUCT DEVELOPMENT DALE LAFOUNTAIN VICE
PRESIDENT OF INFORMATION TECHNOLOGY CARA NIECE VICE PRESIDENT
OF PRODUCTION AND SCHEDULING KEN LIZZI GENERAL COUNSEL DAVEY
ESTRADA EDITORIAL DIRECTOR DAVE MARSHALL EDITOR IN CHIEF SCOTT
ALLIE EXECUTIVE SENIOR EDITOR CHRIS WARNER SENIOR BOOKS EDITOR
CARY GRAZZINI DIRECTOR OF PRINT AND DEVELOPMENT LIA RIBACCHI
ART DIRECTOR MARK BERNARDI DIRECTOR OF DIGITAL PUBLISHING

---

*THIS VOLUME COLLECTS THE COMIC BOOK SERIES REBELS #1–#10 FROM
DARK HORSE COMICS.*

I was born and grew up in Essex Junction, Vermont, about a mile as the crow flies from Fort Ethan Allen. I would walk to my school, Hiawatha Elementary, by way of streets named Cascadnac, Wenonah, Owaissa, and Abenaki. We were taught local history with a focus and depth that I have to assume doesn't happen anymore. Living an hour from Canada, we were also taught colonial-era Canadian history. We took field trips to Fort Ticonderoga and Mount Independence. We learned American folk songs in music class. My friends and I would scour the woods hoping to find arrowheads and musket balls. It was a picture-book setting completely steeped in local history, the sort of thing you don't appreciate until much later in life, usually after you've moved away.

The idea to write something on this subject came to me a few years ago in a conversation with a friend. We were talking about the need for a retelling of the Founding Fathers story—not as elder statesmen, but as young firebrands, flaws and all. I liked that idea, but my interest went not to Washington and Adams and Ben Franklin, but to Ethan Allen, Seth Warner, and the Green Mountain Boys, the heroes of Vermont. Once I happened upon the phrase "America's first militia," I had my book idea.

I've written historical fiction in comics before, stories of wilderness, hardships, violence, and tragedy, and the trick has always been to find a way to connect it to modern life, to the lives of the readers. With my Viking book *Northlanders*, this was a little difficult, but with Revolutionary America? The parallels are right there on the surface. You haven't lived through an election season without seeing and hearing this history evoked on a daily basis. A quick browse through the new-releases section of a bookstore proves this material is timely and resonant. The *Assassin's Creed* video game series allows you to participate in the famous battles of that war. And the smash Broadway musical *Hamilton* proves it has mass appeal.

My angle on this is to largely avoid the most familiar people and events of the time period and think about a kid in northern Vermont playing in the woods. The first few pages of *Rebels* puts us in young Seth Abbott's shoes as he plays with his sister, reads with his mother, swims in the gorge, chops wood, does his chores, and looks up to his woodsman father with a mixture of fear and awe. This is essentially my story, and overall this series is shot through with details of rural New England living, but in the 1770s, not my own 1970s.

Beyond that, *Rebels* tells the story of the war, from that first spark of rebellion up to and including Bunker Hill and Dorchester Heights. We skip around and tell one-off tales that round out the era, including stories about Native Americans, urban living at that time, and the war through the eyes of a redcoat, and a rather heartbreaking retelling of the Molly Pitcher folktale.

As someone who has, in the pages of past comics series, taken a rather scorched-earth approach to American politics and social criticism, I've had a great experience showing this other side of America: the emergence of a new nation from chaos, and all the hope and urgency and excitement that came with it. I'm not afraid to call myself a patriot, and I became one sitting in the library at Hiawatha Elementary reading about the Green Mountain Boys.

—Brian Wood

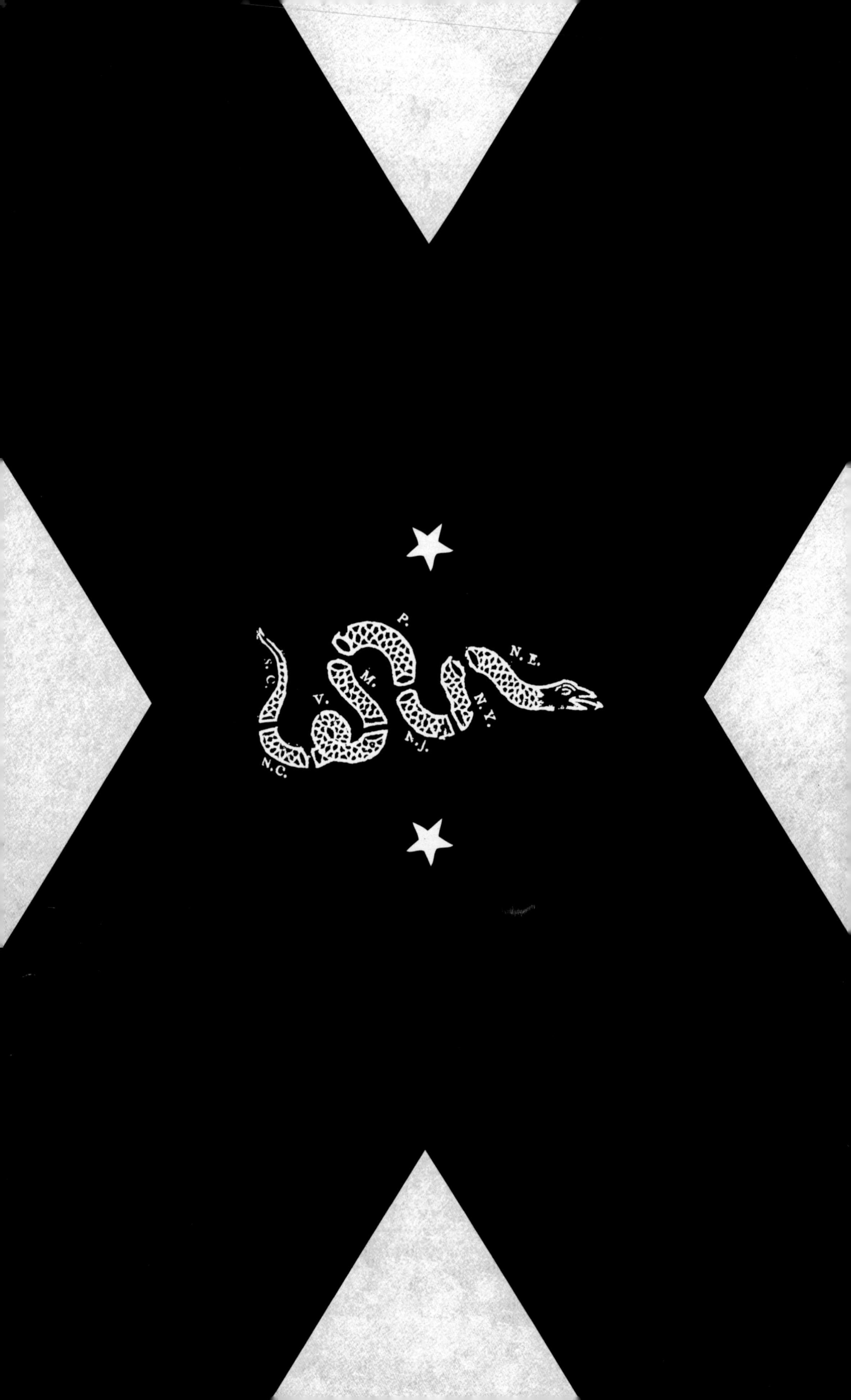
S.C.
N.C.
V.
M.
P.
N.J.
N.Y.
N.E.

TABLE OF CONTENTS

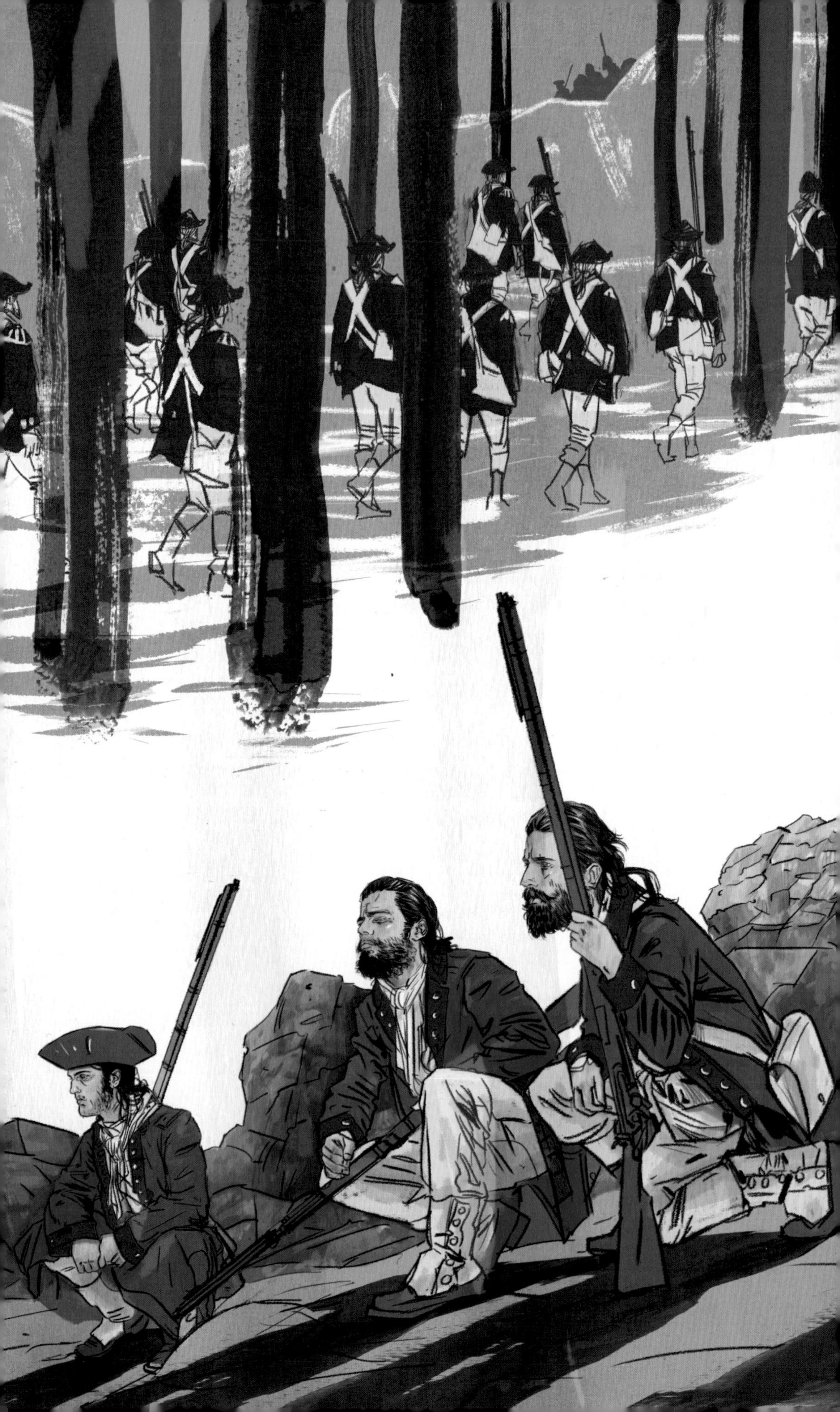

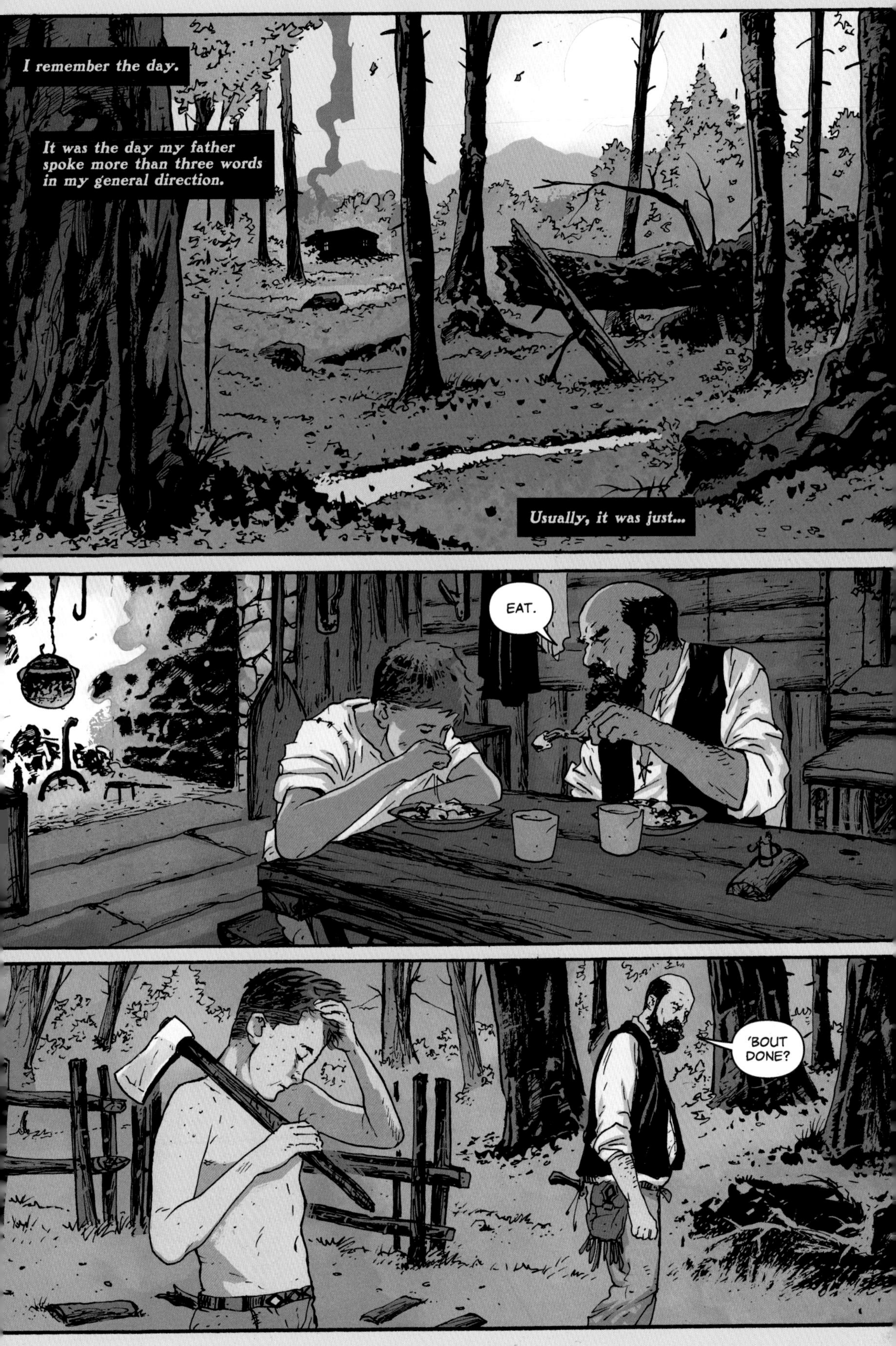
I remember the day.
It was the day my father spoke more than three words in my general direction.
Usually, it was just...
EAT.
'BOUT DONE?

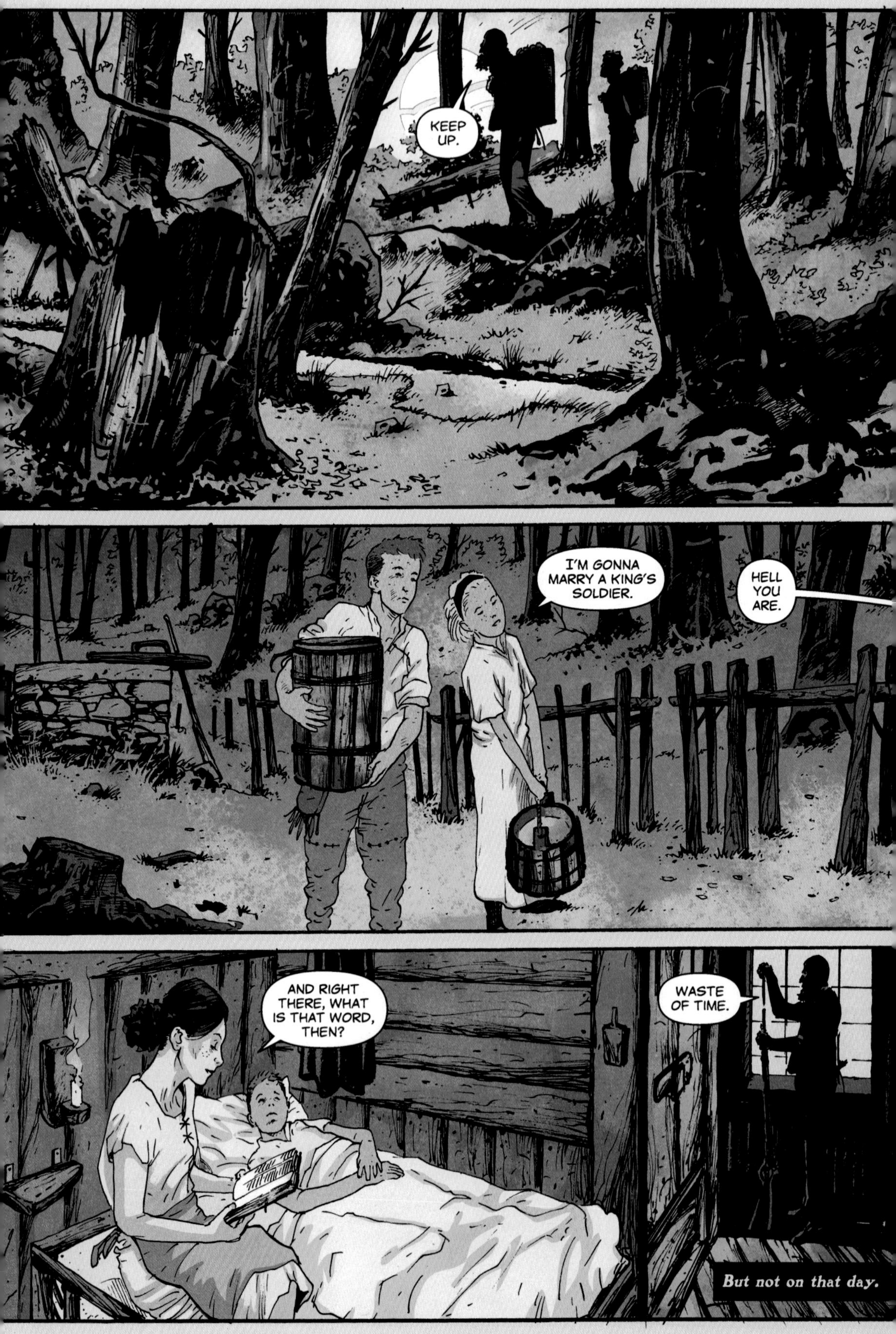
KEEP UP.
I'M GONNA MARRY A KING'S SOLDIER.
HELL YOU ARE.
AND RIGHT THERE, WHAT IS THAT WORD, THEN?
WASTE OF TIME.
But not on that day.

THE TRICK, SON, IS TO CONSIDER THE ORIENTATION OF THE FOREST.

WHAT *IS* THE ORIENTATION OF THE FOREST, SETH?

VERTICAL.

EXACTLY. THE FOREST IS VERTICAL, BUT A *GOOD* WOODSMAN AND HUNTER TRAINS THE EYE TO SEEK OUT ONLY THE HORIZONTAL SHAPES WITHIN. TELL ME, WHAT DO YOU SEE?

I JUST SEE TREES.

TRY AGAIN. ADJUST THE EYES, SO THEY ONLY RECOGNIZE WHAT IS *NOT* A TREE.

...

I SEE A MMMMMAN.

MEN. I SEE *MEN*.

WHAT SORT OF MEN?

BRITISH SOLDIERS. REDCOATS.

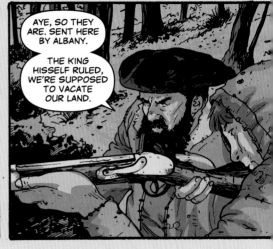

AYE, SO THEY ARE. SENT HERE BY ALBANY.

THE KING HISSELF RULED, WE'RE SUPPOSED TO VACATE OUR LAND.

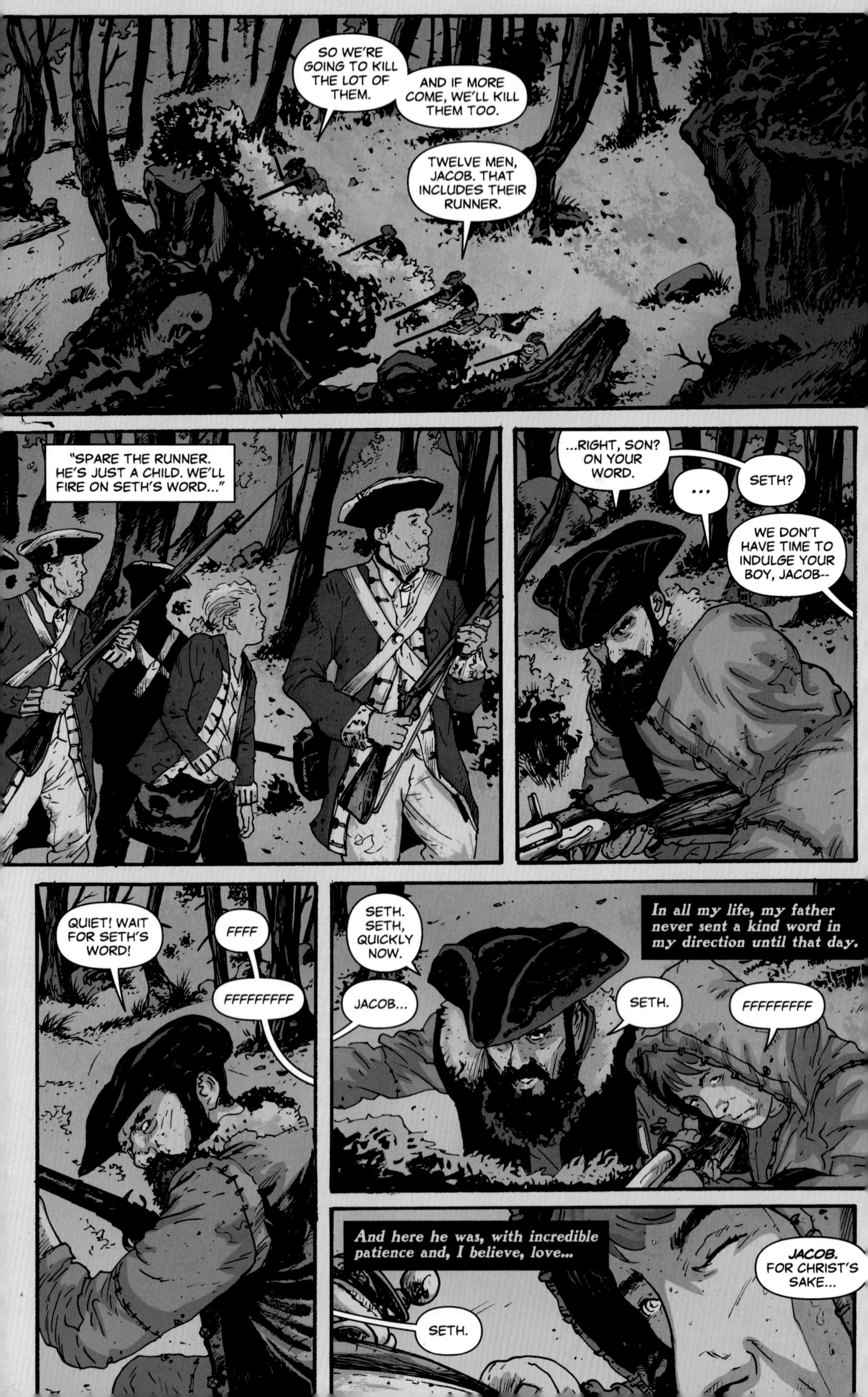
SO WE'RE GOING TO KILL THE LOT OF THEM.
AND IF MORE COME, WE'LL KILL THEM TOO.
TWELVE MEN, JACOB. THAT INCLUDES THEIR RUNNER.
"SPARE THE RUNNER. HE'S JUST A CHILD. WE'LL FIRE ON SETH'S WORD..."
...RIGHT, SON? ON YOUR WORD.
SETH?
...
WE DON'T HAVE TIME TO INDULGE YOUR BOY, JACOB--
QUIET! WAIT FOR SETH'S WORD!
FFFF
FFFFFFFFF
SETH. SETH, QUICKLY NOW.
In all my life, my father never sent a kind word in my direction until that day.
JACOB...
SETH.
FFFFFFFFF
And here he was, with incredible patience and, I believe, love...
JACOB. FOR CHRIST'S SAKE...
SETH.

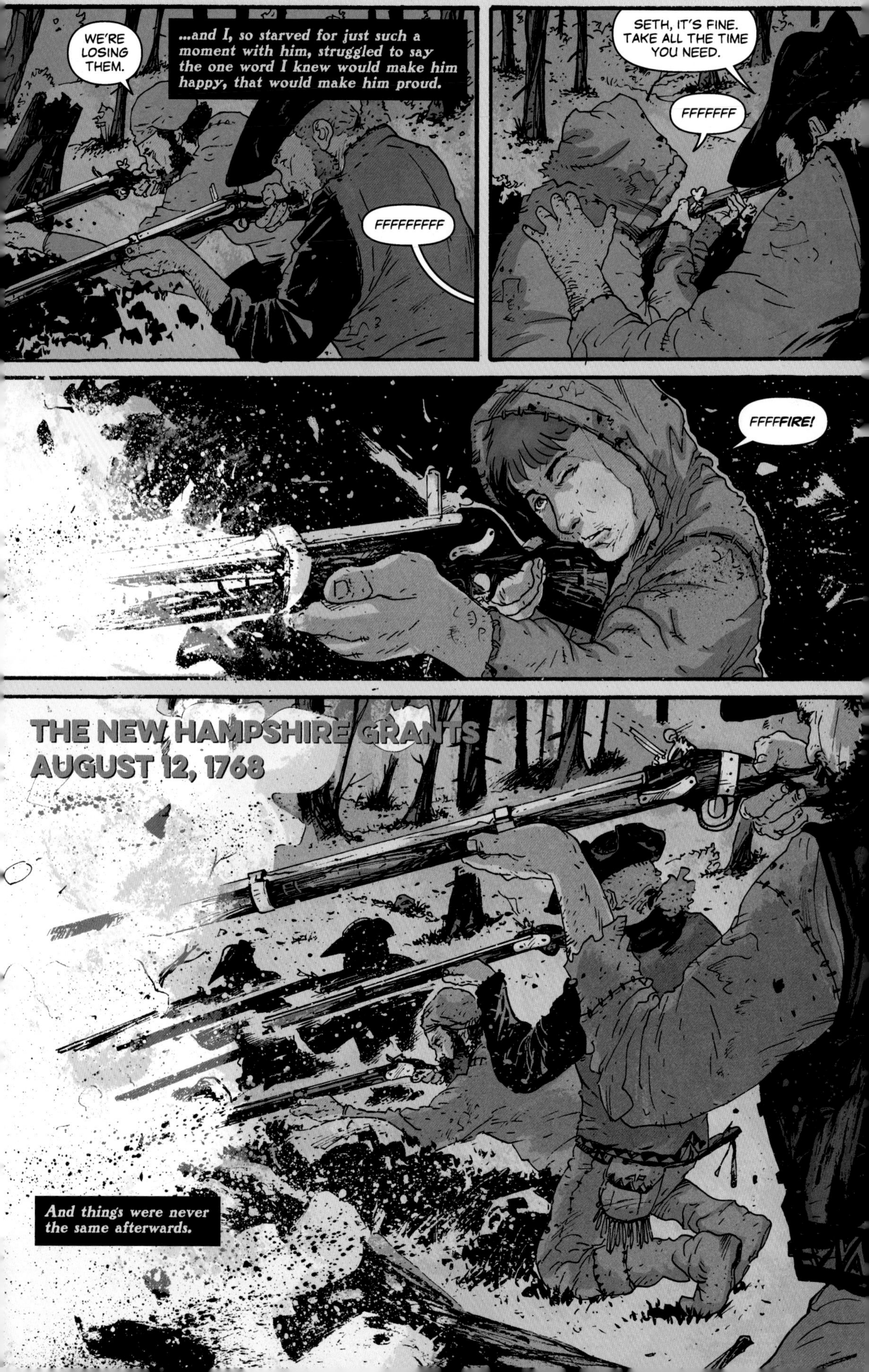

WE'RE LOSING THEM.
...and I, so starved for just such a moment with him, struggled to say the one word I knew would make him happy, that would make him proud.
FFFFFFFFF
SETH, IT'S FINE. TAKE ALL THE TIME YOU NEED.
FFFFFFF
FFFFFIRE!
THE NEW HAMPSHIRE GRANTS
AUGUST 12, 1768
And things were never the same afterwards.

By the time I spoke the order to fire, the redcoats were mostly out of range. We wounded three, but they escaped into the woods.

My father never showed his anger to me, but he lost the respect of the others. Never really recovered from that. Died the following winter.

So I vowed from that point on to let my rifle, my hands, and my courage do the talking for me. Never much trusted my voice after that.

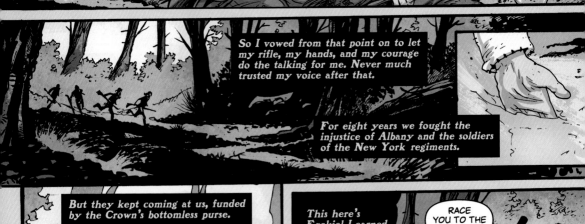

For eight years we fought the injustice of Albany and the soldiers of the New York regiments.

But they kept coming at us, funded by the Crown's bottomless purse.

SETH ABBOTT!

This here's Ezekiel Learned, my best friend.

RACE YOU TO THE STILE?

He'd been a runner with the regimentals, the very same boy we saw that day.

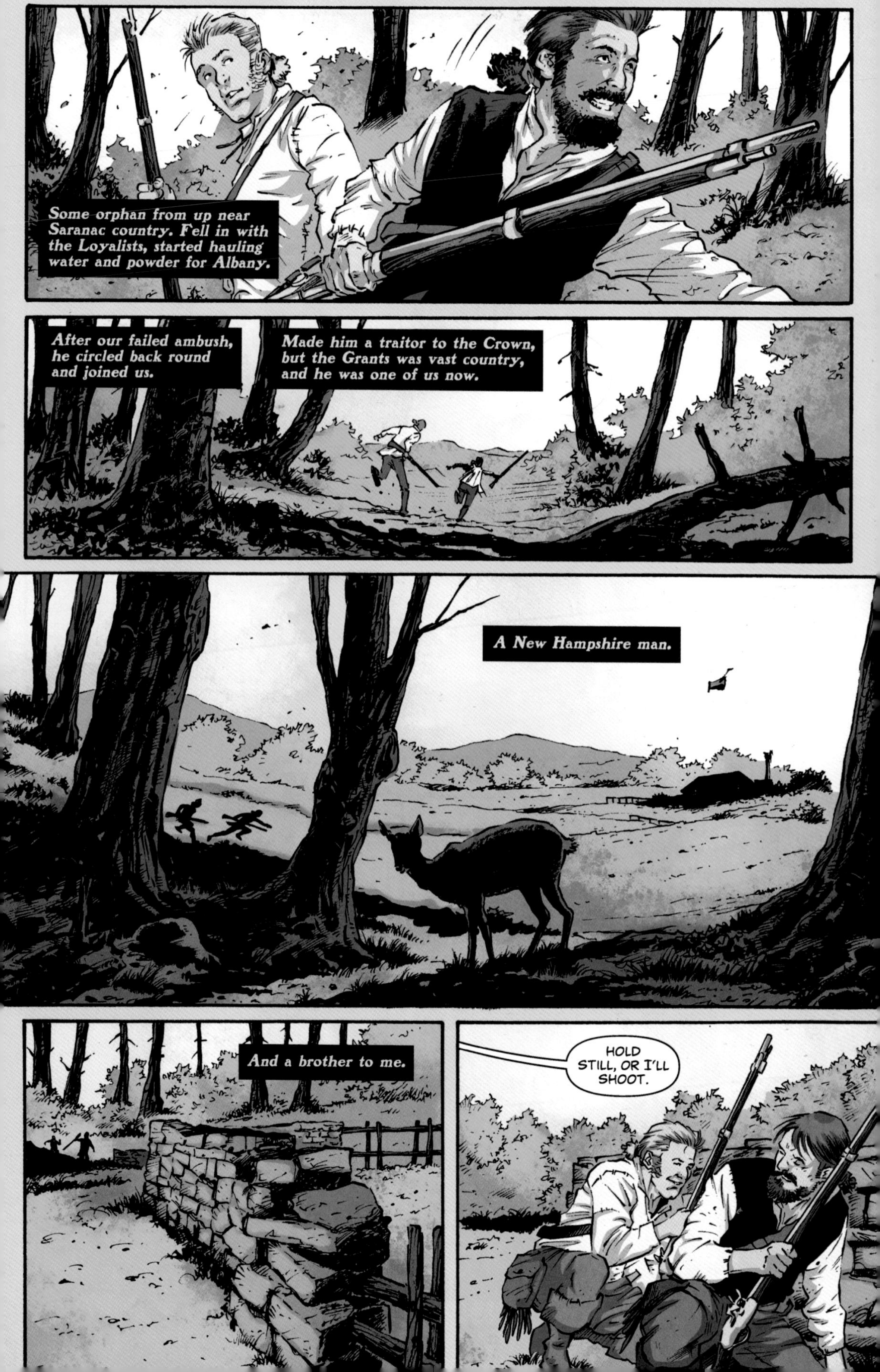

Some orphan from up near Saranac country. Fell in with the Loyalists, started hauling water and powder for Albany.
After our failed ambush, he circled back round and joined us.
Made him a traitor to the Crown, but the Grants was vast country, and he was one of us now.
A New Hampshire man.
And a brother to me.
HOLD STILL, OR I'LL SHOOT.

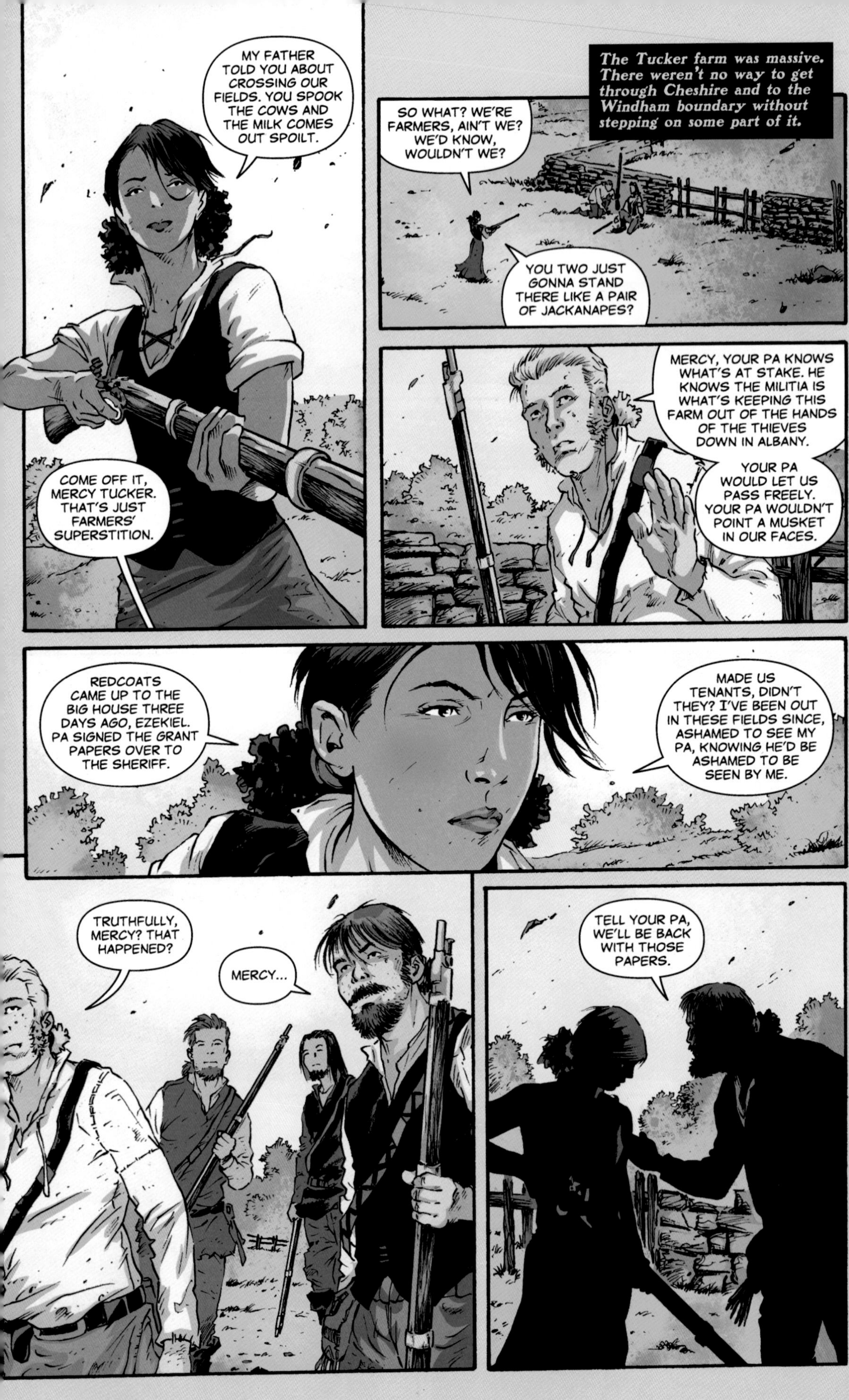
MY FATHER TOLD YOU ABOUT CROSSING OUR FIELDS. YOU SPOOK THE COWS AND THE MILK COMES OUT SPOILT.
COME OFF IT, MERCY TUCKER. THAT'S JUST FARMERS' SUPERSTITION.
The Tucker farm was massive. There weren't no way to get through Cheshire and to the Windham boundary without stepping on some part of it.
SO WHAT? WE'RE FARMERS, AIN'T WE? WE'D KNOW, WOULDN'T WE?
YOU TWO JUST GONNA STAND THERE LIKE A PAIR OF JACKANAPES?
MERCY, YOUR PA KNOWS WHAT'S AT STAKE. HE KNOWS THE MILITIA IS WHAT'S KEEPING THIS FARM OUT OF THE HANDS OF THE THIEVES DOWN IN ALBANY.
YOUR PA WOULD LET US PASS FREELY. YOUR PA WOULDN'T POINT A MUSKET IN OUR FACES.
REDCOATS CAME UP TO THE BIG HOUSE THREE DAYS AGO, EZEKIEL. PA SIGNED THE GRANT PAPERS OVER TO THE SHERIFF.
MADE US TENANTS, DIDN'T THEY? I'VE BEEN OUT IN THESE FIELDS SINCE, ASHAMED TO SEE MY PA, KNOWING HE'D BE ASHAMED TO BE SEEN BY ME.
TRUTHFULLY, MERCY? THAT HAPPENED?
MERCY...
TELL YOUR PA, WE'LL BE BACK WITH THOSE PAPERS.

WESTMINSTER
MARCH 13, 1775

By this time, the massacre in Boston was five years past, the "tea party" was two, and men, representatives from all the colonies, were gathered in Philadelphia.

The farmers of the New Hampshire Grants were fighting their own battle: land rents having come due well before harvest time, a deliberate move to force them into forfeiture.

Land that, just like Caleb Tucker's, was stolen by New York.

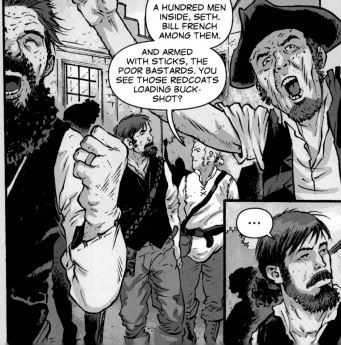

A HUNDRED MEN INSIDE, SETH. BILL FRENCH AMONG THEM.

AND ARMED WITH STICKS, THE POOR BASTARDS. YOU SEE THOSE REDCOATS LOADING BUCK-SHOT?

...

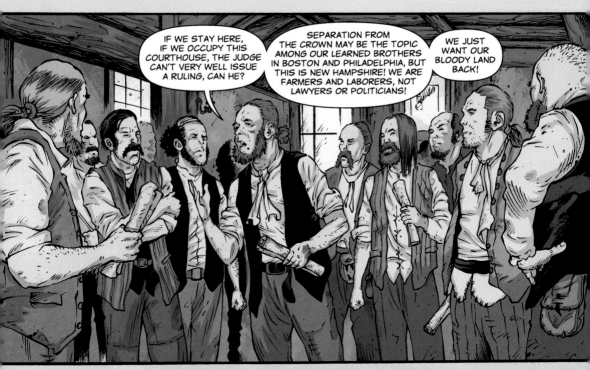

IF WE STAY HERE, IF WE OCCUPY THIS COURTHOUSE, THE JUDGE CAN'T VERY WELL ISSUE A RULING, CAN HE?

SEPARATION FROM THE CROWN MAY BE THE TOPIC AMONG OUR LEARNED BROTHERS IN BOSTON AND PHILADELPHIA, BUT THIS IS NEW HAMPSHIRE! WE ARE FARMERS AND LABORERS, NOT LAWYERS OR POLITICIANS!

WE JUST WANT OUR BLOODY LAND BACK!

AND A *RIDDANCE* OF THE INJUSTICE OF TAXING US FOR WHAT IS RIGHTFULLY AND MORALLY OUR PROPERTY!

AND WE'LL STAY HERE, IN THIS COURTHOUSE, FOR AS LONG AS IT TAKES FOR ALBANY TO SEE SOME SENSE ON THIS ISSUE!

WE ALL HAVE DOCUMENTATION!

TOO RIGHT, AND IT CUTS RIGHT TO THE POINT, DOESN'T IT?

WE ARE NOT REVOLUTIONARIES. WE SEEK ONLY WHAT WE HAVE ALREADY BEEN GRANTED...

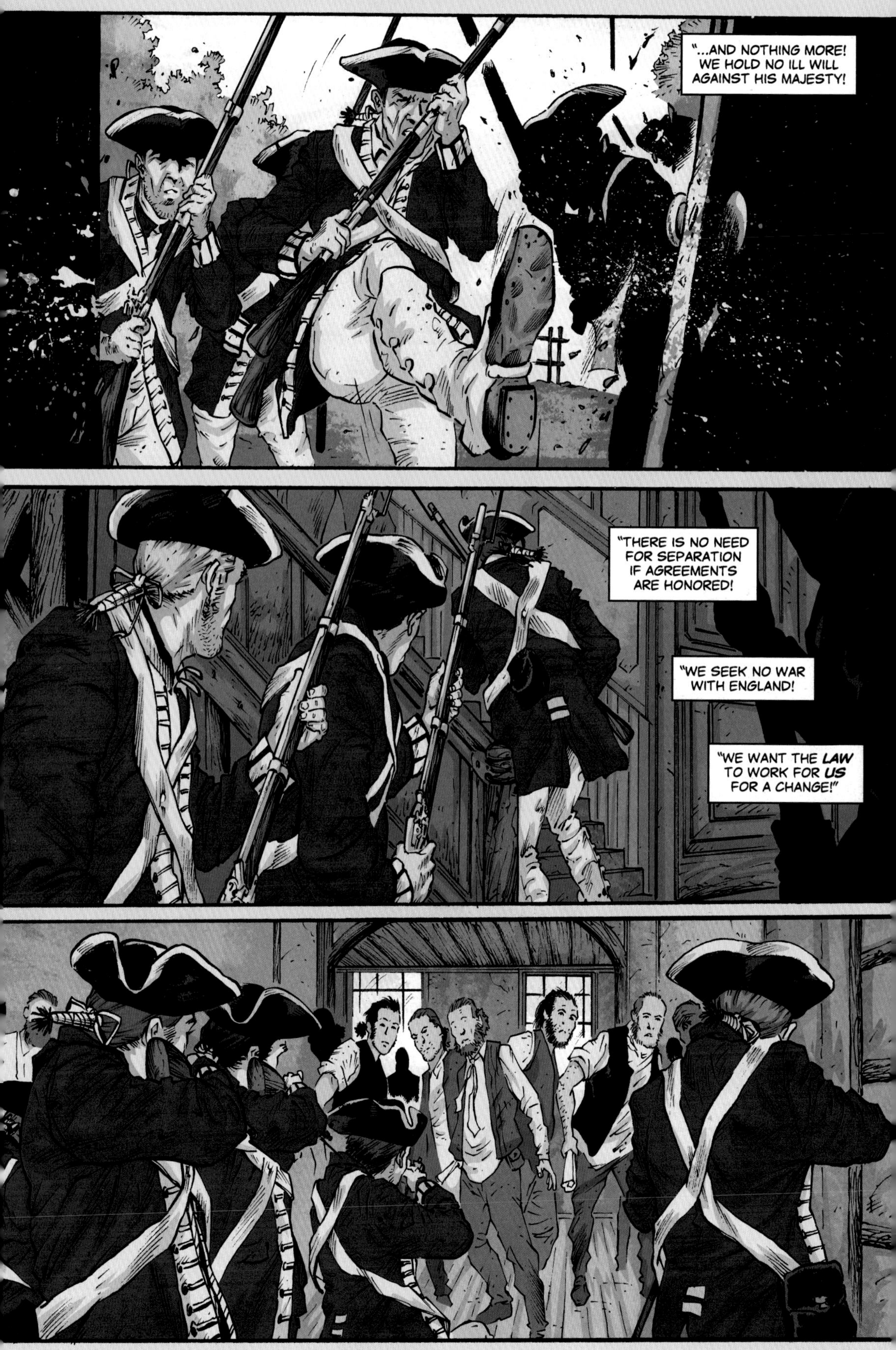
"...AND NOTHING MORE! WE HOLD NO ILL WILL AGAINST HIS MAJESTY!
"THERE IS NO NEED FOR SEPARATION IF AGREEMENTS ARE HONORED!
"WE SEEK NO WAR WITH ENGLAND!
"WE WANT THE ***LAW*** TO WORK FOR ***US*** FOR A CHANGE!"

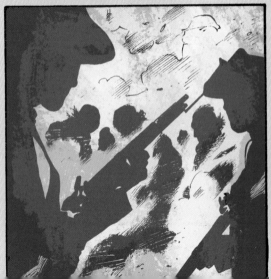

RUSH 'EM! QUICK, BEFORE THEY CAN RELOAD! OUT THE DOOR!

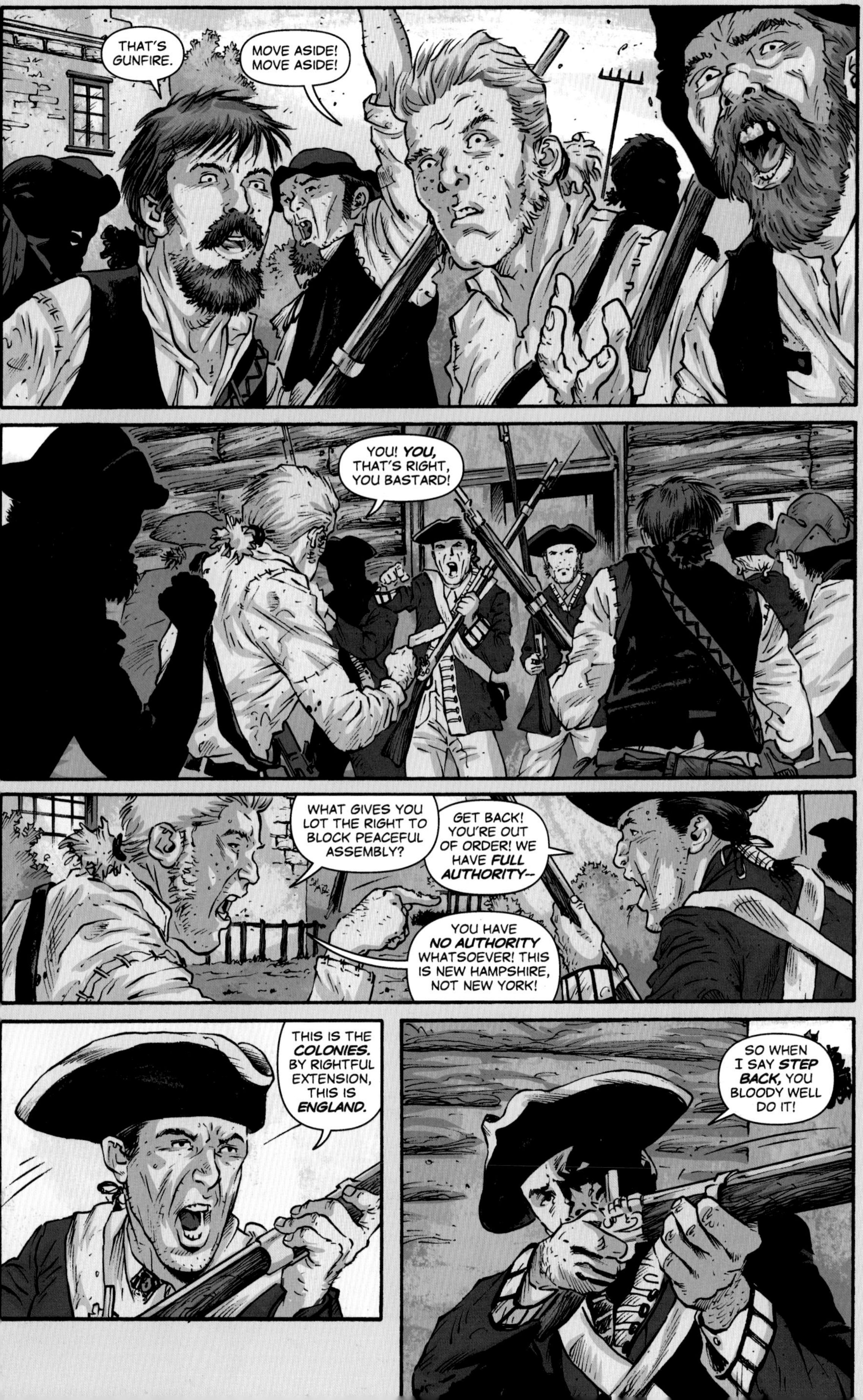
THAT'S GUNFIRE.
MOVE ASIDE! MOVE ASIDE!
YOU! ***YOU,*** THAT'S RIGHT, YOU BASTARD!
WHAT GIVES YOU LOT THE RIGHT TO BLOCK PEACEFUL ASSEMBLY?
GET BACK! YOU'RE OUT OF ORDER! WE HAVE ***FULL AUTHORITY--***
YOU HAVE ***NO AUTHORITY*** WHATSOEVER! THIS IS NEW HAMPSHIRE, NOT NEW YORK!
THIS IS THE ***COLONIES.*** BY RIGHTFUL EXTENSION, THIS IS ***ENGLAND.***
SO WHEN I SAY ***STEP BACK,*** YOU BLOODY WELL DO IT!

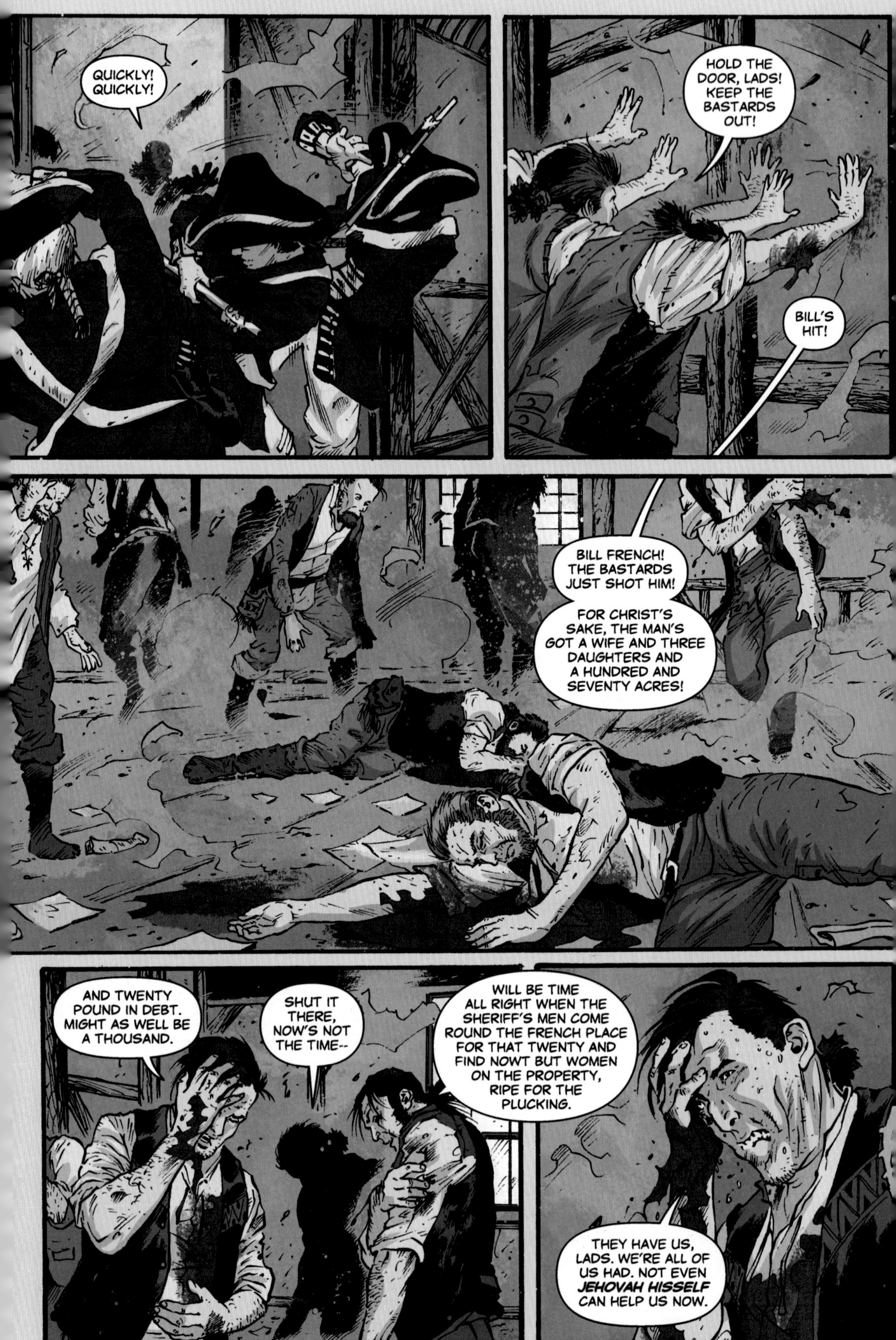
QUICKLY! QUICKLY!
HOLD THE DOOR, LADS! KEEP THE BASTARDS OUT!
BILL'S HIT!
BILL FRENCH! THE BASTARDS JUST SHOT HIM!
FOR CHRIST'S SAKE, THE MAN'S GOT A WIFE AND THREE DAUGHTERS AND A HUNDRED AND SEVENTY ACRES!
AND TWENTY POUND IN DEBT. MIGHT AS WELL BE A THOUSAND.
SHUT IT THERE, NOW'S NOT THE TIME--
WILL BE TIME ALL RIGHT WHEN THE SHERIFF'S MEN COME ROUND THE FRENCH PLACE FOR THAT TWENTY AND FIND NOWT BUT WOMEN ON THE PROPERTY, RIPE FOR THE PLUCKING.
THEY HAVE US, LADS. WE'RE ALL OF US HAD. NOT EVEN *JEHOVAH HISSELF* CAN HELP US NOW.

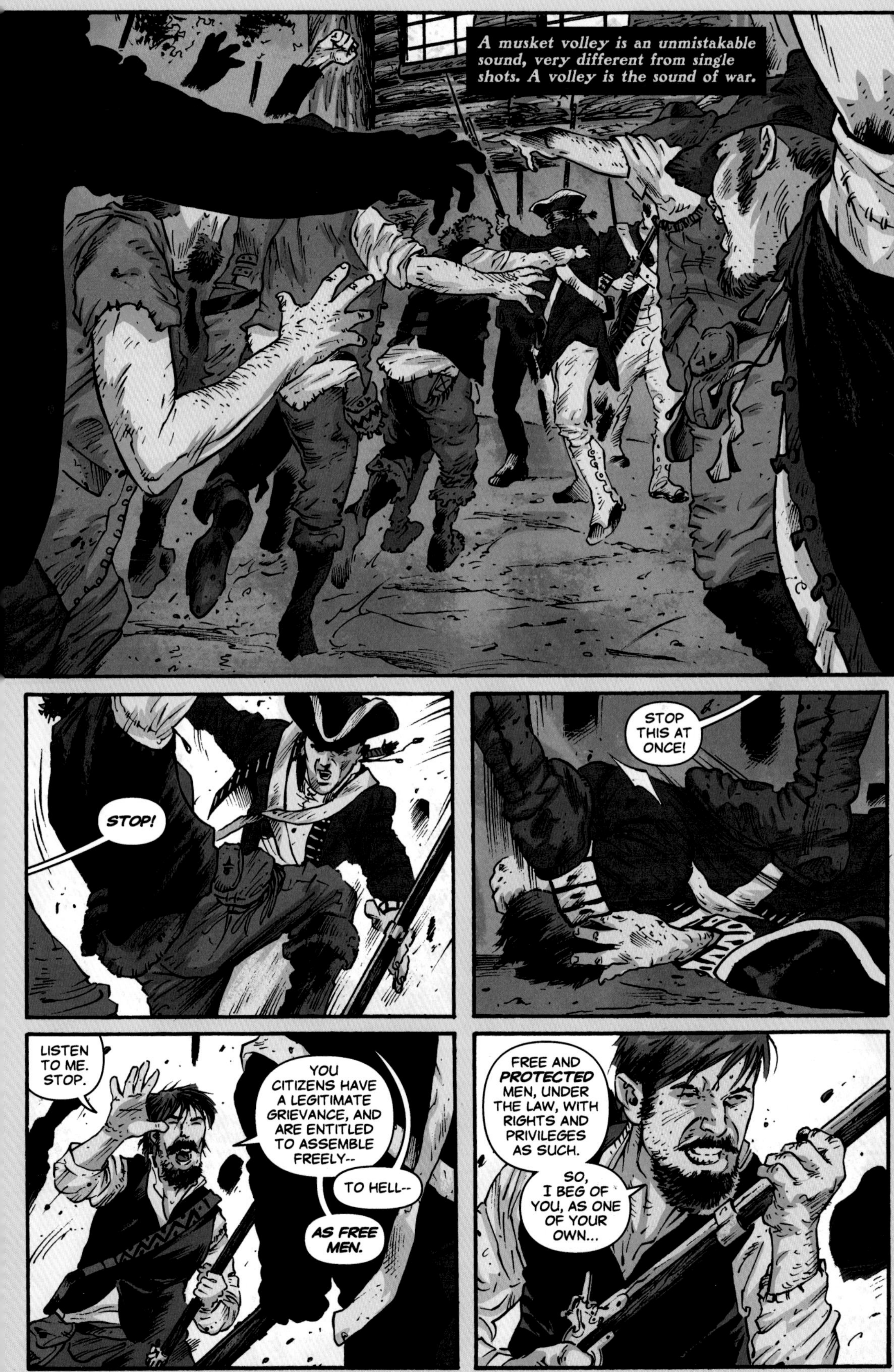
A musket volley is an unmistakable sound, very different from single shots. A volley is the sound of war.
STOP!
STOP THIS AT ONCE!
LISTEN TO ME. STOP.
YOU CITIZENS HAVE A LEGITIMATE GRIEVANCE, AND ARE ENTITLED TO ASSEMBLE FREELY--
TO HELL--
AS FREE MEN.
FREE AND PROTECTED MEN, UNDER THE LAW, WITH RIGHTS AND PRIVILEGES AS SUCH.
SO, I BEG OF YOU, AS ONE OF YOUR OWN...

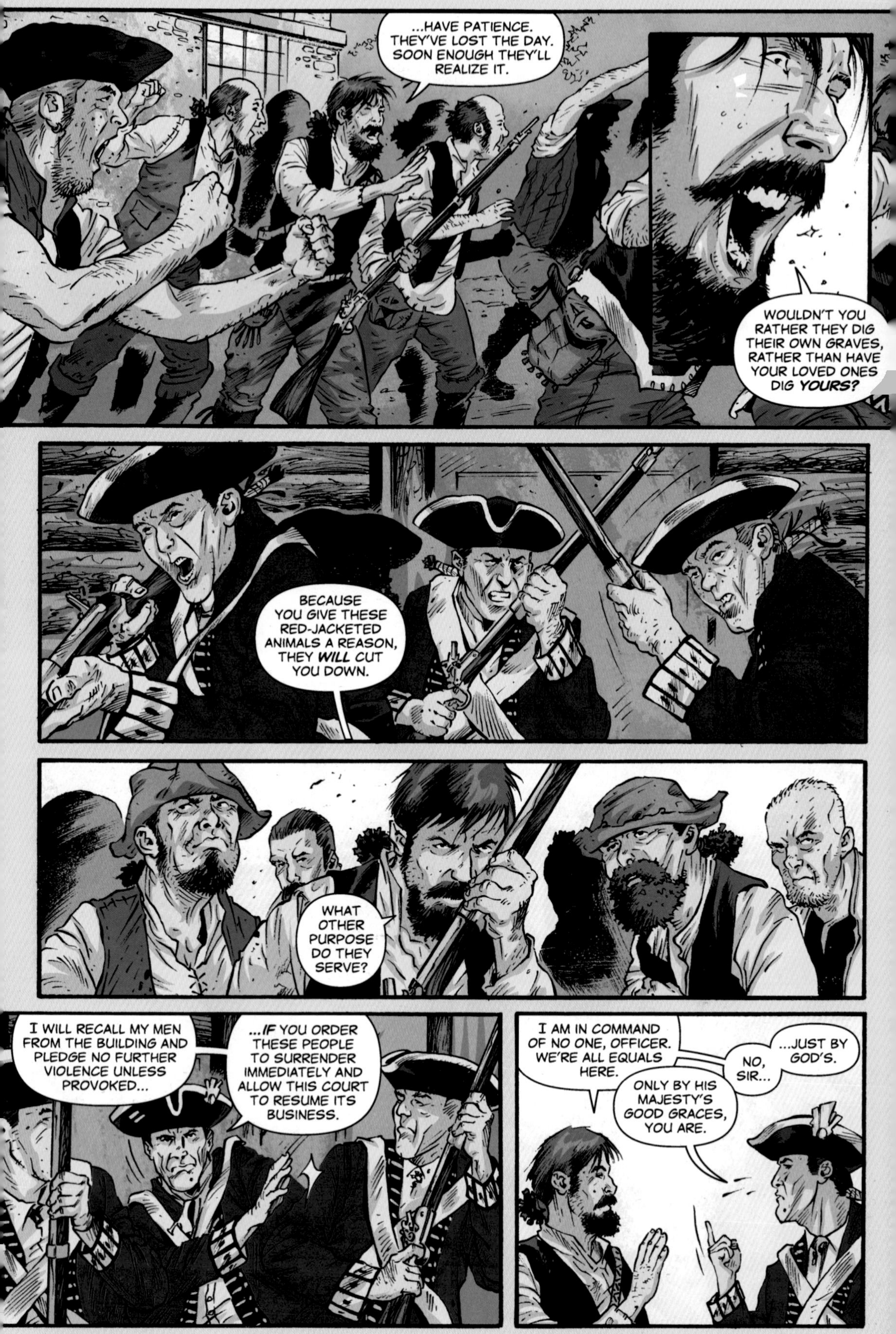
...HAVE PATIENCE. THEY'VE LOST THE DAY. SOON ENOUGH THEY'LL REALIZE IT.
WOULDN'T YOU RATHER THEY DIG THEIR OWN GRAVES, RATHER THAN HAVE YOUR LOVED ONES DIG *YOURS?*
BECAUSE YOU GIVE THESE RED-JACKETED ANIMALS A REASON, THEY *WILL* CUT YOU DOWN.
WHAT OTHER PURPOSE DO THEY SERVE?
I WILL RECALL MY MEN FROM THE BUILDING AND PLEDGE NO FURTHER VIOLENCE UNLESS PROVOKED...
...*IF* YOU ORDER THESE PEOPLE TO SURRENDER IMMEDIATELY AND ALLOW THIS COURT TO RESUME ITS BUSINESS.
I AM IN COMMAND OF NO ONE, OFFICER. WE'RE ALL EQUALS HERE.
ONLY BY HIS MAJESTY'S GOOD GRACES, YOU ARE.
NO, SIR...
...JUST BY GOD'S.

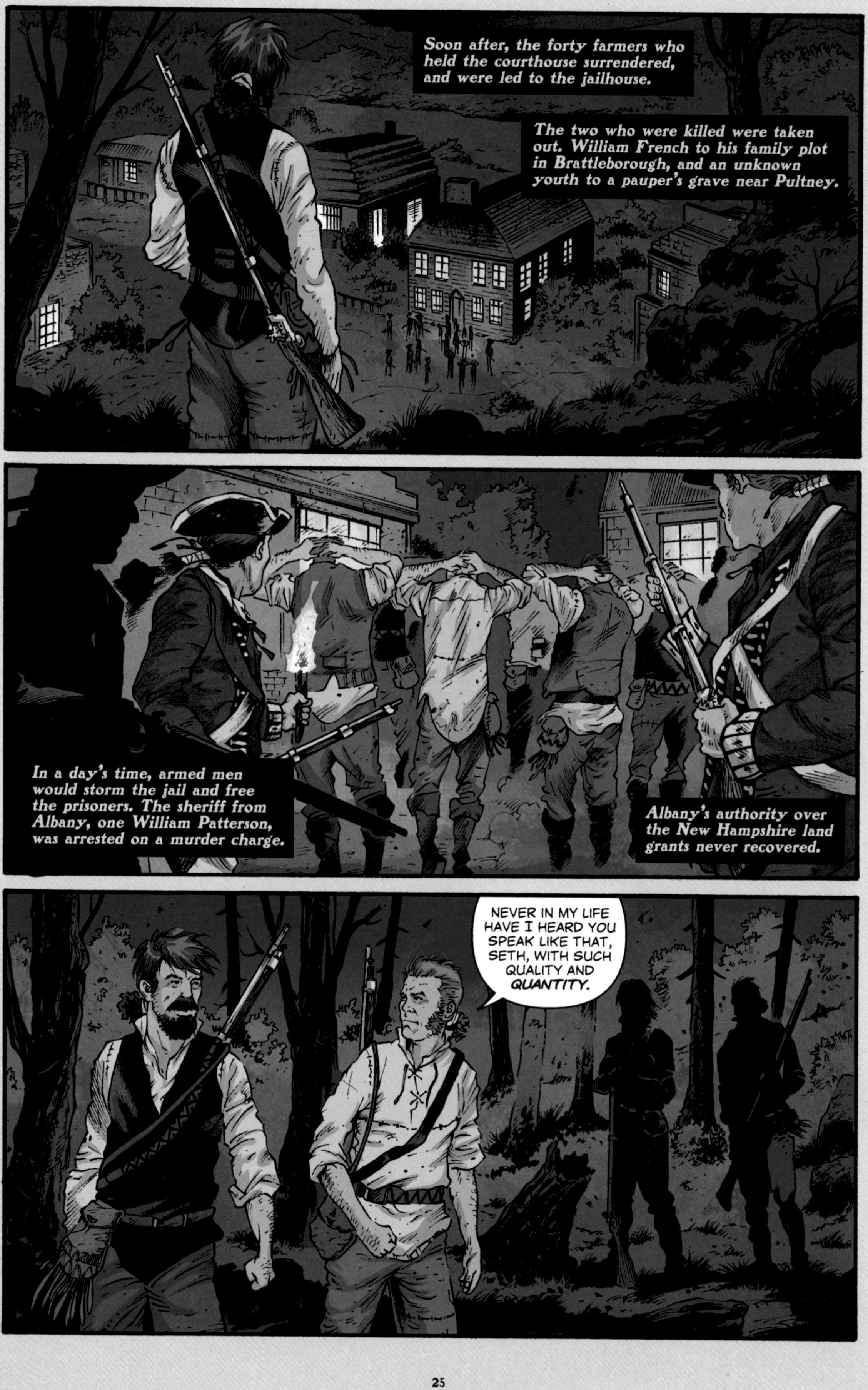
Soon after, the forty farmers who held the courthouse surrendered, and were led to the jailhouse.
The two who were killed were taken out. William French to his family plot in Brattleborough, and an unknown youth to a pauper's grave near Pultney.
In a day's time, armed men would storm the jail and free the prisoners. The sheriff from Albany, one William Patterson, was arrested on a murder charge.
Albany's authority over the New Hampshire land grants never recovered.
NEVER IN MY LIFE HAVE I HEARD YOU SPEAK LIKE THAT, SETH, WITH SUCH QUALITY AND *QUANTITY.*

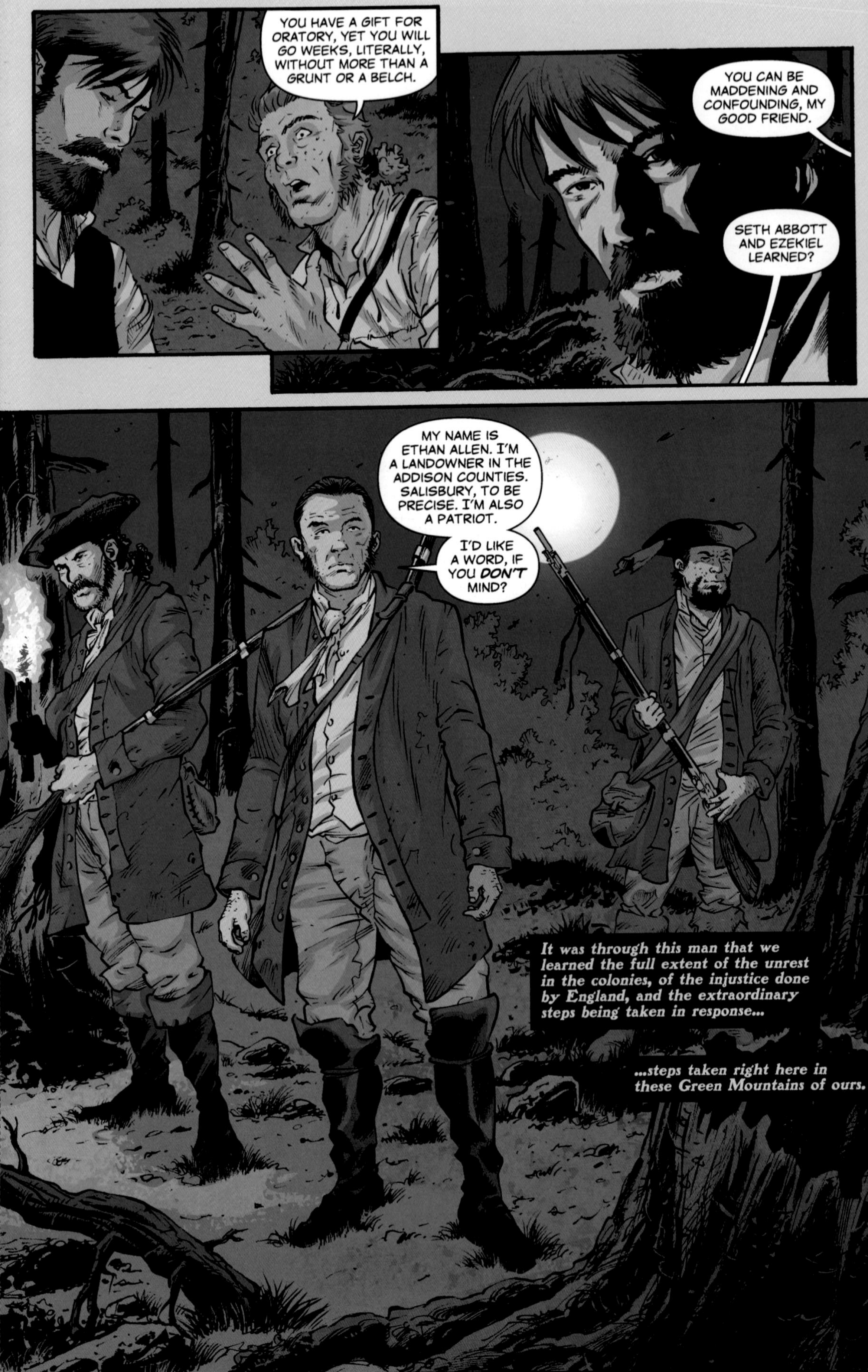
YOU HAVE A GIFT FOR ORATORY, YET YOU WILL GO WEEKS, LITERALLY, WITHOUT MORE THAN A GRUNT OR A BELCH.
YOU CAN BE MADDENING AND CONFOUNDING, MY GOOD FRIEND.
SETH ABBOTT AND EZEKIEL LEARNED?
MY NAME IS ETHAN ALLEN. I'M A LANDOWNER IN THE ADDISON COUNTIES. SALISBURY, TO BE PRECISE. I'M ALSO A PATRIOT.
I'D LIKE A WORD, IF YOU DON'T MIND?
It was through this man that we learned the full extent of the unrest in the colonies, of the injustice done by England, and the extraordinary steps being taken in response...
...steps taken right here in these Green Mountains of ours.

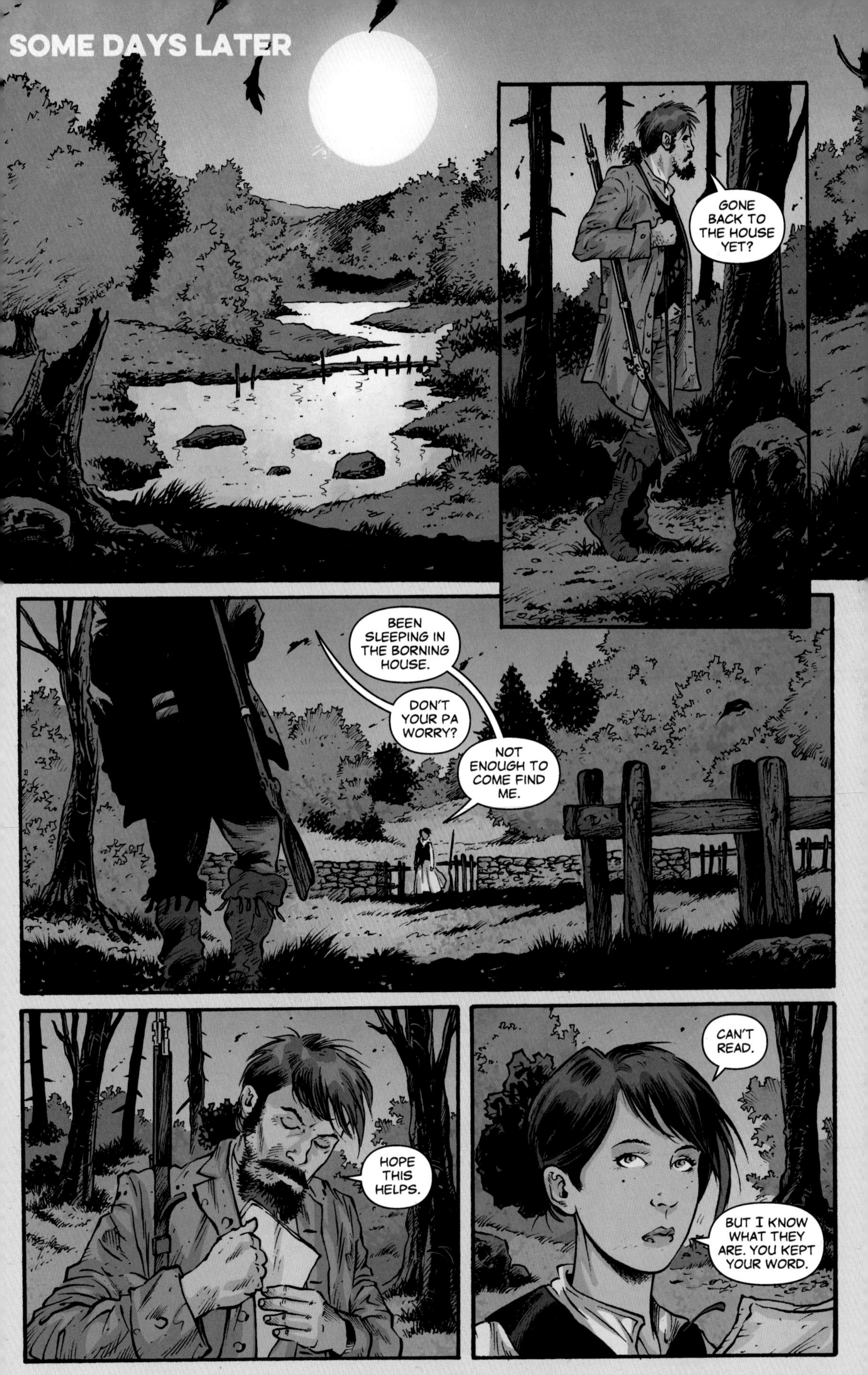
SOME DAYS LATER
GONE BACK TO THE HOUSE YET?
BEEN SLEEPING IN THE BORNING HOUSE.
DON'T YOUR PA WORRY?
NOT ENOUGH TO COME FIND ME.
HOPE THIS HELPS.
CAN'T READ.
BUT I KNOW WHAT THEY ARE. YOU KEPT YOUR WORD.

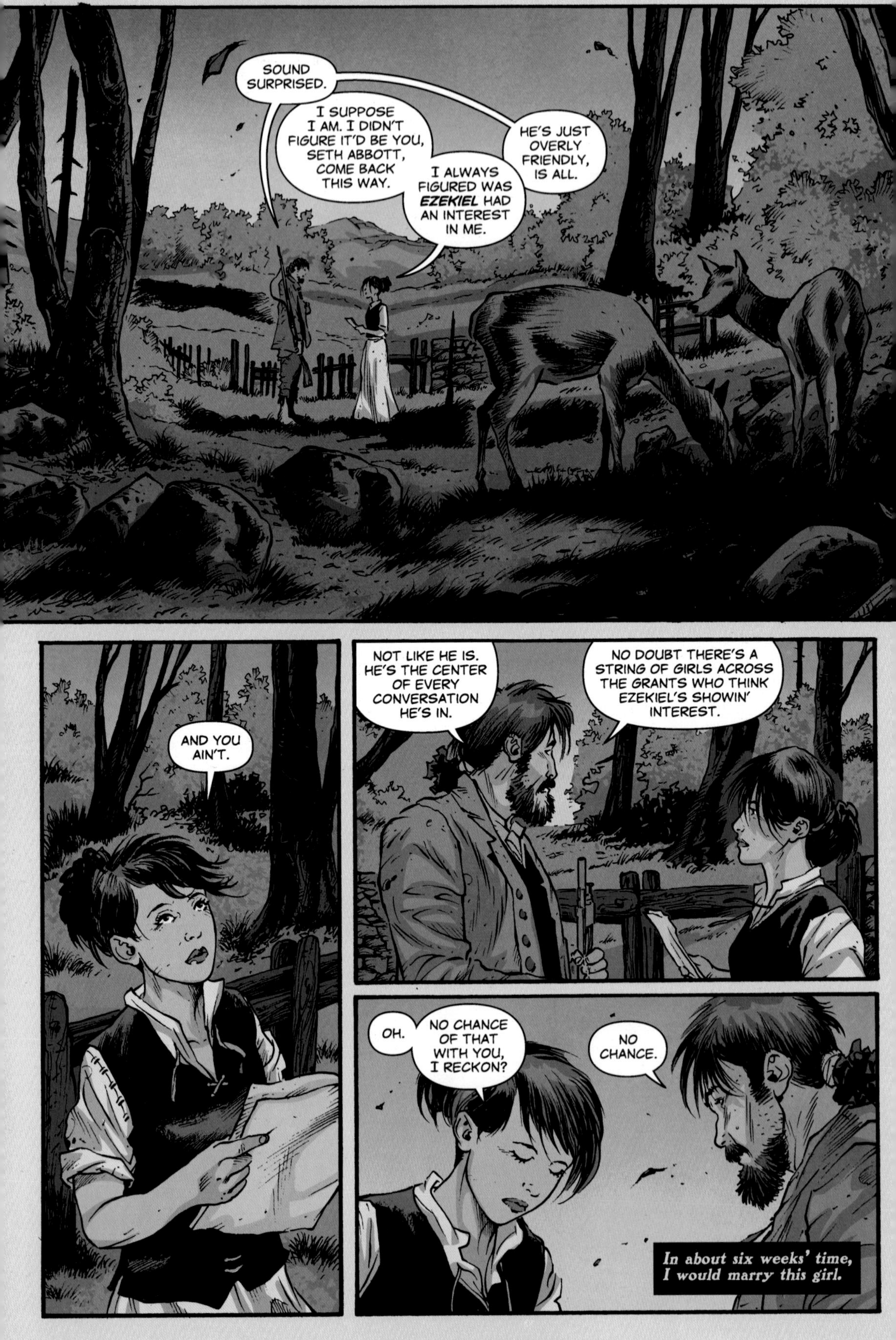

SOUND SURPRISED.
I SUPPOSE I AM. I DIDN'T FIGURE IT'D BE YOU, SETH ABBOTT, COME BACK THIS WAY.
I ALWAYS FIGURED WAS EZEKIEL HAD AN INTEREST IN ME.
HE'S JUST OVERLY FRIENDLY, IS ALL.
AND YOU AIN'T.
NOT LIKE HE IS. HE'S THE CENTER OF EVERY CONVERSATION HE'S IN.
NO DOUBT THERE'S A STRING OF GIRLS ACROSS THE GRANTS WHO THINK EZEKIEL'S SHOWIN' INTEREST.
OH.
NO CHANCE OF THAT WITH YOU, I RECKON?
NO CHANCE.
In about six weeks' time, I would marry this girl.

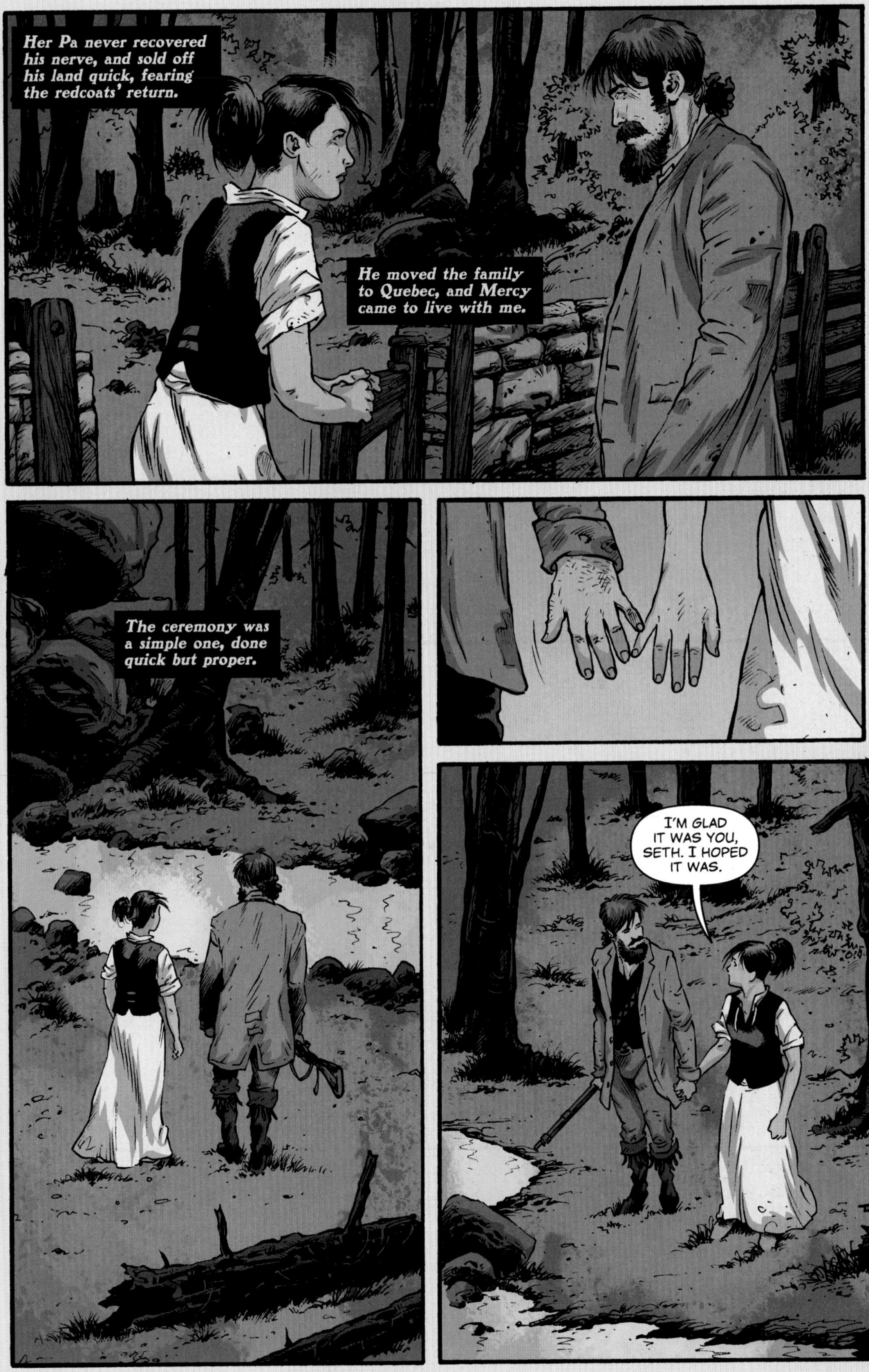
Her Pa never recovered his nerve, and sold off his land quick, fearing the redcoats' return.
He moved the family to Quebec, and Mercy came to live with me.
The ceremony was a simple one, done quick but proper.
I'M GLAD IT WAS YOU, SETH. I HOPED IT WAS.

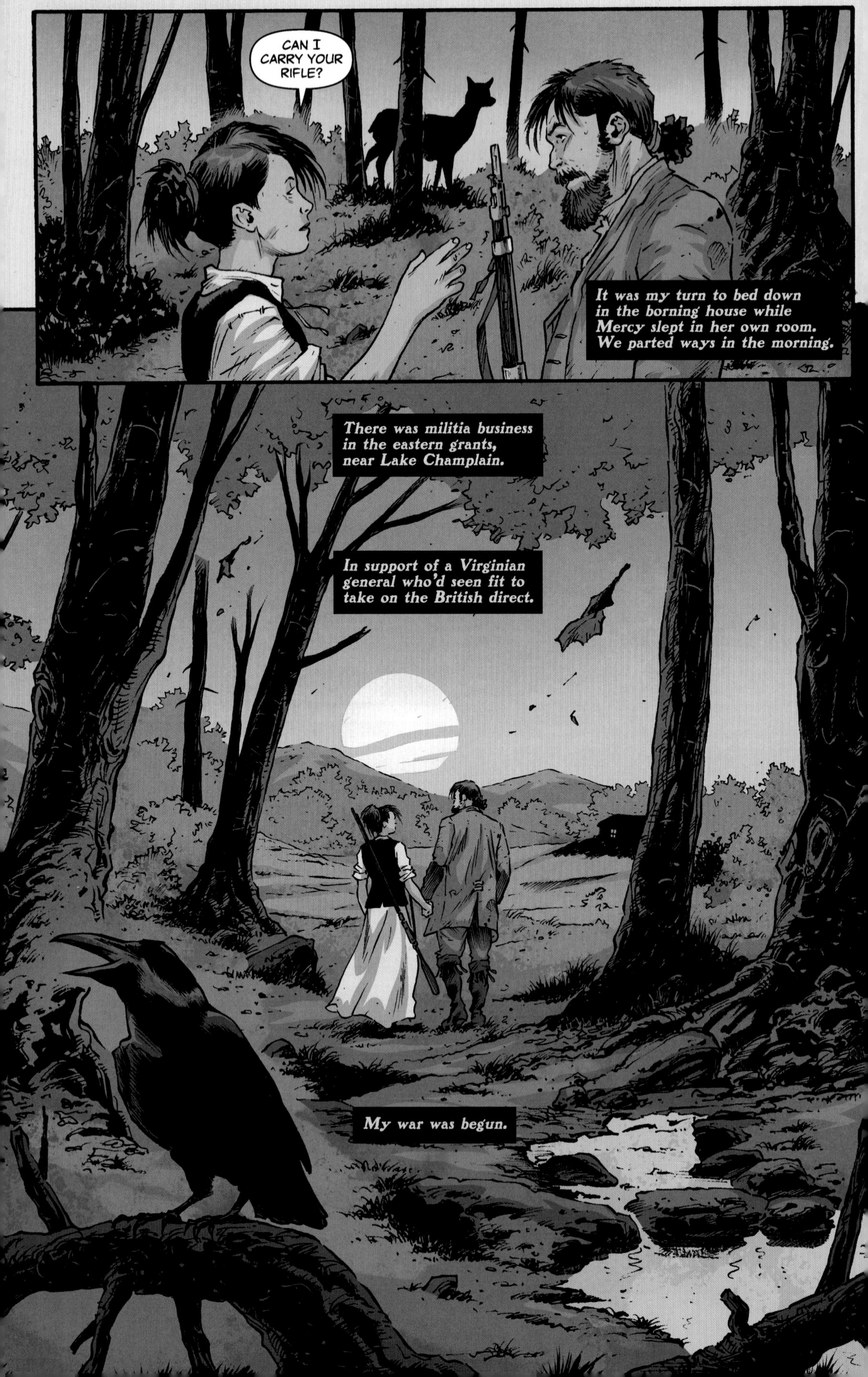
CAN I CARRY YOUR RIFLE?
It was my turn to bed down in the borning house while Mercy slept in her own room. We parted ways in the morning.
There was militia business in the eastern grants, near Lake Champlain.
In support of a Virginian general who'd seen fit to take on the British direct.
My war was begun.

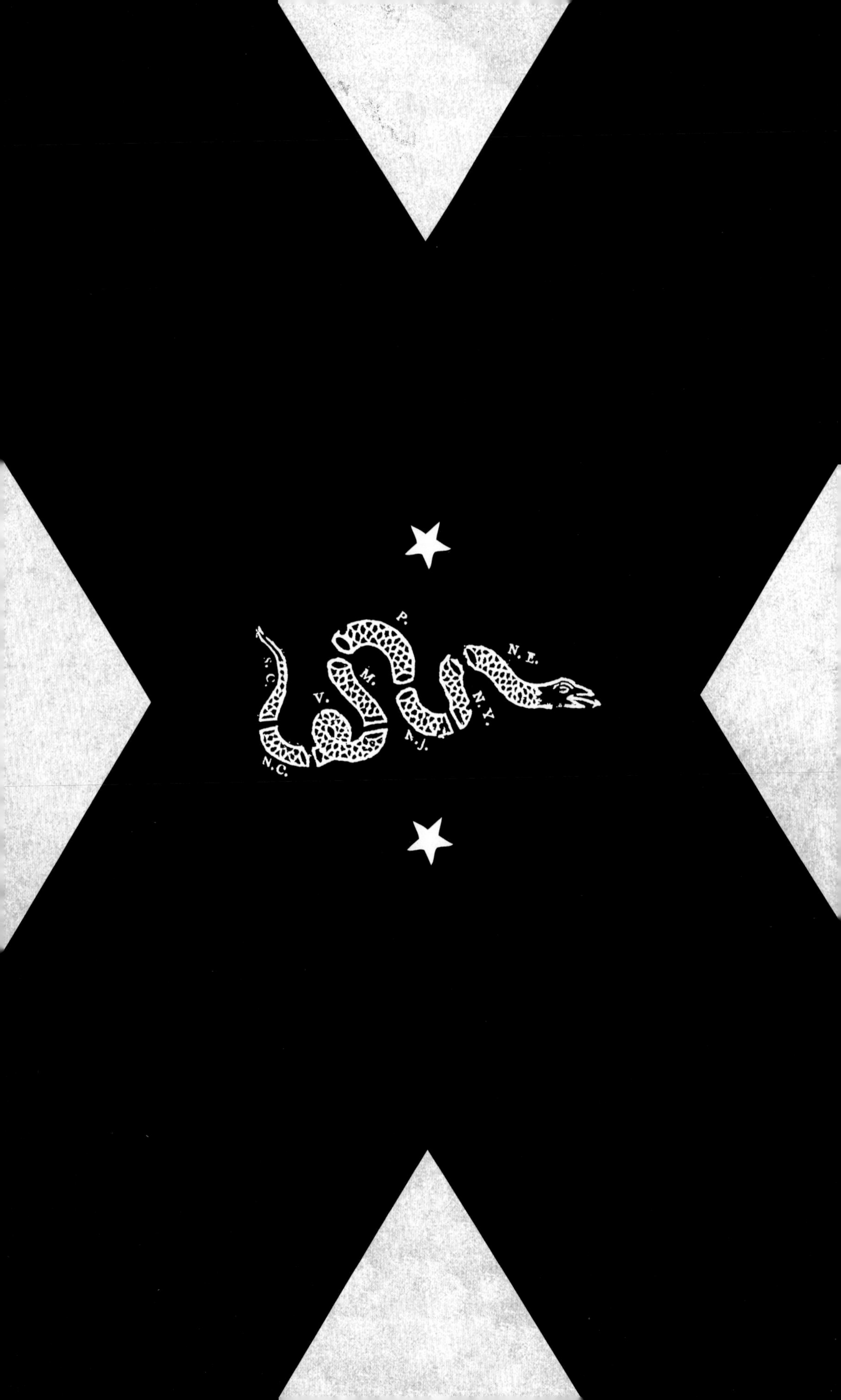
S.C.
N.C.
V.
M.
P.
N.J.
N.Y.
N.E.

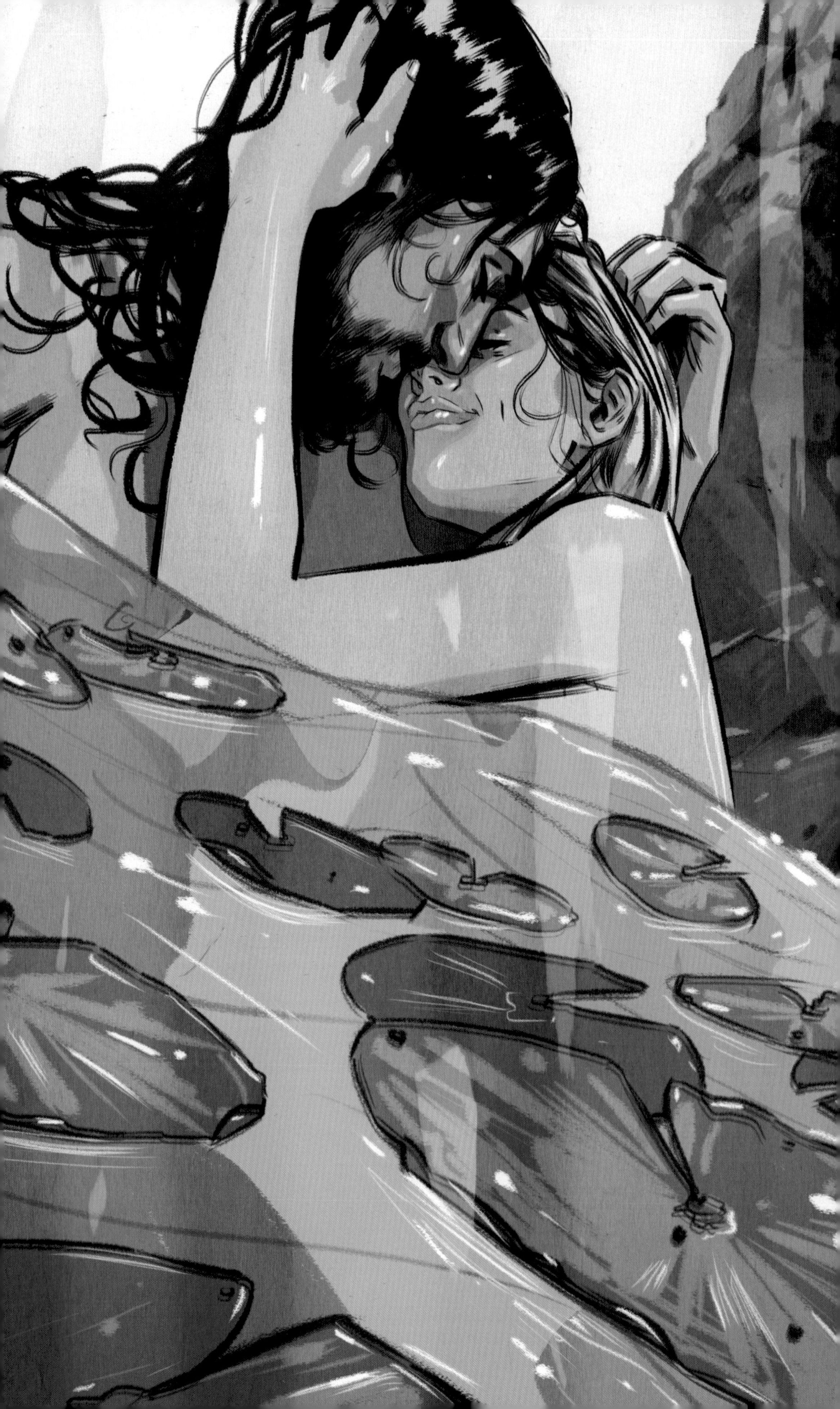

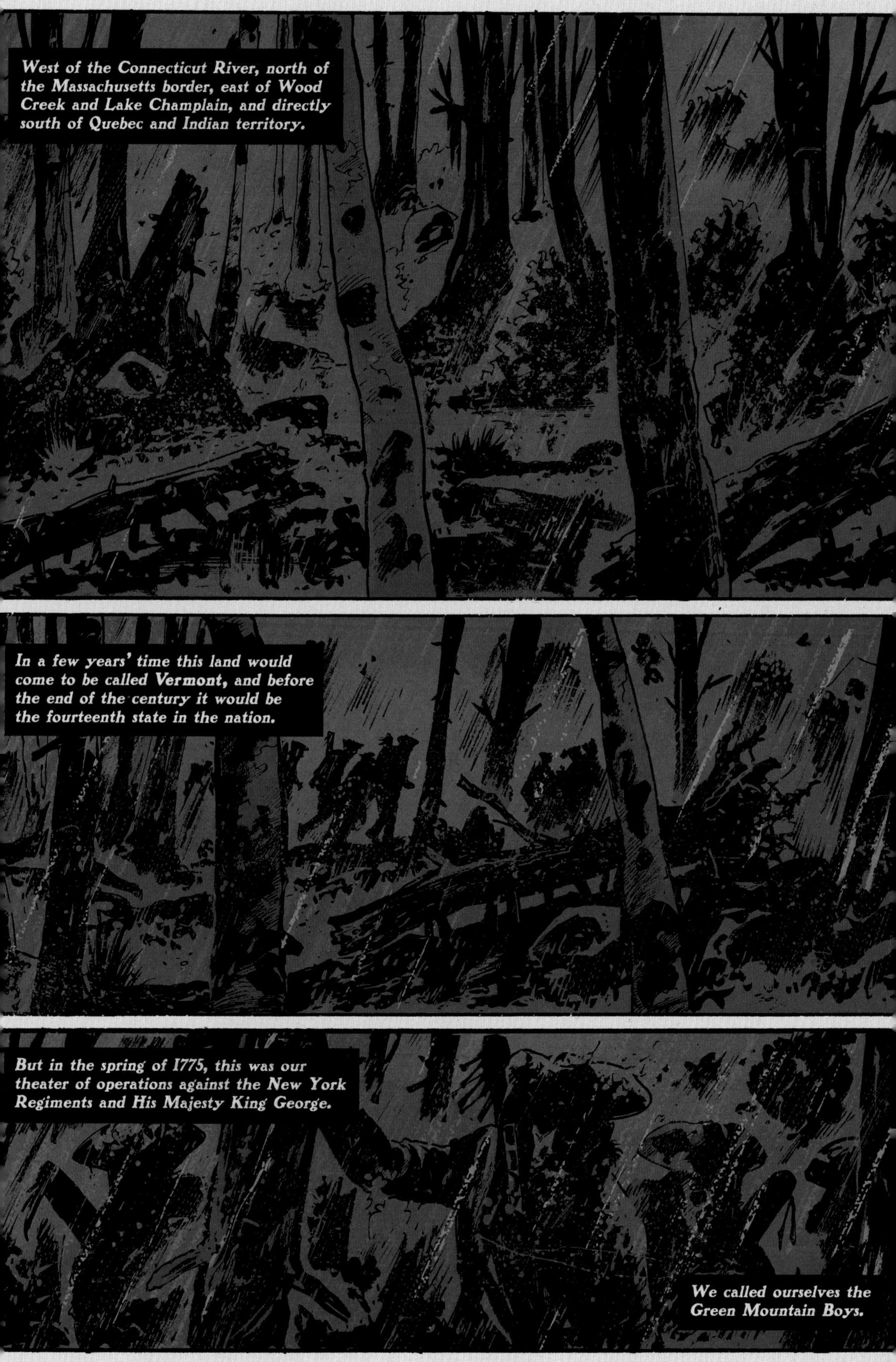
West of the Connecticut River, north of the Massachusetts border, east of Wood Creek and Lake Champlain, and directly south of Quebec and Indian territory.
In a few years' time this land would come to be called Vermont, and before the end of the century it would be the fourteenth state in the nation.
But in the spring of 1775, this was our theater of operations against the New York Regiments and His Majesty King George.
We called ourselves the Green Mountain Boys.

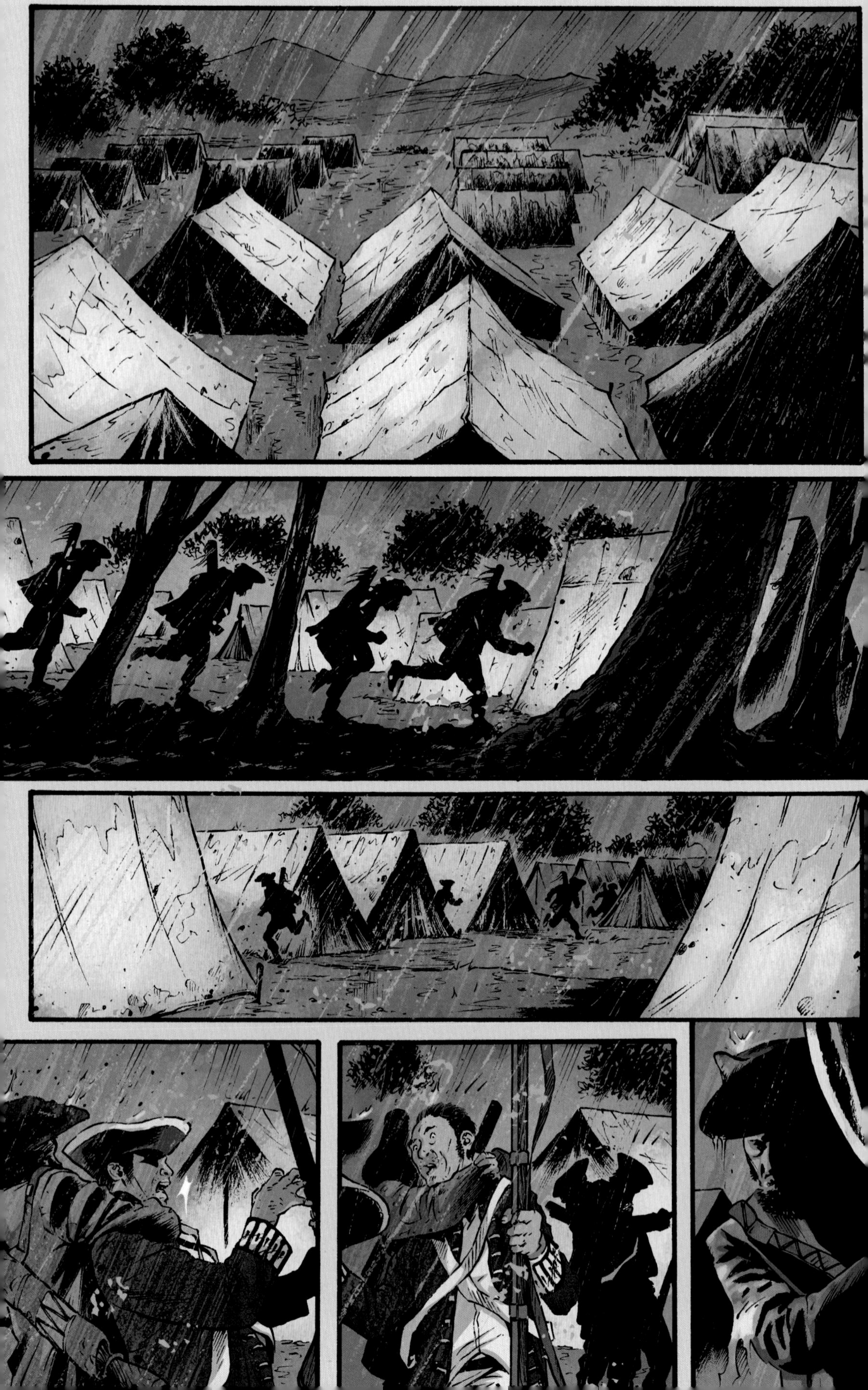

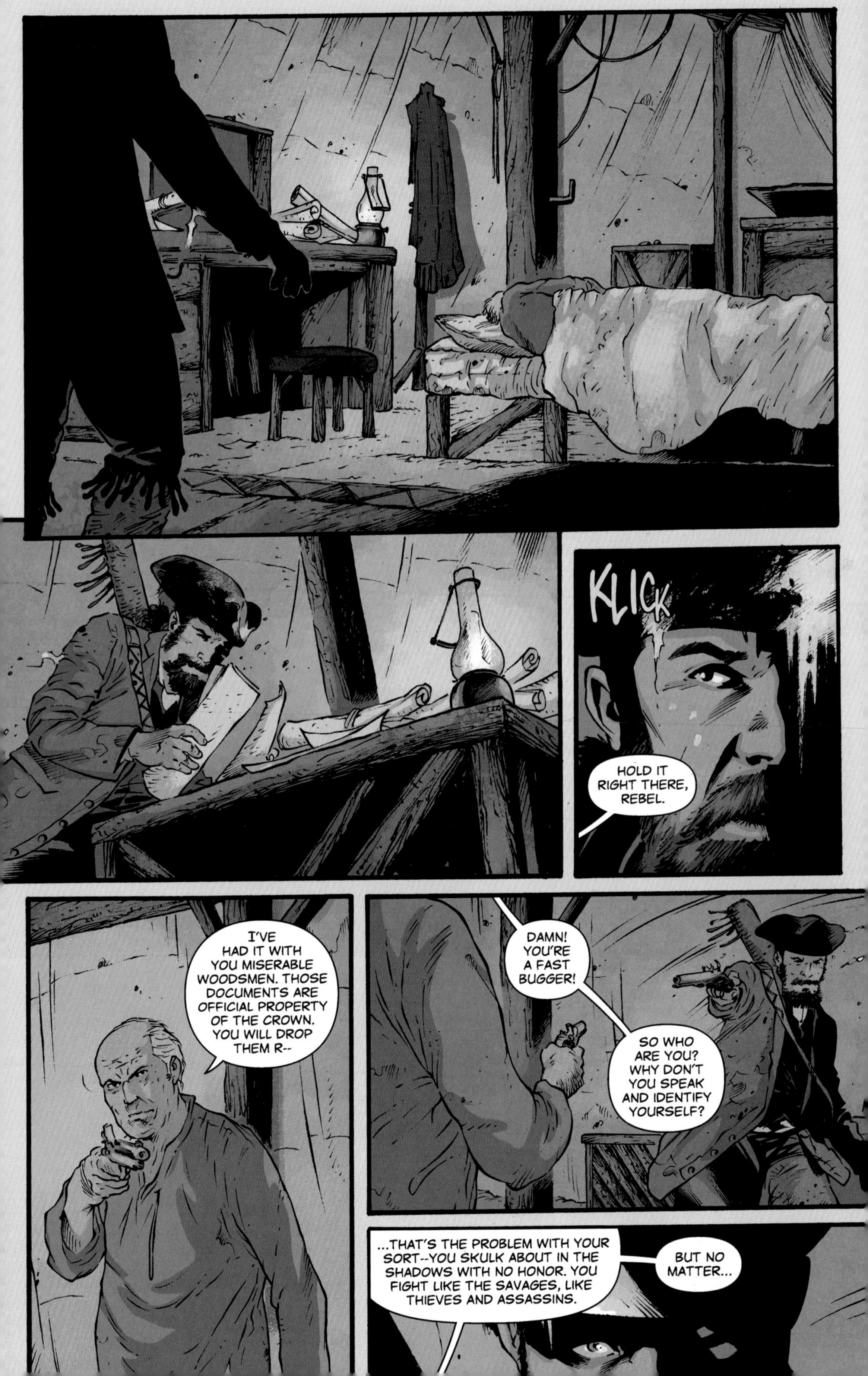
KLICK
HOLD IT RIGHT THERE, REBEL.
I'VE HAD IT WITH YOU MISERABLE WOODSMEN. THOSE DOCUMENTS ARE OFFICIAL PROPERTY OF THE CROWN. YOU WILL DROP THEM R--
DAMN! YOU'RE A FAST BUGGER!
SO WHO ARE YOU? WHY DON'T YOU SPEAK AND IDENTIFY YOURSELF?
...THAT'S THE PROBLEM WITH YOUR SORT--YOU SKULK ABOUT IN THE SHADOWS WITH NO HONOR. YOU FIGHT LIKE THE SAVAGES, LIKE THIEVES AND ASSASSINS.
BUT NO MATTER...

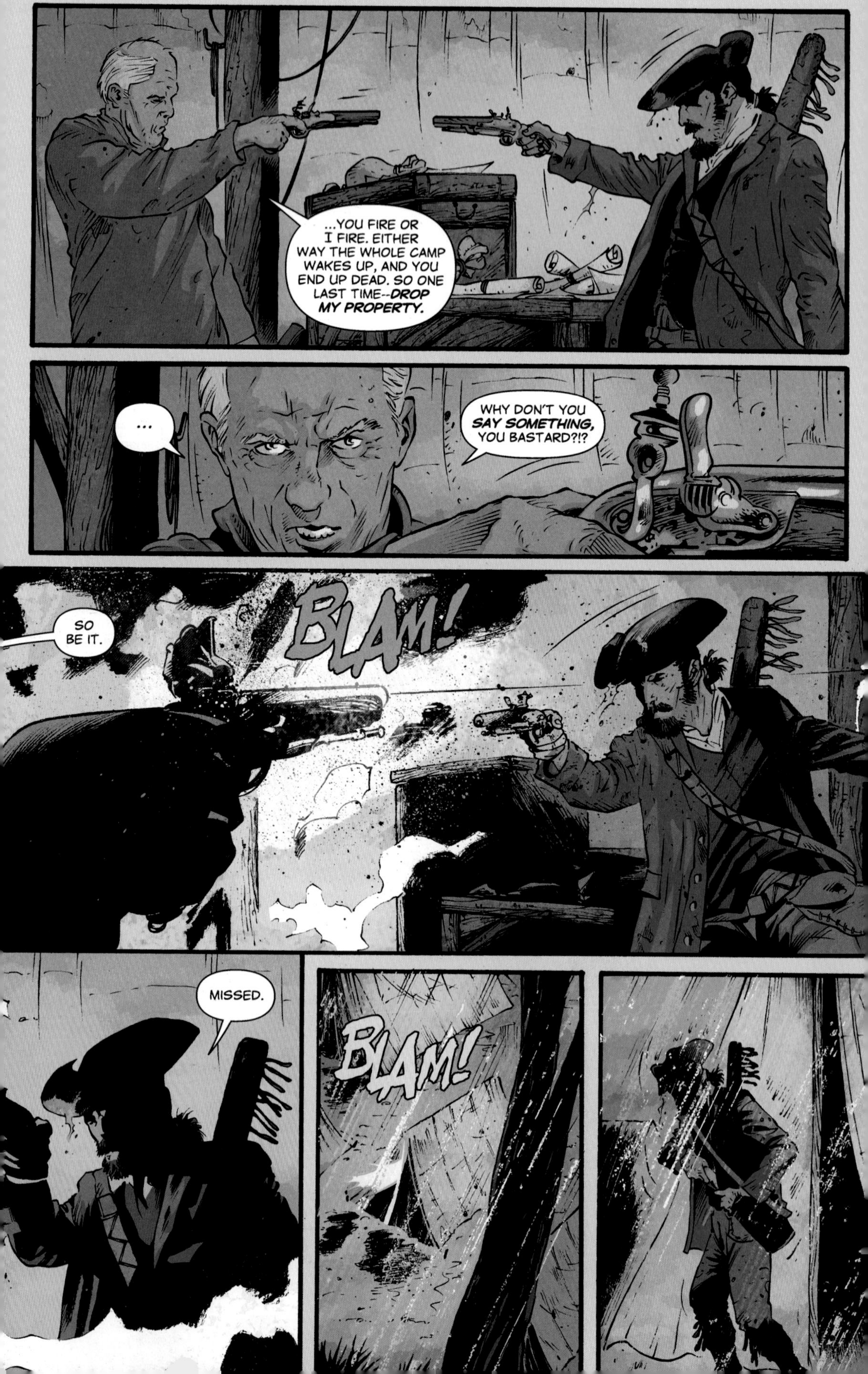
...YOU FIRE OR I FIRE. EITHER WAY THE WHOLE CAMP WAKES UP, AND YOU END UP DEAD. SO ONE LAST TIME--DROP MY PROPERTY.
...
WHY DON'T YOU SAY SOMETHING, YOU BASTARD?!?
SO BE IT.
BLAM!
MISSED.
BLAM!

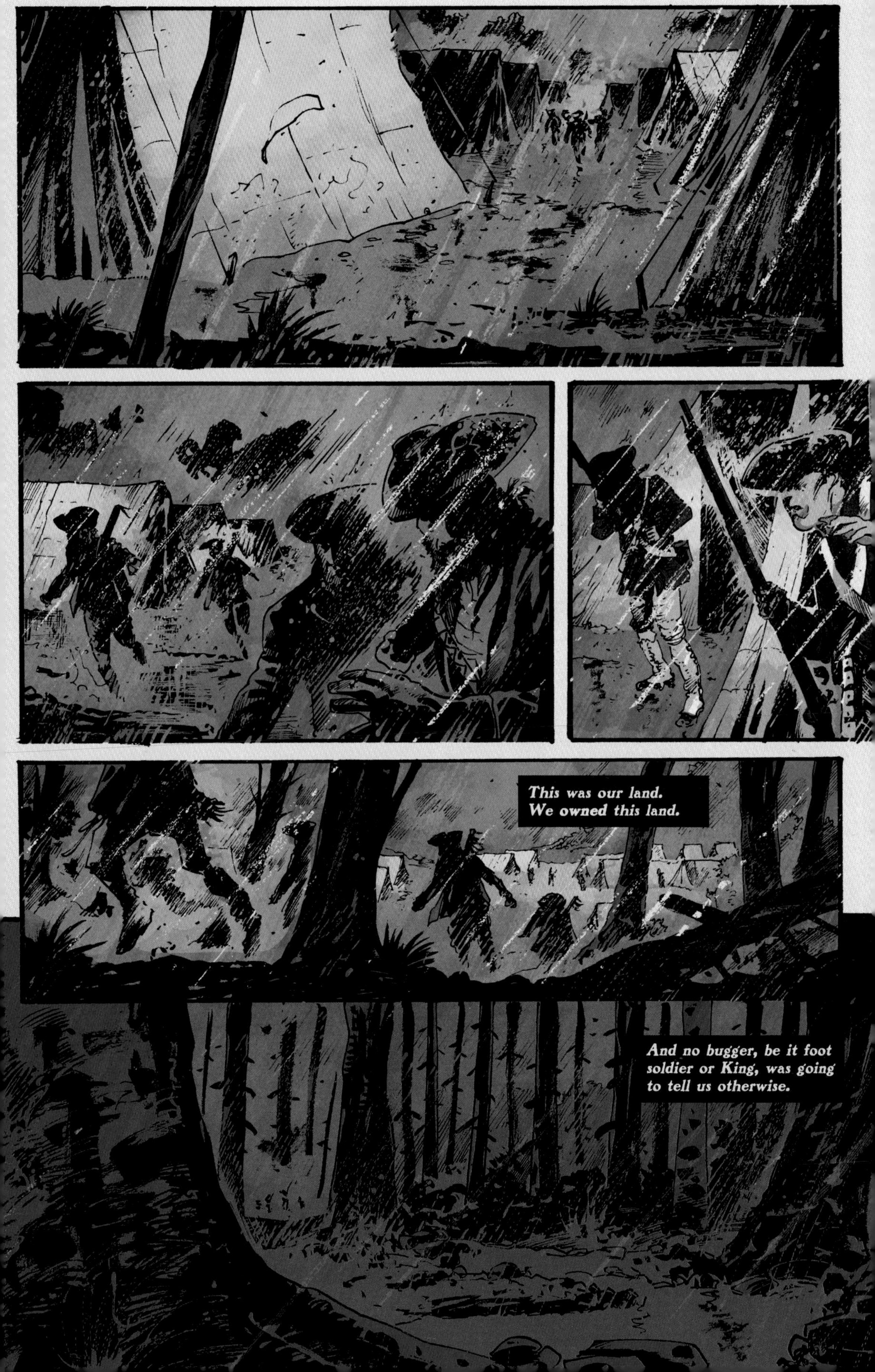
This was our land.
We owned this land.
And no bugger, be it foot soldier or King, was going to tell us otherwise.

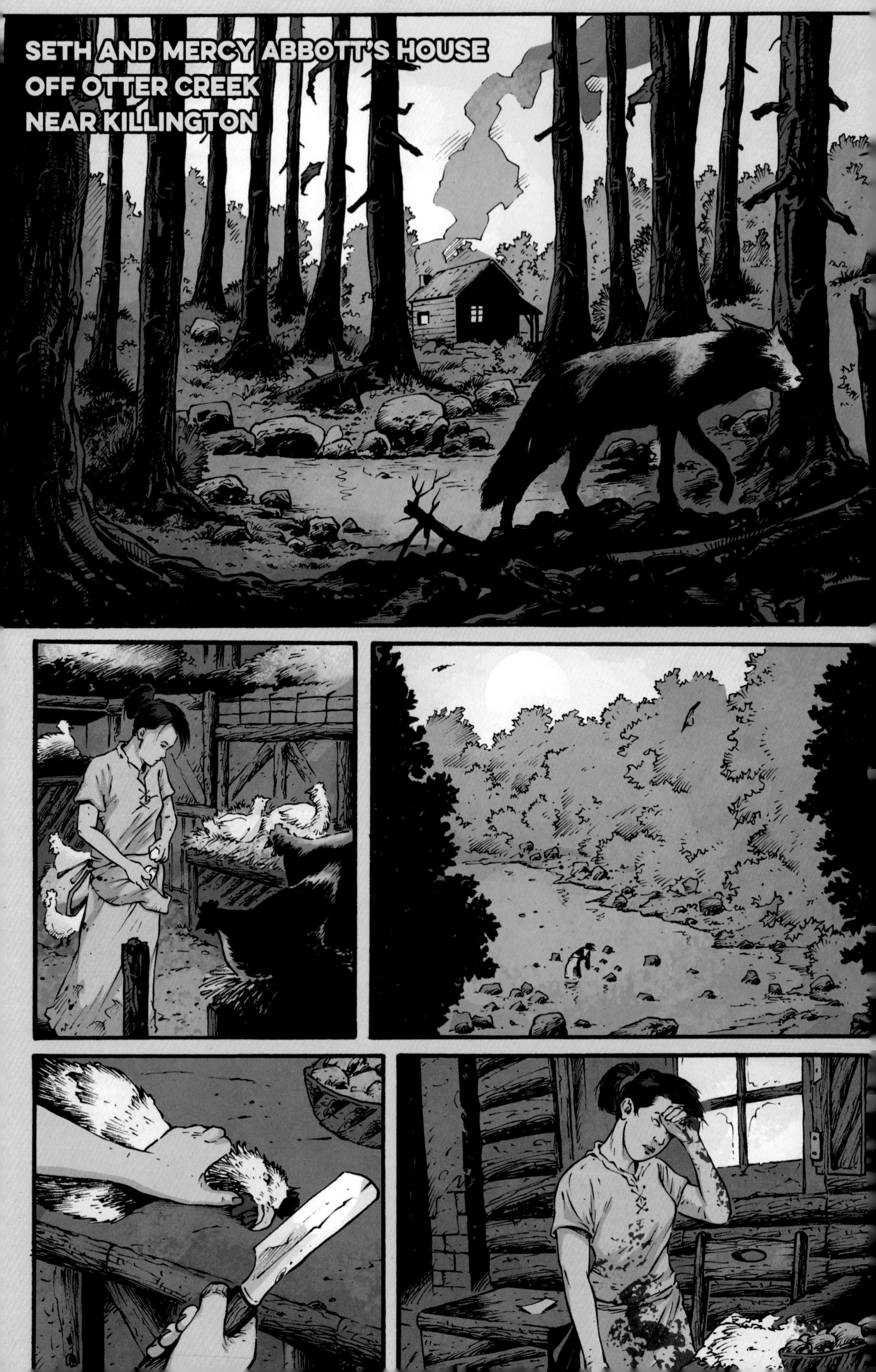
SETH AND MERCY ABBOTT'S HOUSE
OFF OTTER CREEK
NEAR KILLINGTON

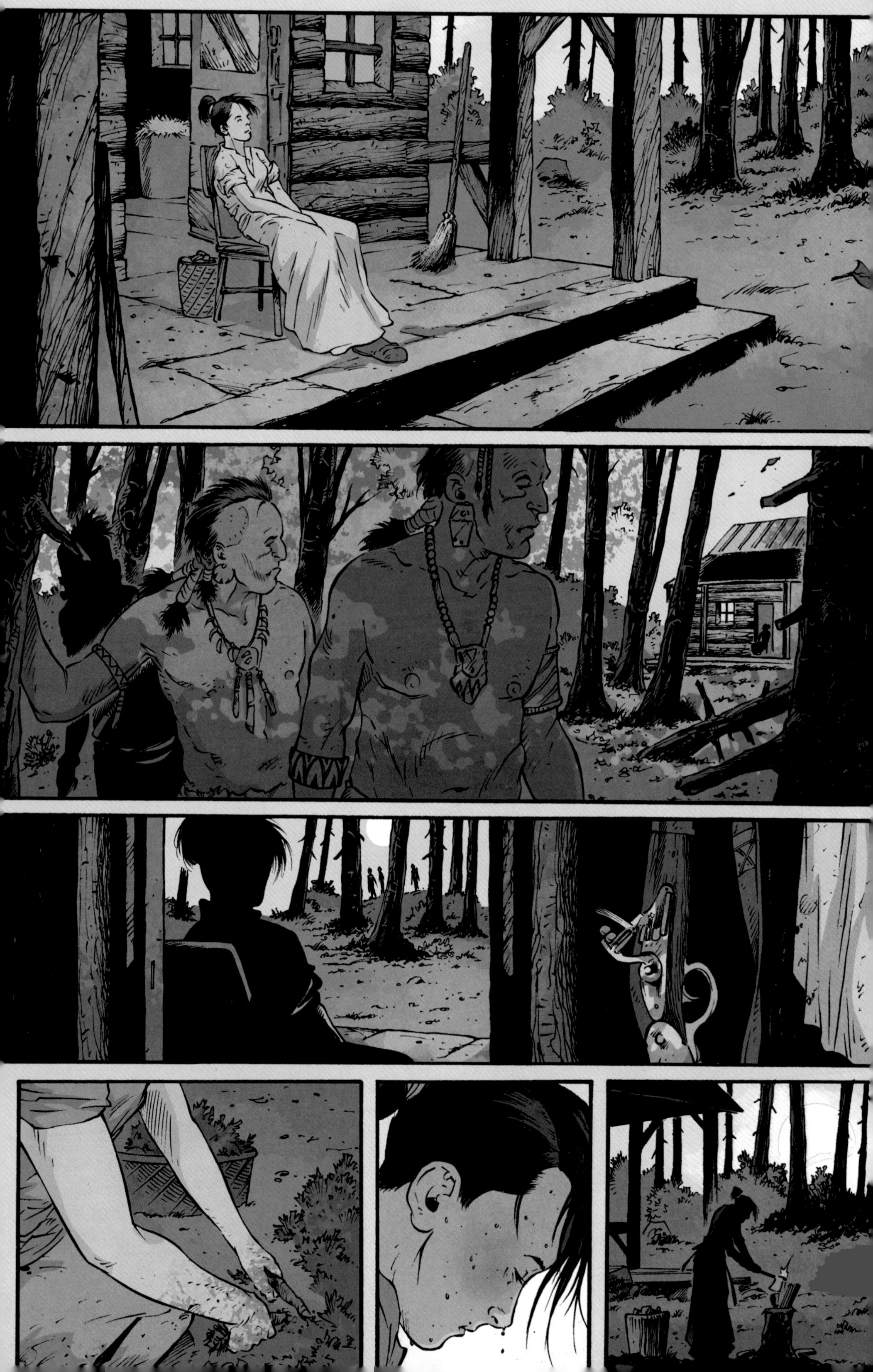

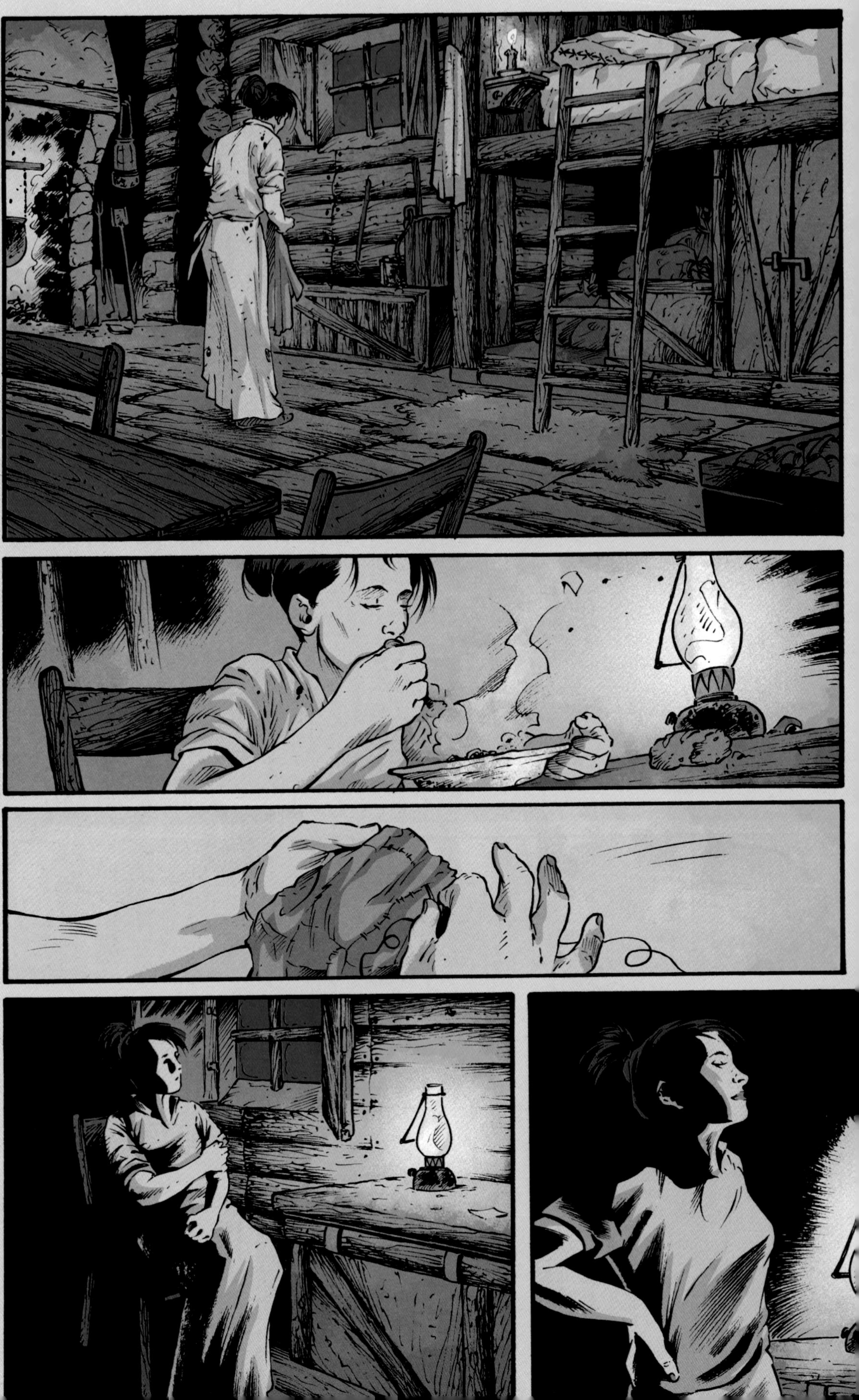

I left Ezekiel and the others at the Old Canada Road and walked the rest of the way home alone.

It was already late, and even had I run, I would still have missed suppertime.

Unlike most of the men in our group, I was newly married. And so I was keenly aware of the responsibilities of the home.

A home gifted to us by Ethan Allen, one of his many land holdings, in exchange for two years' service. It was small but required constant tending all the same.

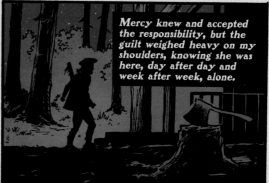

Mercy knew and accepted the responsibility, but the guilt weighed heavy on my shoulders, knowing she was here, day after day and week after week, alone.

I'd have blamed the British for bullying us into this conflict. That's surely what Ethan would have done.

But my father taught me there is no higher honor than the crafting of home and hearth, and in that maddening space of split loyalties...

...I entered my seventeenth year of life, too heartsore to join my wife in bed, lest I disturb her rest.

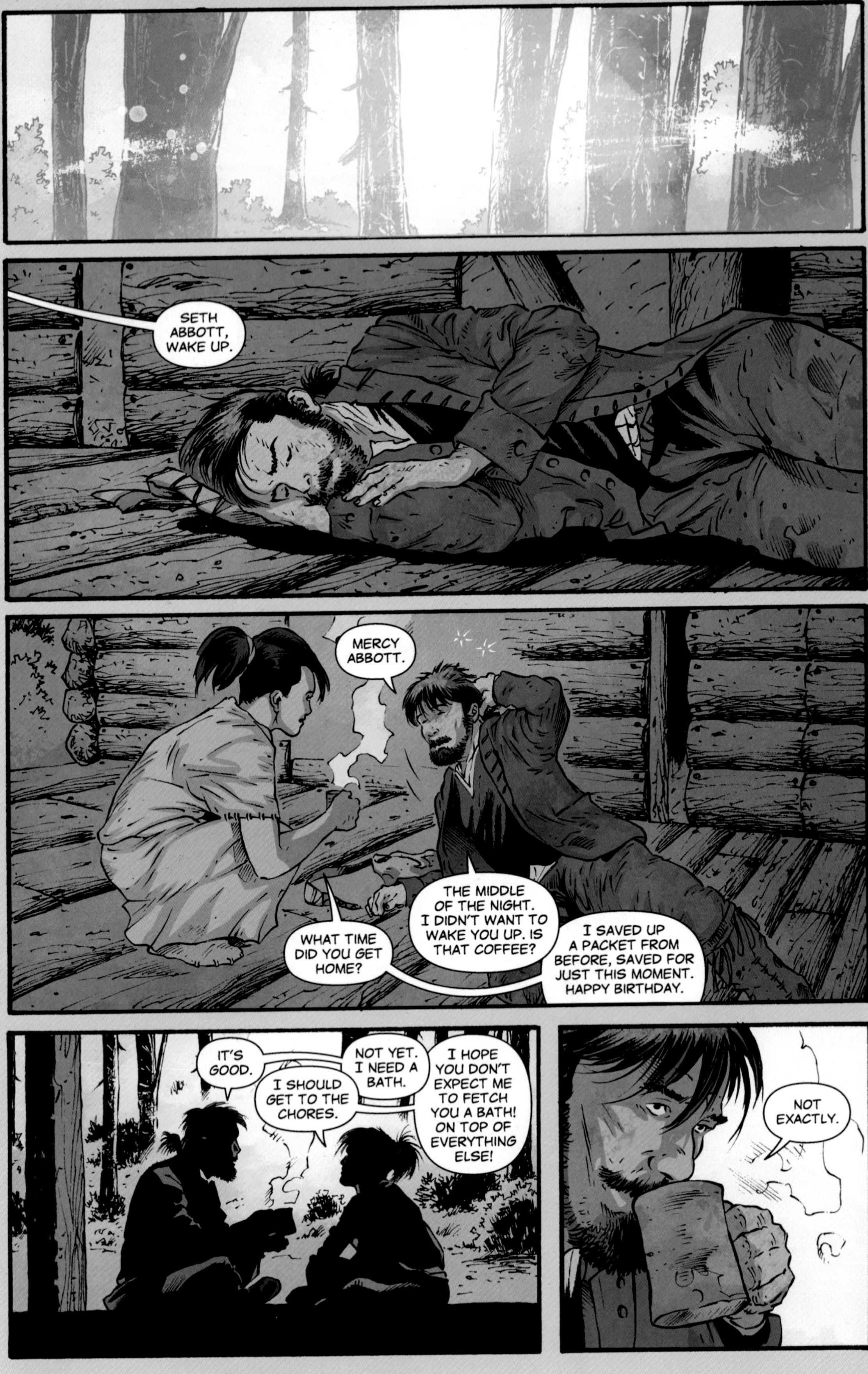
SETH ABBOTT, WAKE UP.
MERCY ABBOTT.
WHAT TIME DID YOU GET HOME?
THE MIDDLE OF THE NIGHT. I DIDN'T WANT TO WAKE YOU UP. IS THAT COFFEE?
I SAVED UP A PACKET FROM BEFORE, SAVED FOR JUST THIS MOMENT. HAPPY BIRTHDAY.
IT'S GOOD.
I SHOULD GET TO THE CHORES.
NOT YET. I NEED A BATH.
I HOPE YOU DON'T EXPECT ME TO FETCH YOU A BATH! ON TOP OF EVERYTHING ELSE!
NOT EXACTLY.

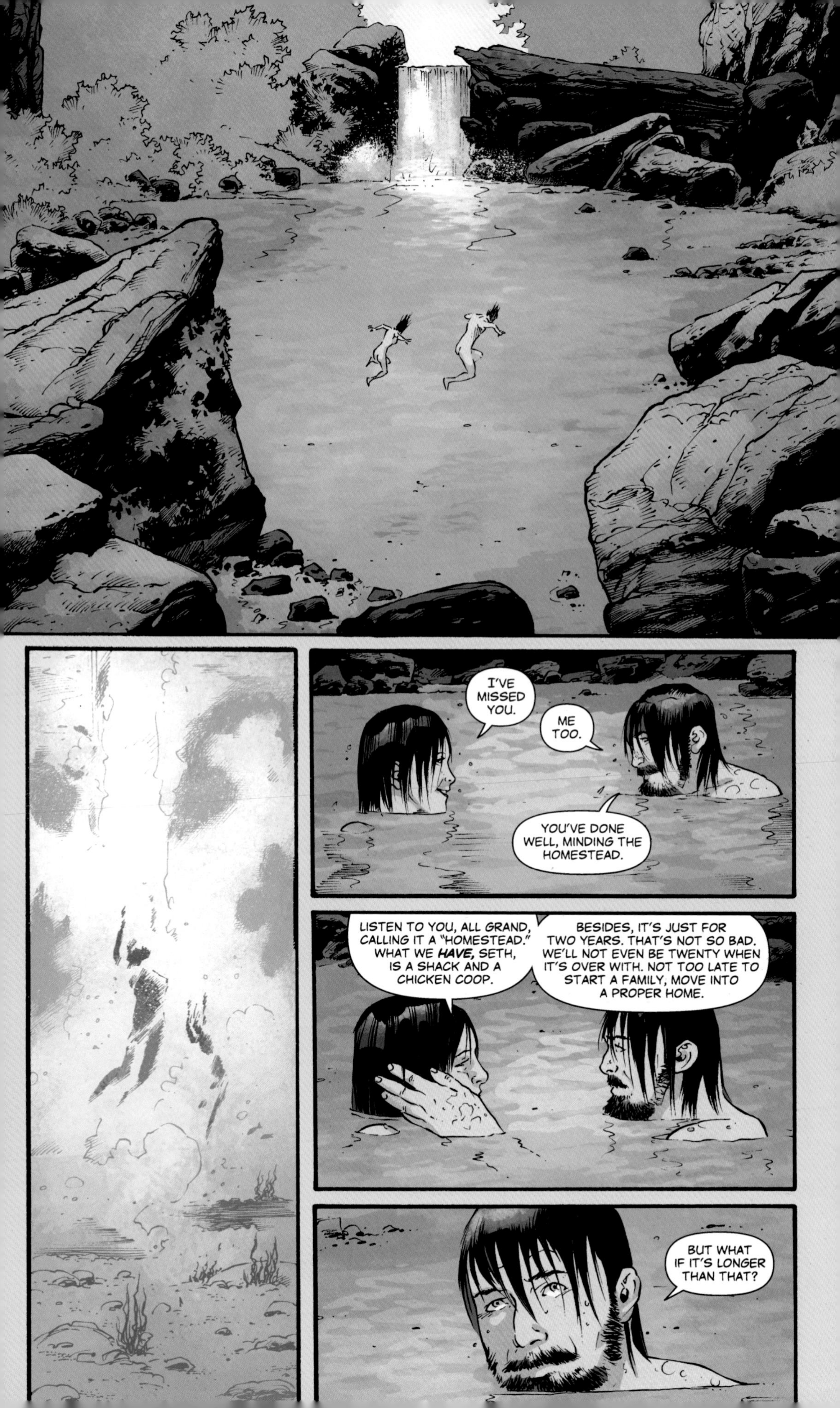
I'VE MISSED YOU.
ME TOO.
YOU'VE DONE WELL, MINDING THE HOMESTEAD.
LISTEN TO YOU, ALL GRAND, CALLING IT A "HOMESTEAD." WHAT WE *HAVE,* SETH, IS A SHACK AND A CHICKEN COOP.
BESIDES, IT'S JUST FOR TWO YEARS. THAT'S NOT SO BAD. WE'LL NOT EVEN BE TWENTY WHEN IT'S OVER WITH. NOT TOO LATE TO START A FAMILY, MOVE INTO A PROPER HOME.
BUT WHAT IF IT'S LONGER THAN THAT?

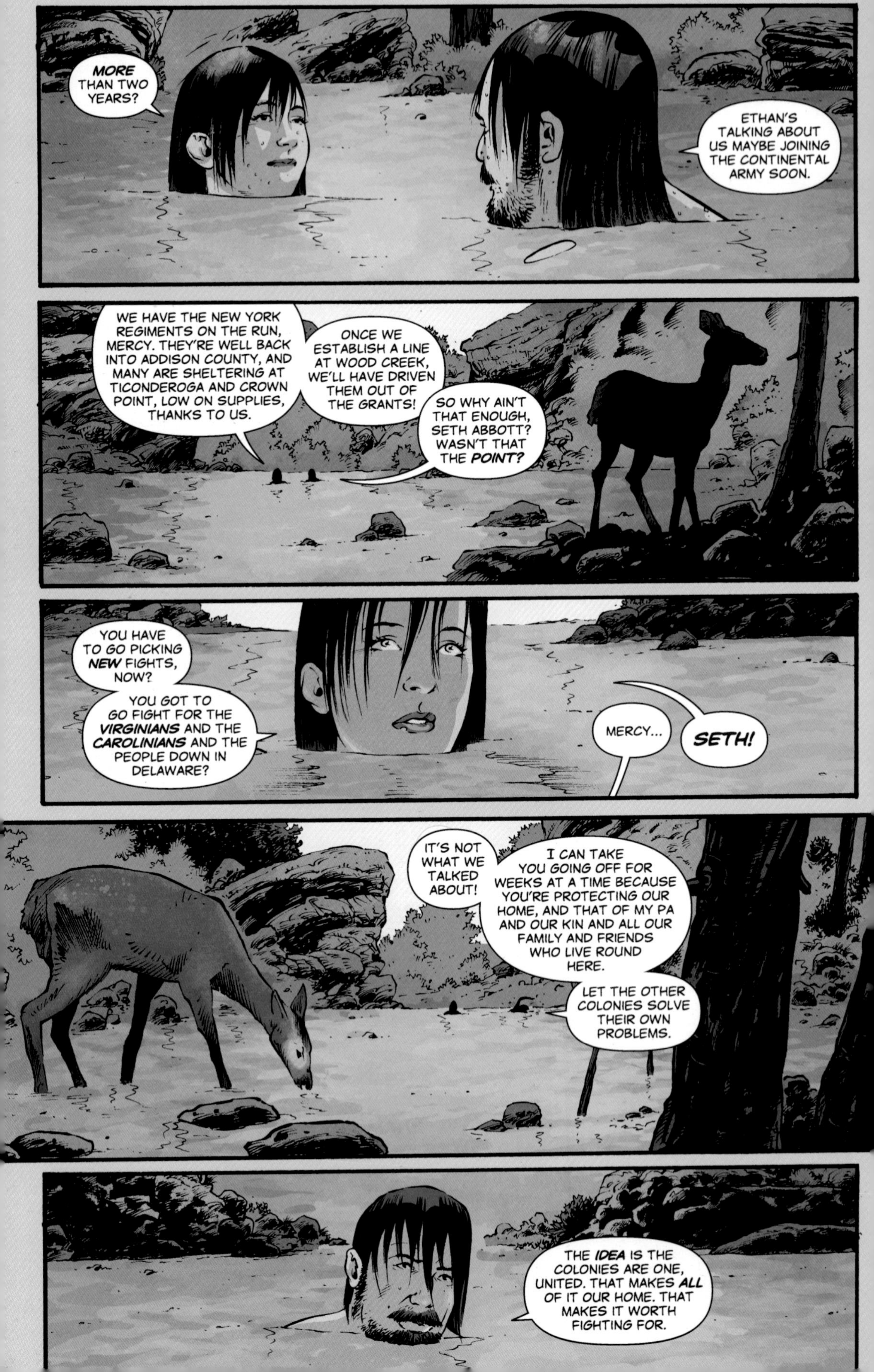

MORE THAN TWO YEARS?
ETHAN'S TALKING ABOUT US MAYBE JOINING THE CONTINENTAL ARMY SOON.
WE HAVE THE NEW YORK REGIMENTS ON THE RUN, MERCY. THEY'RE WELL BACK INTO ADDISON COUNTY, AND MANY ARE SHELTERING AT TICONDEROGA AND CROWN POINT, LOW ON SUPPLIES, THANKS TO US.
ONCE WE ESTABLISH A LINE AT WOOD CREEK, WE'LL HAVE DRIVEN THEM OUT OF THE GRANTS!
SO WHY AIN'T THAT ENOUGH, SETH ABBOTT? WASN'T THAT THE POINT?
YOU HAVE TO GO PICKING NEW FIGHTS, NOW?
YOU GOT TO GO FIGHT FOR THE VIRGINIANS AND THE CAROLINIANS AND THE PEOPLE DOWN IN DELAWARE?
MERCY...
SETH!
IT'S NOT WHAT WE TALKED ABOUT!
I CAN TAKE YOU GOING OFF FOR WEEKS AT A TIME BECAUSE YOU'RE PROTECTING OUR HOME, AND THAT OF MY PA AND OUR KIN AND ALL OUR FAMILY AND FRIENDS WHO LIVE ROUND HERE.
LET THE OTHER COLONIES SOLVE THEIR OWN PROBLEMS.
THE IDEA IS THE COLONIES ARE ONE, UNITED. THAT MAKES ALL OF IT OUR HOME. THAT MAKES IT WORTH FIGHTING FOR.

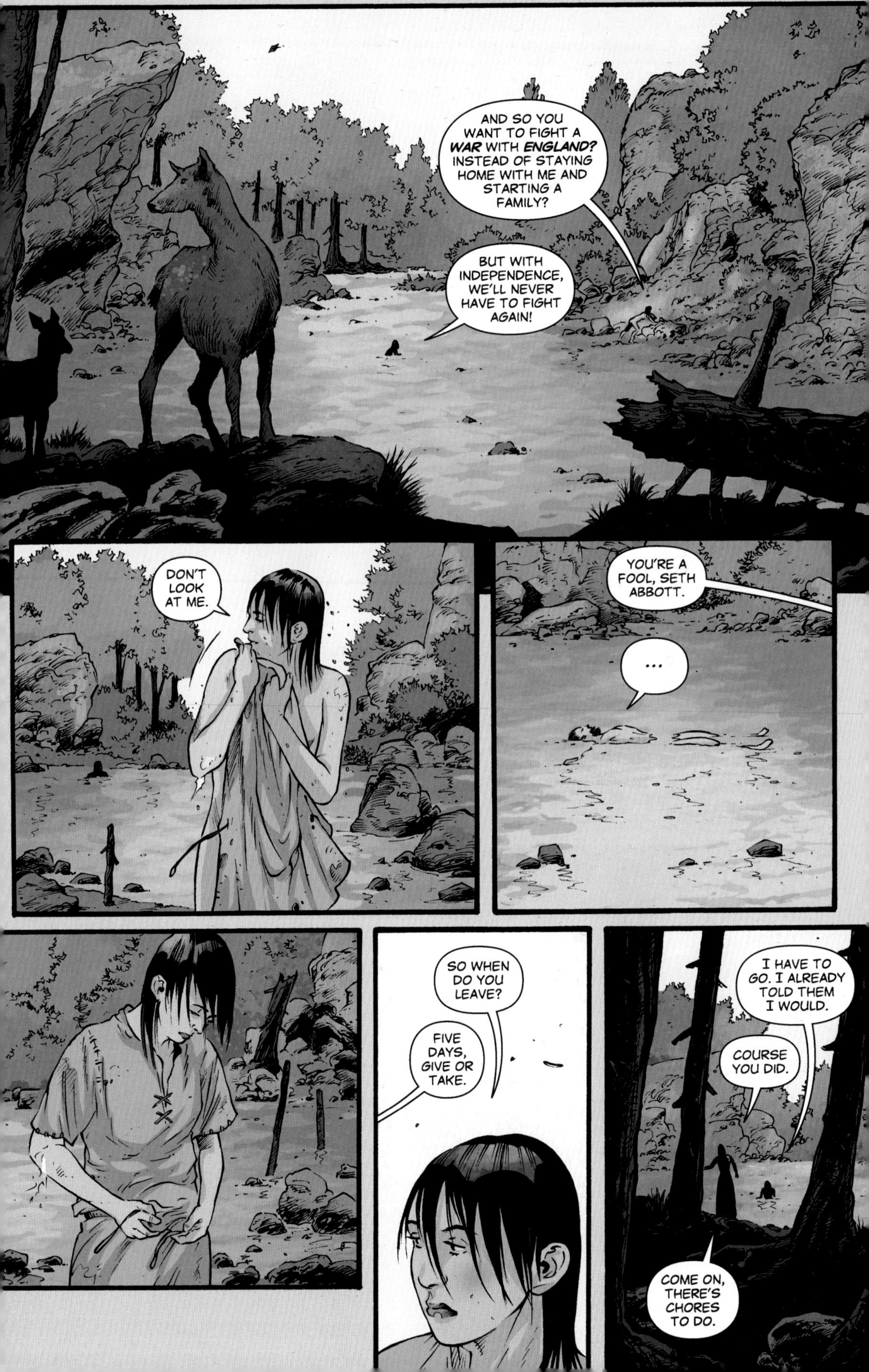
AND SO YOU WANT TO FIGHT A **WAR** WITH **ENGLAND?** INSTEAD OF STAYING HOME WITH ME AND STARTING A FAMILY?
BUT WITH INDEPENDENCE, WE'LL NEVER HAVE TO FIGHT AGAIN!
DON'T LOOK AT ME.
YOU'RE A FOOL, SETH ABBOTT.
...
SO WHEN DO YOU LEAVE?
FIVE DAYS, GIVE OR TAKE.
I HAVE TO GO. I ALREADY TOLD THEM I WOULD.
COURSE YOU DID.
COME ON, THERE'S CHORES TO DO.

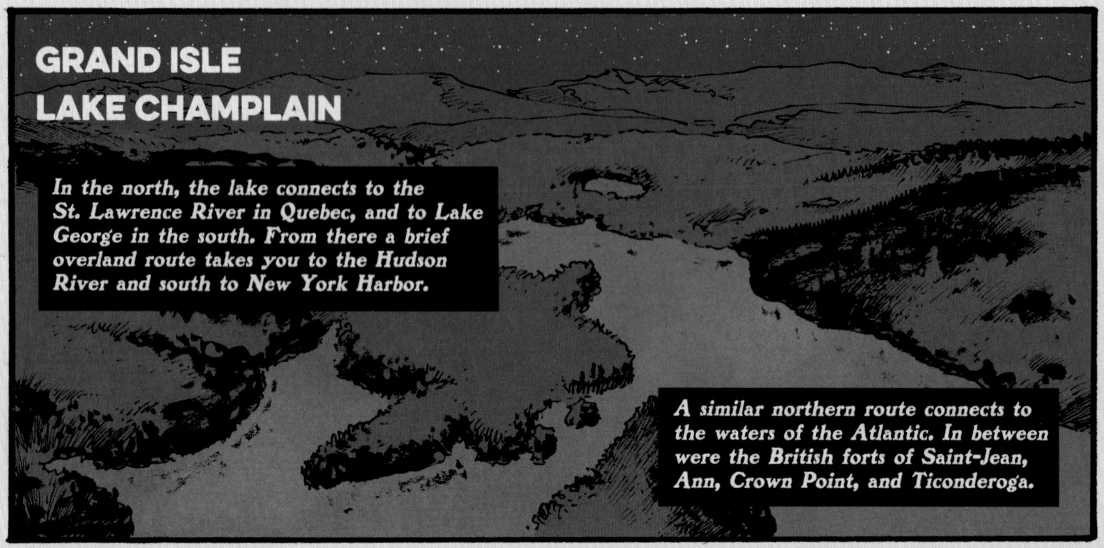
GRAND ISLE
LAKE CHAMPLAIN
In the north, the lake connects to the St. Lawrence River in Quebec, and to Lake George in the south. From there a brief overland route takes you to the Hudson River and south to New York Harbor.
A similar northern route connects to the waters of the Atlantic. In between were the British forts of Saint-Jean, Ann, Crown Point, and Ticonderoga.

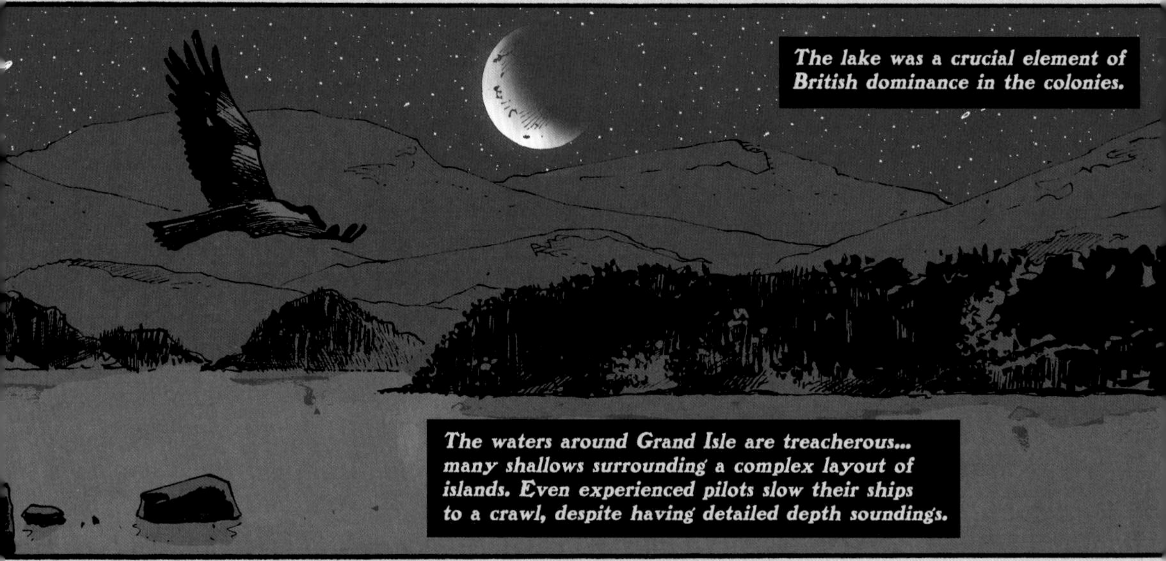
The lake was a crucial element of British dominance in the colonies.
The waters around Grand Isle are treacherous... many shallows surrounding a complex layout of islands. Even experienced pilots slow their ships to a crawl, despite having detailed depth soundings.

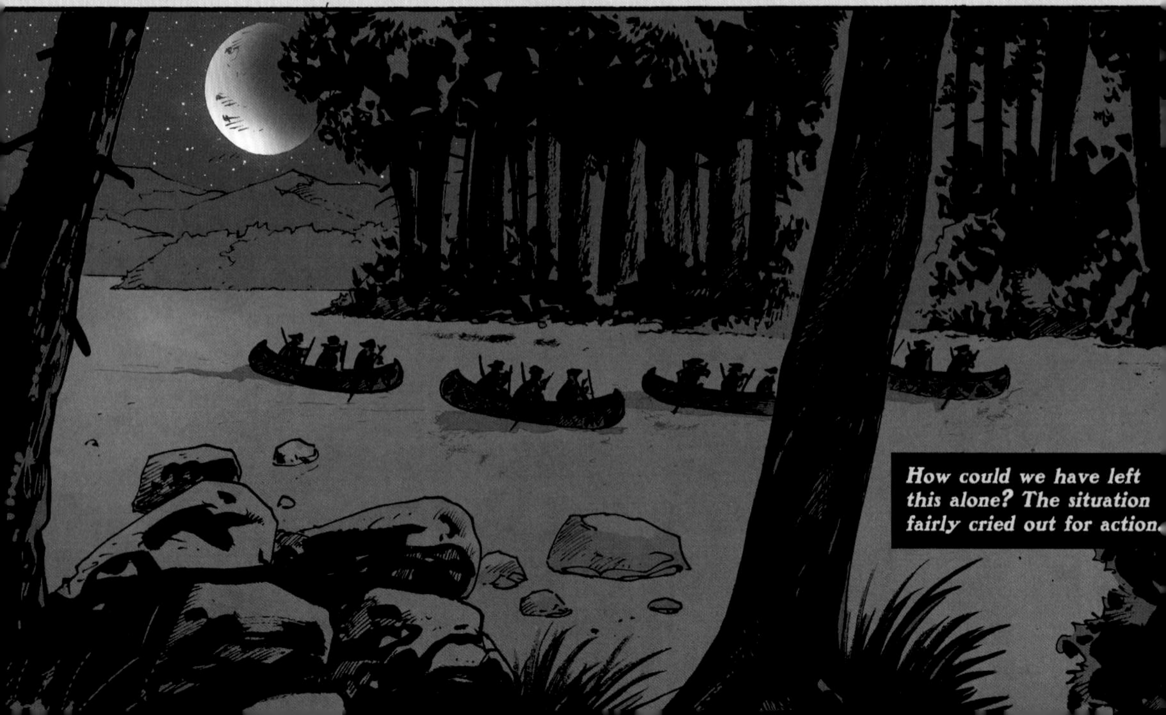
How could we have left this alone? The situation fairly cried out for action.

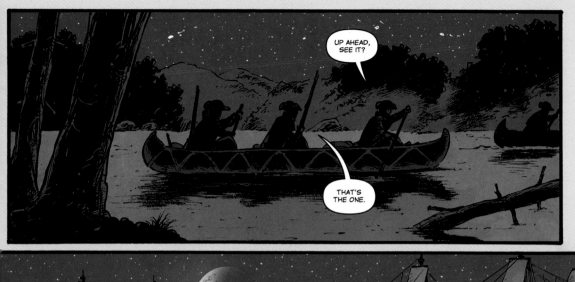

UP AHEAD, SEE IT?

THAT'S THE ONE.

THE ESCORTS'RE BRIT KETCHES, LIKELY TO HAVE A HALF DOZEN LOBSTERS ABOARD, AND FOUR SIX-POUND GUNS. FAST BUGGERS, MORE THAN A LITTLE BIT LETHAL.

Our target was the barge. Those granite blocks were headed south to reinforce existing positions, and, based on the letters I swiped off that officer...

...to build a new fort planned for just south of the Narrows, at Button Mould Bay.

OUR CHIEF CONCERN IS THAT BARGE. WE'LL MEET IT AT TWO BROTHERS AND SINK IT THERE.

THAT AND A COUPLE WELL-PLACED CANNON AT THE HEAD WILL ISOLATE THE FORTS DOWN SOUTH. GENERAL WASHINGTON AND THE ARMY CAN TAKE CARE OF THE HUDSON.

SETH, ADJUST A FEW POINTS TO THE RIGHT.

WE SHOULD WATCH FOR SHARP-SHOOTERS.

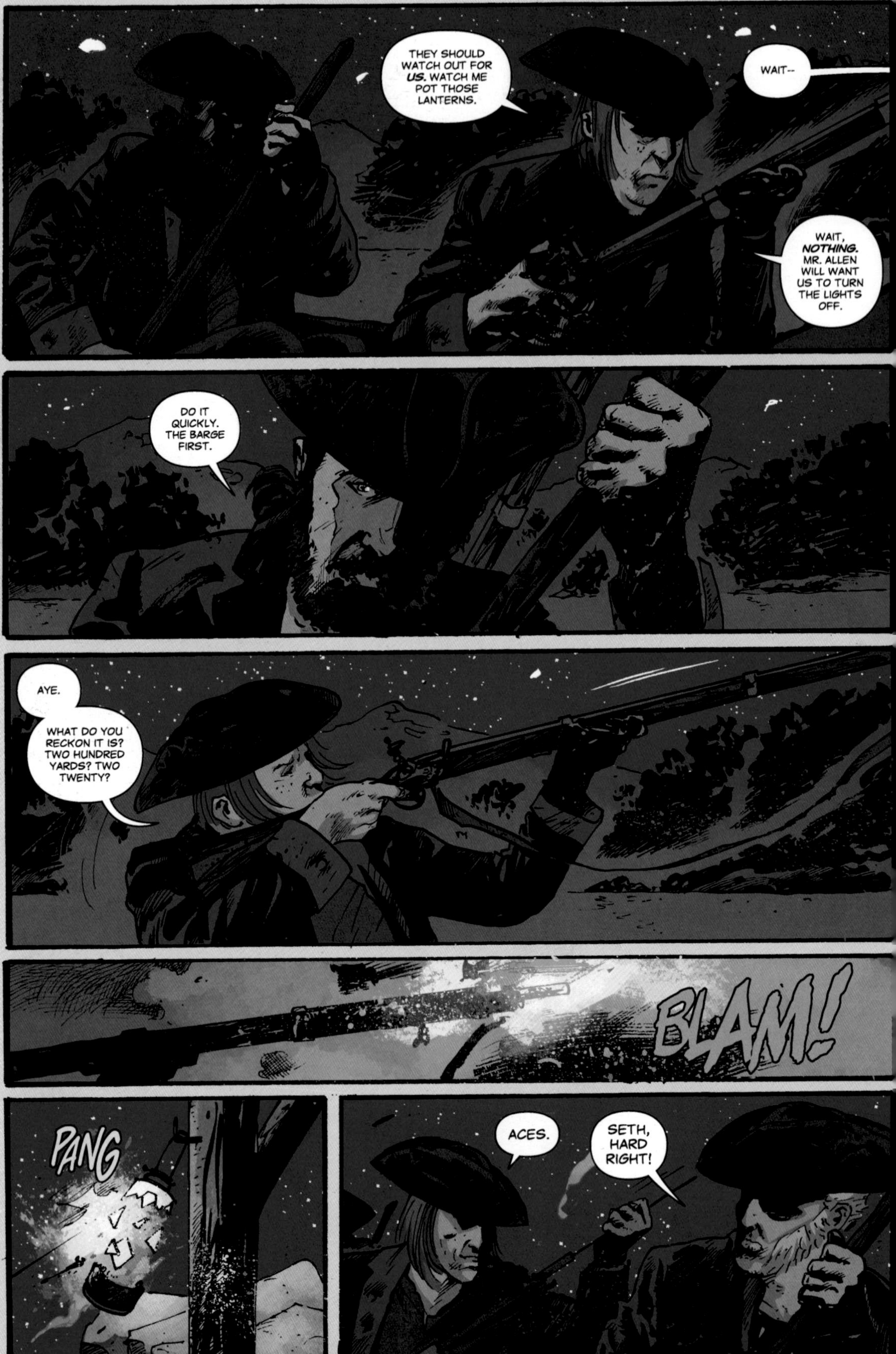
THEY SHOULD WATCH OUT FOR *US.* WATCH ME POT THOSE LANTERNS.
WAIT--
WAIT, *NOTHING.* MR. ALLEN WILL WANT US TO TURN THE LIGHTS OFF.
DO IT QUICKLY. THE BARGE FIRST.
AYE.
WHAT DO YOU RECKON IT IS? TWO HUNDRED YARDS? TWO TWENTY?
BLAM!
PANG
ACES.
SETH, HARD RIGHT!

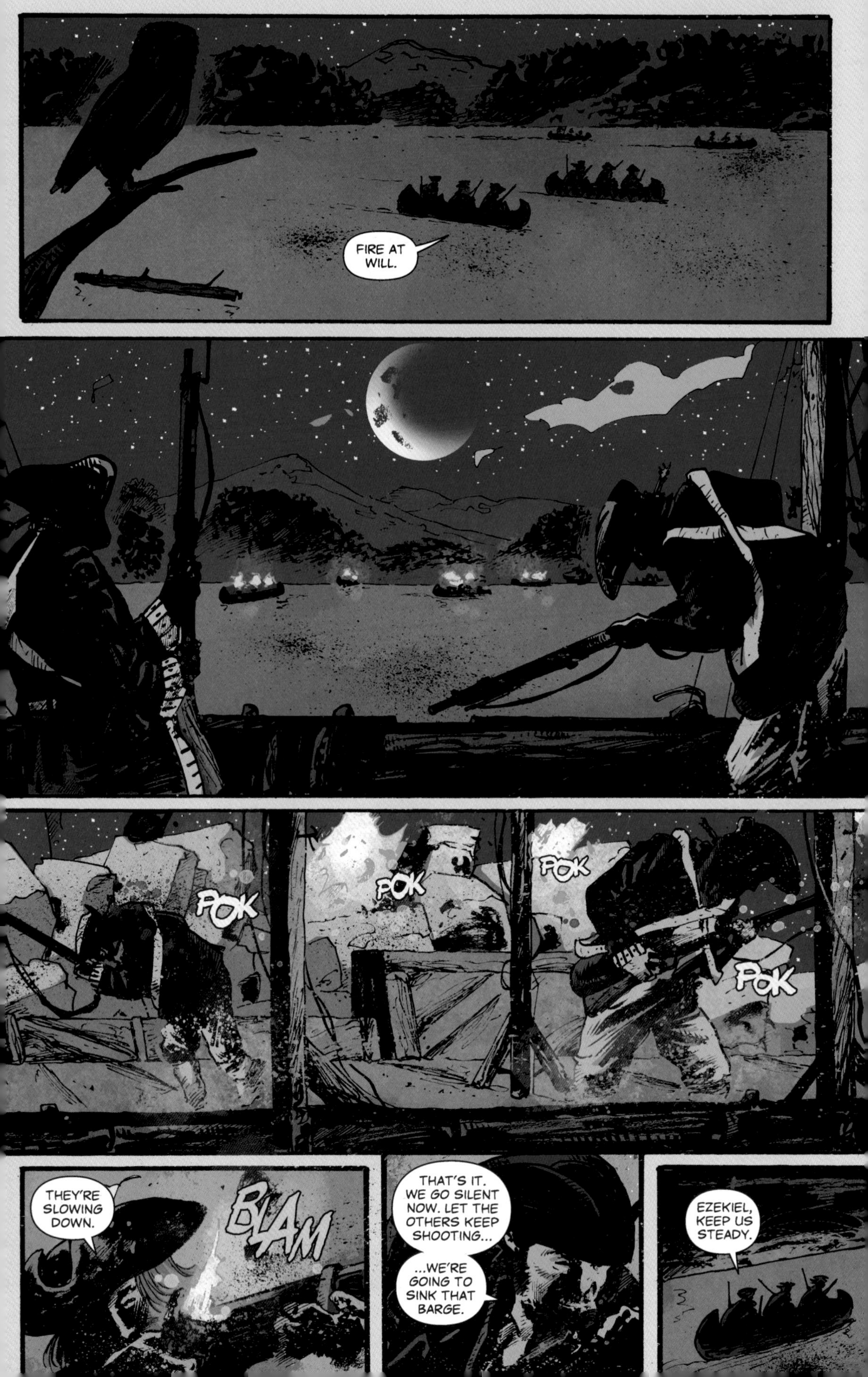

FIRE AT WILL.
POK
POK
POK
POK
THEY'RE SLOWING DOWN.
BLAM
THAT'S IT. WE GO SILENT NOW. LET THE OTHERS KEEP SHOOTING...
...WE'RE GOING TO SINK THAT BARGE.
EZEKIEL, KEEP US STEADY.

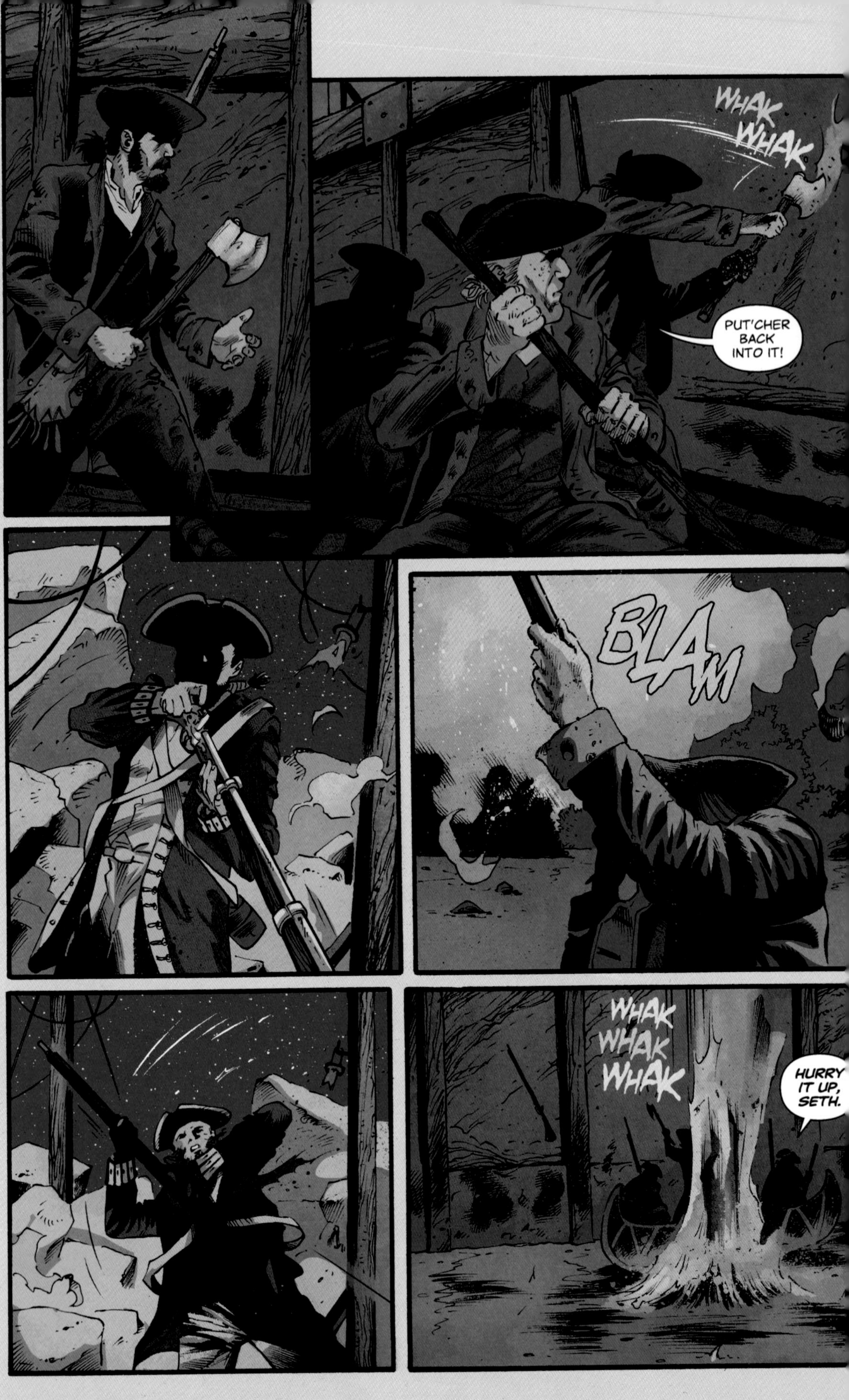
WHAK
WHAK
PUT'CHER BACK INTO IT!
BLAM
WHAK
WHAK
WHAK
HURRY IT UP, SETH.

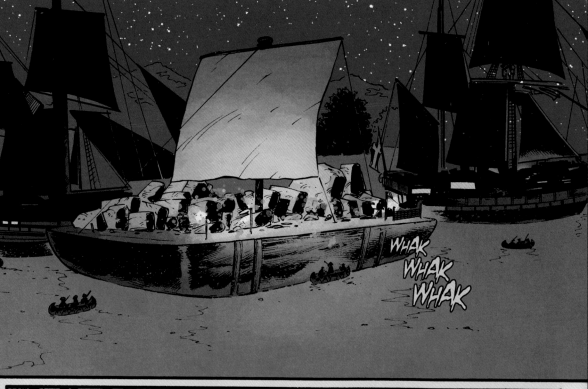

WHAK
WHAK
WHAK

AT THE WATER LINE NOW. SHE'S TAKING IN WATER, BUT NOT FAST ENOUGH.

WHAK

WE'RE COMPLETELY EXPOSED...

OH NO.

BOOM

VVNHHHKKK!

SPLLLLIISSSH

MOTHER OF GOD!

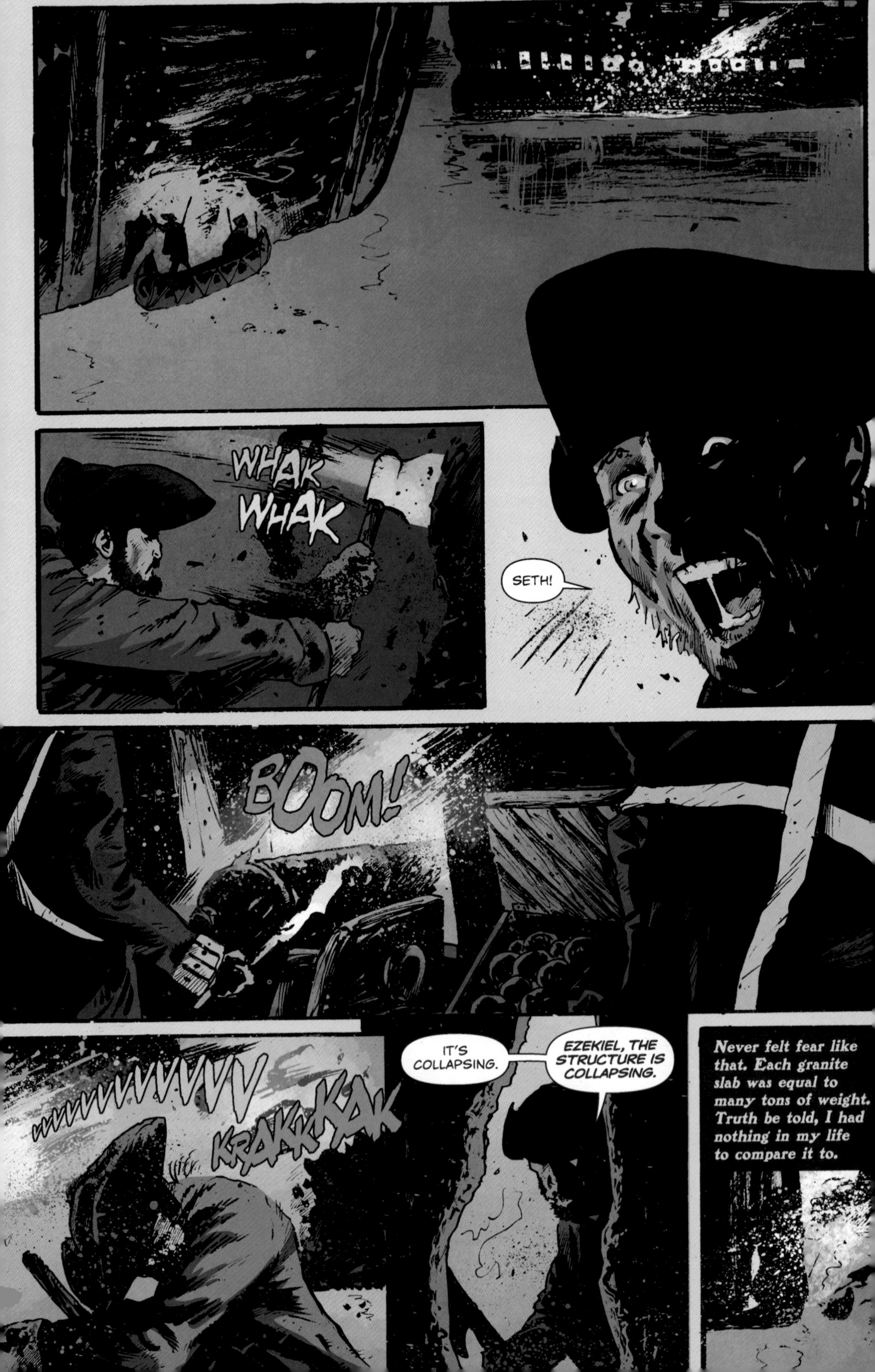
WHAK
WHAK
SETH!
BOOM!
VVVVVVVVVVVV
KRAKKKAK
IT'S COLLAPSING.
EZEKIEL, THE STRUCTURE IS COLLAPSING.
Never felt fear like that. Each granite slab was equal to many tons of weight. Truth be told, I had nothing in my life to compare it to.

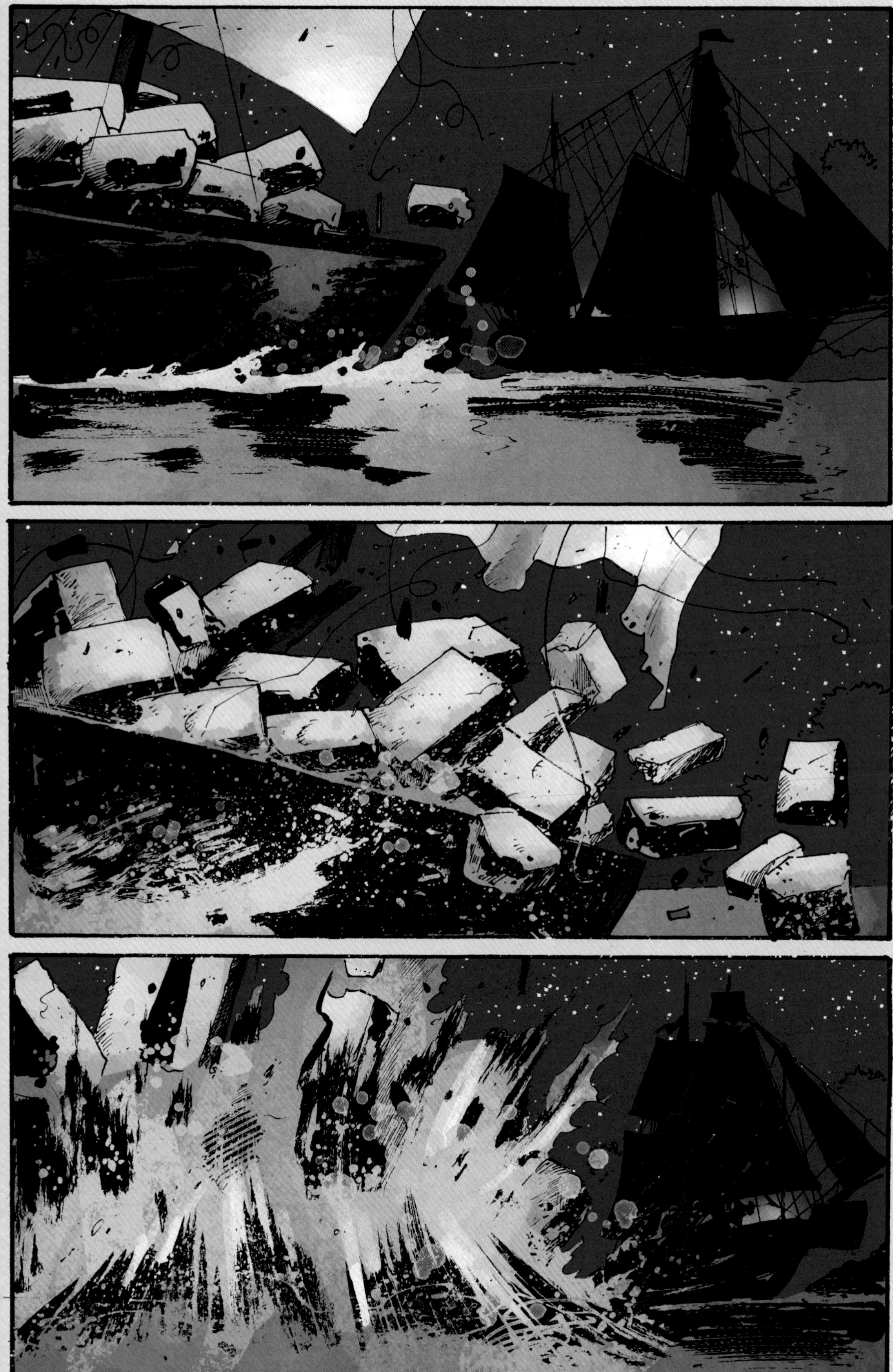

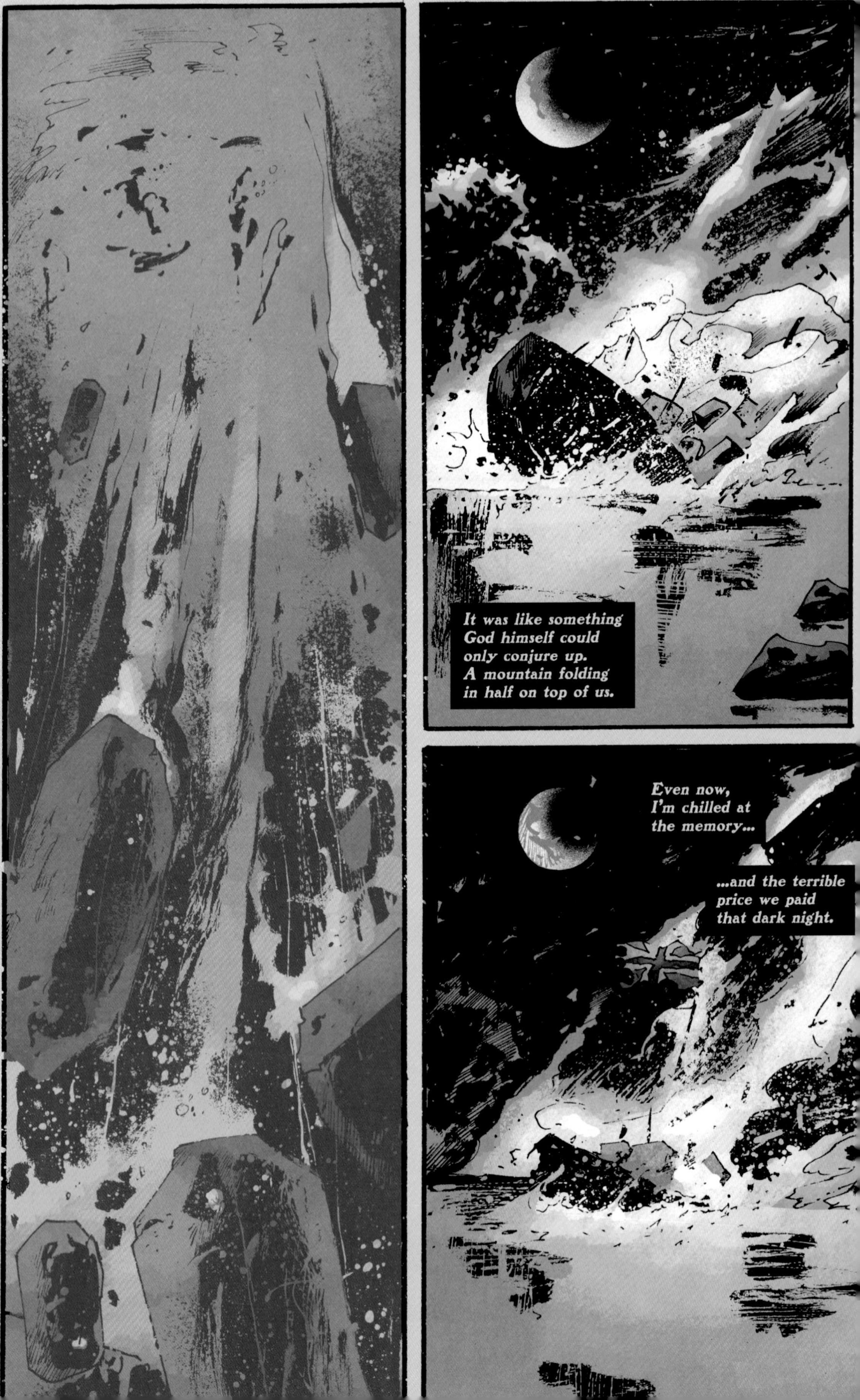
It was like something God himself could only conjure up. A mountain folding in half on top of us.
Even now, I'm chilled at the memory...
...and the terrible price we paid that dark night.

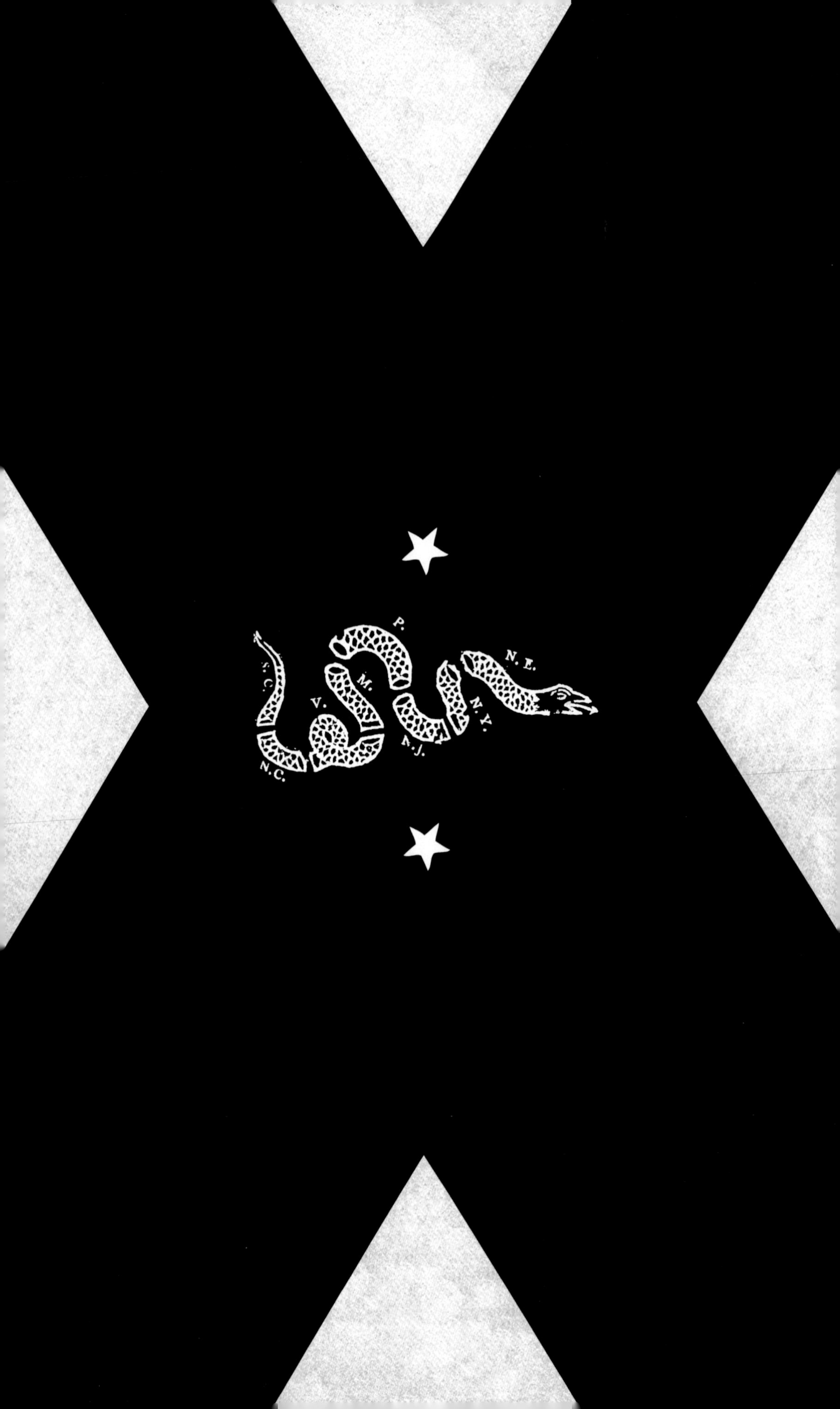

P.
N. E.
S. C.
M.
V.
N. Y.
N. J.
N. C.

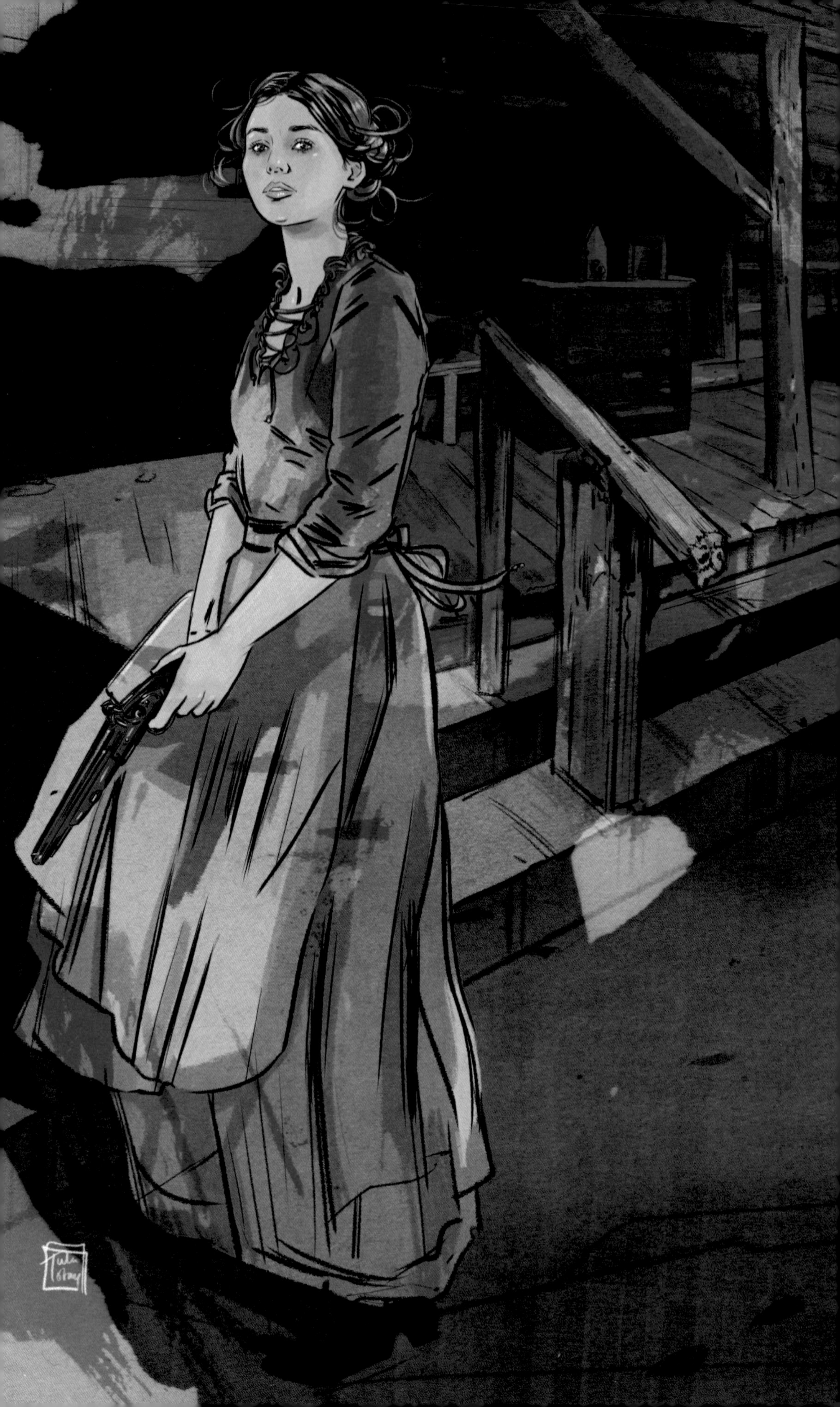

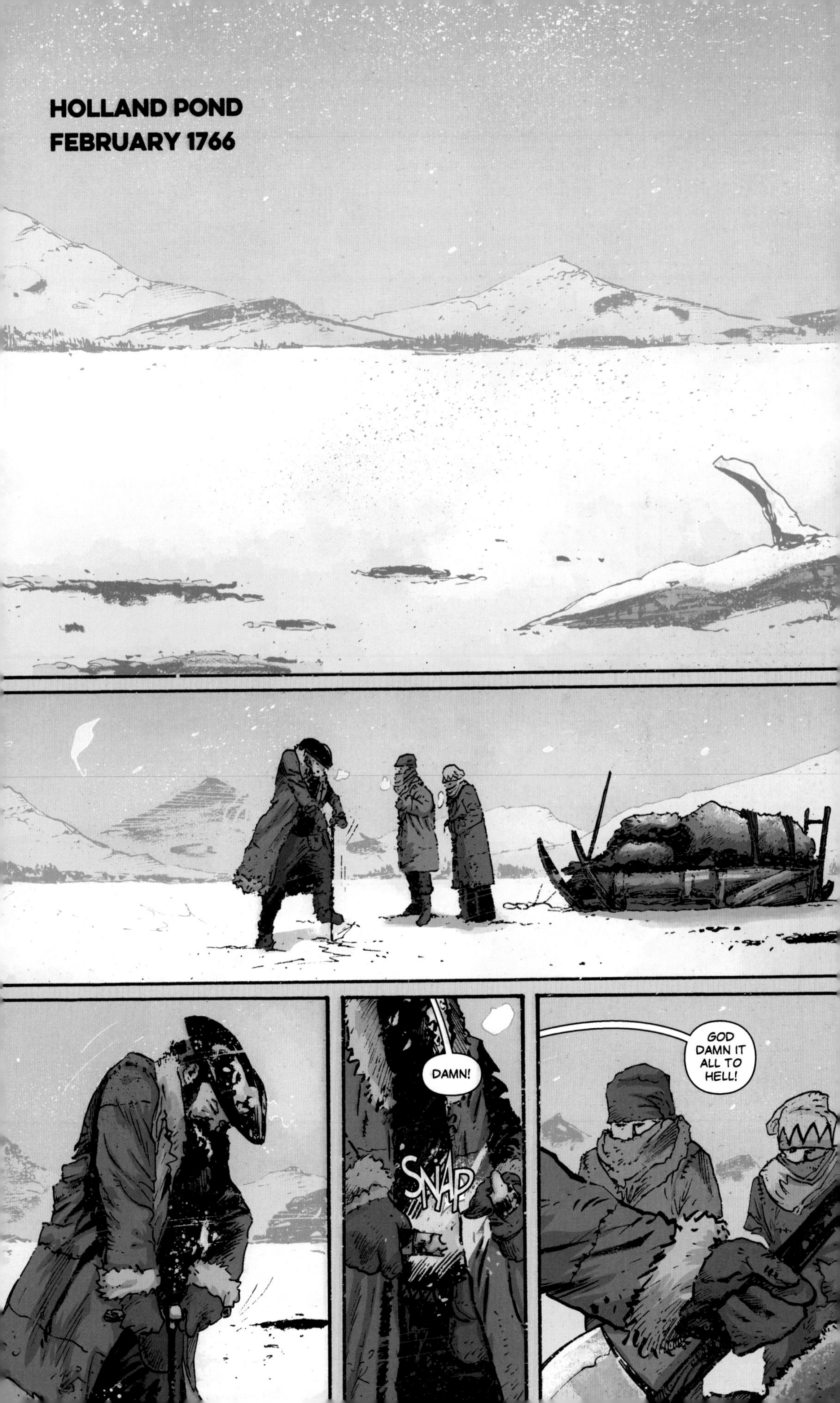
HOLLAND POND
FEBRUARY 1766
DAMN!
SNAP
GOD DAMN IT ALL TO HELL!

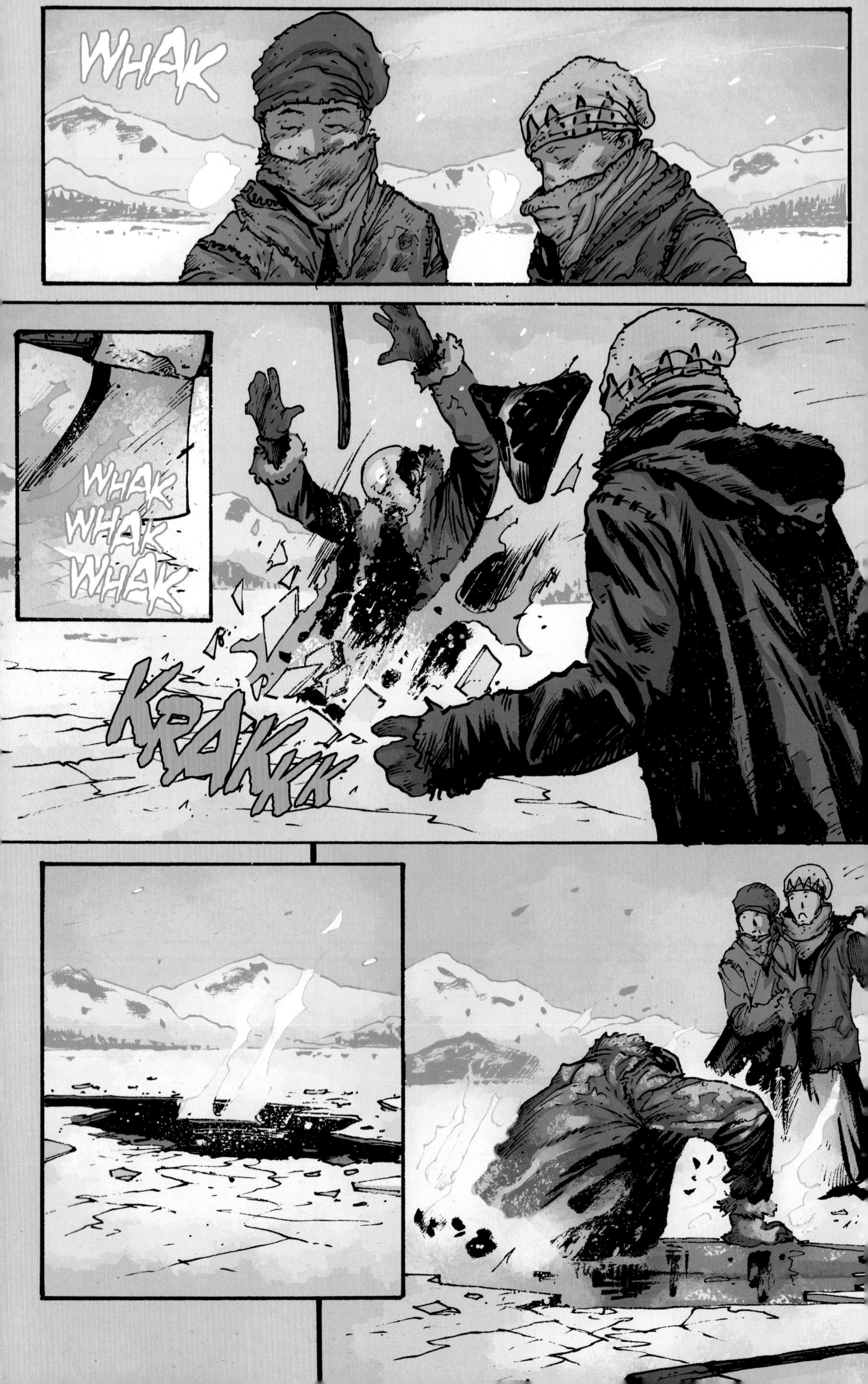
WHAK
WHAK
WHAK
WHAK
KRAKKK

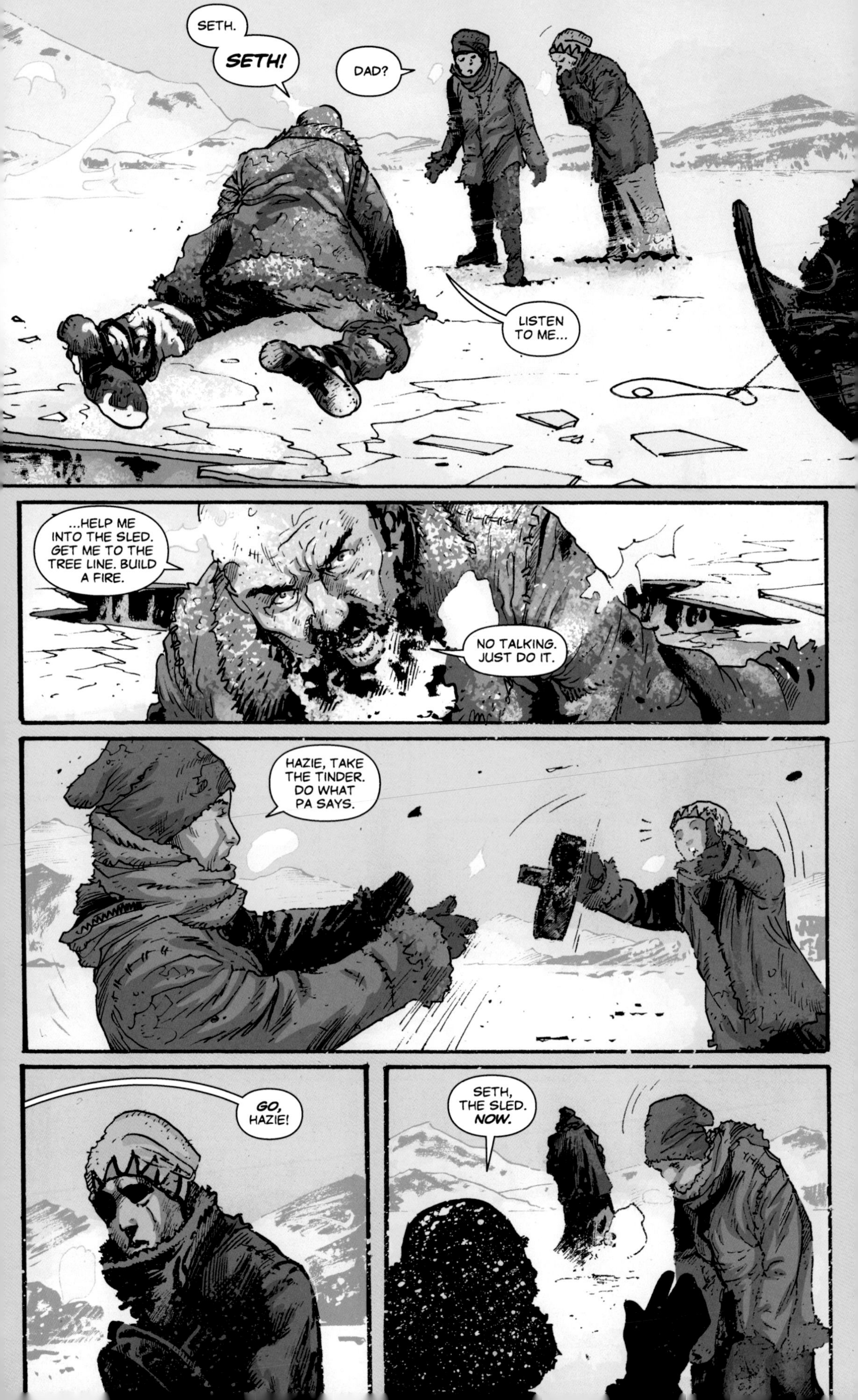
SETH.
SETH!
DAD?
LISTEN TO ME...
...HELP ME INTO THE SLED. GET ME TO THE TREE LINE. BUILD A FIRE.
NO TALKING. JUST DO IT.
HAZIE, TAKE THE TINDER. DO WHAT PA SAYS.
GO, HAZIE!
SETH, THE SLED. NOW.

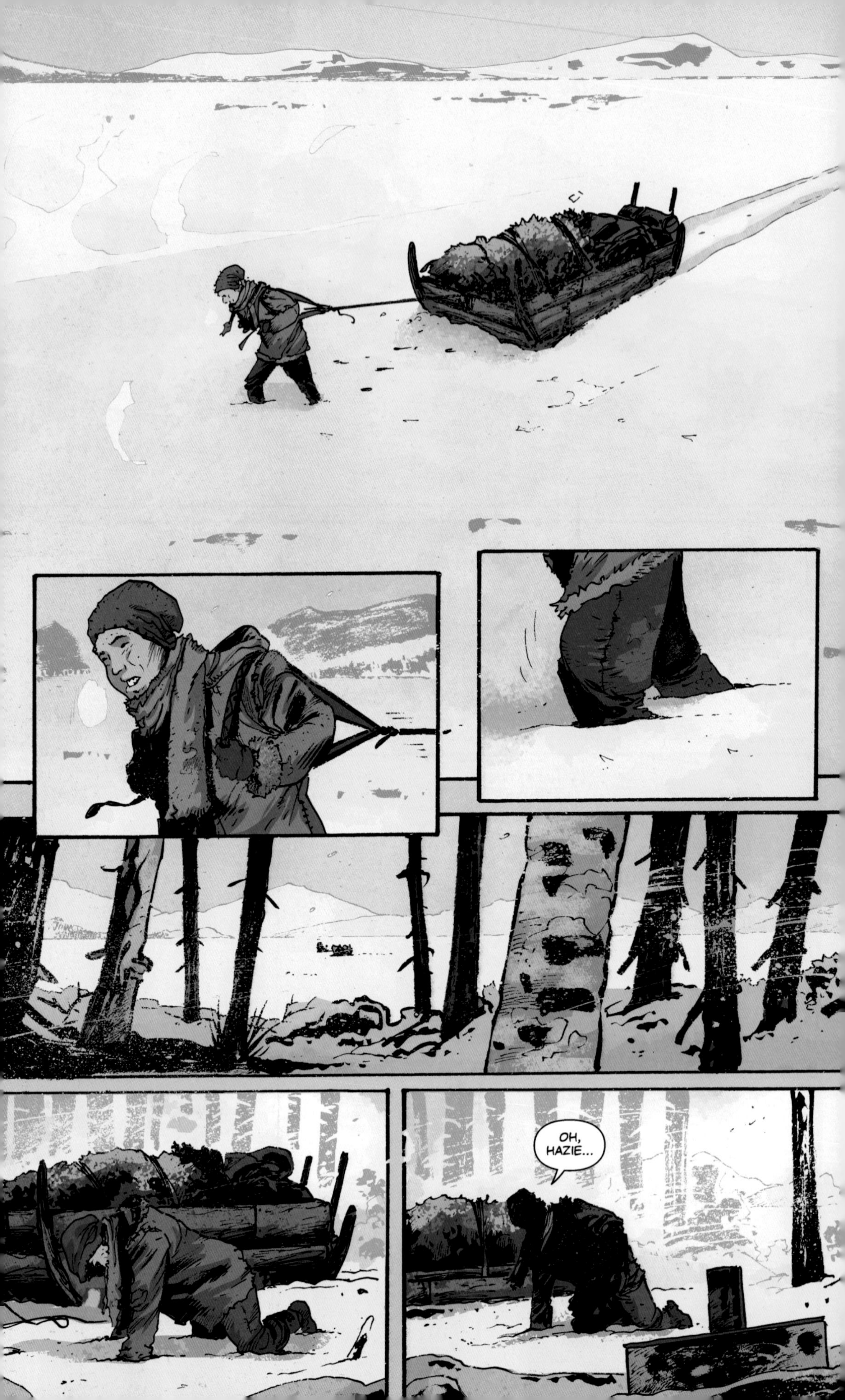
OH, HAZIE...

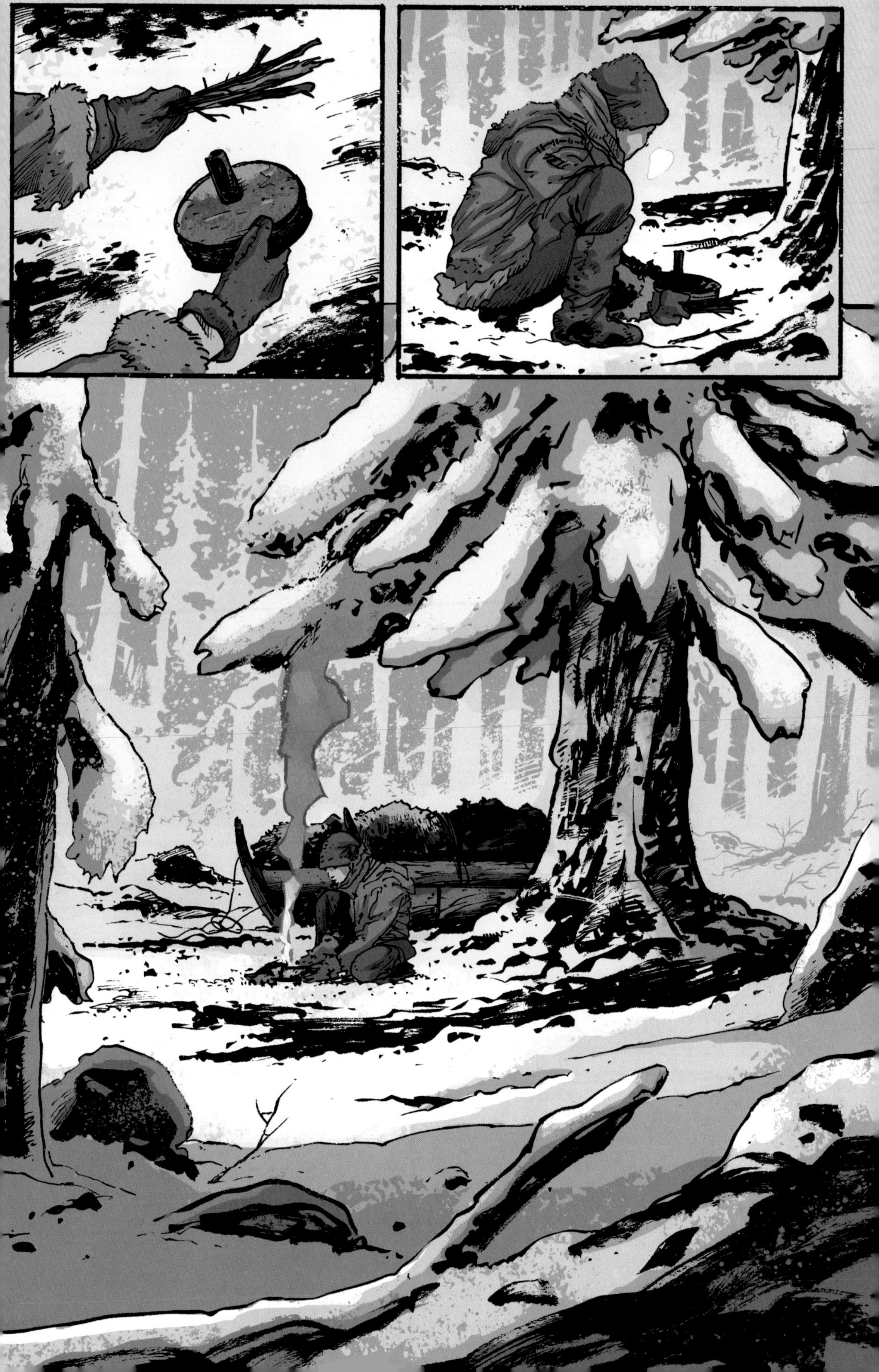

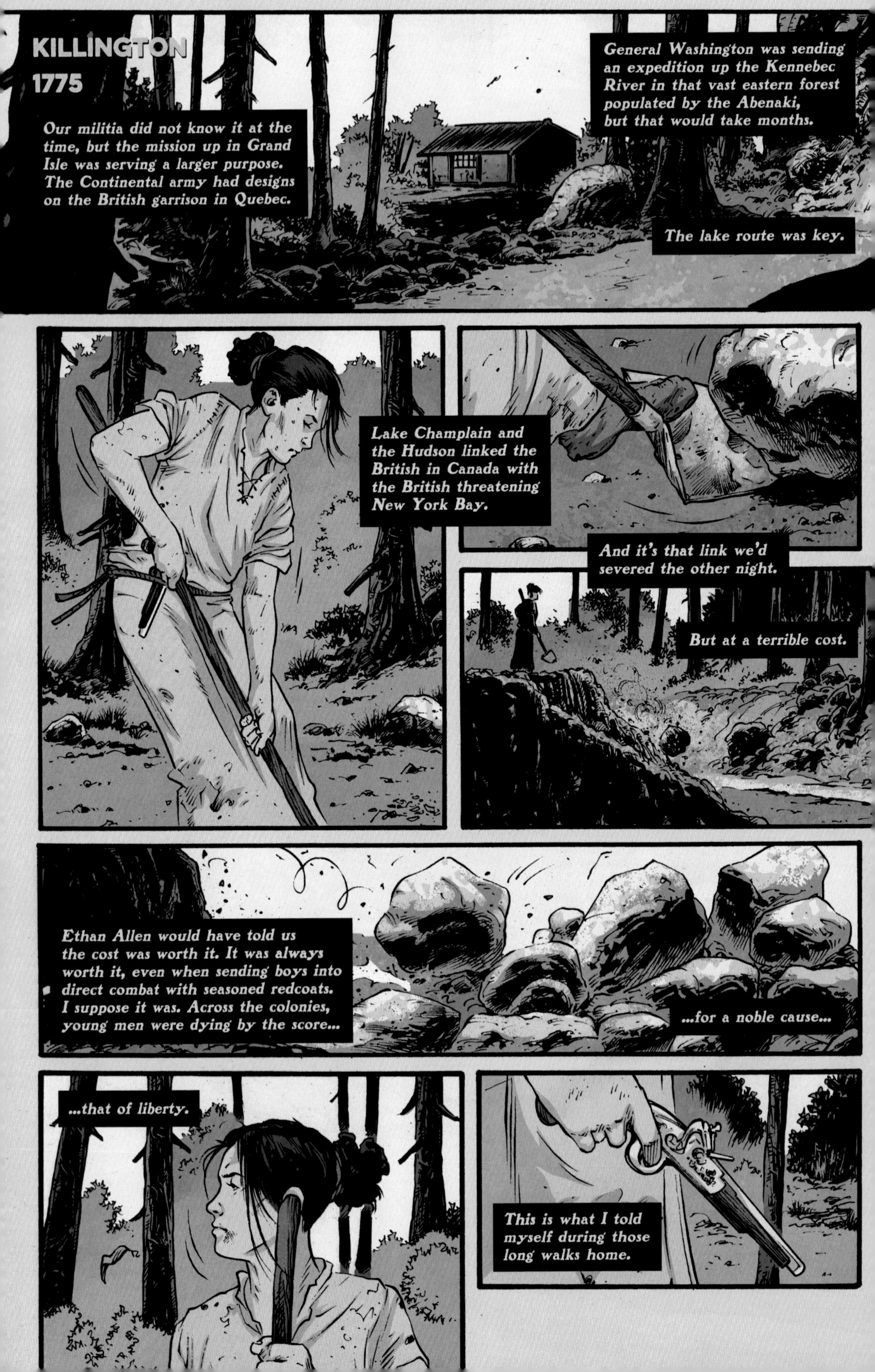
KILLINGTON
1775
Our militia did not know it at the time, but the mission up in Grand Isle was serving a larger purpose. The Continental army had designs on the British garrison in Quebec.
General Washington was sending an expedition up the Kennebec River in that vast eastern forest populated by the Abenaki, but that would take months.
The lake route was key.
Lake Champlain and the Hudson linked the British in Canada with the British threatening New York Bay.
And it's that link we'd severed the other night.
But at a terrible cost.
Ethan Allen would have told us the cost was worth it. It was always worth it, even when sending boys into direct combat with seasoned redcoats. I suppose it was. Across the colonies, young men were dying by the score...
...for a noble cause...
...that of liberty.
This is what I told myself during those long walks home.

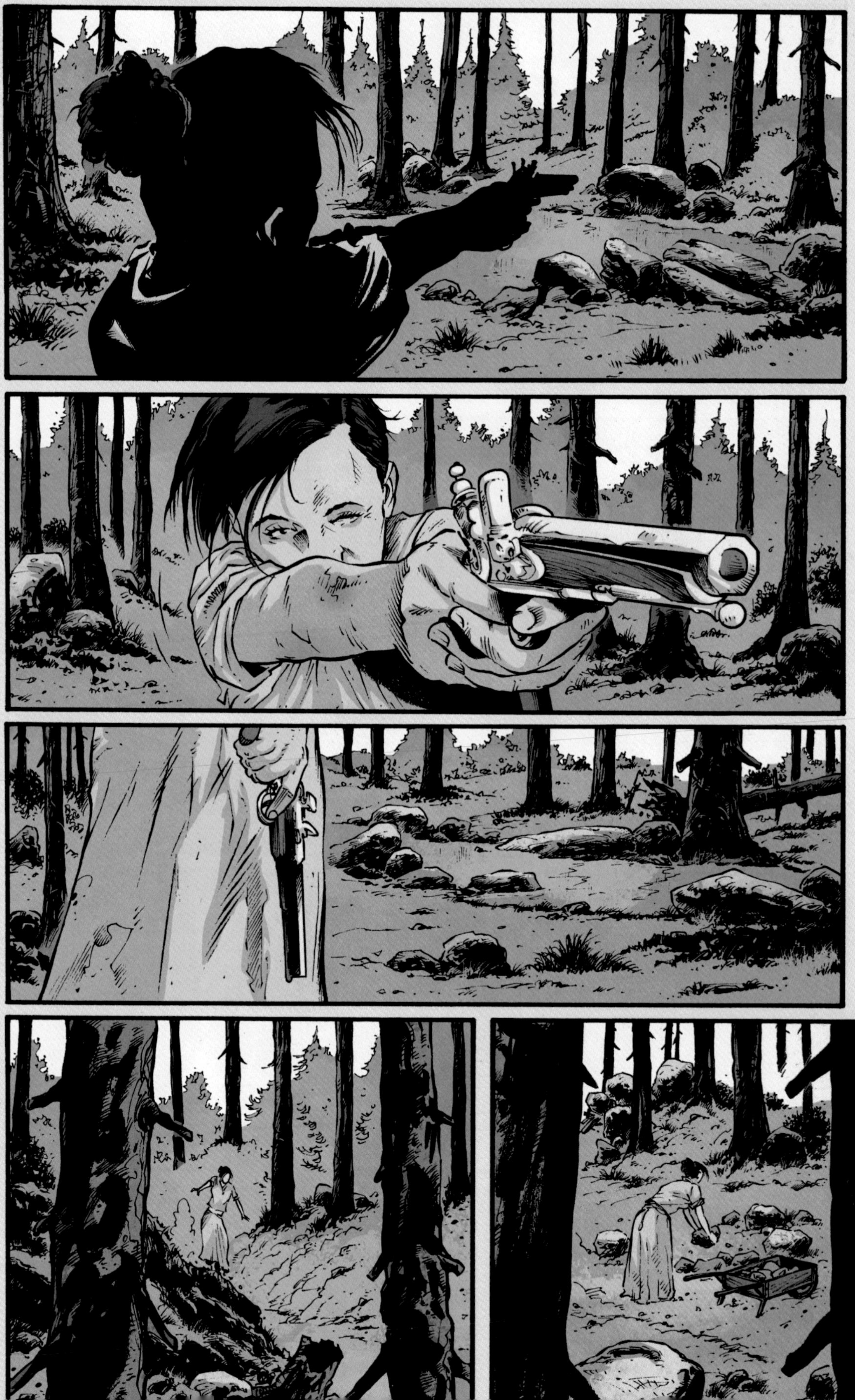

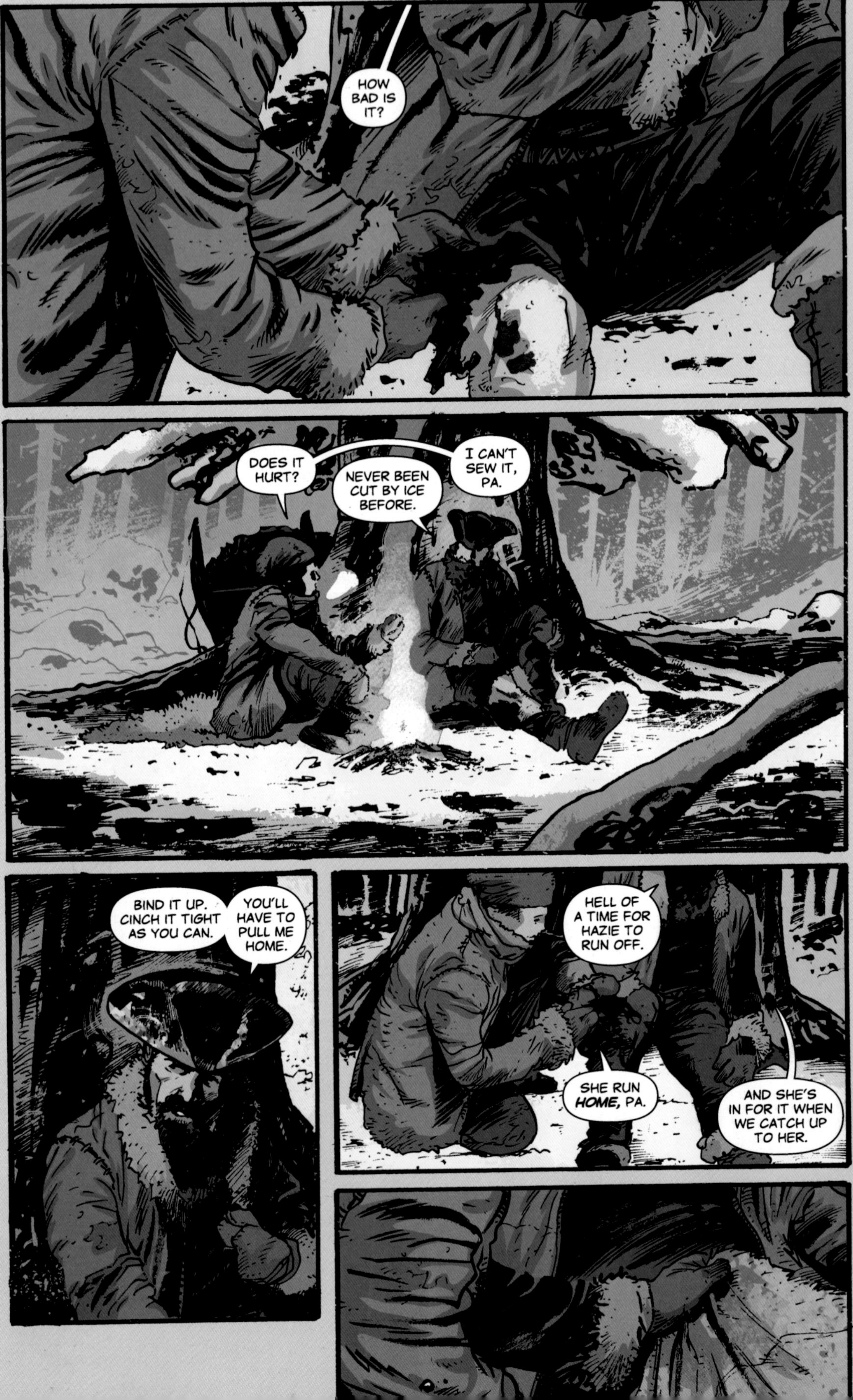

HOW BAD IS IT?
DOES IT HURT?
NEVER BEEN CUT BY ICE BEFORE.
I CAN'T SEW IT, PA.
BIND IT UP. CINCH IT TIGHT AS YOU CAN.
YOU'LL HAVE TO PULL ME HOME.
HELL OF A TIME FOR HAZIE TO RUN OFF.
SHE RUN *HOME,* PA.
AND SHE'S IN FOR IT WHEN WE CATCH UP TO HER.

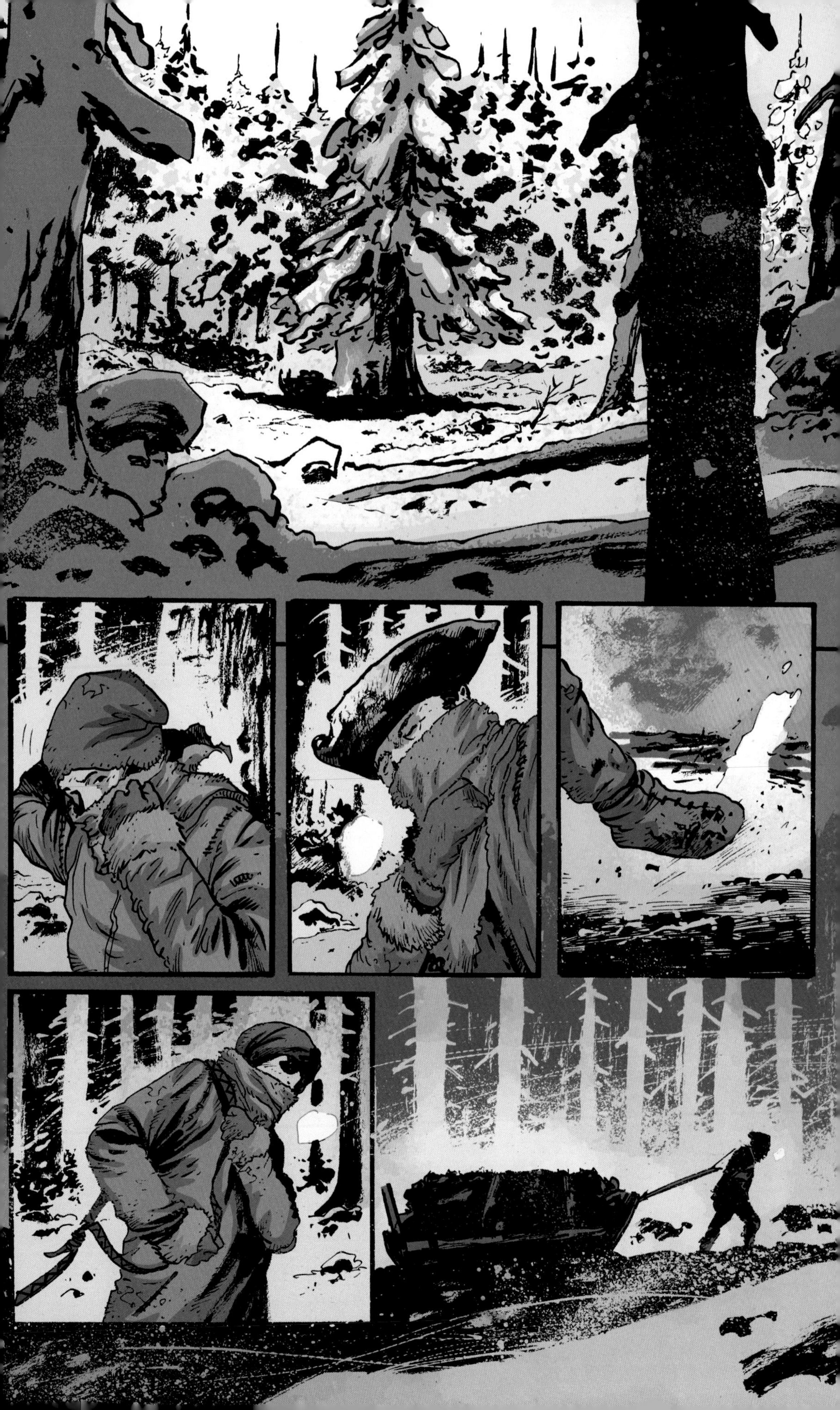

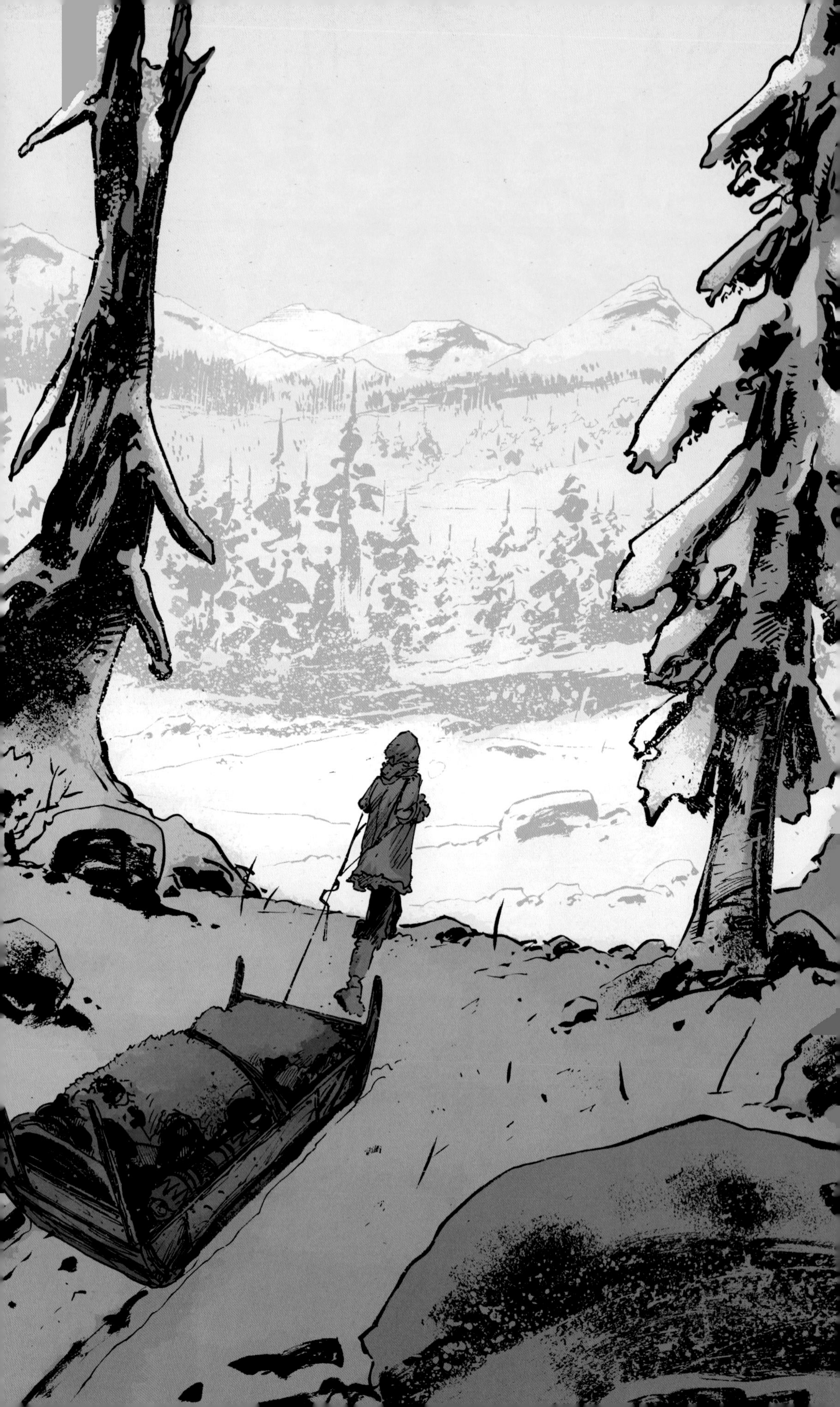

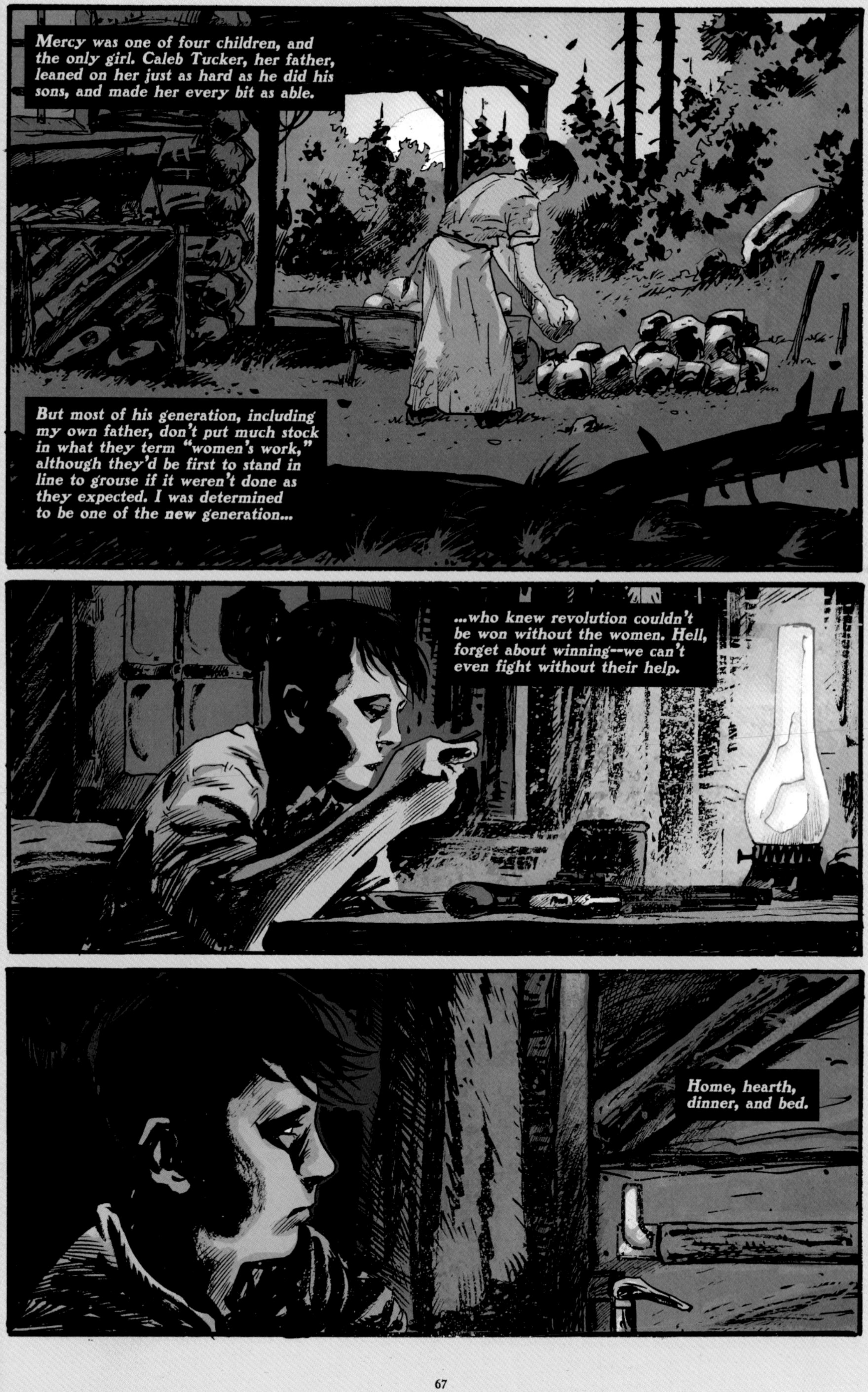
Mercy was one of four children, and the only girl. Caleb Tucker, her father, leaned on her just as hard as he did his sons, and made her every bit as able.
But most of his generation, including my own father, don't put much stock in what they term "women's work," although they'd be first to stand in line to grouse if it weren't done as they expected. I was determined to be one of the new generation...
...who knew revolution couldn't be won without the women. Hell, forget about winning--we can't even fight without their help.
Home, hearth, dinner, and bed.

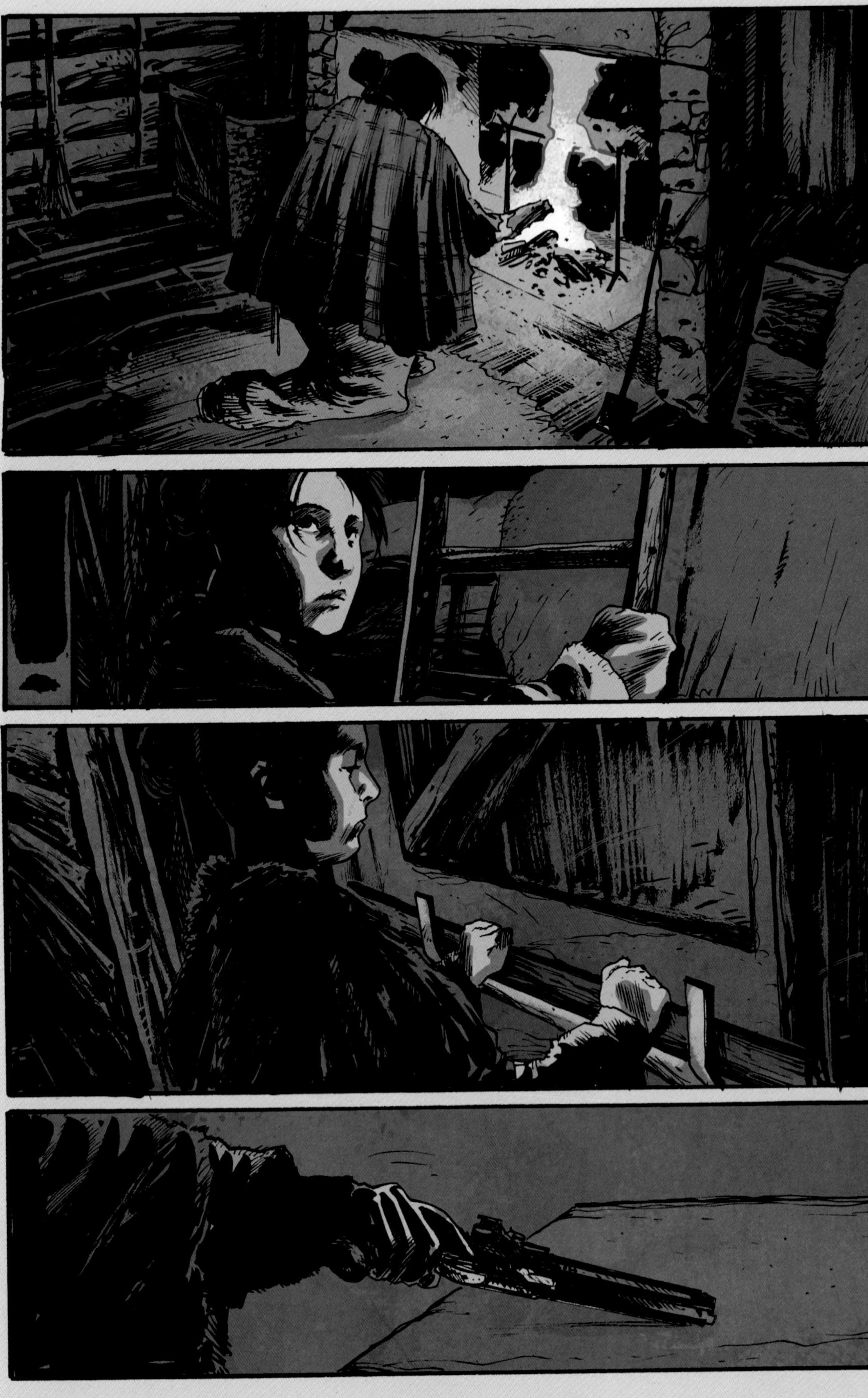

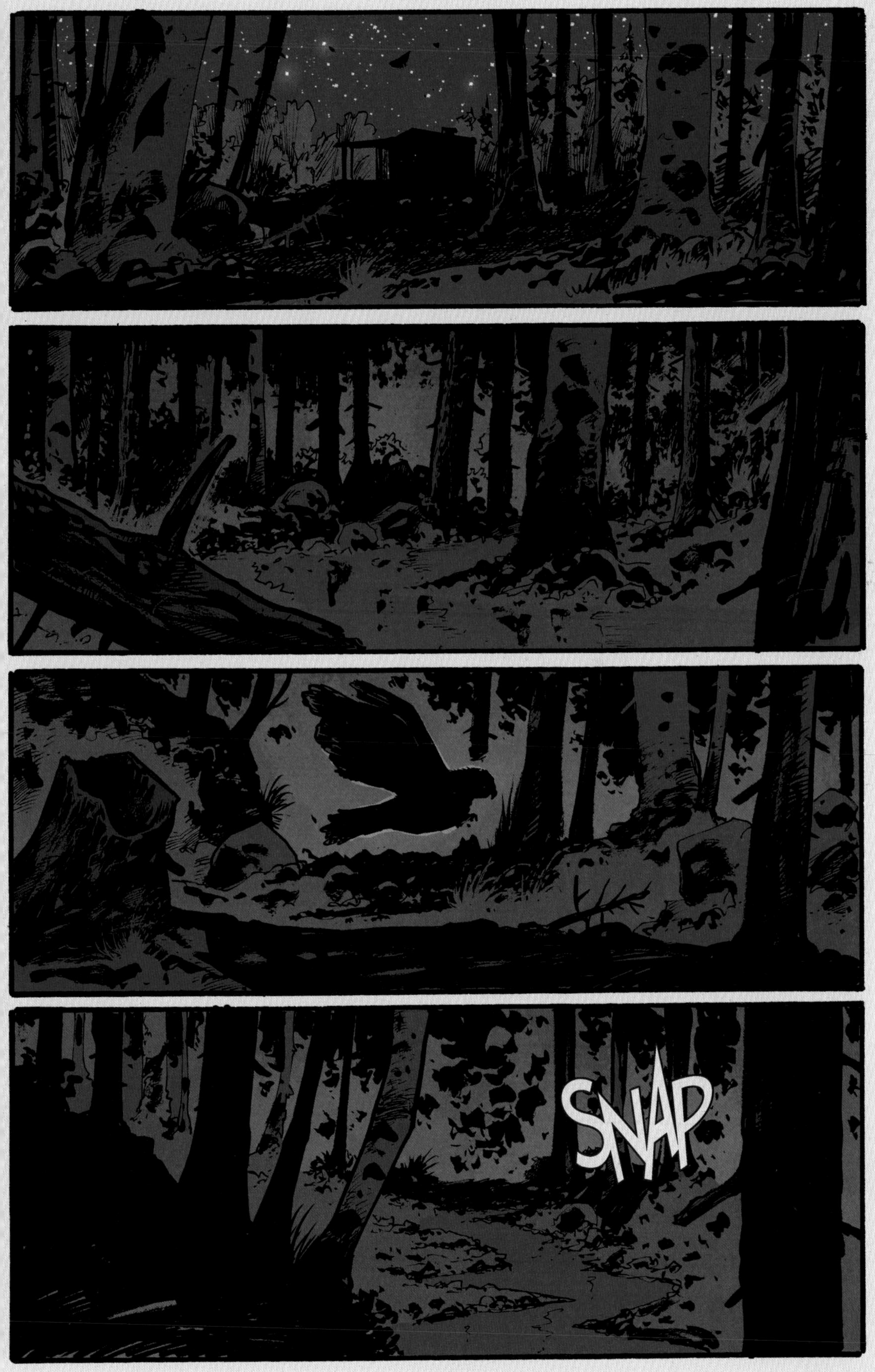
SNAP

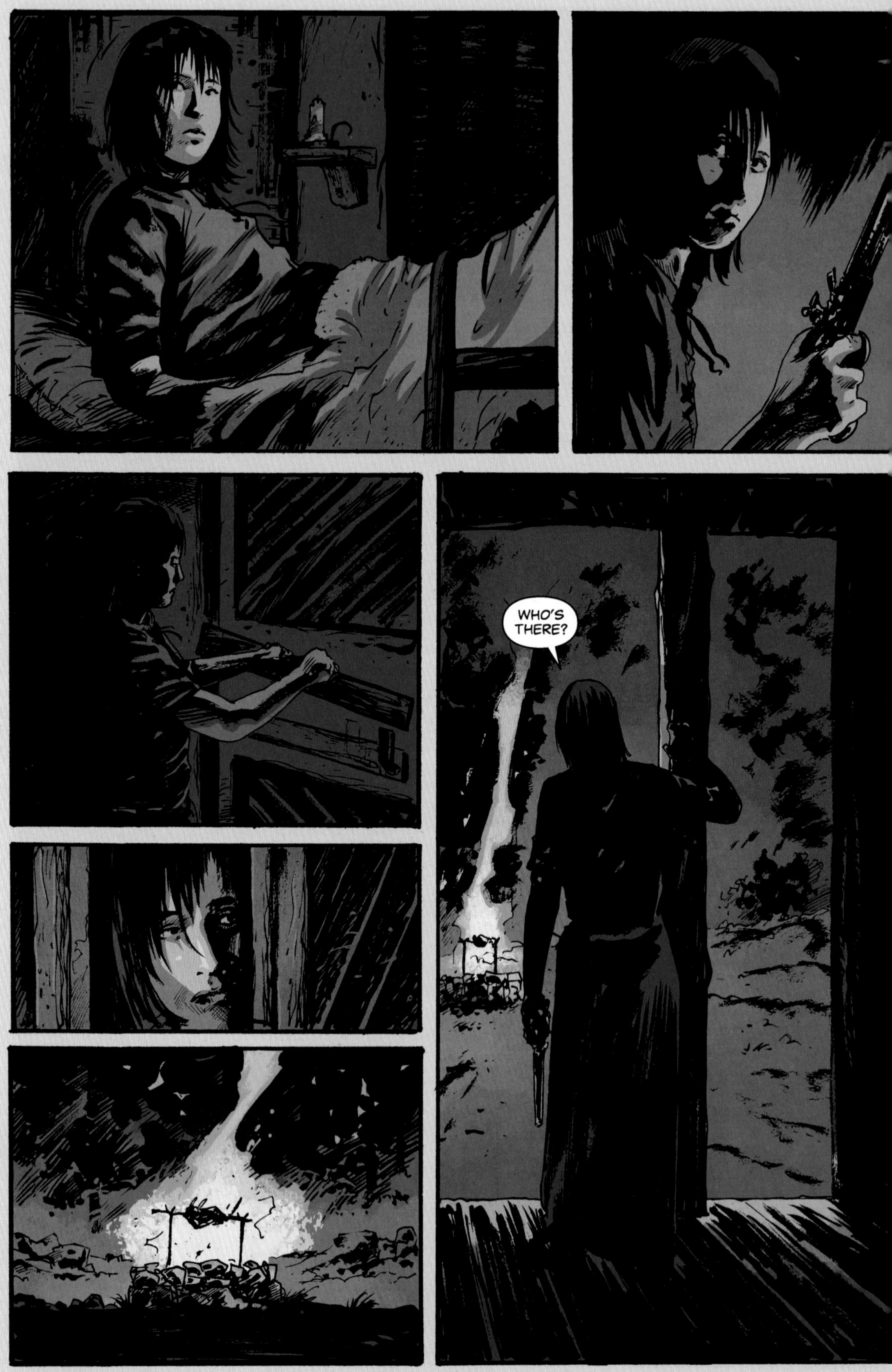
WHO'S THERE?

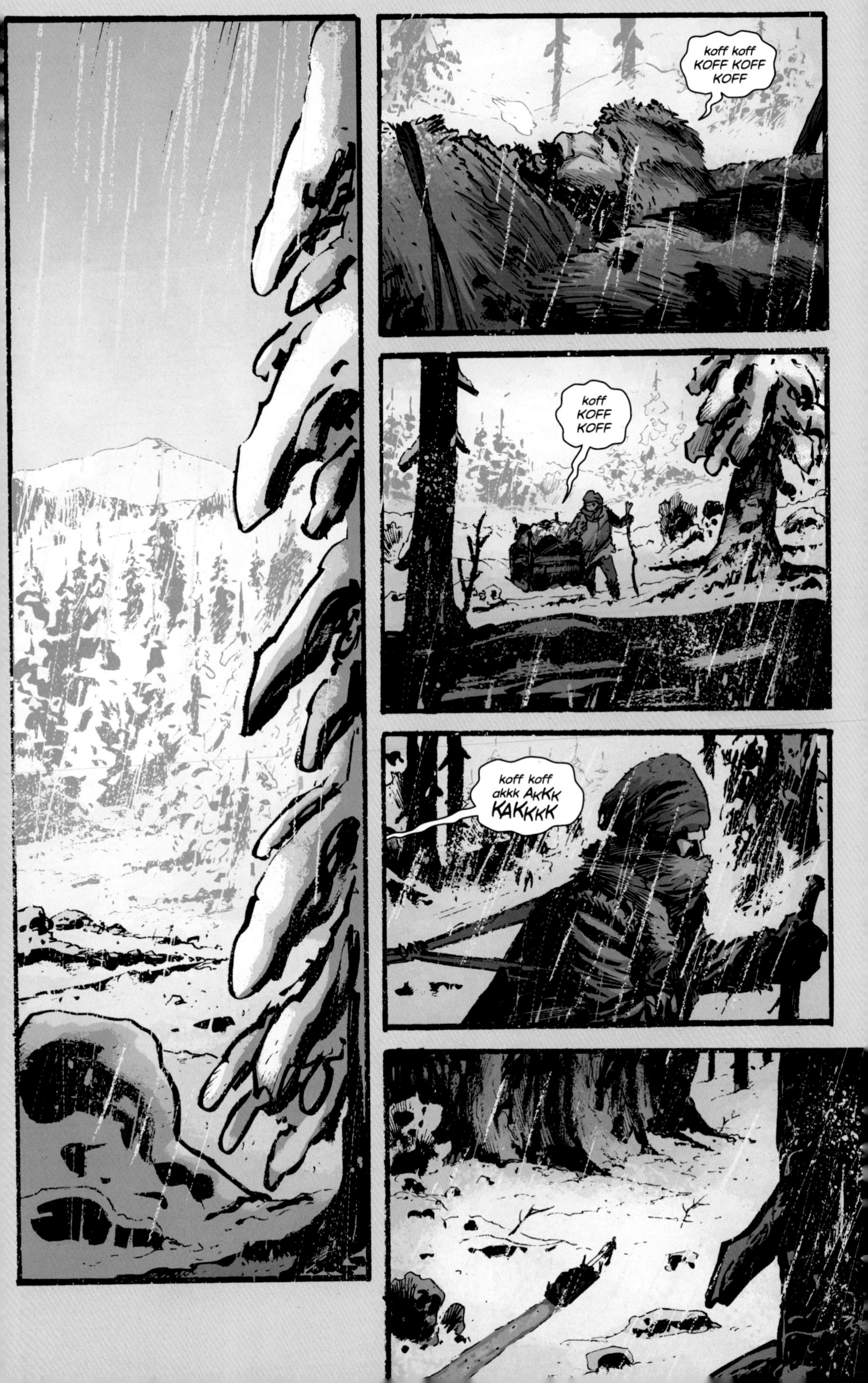
koff koff
KOFF KOFF
KOFF
koff
KOFF
KOFF
koff koff
akkk AKKk
KAKKKK

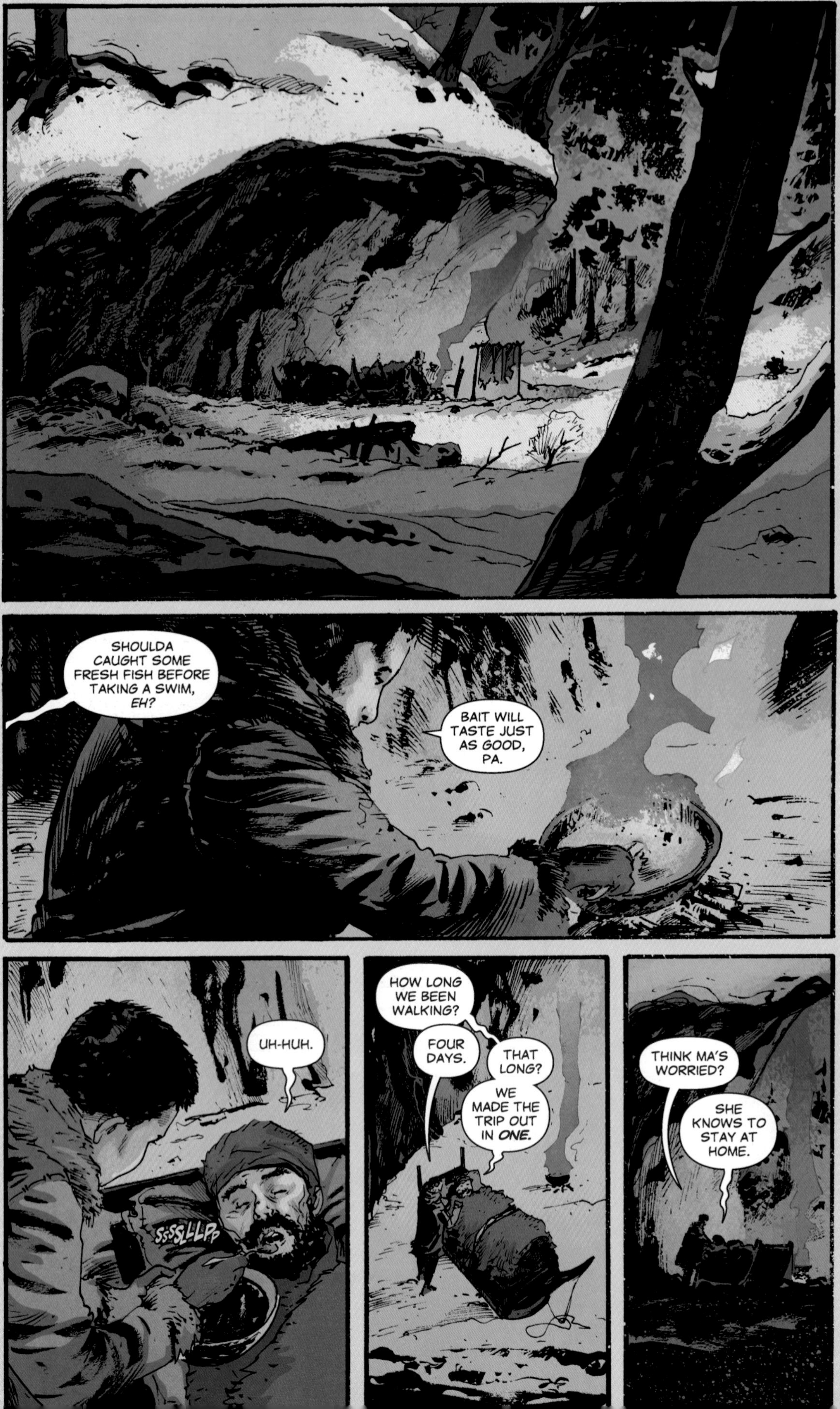
SHOULDA CAUGHT SOME FRESH FISH BEFORE TAKING A SWIM, EH?
BAIT WILL TASTE JUST AS GOOD, PA.
UH-HUH.
SSSSLLLPP
HOW LONG WE BEEN WALKING?
FOUR DAYS.
THAT LONG?
WE MADE THE TRIP OUT IN ONE.
THINK MA'S WORRIED?
SHE KNOWS TO STAY AT HOME.

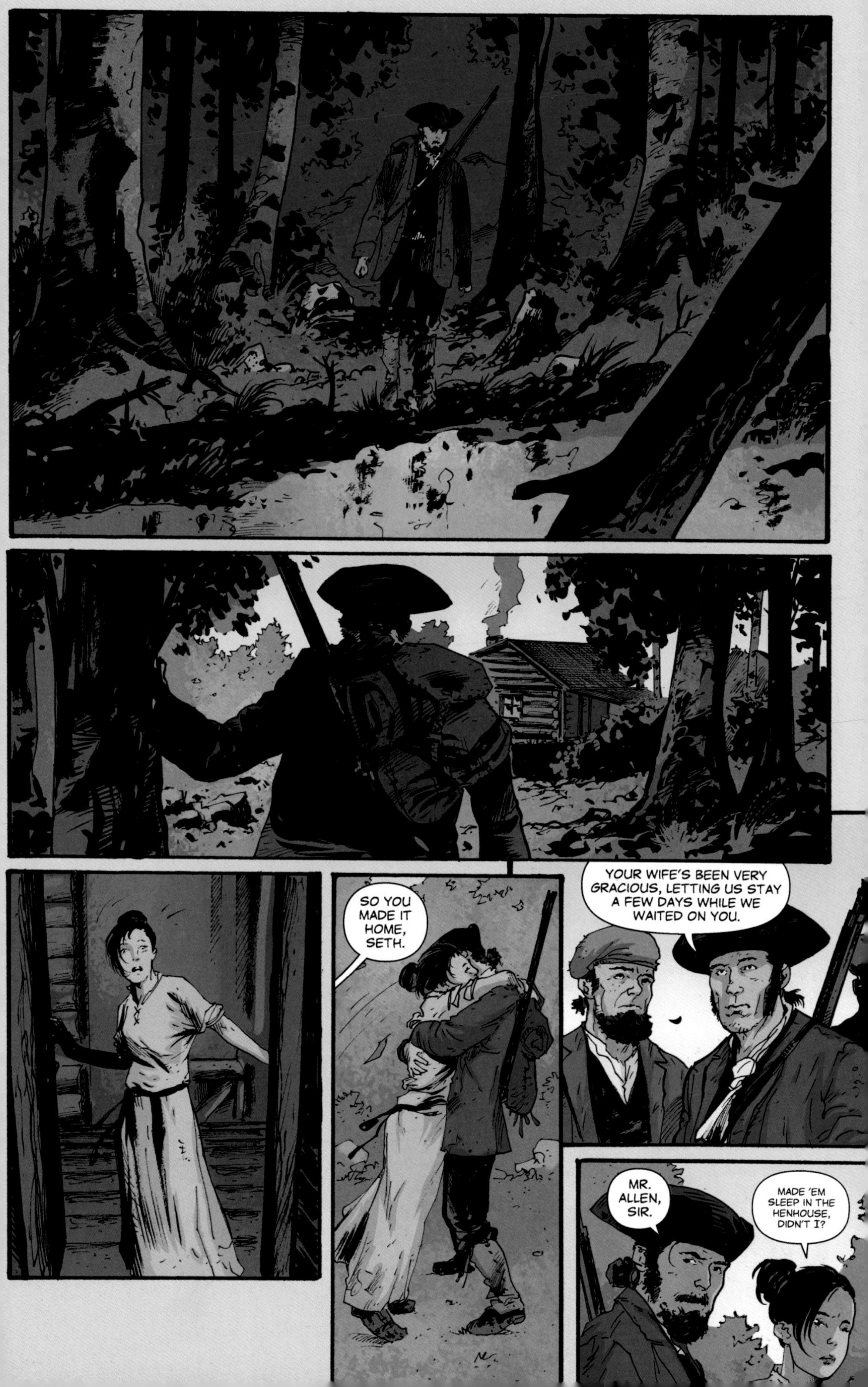
SO YOU MADE IT HOME, SETH.
YOUR WIFE'S BEEN VERY GRACIOUS, LETTING US STAY A FEW DAYS WHILE WE WAITED ON YOU.
MR. ALLEN, SIR.
MADE 'EM SLEEP IN THE HENHOUSE, DIDN'T I?

I had been home all of fifteen minutes. I had not yet changed my clothing, or had a wash.

YOU BLOCKED THE NARROWS, SETH. YOU AND EZEKIEL LEARNED SHOULD BE PROUD OF THAT. THE BRITISH WON'T BE ABLE TO SAIL ANYTHING LARGER THAN A SKIFF THROUGH THERE.

NOW, EXPLAIN TO ME WHAT WENT WRONG.

WE LOST TOO MANY MEN.

IS THAT ALL?

ISN'T THAT ENOUGH?

I KNEW EACH AND EVERY ONE OF THEM. MOST HAVE HOMES WITHIN TWENTY MILES OF HERE.

WAR'S NOT FOR THE SQUEAMISH, ABBOTT.

WEIGH THE COST AND THE REWARD PROPERLY, AND YOU CAN CLAIM A VICTORY EVERY TIME.

SETH'S RIGHT. THE BRITISH CAN THROW MEN AT US BY THE BOATLOAD, BUT OUR STOCKS ARE FINITE. AND A DAMN SIGHT MORE PRECIOUS, IF YOU ASK ME.

THE PLAN WAS SOUND. THE EXECUTION WAS DARING. NEXT TIME, I'LL PUT RIFLEMEN IN THE WOODS.

SIR.

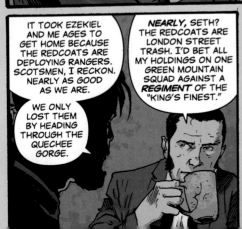

IT TOOK EZEKIEL AND ME AGES TO GET HOME BECAUSE THE REDCOATS ARE DEPLOYING RANGERS. SCOTSMEN, I RECKON. NEARLY AS GOOD AS WE ARE.

WE ONLY LOST THEM BY HEADING THROUGH THE QUECHEE GORGE.

NEARLY, SETH? THE REDCOATS ARE LONDON STREET TRASH. I'D BET ALL MY HOLDINGS ON ONE GREEN MOUNTAIN SQUAD AGAINST A *REGIMENT* OF THE "KING'S FINEST."

MEN, LET'S ALLOW MR. ABBOTT THE REST HE DESERVES, BEFORE HE FALLS ASLEEP IN HIS SOUP BOWL.

He was lying.

The notion of rest, of a few days' downtime with Mercy... That was fiction. They were restless from waiting on me. It was time to go.

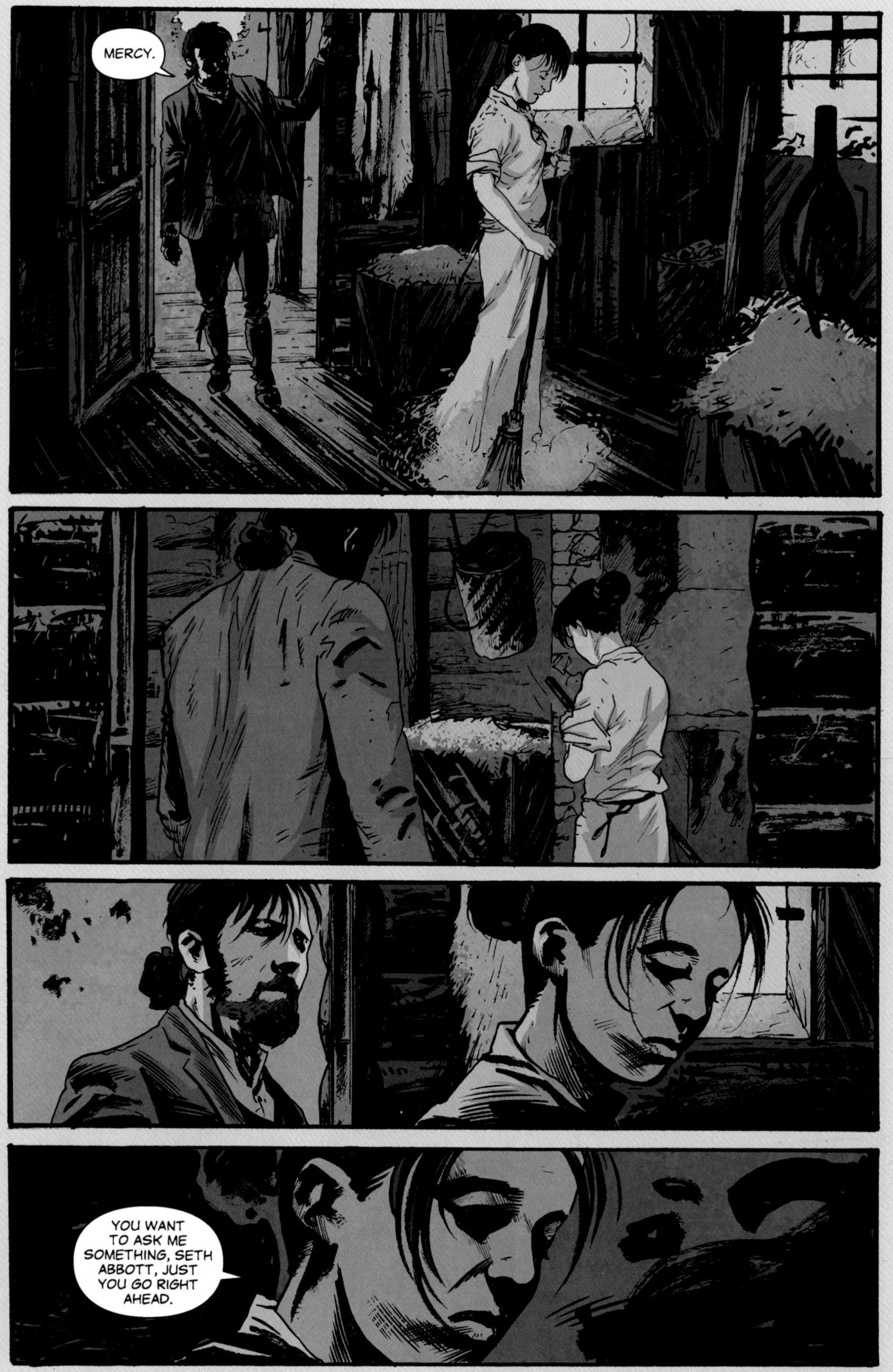
MERCY.
YOU WANT TO ASK ME SOMETHING, SETH ABBOTT, JUST YOU GO RIGHT AHEAD.

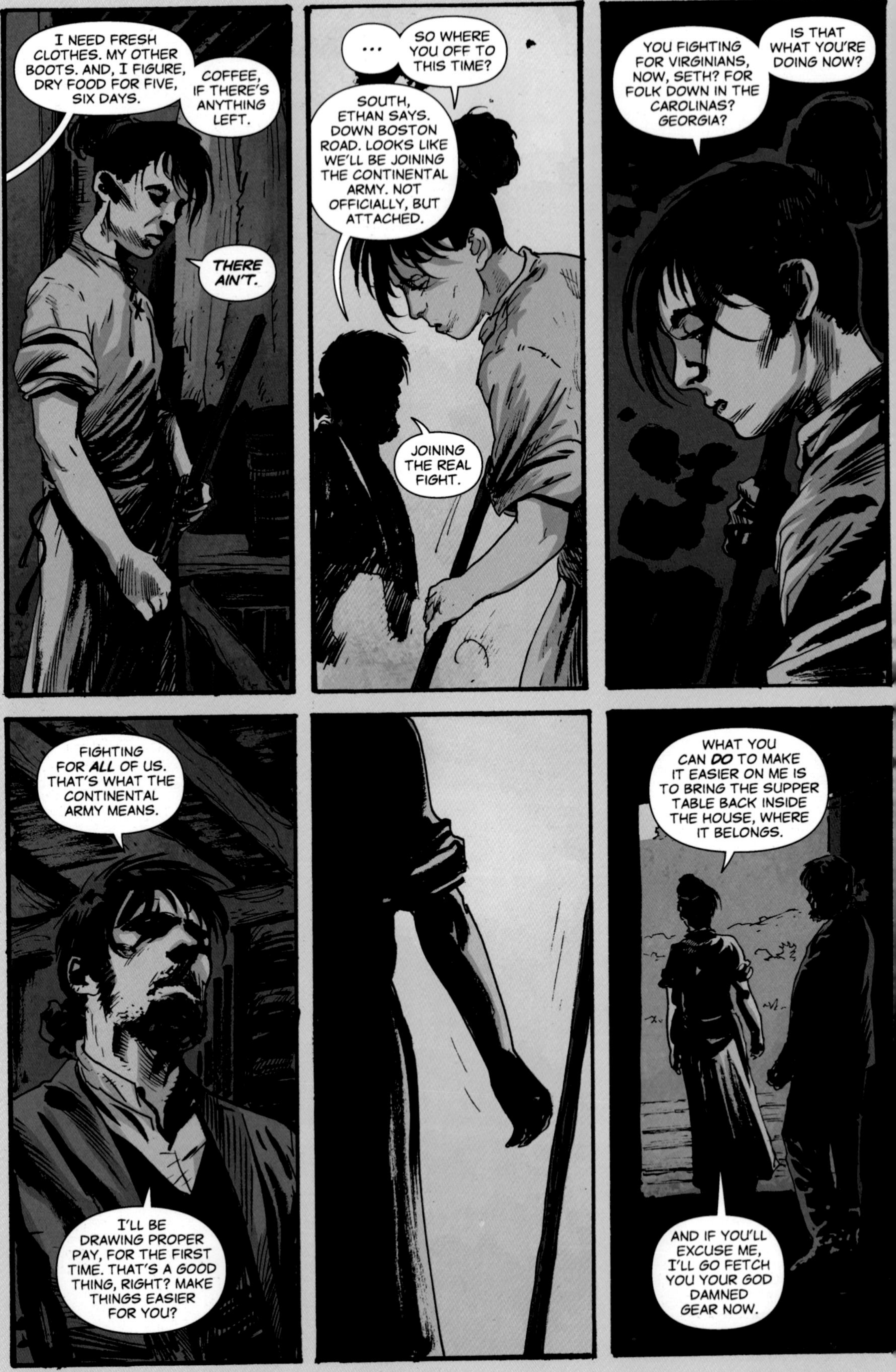
I NEED FRESH CLOTHES. MY OTHER BOOTS. AND, I FIGURE, DRY FOOD FOR FIVE, SIX DAYS.
COFFEE, IF THERE'S ANYTHING LEFT.
THERE AIN'T.
...
SO WHERE YOU OFF TO THIS TIME?
SOUTH, ETHAN SAYS. DOWN BOSTON ROAD. LOOKS LIKE WE'LL BE JOINING THE CONTINENTAL ARMY. NOT OFFICIALLY, BUT ATTACHED.
JOINING THE REAL FIGHT.
YOU FIGHTING FOR VIRGINIANS, NOW, SETH? FOR FOLK DOWN IN THE CAROLINAS? GEORGIA?
IS THAT WHAT YOU'RE DOING NOW?
FIGHTING FOR ALL OF US. THAT'S WHAT THE CONTINENTAL ARMY MEANS.
I'LL BE DRAWING PROPER PAY, FOR THE FIRST TIME. THAT'S A GOOD THING, RIGHT? MAKE THINGS EASIER FOR YOU?
WHAT YOU CAN DO TO MAKE IT EASIER ON ME IS TO BRING THE SUPPER TABLE BACK INSIDE THE HOUSE, WHERE IT BELONGS.
AND IF YOU'LL EXCUSE ME, I'LL GO FETCH YOU YOUR GOD DAMNED GEAR NOW.

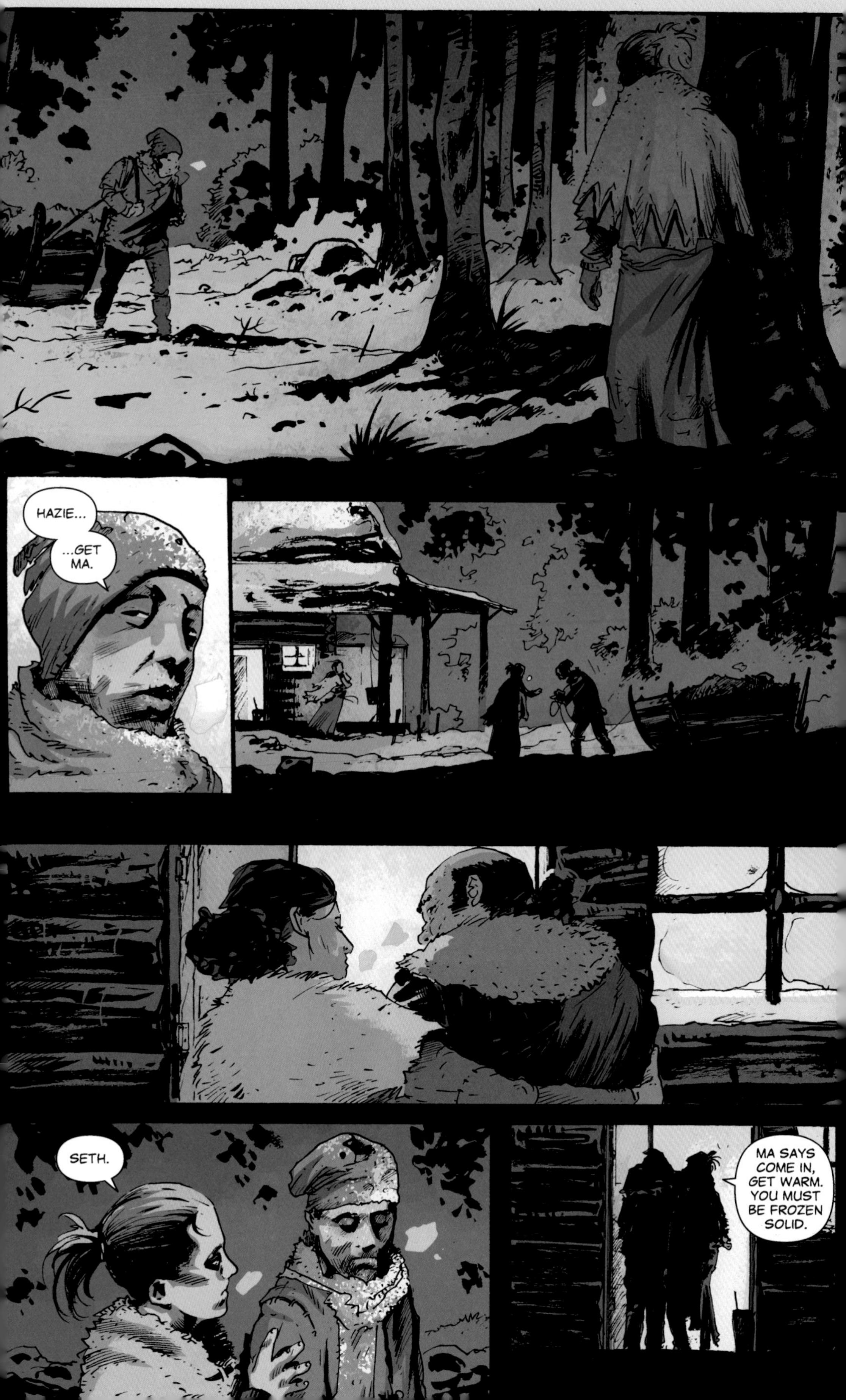
HAZIE...
...GET MA.
SETH.
MA SAYS COME IN, GET WARM. YOU MUST BE FROZEN SOLID.

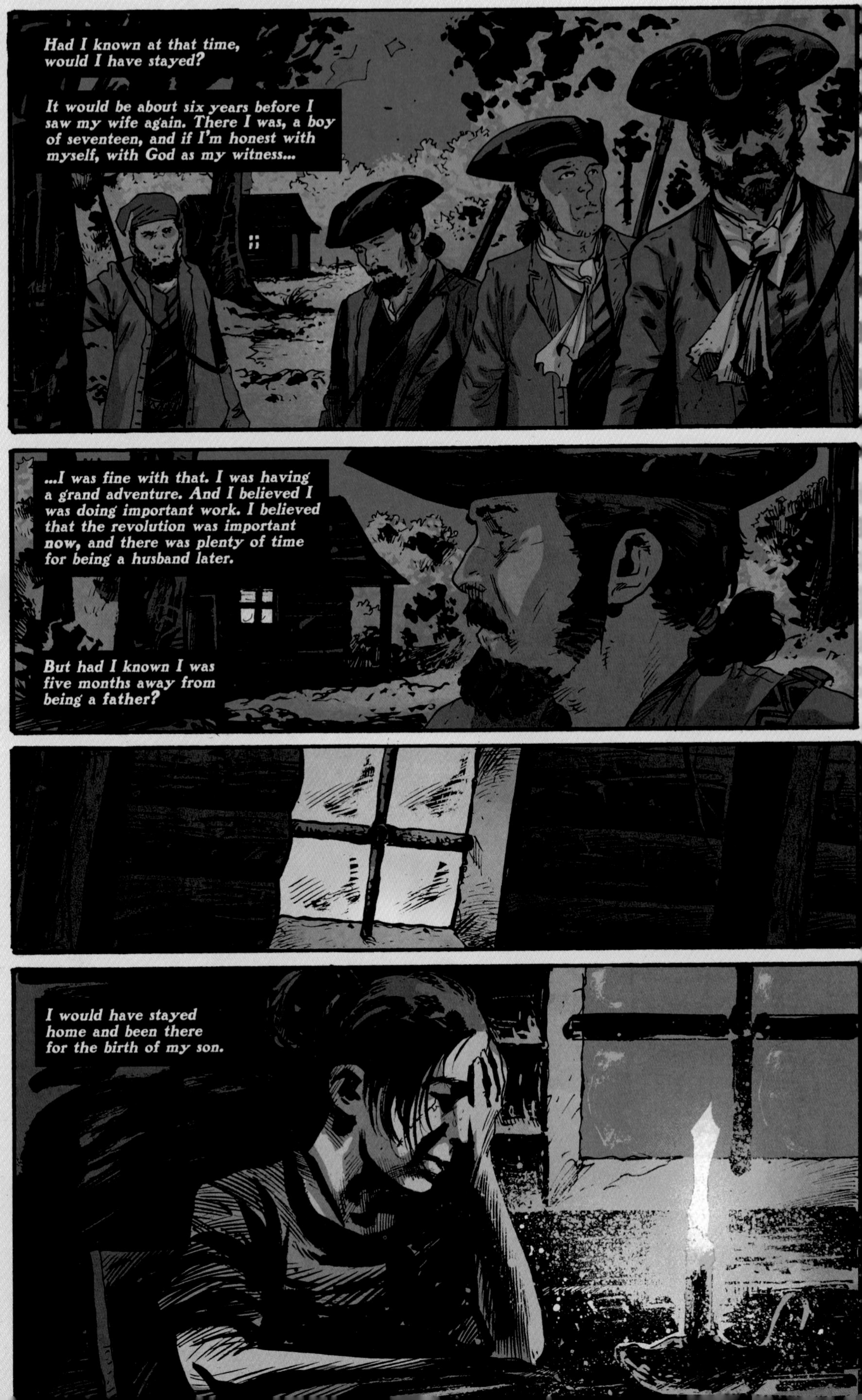
Had I known at that time, would I have stayed?
It would be about six years before I saw my wife again. There I was, a boy of seventeen, and if I'm honest with myself, with God as my witness...
...I was fine with that. I was having a grand adventure. And I believed I was doing important work. I believed that the revolution was important now, and there was plenty of time for being a husband later.
But had I known I was five months away from being a father?
I would have stayed home and been there for the birth of my son.

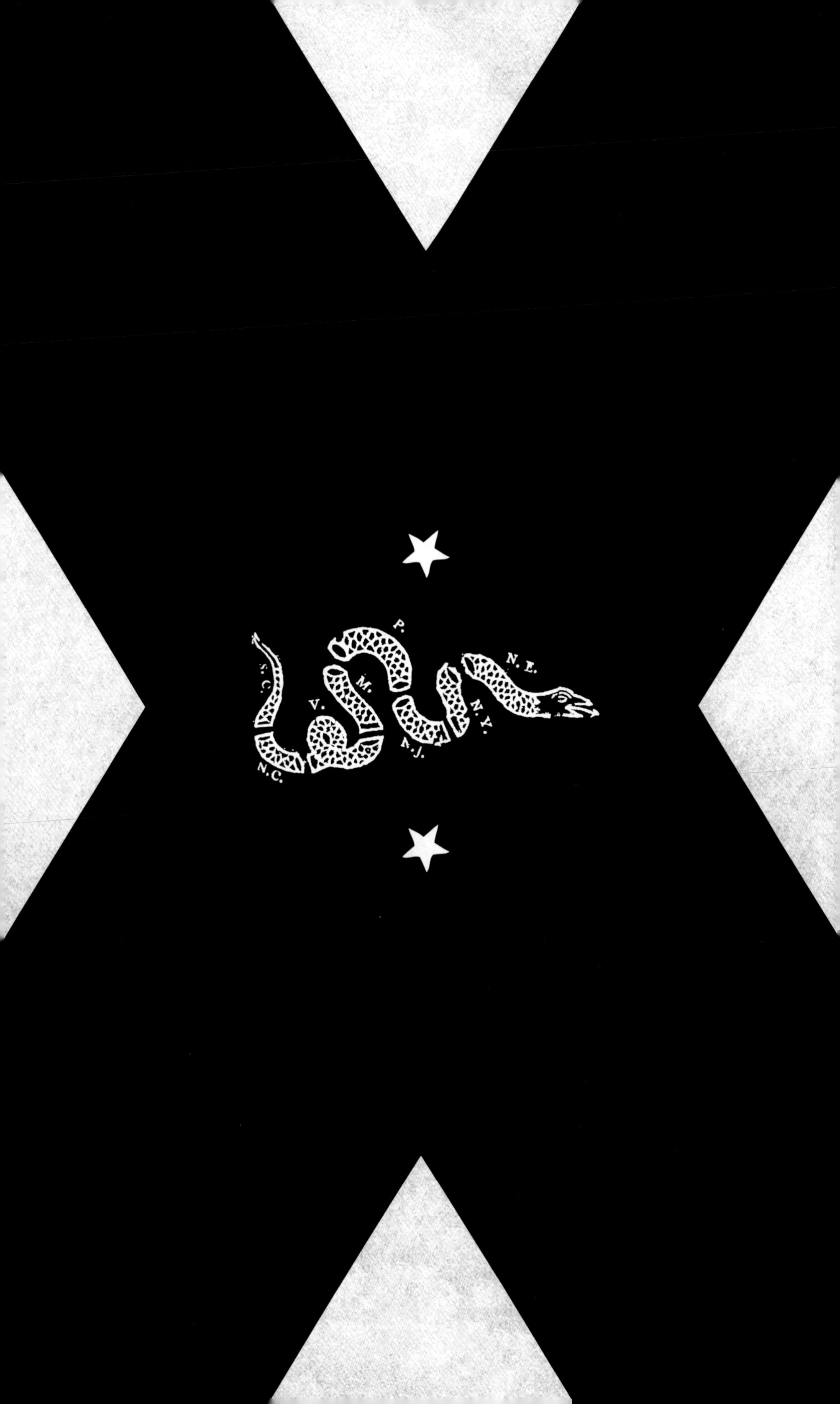
S.C.
N.C.
V.
M.
P.
N.J.
N.Y.
N.E.

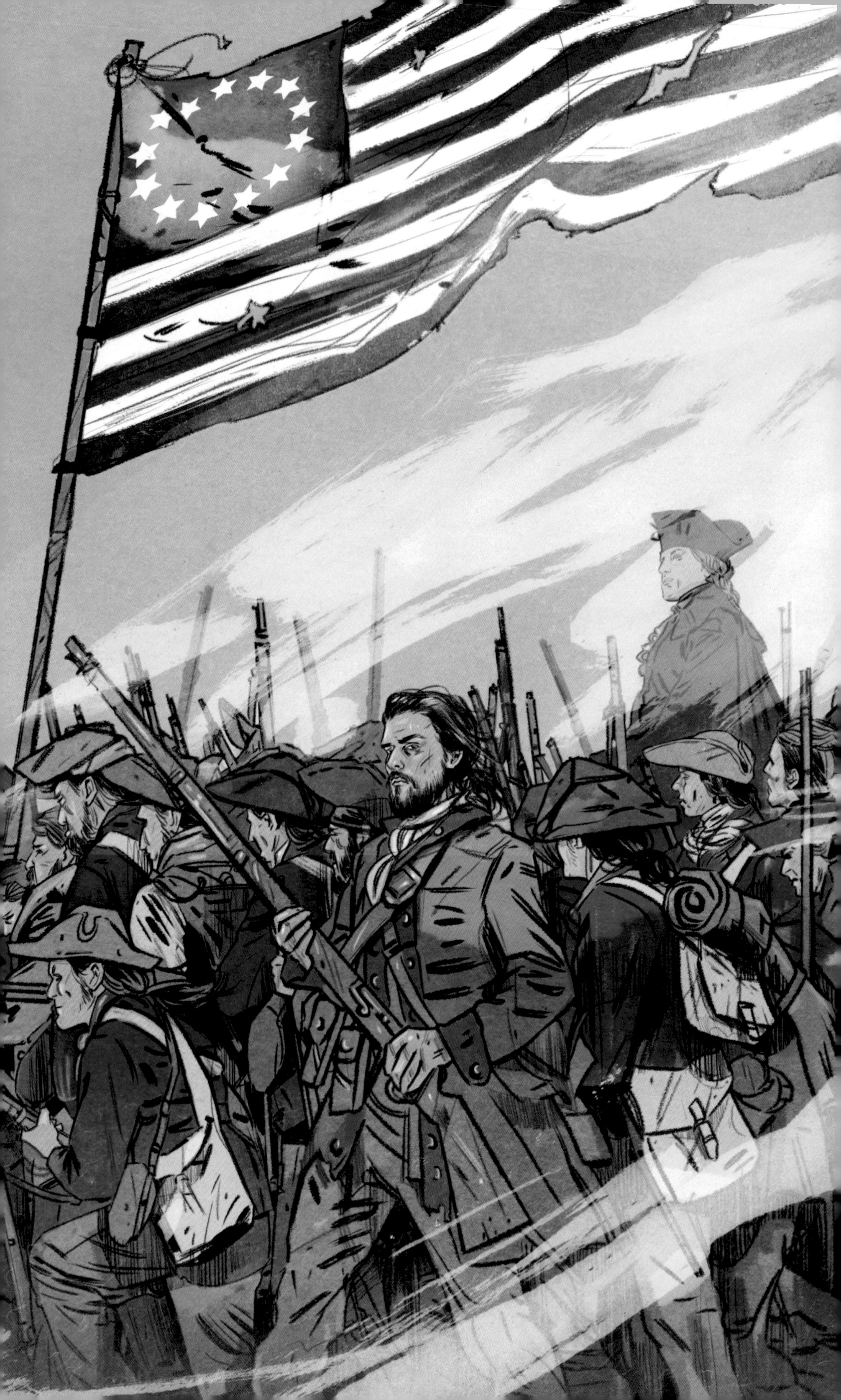

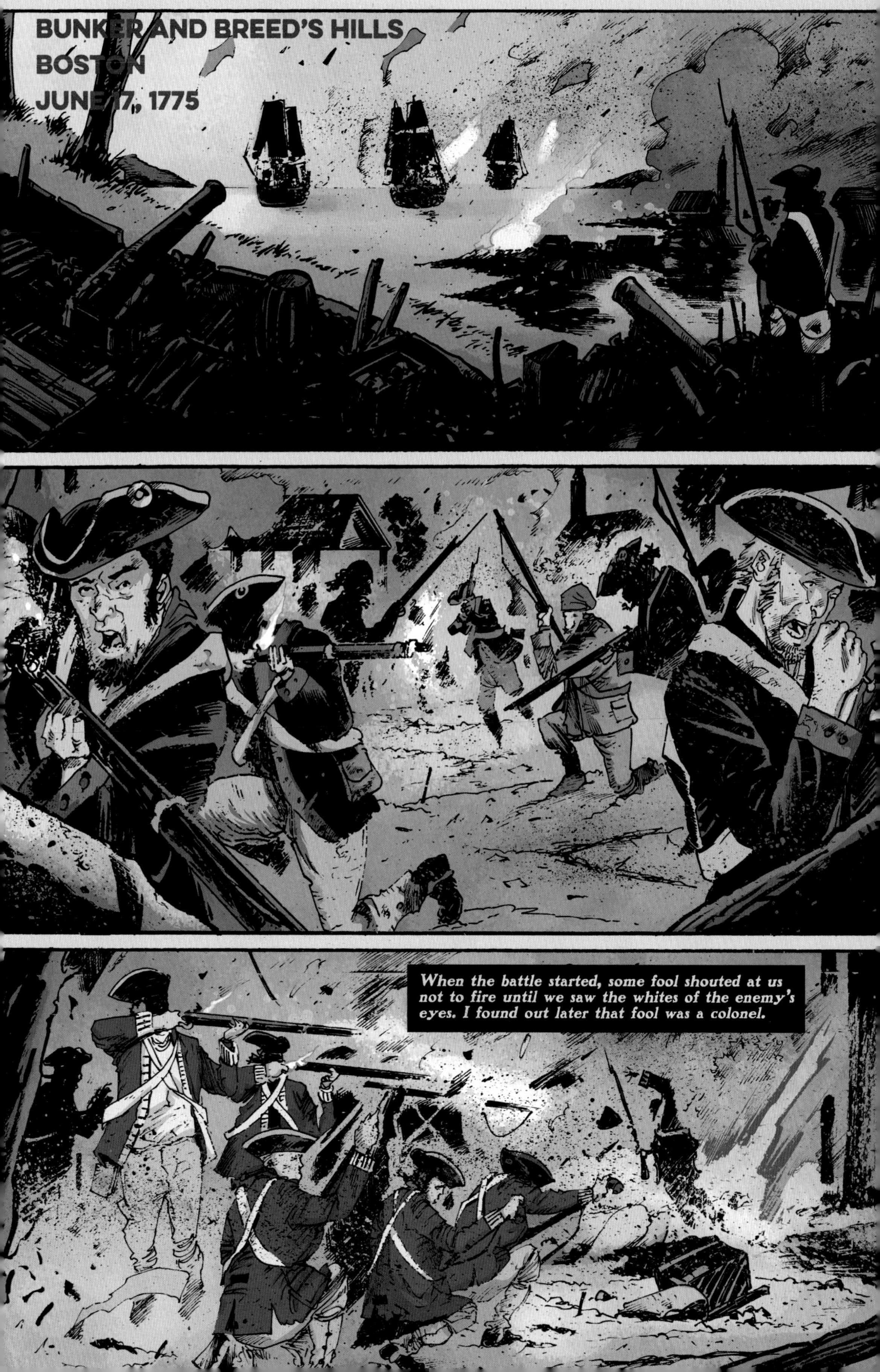
BUNKER AND BREED'S HILLS
BOSTON
JUNE 17, 1775
When the battle started, some fool shouted at us not to fire until we saw the whites of the enemy's eyes. I found out later that fool was a colonel.

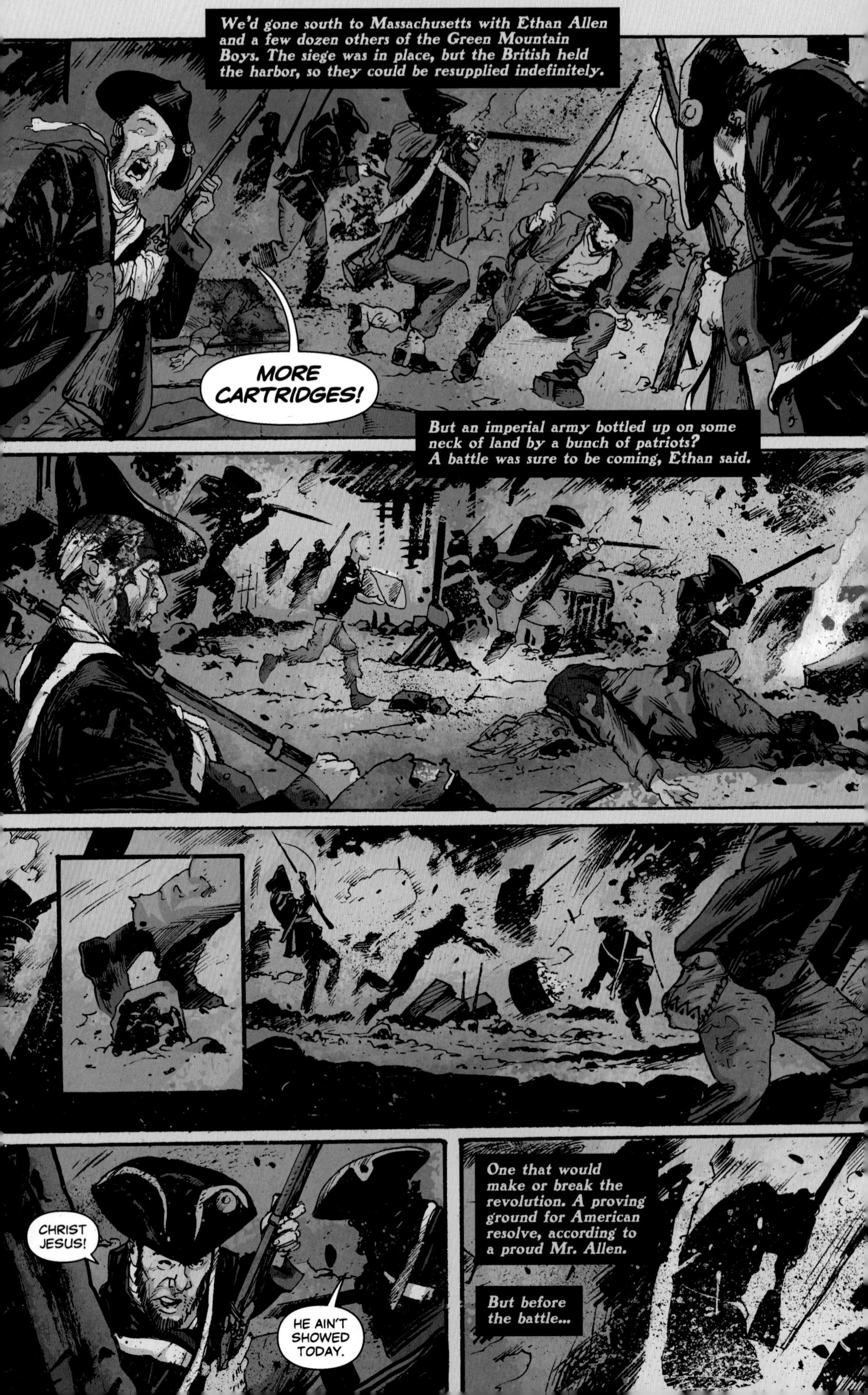
We'd gone south to Massachusetts with Ethan Allen and a few dozen others of the Green Mountain Boys. The siege was in place, but the British held the harbor, so they could be resupplied indefinitely.
MORE CARTRIDGES!
But an imperial army bottled up on some neck of land by a bunch of patriots? A battle was sure to be coming, Ethan said.
CHRIST JESUS!
HE AIN'T SHOWED TODAY.
One that would make or break the revolution. A proving ground for American resolve, according to a proud Mr. Allen.
But before the battle...

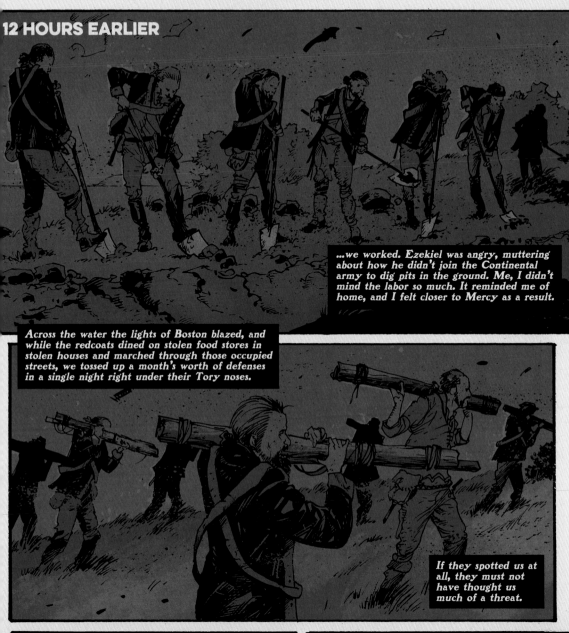

...we worked. Ezekiel was angry, muttering about how he didn't join the Continental army to dig pits in the ground. Me, I didn't mind the labor so much. It reminded me of home, and I felt closer to Mercy as a result.

Across the water the lights of Boston blazed, and while the redcoats dined on stolen food stores in stolen houses and marched through those occupied streets, we tossed up a month's worth of defenses in a single night right under their Tory noses.

If they spotted us at all, they must not have thought us much of a threat.

We dug ditches, built earthen walls, breastworks, gun emplacements, and a small redoubt at the top of Breed's Hill.

And in the morning...

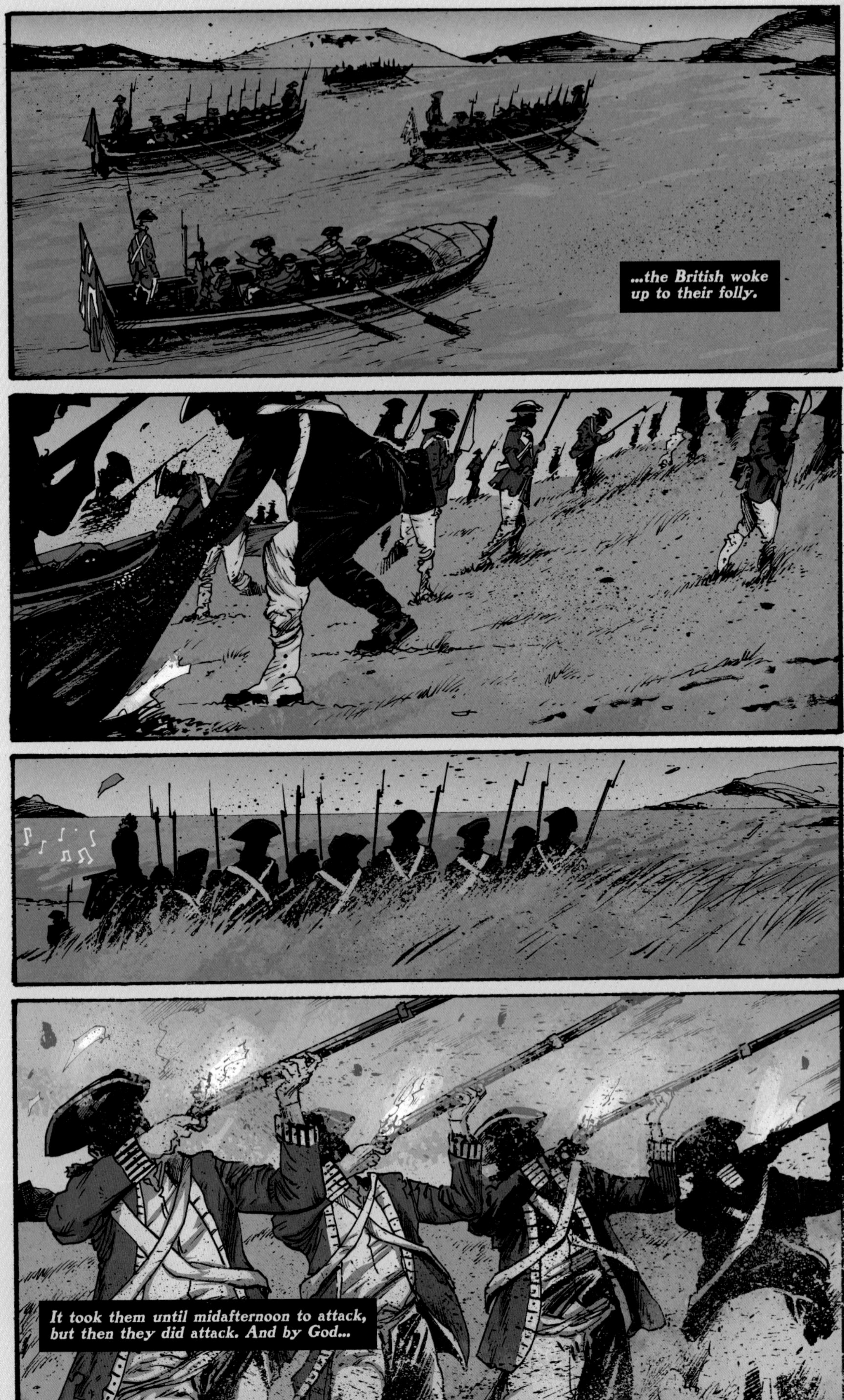
...the British woke up to their folly.
It took them until midafternoon to attack, but then they did attack. And by God...

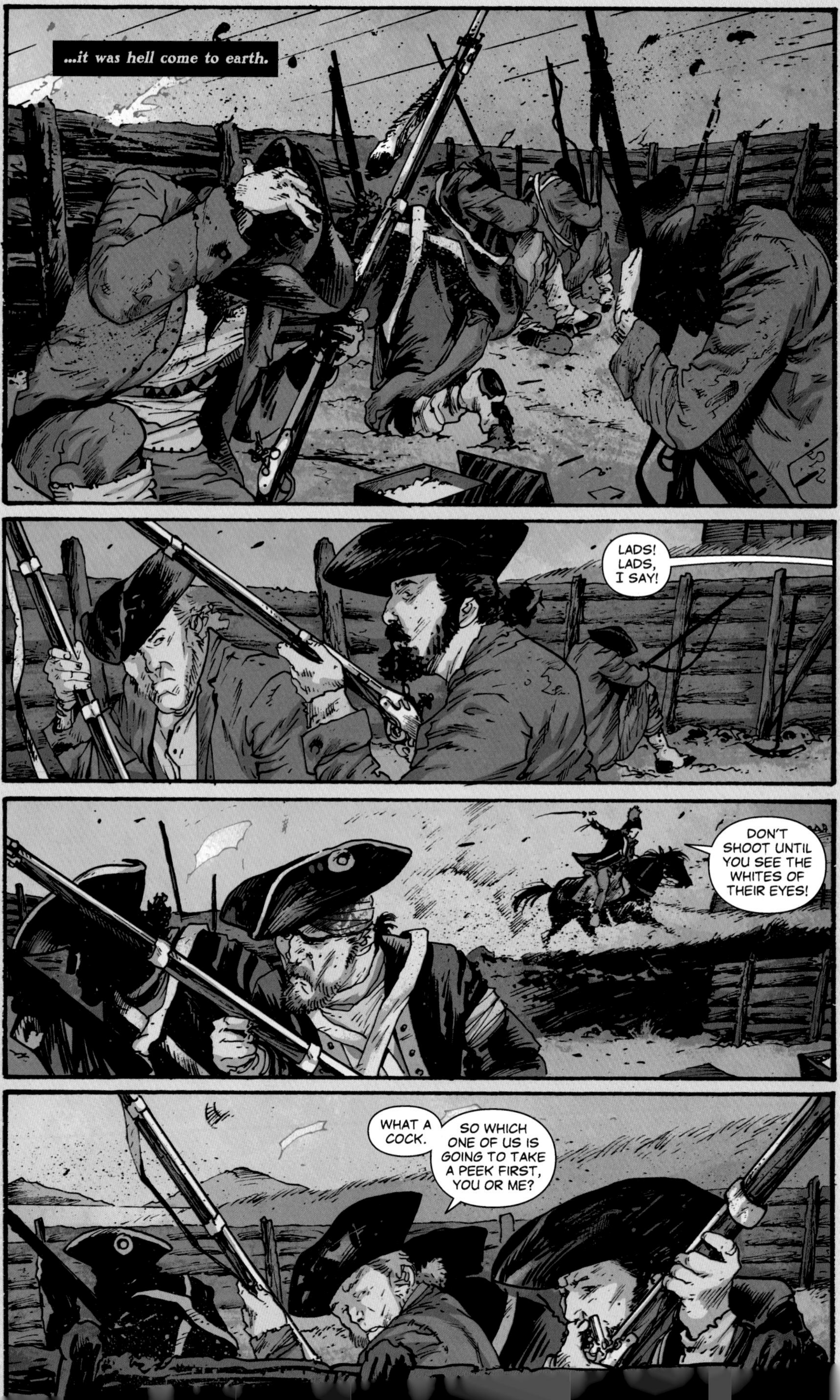
...it was hell come to earth.
LADS! LADS, I SAY!
DON'T SHOOT UNTIL YOU SEE THE WHITES OF THEIR EYES!
WHAT A COCK.
SO WHICH ONE OF US IS GOING TO TAKE A PEEK FIRST, YOU OR ME?

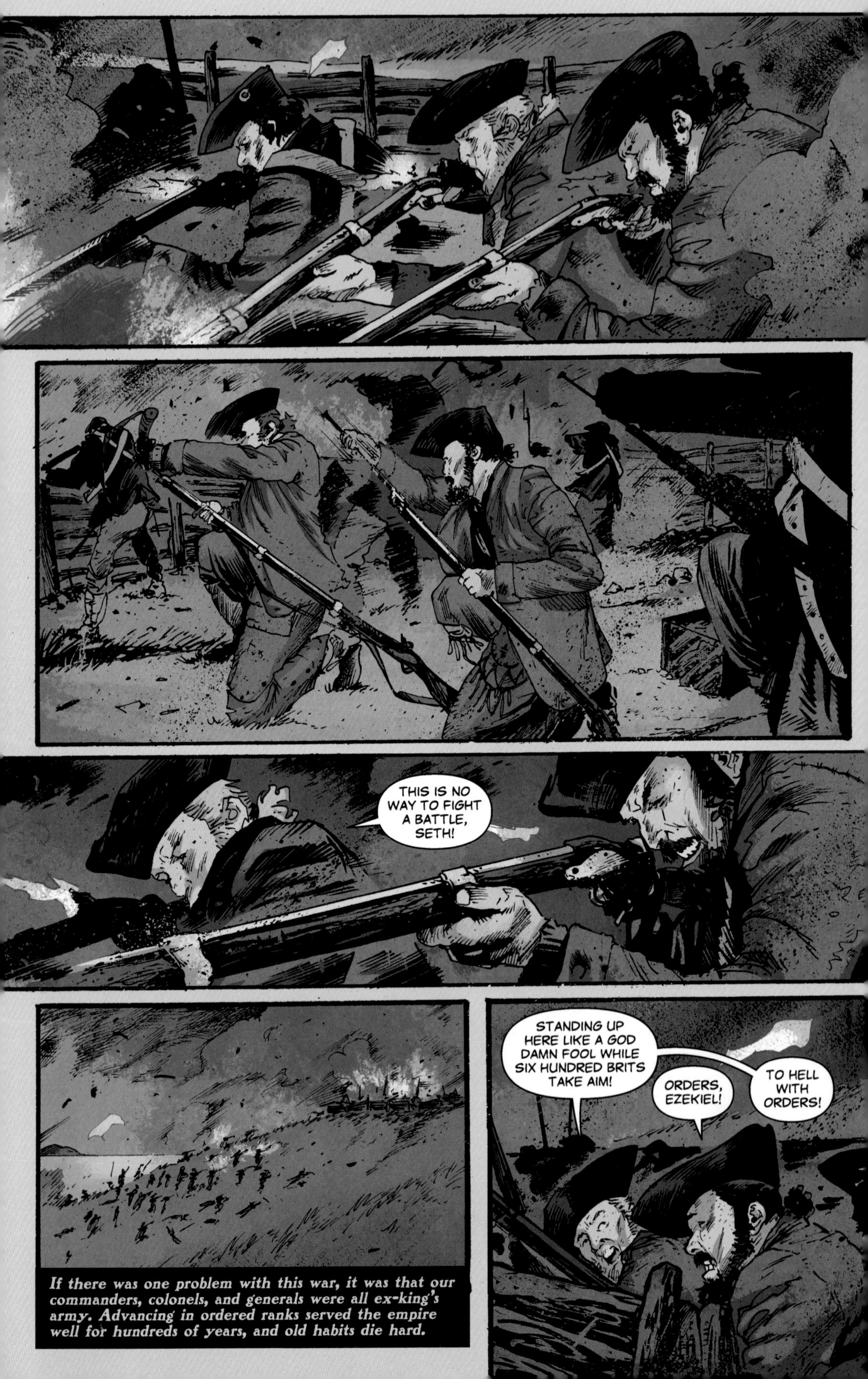

THIS IS NO WAY TO FIGHT A BATTLE, SETH!
If there was one problem with this war, it was that our commanders, colonels, and generals were all ex-king's army. Advancing in ordered ranks served the empire well for hundreds of years, and old habits die hard.
STANDING UP HERE LIKE A GOD DAMN FOOL WHILE SIX HUNDRED BRITS TAKE AIM!
ORDERS, EZEKIEL!
TO HELL WITH ORDERS!

The discipline, the relentlessness of the approach, the sheer terror of the timed volleys...It was nothing any of us had ever faced before.

But we were Green Mountain Boys.

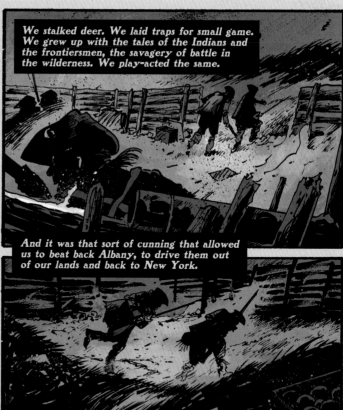

We stalked deer. We laid traps for small game. We grew up with the tales of the Indians and the frontiersmen, the savagery of battle in the wilderness. We play-acted the same.

And it was that sort of cunning that allowed us to beat back Albany, to drive them out of our lands and back to New York.

ONLY THE FIRST TWO ROWS ARE FIRING. THE MEN BEHIND STEP FORWARD WHEN SOMEONE FALLS AND FILL THE GAP LIKE NOTHING HAPPENED.

IT AIN'T HUMAN.

He was right, they ain't.

WATCH THIS.

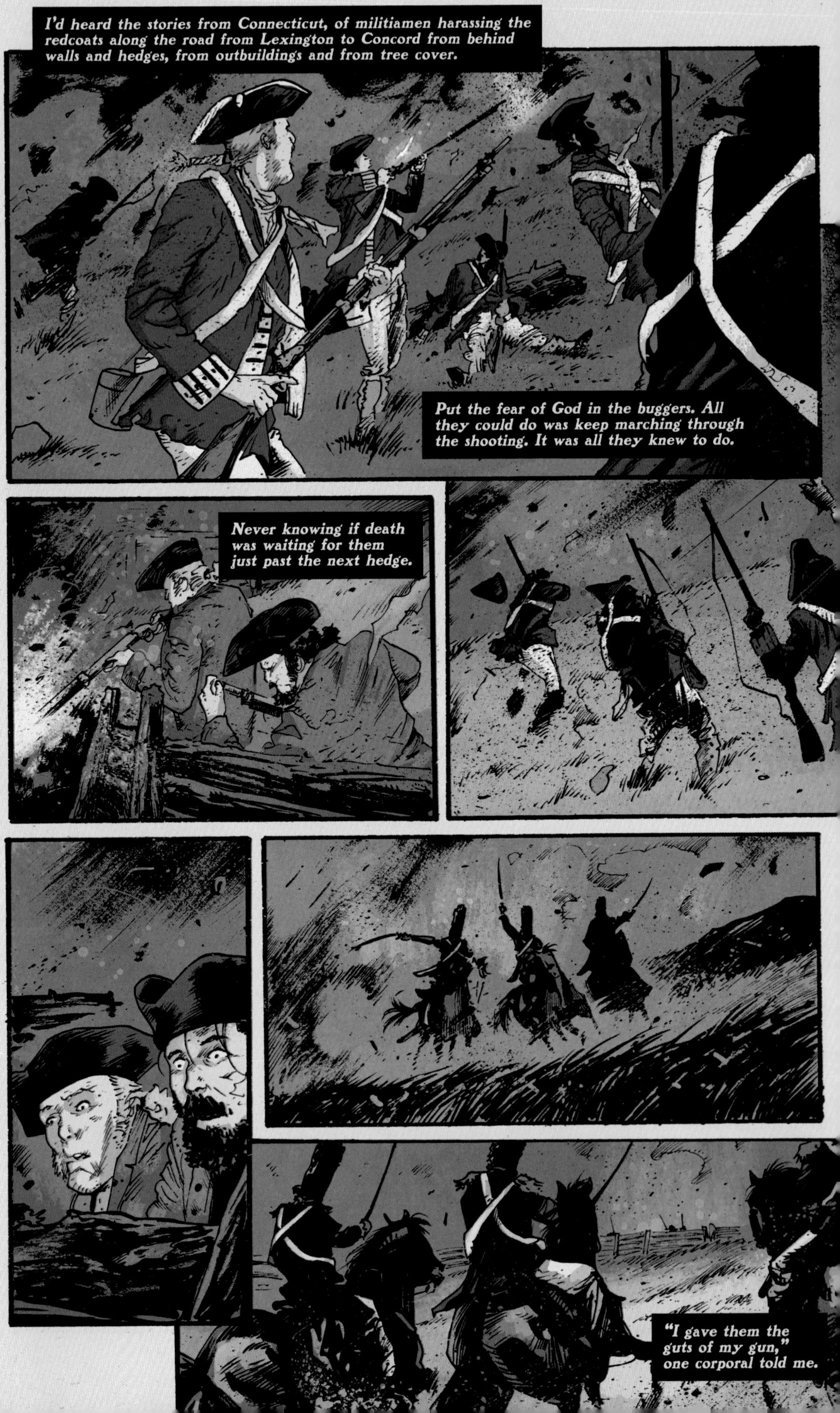

I'd heard the stories from Connecticut, of militiamen harassing the redcoats along the road from Lexington to Concord from behind walls and hedges, from outbuildings and from tree cover.
Put the fear of God in the buggers. All they could do was keep marching through the shooting. It was all they knew to do.
Never knowing if death was waiting for them just past the next hedge.
"I gave them the guts of my gun," one corporal told me.

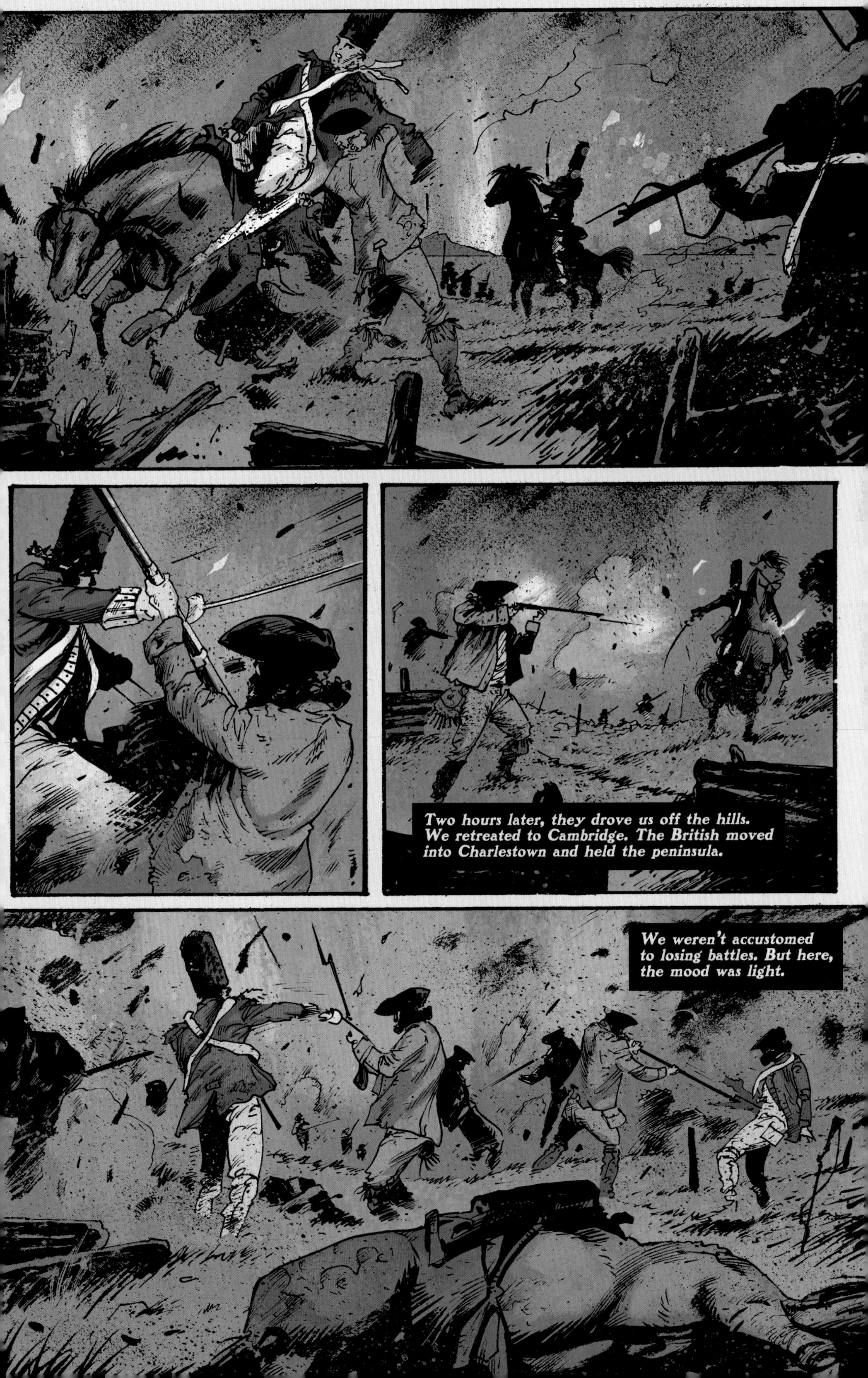

Two hours later, they drove us off the hills. We retreated to Cambridge. The British moved into Charlestown and held the peninsula.
We weren't accustomed to losing battles. But here, the mood was light.

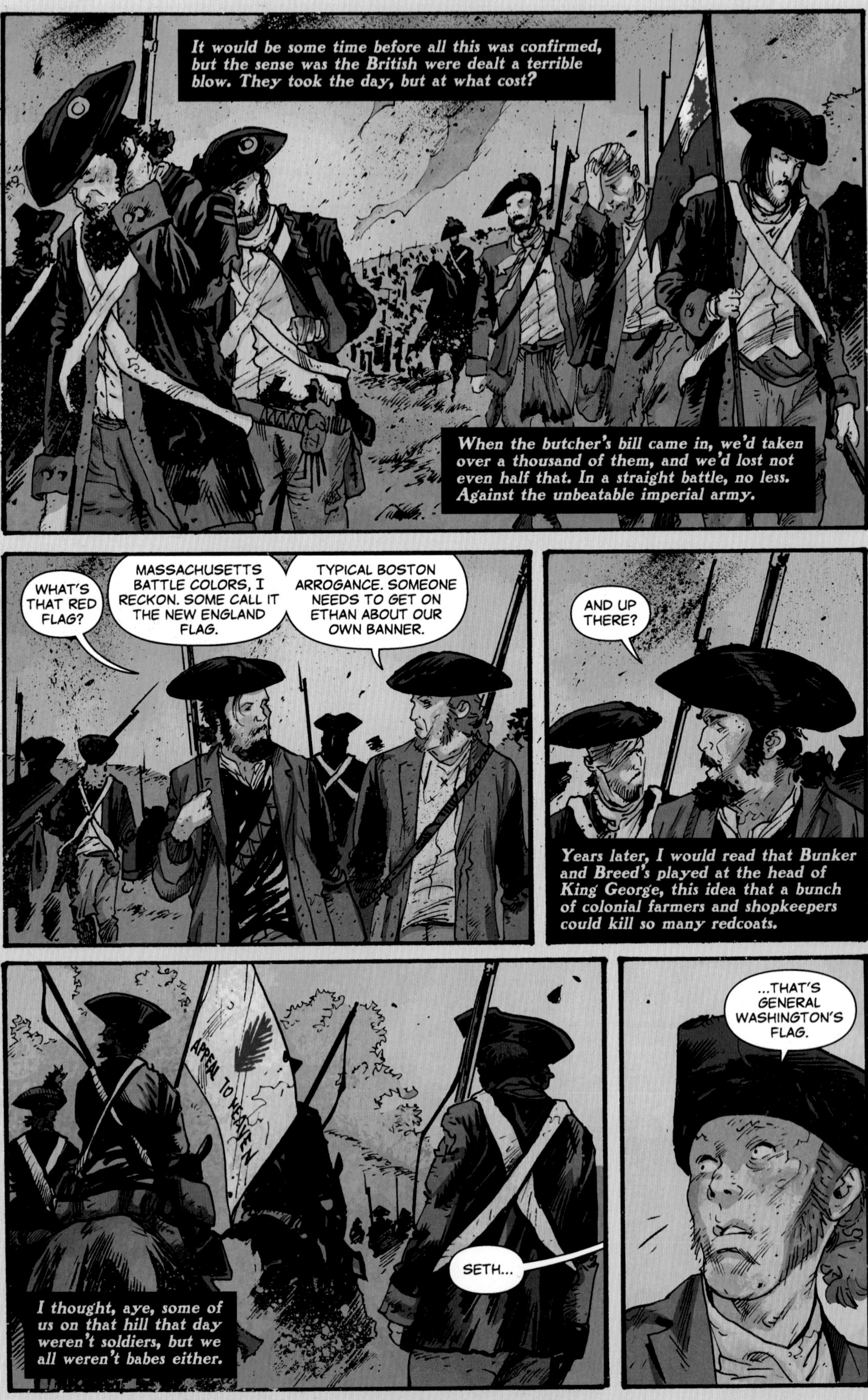
It would be some time before all this was confirmed, but the sense was the British were dealt a terrible blow. They took the day, but at what cost?
When the butcher's bill came in, we'd taken over a thousand of them, and we'd lost not even half that. In a straight battle, no less. Against the unbeatable imperial army.
WHAT'S THAT RED FLAG?
MASSACHUSETTS BATTLE COLORS, I RECKON. SOME CALL IT THE NEW ENGLAND FLAG.
TYPICAL BOSTON ARROGANCE. SOMEONE NEEDS TO GET ON ETHAN ABOUT OUR OWN BANNER.
AND UP THERE?
Years later, I would read that Bunker and Breed's played at the head of King George, this idea that a bunch of colonial farmers and shopkeepers could kill so many redcoats.
APPEAL TO HEAVEN
SETH...
I thought, aye, some of us on that hill that day weren't soldiers, but we all weren't babes either.
...THAT'S GENERAL WASHINGTON'S FLAG.

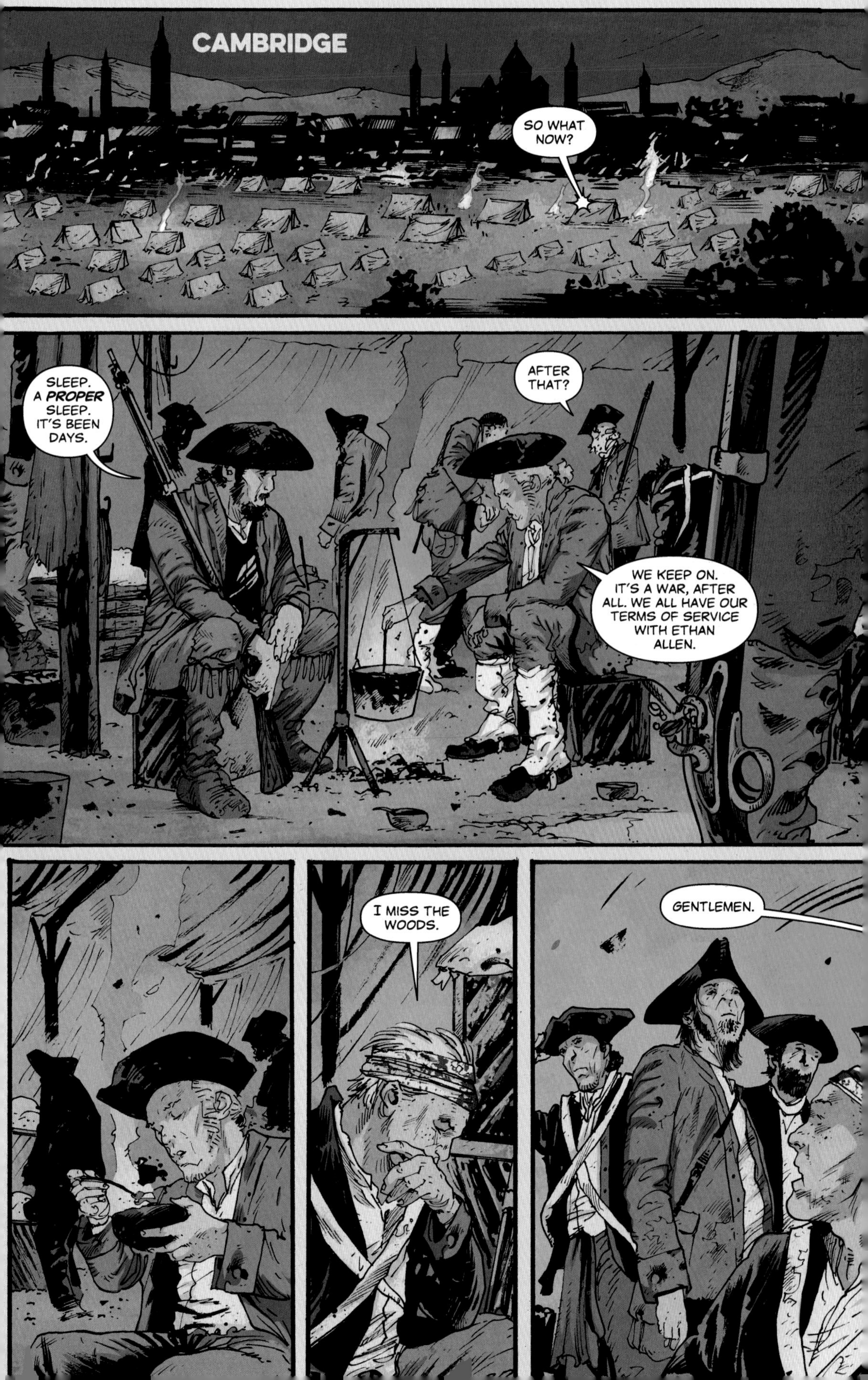
CAMBRIDGE
SO WHAT NOW?
SLEEP. A **PROPER** SLEEP. IT'S BEEN DAYS.
AFTER THAT?
WE KEEP ON. IT'S A WAR, AFTER ALL. WE ALL HAVE OUR TERMS OF SERVICE WITH ETHAN ALLEN.
I MISS THE WOODS.
GENTLEMEN.

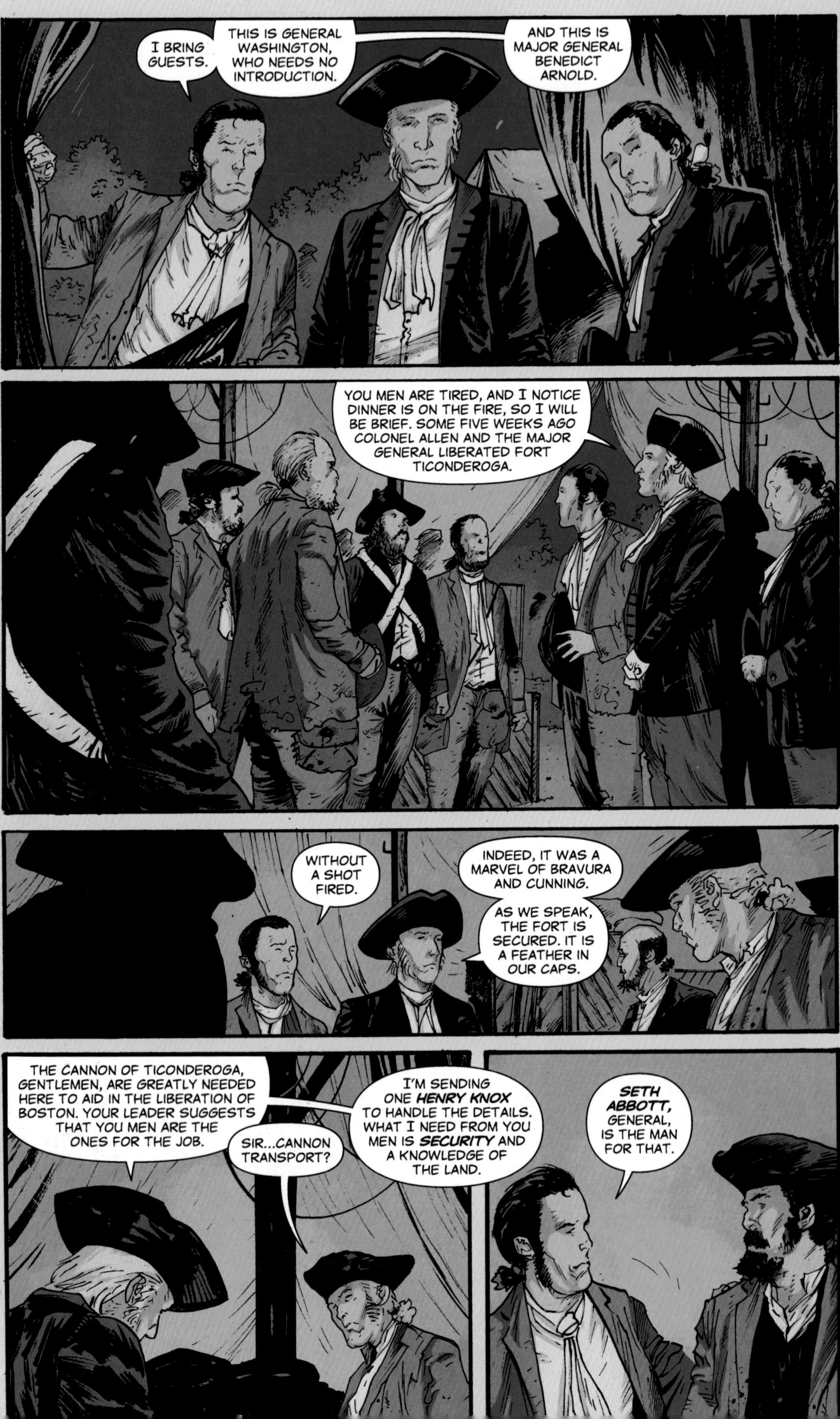

I BRING GUESTS.
THIS IS GENERAL WASHINGTON, WHO NEEDS NO INTRODUCTION.
AND THIS IS MAJOR GENERAL BENEDICT ARNOLD.
YOU MEN ARE TIRED, AND I NOTICE DINNER IS ON THE FIRE, SO I WILL BE BRIEF. SOME FIVE WEEKS AGO COLONEL ALLEN AND THE MAJOR GENERAL LIBERATED FORT TICONDEROGA.
WITHOUT A SHOT FIRED.
INDEED, IT WAS A MARVEL OF BRAVURA AND CUNNING.
AS WE SPEAK, THE FORT IS SECURED. IT IS A FEATHER IN OUR CAPS.
THE CANNON OF TICONDEROGA, GENTLEMEN, ARE GREATLY NEEDED HERE TO AID IN THE LIBERATION OF BOSTON. YOUR LEADER SUGGESTS THAT YOU MEN ARE THE ONES FOR THE JOB.
SIR...CANNON TRANSPORT?
I'M SENDING ONE **HENRY KNOX** TO HANDLE THE DETAILS. WHAT I NEED FROM YOU MEN IS **SECURITY** AND A KNOWLEDGE OF THE LAND.
SETH ABBOTT, GENERAL, IS THE MAN FOR THAT.

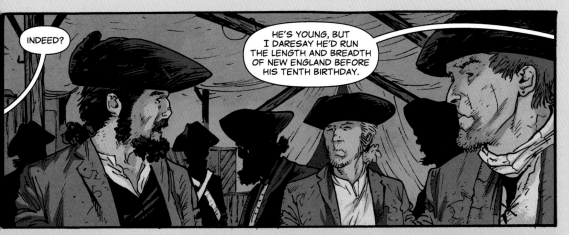

INDEED?

HE'S YOUNG, BUT I DARESAY HE'D RUN THE LENGTH AND BREADTH OF NEW ENGLAND BEFORE HIS TENTH BIRTHDAY.

YOU'VE SEEN THE FORT, MR. ABBOTT?

YES.

...AND?

...

MR. ABBOTT, CAN YOU DO THIS?

I CAN.

SIR. YOU CAN, SIR.

CHRIST ALMIGHTY, ETHAN...

WE'LL DO THE JOB, GENERAL. THERE'S LITERALLY NONE BETTER AT NAVIGATING THOSE WOODS THAN MY MEN. I'LL STAKE MY REPUTATION ON IT.

THAT'S FINE, THEN.

FINE WORK TODAY, BOYS.

MR. ALLEN? A WORD.

SIR--

MR. ALLEN, YOU HAVE MY UTMOST RESPECT FOR YOUR LEADERSHIP AND MY THANKS FOR THE USE OF YOUR MEN. I DON'T NEED TO REMIND YOU HOW IMPORTANT A MISSION THIS IS.

BUT I DON'T WANT THAT MAN, THAT *MR. ABBOTT,* ANYWHERE *NEAR* THIS.

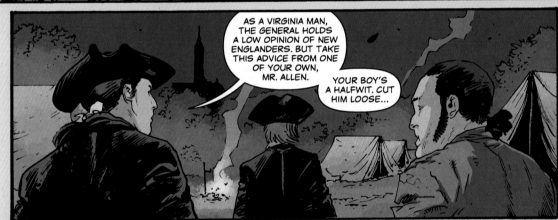

AS A VIRGINIA MAN, THE GENERAL HOLDS A LOW OPINION OF NEW ENGLANDERS. BUT TAKE THIS ADVICE FROM ONE OF YOUR OWN, MR. ALLEN.

YOUR BOY'S A HALFWIT. CUT HIM LOOSE...

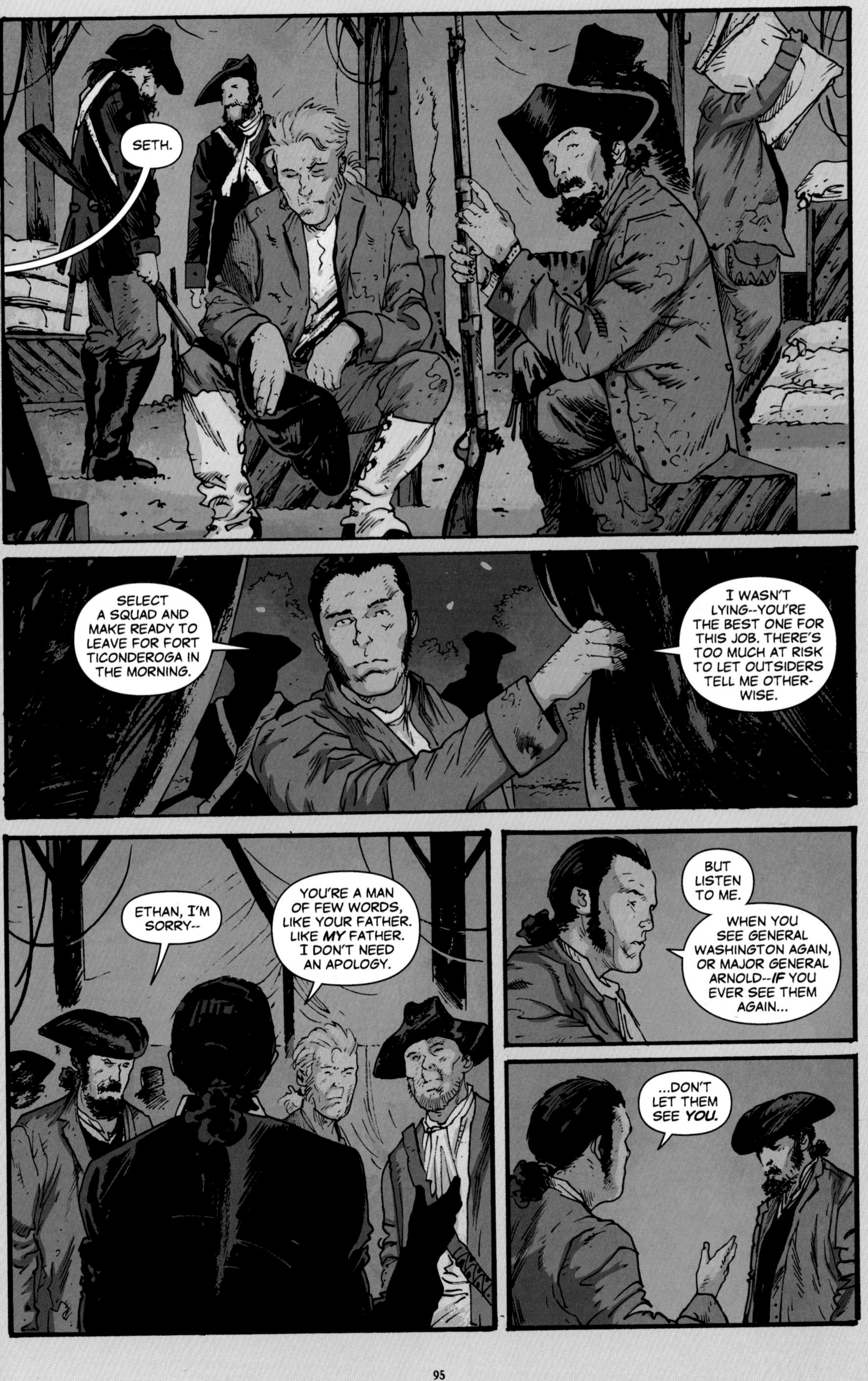
SETH.
SELECT A SQUAD AND MAKE READY TO LEAVE FOR FORT TICONDEROGA IN THE MORNING.
I WASN'T LYING--YOU'RE THE BEST ONE FOR THIS JOB. THERE'S TOO MUCH AT RISK TO LET OUTSIDERS TELL ME OTHER-WISE.
ETHAN, I'M SORRY--
YOU'RE A MAN OF FEW WORDS, LIKE YOUR FATHER. LIKE *MY* FATHER. I DON'T NEED AN APOLOGY.
BUT LISTEN TO ME.
WHEN YOU SEE GENERAL WASHINGTON AGAIN, OR MAJOR GENERAL ARNOLD--*IF* YOU EVER SEE THEM AGAIN...
...DON'T LET THEM SEE *YOU.*

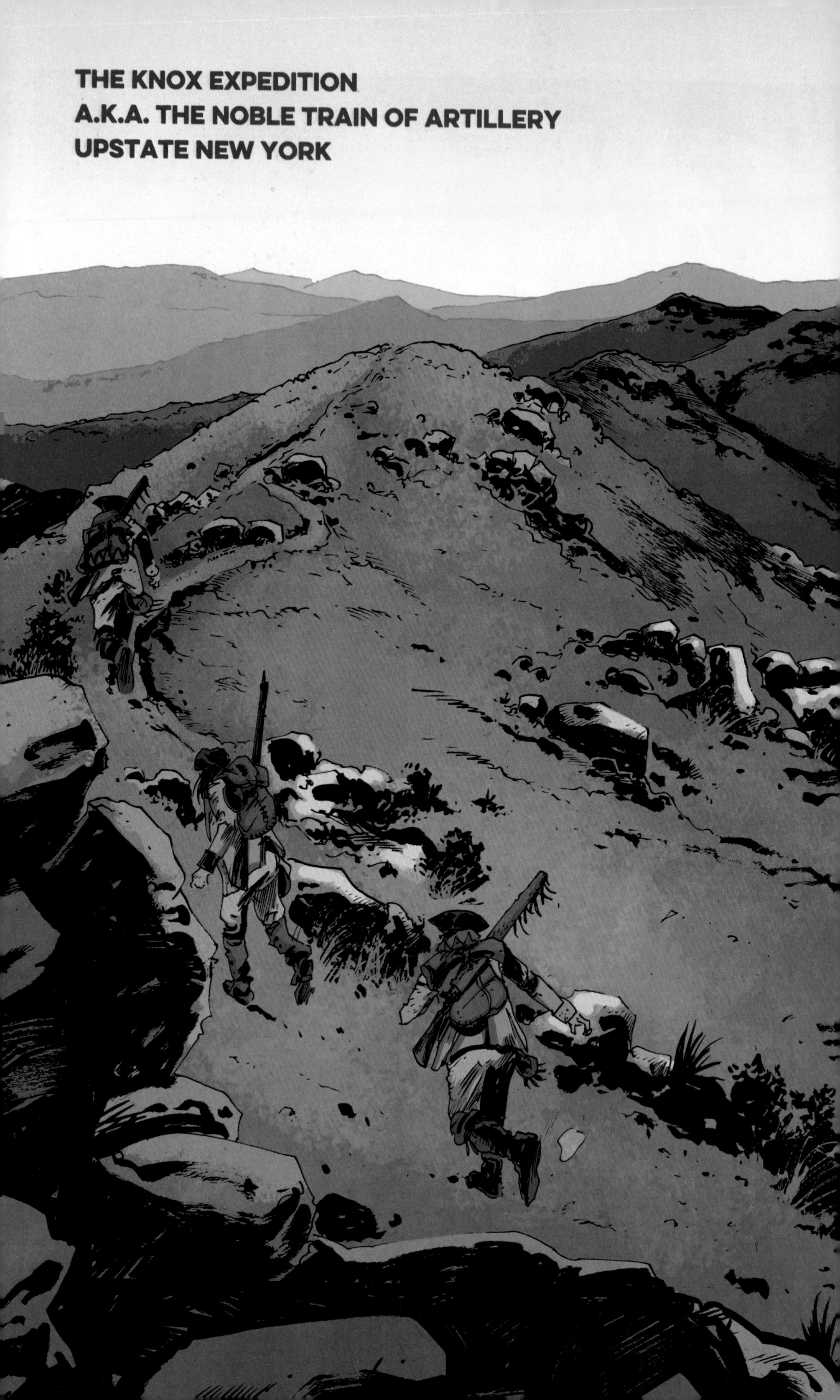
THE KNOX EXPEDITION
A.K.A. THE NOBLE TRAIN OF ARTILLERY
UPSTATE NEW YORK

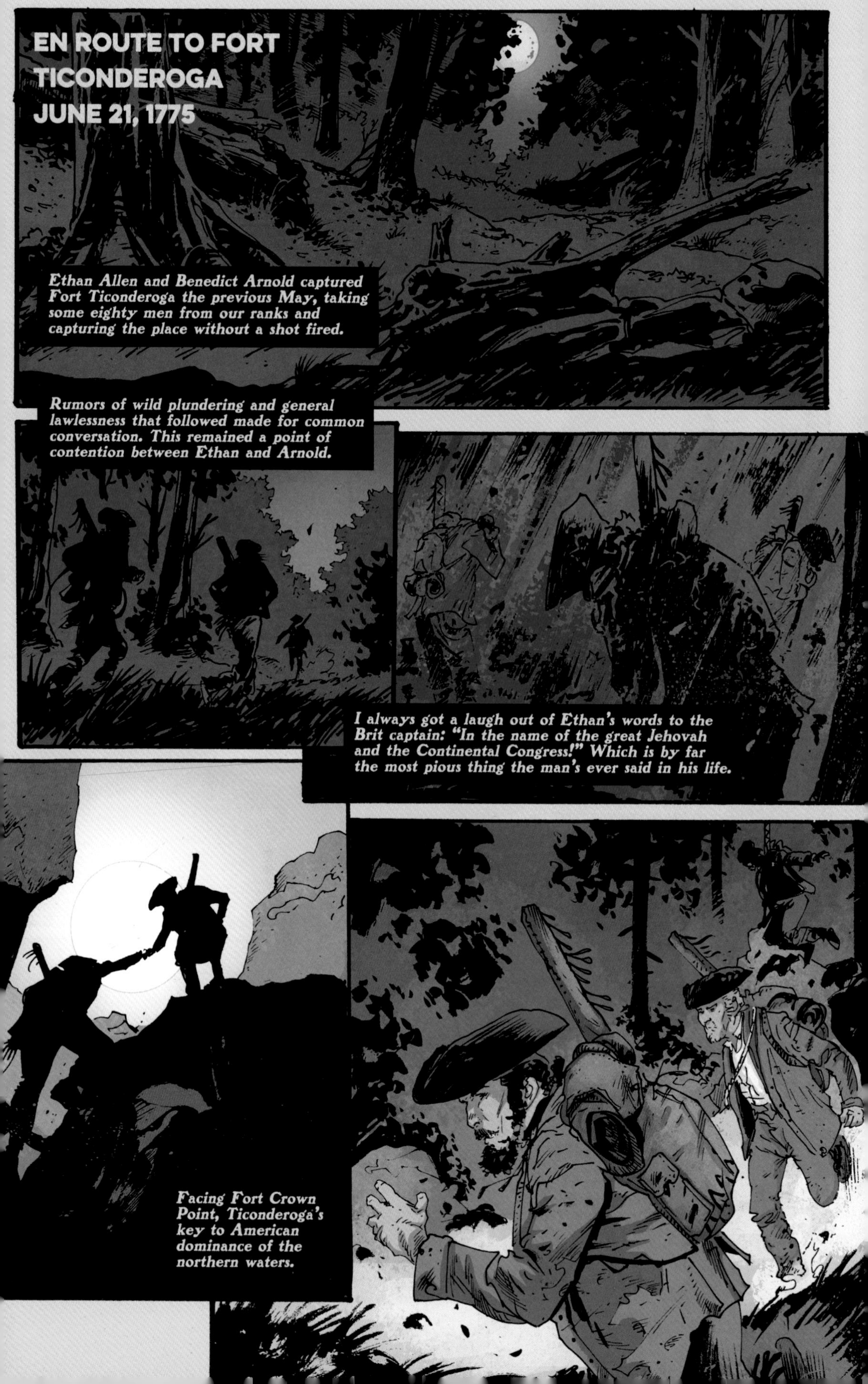
EN ROUTE TO FORT TICONDEROGA JUNE 21, 1775
Ethan Allen and Benedict Arnold captured Fort Ticonderoga the previous May, taking some eighty men from our ranks and capturing the place without a shot fired.
Rumors of wild plundering and general lawlessness that followed made for common conversation. This remained a point of contention between Ethan and Arnold.
I always got a laugh out of Ethan's words to the Brit captain: "In the name of the great Jehovah and the Continental Congress!" Which is by far the most pious thing the man's ever said in his life.
Facing Fort Crown Point, Ticonderoga's key to American dominance of the northern waters.

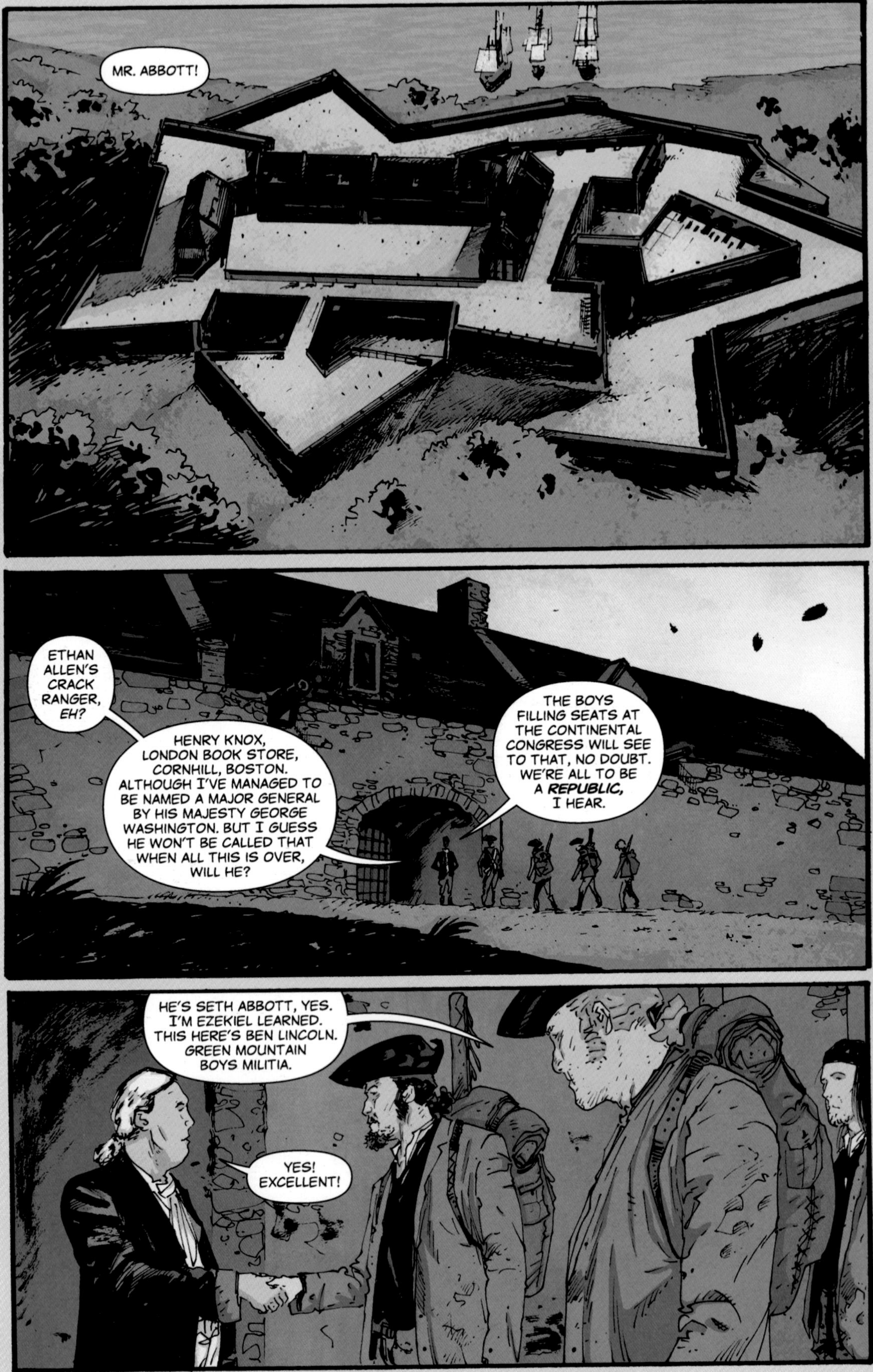
MR. ABBOTT!
ETHAN ALLEN'S CRACK RANGER, EH?
HENRY KNOX, LONDON BOOK STORE, CORNHILL, BOSTON. ALTHOUGH I'VE MANAGED TO BE NAMED A MAJOR GENERAL BY HIS MAJESTY GEORGE WASHINGTON. BUT I GUESS HE WON'T BE CALLED THAT WHEN ALL THIS IS OVER, WILL HE?
THE BOYS FILLING SEATS AT THE CONTINENTAL CONGRESS WILL SEE TO THAT, NO DOUBT. WE'RE ALL TO BE A REPUBLIC, I HEAR.
HE'S SETH ABBOTT, YES. I'M EZEKIEL LEARNED. THIS HERE'S BEN LINCOLN. GREEN MOUNTAIN BOYS MILITIA.
YES! EXCELLENT!

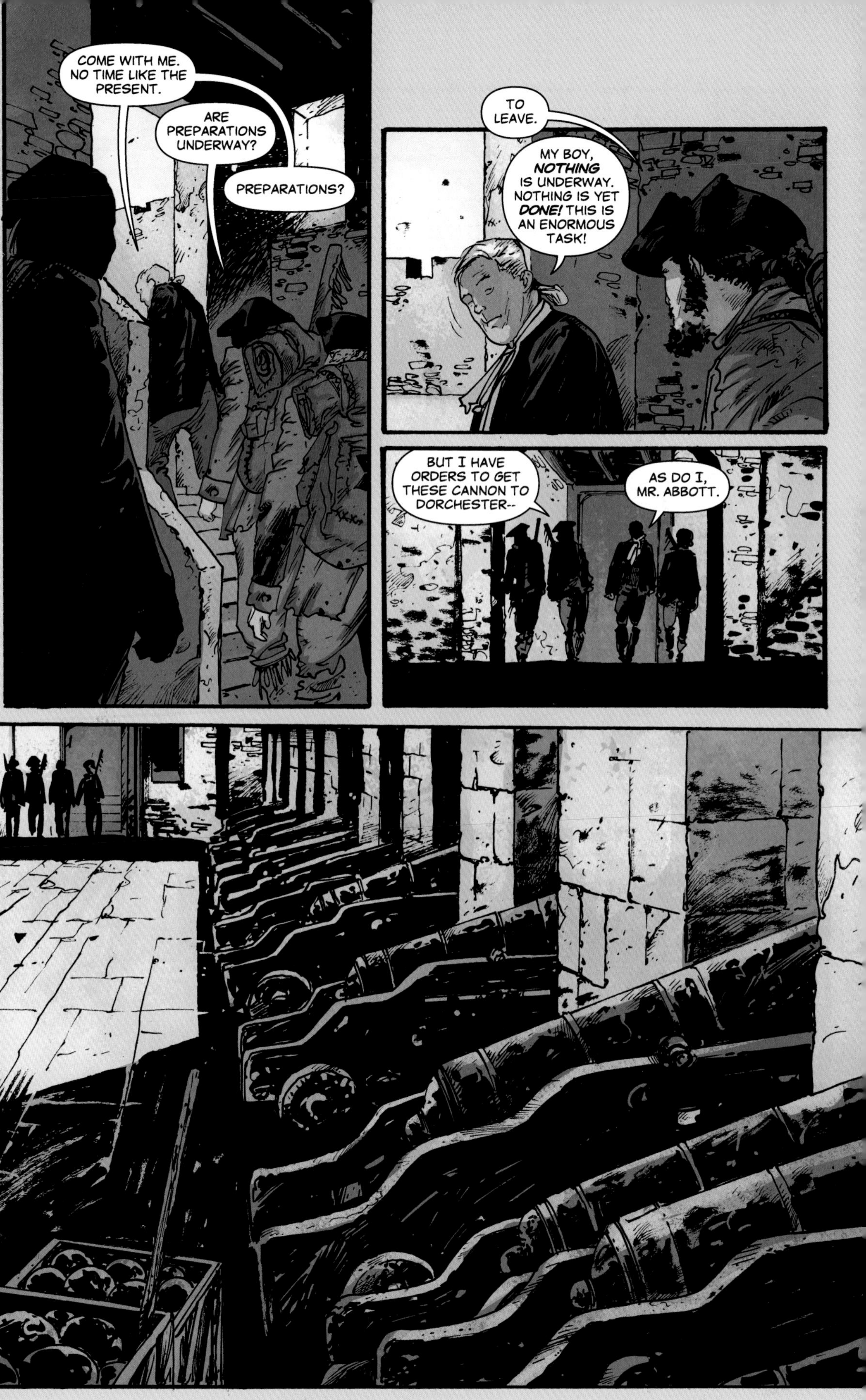

COME WITH ME. NO TIME LIKE THE PRESENT.
ARE PREPARATIONS UNDERWAY?
PREPARATIONS?
TO LEAVE.
MY BOY, NOTHING IS UNDERWAY. NOTHING IS YET DONE! THIS IS AN ENORMOUS TASK!
BUT I HAVE ORDERS TO GET THESE CANNON TO DORCHESTER--
AS DO I, MR. ABBOTT.

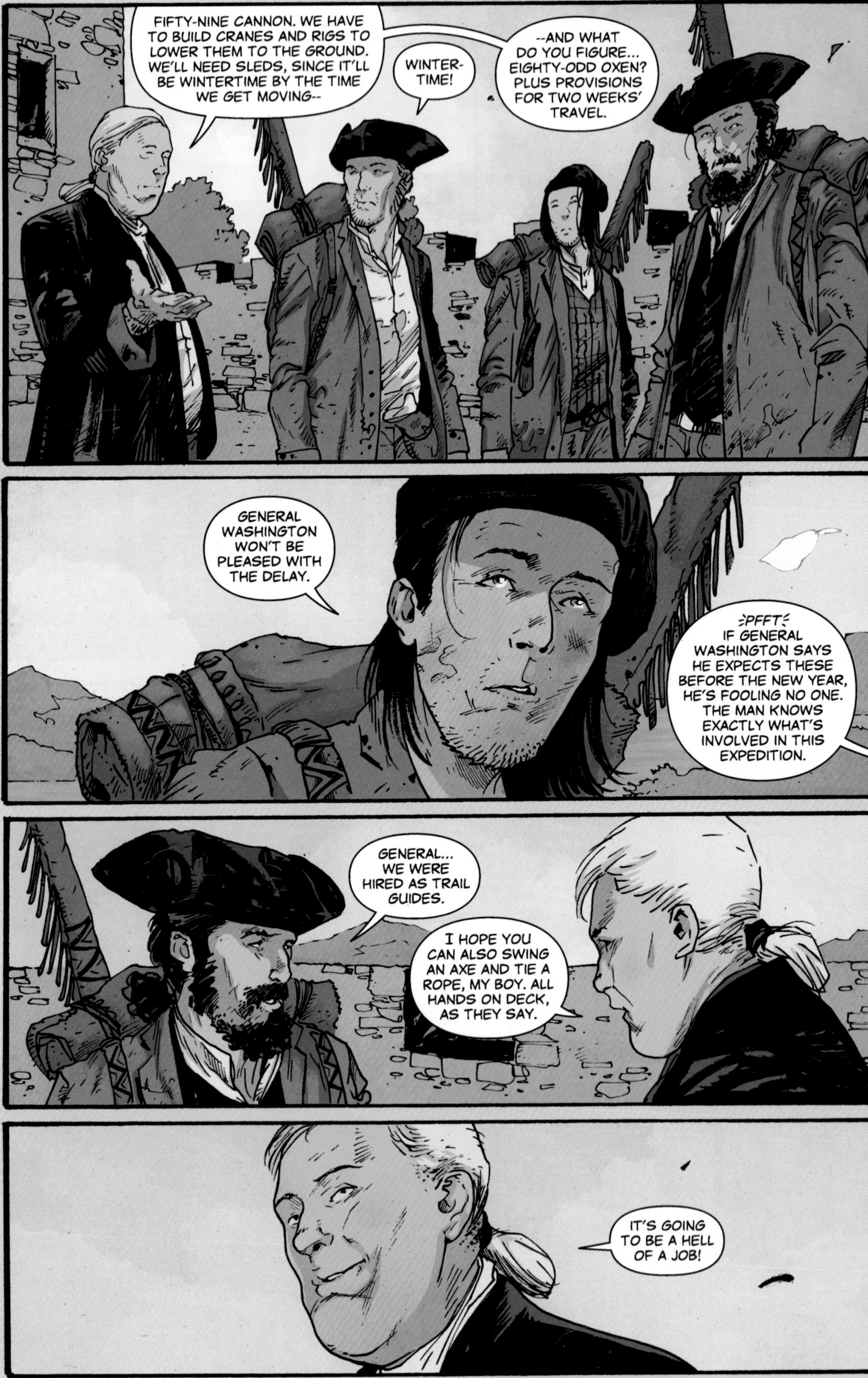
FIFTY-NINE CANNON. WE HAVE TO BUILD CRANES AND RIGS TO LOWER THEM TO THE GROUND. WE'LL NEED SLEDS, SINCE IT'LL BE WINTERTIME BY THE TIME WE GET MOVING--
WINTER-TIME!
--AND WHAT DO YOU FIGURE... EIGHTY-ODD OXEN? PLUS PROVISIONS FOR TWO WEEKS' TRAVEL.
GENERAL WASHINGTON WON'T BE PLEASED WITH THE DELAY.
PFFT
IF GENERAL WASHINGTON SAYS HE EXPECTS THESE BEFORE THE NEW YEAR, HE'S FOOLING NO ONE. THE MAN KNOWS EXACTLY WHAT'S INVOLVED IN THIS EXPEDITION.
GENERAL... WE WERE HIRED AS TRAIL GUIDES.
I HOPE YOU CAN ALSO SWING AN AXE AND TIE A ROPE, MY BOY. ALL HANDS ON DECK, AS THEY SAY.
IT'S GOING TO BE A HELL OF A JOB!

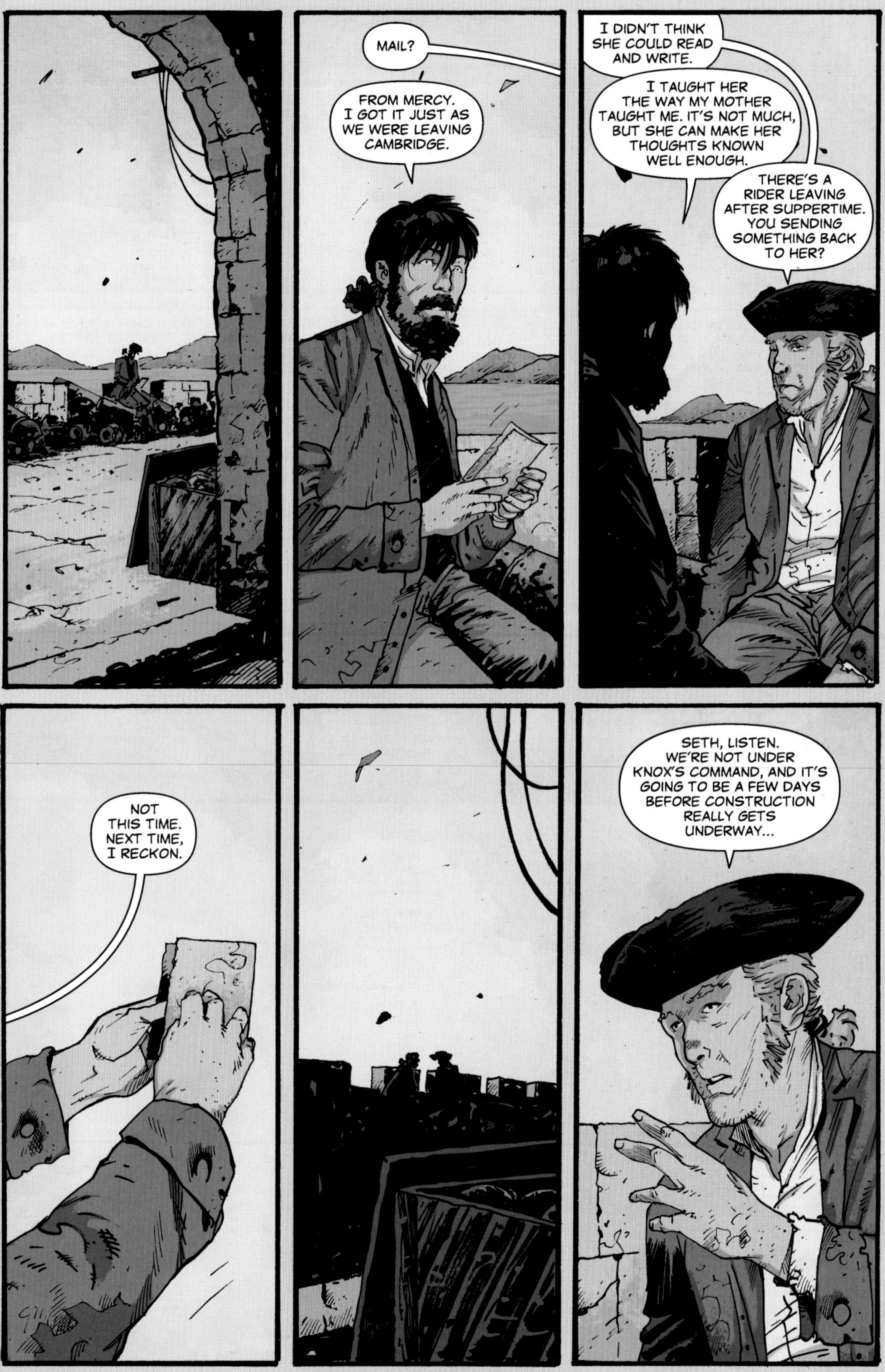
MAIL?
FROM MERCY. I GOT IT JUST AS WE WERE LEAVING CAMBRIDGE.
I DIDN'T THINK SHE COULD READ AND WRITE.
I TAUGHT HER THE WAY MY MOTHER TAUGHT ME. IT'S NOT MUCH, BUT SHE CAN MAKE HER THOUGHTS KNOWN WELL ENOUGH.
THERE'S A RIDER LEAVING AFTER SUPPERTIME. YOU SENDING SOMETHING BACK TO HER?
NOT THIS TIME. NEXT TIME, I RECKON.
SETH, LISTEN. WE'RE NOT UNDER KNOX'S COMMAND, AND IT'S GOING TO BE A FEW DAYS BEFORE CONSTRUCTION REALLY GETS UNDERWAY...

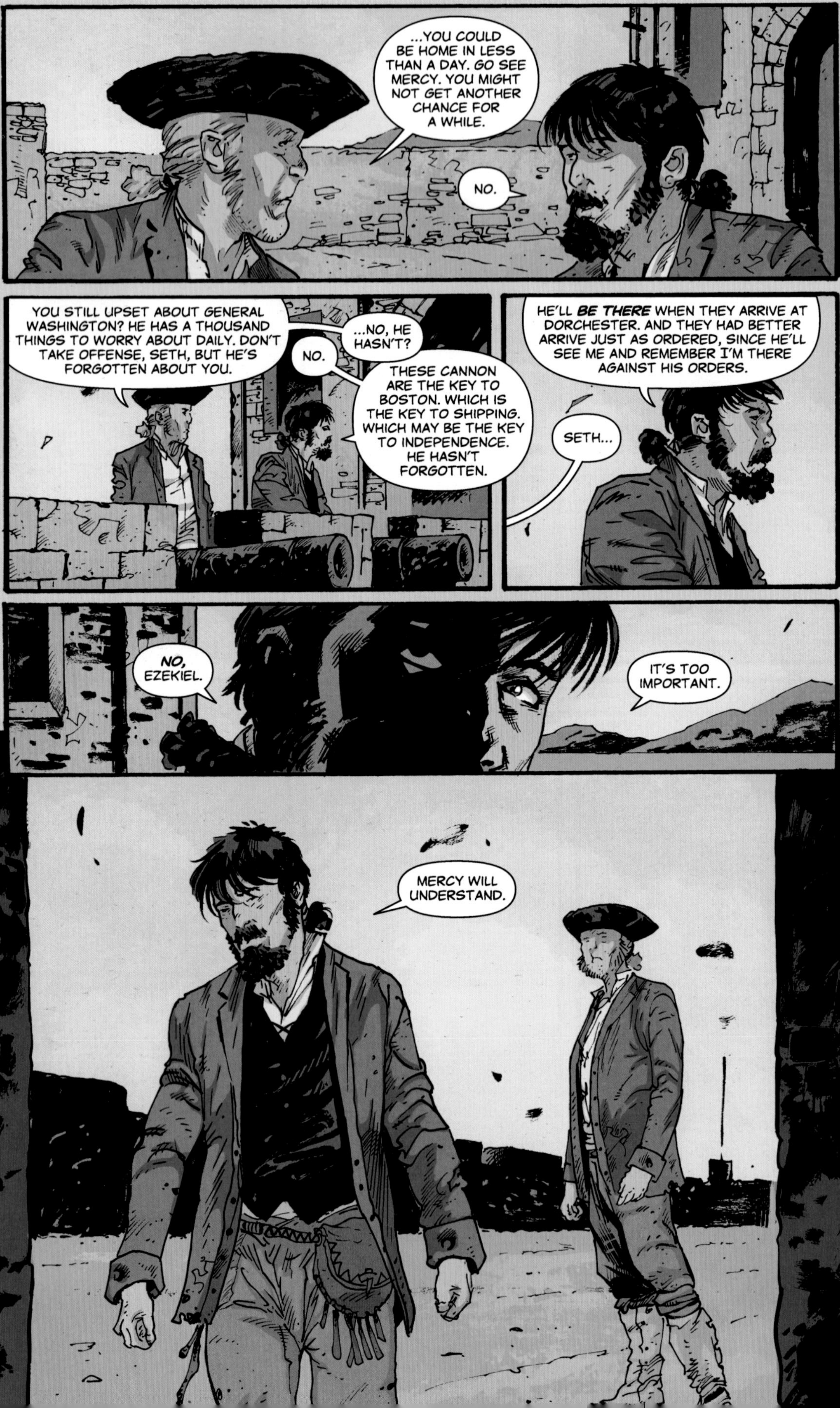
...YOU COULD BE HOME IN LESS THAN A DAY. GO SEE MERCY. YOU MIGHT NOT GET ANOTHER CHANCE FOR A WHILE.
NO.
YOU STILL UPSET ABOUT GENERAL WASHINGTON? HE HAS A THOUSAND THINGS TO WORRY ABOUT DAILY. DON'T TAKE OFFENSE, SETH, BUT HE'S FORGOTTEN ABOUT YOU.
NO.
...NO, HE HASN'T?
THESE CANNON ARE THE KEY TO BOSTON. WHICH IS THE KEY TO SHIPPING. WHICH MAY BE THE KEY TO INDEPENDENCE. HE HASN'T FORGOTTEN.
HE'LL *BE THERE* WHEN THEY ARRIVE AT DORCHESTER. AND THEY HAD BETTER ARRIVE JUST AS ORDERED, SINCE HE'LL SEE ME AND REMEMBER I'M THERE AGAINST HIS ORDERS.
SETH...
NO, EZEKIEL.
IT'S TOO IMPORTANT.
MERCY WILL UNDERSTAND.

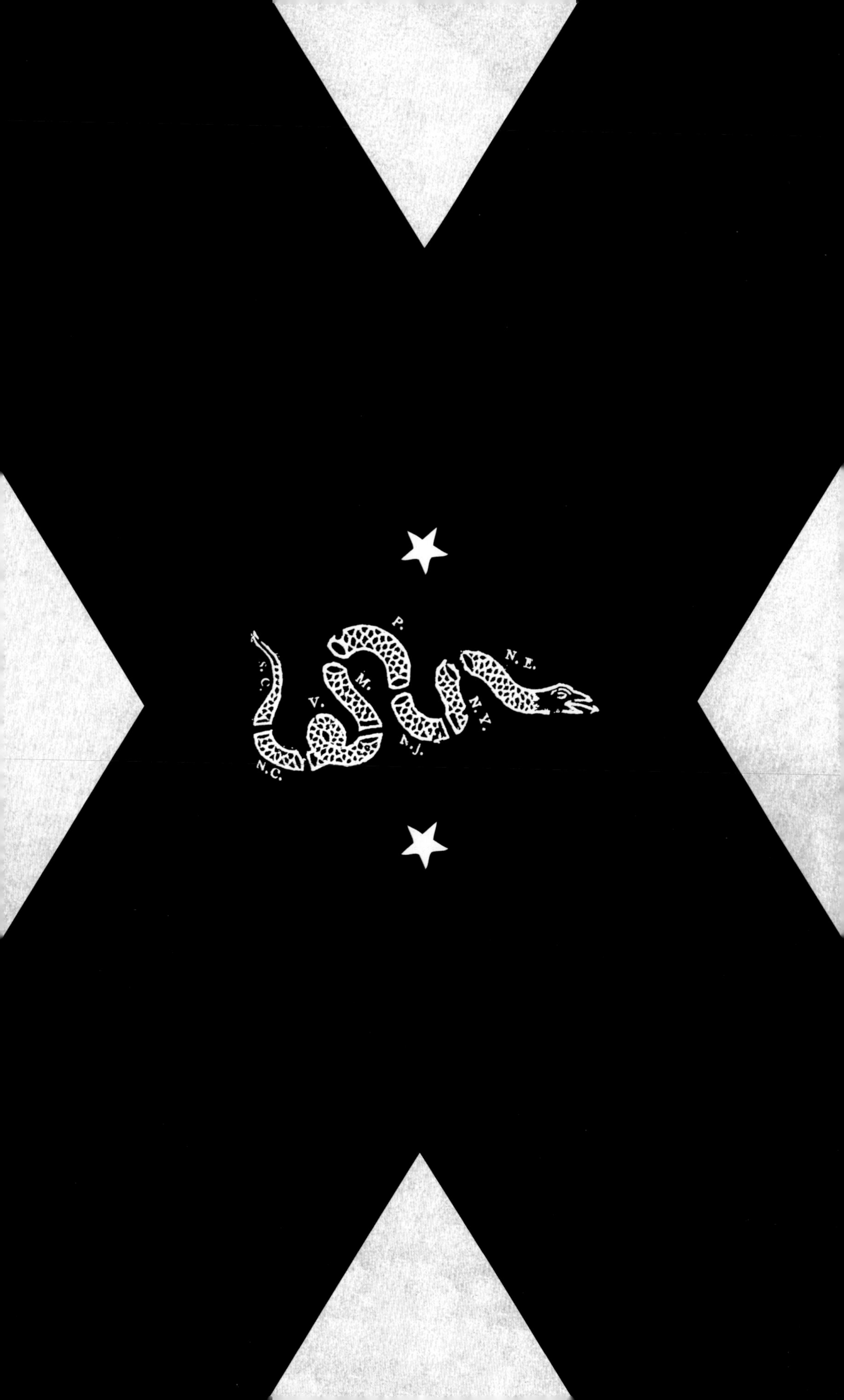
S.C.
N.C.
V.
M.
P.
N.J.
N.Y.
N.E.

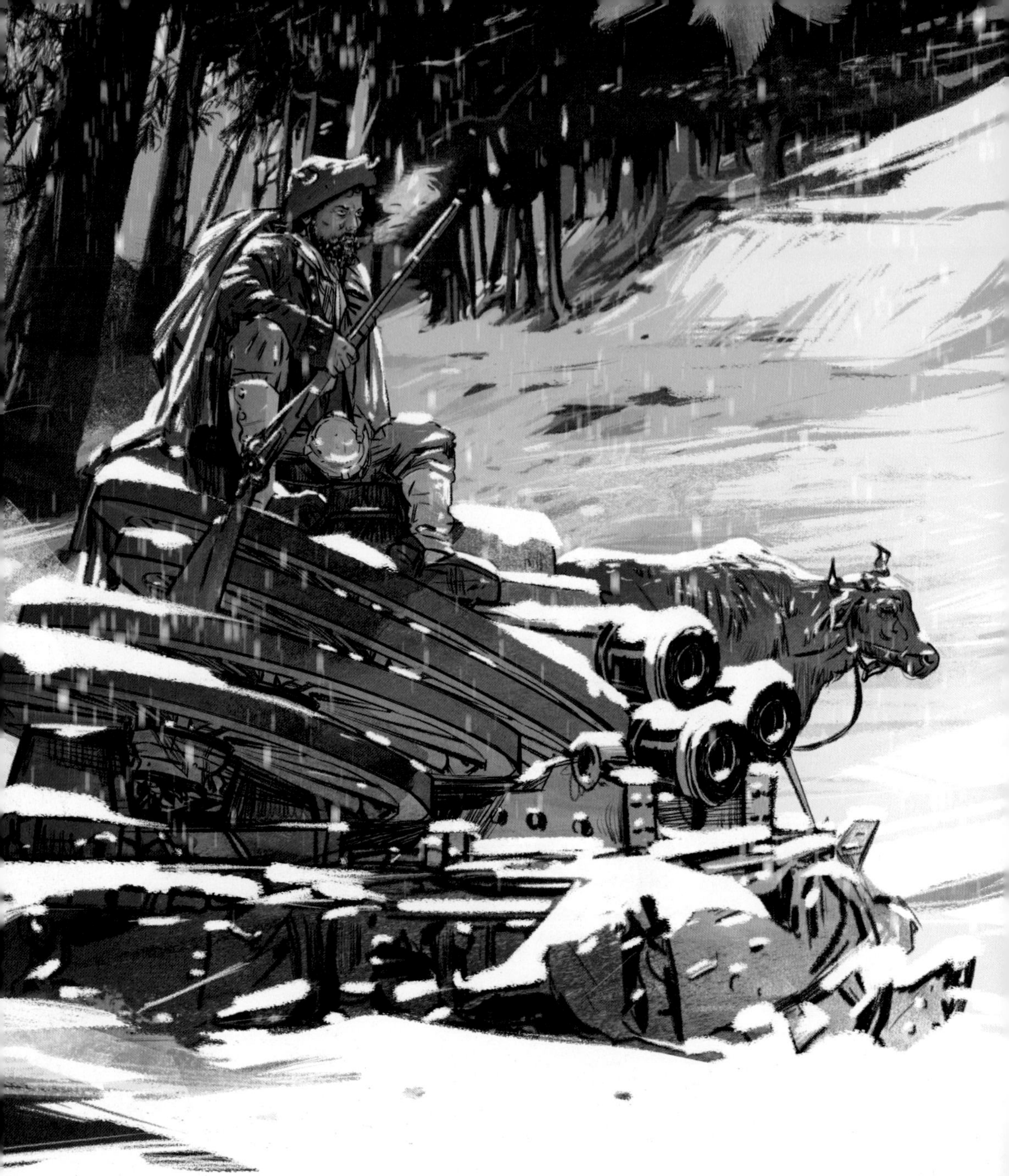

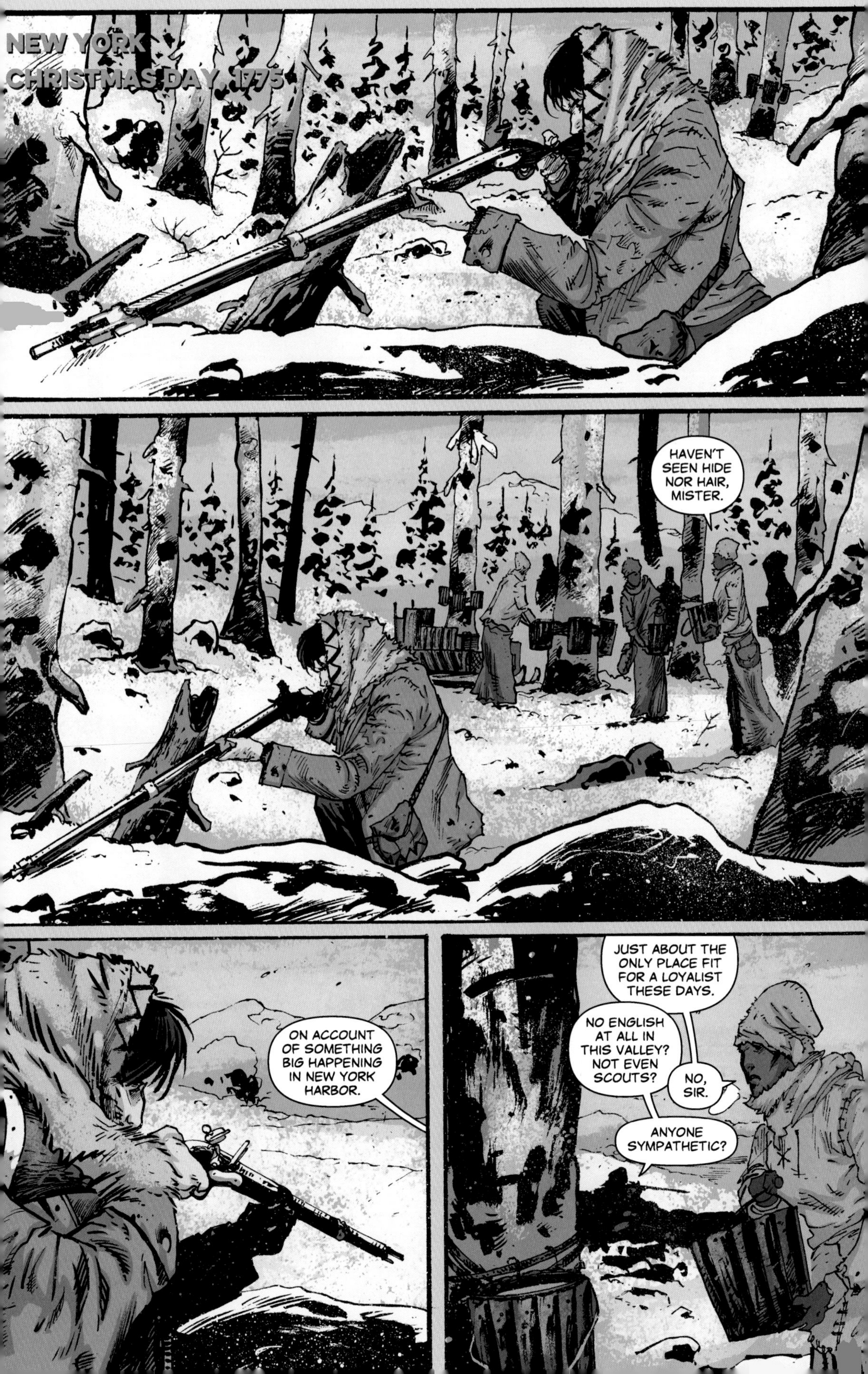
NEW YORK
CHRISTMAS DAY, 1775
HAVEN'T SEEN HIDE NOR HAIR, MISTER.
ON ACCOUNT OF SOMETHING BIG HAPPENING IN NEW YORK HARBOR.
JUST ABOUT THE ONLY PLACE FIT FOR A LOYALIST THESE DAYS.
NO ENGLISH AT ALL IN THIS VALLEY? NOT EVEN SCOUTS?
NO, SIR.
ANYONE SYMPATHETIC?

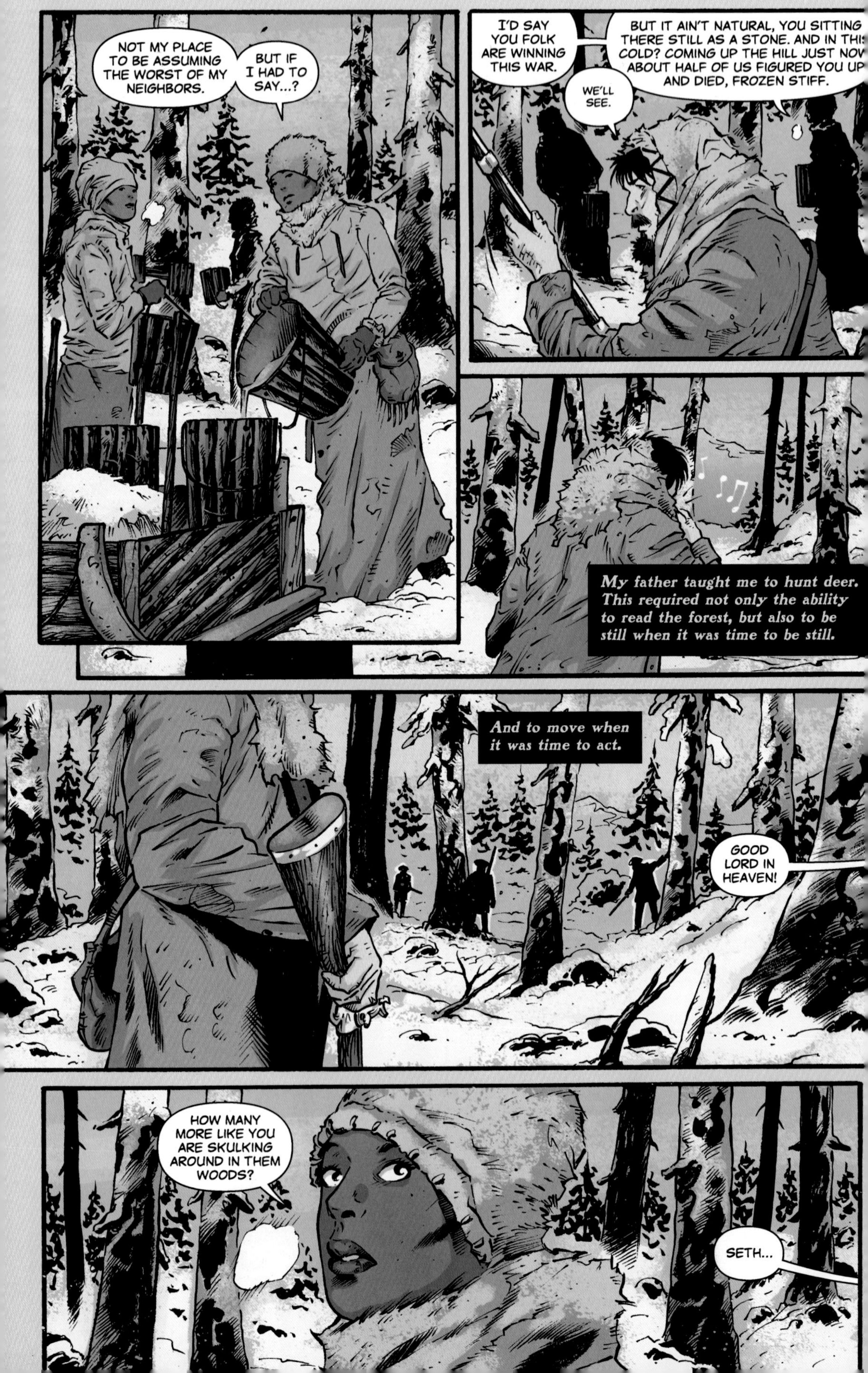
NOT MY PLACE TO BE ASSUMING THE WORST OF MY NEIGHBORS.
BUT IF I HAD TO SAY...?
I'D SAY YOU FOLK ARE WINNING THIS WAR.
BUT IT AIN'T NATURAL, YOU SITTING THERE STILL AS A STONE. AND IN THIS COLD? COMING UP THE HILL JUST NOW ABOUT HALF OF US FIGURED YOU UP AND DIED, FROZEN STIFF.
WE'LL SEE.
My father taught me to hunt deer. This required not only the ability to read the forest, but also to be still when it was time to be still.
And to move when it was time to act.
GOOD LORD IN HEAVEN!
HOW MANY MORE LIKE YOU ARE SKULKING AROUND IN THEM WOODS?
SETH...

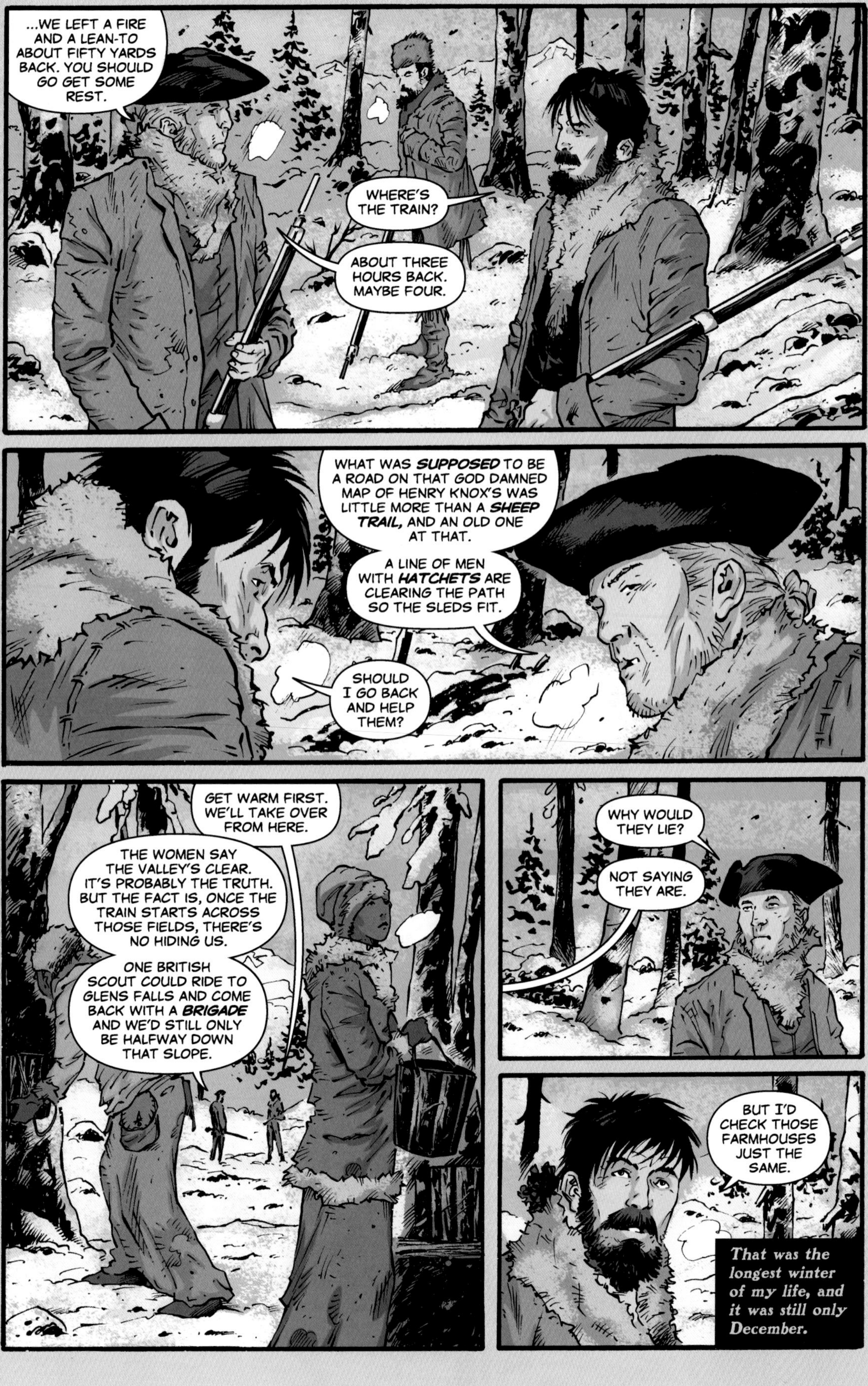
...WE LEFT A FIRE AND A LEAN-TO ABOUT FIFTY YARDS BACK. YOU SHOULD GO GET SOME REST.
WHERE'S THE TRAIN?
ABOUT THREE HOURS BACK. MAYBE FOUR.
WHAT WAS SUPPOSED TO BE A ROAD ON THAT GOD DAMNED MAP OF HENRY KNOX'S WAS LITTLE MORE THAN A SHEEP TRAIL, AND AN OLD ONE AT THAT.
A LINE OF MEN WITH HATCHETS ARE CLEARING THE PATH SO THE SLEDS FIT.
SHOULD I GO BACK AND HELP THEM?
GET WARM FIRST. WE'LL TAKE OVER FROM HERE.
THE WOMEN SAY THE VALLEY'S CLEAR. IT'S PROBABLY THE TRUTH. BUT THE FACT IS, ONCE THE TRAIN STARTS ACROSS THOSE FIELDS, THERE'S NO HIDING US.
ONE BRITISH SCOUT COULD RIDE TO GLENS FALLS AND COME BACK WITH A BRIGADE AND WE'D STILL ONLY BE HALFWAY DOWN THAT SLOPE.
WHY WOULD THEY LIE?
NOT SAYING THEY ARE.
BUT I'D CHECK THOSE FARMHOUSES JUST THE SAME.
That was the longest winter of my life, and it was still only December.

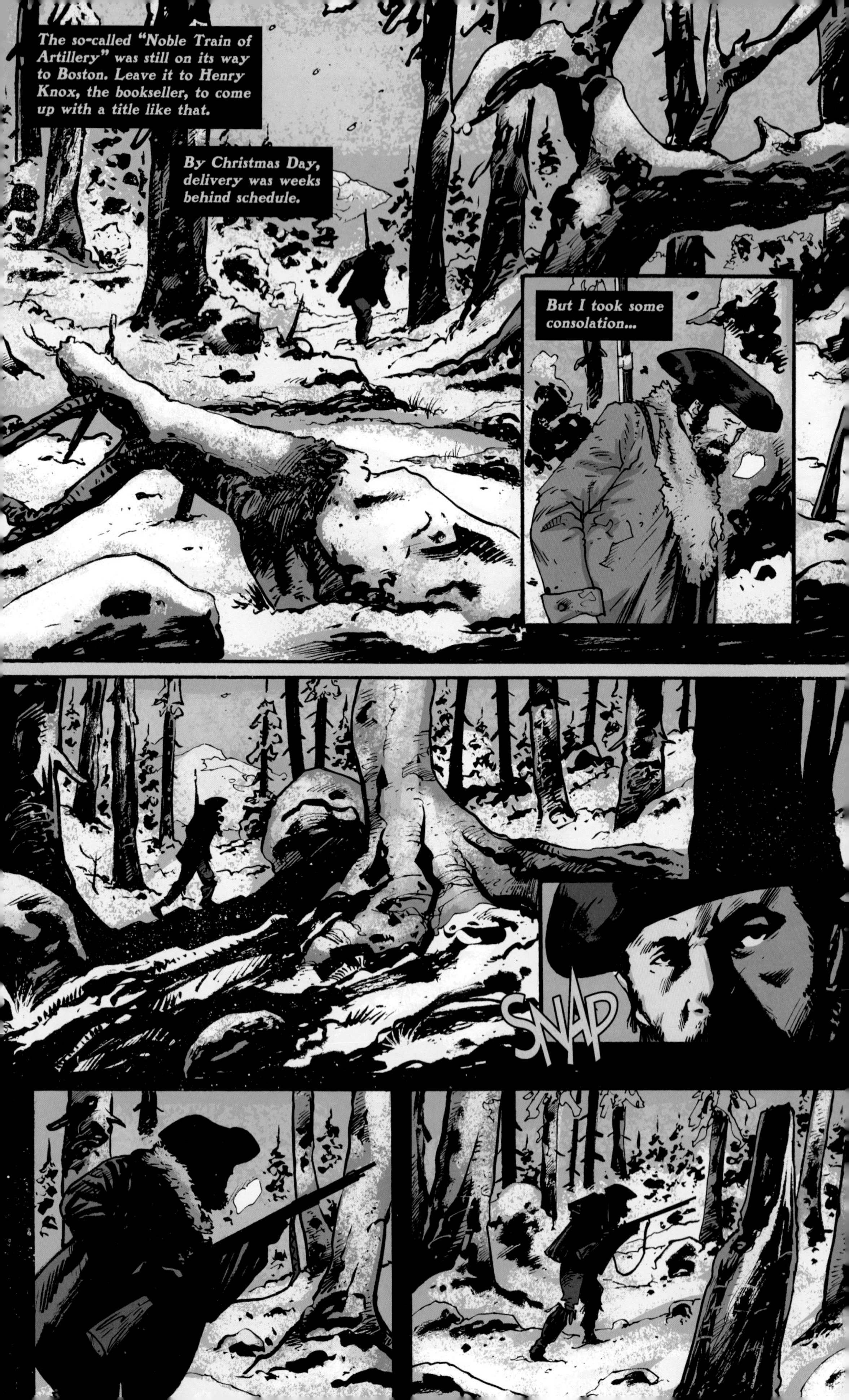
The so-called "Noble Train of Artillery" was still on its way to Boston. Leave it to Henry Knox, the bookseller, to come up with a title like that.
By Christmas Day, delivery was weeks behind schedule.
But I took some consolation...
SNAP

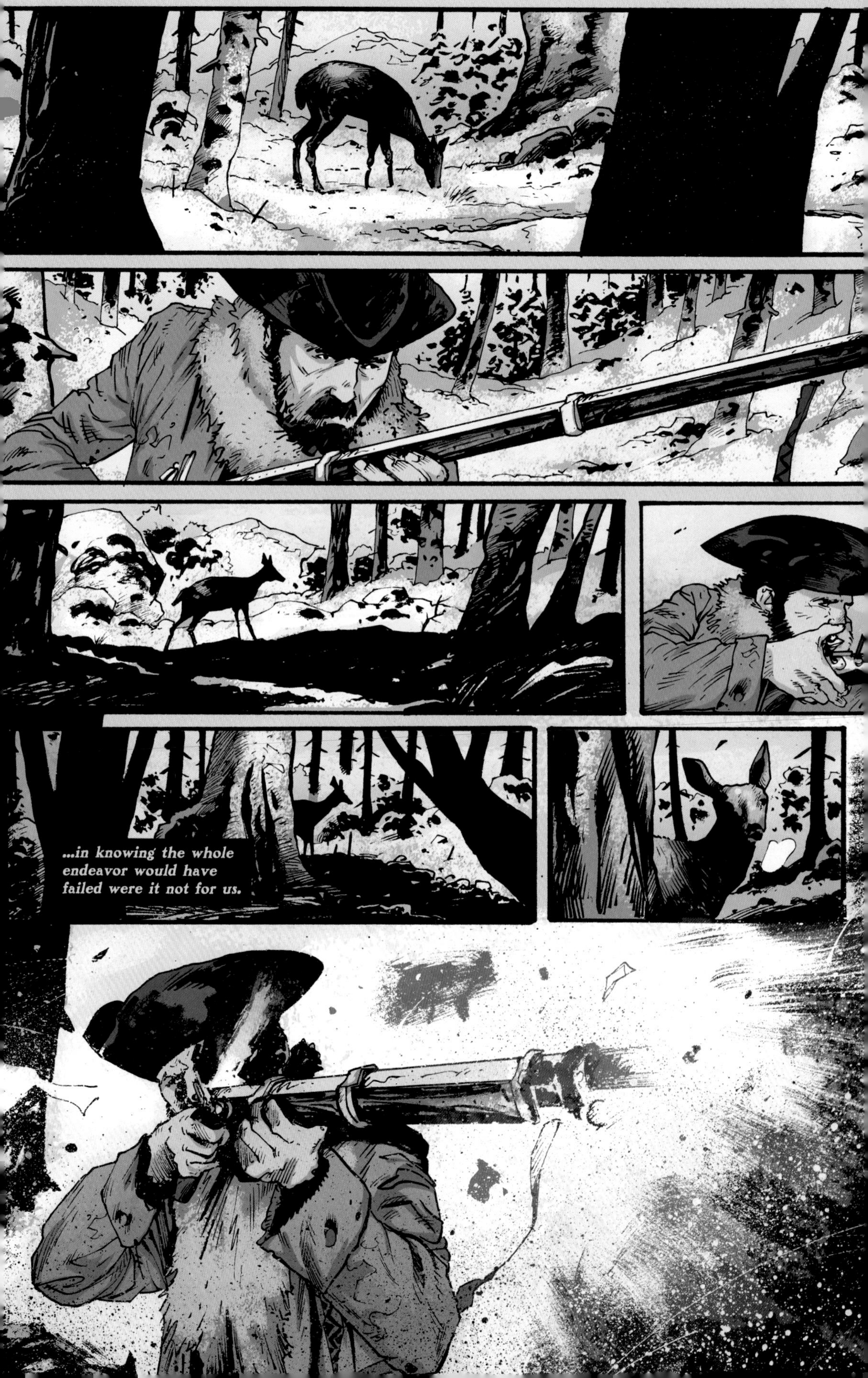
...in knowing the whole endeavor would have failed were it not for us.

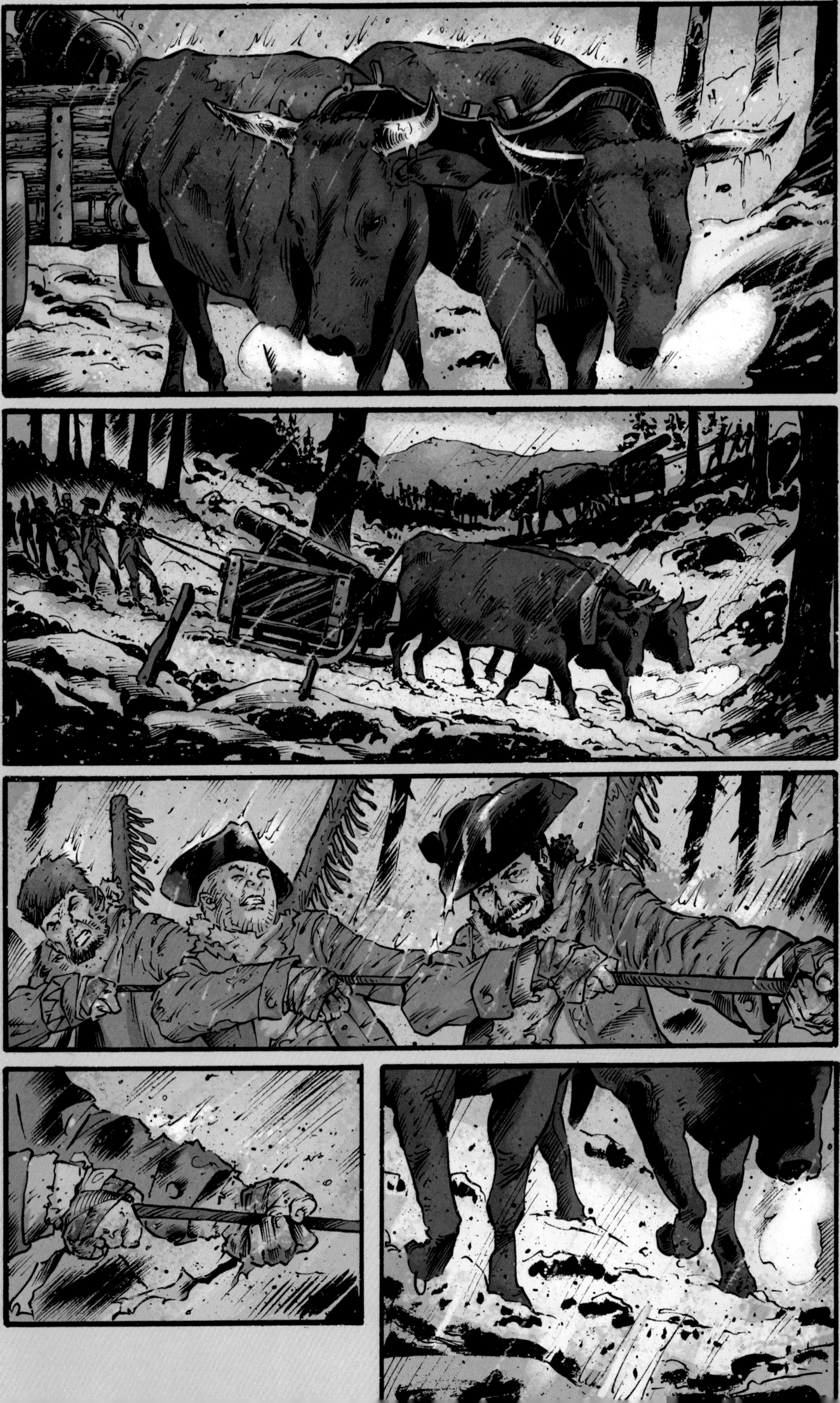

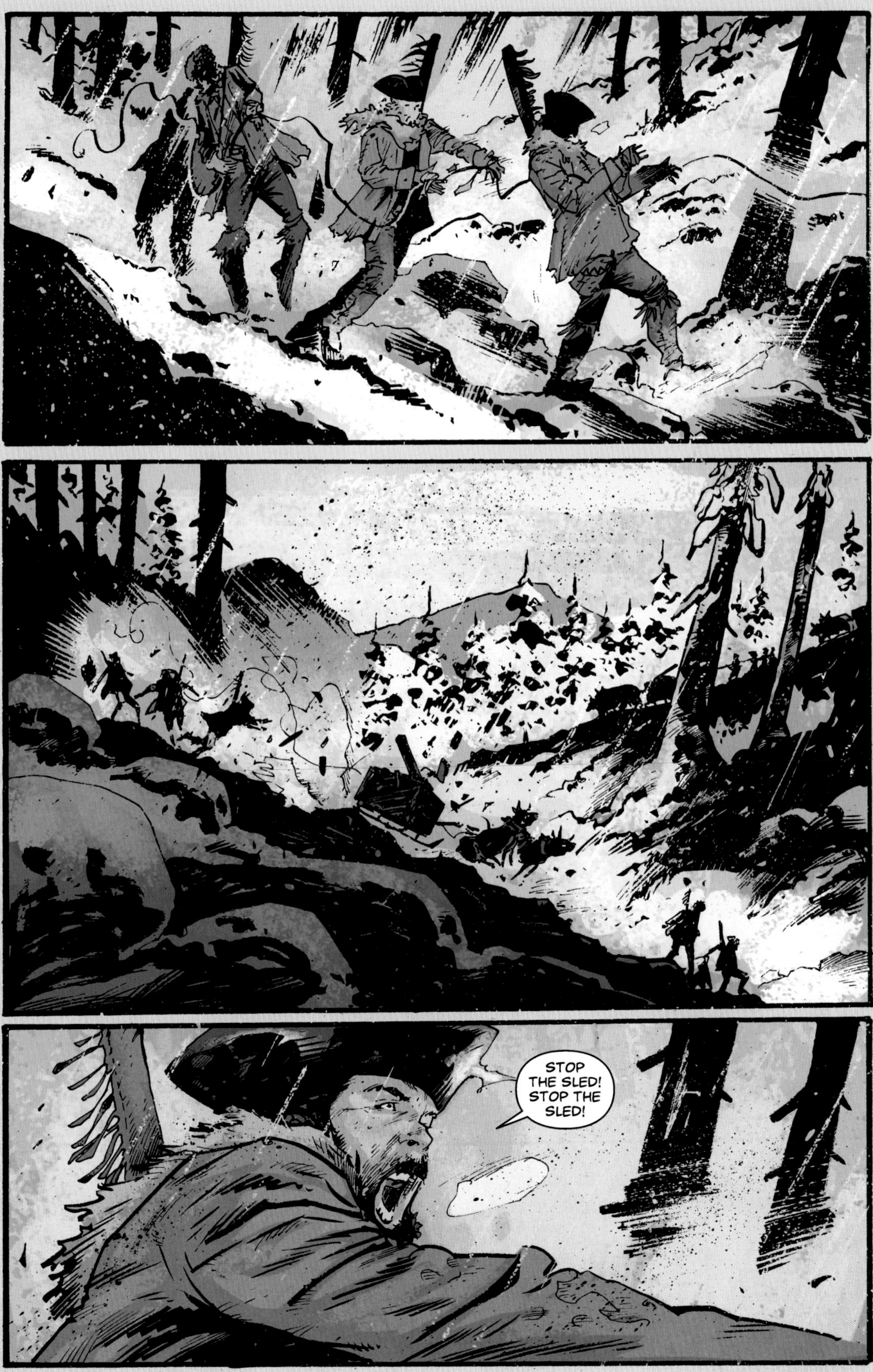
STOP THE SLED! STOP THE SLED!

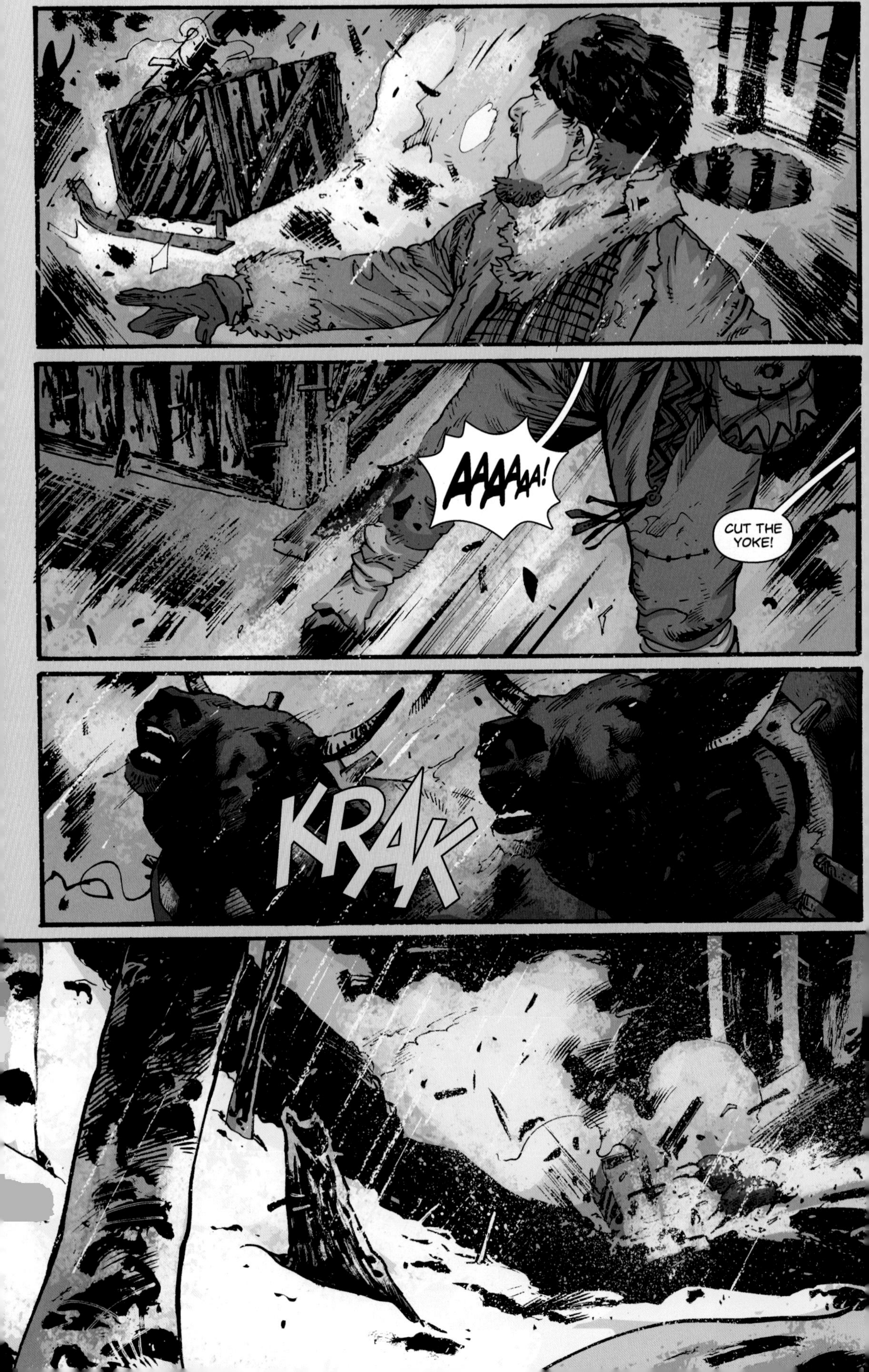
AAAAAA!
CUT THE YOKE!
KRAK

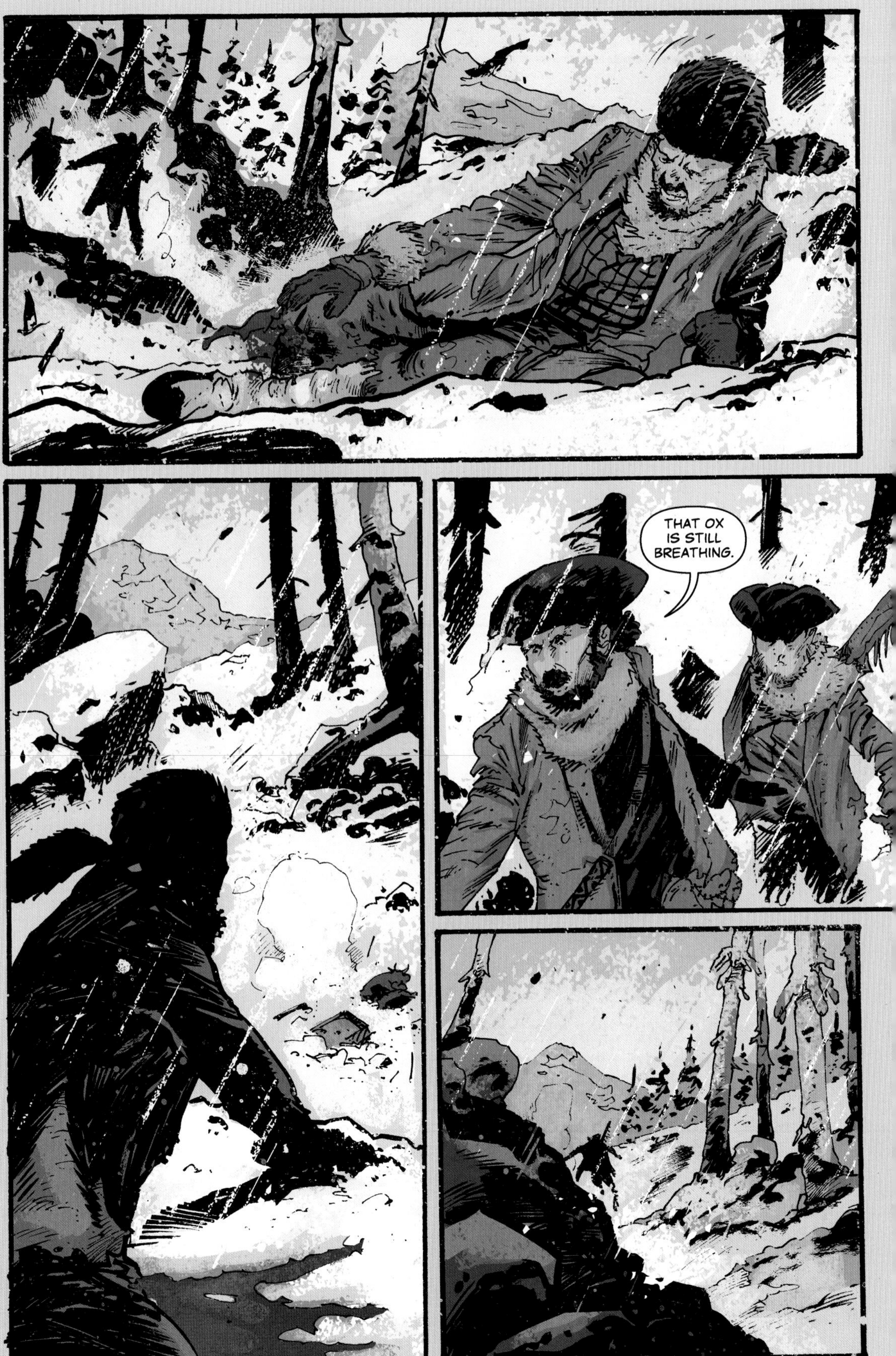
THAT OX IS STILL BREATHING.

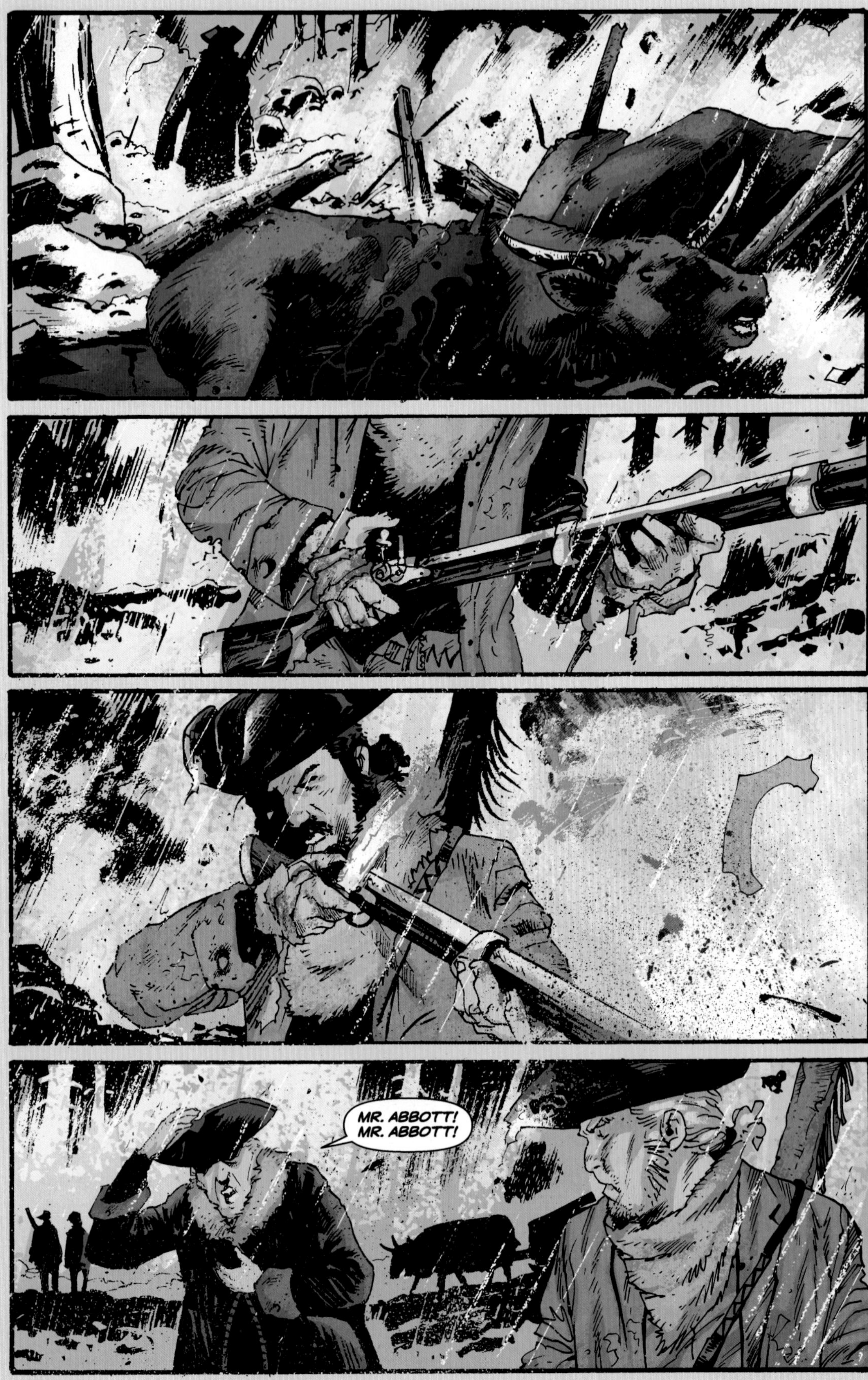
MR. ABBOTT! MR. ABBOTT!

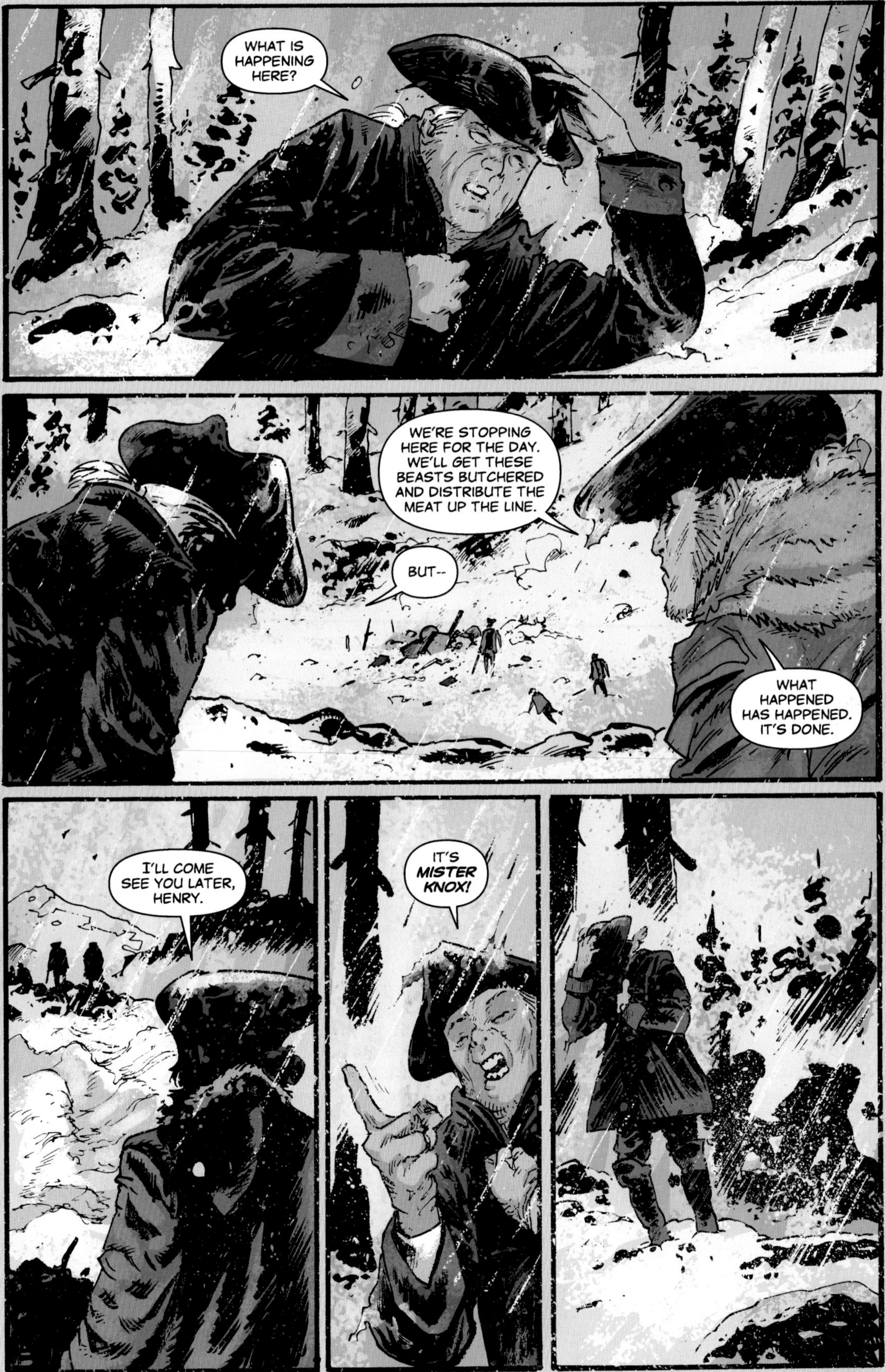
WHAT IS HAPPENING HERE?
WE'RE STOPPING HERE FOR THE DAY. WE'LL GET THESE BEASTS BUTCHERED AND DISTRIBUTE THE MEAT UP THE LINE.
BUT--
WHAT HAPPENED HAS HAPPENED. IT'S DONE.
I'LL COME SEE YOU LATER, HENRY.
IT'S *MISTER KNOX!*

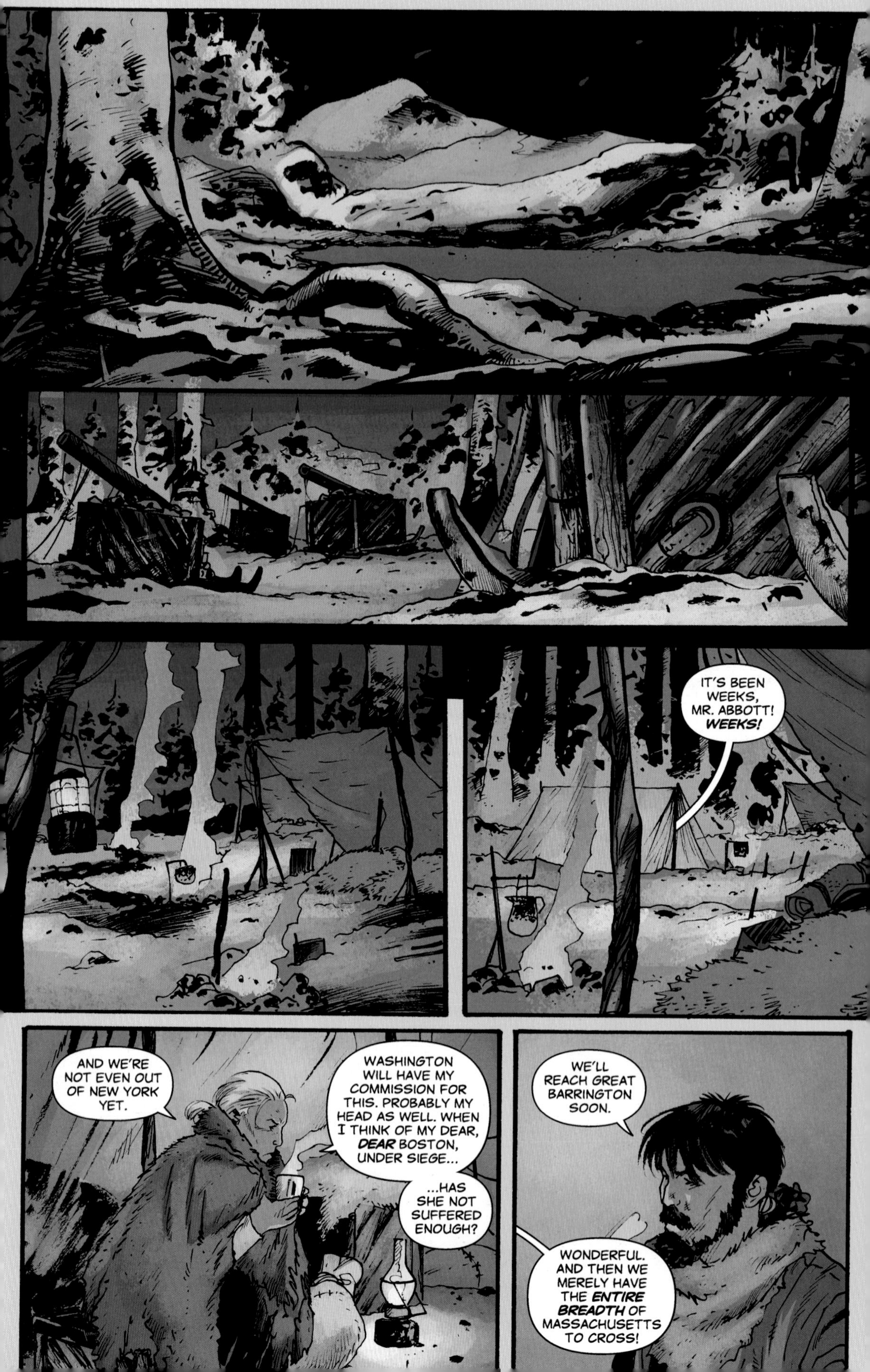
IT'S BEEN WEEKS, MR. ABBOTT! **WEEKS!**
AND WE'RE NOT EVEN OUT OF NEW YORK YET.
WASHINGTON WILL HAVE MY COMMISSION FOR THIS. PROBABLY MY HEAD AS WELL. WHEN I THINK OF MY DEAR, **DEAR** BOSTON, UNDER SIEGE...
...HAS SHE NOT SUFFERED ENOUGH?
WE'LL REACH GREAT BARRINGTON SOON.
WONDERFUL. AND THEN WE MERELY HAVE THE **ENTIRE BREADTH** OF MASSACHUSETTS TO CROSS!

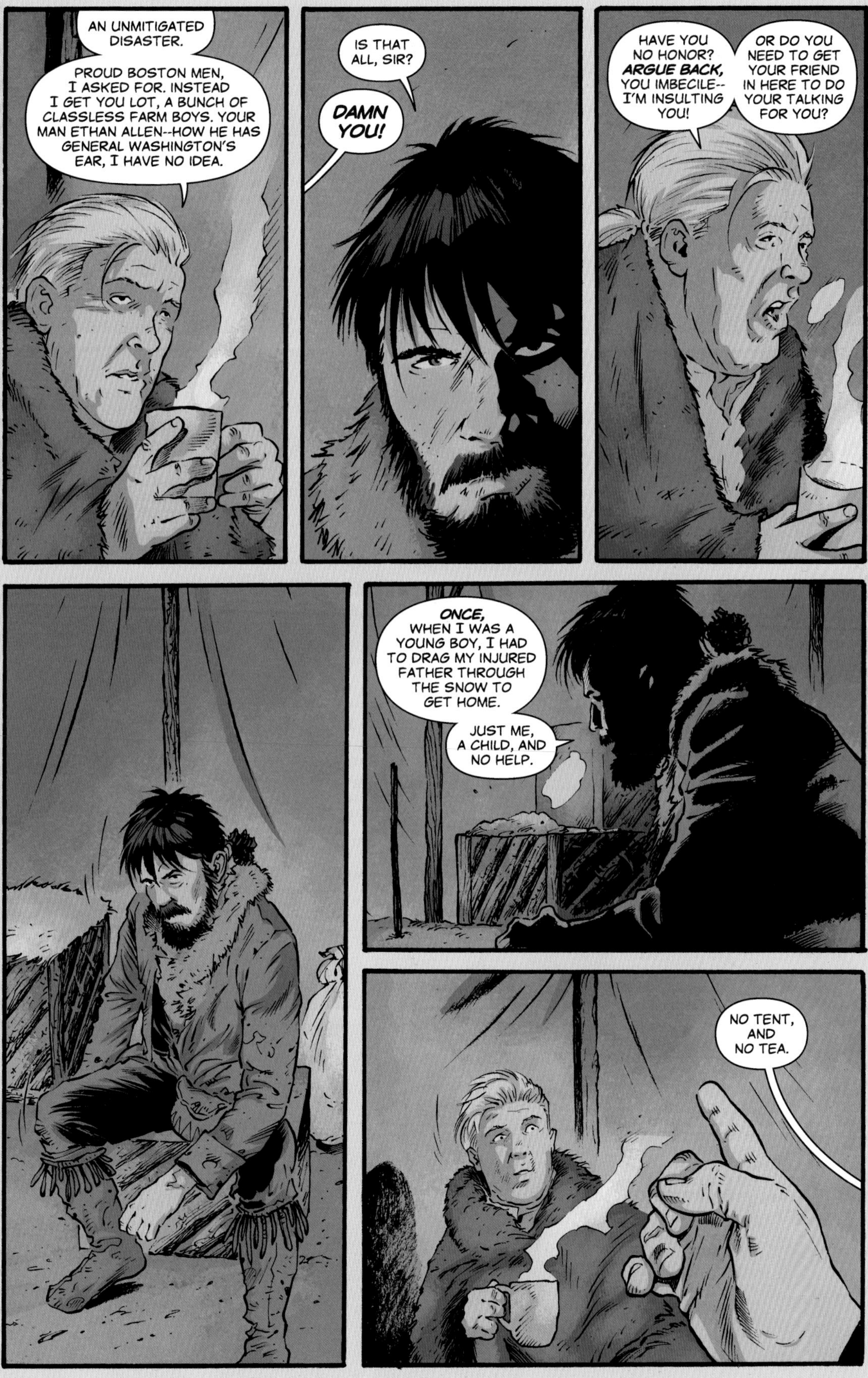
AN UNMITIGATED DISASTER.
PROUD BOSTON MEN, I ASKED FOR. INSTEAD I GET YOU LOT, A BUNCH OF CLASSLESS FARM BOYS. YOUR MAN ETHAN ALLEN--HOW HE HAS GENERAL WASHINGTON'S EAR, I HAVE NO IDEA.
IS THAT ALL, SIR?
DAMN YOU!
HAVE YOU NO HONOR? ARGUE BACK, YOU IMBECILE--I'M INSULTING YOU!
OR DO YOU NEED TO GET YOUR FRIEND IN HERE TO DO YOUR TALKING FOR YOU?
ONCE, WHEN I WAS A YOUNG BOY, I HAD TO DRAG MY INJURED FATHER THROUGH THE SNOW TO GET HOME.
JUST ME, A CHILD, AND NO HELP.
NO TENT, AND NO TEA.

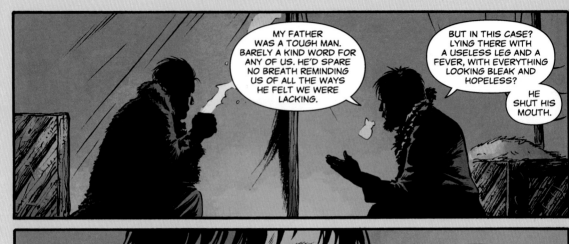

MY FATHER WAS A TOUGH MAN. BARELY A KIND WORD FOR ANY OF US. HE'D SPARE NO BREATH REMINDING US OF ALL THE WAYS HE FELT WE WERE LACKING.

BUT IN THIS CASE? LYING THERE WITH A USELESS LEG AND A FEVER, WITH EVERYTHING LOOKING BLEAK AND HOPELESS?

HE SHUT HIS MOUTH.

MAYBE NOT AT FIRST. HE GOT A COUPLE INSULTS IN.

BUT ALL THAT STOPPED SOON ENOUGH, AFTER HE REALIZED A FEW THINGS. I'M GOING TO TELL YOU WHAT THOSE FEW THINGS ARE WHILE YOU FINISH YOUR TEA.

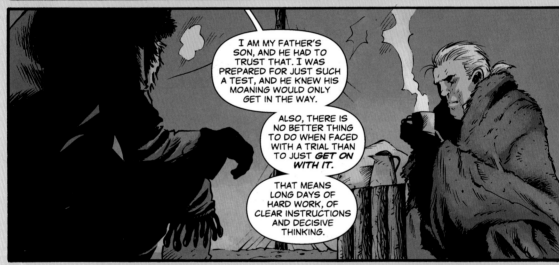

I AM MY FATHER'S SON, AND HE HAD TO TRUST THAT. I WAS PREPARED FOR JUST SUCH A TEST, AND HE KNEW HIS MOANING WOULD ONLY GET IN THE WAY.

ALSO, THERE IS NO BETTER THING TO DO WHEN FACED WITH A TRIAL THAN TO JUST *GET ON WITH IT.*

THAT MEANS LONG DAYS OF HARD WORK, OF CLEAR INSTRUCTIONS AND DECISIVE THINKING.

IT MEANS LITTLE TALKING AND NO COMPLAINING.

A TASK ONLY TAKES AS LONG AS IT TAKES. MY FATHER TAUGHT ME THAT, AND WHILE IT WAS NOT ENJOYABLE FOR HIM TO BE DRAGGED FOR DAYS ON A SLED WITH A TERRIBLE INJURY, HE KNEW I WAS HIS ONLY CHANCE AT GETTING THROUGH IT.

I'M MY FATHER'S SON, AND I'M ALSO ETHAN ALLEN'S MAN. I EARNED BOTH MEN'S TRUST. I CAN GET US THROUGH THIS. I'VE DONE IT BEFORE.

UNDERSTAND?

BUT--

NO MORE OF YOUR MAPS AND PLANS. I WANT YOU TO STOP THINKING FOR US. STOP MANAGING US. FROM THIS POINT ON, YOU WILL ONLY *LISTEN* AND *OBEY.*

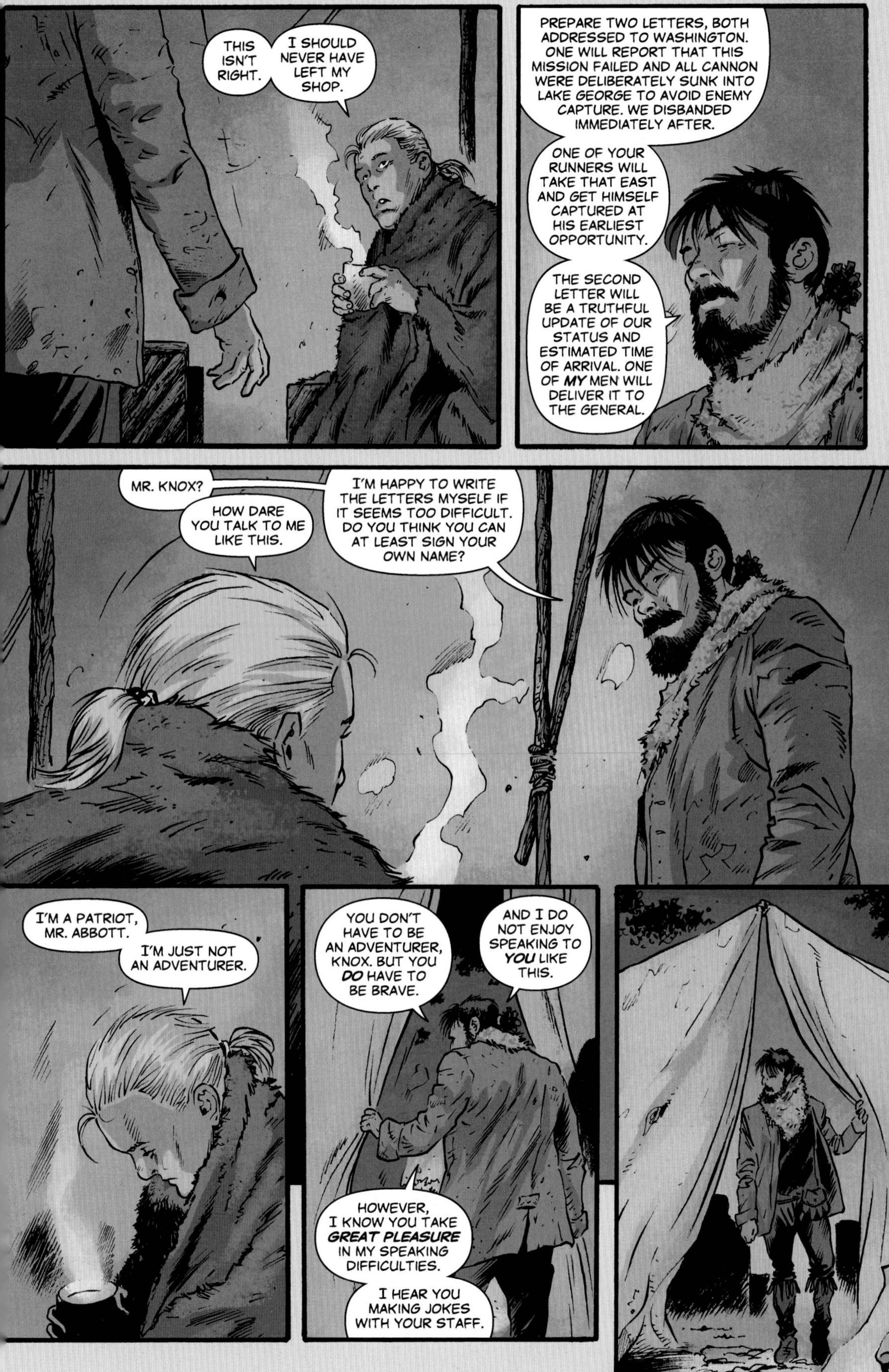
THIS ISN'T RIGHT.
I SHOULD NEVER HAVE LEFT MY SHOP.
PREPARE TWO LETTERS, BOTH ADDRESSED TO WASHINGTON. ONE WILL REPORT THAT THIS MISSION FAILED AND ALL CANNON WERE DELIBERATELY SUNK INTO LAKE GEORGE TO AVOID ENEMY CAPTURE. WE DISBANDED IMMEDIATELY AFTER.
ONE OF YOUR RUNNERS WILL TAKE THAT EAST AND GET HIMSELF CAPTURED AT HIS EARLIEST OPPORTUNITY.
THE SECOND LETTER WILL BE A TRUTHFUL UPDATE OF OUR STATUS AND ESTIMATED TIME OF ARRIVAL. ONE OF *MY* MEN WILL DELIVER IT TO THE GENERAL.
MR. KNOX?
HOW DARE YOU TALK TO ME LIKE THIS.
I'M HAPPY TO WRITE THE LETTERS MYSELF IF IT SEEMS TOO DIFFICULT. DO YOU THINK YOU CAN AT LEAST SIGN YOUR OWN NAME?
I'M A PATRIOT, MR. ABBOTT.
I'M JUST NOT AN ADVENTURER.
YOU DON'T HAVE TO BE AN ADVENTURER, KNOX. BUT YOU *DO* HAVE TO BE BRAVE.
AND I DO NOT ENJOY SPEAKING TO *YOU* LIKE THIS.
HOWEVER, I KNOW YOU TAKE ***GREAT PLEASURE*** IN MY SPEAKING DIFFICULTIES.
I HEAR YOU MAKING JOKES WITH YOUR STAFF.

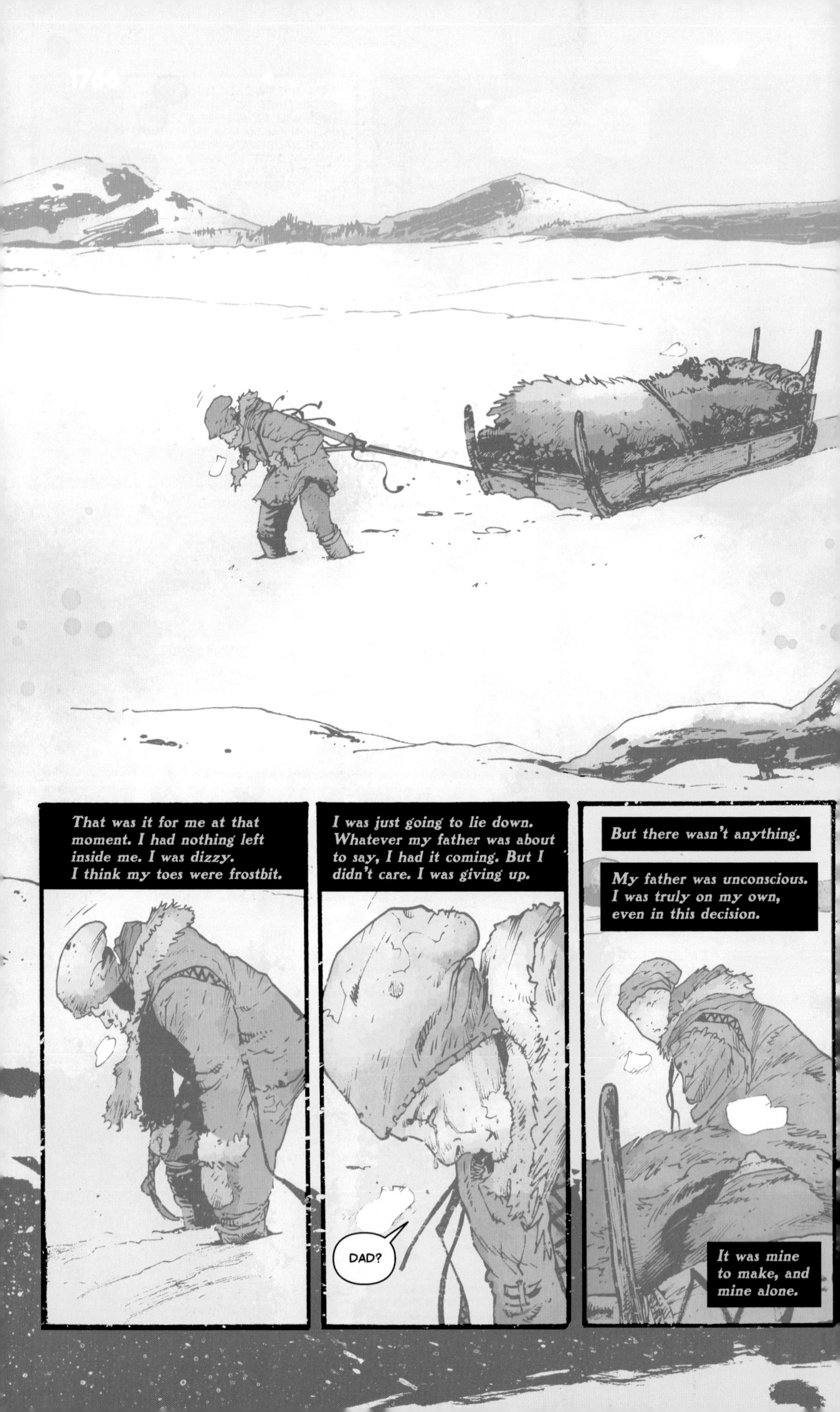
1766
That was it for me at that moment. I had nothing left inside me. I was dizzy. I think my toes were frostbit.
I was just going to lie down. Whatever my father was about to say, I had it coming. But I didn't care. I was giving up.
DAD?
But there wasn't anything.
My father was unconscious. I was truly on my own, even in this decision.
It was mine to make, and mine alone.

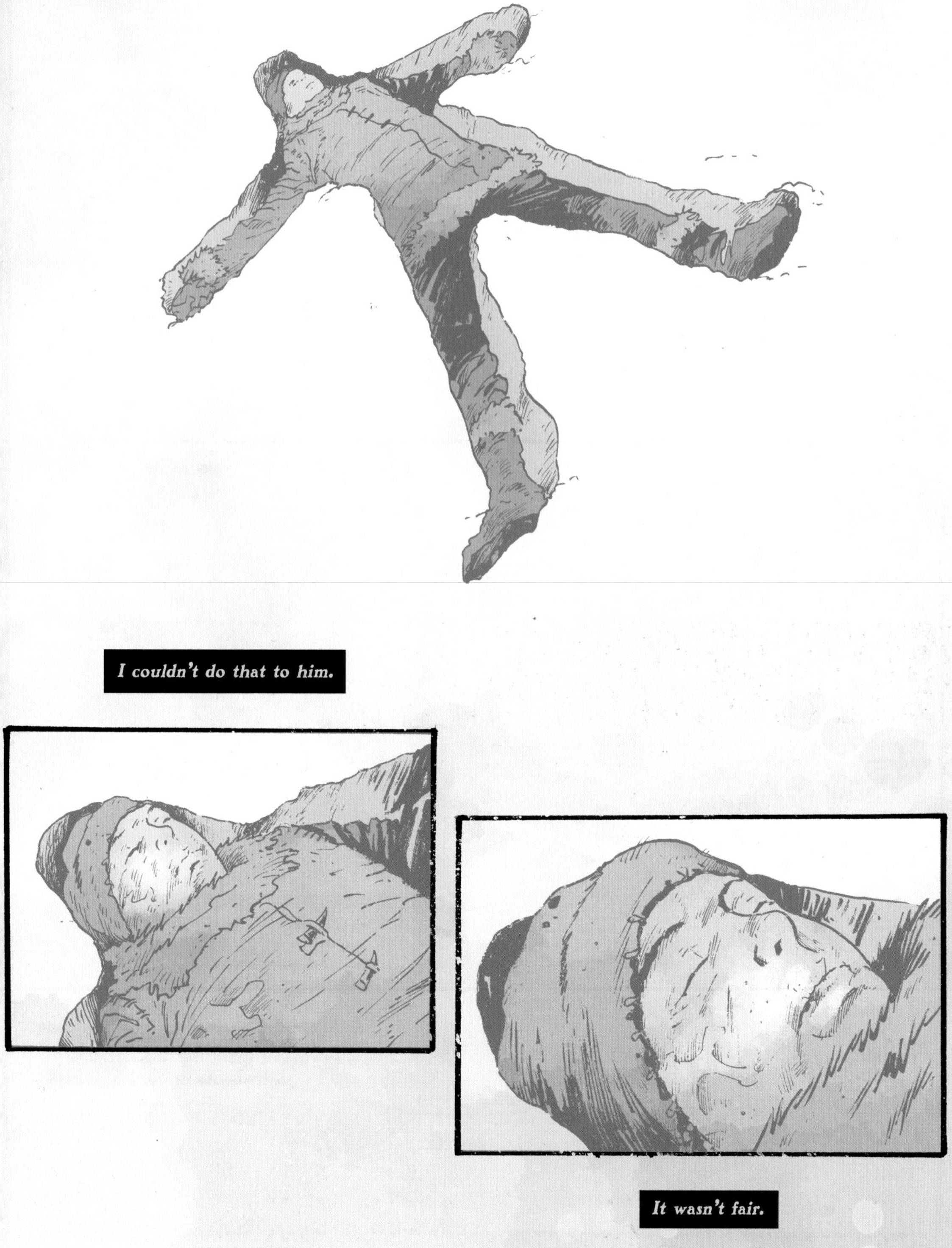
I couldn't do that to him.
It wasn't fair.

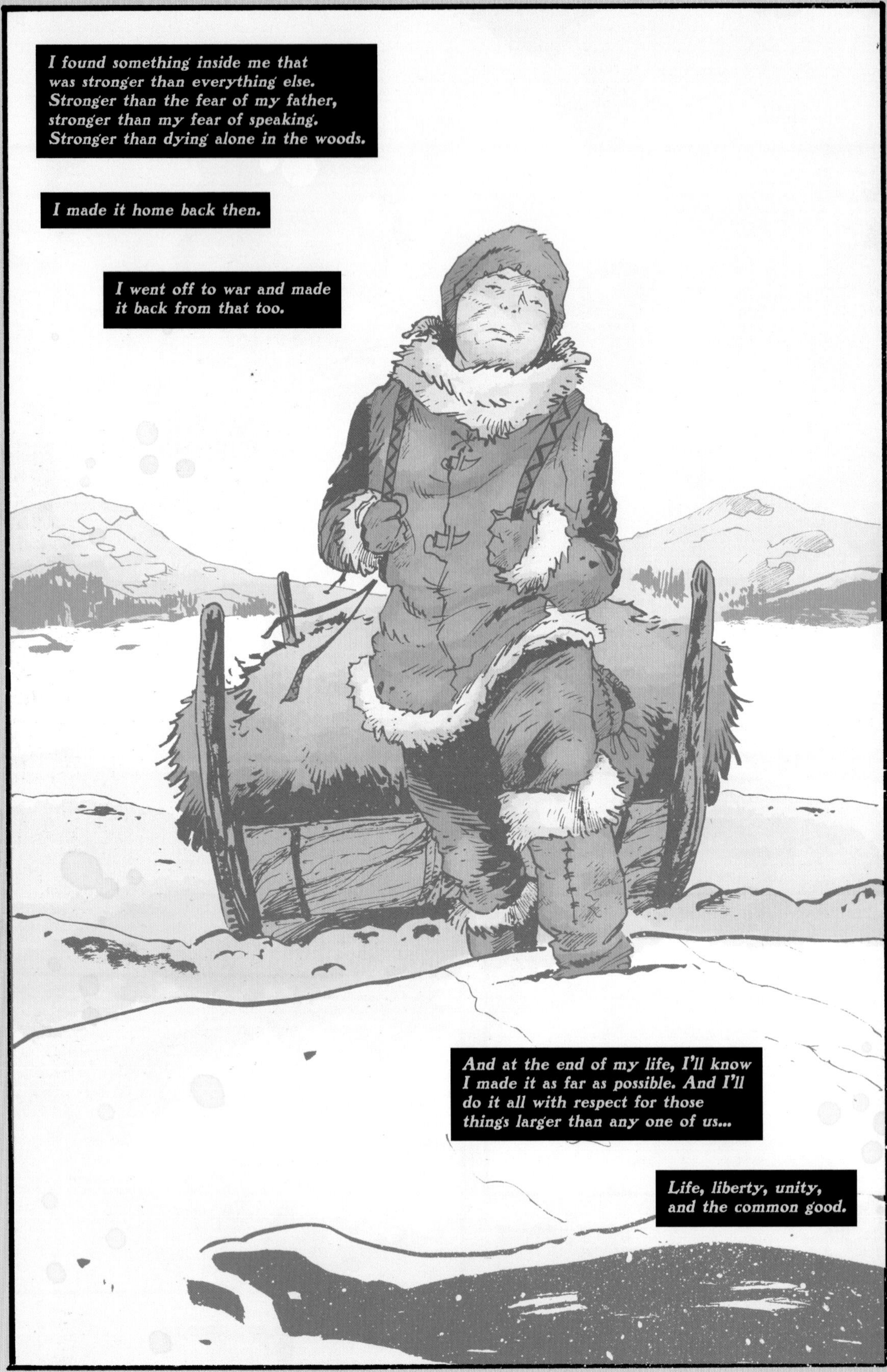
I found something inside me that was stronger than everything else. Stronger than the fear of my father, stronger than my fear of speaking. Stronger than dying alone in the woods.
I made it home back then.
I went off to war and made it back from that too.
And at the end of my life, I'll know I made it as far as possible. And I'll do it all with respect for those things larger than any one of us...
Life, liberty, unity, and the common good.

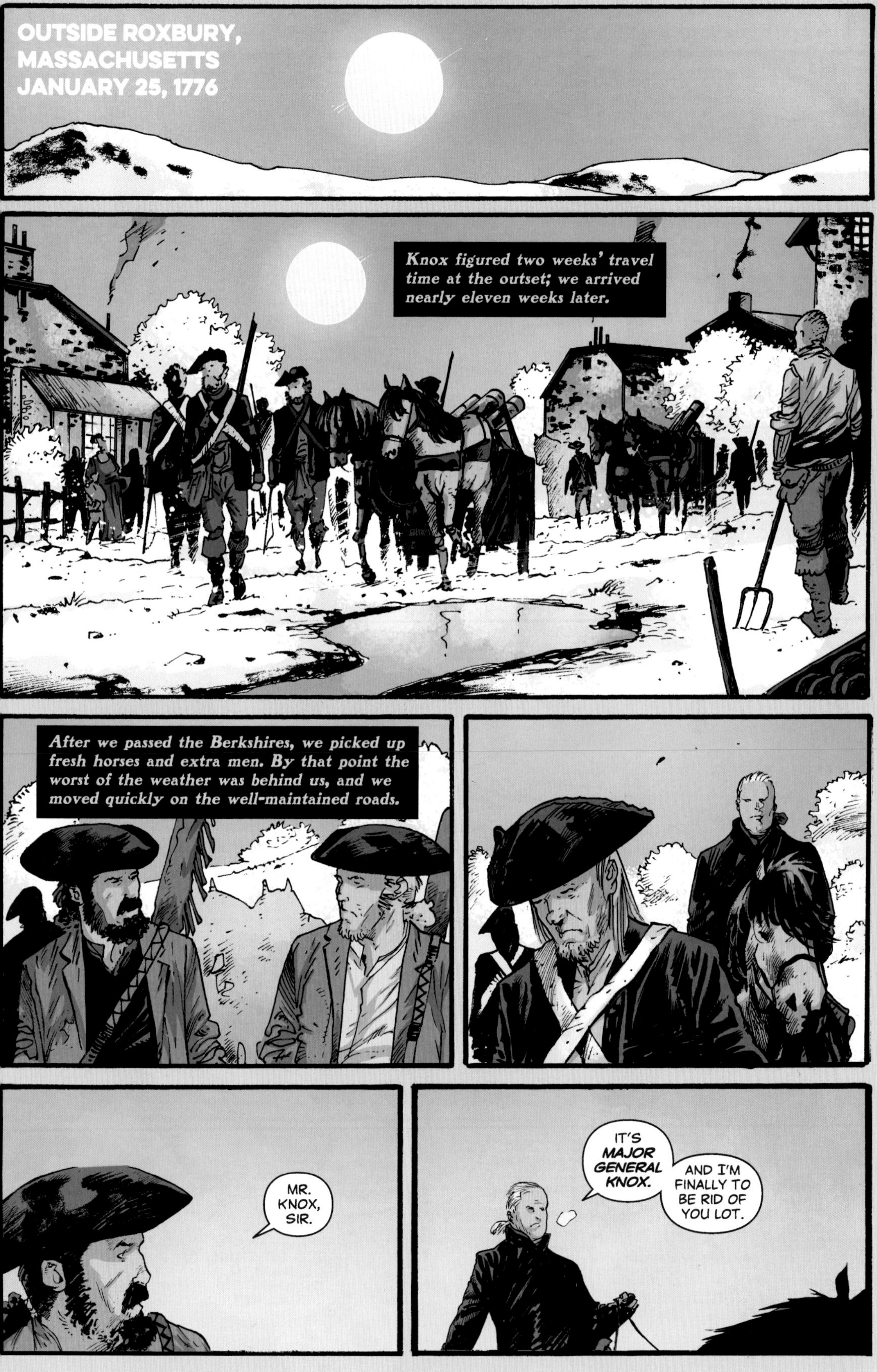
OUTSIDE ROXBURY, MASSACHUSETTS JANUARY 25, 1776
Knox figured two weeks' travel time at the outset; we arrived nearly eleven weeks later.
After we passed the Berkshires, we picked up fresh horses and extra men. By that point the worst of the weather was behind us, and we moved quickly on the well-maintained roads.
MR. KNOX, SIR.
IT'S *MAJOR GENERAL* KNOX.
AND I'M FINALLY TO BE RID OF YOU LOT.

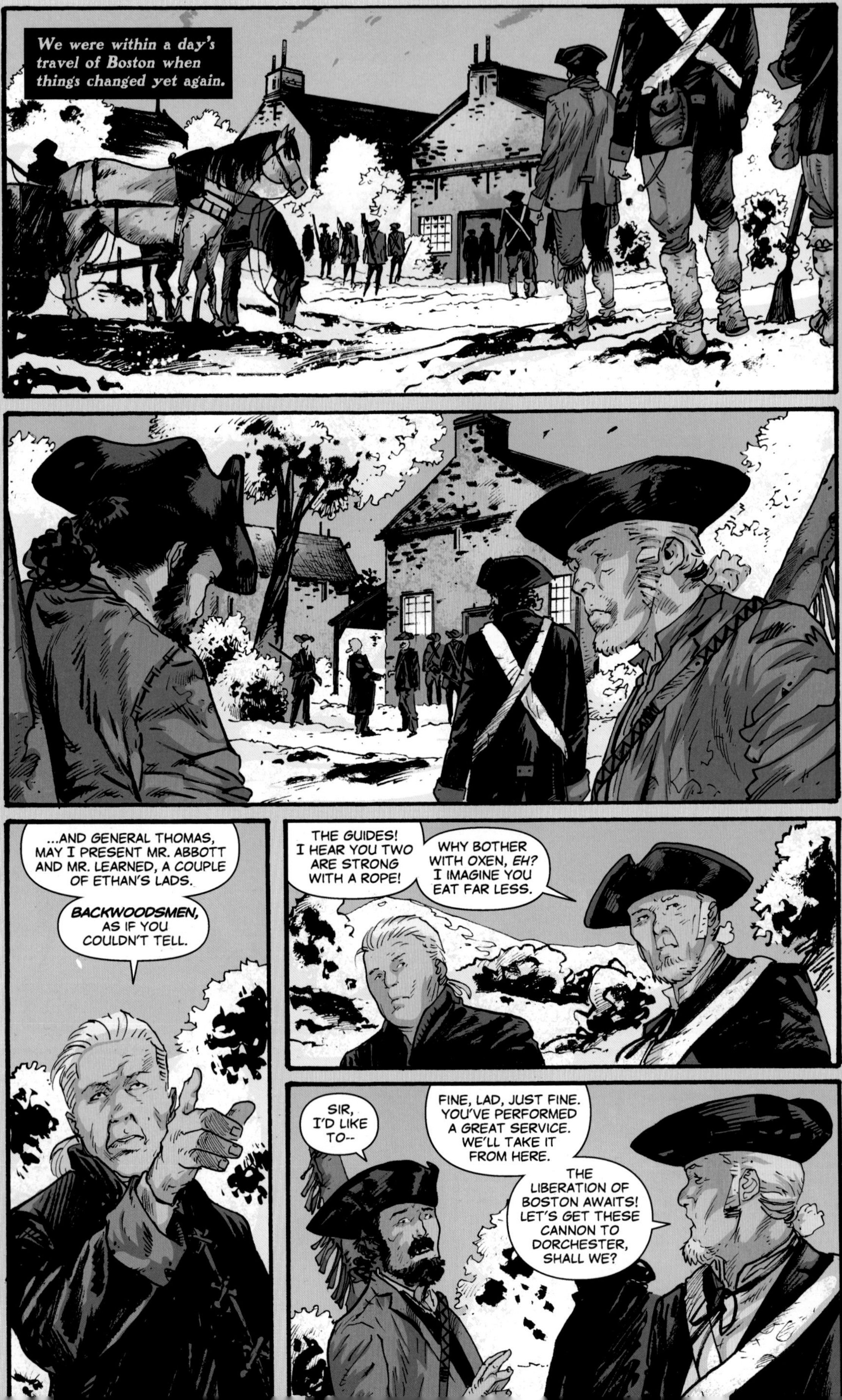
We were within a day's travel of Boston when things changed yet again.
...AND GENERAL THOMAS, MAY I PRESENT MR. ABBOTT AND MR. LEARNED, A COUPLE OF ETHAN'S LADS.
BACKWOODSMEN, AS IF YOU COULDN'T TELL.
THE GUIDES! I HEAR YOU TWO ARE STRONG WITH A ROPE!
WHY BOTHER WITH OXEN, EH? I IMAGINE YOU EAT FAR LESS.
SIR, I'D LIKE TO--
FINE, LAD, JUST FINE. YOU'VE PERFORMED A GREAT SERVICE. WE'LL TAKE IT FROM HERE.
THE LIBERATION OF BOSTON AWAITS! LET'S GET THESE CANNON TO DORCHESTER, SHALL WE?

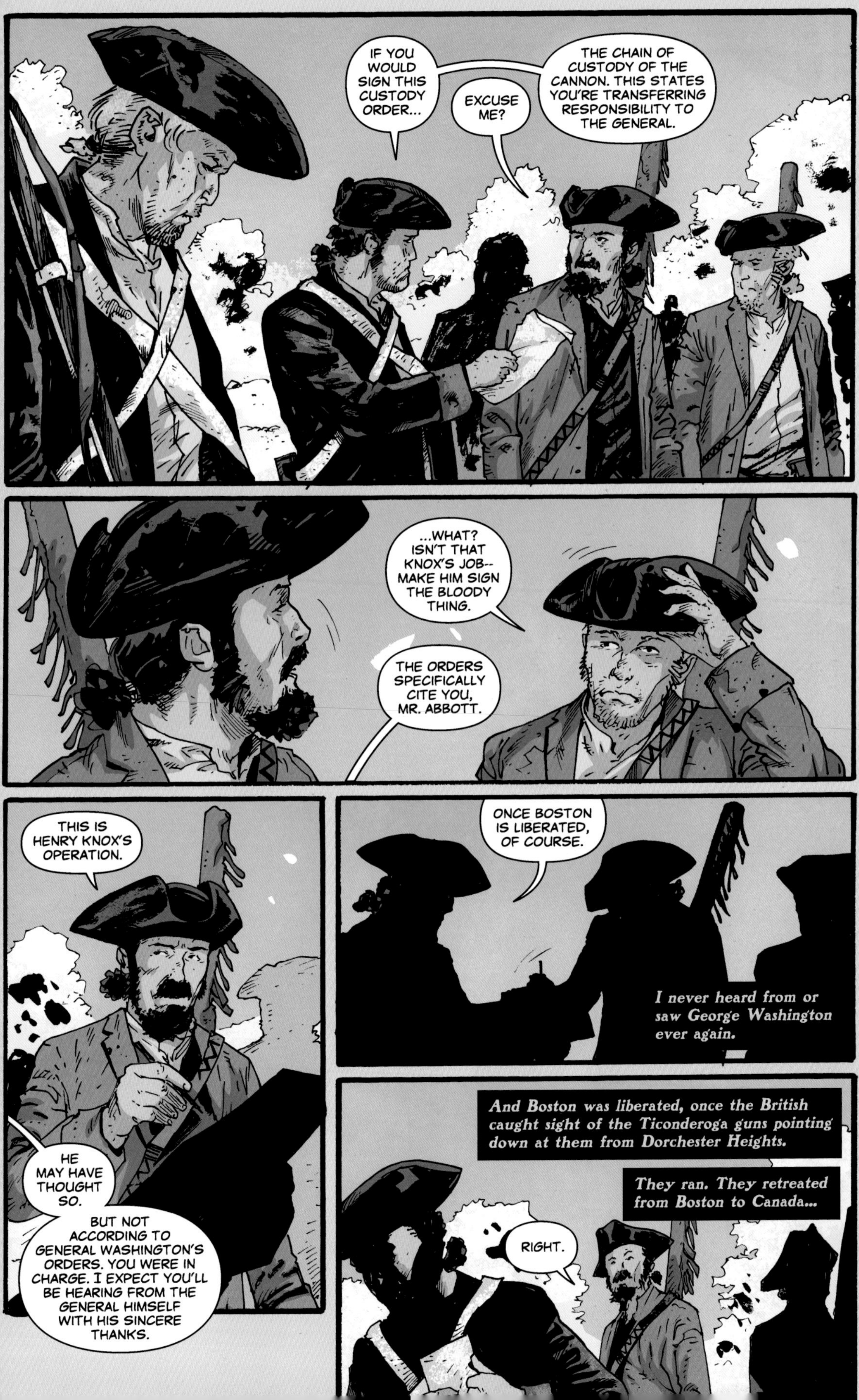
IF YOU WOULD SIGN THIS CUSTODY ORDER...
EXCUSE ME?
THE CHAIN OF CUSTODY OF THE CANNON. THIS STATES YOU'RE TRANSFERRING RESPONSIBILITY TO THE GENERAL.
...WHAT? ISN'T THAT KNOX'S JOB-- MAKE HIM SIGN THE BLOODY THING.
THE ORDERS SPECIFICALLY CITE YOU, MR. ABBOTT.
THIS IS HENRY KNOX'S OPERATION.
HE MAY HAVE THOUGHT SO.
BUT NOT ACCORDING TO GENERAL WASHINGTON'S ORDERS. YOU WERE IN CHARGE. I EXPECT YOU'LL BE HEARING FROM THE GENERAL HIMSELF WITH HIS SINCERE THANKS.
ONCE BOSTON IS LIBERATED, OF COURSE.
I never heard from or saw George Washington ever again.
And Boston was liberated, once the British caught sight of the Ticonderoga guns pointing down at them from Dorchester Heights.
They ran. They retreated from Boston to Canada...
RIGHT.

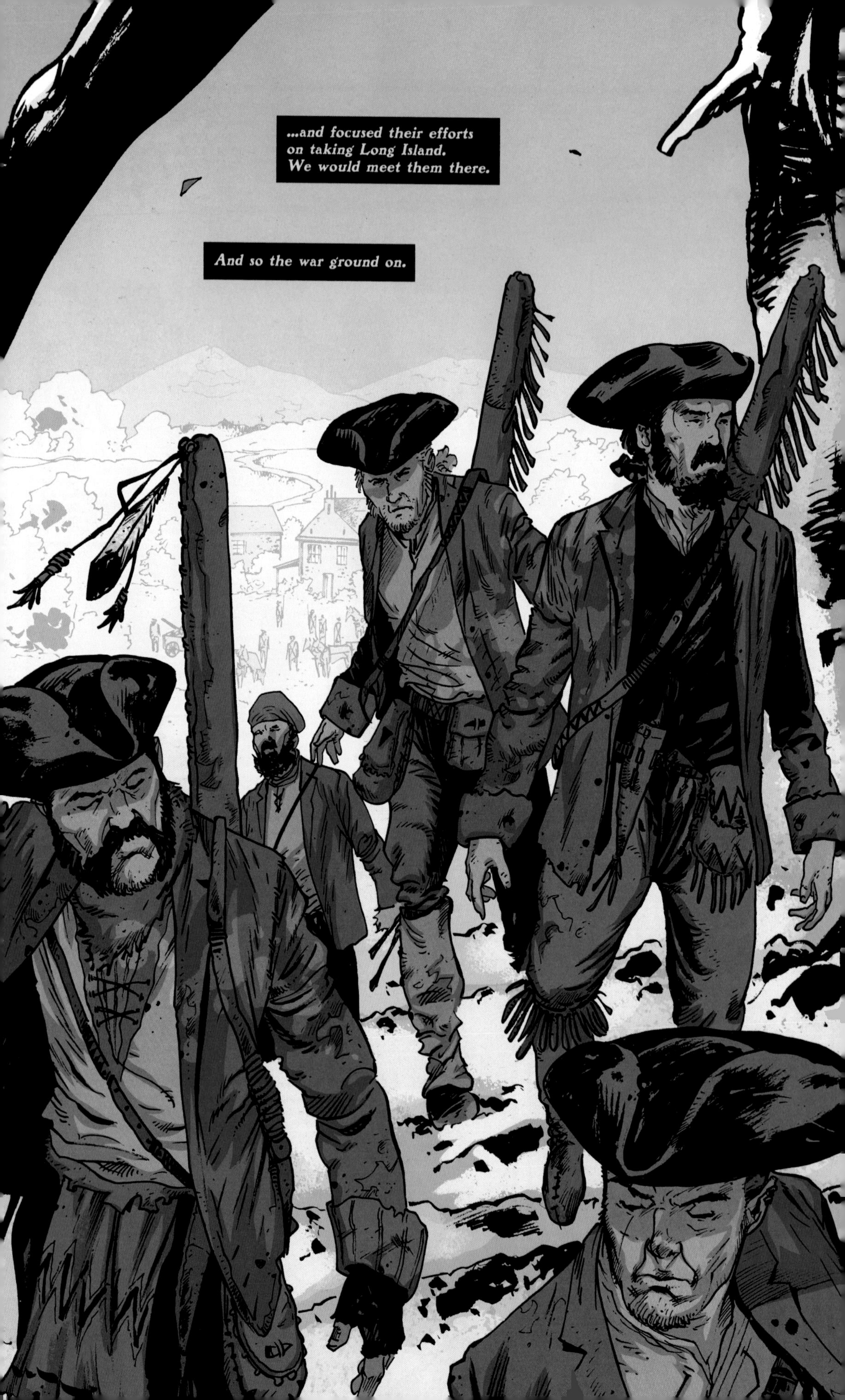
...and focused their efforts on taking Long Island. We would meet them there.
And so the war ground on.

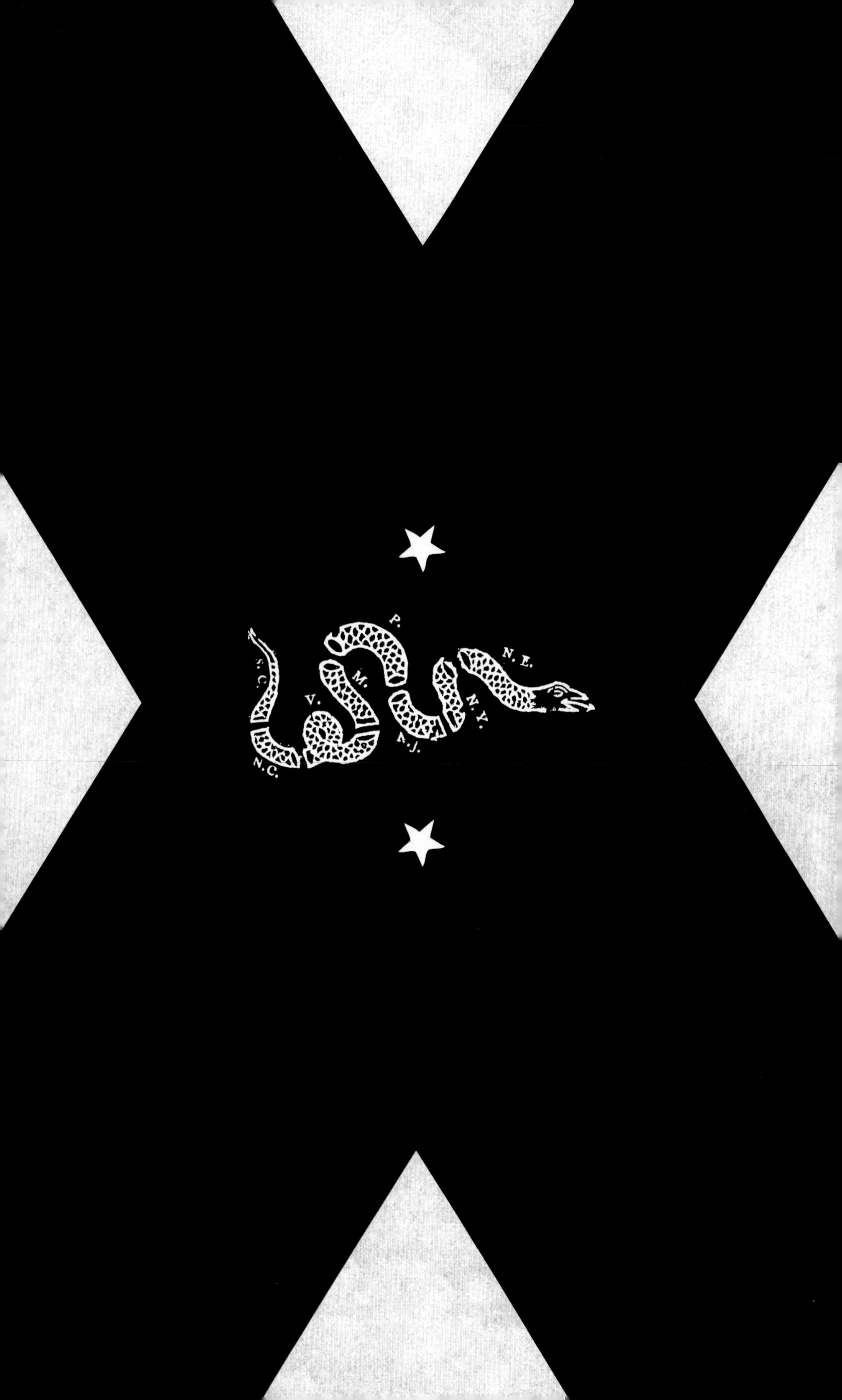
S.C.
N.C.
V.
M.
P.
N.J.
N.Y.
N.E.

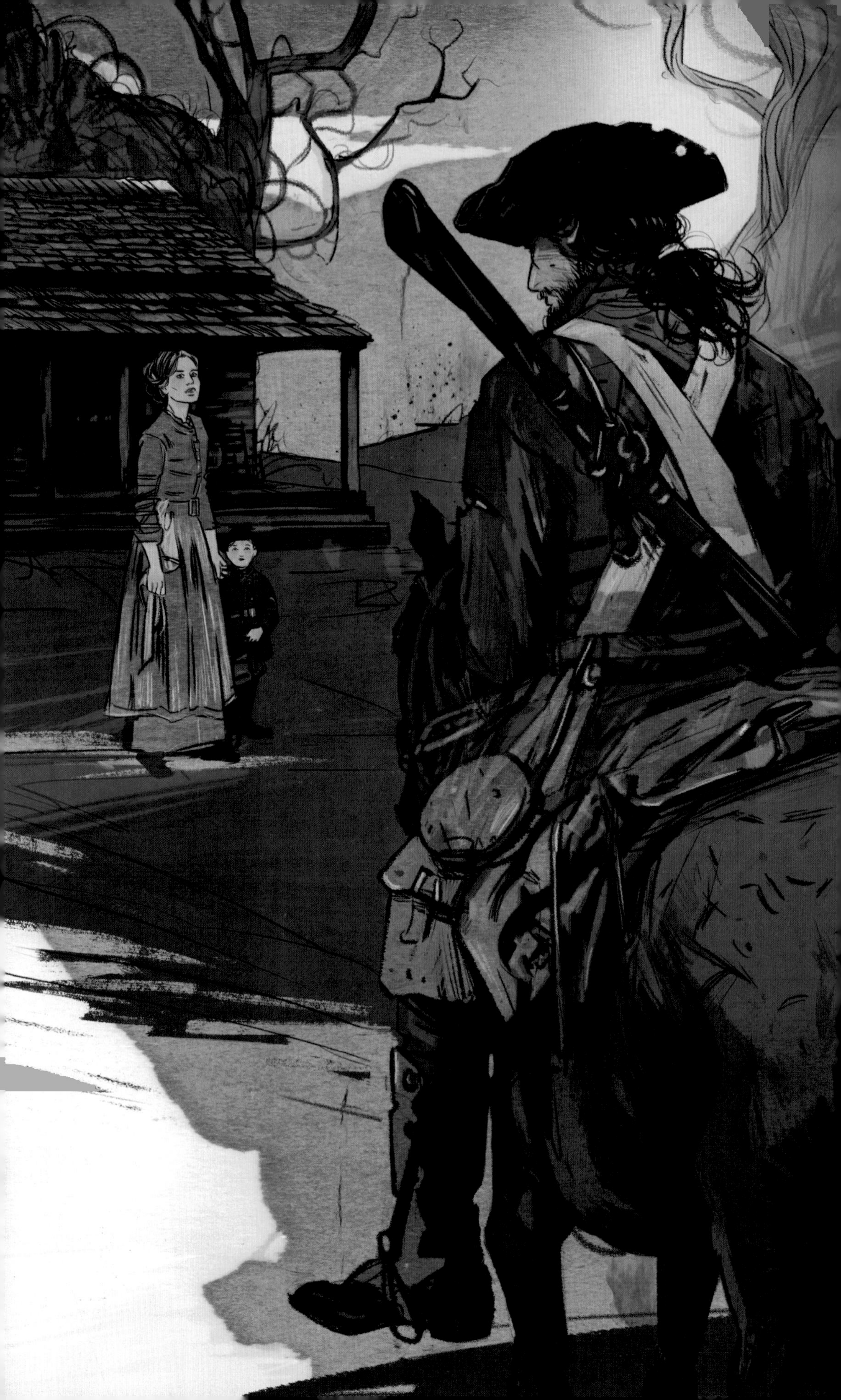

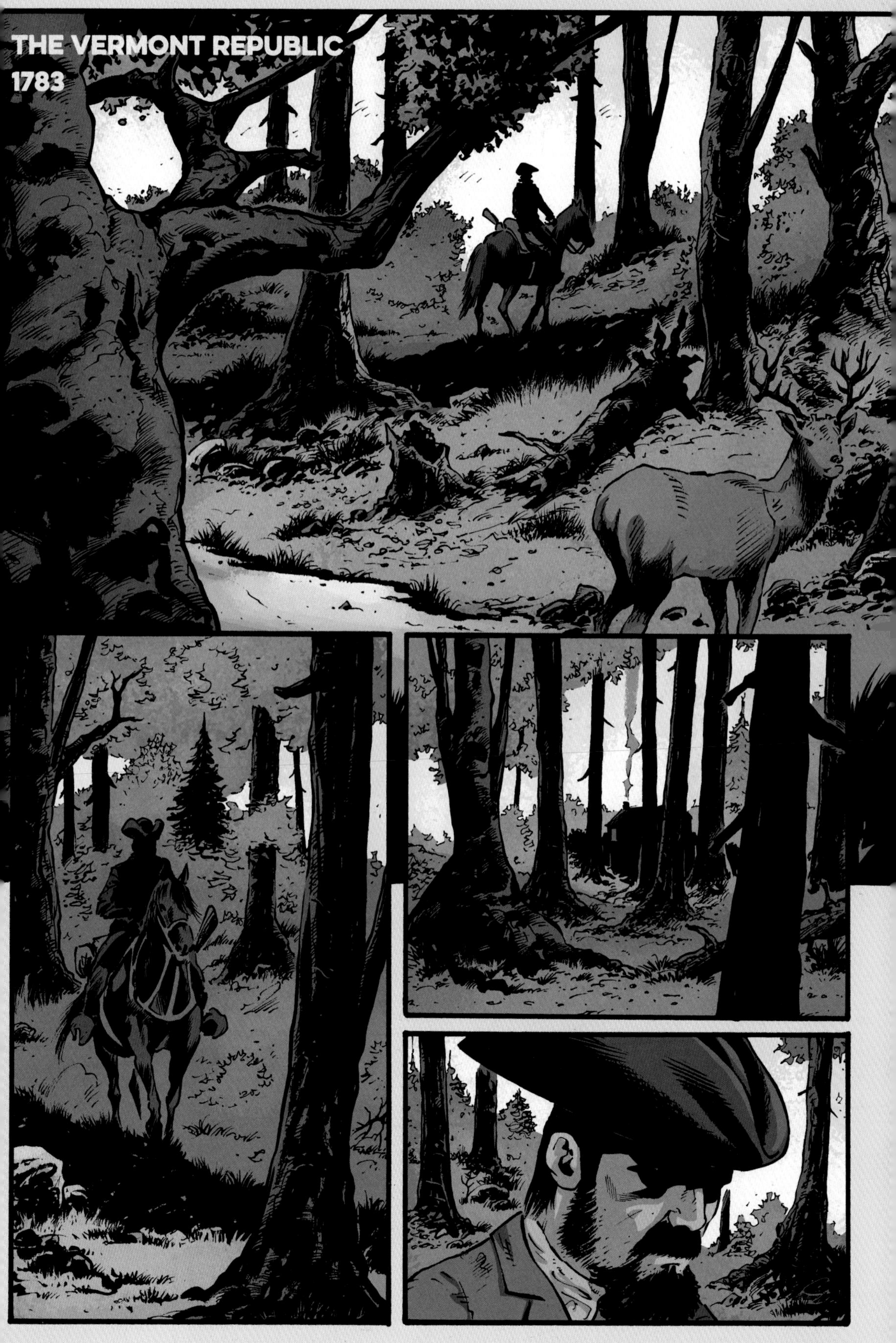
THE VERMONT REPUBLIC
1783

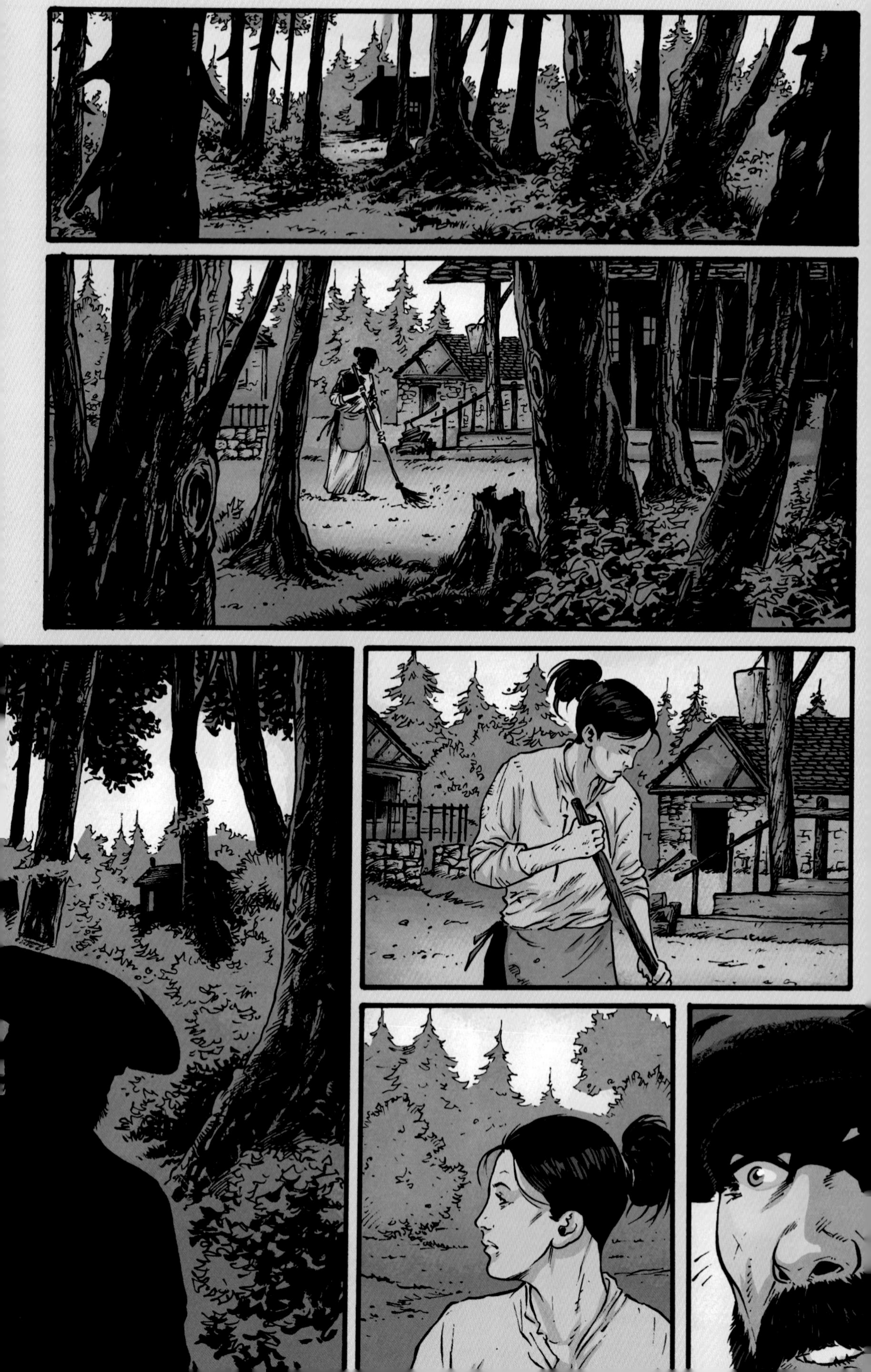

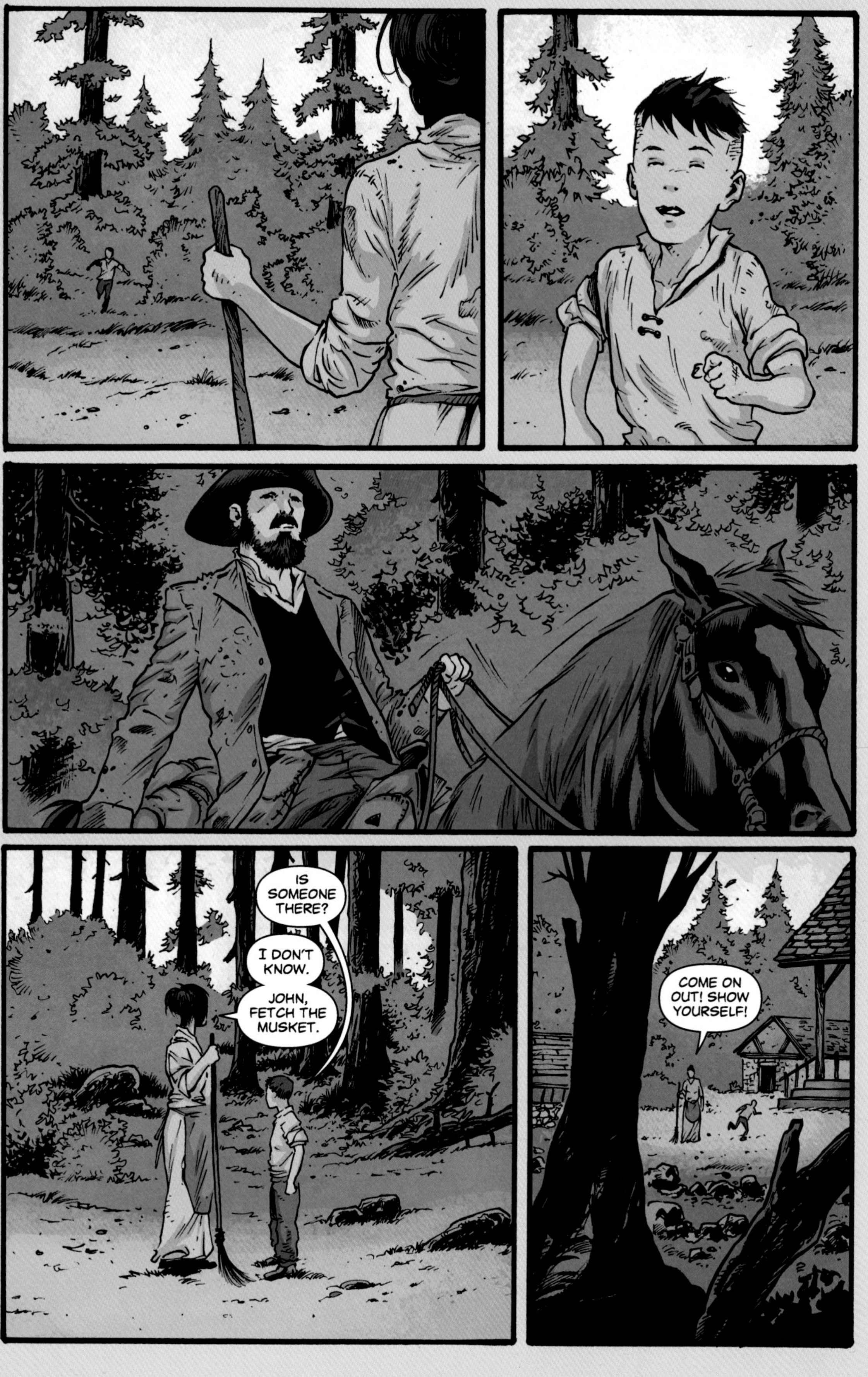
IS SOMEONE THERE?
I DON'T KNOW.
JOHN, FETCH THE MUSKET.
COME ON OUT! SHOW YOURSELF!

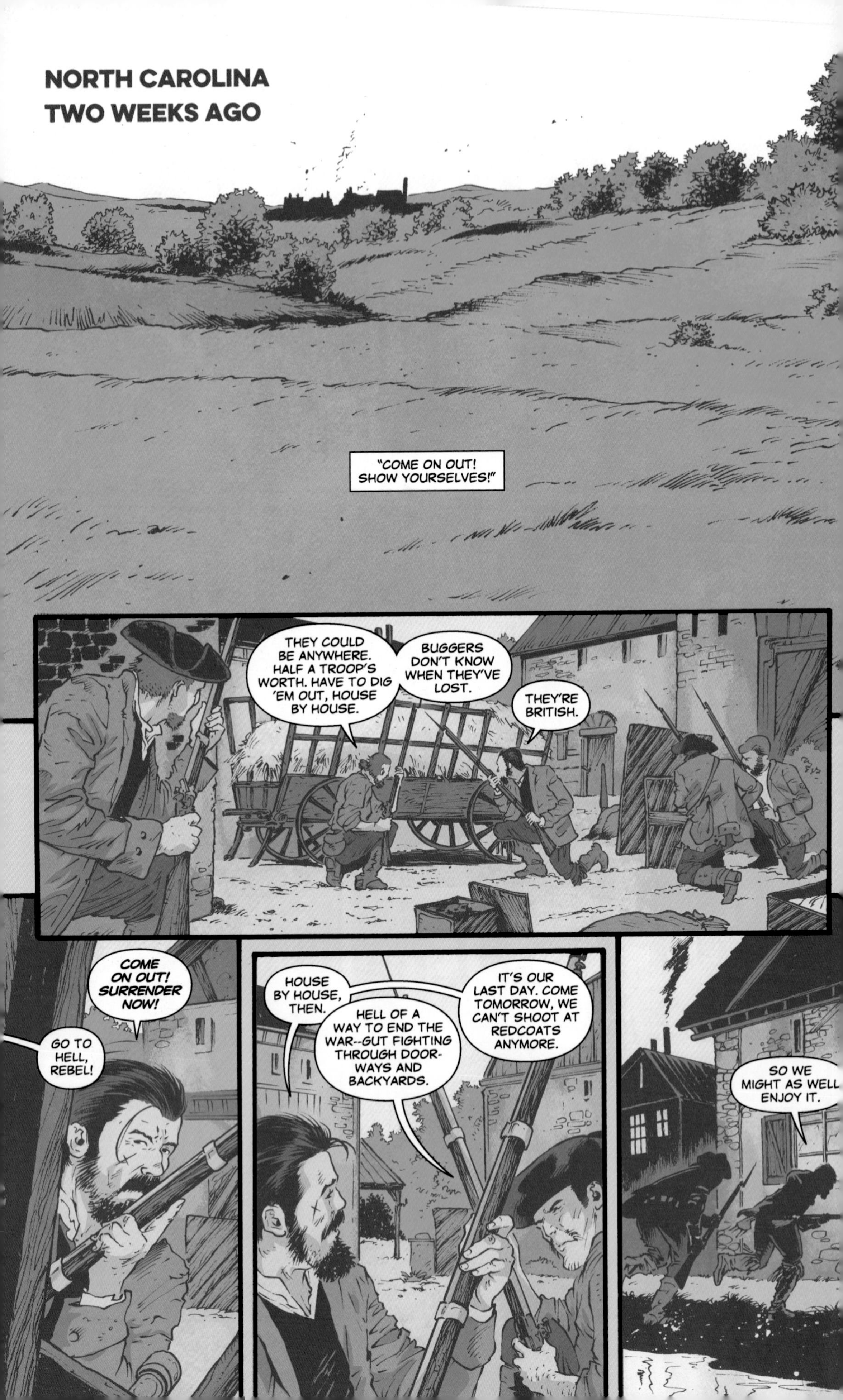
NORTH CAROLINA
TWO WEEKS AGO
"COME ON OUT! SHOW YOURSELVES!"
THEY COULD BE ANYWHERE. HALF A TROOP'S WORTH. HAVE TO DIG 'EM OUT, HOUSE BY HOUSE.
BUGGERS DON'T KNOW WHEN THEY'VE LOST.
THEY'RE BRITISH.
COME ON OUT! SURRENDER NOW!
GO TO HELL, REBEL!
HOUSE BY HOUSE, THEN.
HELL OF A WAY TO END THE WAR--GUT FIGHTING THROUGH DOORWAYS AND BACKYARDS.
IT'S OUR LAST DAY. COME TOMORROW, WE CAN'T SHOOT AT REDCOATS ANYMORE.
SO WE MIGHT AS WELL ENJOY IT.

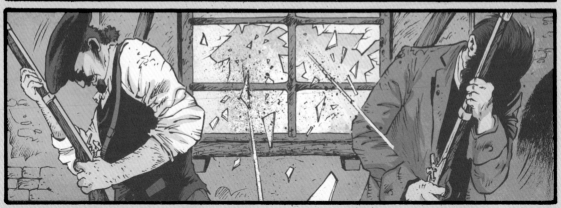

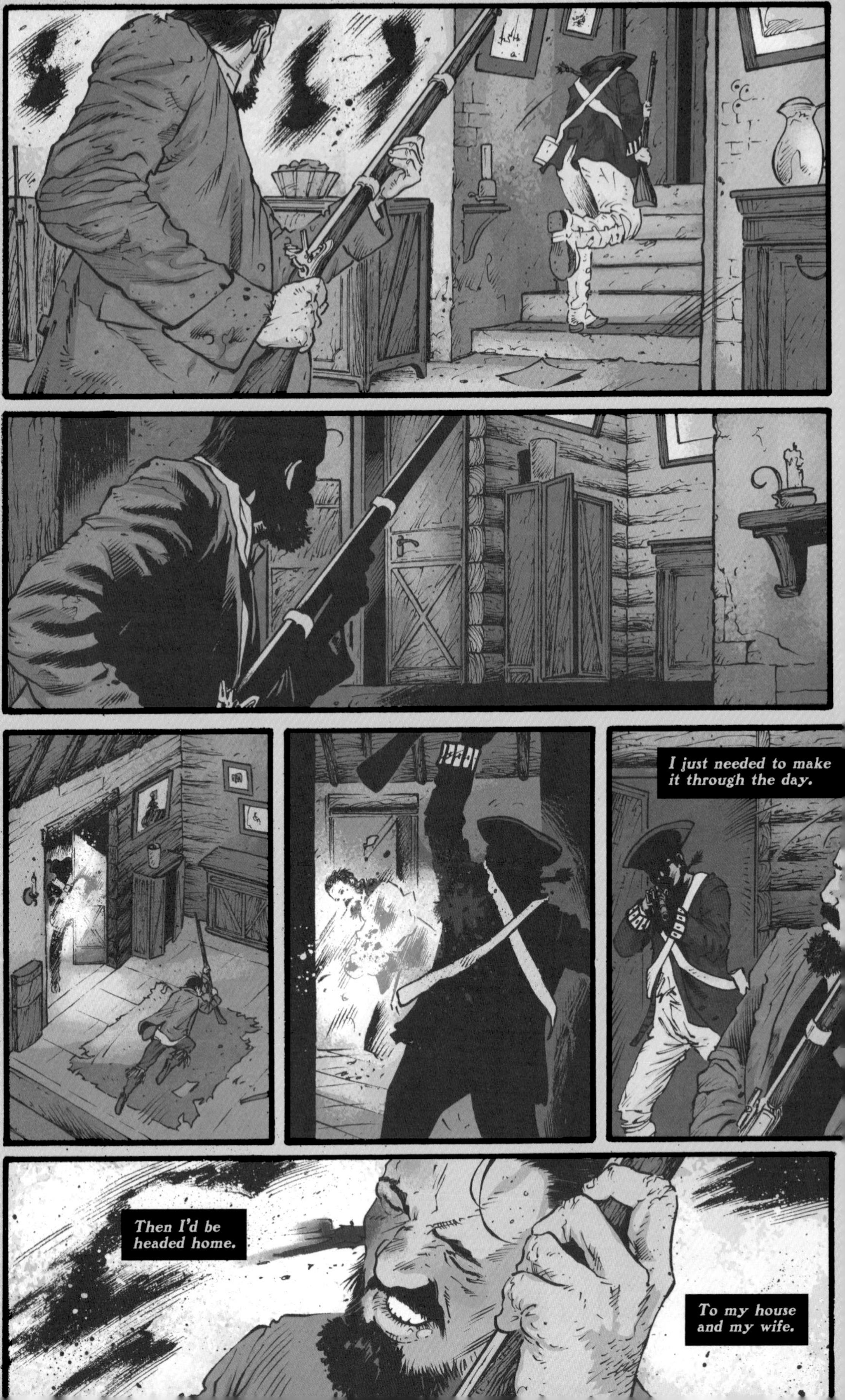
I just needed to make it through the day.
Then I'd be headed home.
To my house and my wife.

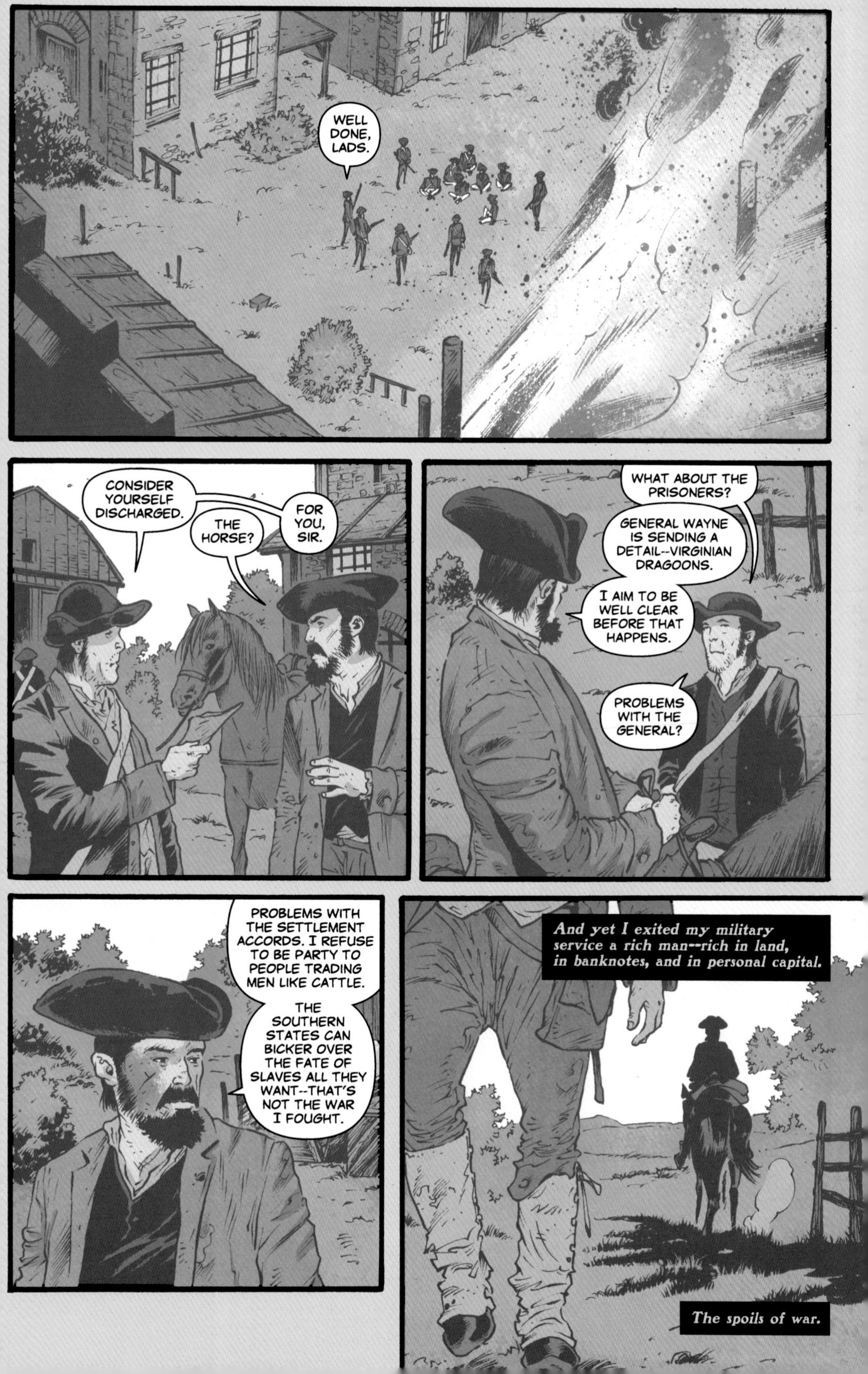

WELL DONE, LADS.
CONSIDER YOURSELF DISCHARGED.
FOR YOU, SIR.
THE HORSE?
WHAT ABOUT THE PRISONERS?
GENERAL WAYNE IS SENDING A DETAIL--VIRGINIAN DRAGOONS.
I AIM TO BE WELL CLEAR BEFORE THAT HAPPENS.
PROBLEMS WITH THE GENERAL?
PROBLEMS WITH THE SETTLEMENT ACCORDS. I REFUSE TO BE PARTY TO PEOPLE TRADING MEN LIKE CATTLE.
THE SOUTHERN STATES CAN BICKER OVER THE FATE OF SLAVES ALL THEY WANT--THAT'S NOT THE WAR I FOUGHT.
And yet I exited my military service a rich man--rich in land, in banknotes, and in personal capital.
The spoils of war.

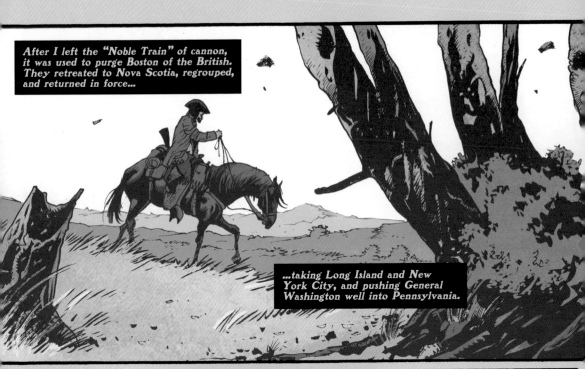

After I left the "Noble Train" of cannon, it was used to purge Boston of the British. They retreated to Nova Scotia, regrouped, and returned in force...

...taking Long Island and New York City, and pushing General Washington well into Pennsylvania.

I was there. Ethan Allen spent a lot of money creating the Green Mountain militia, and he made sure we were put to use.

At the start of hostilities, the southern states felt to me about as far away as England and France.

Yet for the last year or two of the war, I fought for their freedom as well. I bled into the ground.

I cried into it too.

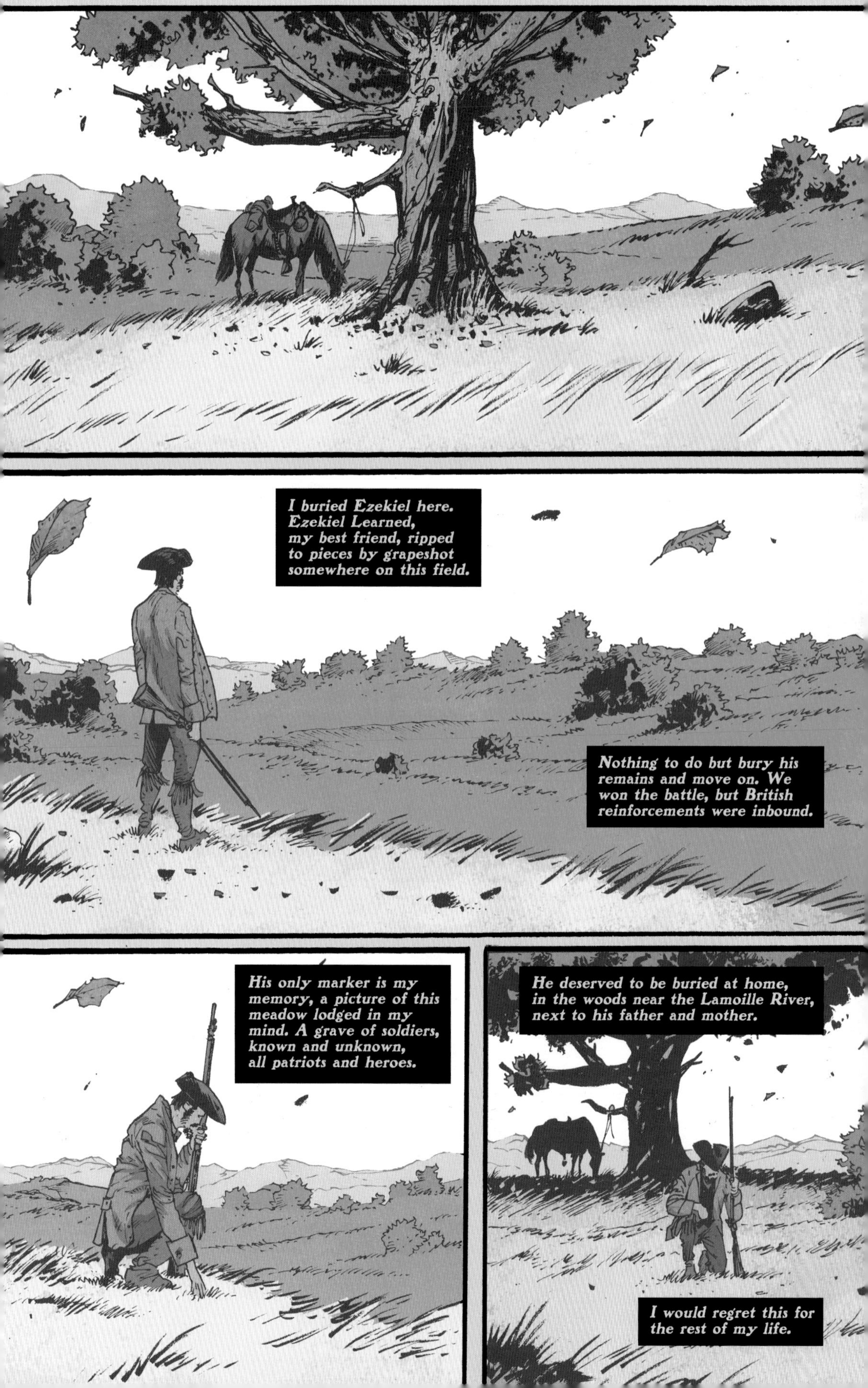
I buried Ezekiel here. Ezekiel Learned, my best friend, ripped to pieces by grapeshot somewhere on this field.
Nothing to do but bury his remains and move on. We won the battle, but British reinforcements were inbound.
His only marker is my memory, a picture of this meadow lodged in my mind. A grave of soldiers, known and unknown, all patriots and heroes.
He deserved to be buried at home, in the woods near the Lamoille River, next to his father and mother.
I would regret this for the rest of my life.

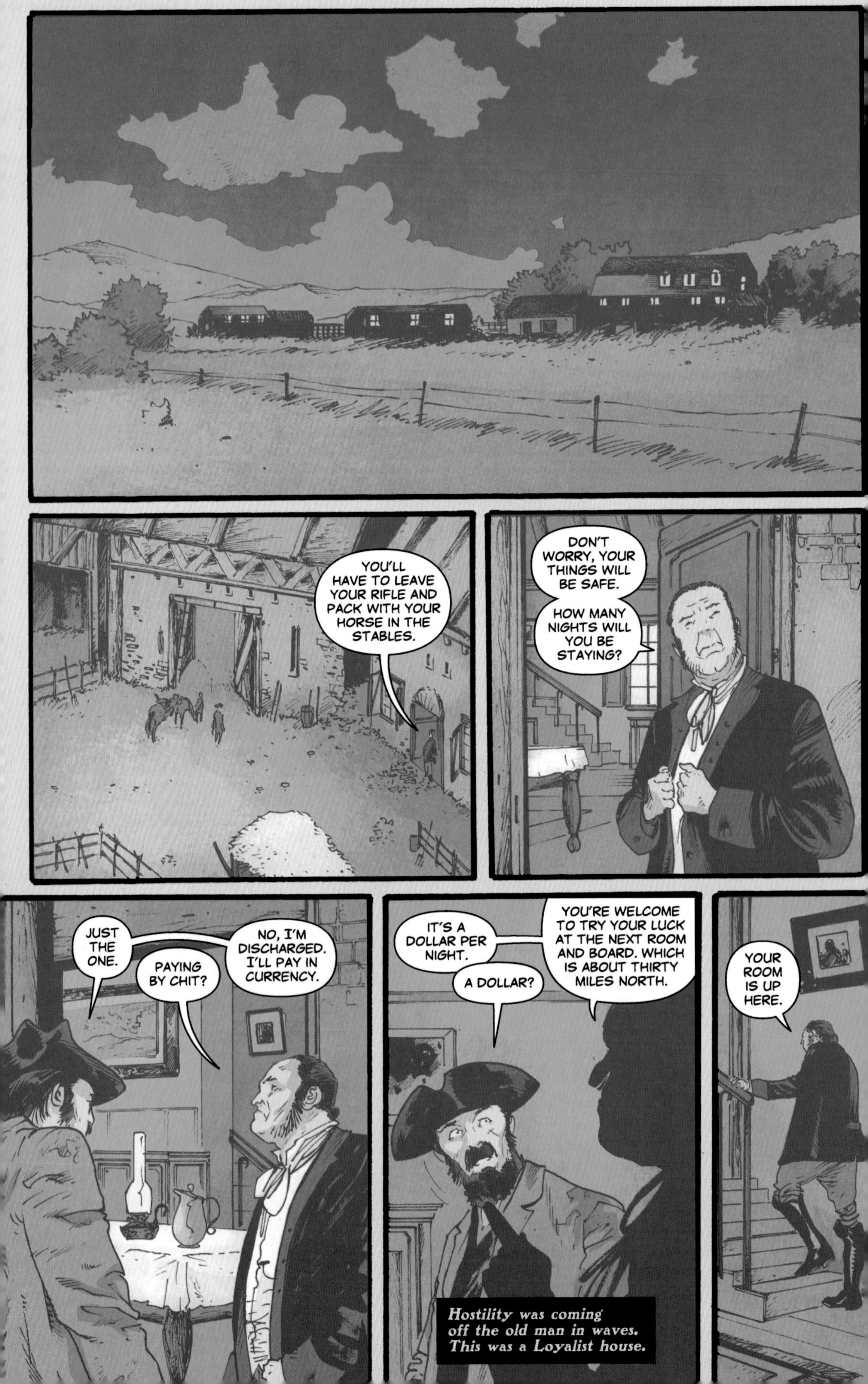
YOU'LL HAVE TO LEAVE YOUR RIFLE AND PACK WITH YOUR HORSE IN THE STABLES.
DON'T WORRY, YOUR THINGS WILL BE SAFE.
HOW MANY NIGHTS WILL YOU BE STAYING?
JUST THE ONE.
PAYING BY CHIT?
NO, I'M DISCHARGED. I'LL PAY IN CURRENCY.
IT'S A DOLLAR PER NIGHT.
A DOLLAR?
YOU'RE WELCOME TO TRY YOUR LUCK AT THE NEXT ROOM AND BOARD. WHICH IS ABOUT THIRTY MILES NORTH.
Hostility was coming off the old man in waves. This was a Loyalist house.
YOUR ROOM IS UP HERE.

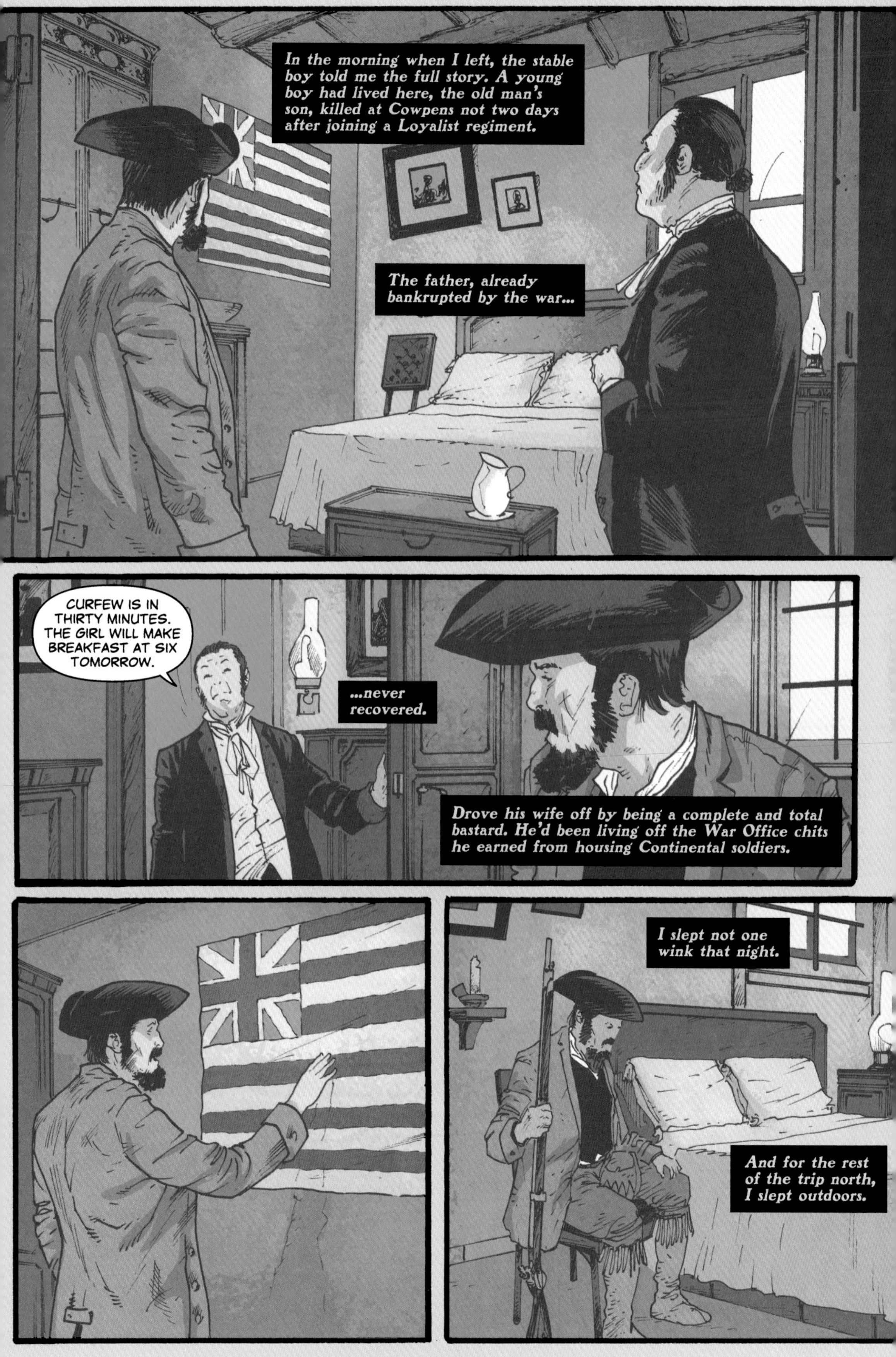
In the morning when I left, the stable boy told me the full story. A young boy had lived here, the old man's son, killed at Cowpens not two days after joining a Loyalist regiment.
The father, already bankrupted by the war...
CURFEW IS IN THIRTY MINUTES. THE GIRL WILL MAKE BREAKFAST AT SIX TOMORROW.
...never recovered.
Drove his wife off by being a complete and total bastard. He'd been living off the War Office chits he earned from housing Continental soldiers.
I slept not one wink that night.
And for the rest of the trip north, I slept outdoors.

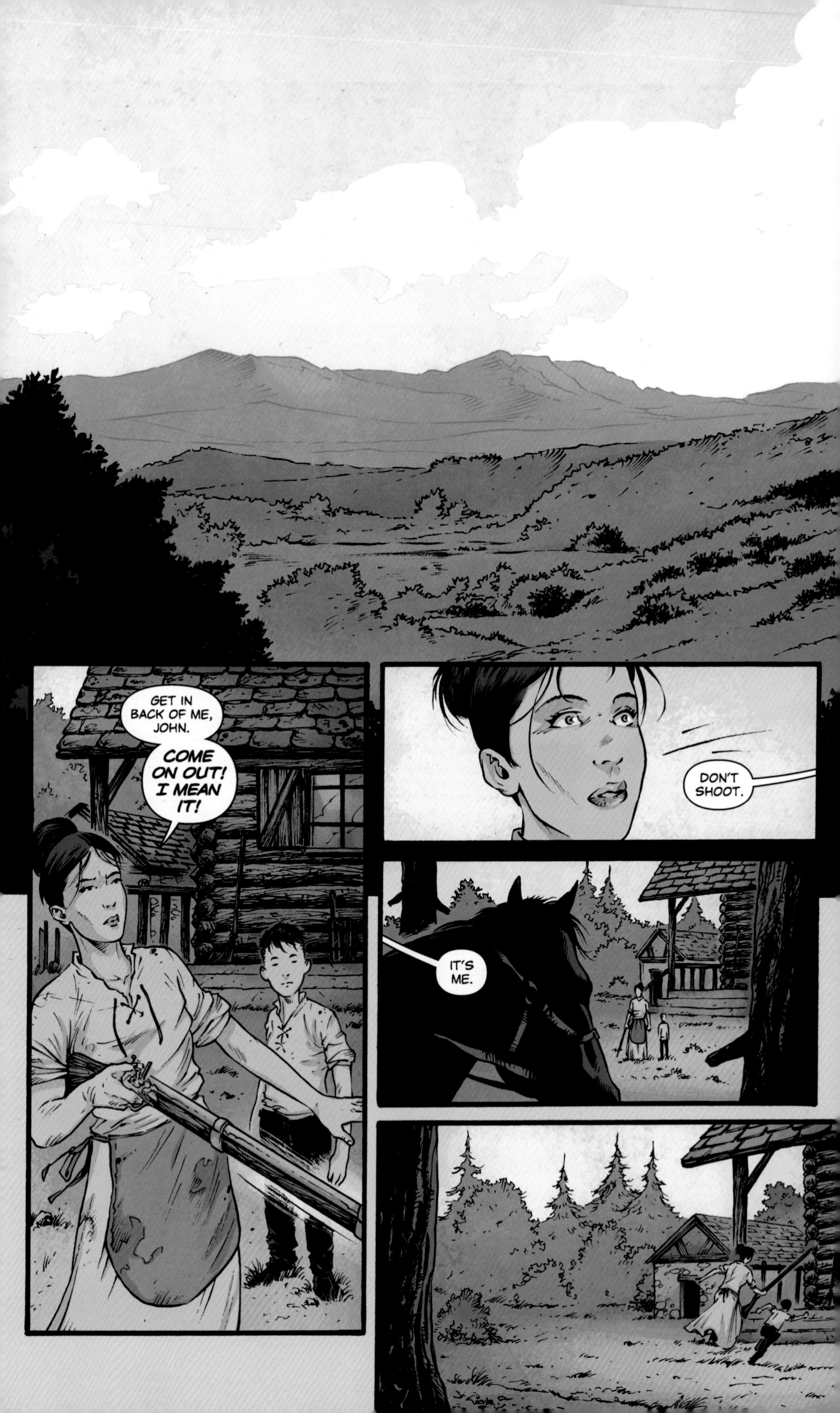
GET IN BACK OF ME, JOHN.
COME ON OUT! I MEAN IT!
DON'T SHOOT.
IT'S ME.

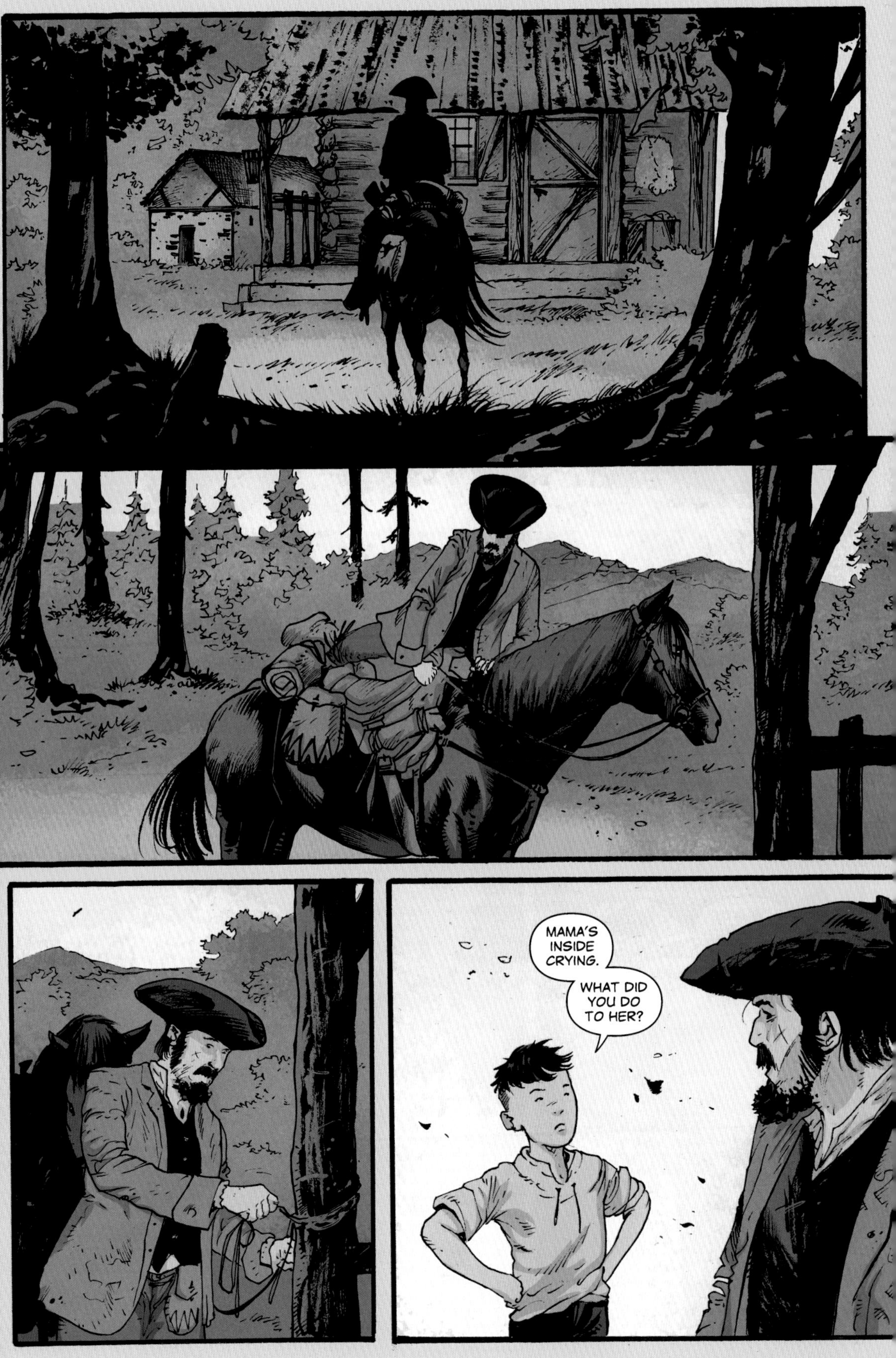
MAMA'S INSIDE CRYING.
WHAT DID YOU DO TO HER?

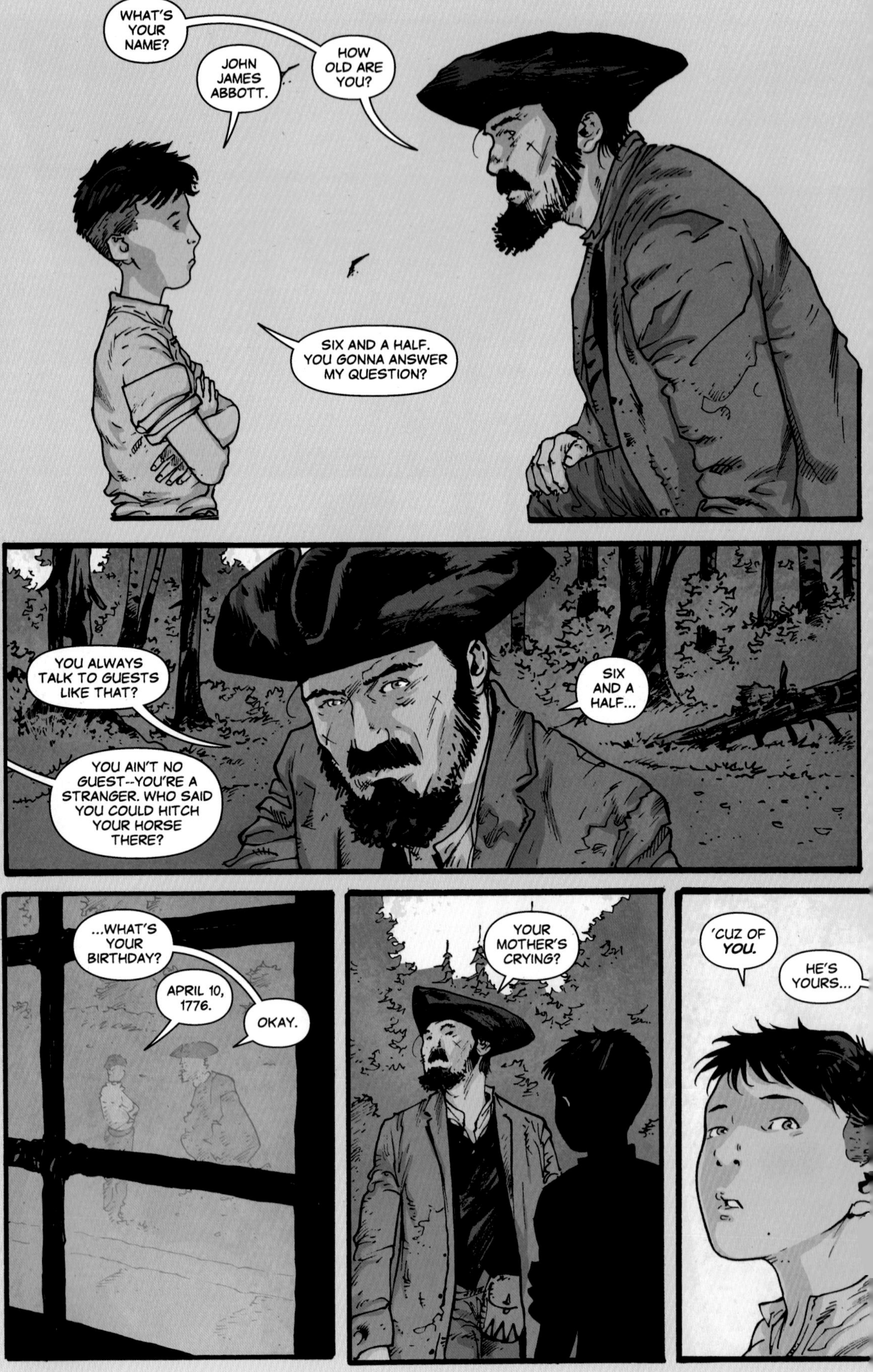
WHAT'S YOUR NAME?
JOHN JAMES ABBOTT.
HOW OLD ARE YOU?
SIX AND A HALF. YOU GONNA ANSWER MY QUESTION?
YOU ALWAYS TALK TO GUESTS LIKE THAT?
SIX AND A HALF...
YOU AIN'T NO GUEST--YOU'RE A STRANGER. WHO SAID YOU COULD HITCH YOUR HORSE THERE?
...WHAT'S YOUR BIRTHDAY?
APRIL 10, 1776.
OKAY.
YOUR MOTHER'S CRYING?
'CUZ OF *YOU.*
HE'S YOURS...

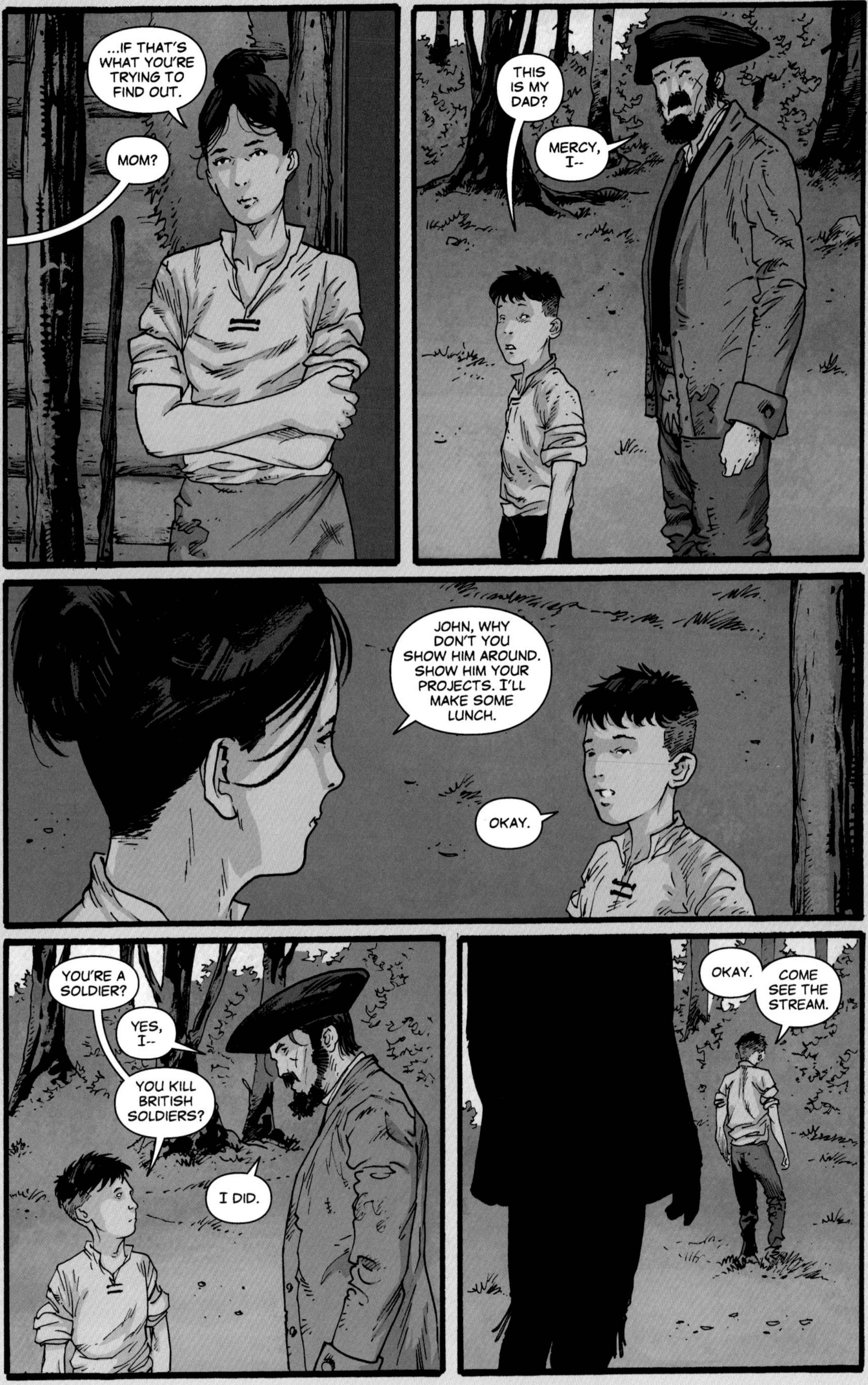
...IF THAT'S WHAT YOU'RE TRYING TO FIND OUT.
MOM?
THIS IS MY DAD?
MERCY, I--
JOHN, WHY DON'T YOU SHOW HIM AROUND. SHOW HIM YOUR PROJECTS. I'LL MAKE SOME LUNCH.
OKAY.
YOU'RE A SOLDIER?
YES, I--
YOU KILL BRITISH SOLDIERS?
I DID.
OKAY.
COME SEE THE STREAM.

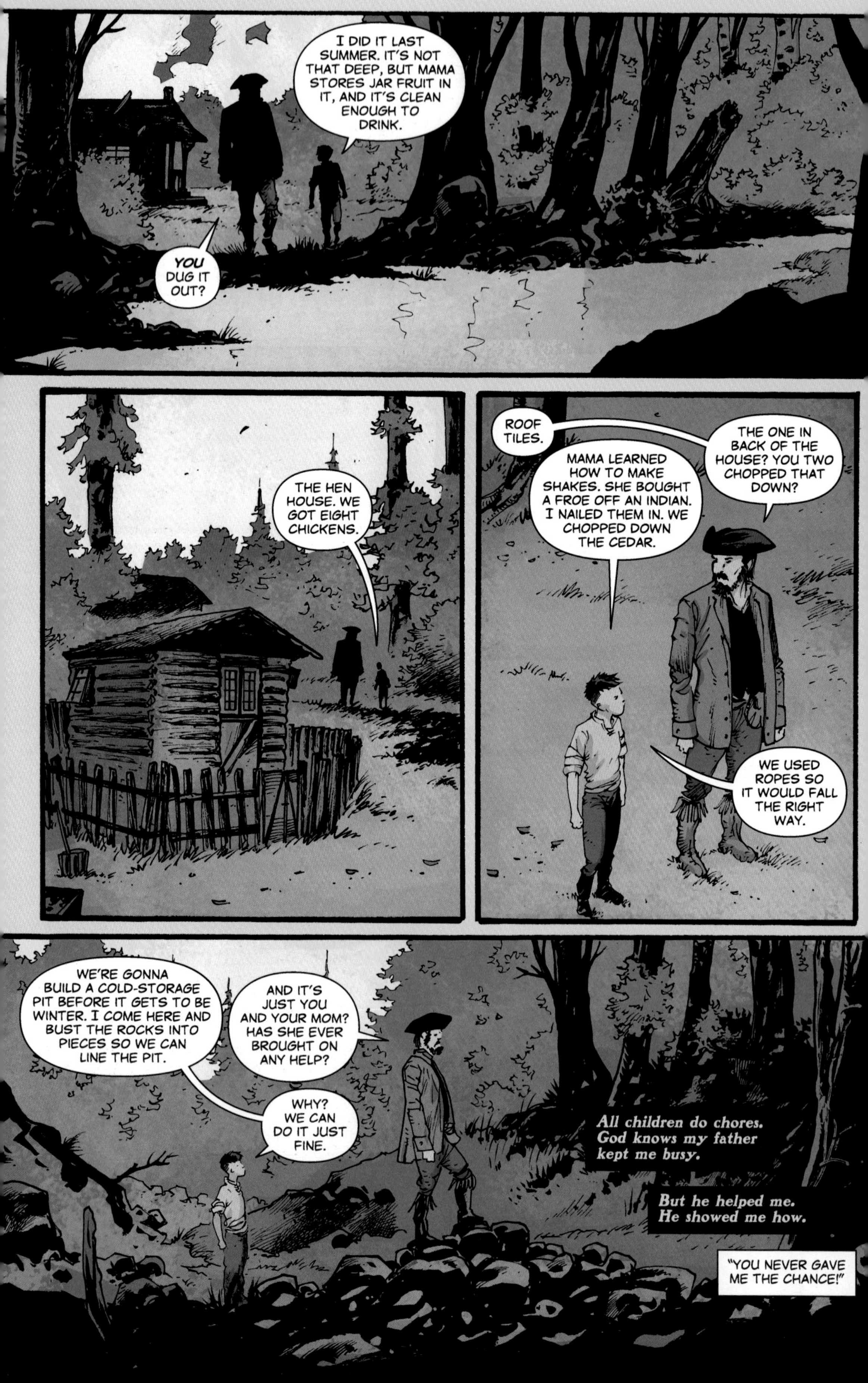

I DID IT LAST SUMMER. IT'S NOT THAT DEEP, BUT MAMA STORES JAR FRUIT IN IT, AND IT'S CLEAN ENOUGH TO DRINK.
YOU DUG IT OUT?
THE HEN HOUSE. WE GOT EIGHT CHICKENS.
ROOF TILES.
THE ONE IN BACK OF THE HOUSE? YOU TWO CHOPPED THAT DOWN?
MAMA LEARNED HOW TO MAKE SHAKES. SHE BOUGHT A FROE OFF AN INDIAN. I NAILED THEM IN. WE CHOPPED DOWN THE CEDAR.
WE USED ROPES SO IT WOULD FALL THE RIGHT WAY.
WE'RE GONNA BUILD A COLD-STORAGE PIT BEFORE IT GETS TO BE WINTER. I COME HERE AND BUST THE ROCKS INTO PIECES SO WE CAN LINE THE PIT.
AND IT'S JUST YOU AND YOUR MOM? HAS SHE EVER BROUGHT ON ANY HELP?
WHY? WE CAN DO IT JUST FINE.
All children do chores. God knows my father kept me busy.
But he helped me. He showed me how.
"YOU NEVER GAVE ME THE CHANCE!"

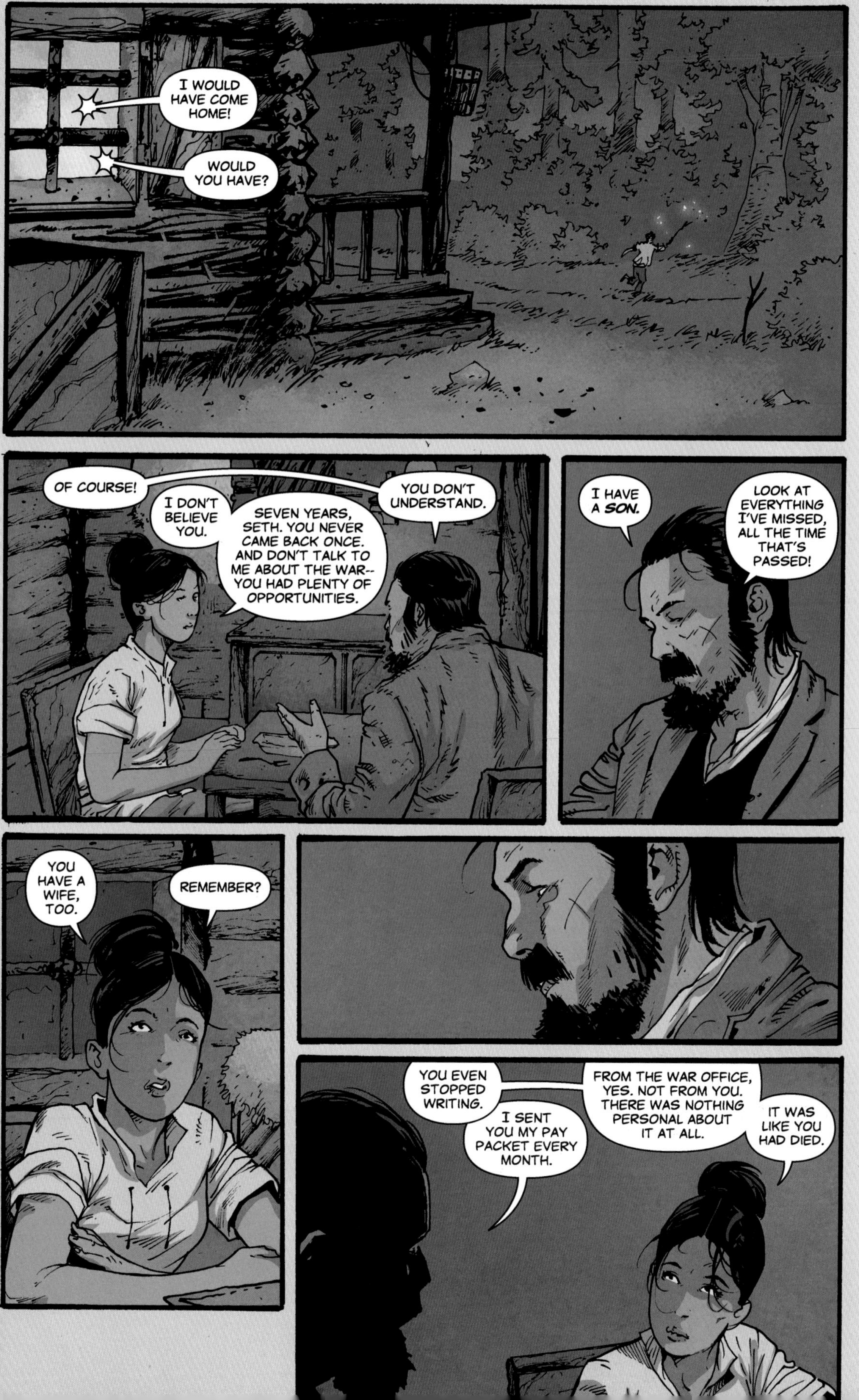
I WOULD HAVE COME HOME!
WOULD YOU HAVE?
OF COURSE!
YOU DON'T UNDERSTAND.
I DON'T BELIEVE YOU.
SEVEN YEARS, SETH. YOU NEVER CAME BACK ONCE. AND DON'T TALK TO ME ABOUT THE WAR-- YOU HAD PLENTY OF OPPORTUNITIES.
I HAVE A SON.
LOOK AT EVERYTHING I'VE MISSED, ALL THE TIME THAT'S PASSED!
YOU HAVE A WIFE, TOO.
REMEMBER?
YOU EVEN STOPPED WRITING.
I SENT YOU MY PAY PACKET EVERY MONTH.
FROM THE WAR OFFICE, YES. NOT FROM YOU. THERE WAS NOTHING PERSONAL ABOUT IT AT ALL.
IT WAS LIKE YOU HAD DIED.

YOU DID MISS A LOT. MY PREGNANCY, JOHN BEING BORN--I DID THAT ALONE, BY THE WAY. HE WAS EARLY, AND SO THE MIDWIFE HADN'T ARRIVED.

I WAS SO SCARED.

BUT, MERCY, IF YOU HAD JUST--

STOP. JUST LISTEN.

HE HAD FEVER TWICE. THE SECOND TIME WAS BAD ENOUGH FOR ME TO CARRY HIM TO THE TRIBES FOR HELP. HE WAS SO HOT, IT WAS HARD TO EVEN HOLD HIM.

THEN THERE WERE THE POACHERS, THE THIEVES...WORD GETS AROUND ABOUT A LONE WOMAN AND A SMALL CHILD. PEOPLE COME TO TAKE ADVANTAGE.

ETHAN SAID HE HAS MILITIA GO AROUND TO ALL THE HOMESTEADS REGULARLY, TO ASSIST.

TO POACH AND THIEVE. JUST BECAUSE THEY WEAR A GREEN COAT DOESN'T MAKE THEM SAINTS.

I HAD TO GROW HIM UP FAST, SETH. I NEEDED HELP.

HE'S A GOOD BOY. HE'S BRAVE AND LEARNS QUICK AND LISTENS TO ME.

WE'VE DONE WELL.

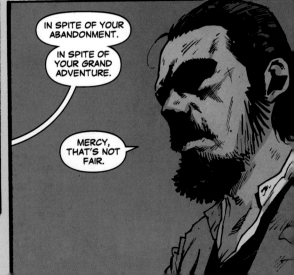

IN SPITE OF YOUR ABANDONMENT.

IN SPITE OF YOUR GRAND ADVENTURE.

MERCY, THAT'S NOT FAIR.

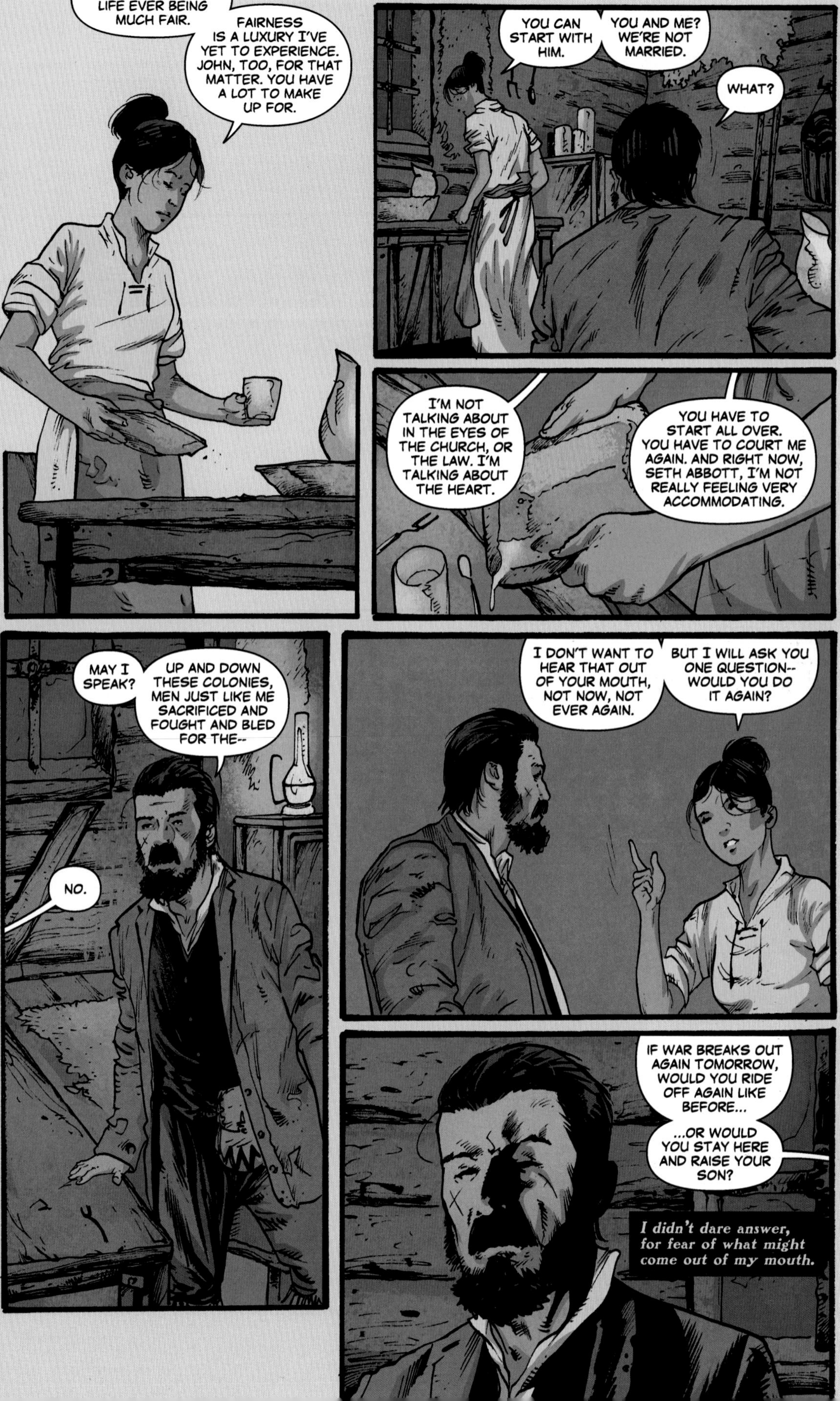
PERHAPS NOT, BUT I DON'T RECALL LIFE EVER BEING MUCH FAIR.
FAIRNESS IS A LUXURY I'VE YET TO EXPERIENCE. JOHN, TOO, FOR THAT MATTER. YOU HAVE A LOT TO MAKE UP FOR.
YOU CAN START WITH HIM.
YOU AND ME? WE'RE NOT MARRIED.
WHAT?
I'M NOT TALKING ABOUT IN THE EYES OF THE CHURCH, OR THE LAW. I'M TALKING ABOUT THE HEART.
YOU HAVE TO START ALL OVER. YOU HAVE TO COURT ME AGAIN. AND RIGHT NOW, SETH ABBOTT, I'M NOT REALLY FEELING VERY ACCOMMODATING.
MAY I SPEAK?
UP AND DOWN THESE COLONIES, MEN JUST LIKE ME SACRIFICED AND FOUGHT AND BLED FOR THE--
NO.
I DON'T WANT TO HEAR THAT OUT OF YOUR MOUTH, NOT NOW, NOT EVER AGAIN.
BUT I WILL ASK YOU ONE QUESTION-- WOULD YOU DO IT AGAIN?
IF WAR BREAKS OUT AGAIN TOMORROW, WOULD YOU RIDE OFF AGAIN LIKE BEFORE...
...OR WOULD YOU STAY HERE AND RAISE YOUR SON?
I didn't dare answer, for fear of what might come out of my mouth.

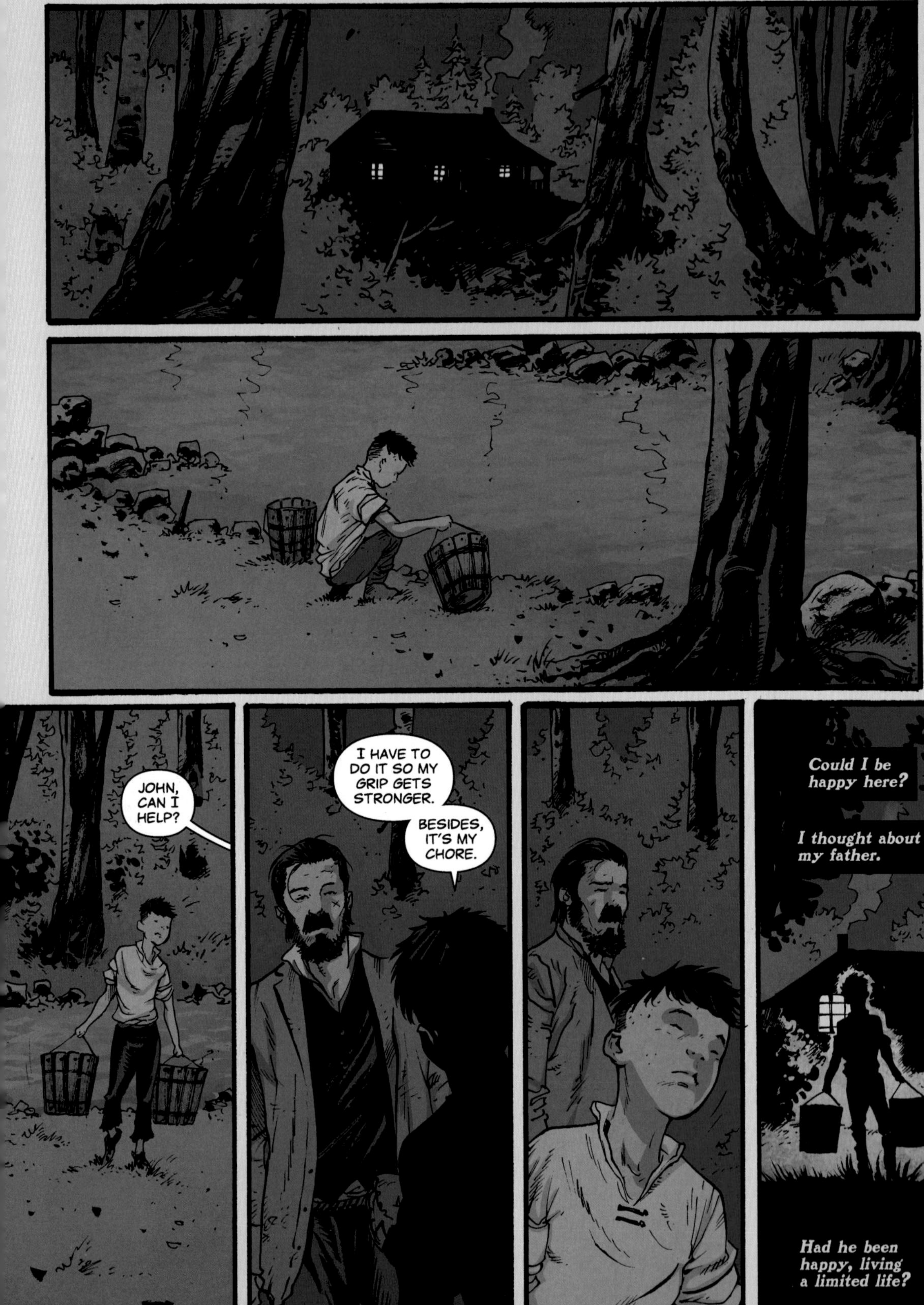
JOHN, CAN I HELP?
I HAVE TO DO IT SO MY GRIP GETS STRONGER.
BESIDES, IT'S MY CHORE.
Could I be happy here?
I thought about my father.
Had he been happy, living a limited life?

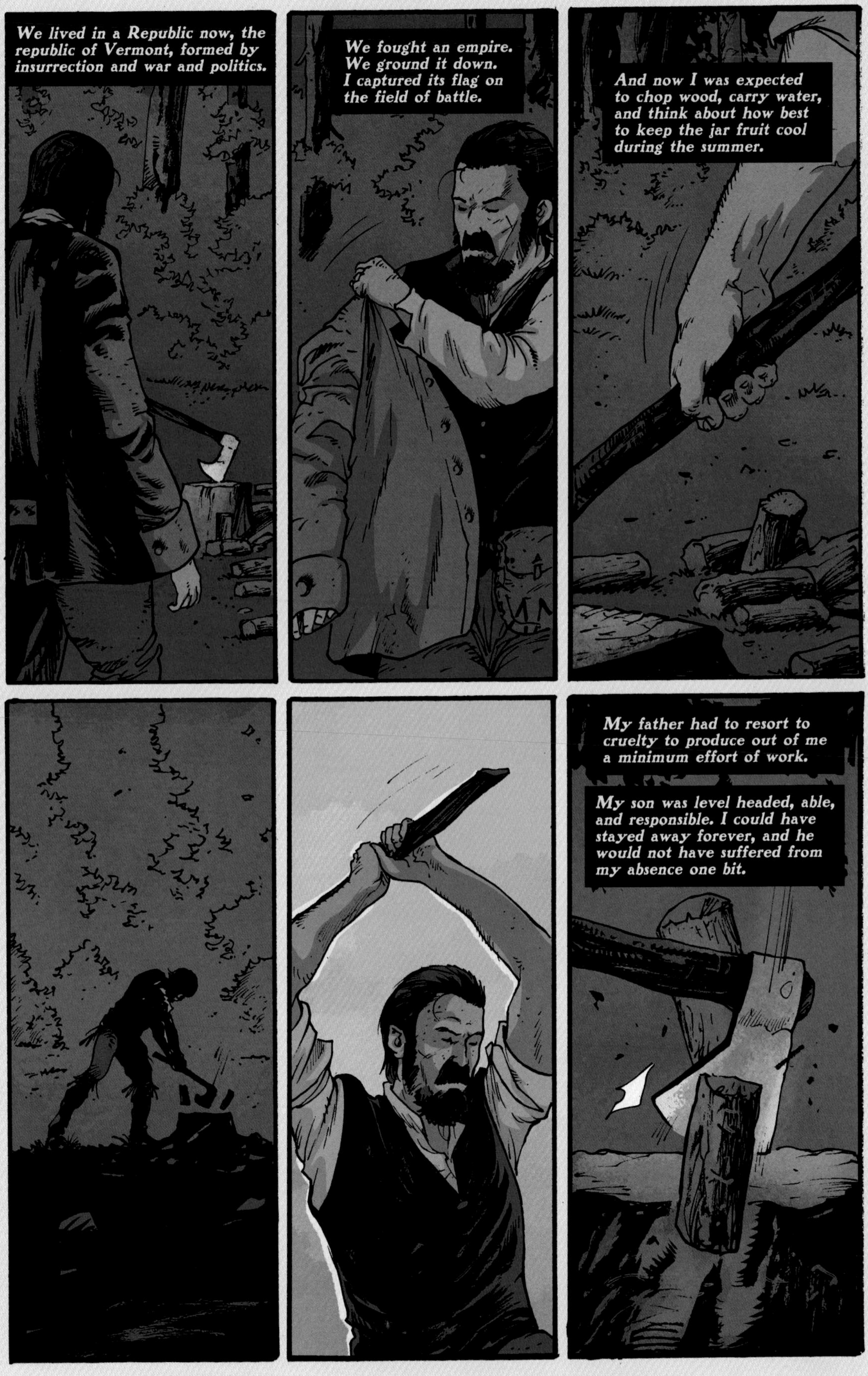

We lived in a Republic now, the republic of Vermont, formed by insurrection and war and politics.
We fought an empire. We ground it down. I captured its flag on the field of battle.
And now I was expected to chop wood, carry water, and think about how best to keep the jar fruit cool during the summer.
My father had to resort to cruelty to produce out of me a minimum effort of work.
My son was level headed, able, and responsible. I could have stayed away forever, and he would not have suffered from my absence one bit.

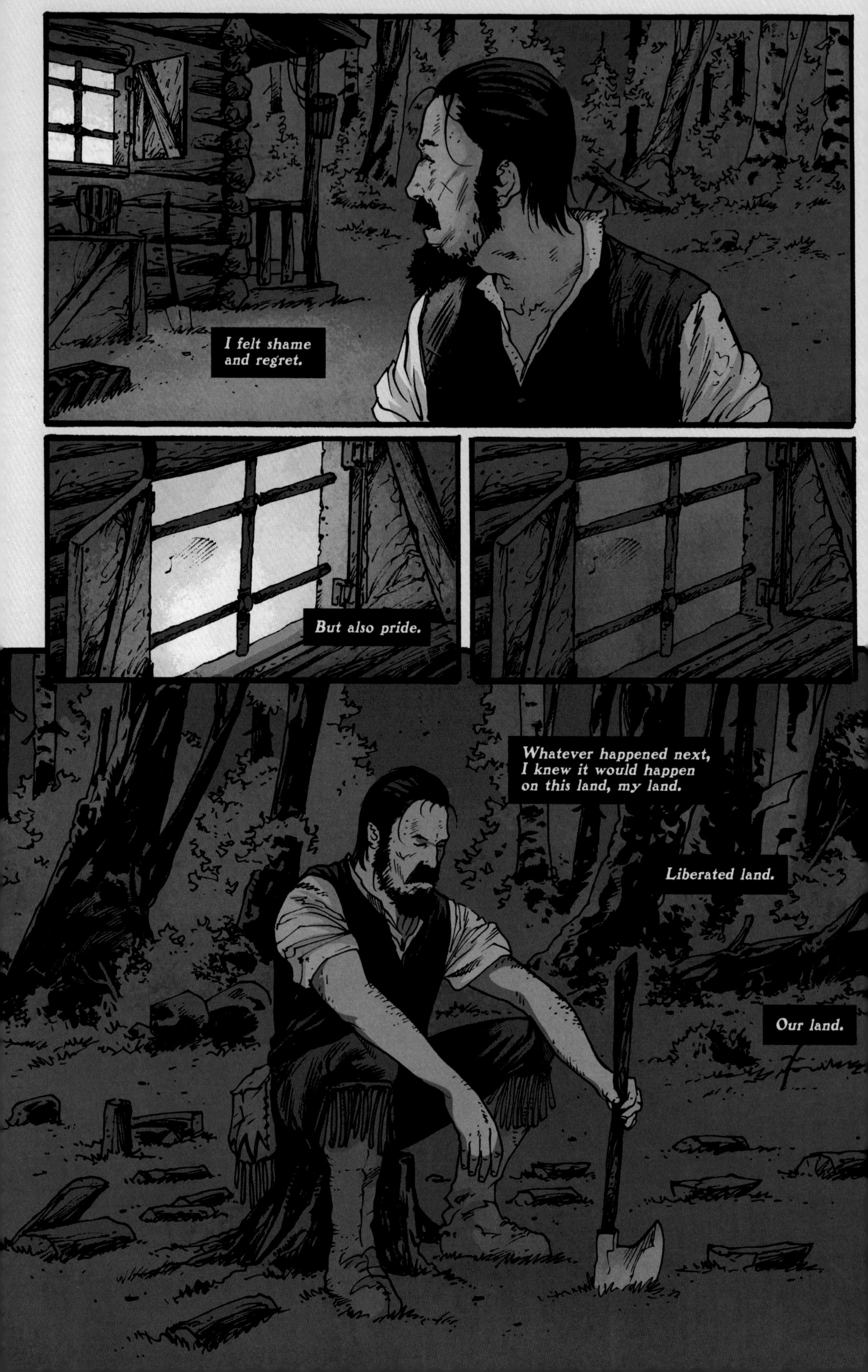
I felt shame and regret.
But also pride.
Whatever happened next, I knew it would happen on this land, my land.
Liberated land.
Our land.

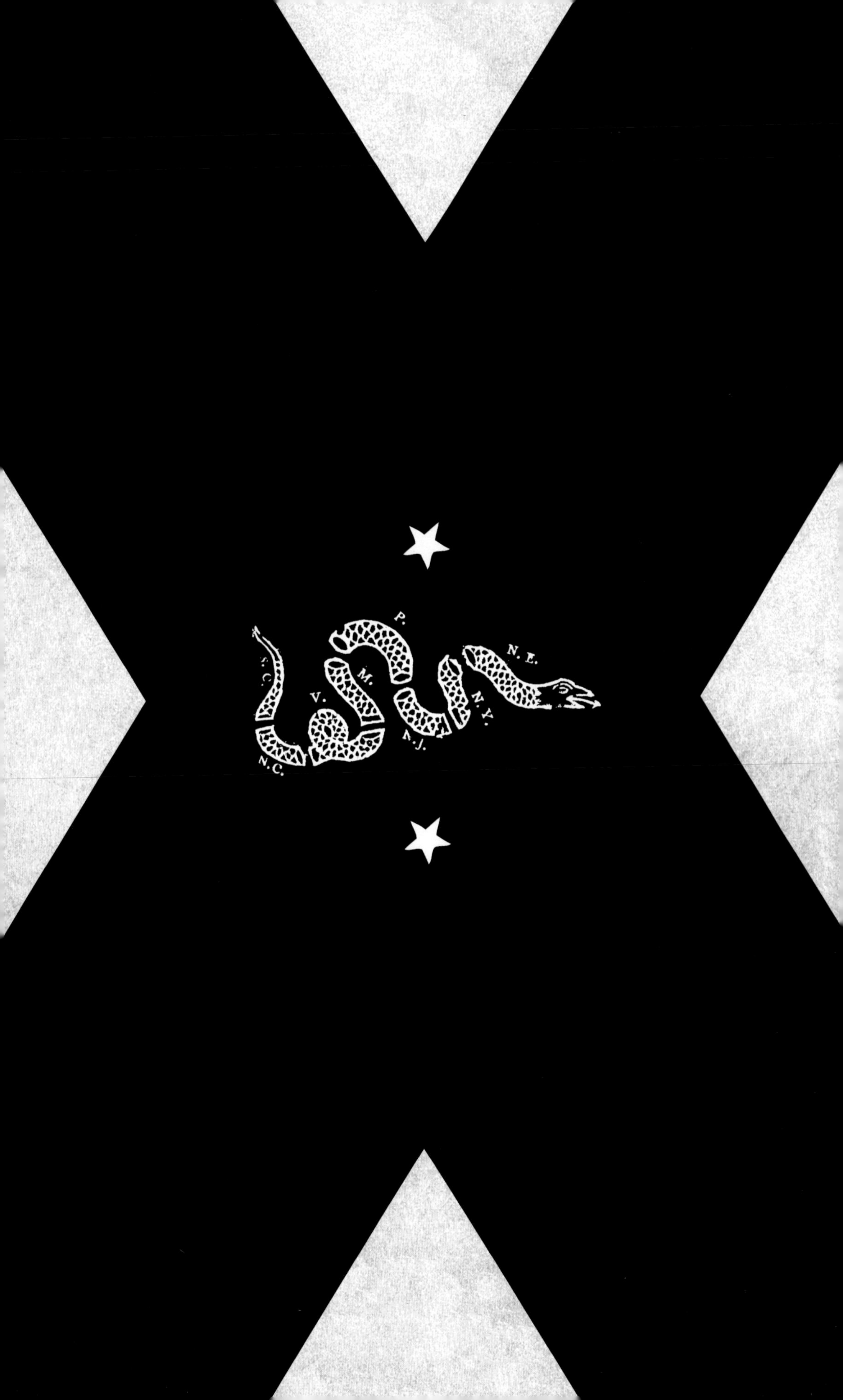
S.C.
N.C.
V.
M.
P.
N.J.
N.Y.
N.E.

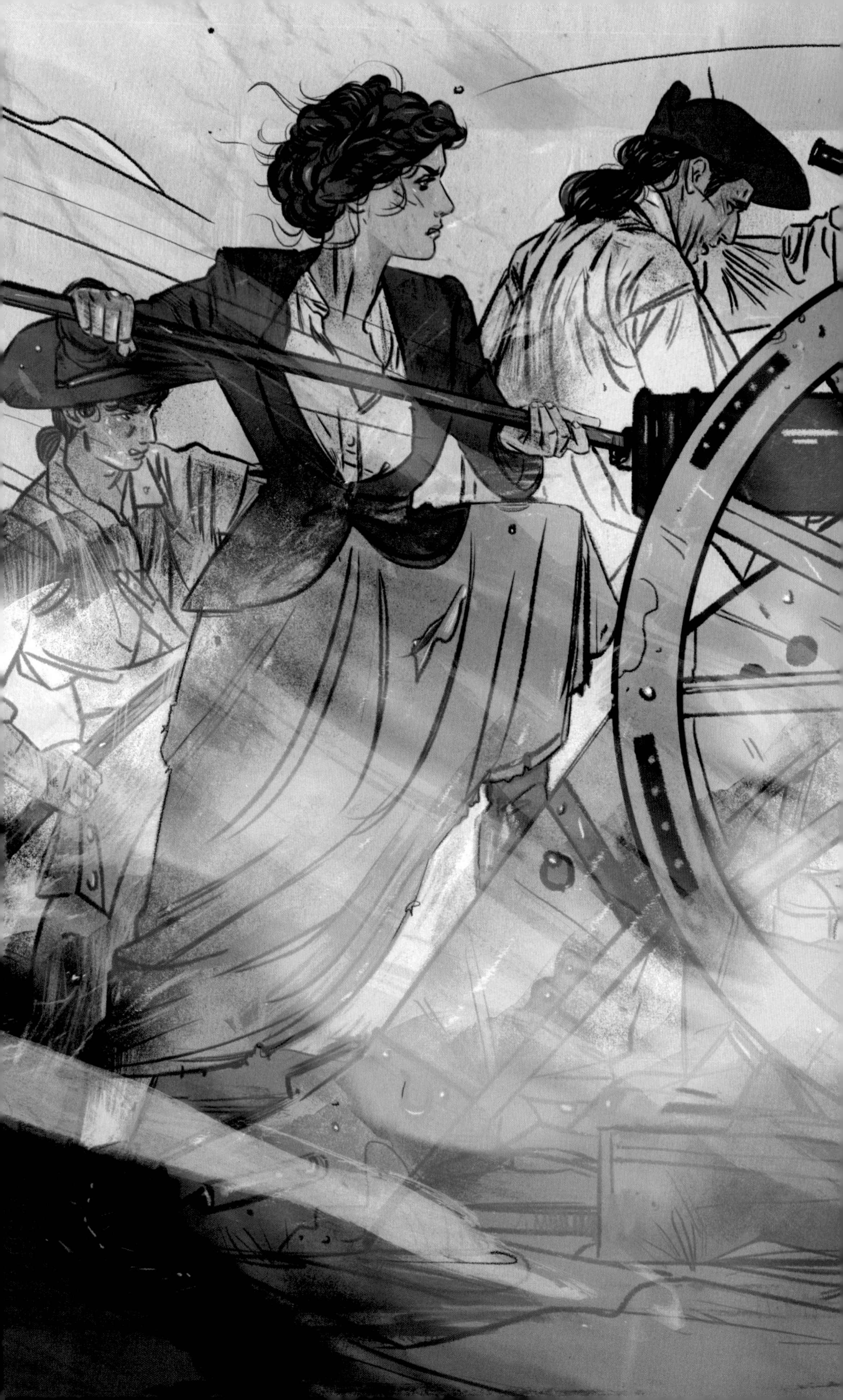

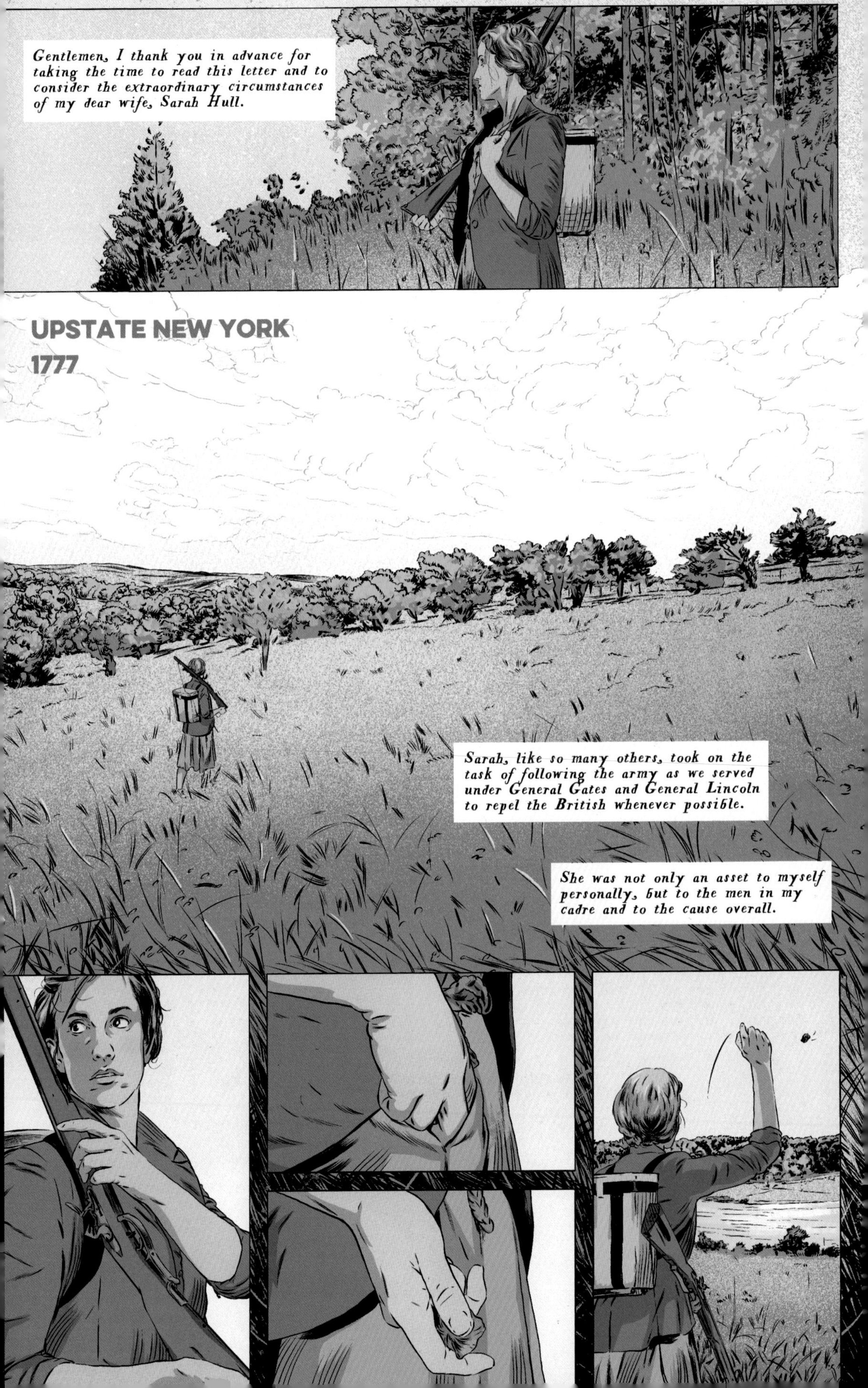
Gentlemen, I thank you in advance for taking the time to read this letter and to consider the extraordinary circumstances of my dear wife, Sarah Hull.
UPSTATE NEW YORK
1777
Sarah, like so many others, took on the task of following the army as we served under General Gates and General Lincoln to repel the British whenever possible.
She was not only an asset to myself personally, but to the men in my cadre and to the cause overall.

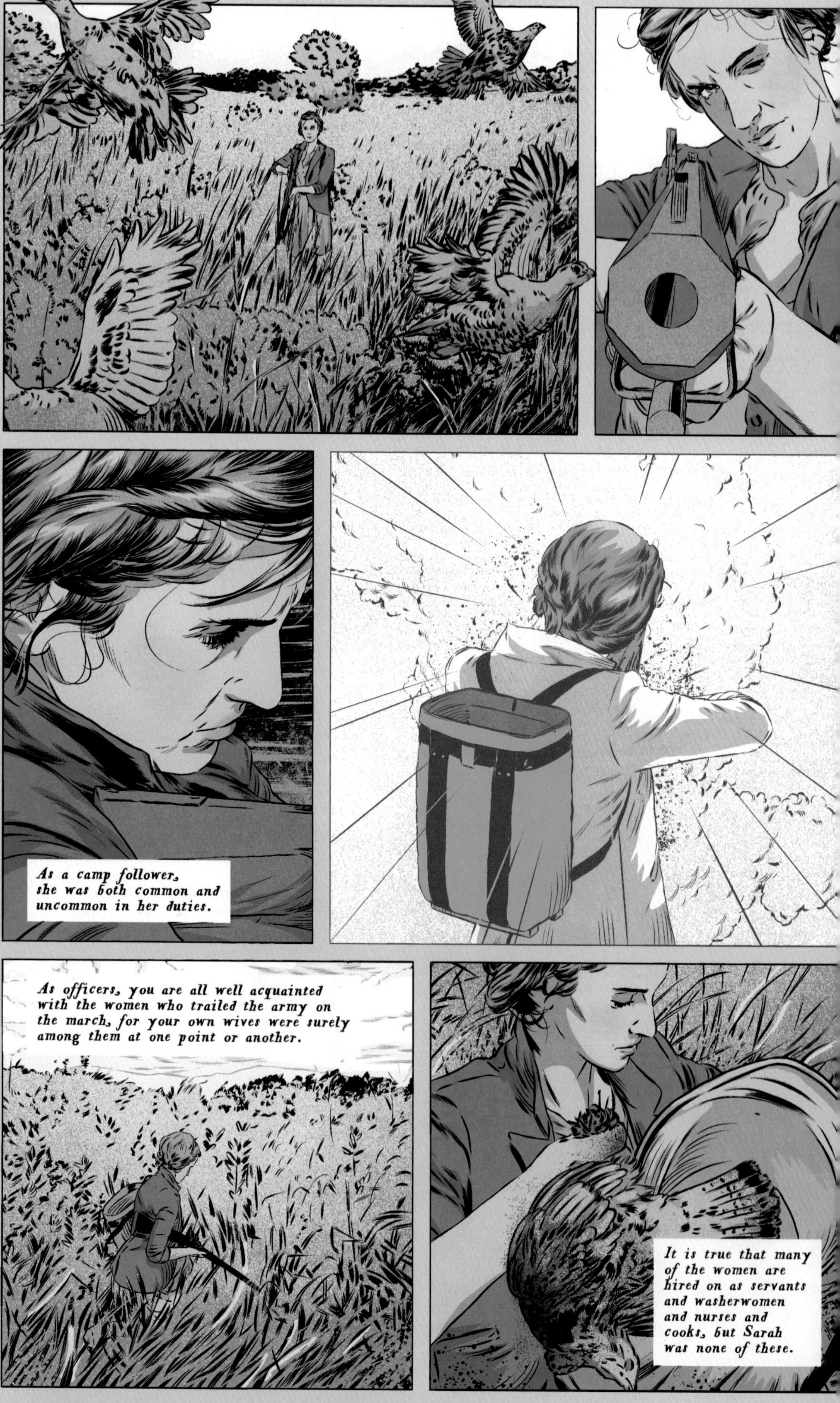
As a camp follower, she was both common and uncommon in her duties.
As officers, you are all well acquainted with the women who trailed the army on the march, for your own wives were surely among them at one point or another.
It is true that many of the women are hired on as servants and washerwomen and nurses and cooks, but Sarah was none of these.

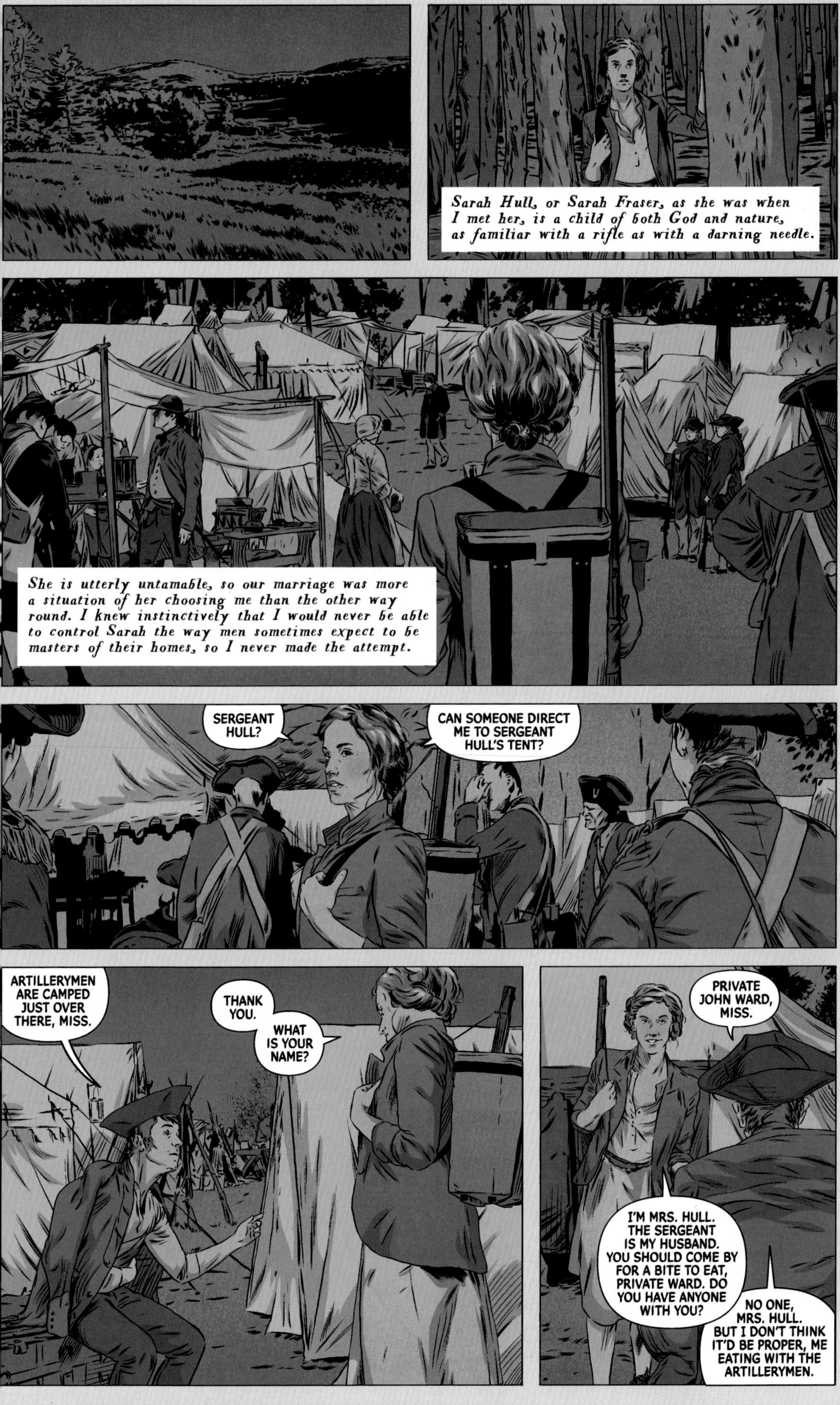
Sarah Hull, or Sarah Fraser, as she was when I met her, is a child of both God and nature, as familiar with a rifle as with a darning needle.
She is utterly untamable, so our marriage was more a situation of her choosing me than the other way round. I knew instinctively that I would never be able to control Sarah the way men sometimes expect to be masters of their homes, so I never made the attempt.
SERGEANT HULL?
CAN SOMEONE DIRECT ME TO SERGEANT HULL'S TENT?
ARTILLERYMEN ARE CAMPED JUST OVER THERE, MISS.
THANK YOU.
WHAT IS YOUR NAME?
PRIVATE JOHN WARD, MISS.
I'M MRS. HULL. THE SERGEANT IS MY HUSBAND. YOU SHOULD COME BY FOR A BITE TO EAT, PRIVATE WARD. DO YOU HAVE ANYONE WITH YOU?
NO ONE, MRS. HULL. BUT I DON'T THINK IT'D BE PROPER, ME EATING WITH THE ARTILLERYMEN.

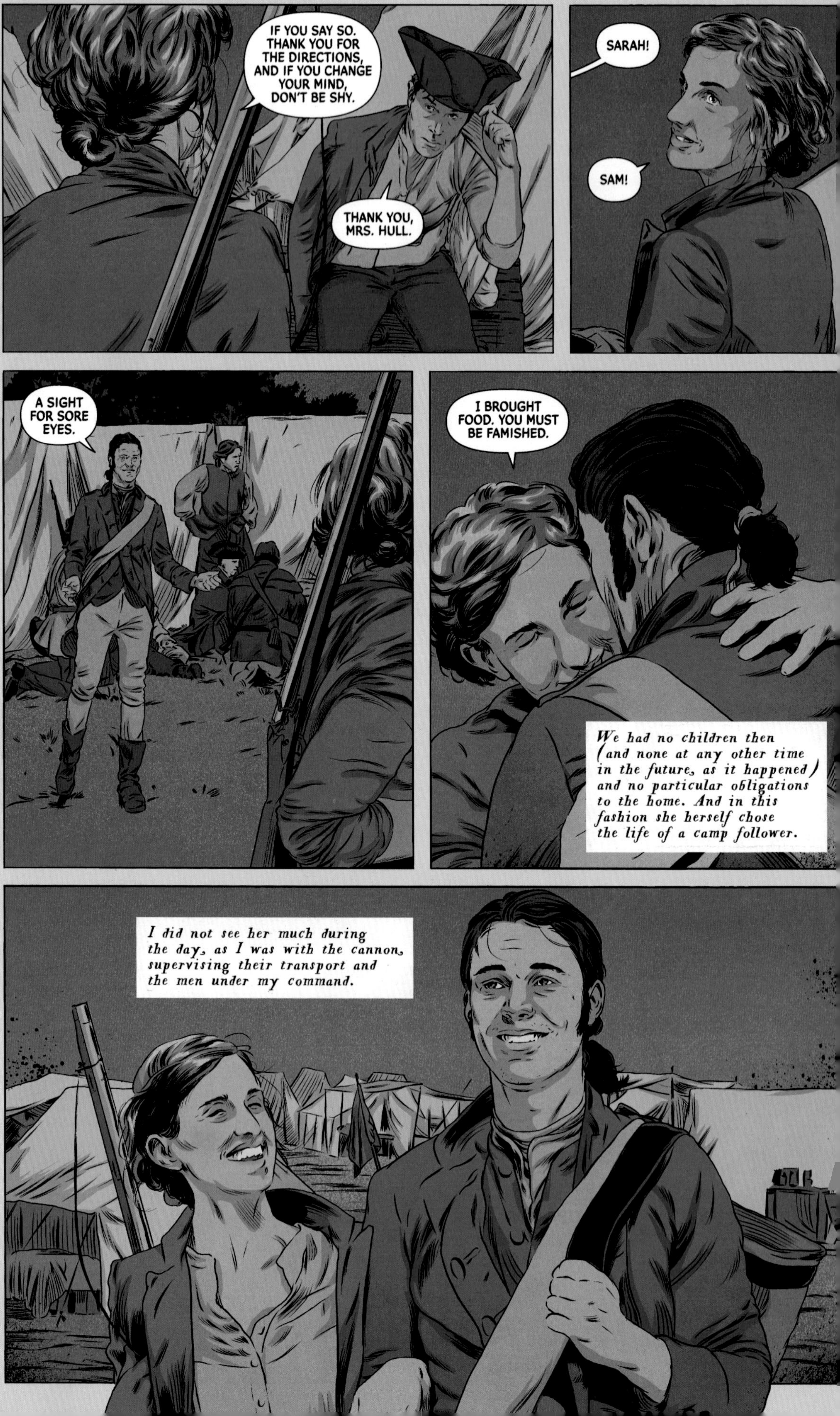
IF YOU SAY SO. THANK YOU FOR THE DIRECTIONS, AND IF YOU CHANGE YOUR MIND, DON'T BE SHY.
THANK YOU, MRS. HULL.
SARAH!
SAM!
A SIGHT FOR SORE EYES.
I BROUGHT FOOD. YOU MUST BE FAMISHED.
We had no children then (and none at any other time in the future, as it happened) and no particular obligations to the home. And in this fashion she herself chose the life of a camp follower.
I did not see her much during the day, as I was with the cannon, supervising their transport and the men under my command.

She would range far from the army train, hunting and trapping and foraging as required...

...and reappear at dinner with enough food for my entire cadre. She would then work well into the night, and at some point before dawn, I would feel her lie down beside me and rest.

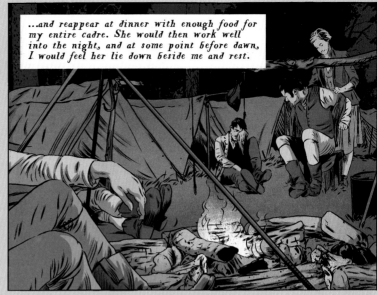

I viewed my husbandly obligation in this most unusual of marriages to always be a positive and joyous presence around her, to be gracious and thankful and respectful of her time and talents, to never overburden her or take her for granted.

I continued this in our postwar life as well, and I believe we've had a happier marriage than most as a result.

She is, as I have stated, a most extraordinary woman.

Speaking specifically of the Saratoga campaign, of the battles of 19 September and 7 October, 1777, she was utterly indispensable, and it is to that point that I direct my energies in writing to you.

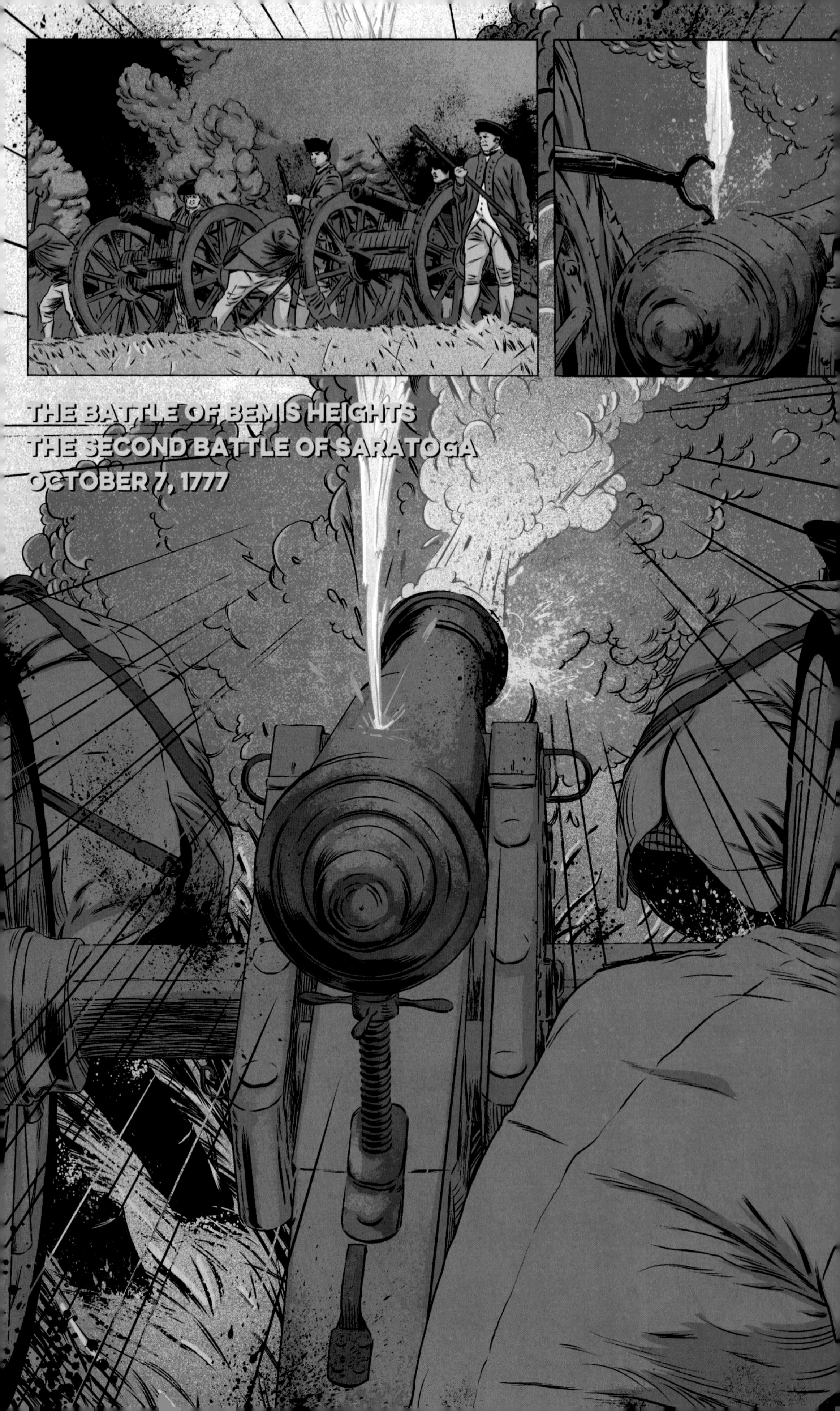
THE BATTLE OF BEMIS HEIGHTS
THE SECOND BATTLE OF SARATOGA
OCTOBER 7, 1777

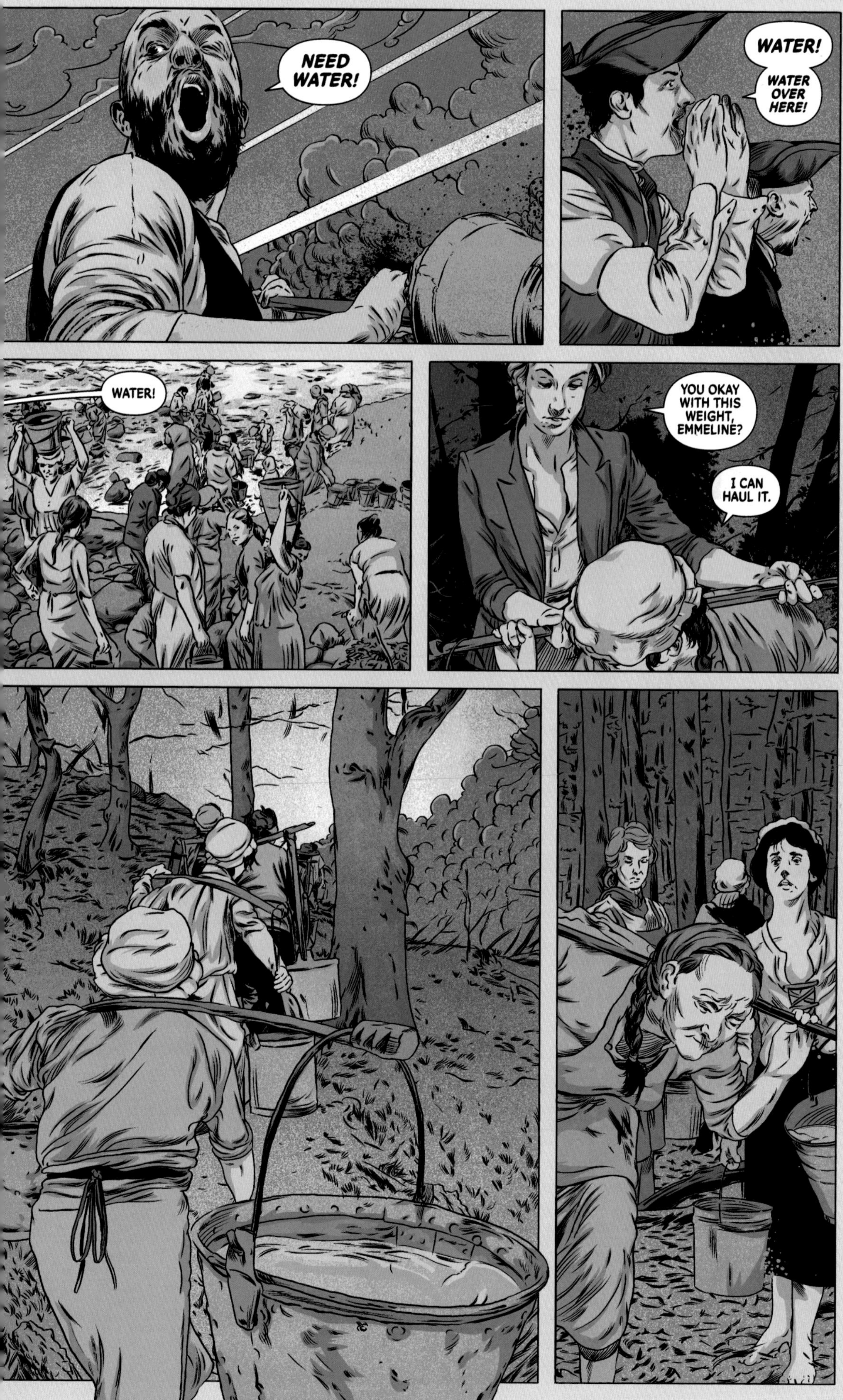
NEED WATER!
WATER!
WATER OVER HERE!
WATER!
YOU OKAY WITH THIS WEIGHT, EMMELINE?
I CAN HAUL IT.

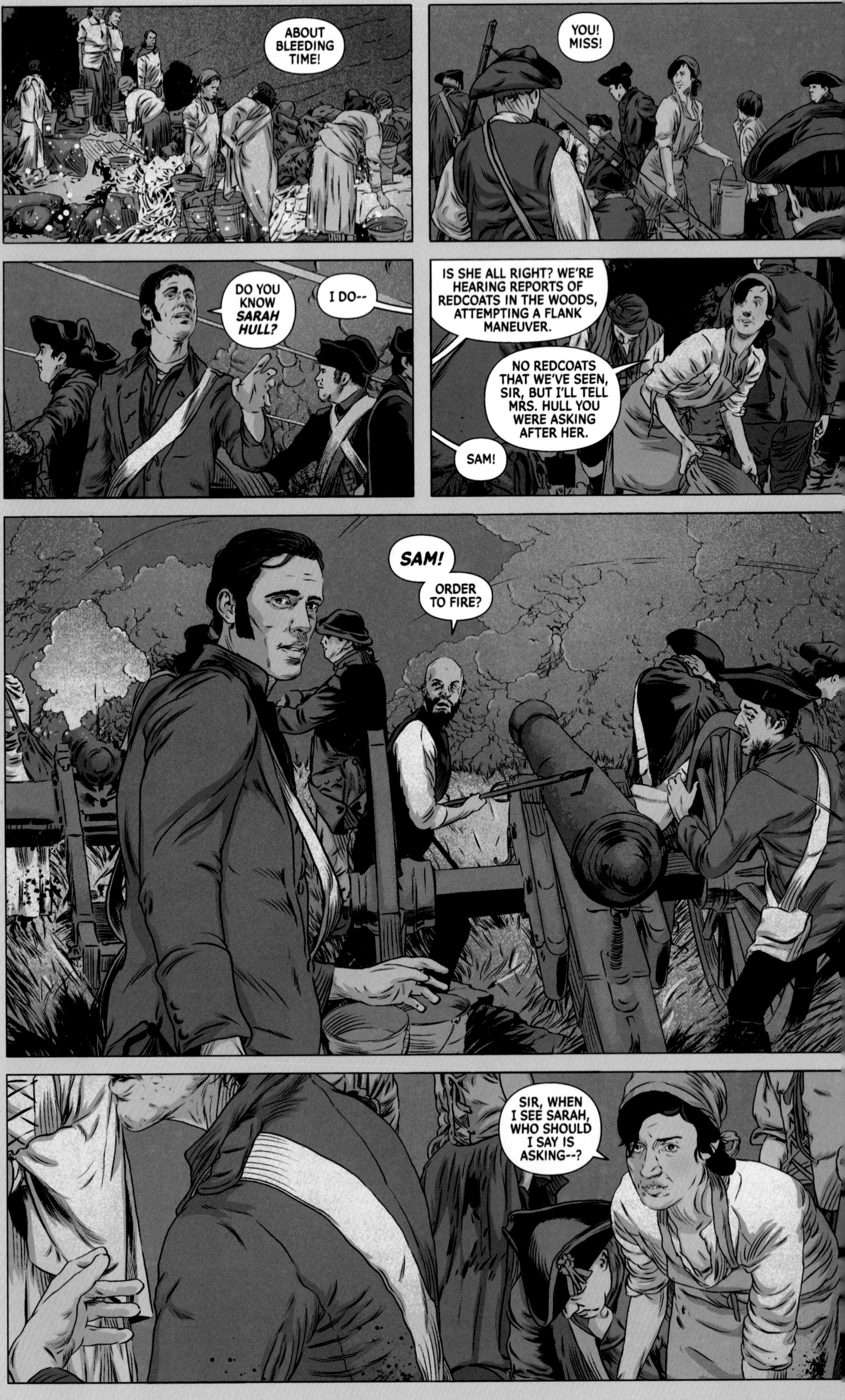
ABOUT BLEEDING TIME!
YOU! MISS!
DO YOU KNOW *SARAH HULL?*
I DO--
IS SHE ALL RIGHT? WE'RE HEARING REPORTS OF REDCOATS IN THE WOODS, ATTEMPTING A FLANK MANEUVER.
NO REDCOATS THAT WE'VE SEEN, SIR, BUT I'LL TELL MRS. HULL YOU WERE ASKING AFTER HER.
SAM!
SAM!
ORDER TO FIRE?
SIR, WHEN I SEE SARAH, WHO SHOULD I SAY IS ASKING--?

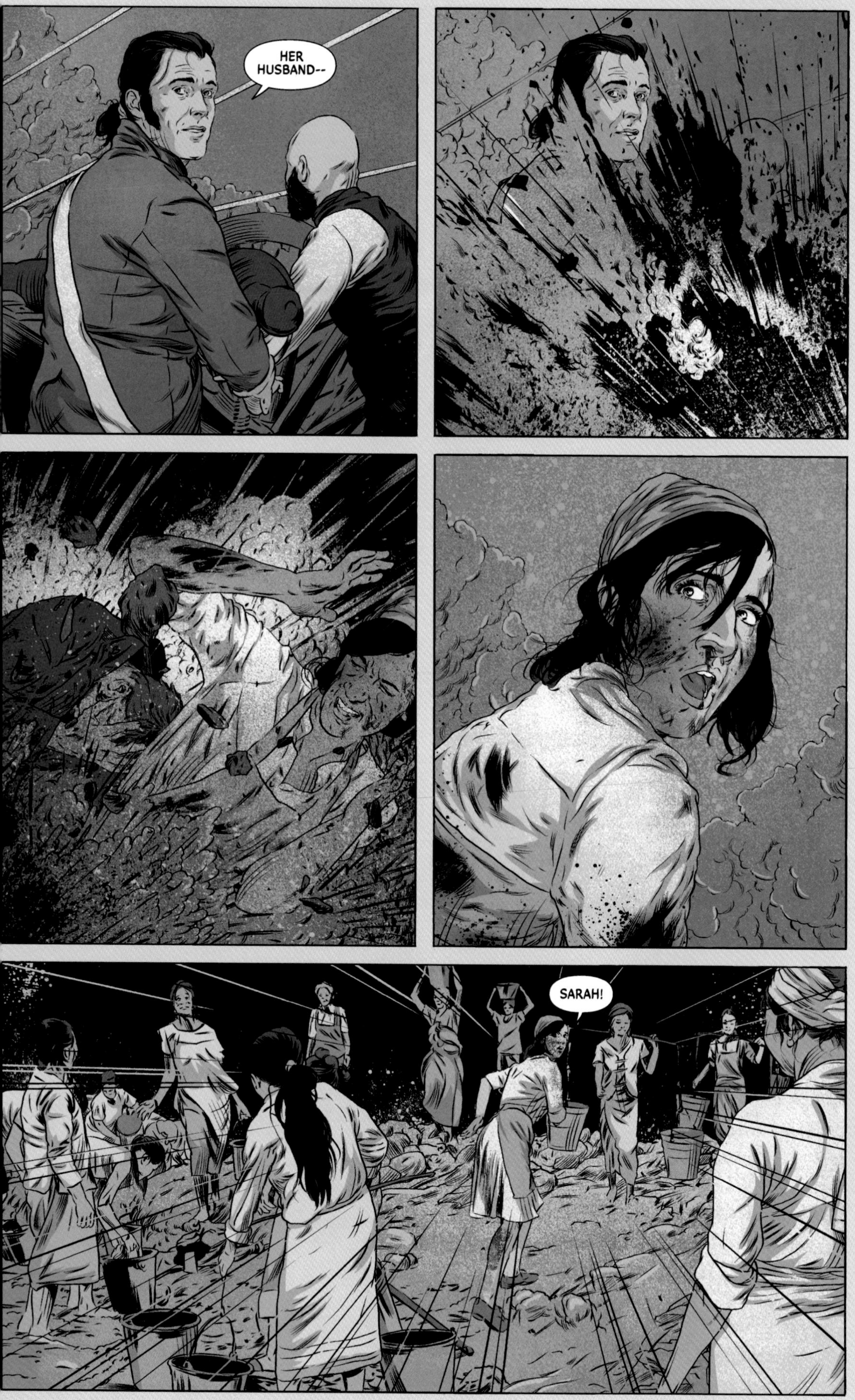
HER HUSBAND--
SARAH!

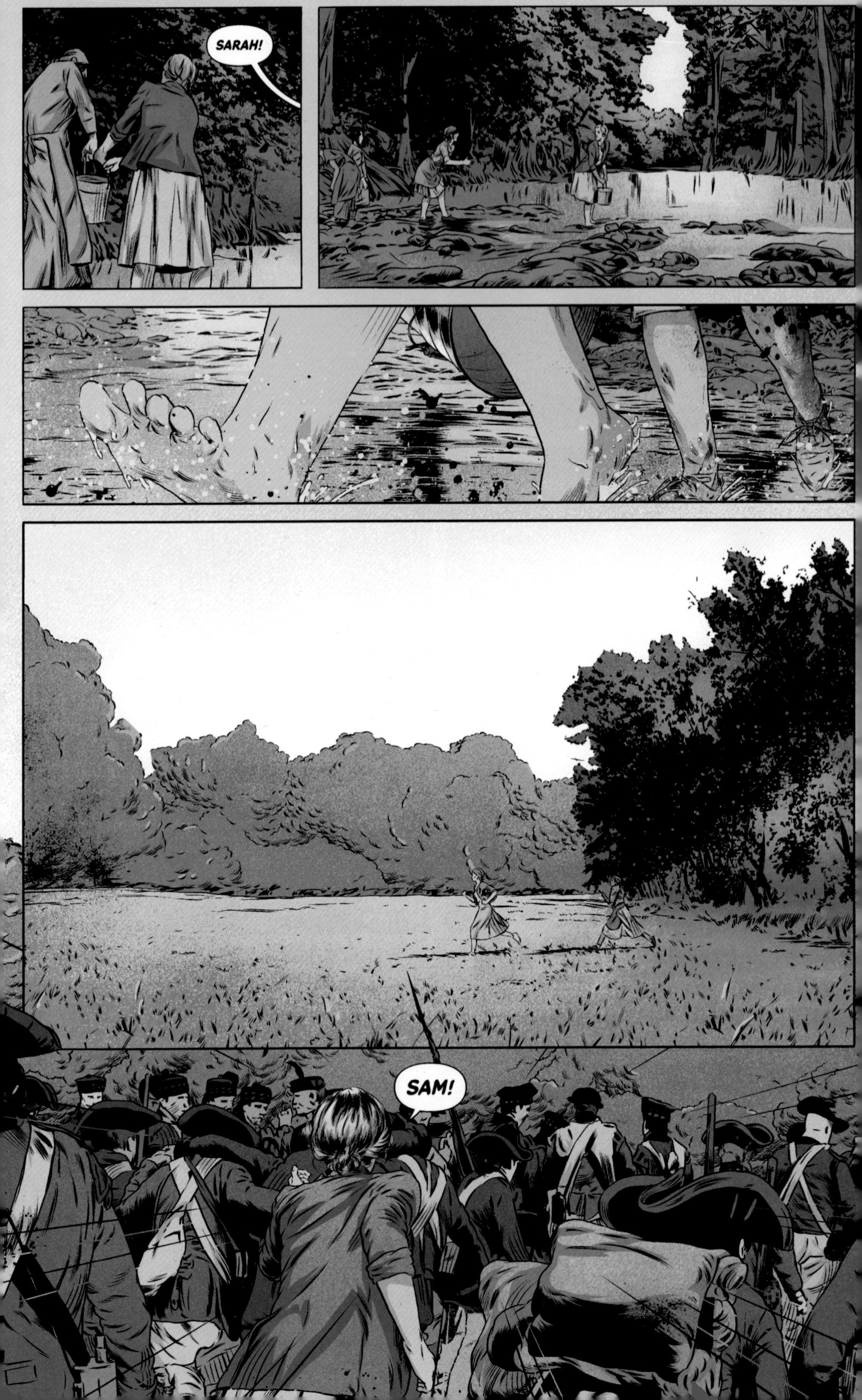
SARAH!
SAM!

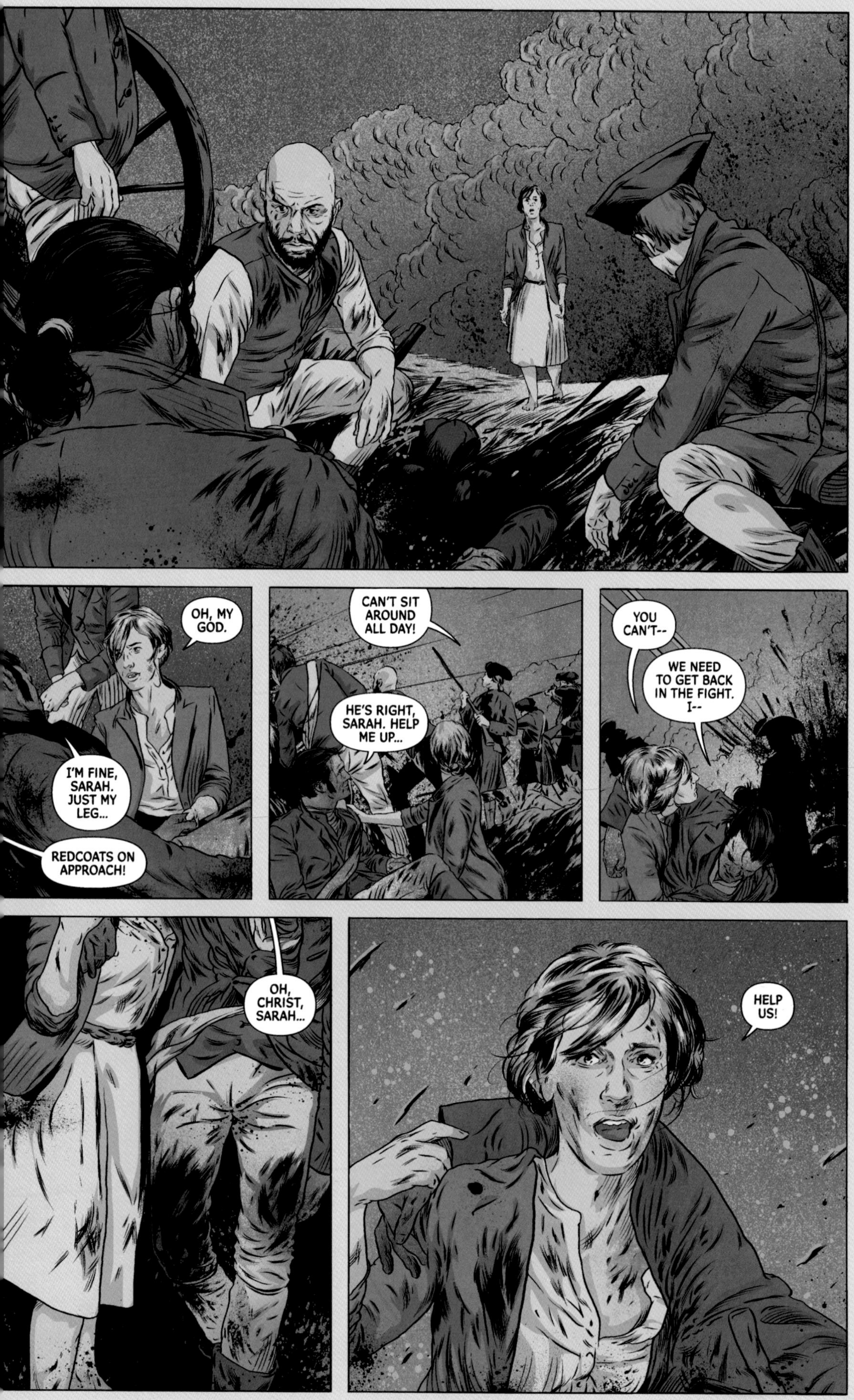
OH, MY GOD.
I'M FINE, SARAH. JUST MY LEG...
REDCOATS ON APPROACH!
CAN'T SIT AROUND ALL DAY!
HE'S RIGHT, SARAH. HELP ME UP...
YOU CAN'T--
WE NEED TO GET BACK IN THE FIGHT. I--
OH, CHRIST, SARAH...
HELP US!

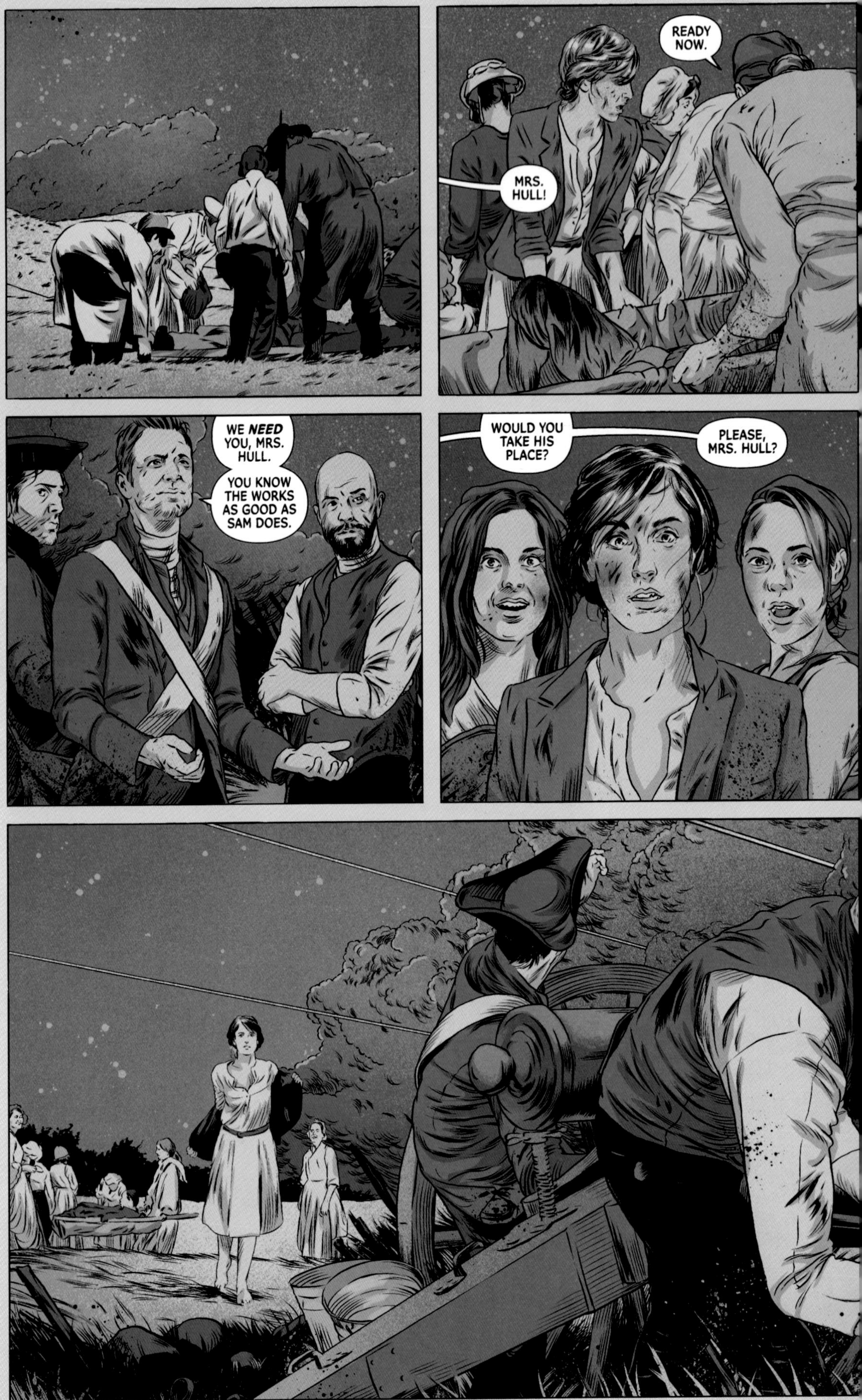
READY NOW.
MRS. HULL!
WE NEED YOU, MRS. HULL.
YOU KNOW THE WORKS AS GOOD AS SAM DOES.
WOULD YOU TAKE HIS PLACE?
PLEASE, MRS. HULL?

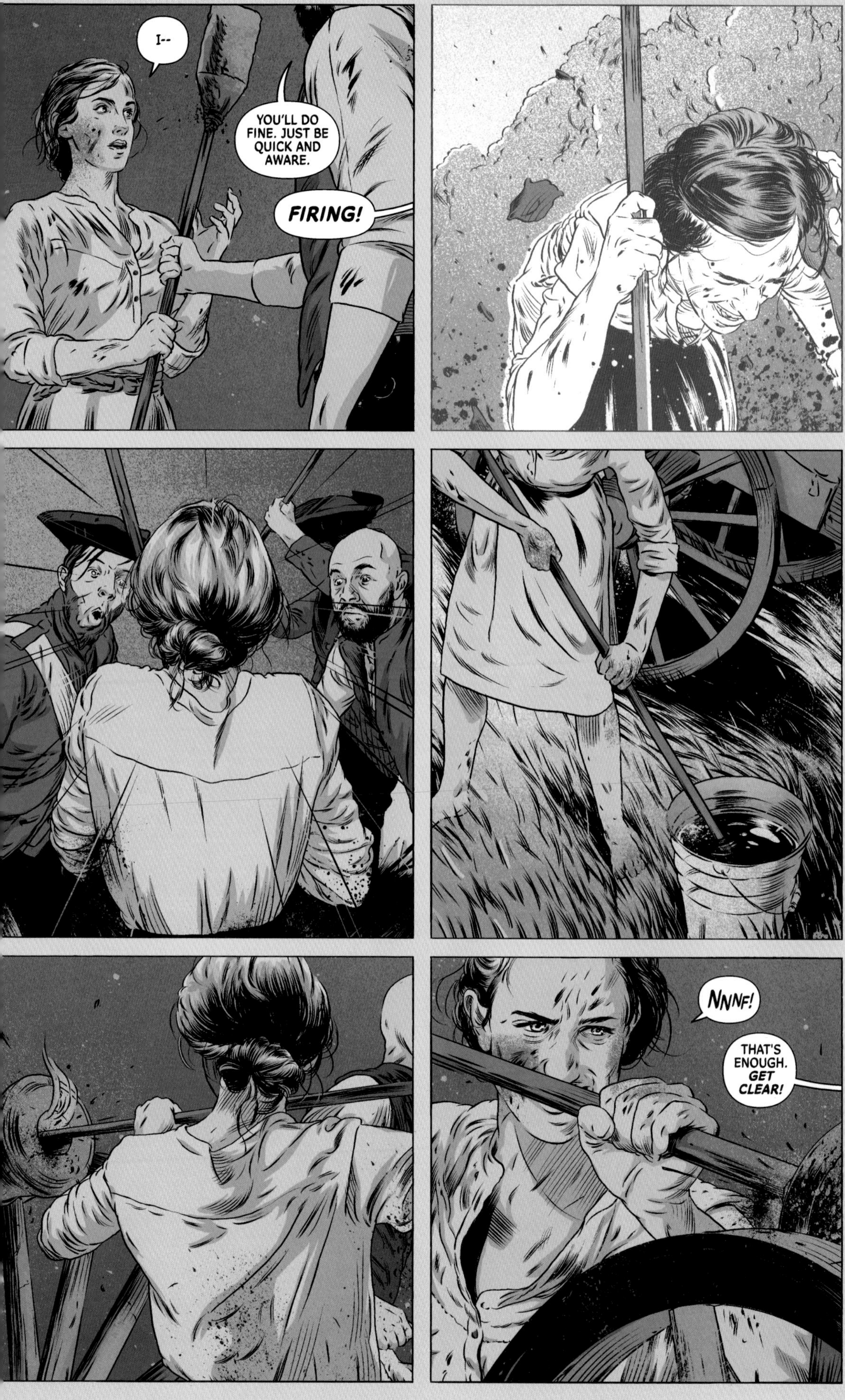
I--
YOU'LL DO FINE. JUST BE QUICK AND AWARE.
FIRING!
NNNF!
THAT'S ENOUGH. GET CLEAR!

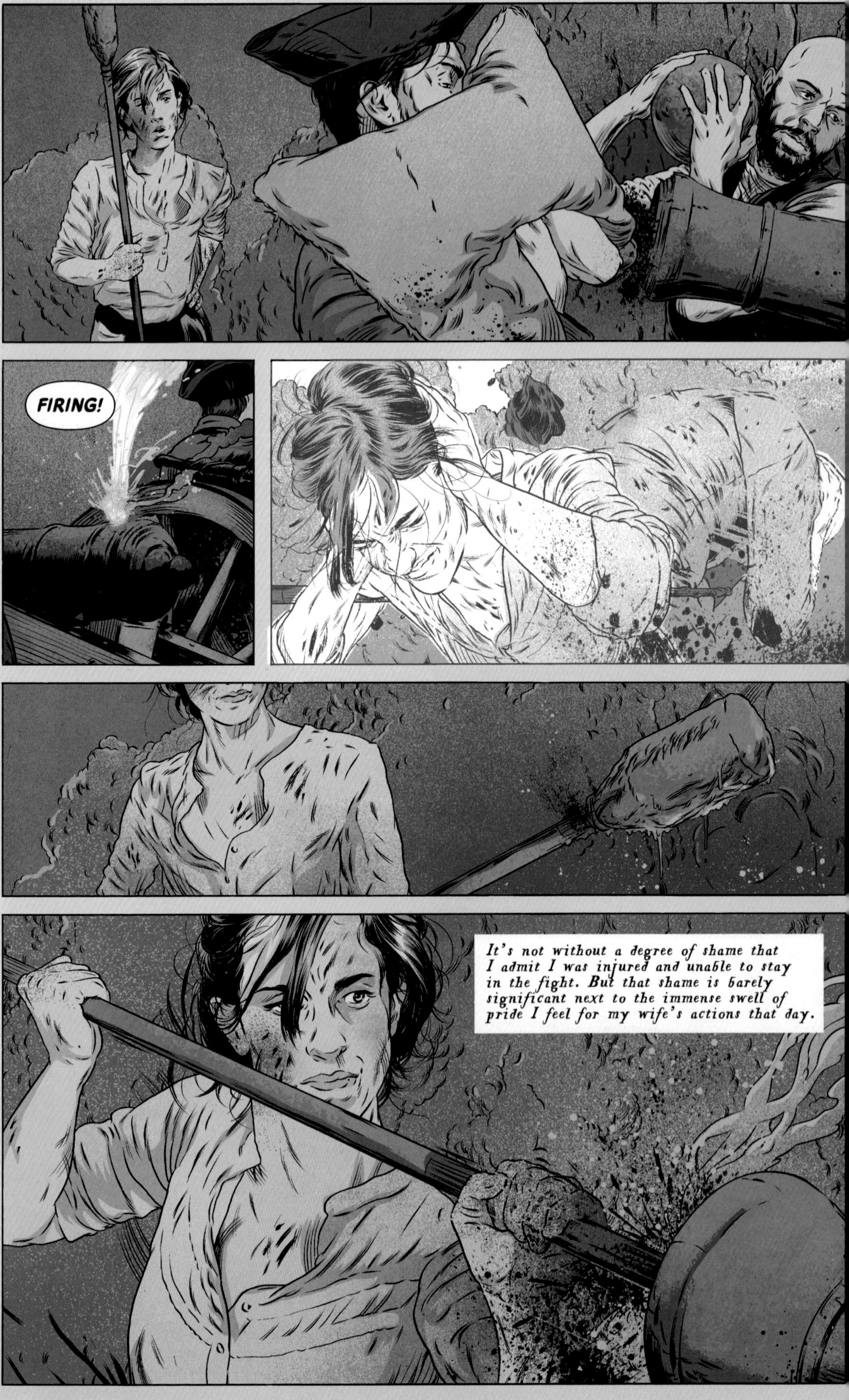
FIRING!
It's not without a degree of shame that I admit I was injured and unable to stay in the fight. But that shame is barely significant next to the immense swell of pride I feel for my wife's actions that day.

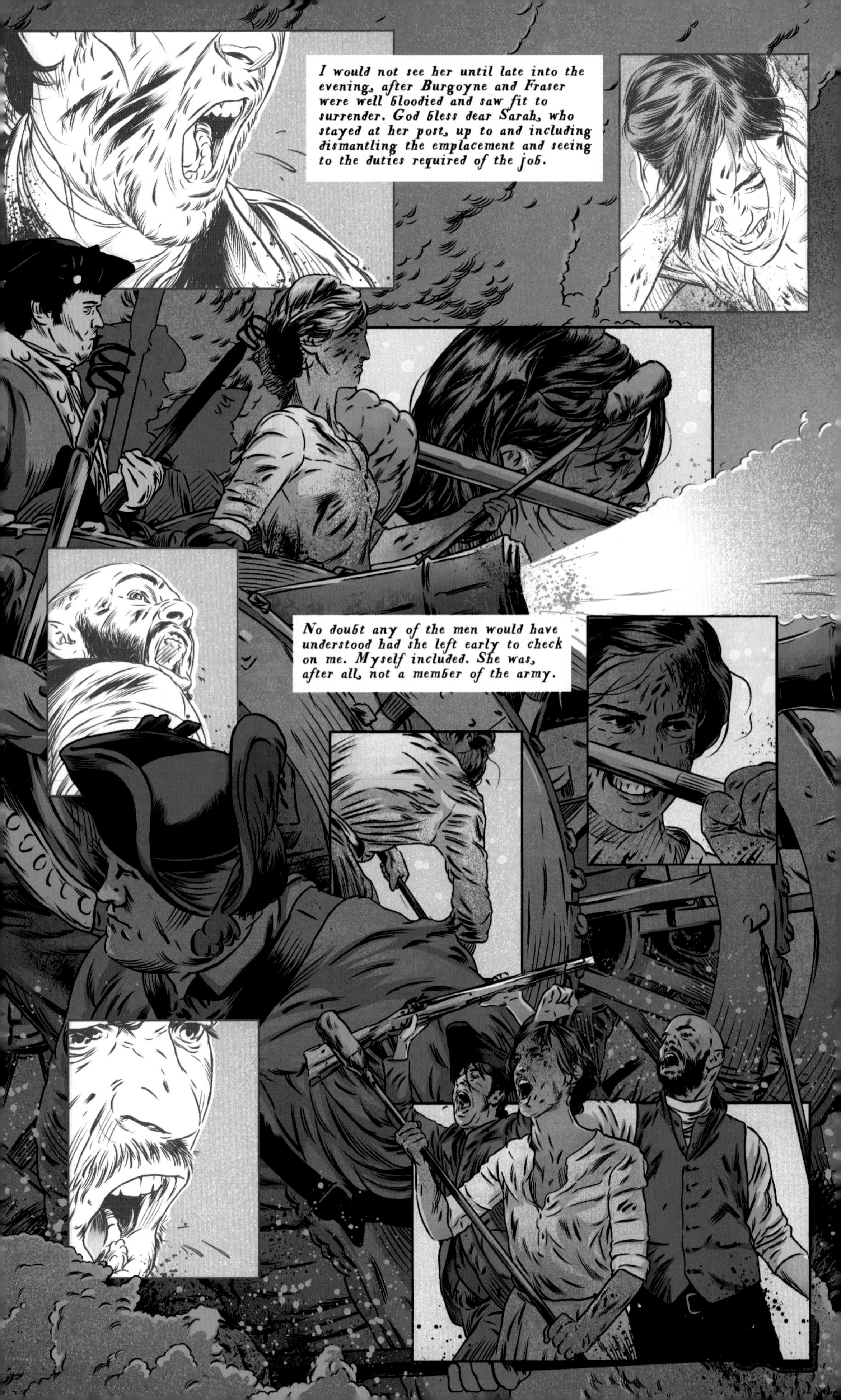
I would not see her until late into the evening, after Burgoyne and Fraser were well bloodied and saw fit to surrender. God bless dear Sarah, who stayed at her post, up to and including dismantling the emplacement and seeing to the duties required of the job.
No doubt any of the men would have understood had she left early to check on me. Myself included. She was, after all, not a member of the army.

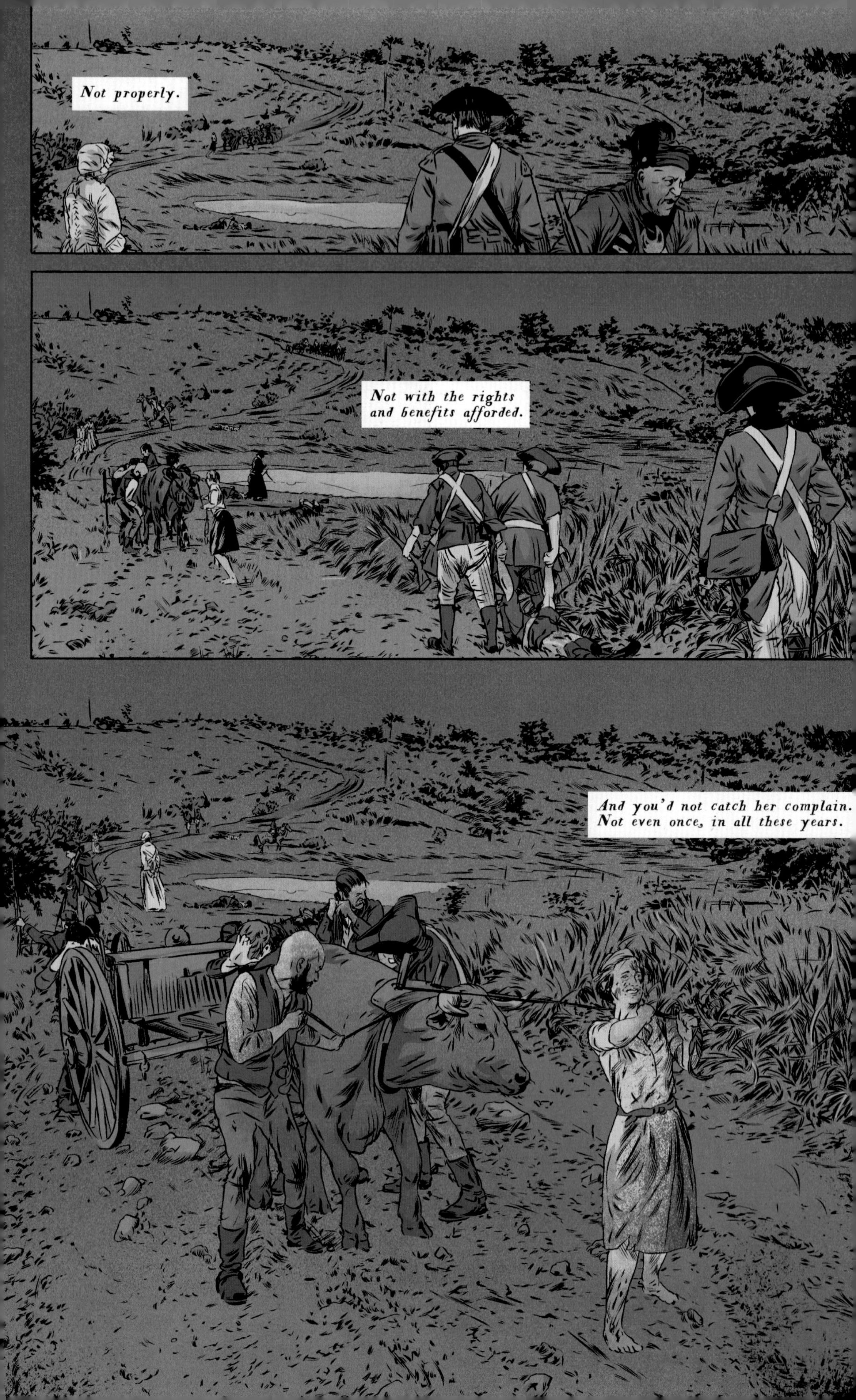
Not properly.
Not with the rights and benefits afforded.
And you'd not catch her complain. Not even once, in all these years.

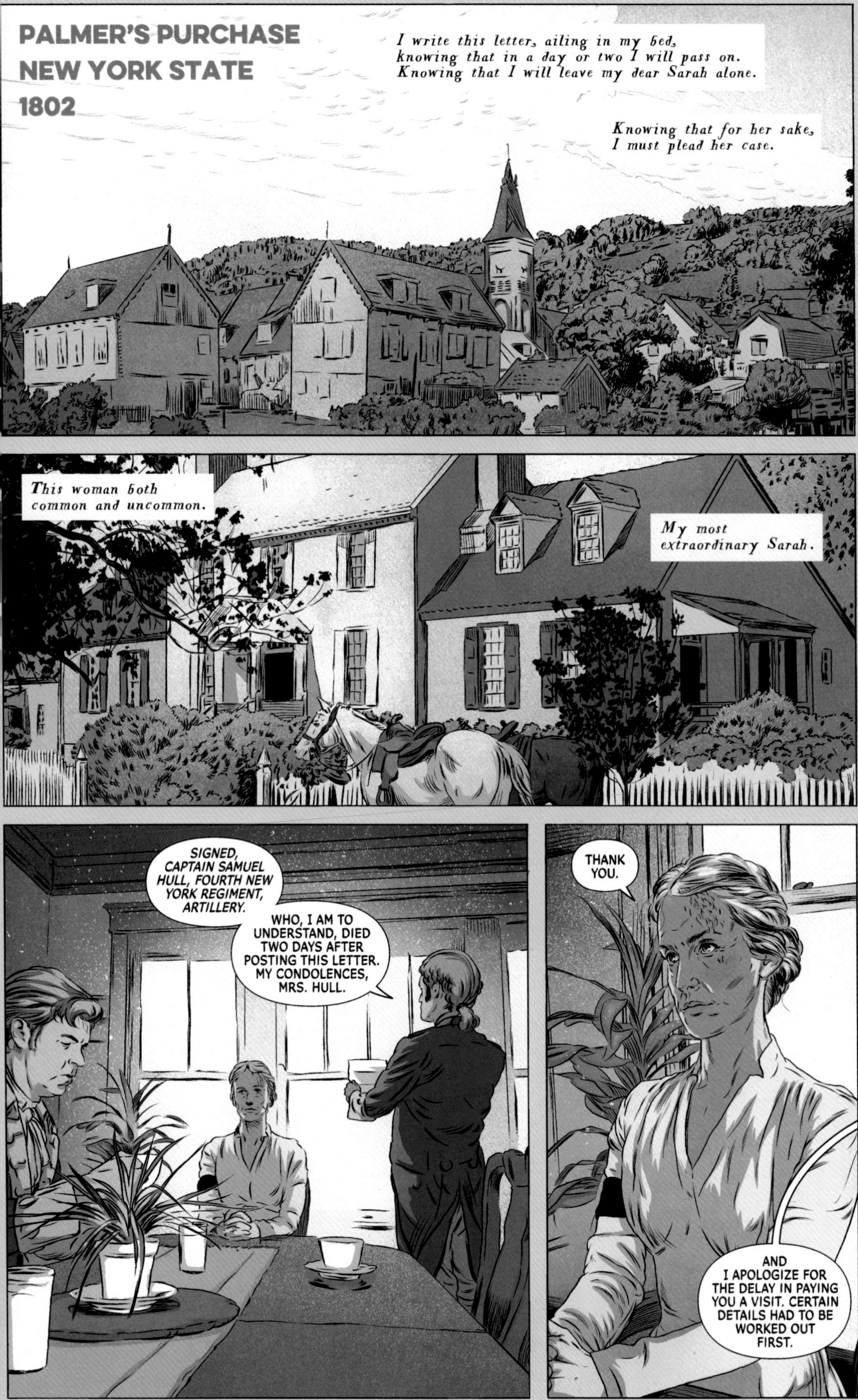

PALMER'S PURCHASE
NEW YORK STATE
1802
I write this letter, ailing in my bed, knowing that in a day or two I will pass on. Knowing that I will leave my dear Sarah alone.
Knowing that for her sake, I must plead her case.
This woman both common and uncommon.
My most extraordinary Sarah.
SIGNED, CAPTAIN SAMUEL HULL, FOURTH NEW YORK REGIMENT, ARTILLERY.
WHO, I AM TO UNDERSTAND, DIED TWO DAYS AFTER POSTING THIS LETTER. MY CONDOLENCES, MRS. HULL.
THANK YOU.
AND I APOLOGIZE FOR THE DELAY IN PAYING YOU A VISIT. CERTAIN DETAILS HAD TO BE WORKED OUT FIRST.

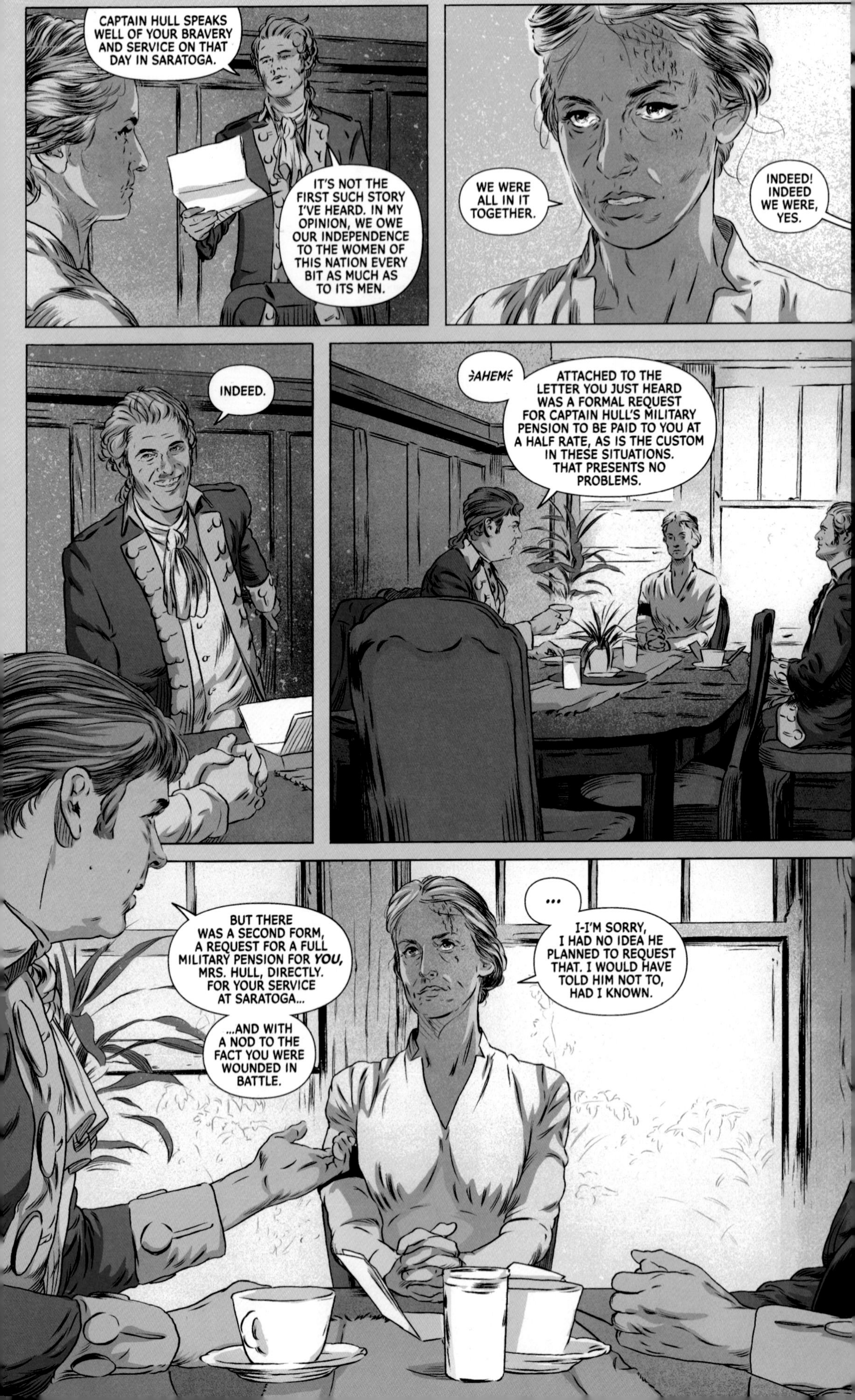
CAPTAIN HULL SPEAKS WELL OF YOUR BRAVERY AND SERVICE ON THAT DAY IN SARATOGA.
IT'S NOT THE FIRST SUCH STORY I'VE HEARD. IN MY OPINION, WE OWE OUR INDEPENDENCE TO THE WOMEN OF THIS NATION EVERY BIT AS MUCH AS TO ITS MEN.
WE WERE ALL IN IT TOGETHER.
INDEED! INDEED WE WERE, YES.
INDEED.
AHEM
ATTACHED TO THE LETTER YOU JUST HEARD WAS A FORMAL REQUEST FOR CAPTAIN HULL'S MILITARY PENSION TO BE PAID TO YOU AT A HALF RATE, AS IS THE CUSTOM IN THESE SITUATIONS. THAT PRESENTS NO PROBLEMS.
BUT THERE WAS A SECOND FORM, A REQUEST FOR A FULL MILITARY PENSION FOR *YOU,* MRS. HULL, DIRECTLY. FOR YOUR SERVICE AT SARATOGA...
...AND WITH A NOD TO THE FACT YOU WERE WOUNDED IN BATTLE.
...
I-I'M SORRY, I HAD NO IDEA HE PLANNED TO REQUEST THAT. I WOULD HAVE TOLD HIM NOT TO, HAD I KNOWN.

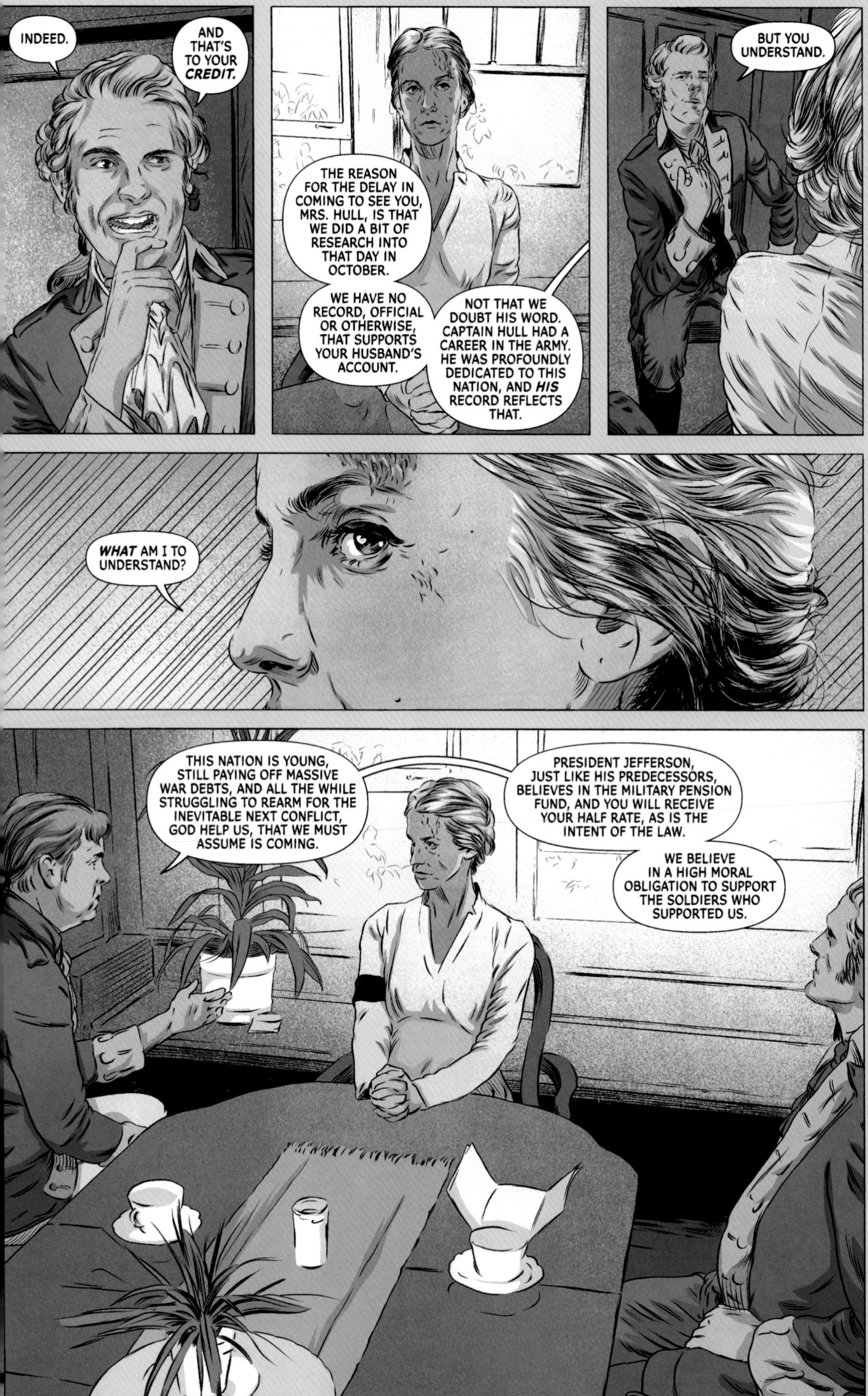
INDEED.
AND THAT'S TO YOUR *CREDIT.*
THE REASON FOR THE DELAY IN COMING TO SEE YOU, MRS. HULL, IS THAT WE DID A BIT OF RESEARCH INTO THAT DAY IN OCTOBER.
WE HAVE NO RECORD, OFFICIAL OR OTHERWISE, THAT SUPPORTS YOUR HUSBAND'S ACCOUNT.
NOT THAT WE DOUBT HIS WORD. CAPTAIN HULL HAD A CAREER IN THE ARMY. HE WAS PROFOUNDLY DEDICATED TO THIS NATION, AND *HIS* RECORD REFLECTS THAT.
BUT YOU UNDERSTAND.
WHAT AM I TO UNDERSTAND?
THIS NATION IS YOUNG, STILL PAYING OFF MASSIVE WAR DEBTS, AND ALL THE WHILE STRUGGLING TO REARM FOR THE INEVITABLE NEXT CONFLICT, GOD HELP US, THAT WE MUST ASSUME IS COMING.
PRESIDENT JEFFERSON, JUST LIKE HIS PREDECESSORS, BELIEVES IN THE MILITARY PENSION FUND, AND YOU WILL RECEIVE YOUR HALF RATE, AS IS THE INTENT OF THE LAW.
WE BELIEVE IN A HIGH MORAL OBLIGATION TO SUPPORT THE SOLDIERS WHO SUPPORTED US.

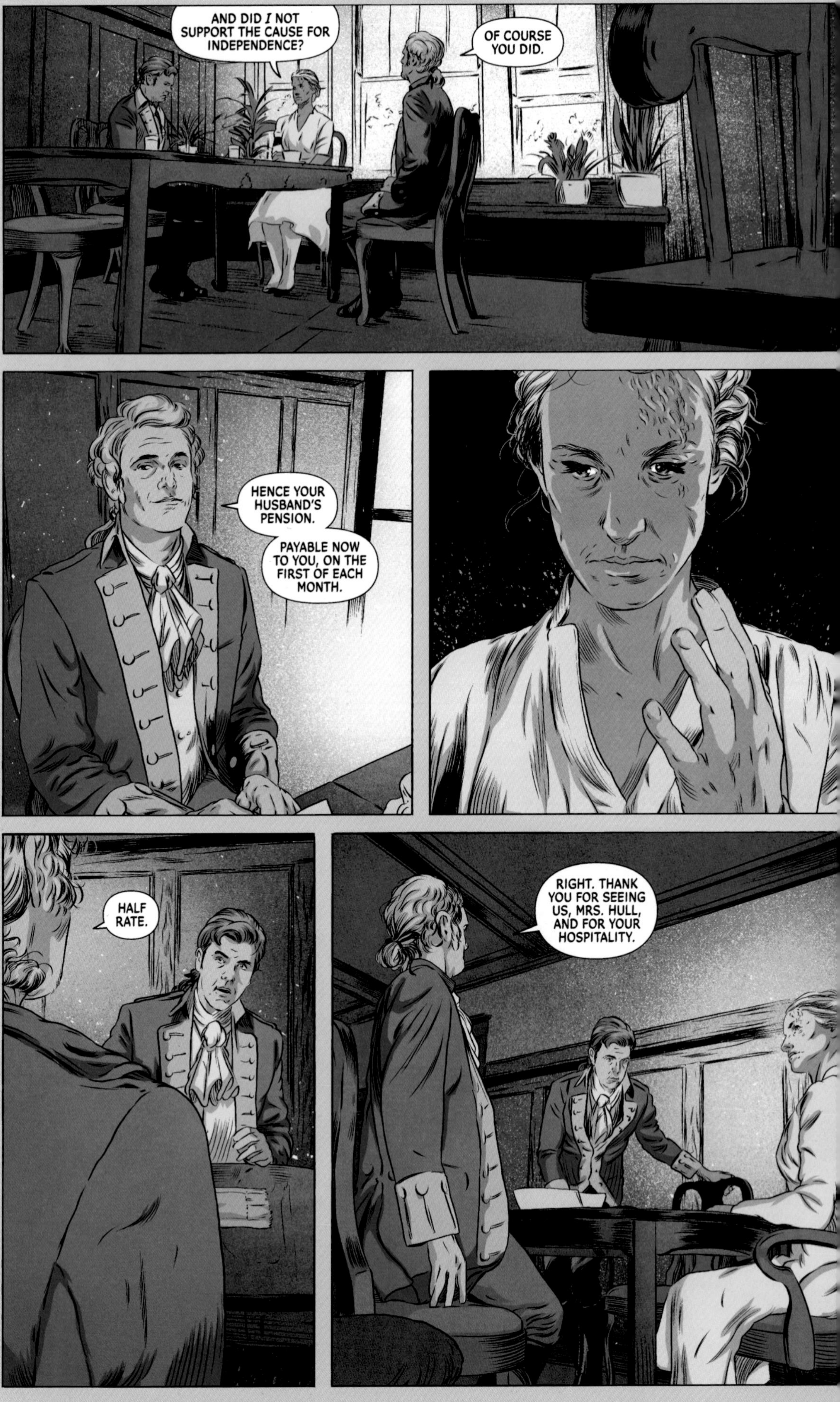
AND DID *I* NOT SUPPORT THE CAUSE FOR INDEPENDENCE?
OF COURSE YOU DID.
HENCE YOUR HUSBAND'S PENSION.
PAYABLE NOW TO YOU, ON THE FIRST OF EACH MONTH.
HALF RATE.
RIGHT. THANK YOU FOR SEEING US, MRS. HULL, AND FOR YOUR HOSPITALITY.

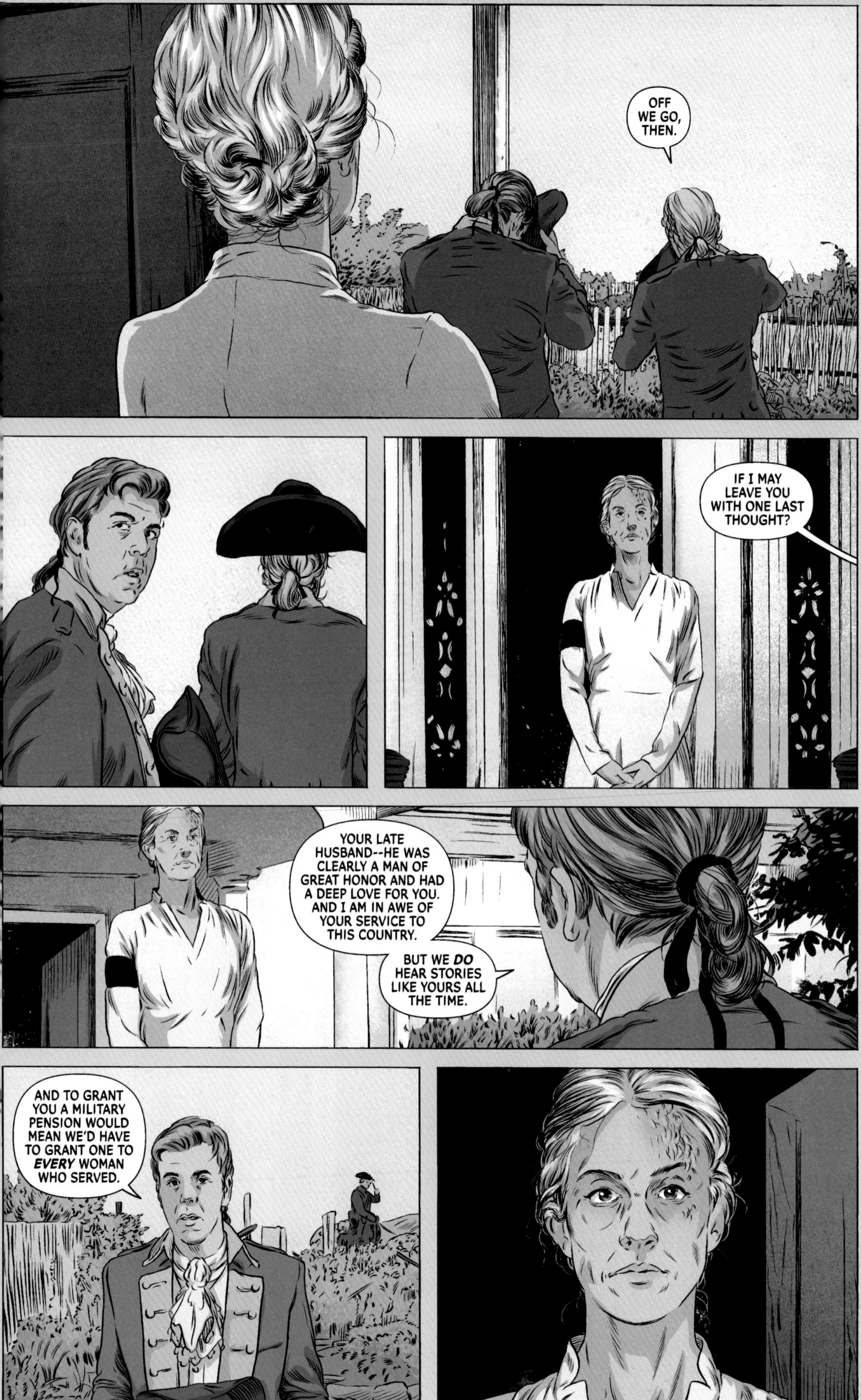
OFF WE GO, THEN.
IF I MAY LEAVE YOU WITH ONE LAST THOUGHT?
YOUR LATE HUSBAND--HE WAS CLEARLY A MAN OF GREAT HONOR AND HAD A DEEP LOVE FOR YOU. AND I AM IN AWE OF YOUR SERVICE TO THIS COUNTRY.
BUT WE *DO* HEAR STORIES LIKE YOURS ALL THE TIME.
AND TO GRANT YOU A MILITARY PENSION WOULD MEAN WE'D HAVE TO GRANT ONE TO *EVERY* WOMAN WHO SERVED.

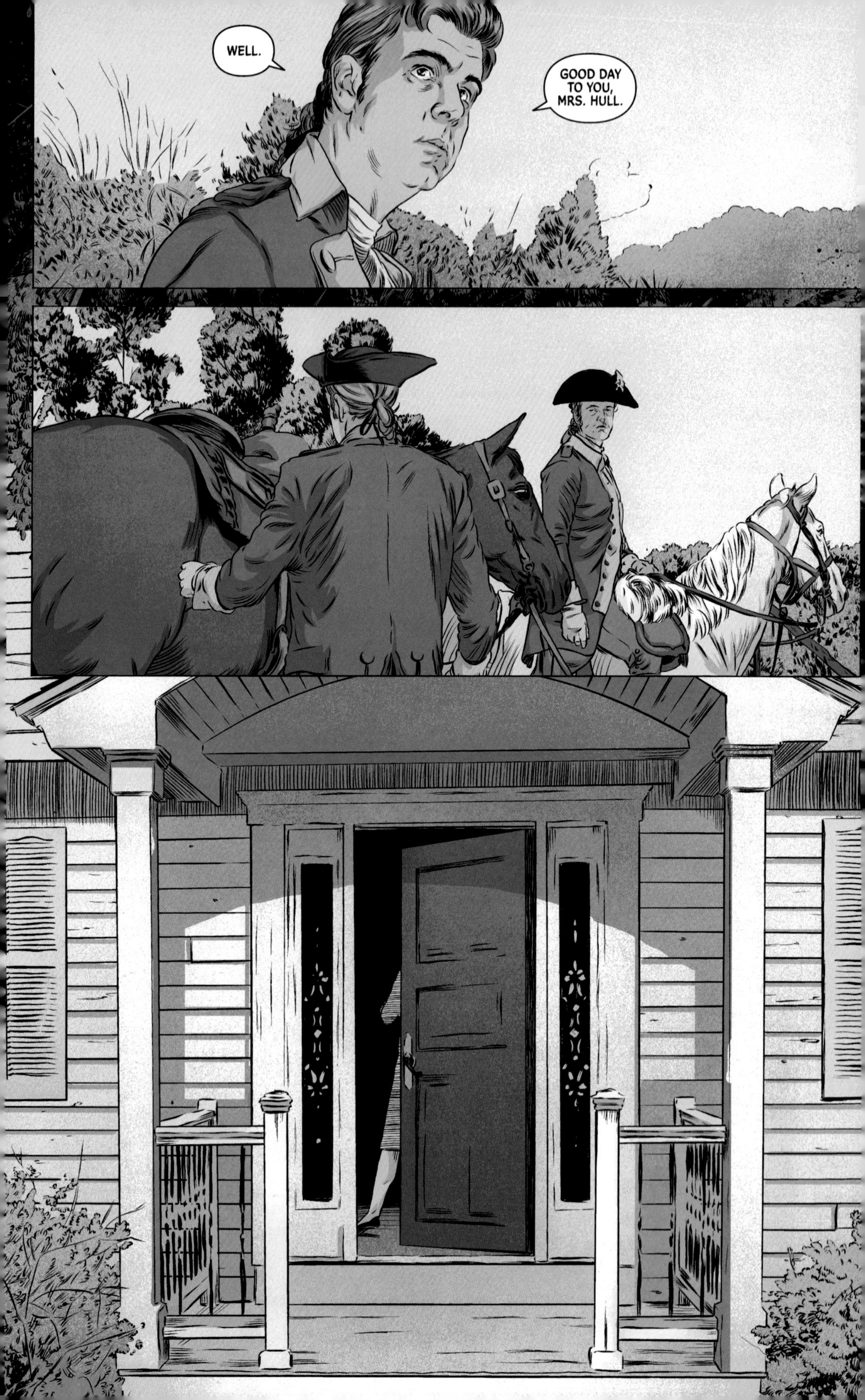
WELL.
GOOD DAY TO YOU, MRS. HULL.

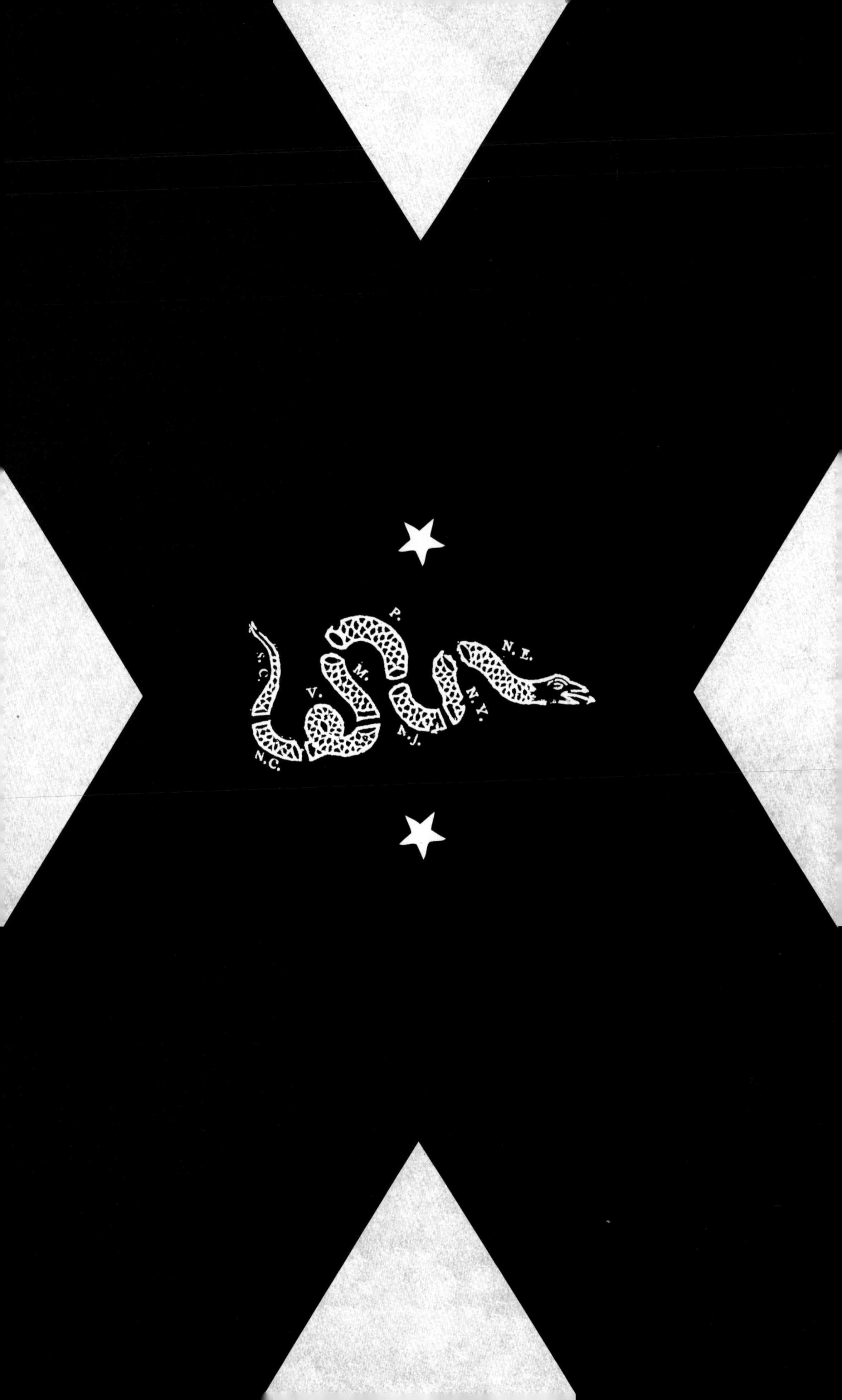
S.C.
N.C.
V.
M.
P.
N.J.
N.Y.
N.E.

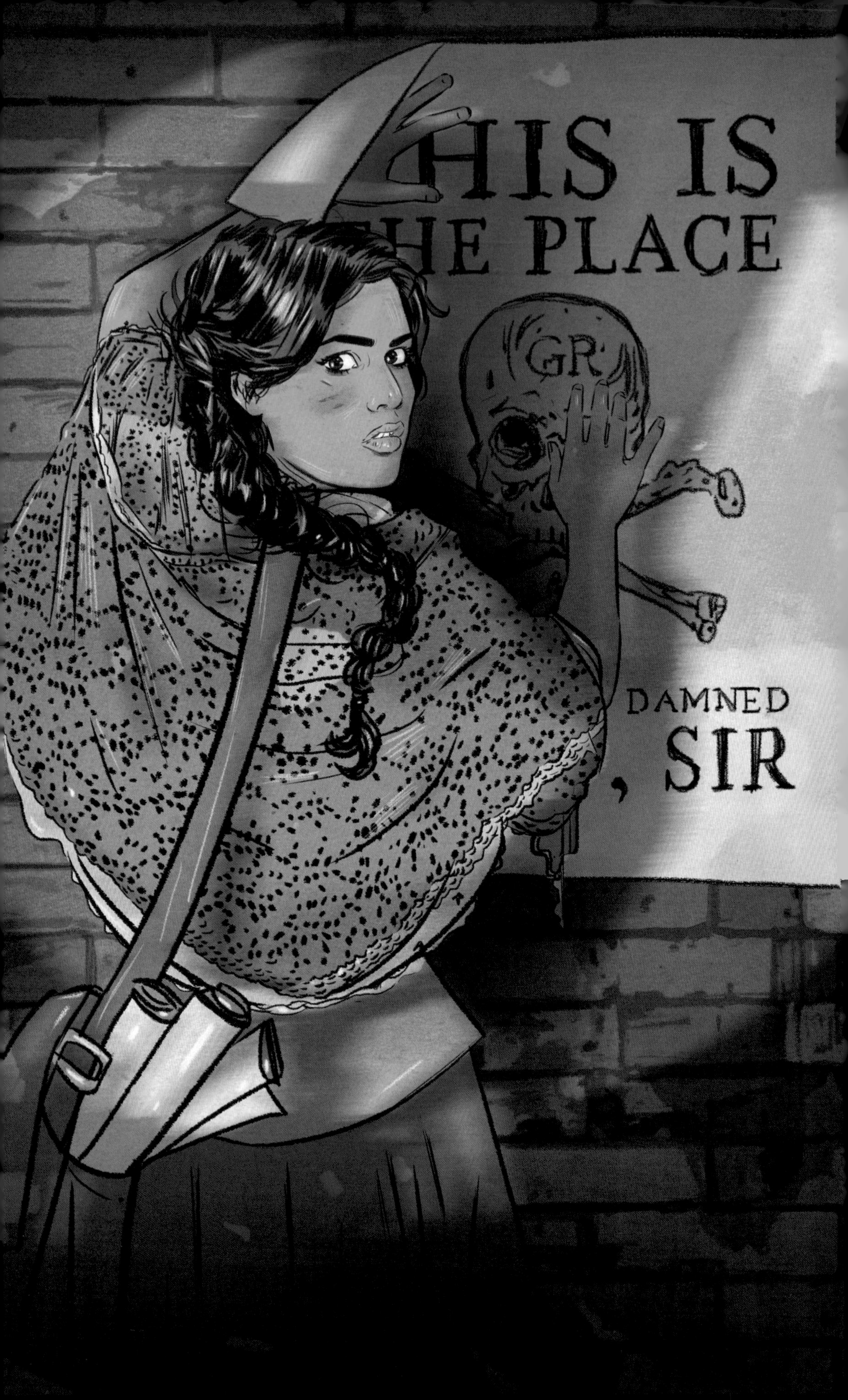
HIS IS
HE PLACE
GR
DAMNED
, SIR

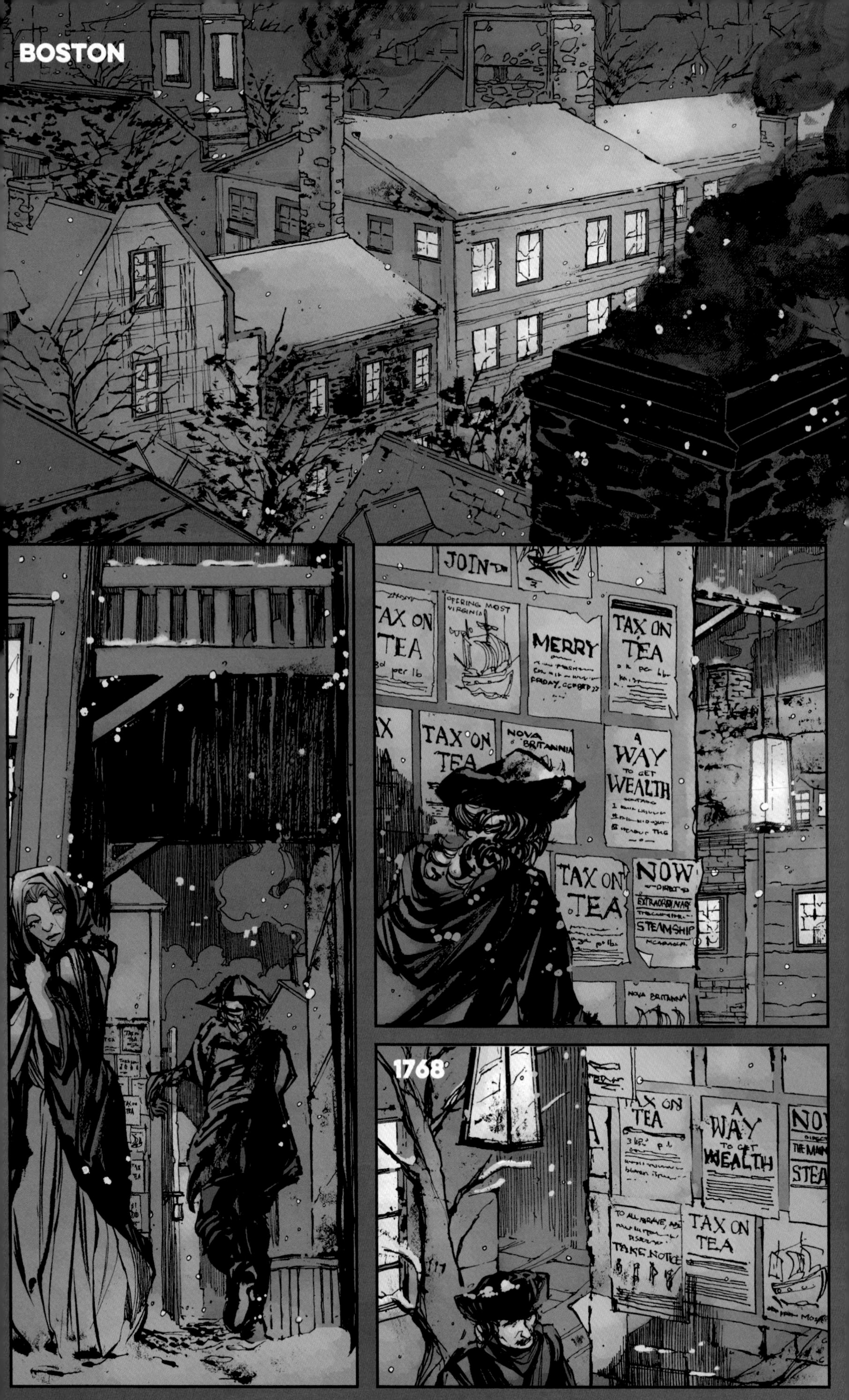
BOSTON
JOIN
TAX ON TEA
OFFERING MOST VIRGINIA
MERRY
TAX ON TEA
TAX ON TEA
NOVA BRITANNIA
A WAY TO GET WEALTH
TAX ON TEA
NOW
EXTRAORDINARY
STEAMSHIP
NOVA BRITANNIA
1768
TAX ON TEA
A WAY TO GET WEALTH
TAKE NOTICE
TAX ON TEA

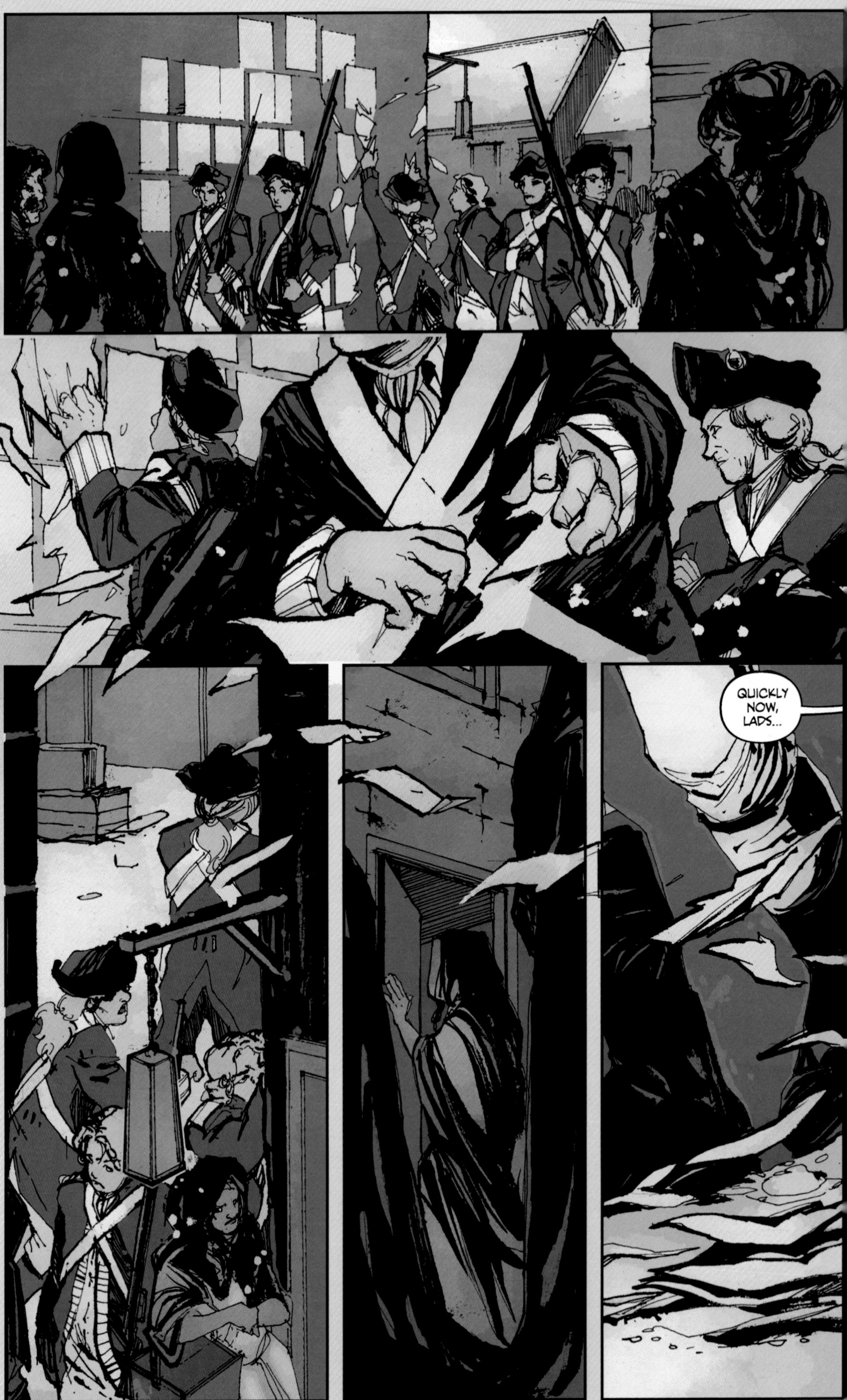
QUICKLY NOW, LADS...

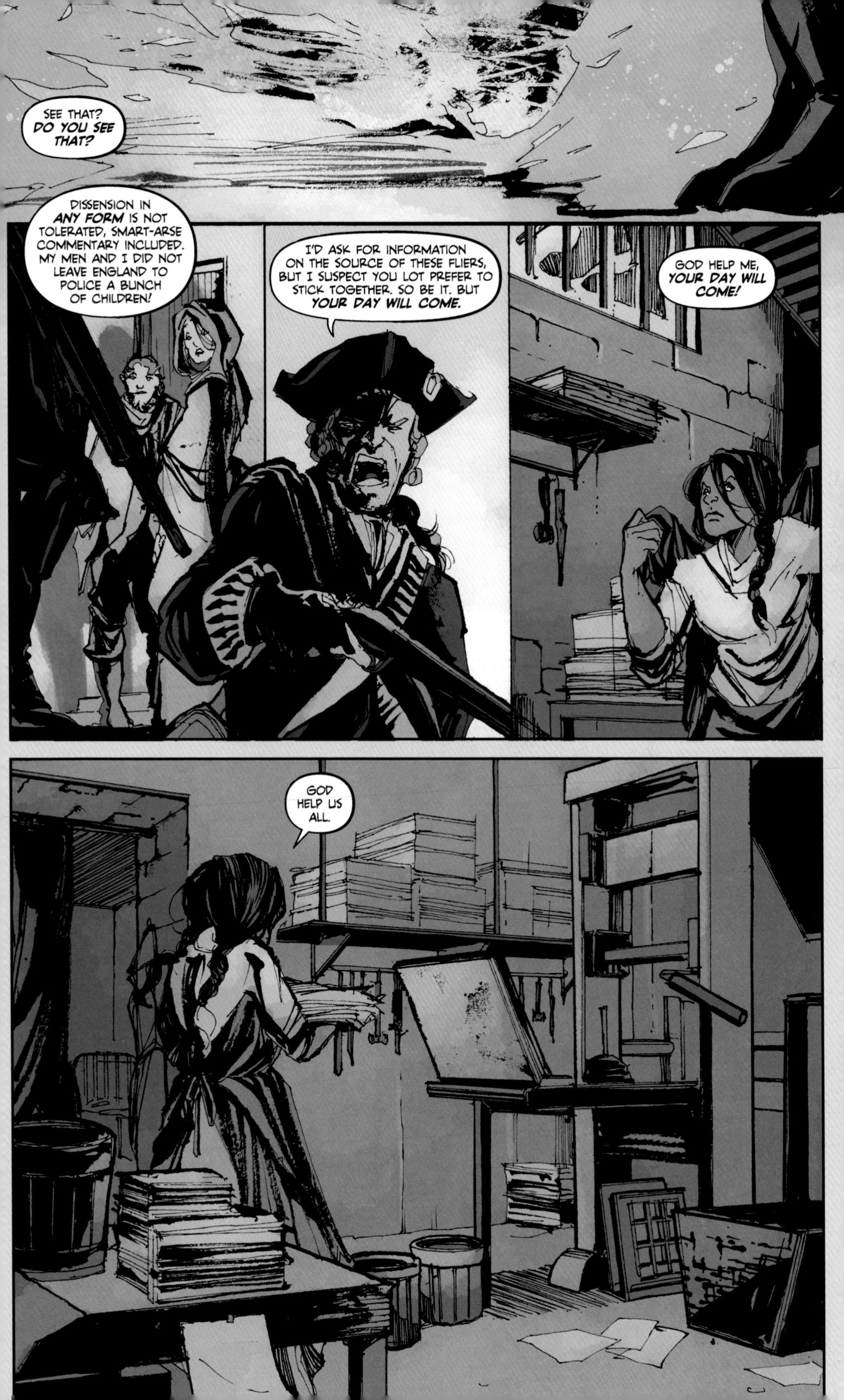
SEE THAT? DO YOU SEE THAT?
DISSENSION IN ANY FORM IS NOT TOLERATED, SMART-ARSE COMMENTARY INCLUDED. MY MEN AND I DID NOT LEAVE ENGLAND TO POLICE A BUNCH OF CHILDREN!
I'D ASK FOR INFORMATION ON THE SOURCE OF THESE FLIERS, BUT I SUSPECT YOU LOT PREFER TO STICK TOGETHER. SO BE IT. BUT YOUR DAY WILL COME.
GOD HELP ME, YOUR DAY WILL COME!
GOD HELP US ALL.

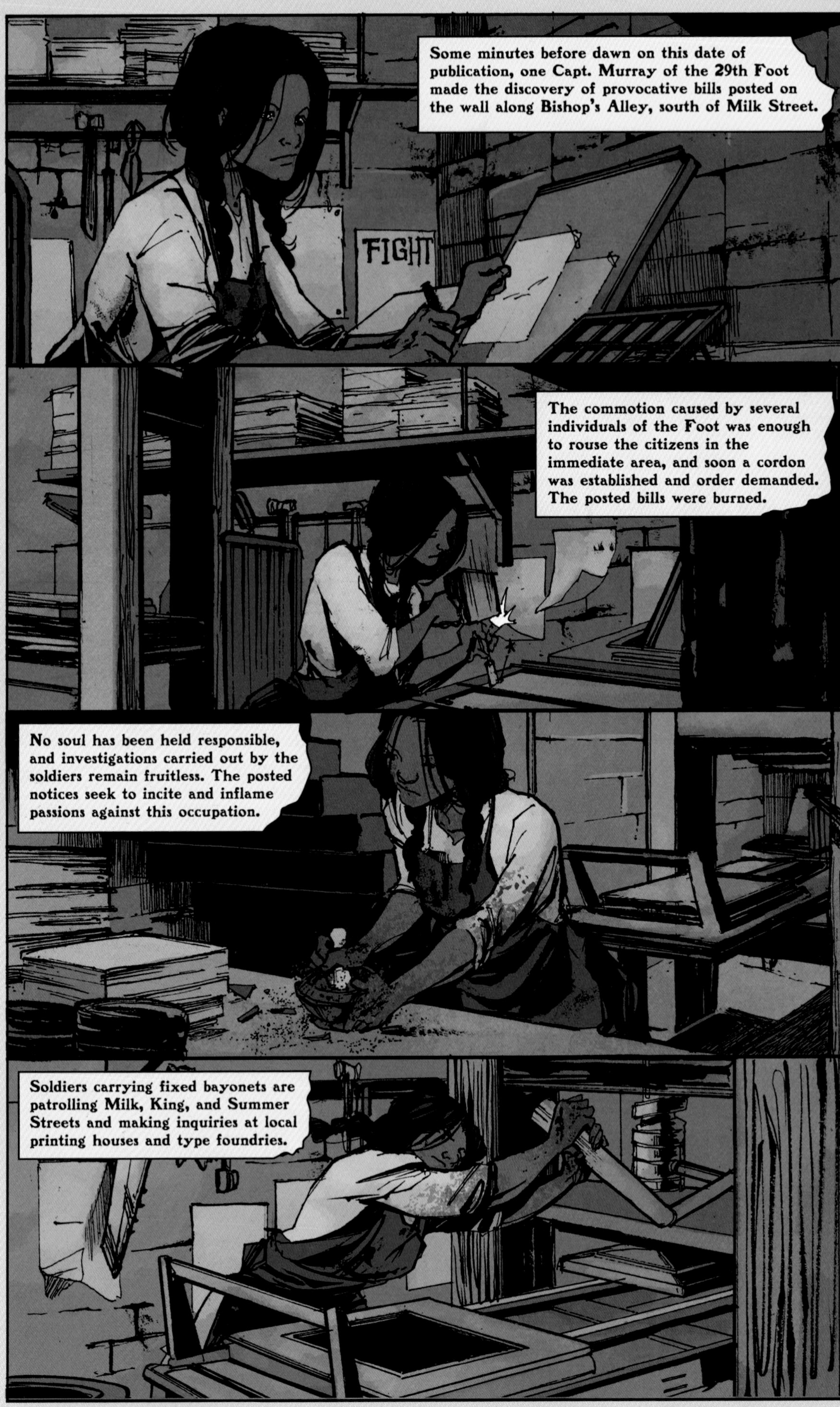

Some minutes before dawn on this date of publication, one Capt. Murray of the 29th Foot made the discovery of provocative bills posted on the wall along Bishop's Alley, south of Milk Street.
FIGHT
The commotion caused by several individuals of the Foot was enough to rouse the citizens in the immediate area, and soon a cordon was established and order demanded. The posted bills were burned.
No soul has been held responsible, and investigations carried out by the soldiers remain fruitless. The posted notices seek to incite and inflame passions against this occupation.
Soldiers carrying fixed bayonets are patrolling Milk, King, and Summer Streets and making inquiries at local printing houses and type foundries.

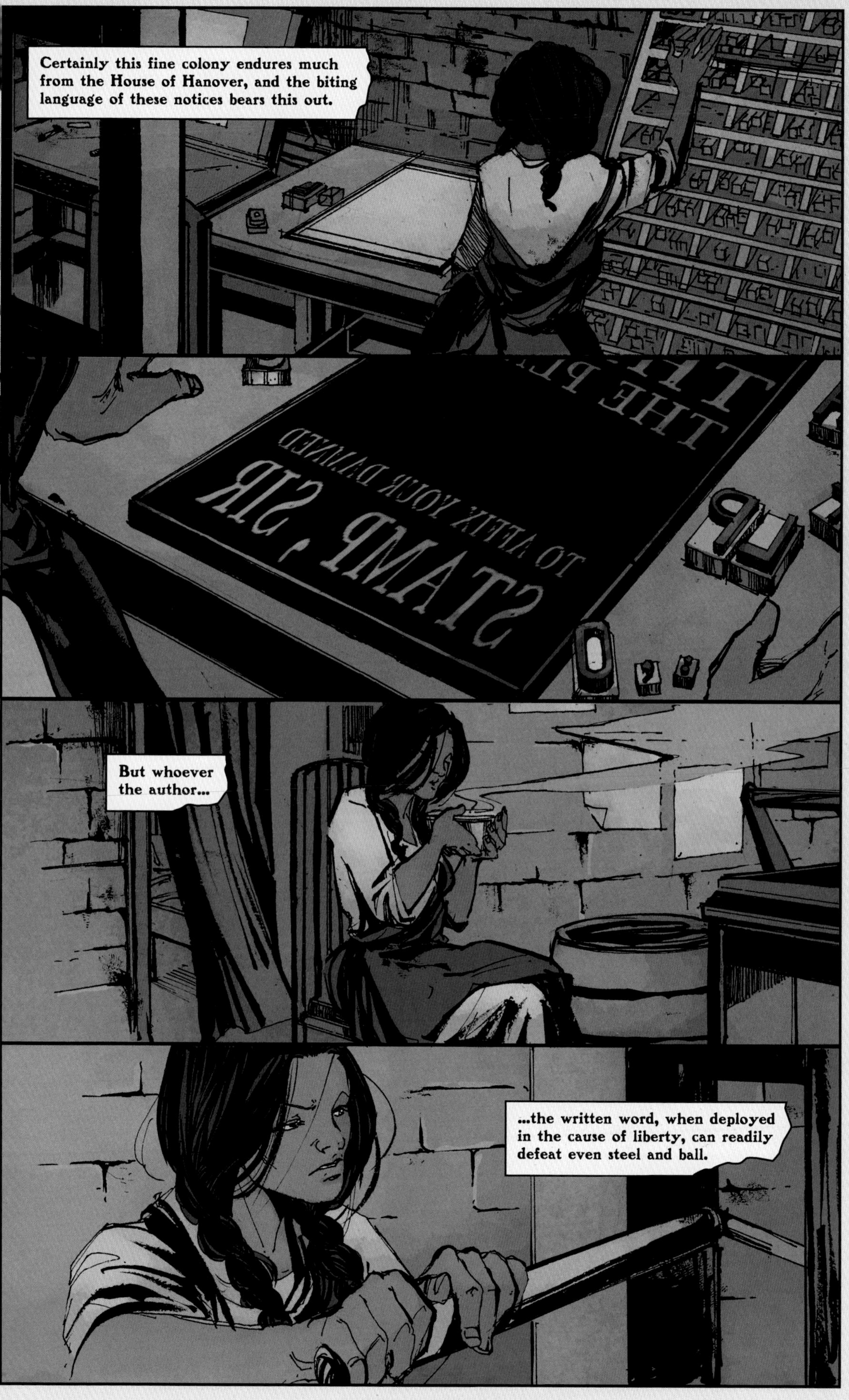
Certainly this fine colony endures much from the House of Hanover, and the biting language of these notices bears this out.
TO AFFIX YOUR DAMNED
STAMP, SIR
But whoever the author...
...the written word, when deployed in the cause of liberty, can readily defeat even steel and ball.

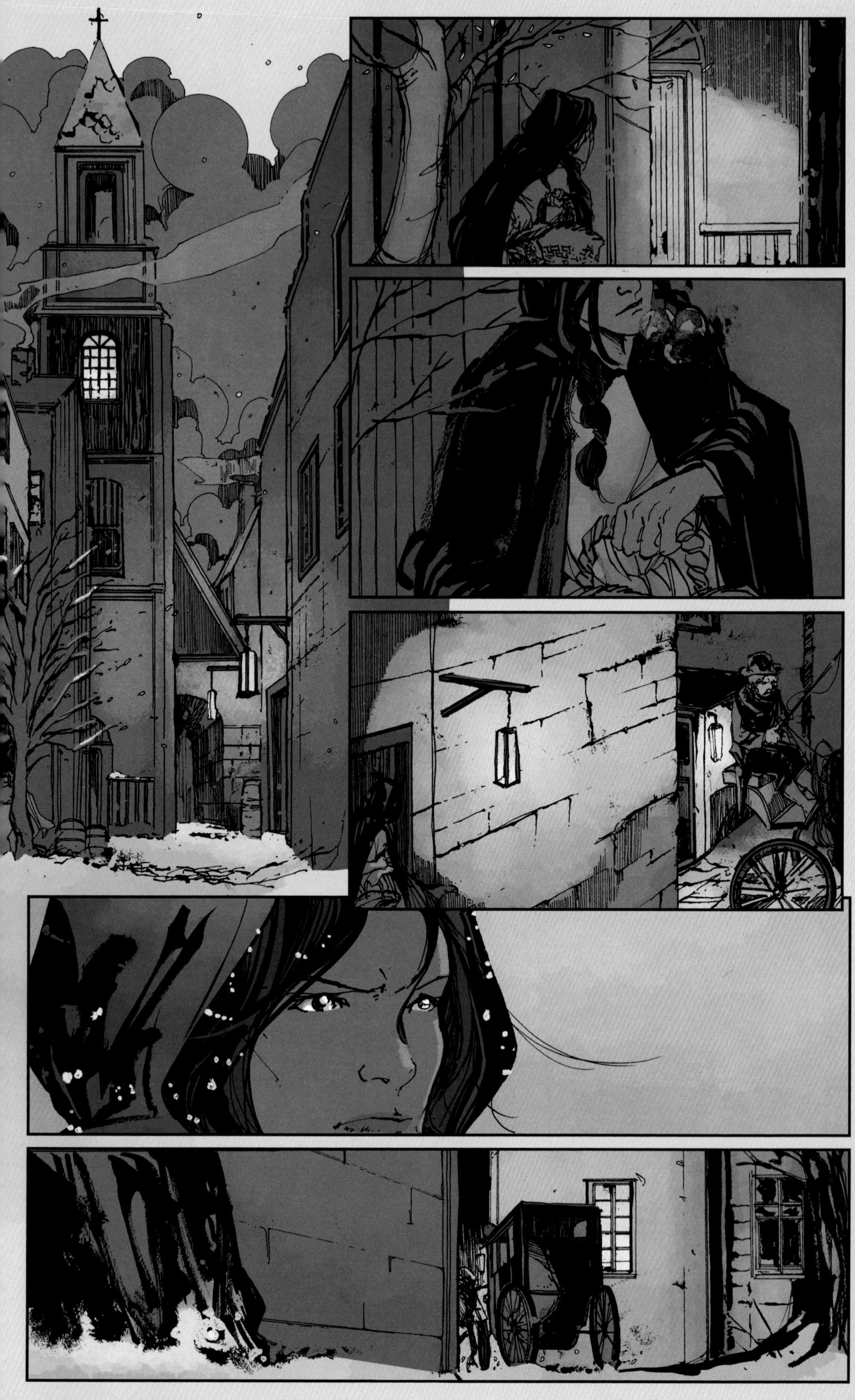

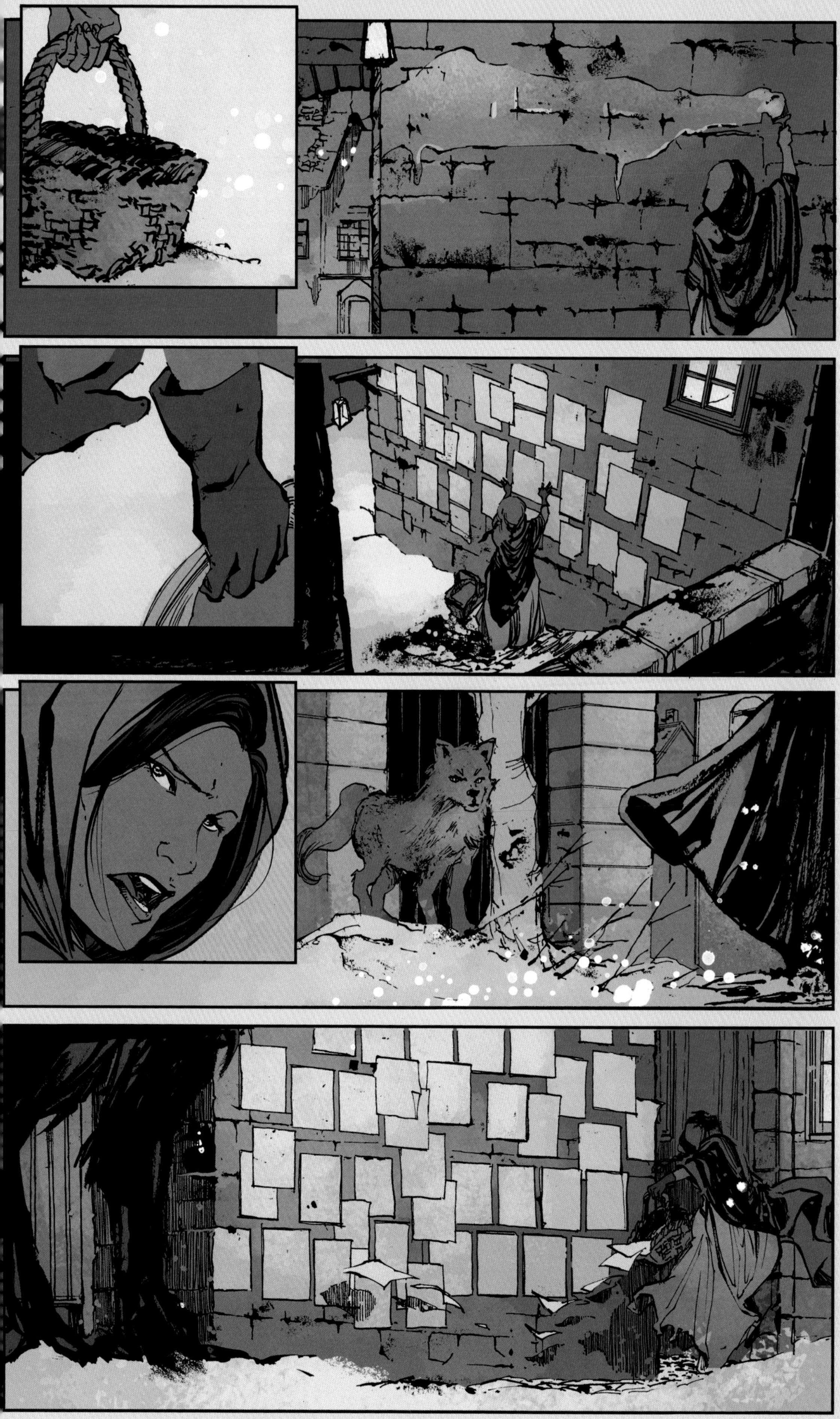

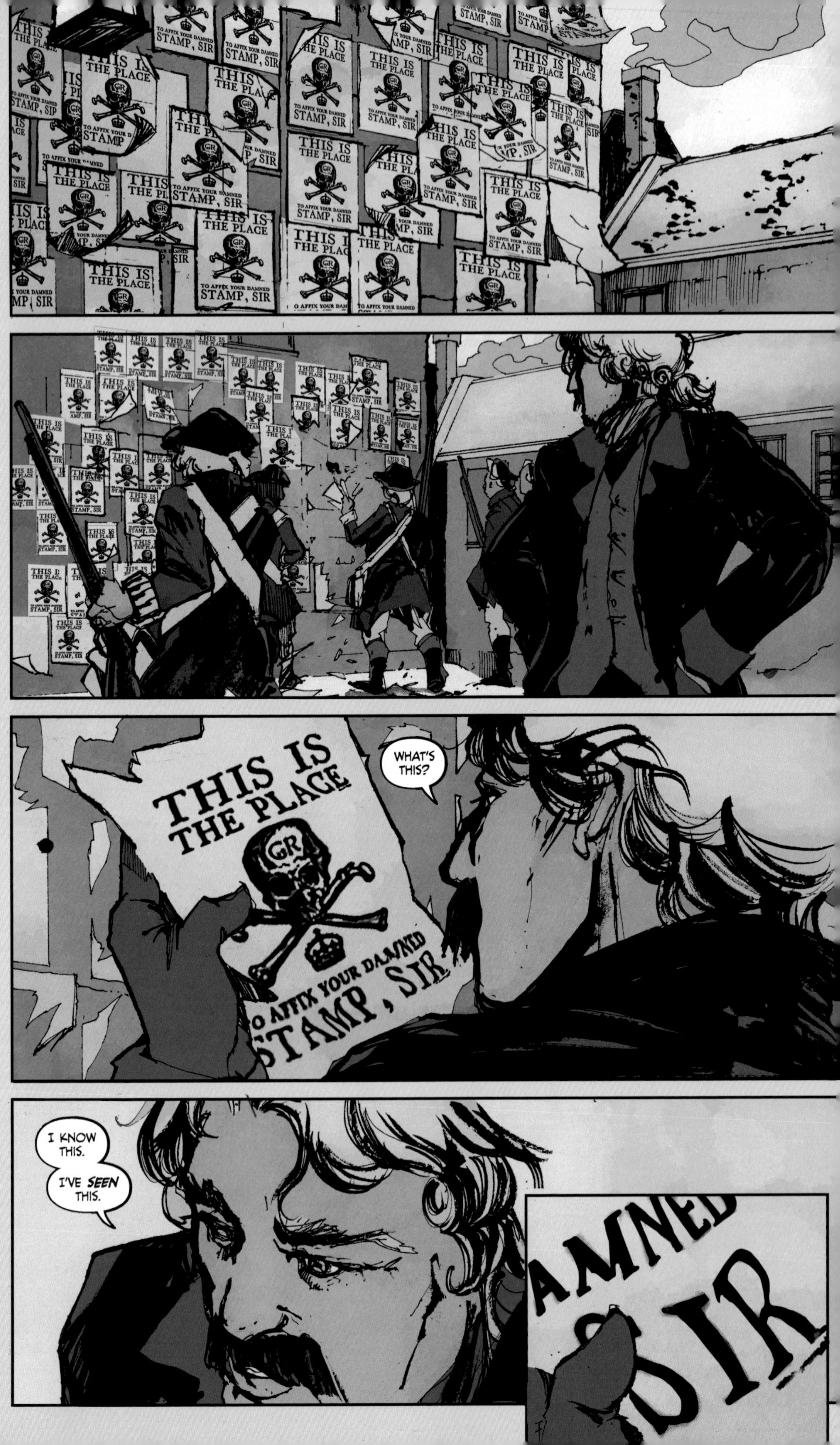
THIS IS THE PLACE
TO AFFIX YOUR DAMNED
STAMP, SIR
WHAT'S THIS?
THIS IS THE PLACE
TO AFFIX YOUR DAMNED
STAMP, SIR
I KNOW THIS.
I'VE *SEEN* THIS.
AMNED
SIR

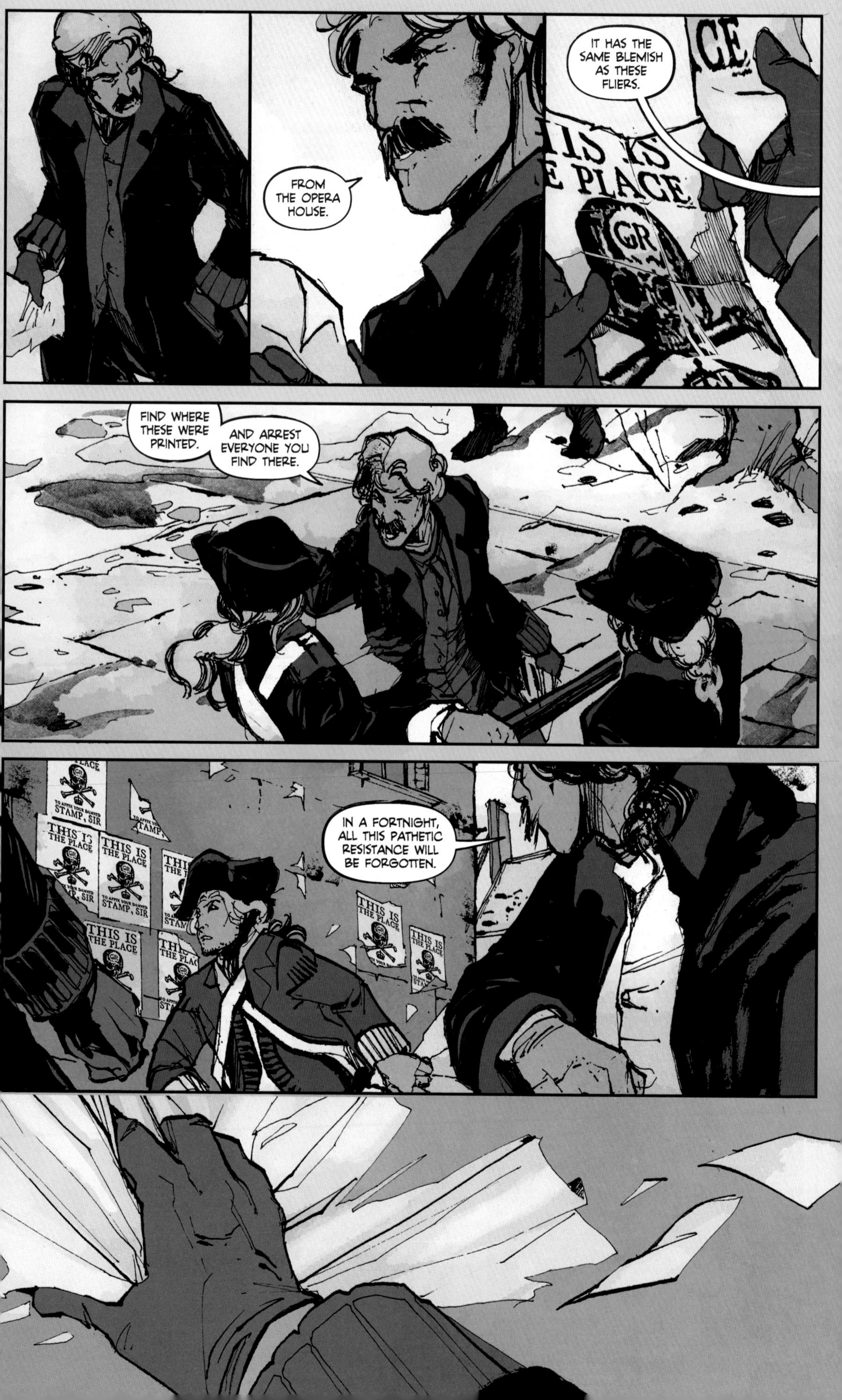
FROM THE OPERA HOUSE.
IT HAS THE SAME BLEMISH AS THESE FLIERS.
FIND WHERE THESE WERE PRINTED.
AND ARREST EVERYONE YOU FIND THERE.
THIS IS THE PLACE
STAMP, SIR
IN A FORTNIGHT, ALL THIS PATHETIC RESISTANCE WILL BE FORGOTTEN.

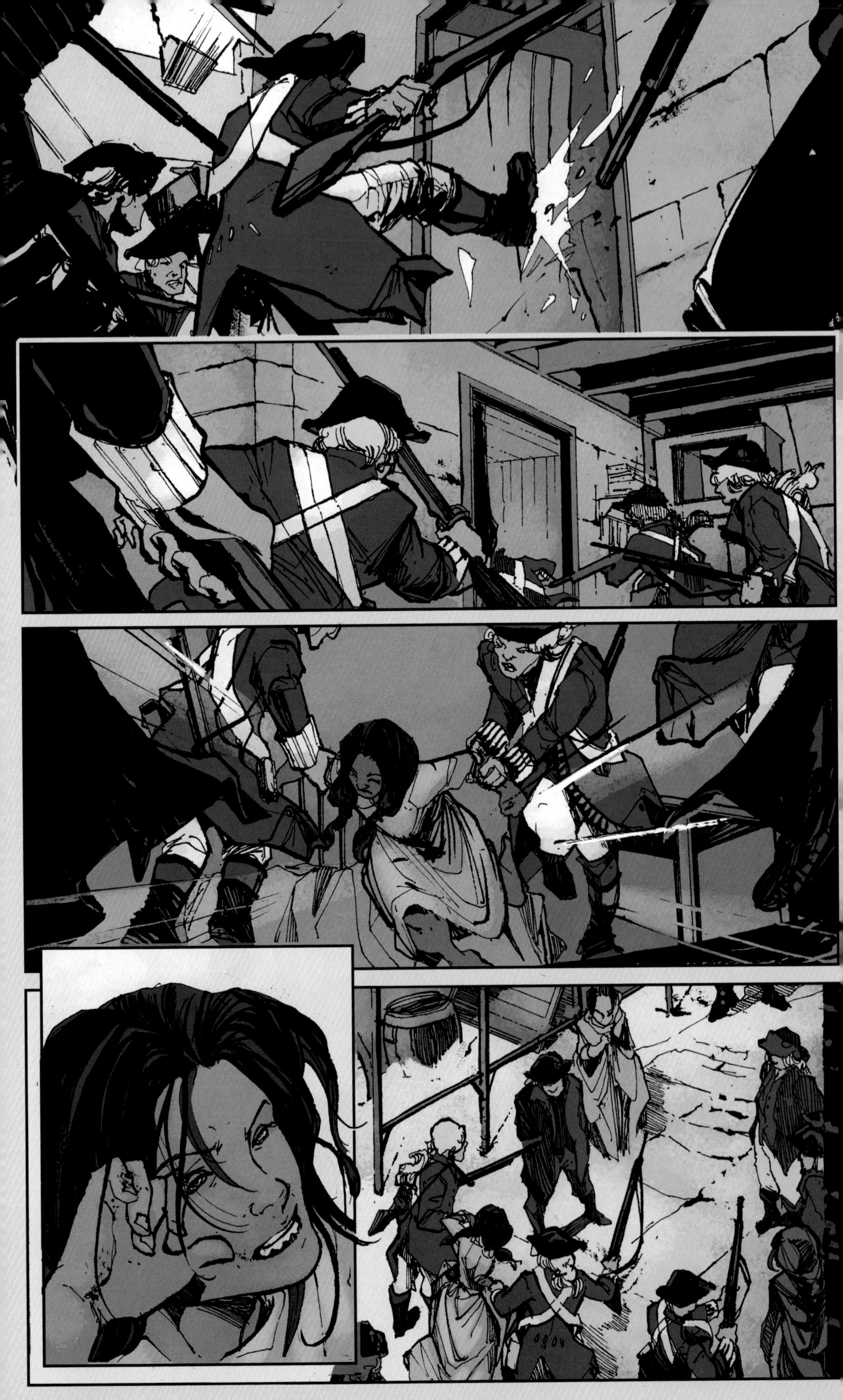

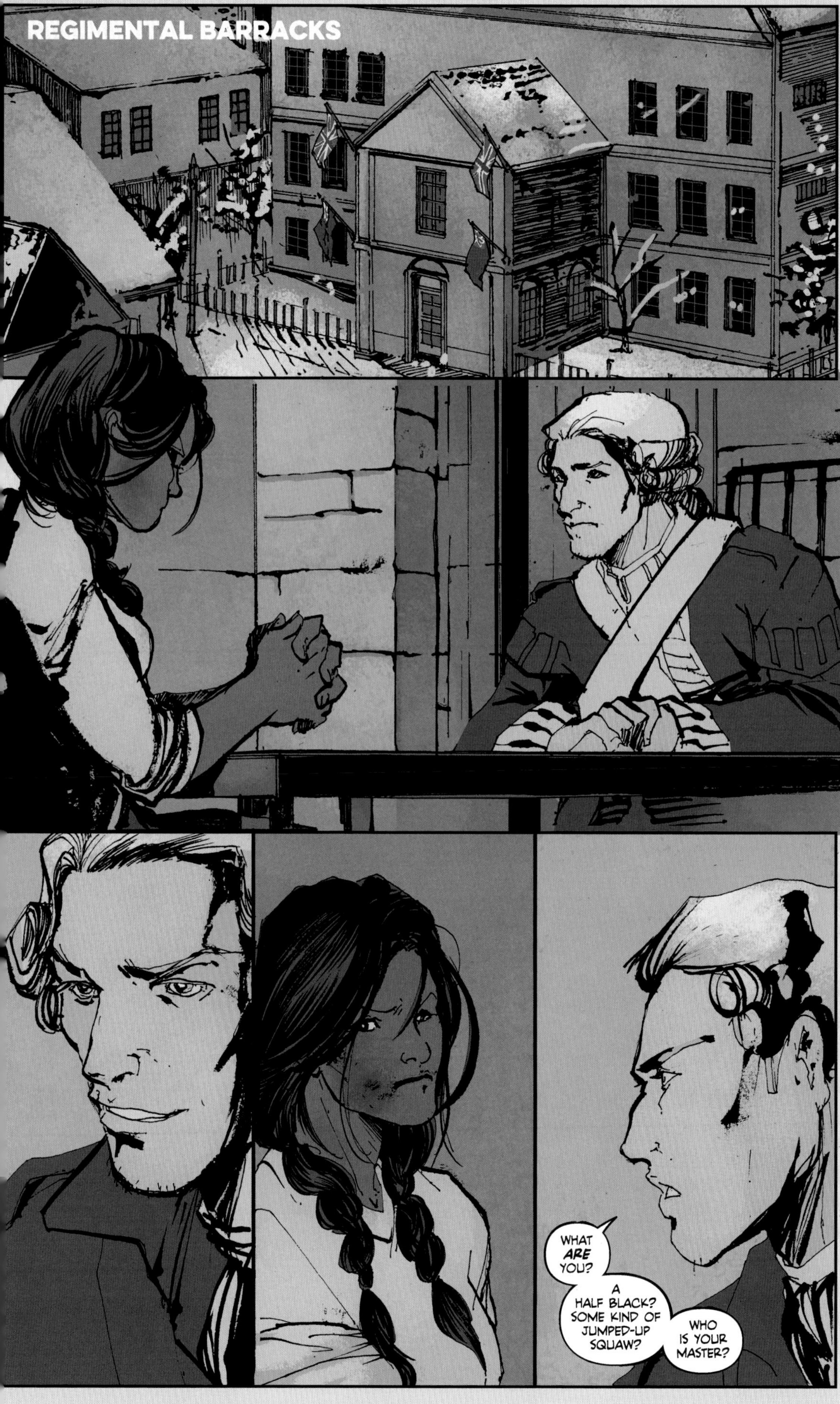

REGIMENTAL BARRACKS
WHAT ARE YOU?
A HALF BLACK? SOME KIND OF JUMPED-UP SQUAW?
WHO IS YOUR MASTER?

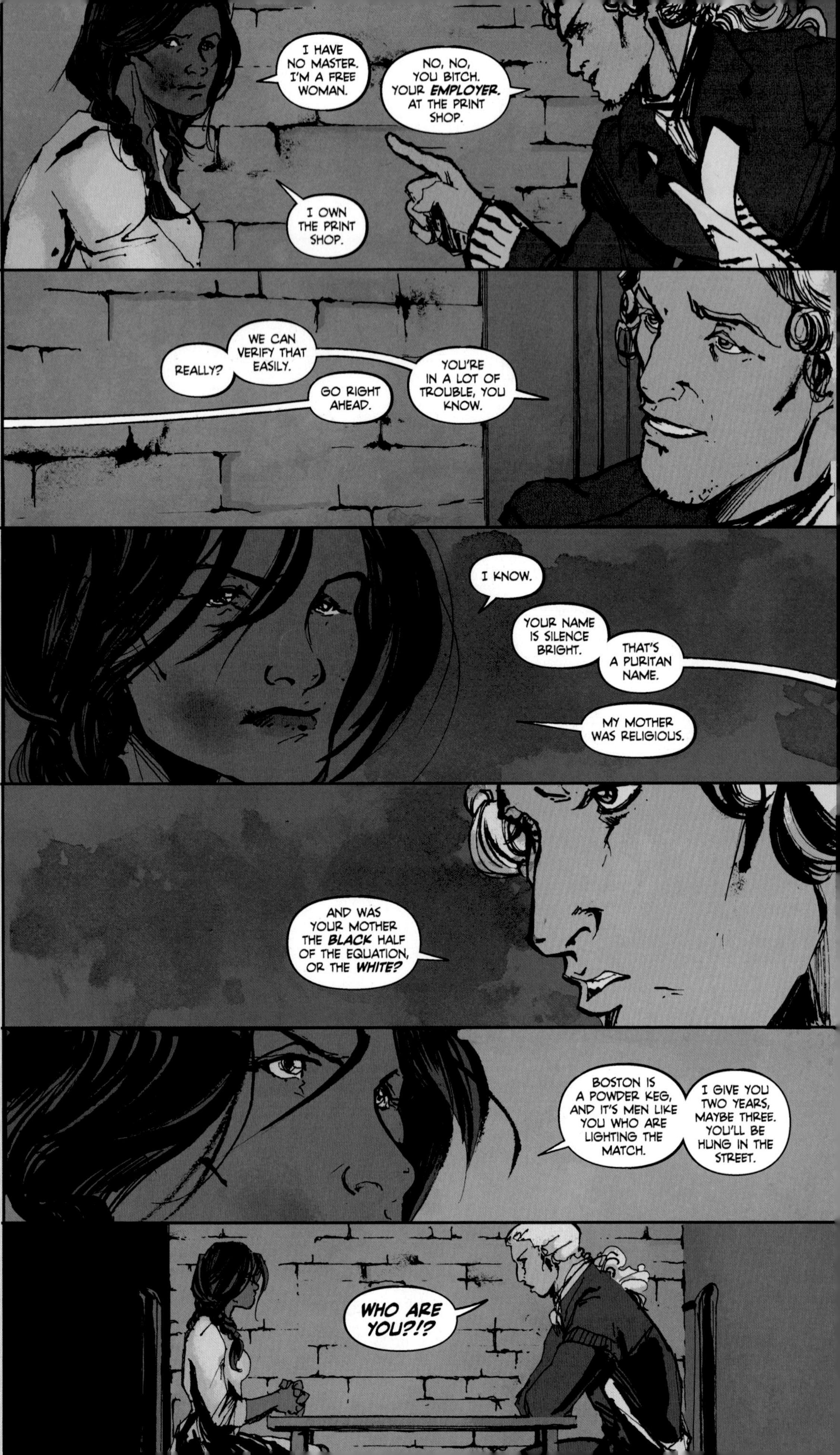

I HAVE NO MASTER. I'M A FREE WOMAN.
NO, NO, YOU BITCH. YOUR EMPLOYER. AT THE PRINT SHOP.
I OWN THE PRINT SHOP.
REALLY?
WE CAN VERIFY THAT EASILY.
GO RIGHT AHEAD.
YOU'RE IN A LOT OF TROUBLE, YOU KNOW.
I KNOW.
YOUR NAME IS SILENCE BRIGHT.
THAT'S A PURITAN NAME.
MY MOTHER WAS RELIGIOUS.
AND WAS YOUR MOTHER THE BLACK HALF OF THE EQUATION, OR THE WHITE?
BOSTON IS A POWDER KEG, AND IT'S MEN LIKE YOU WHO ARE LIGHTING THE MATCH.
I GIVE YOU TWO YEARS, MAYBE THREE. YOU'LL BE HUNG IN THE STREET.
WHO ARE YOU?!?

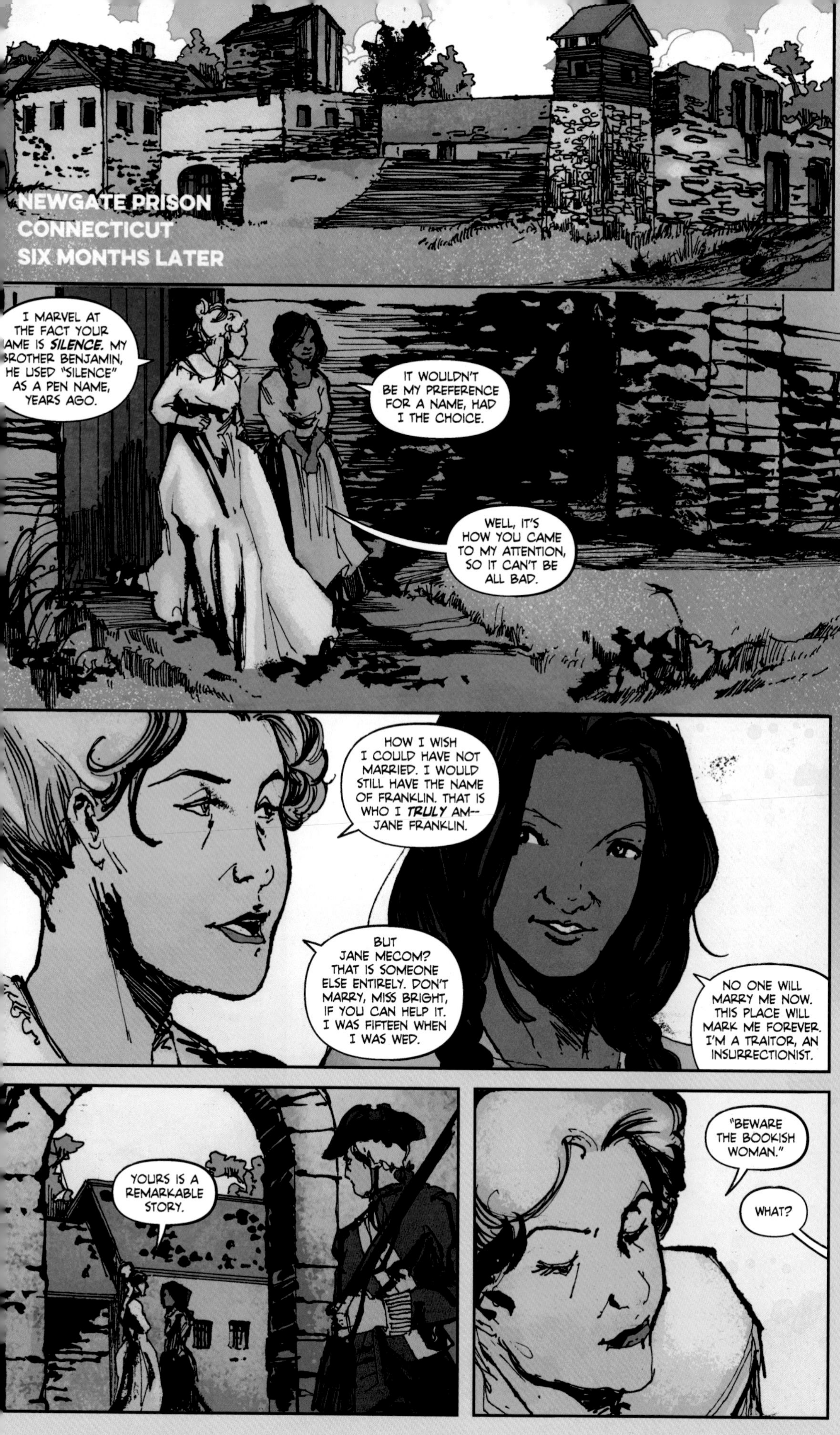
NEWGATE PRISON
CONNECTICUT
SIX MONTHS LATER
I MARVEL AT THE FACT YOUR NAME IS *SILENCE.* MY BROTHER BENJAMIN, HE USED "SILENCE" AS A PEN NAME, YEARS AGO.
IT WOULDN'T BE MY PREFERENCE FOR A NAME, HAD I THE CHOICE.
WELL, IT'S HOW YOU CAME TO MY ATTENTION, SO IT CAN'T BE ALL BAD.
HOW I WISH I COULD HAVE NOT MARRIED. I WOULD STILL HAVE THE NAME OF FRANKLIN. THAT IS WHO I *TRULY* AM-- JANE FRANKLIN.
BUT JANE MECOM? THAT IS SOMEONE ELSE ENTIRELY. DON'T MARRY, MISS BRIGHT, IF YOU CAN HELP IT. I WAS FIFTEEN WHEN I WAS WED.
NO ONE WILL MARRY ME NOW. THIS PLACE WILL MARK ME FOREVER. I'M A TRAITOR, AN INSURRECTIONIST.
YOURS IS A REMARKABLE STORY.
"BEWARE THE BOOKISH WOMAN."
WHAT?

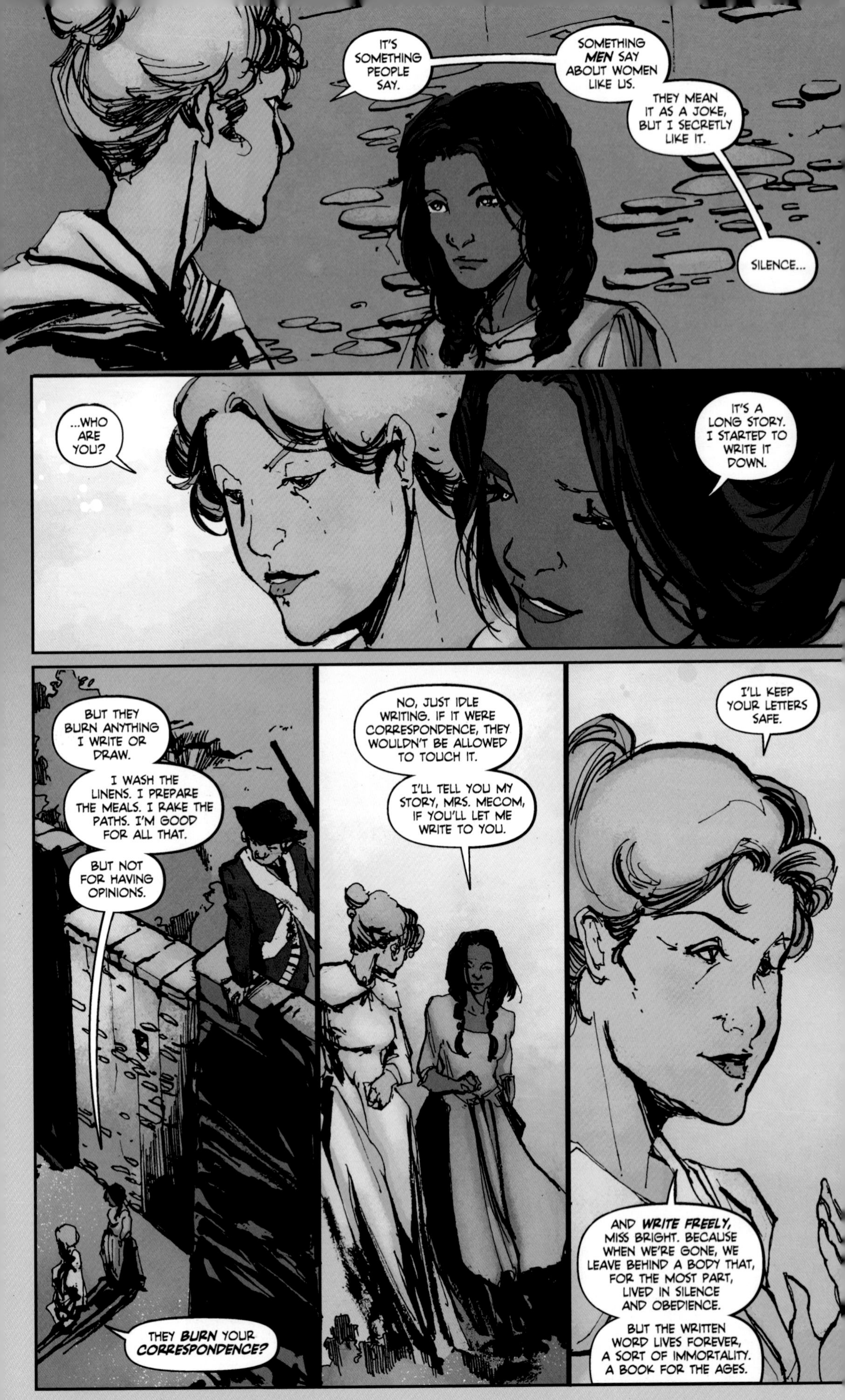

IT'S SOMETHING PEOPLE SAY.
SOMETHING MEN SAY ABOUT WOMEN LIKE US.
THEY MEAN IT AS A JOKE, BUT I SECRETLY LIKE IT.
SILENCE...
...WHO ARE YOU?
IT'S A LONG STORY. I STARTED TO WRITE IT DOWN.
BUT THEY BURN ANYTHING I WRITE OR DRAW.
I WASH THE LINENS. I PREPARE THE MEALS. I RAKE THE PATHS. I'M GOOD FOR ALL THAT.
BUT NOT FOR HAVING OPINIONS.
THEY BURN YOUR CORRESPONDENCE?
NO, JUST IDLE WRITING. IF IT WERE CORRESPONDENCE, THEY WOULDN'T BE ALLOWED TO TOUCH IT.
I'LL TELL YOU MY STORY, MRS. MECOM, IF YOU'LL LET ME WRITE TO YOU.
I'LL KEEP YOUR LETTERS SAFE.
AND WRITE FREELY, MISS BRIGHT. BECAUSE WHEN WE'RE GONE, WE LEAVE BEHIND A BODY THAT, FOR THE MOST PART, LIVED IN SILENCE AND OBEDIENCE.
BUT THE WRITTEN WORD LIVES FOREVER, A SORT OF IMMORTALITY. A BOOK FOR THE AGES.

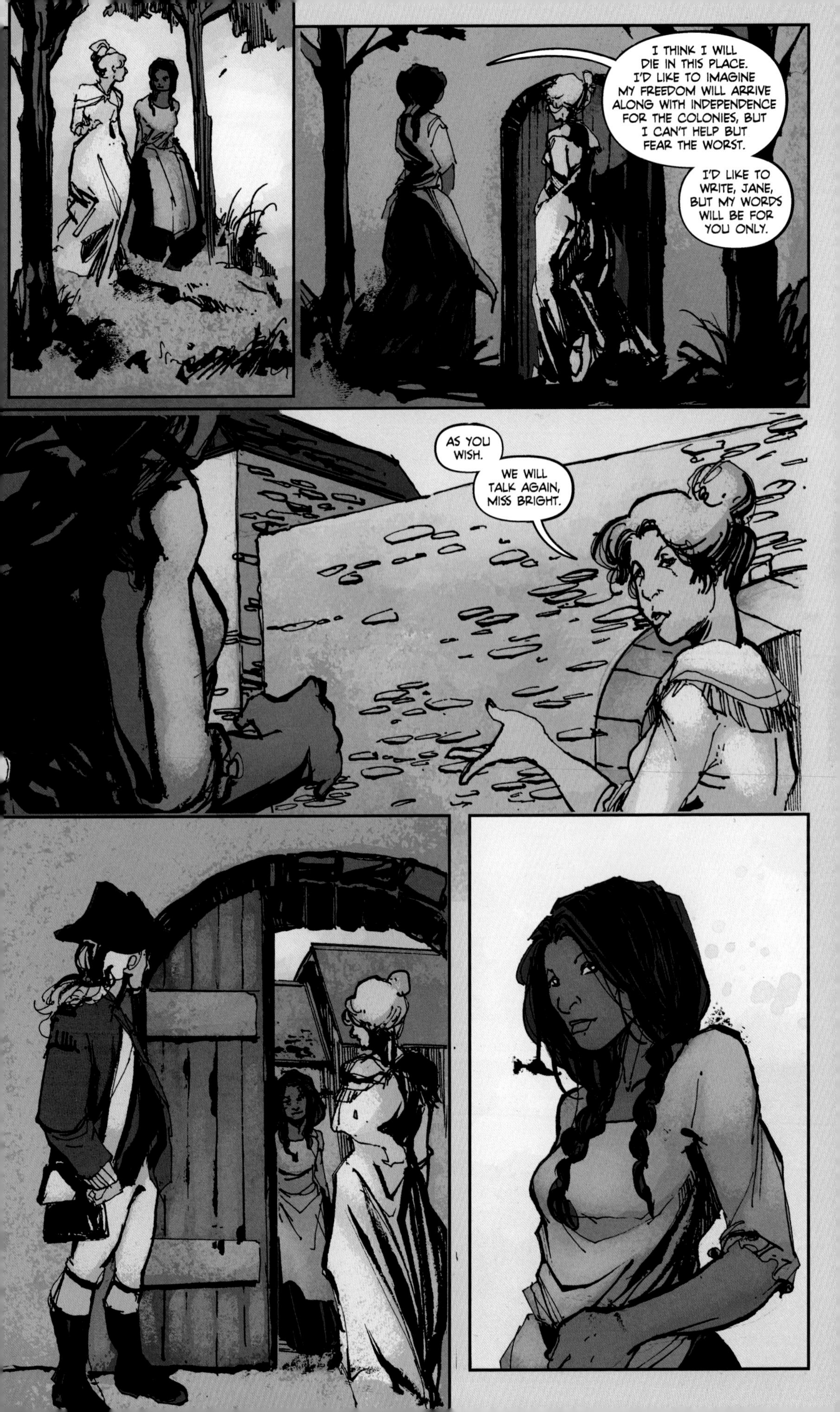
I THINK I WILL DIE IN THIS PLACE. I'D LIKE TO IMAGINE MY FREEDOM WILL ARRIVE ALONG WITH INDEPENDENCE FOR THE COLONIES, BUT I CAN'T HELP BUT FEAR THE WORST.
I'D LIKE TO WRITE, JANE, BUT MY WORDS WILL BE FOR YOU ONLY.
AS YOU WISH.
WE WILL TALK AGAIN, MISS BRIGHT.

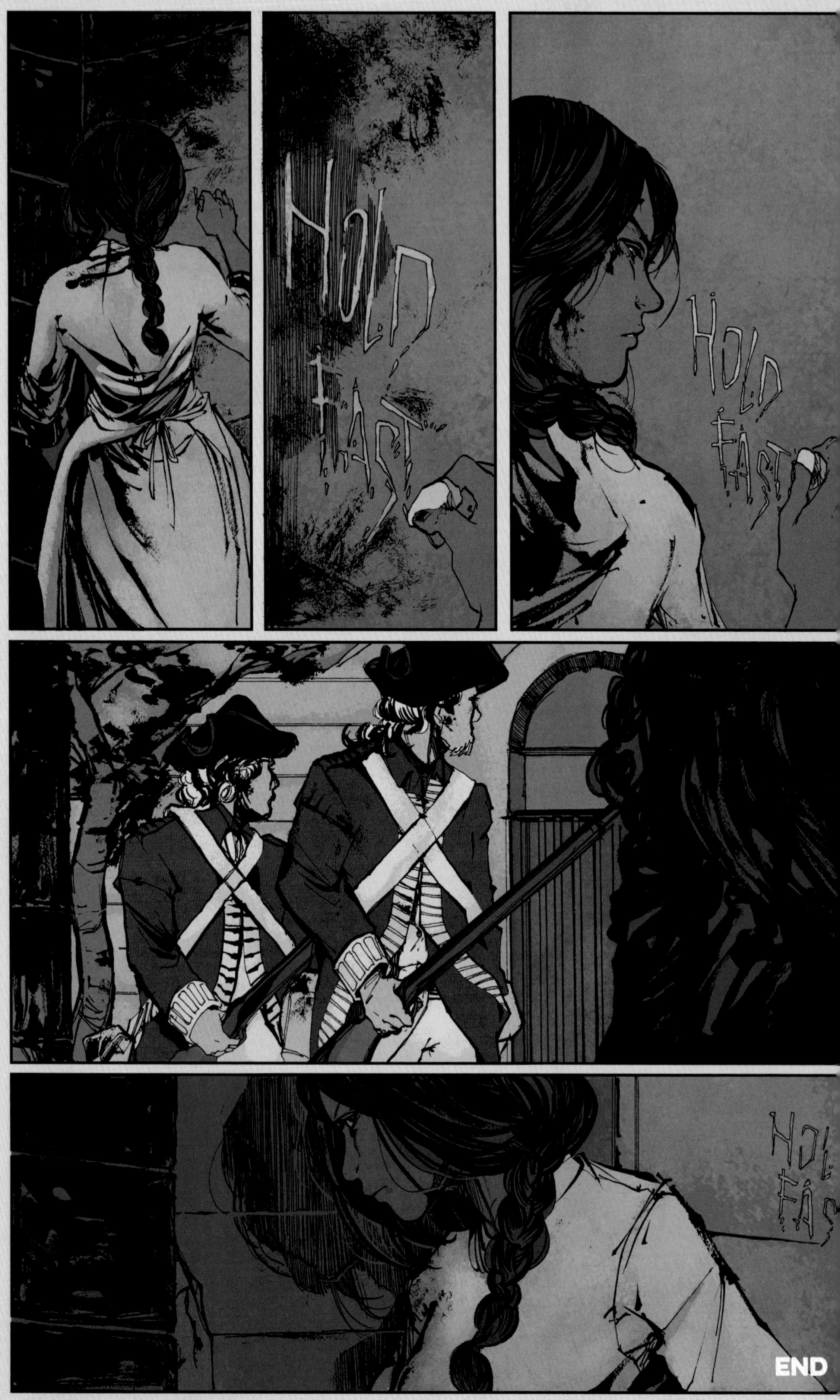
HOLD FAST
HOLD FAST
HOLD FAS
END

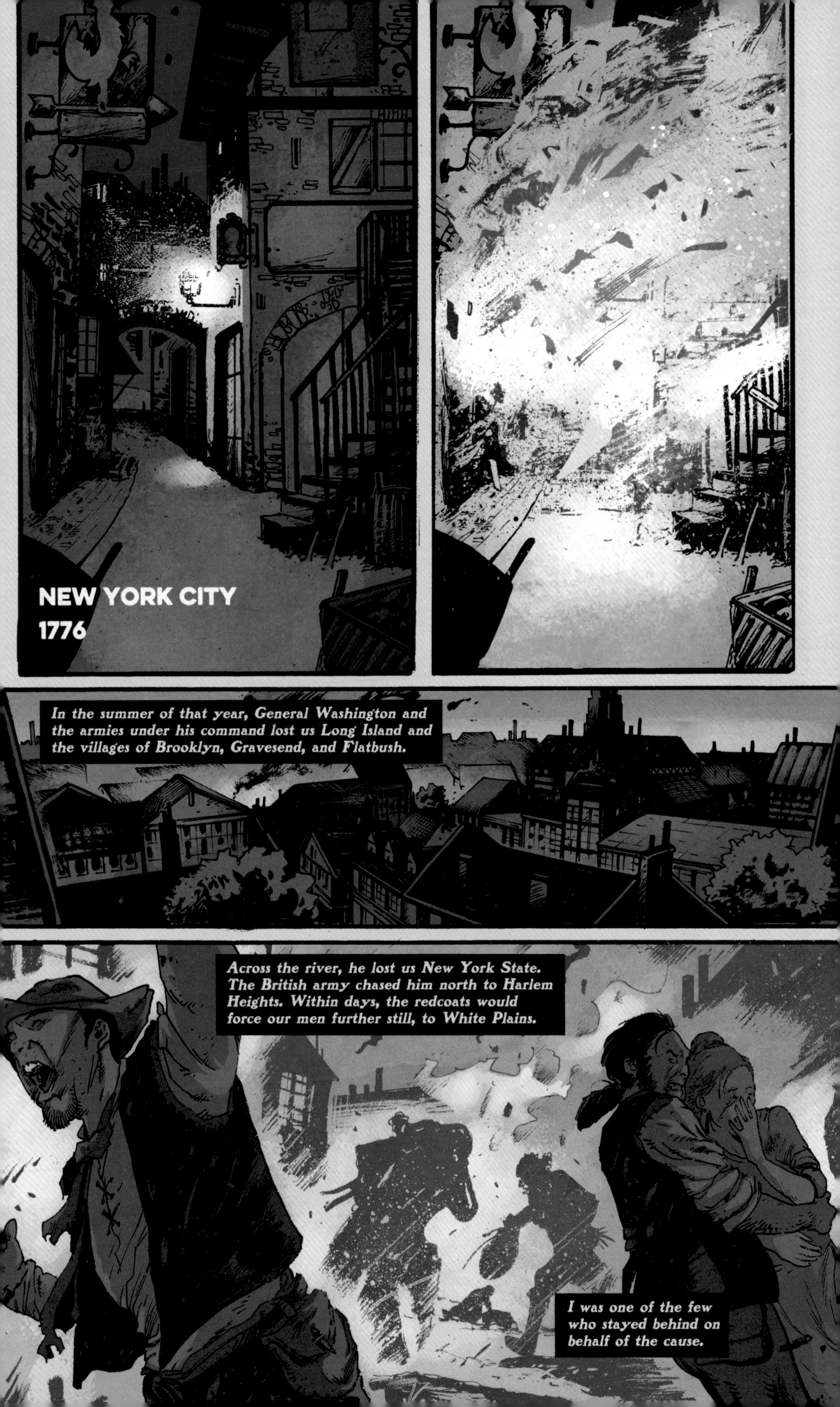
NEW YORK CITY
1776
In the summer of that year, General Washington and the armies under his command lost us Long Island and the villages of Brooklyn, Gravesend, and Flatbush.
Across the river, he lost us New York State. The British army chased him north to Harlem Heights. Within days, the redcoats would force our men further still, to White Plains.
I was one of the few who stayed behind on behalf of the cause.

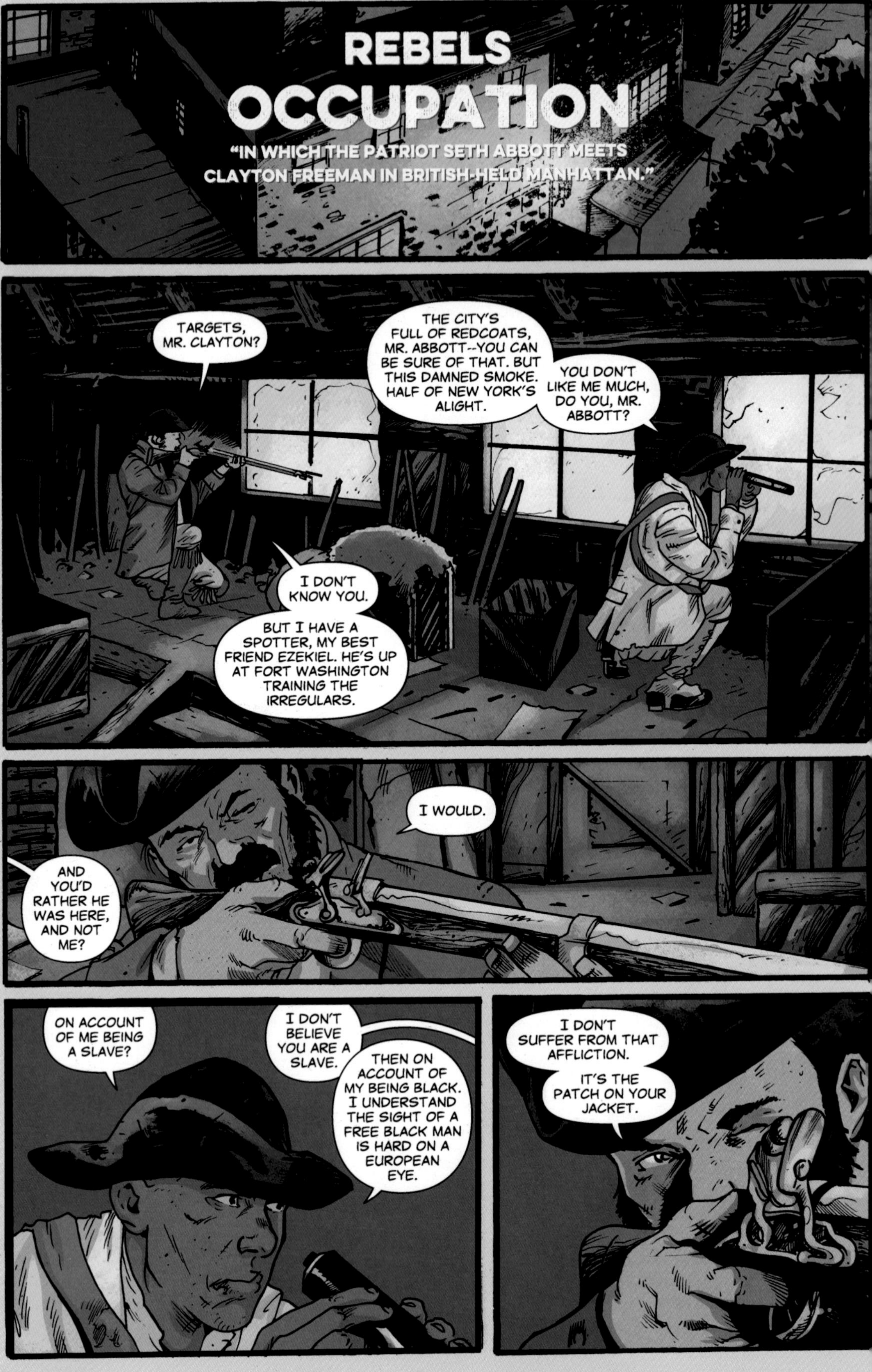
REBELS
OCCUPATION
"IN WHICH THE PATRIOT SETH ABBOTT MEETS CLAYTON FREEMAN IN BRITISH-HELD MANHATTAN."
TARGETS, MR. CLAYTON?
THE CITY'S FULL OF REDCOATS, MR. ABBOTT--YOU CAN BE SURE OF THAT. BUT THIS DAMNED SMOKE. HALF OF NEW YORK'S ALIGHT.
YOU DON'T LIKE ME MUCH, DO YOU, MR. ABBOTT?
I DON'T KNOW YOU.
BUT I HAVE A SPOTTER, MY BEST FRIEND EZEKIEL. HE'S UP AT FORT WASHINGTON TRAINING THE IRREGULARS.
AND YOU'D RATHER HE WAS HERE, AND NOT ME?
I WOULD.
ON ACCOUNT OF ME BEING A SLAVE?
I DON'T BELIEVE YOU ARE A SLAVE.
THEN ON ACCOUNT OF MY BEING BLACK. I UNDERSTAND THE SIGHT OF A FREE BLACK MAN IS HARD ON A EUROPEAN EYE.
I DON'T SUFFER FROM THAT AFFLICTION.
IT'S THE PATCH ON YOUR JACKET.

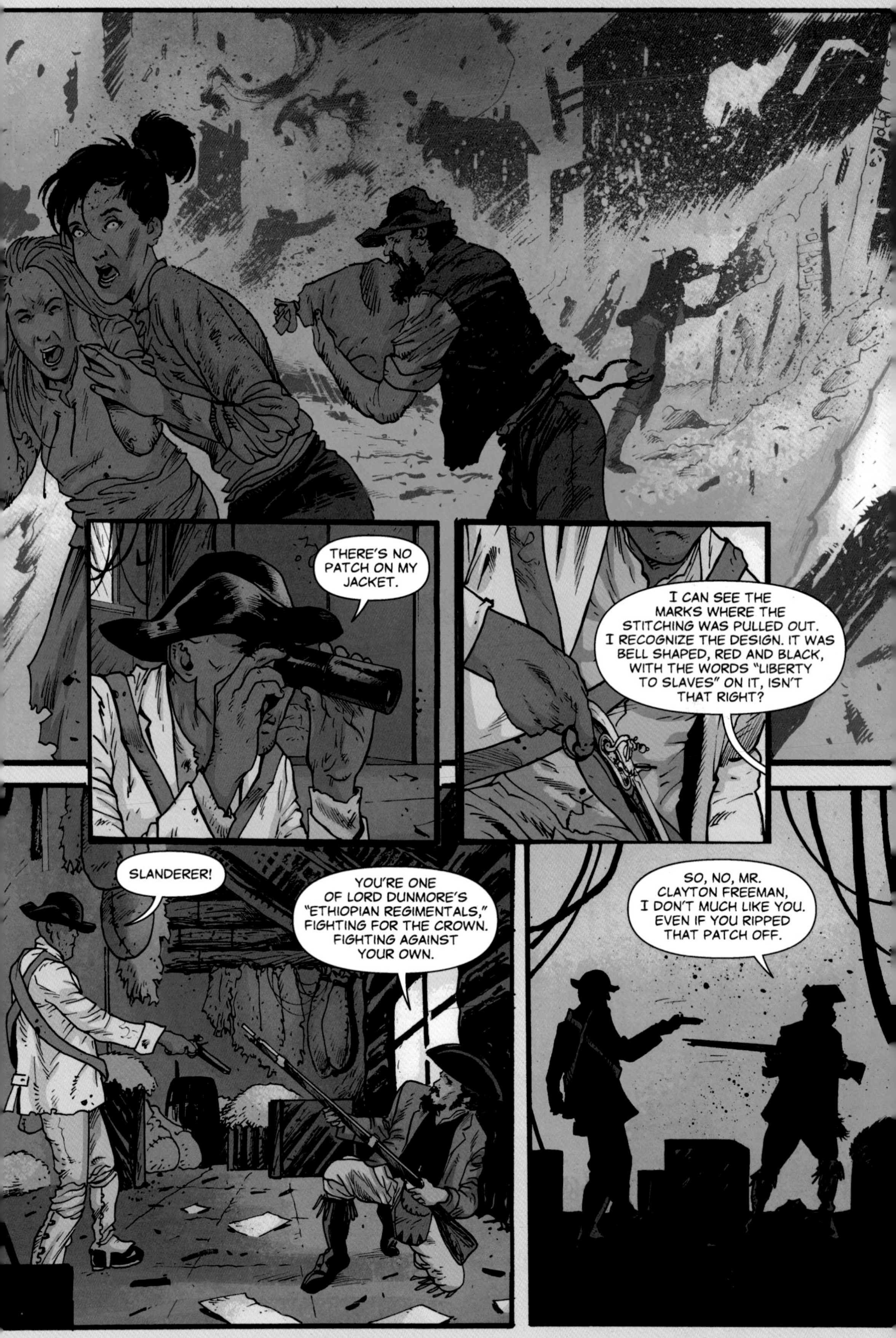
THERE'S NO PATCH ON MY JACKET.
I CAN SEE THE MARKS WHERE THE STITCHING WAS PULLED OUT. I RECOGNIZE THE DESIGN. IT WAS BELL SHAPED, RED AND BLACK, WITH THE WORDS "LIBERTY TO SLAVES" ON IT, ISN'T THAT RIGHT?
SLANDERER!
YOU'RE ONE OF LORD DUNMORE'S "ETHIOPIAN REGIMENTALS," FIGHTING FOR THE CROWN. FIGHTING AGAINST YOUR OWN.
SO, NO, MR. CLAYTON FREEMAN, I DON'T MUCH LIKE YOU. EVEN IF YOU RIPPED THAT PATCH OFF.

YOU AREN'T HERE TO HARRY THE BRITISH PATROLS.

NO.

YOU'RE HERE FOR ME.

AND OTHERS LIKE YOU. LOYALISTS. TRAITORS. WHO SET THAT FIRE, CLAYTON?

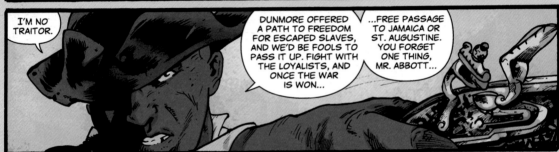

I'M NO TRAITOR.

DUNMORE OFFERED A PATH TO FREEDOM FOR ESCAPED SLAVES, AND WE'D BE FOOLS TO PASS IT UP. FIGHT WITH THE LOYALISTS, AND ONCE THE WAR IS WON...

...FREE PASSAGE TO JAMAICA OR ST. AUGUSTINE. YOU FORGET ONE THING, MR. ABBOTT...

...YOU ALL FORGET ONE THING...

US.

HOW ARE WE TO UNDERSTAND A DECLARATION OF THE RIGHTS OF ALL MEN TO BE FREE, WHEN THE VERY HANDS THAT SIGNED THAT DOCUMENT ARE THE SAME HANDS THAT BIND PEOPLE LIKE US?

TELL ME AGAIN ABOUT HOW I'M A TRAITOR?

YOU AREN'T SEEING THE BIG PICTURE! UNDER THE THUMB OF THE CROWN, ALL MEN OF THE COLONIES ARE AS SLAVES!

NO, MR. ABBOTT.

YOU REALLY AREN'T.

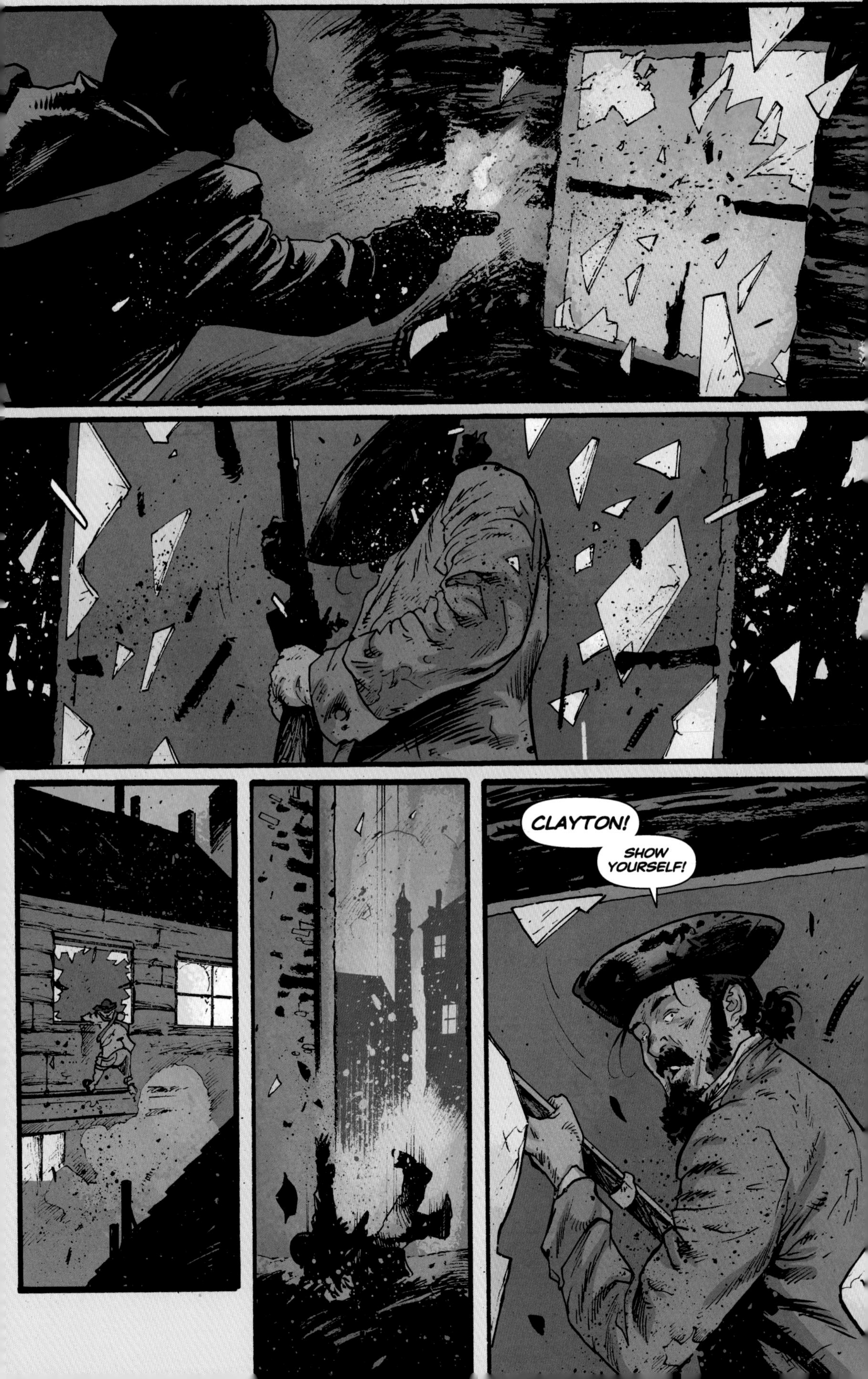
CLAYTON!
SHOW YOURSELF!

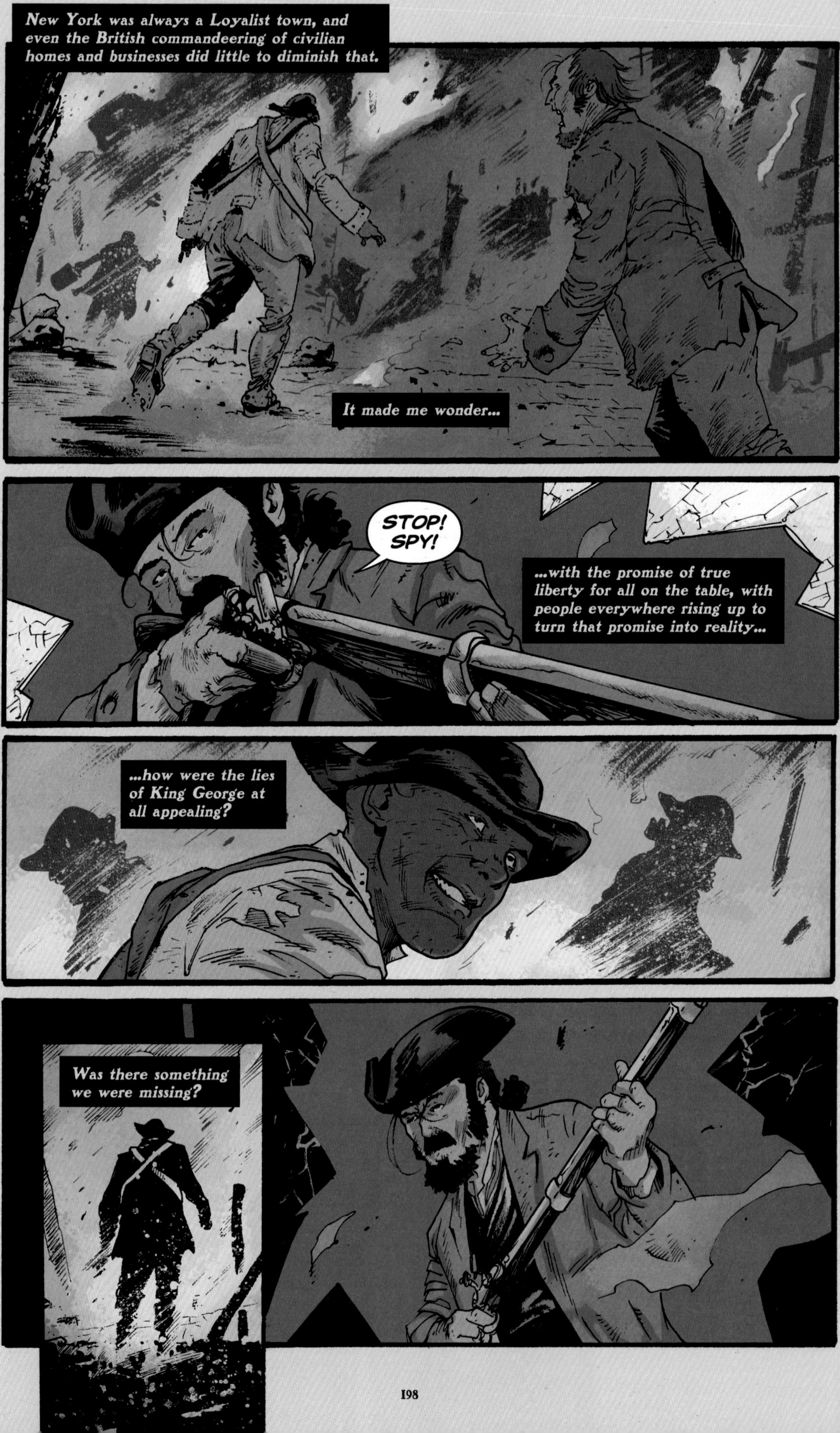
New York was always a Loyalist town, and even the British commandeering of civilian homes and businesses did little to diminish that.
It made me wonder...
STOP! SPY!
...with the promise of true liberty for all on the table, with people everywhere rising up to turn that promise into reality...
...how were the lies of King George at all appealing?
Was there something we were missing?

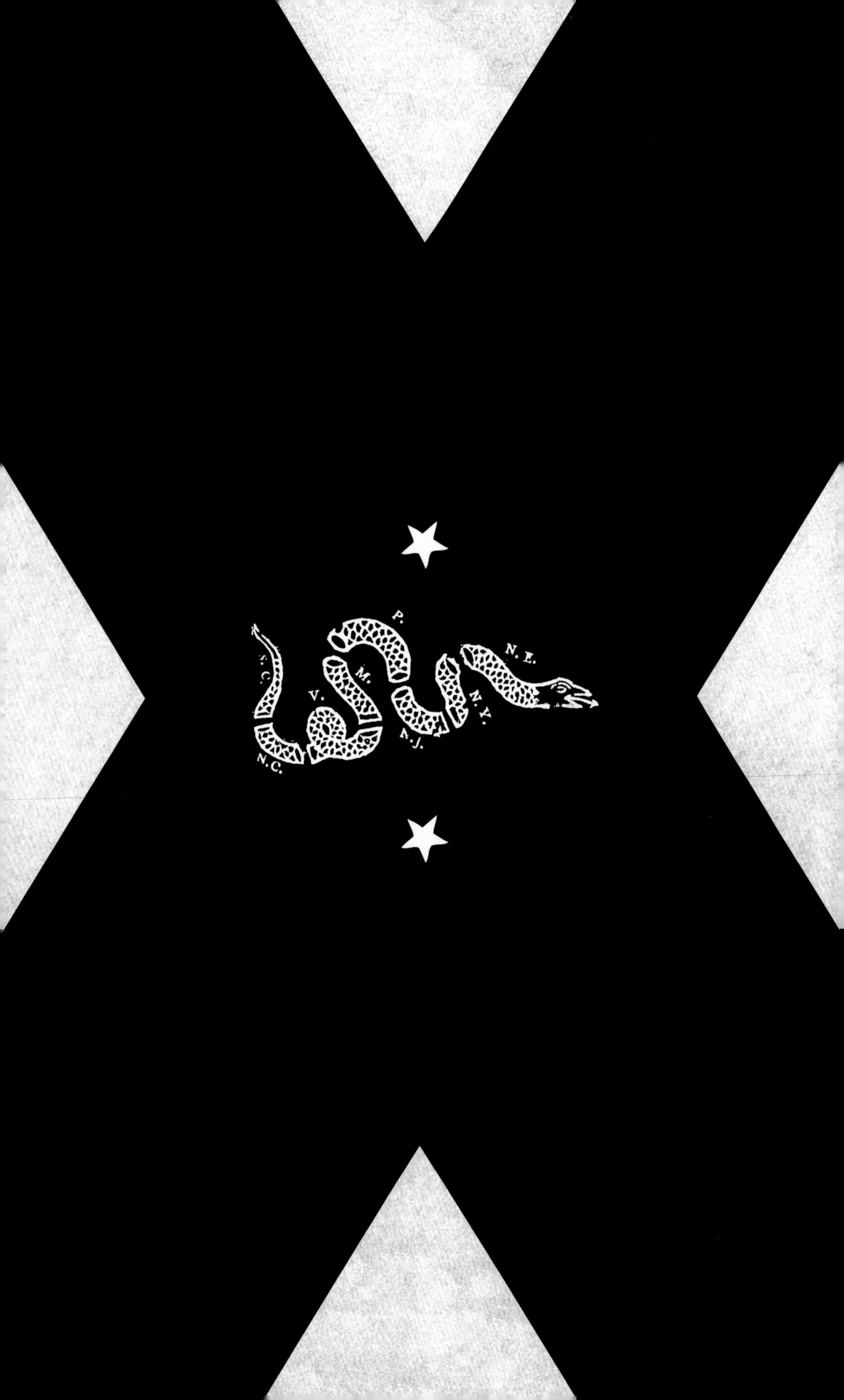

S.C.
N.C.
V.
M.
P.
N.J.
N.Y.
N.E.

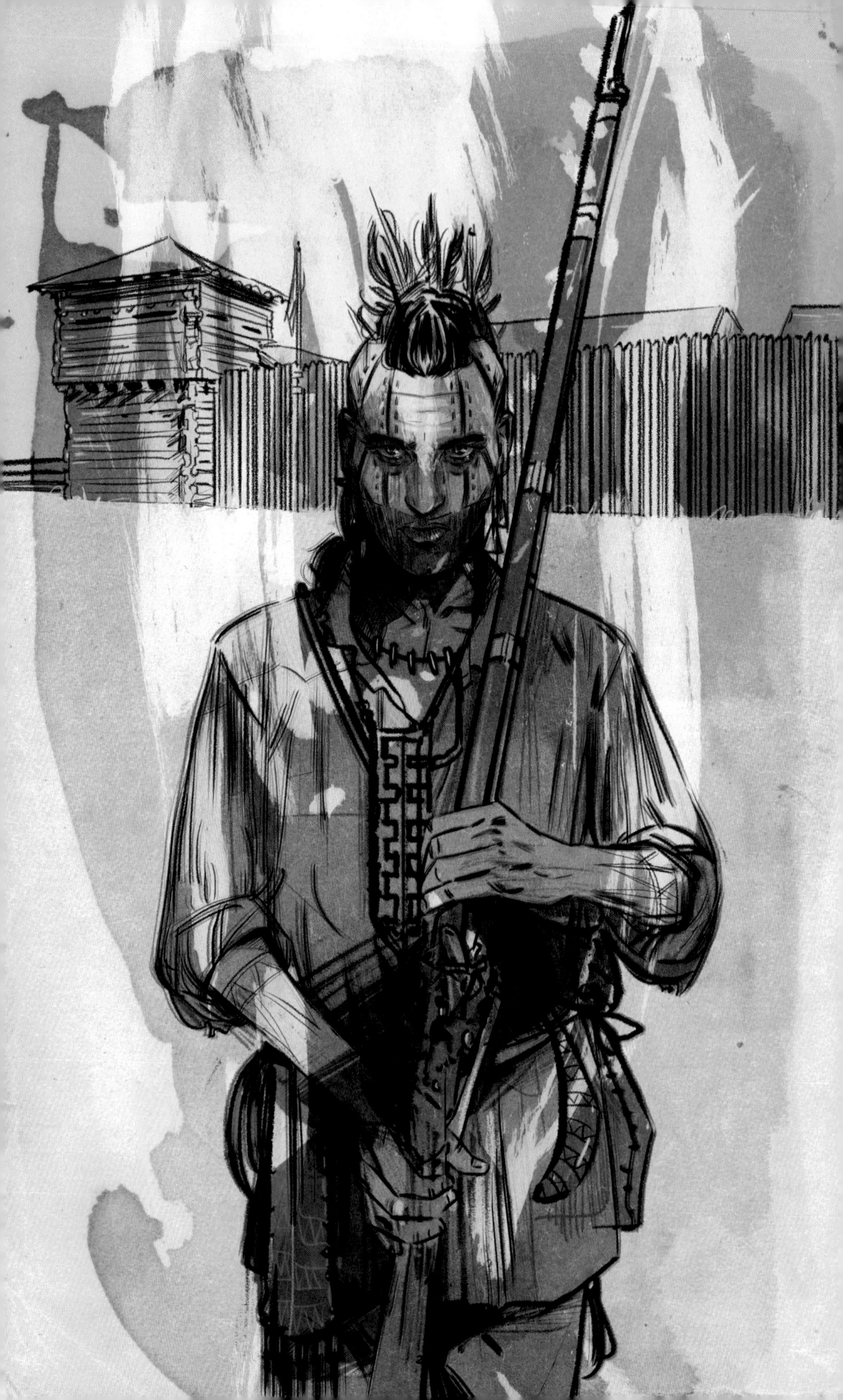

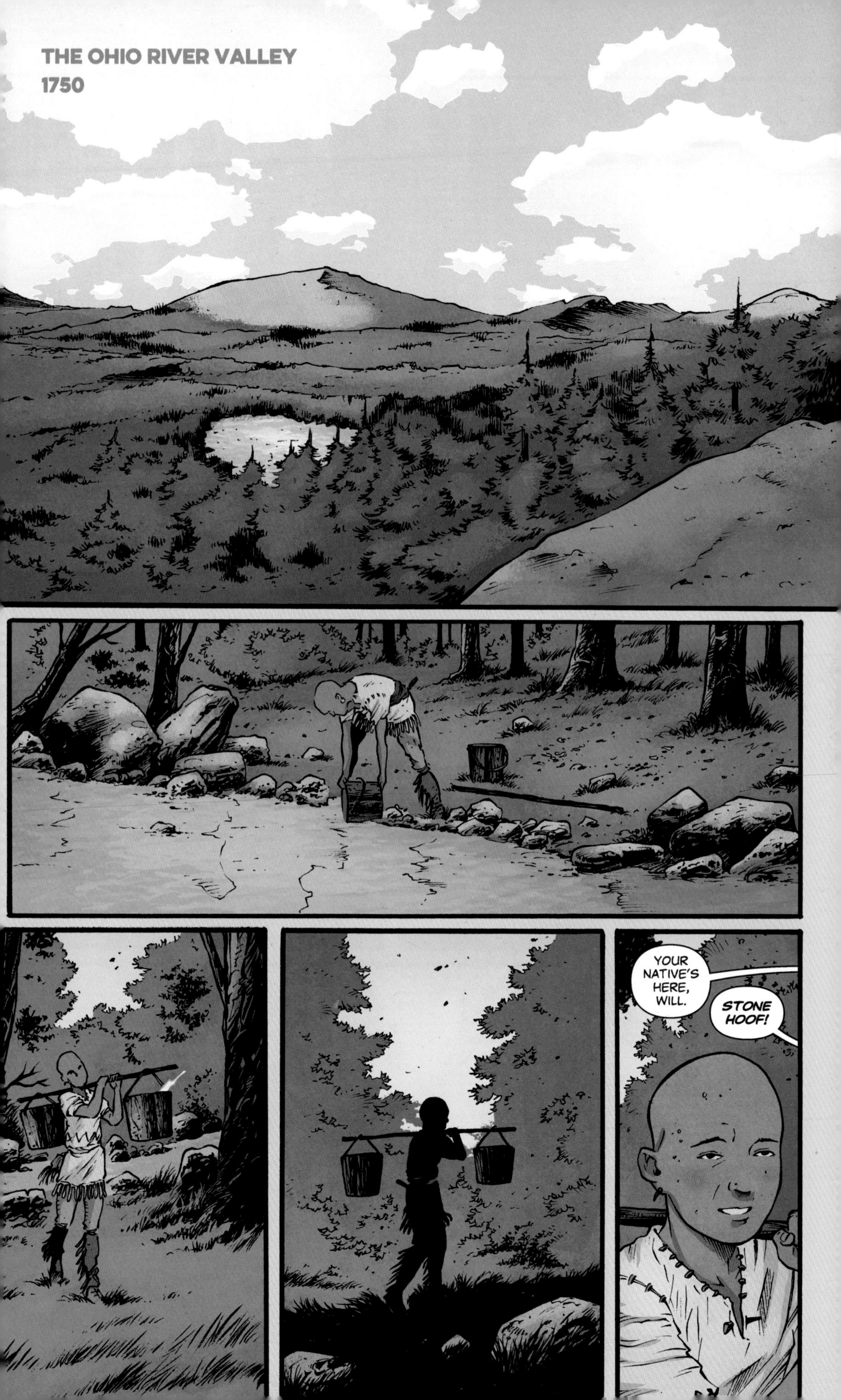
THE OHIO RIVER VALLEY
1750
YOUR NATIVE'S HERE, WILL.
STONE HOOF!

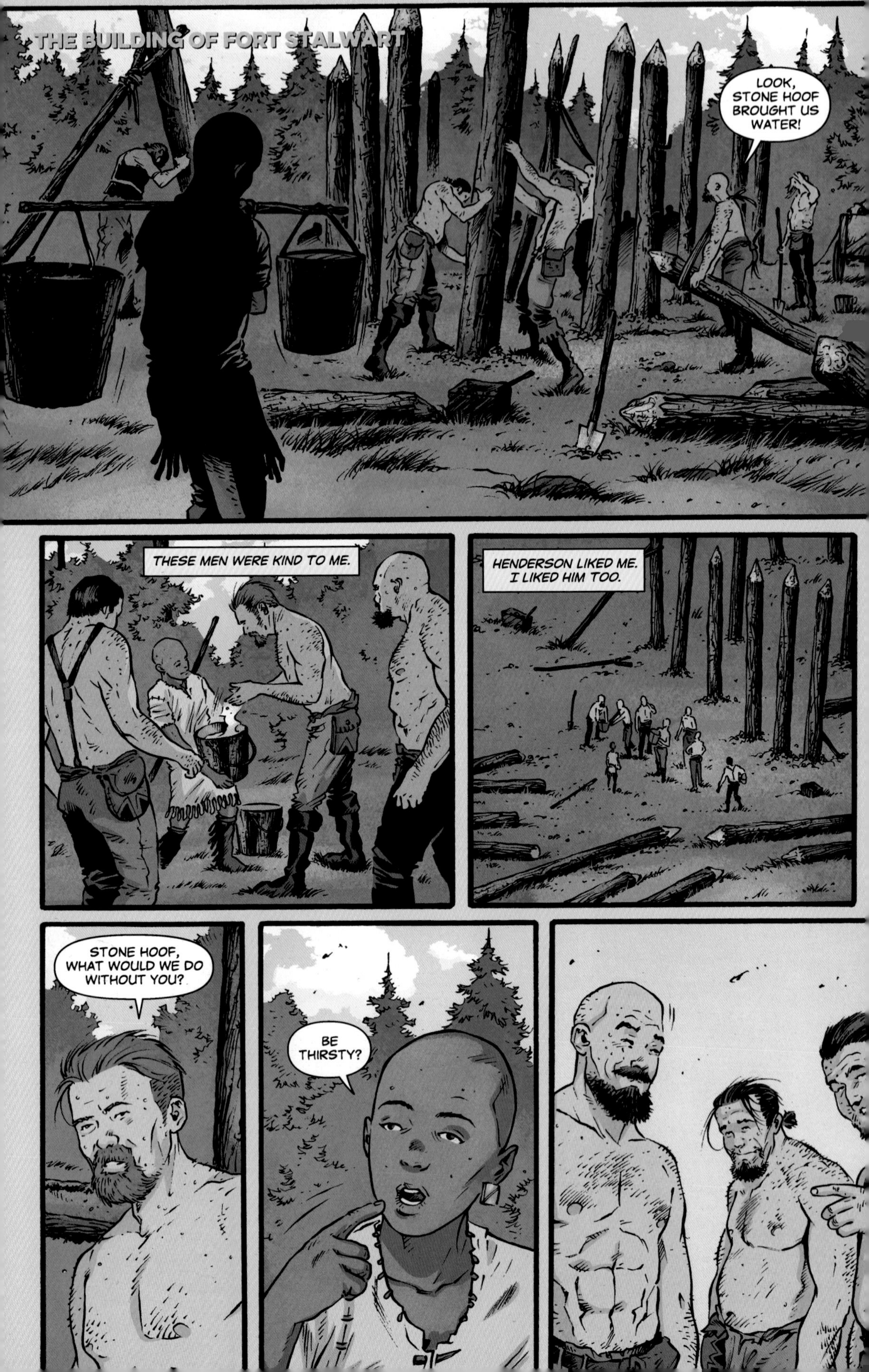
THE BUILDING OF FORT STALWART
LOOK, STONE HOOF BROUGHT US WATER!
THESE MEN WERE KIND TO ME.
HENDERSON LIKED ME. I LIKED HIM TOO.
STONE HOOF, WHAT WOULD WE DO WITHOUT YOU?
BE THIRSTY?

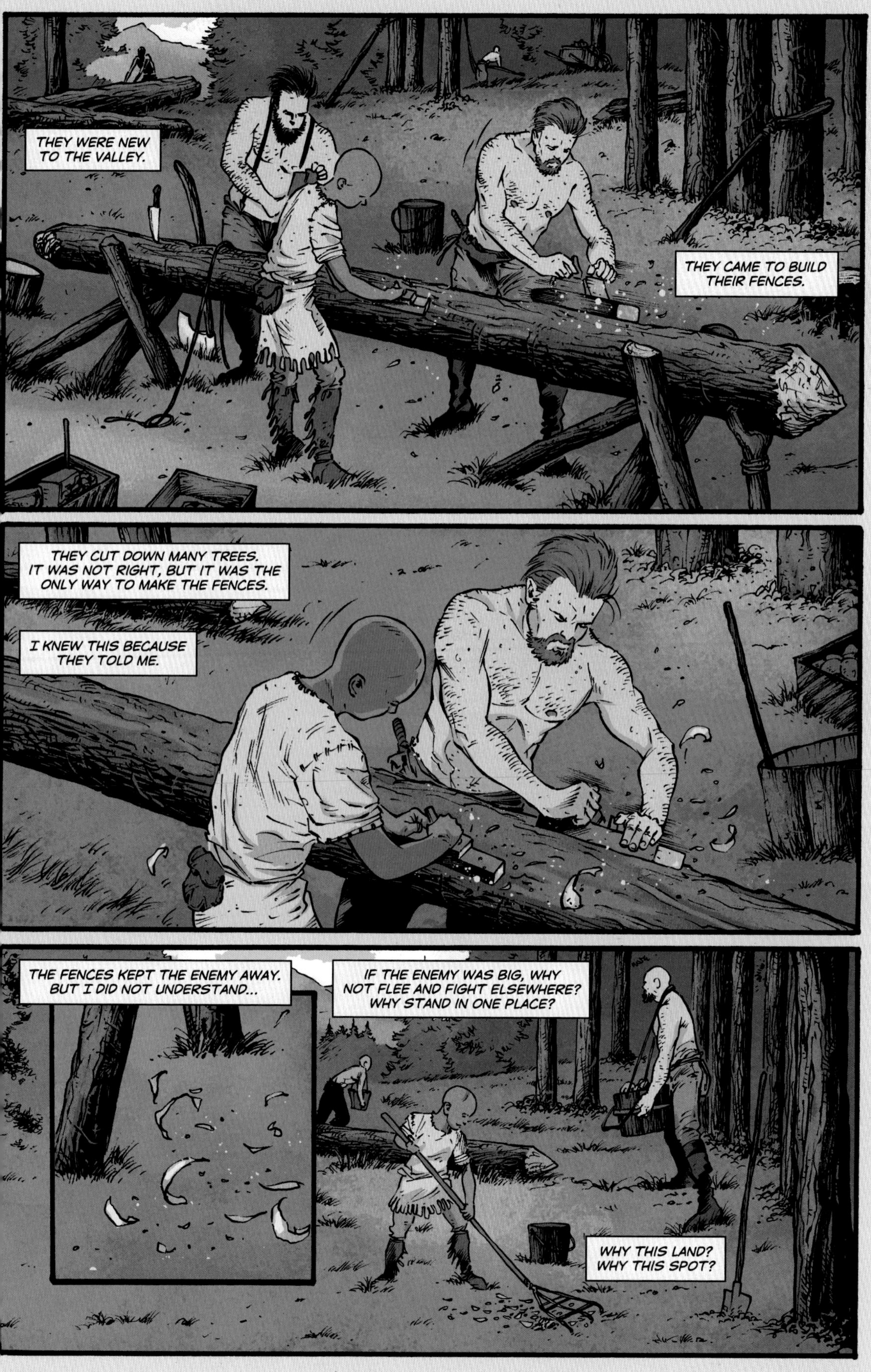
THEY WERE NEW TO THE VALLEY.
THEY CAME TO BUILD THEIR FENCES.
THEY CUT DOWN MANY TREES. IT WAS NOT RIGHT, BUT IT WAS THE ONLY WAY TO MAKE THE FENCES.
I KNEW THIS BECAUSE THEY TOLD ME.
THE FENCES KEPT THE ENEMY AWAY. BUT I DID NOT UNDERSTAND...
IF THE ENEMY WAS BIG, WHY NOT FLEE AND FIGHT ELSEWHERE? WHY STAND IN ONE PLACE?
WHY THIS LAND? WHY THIS SPOT?

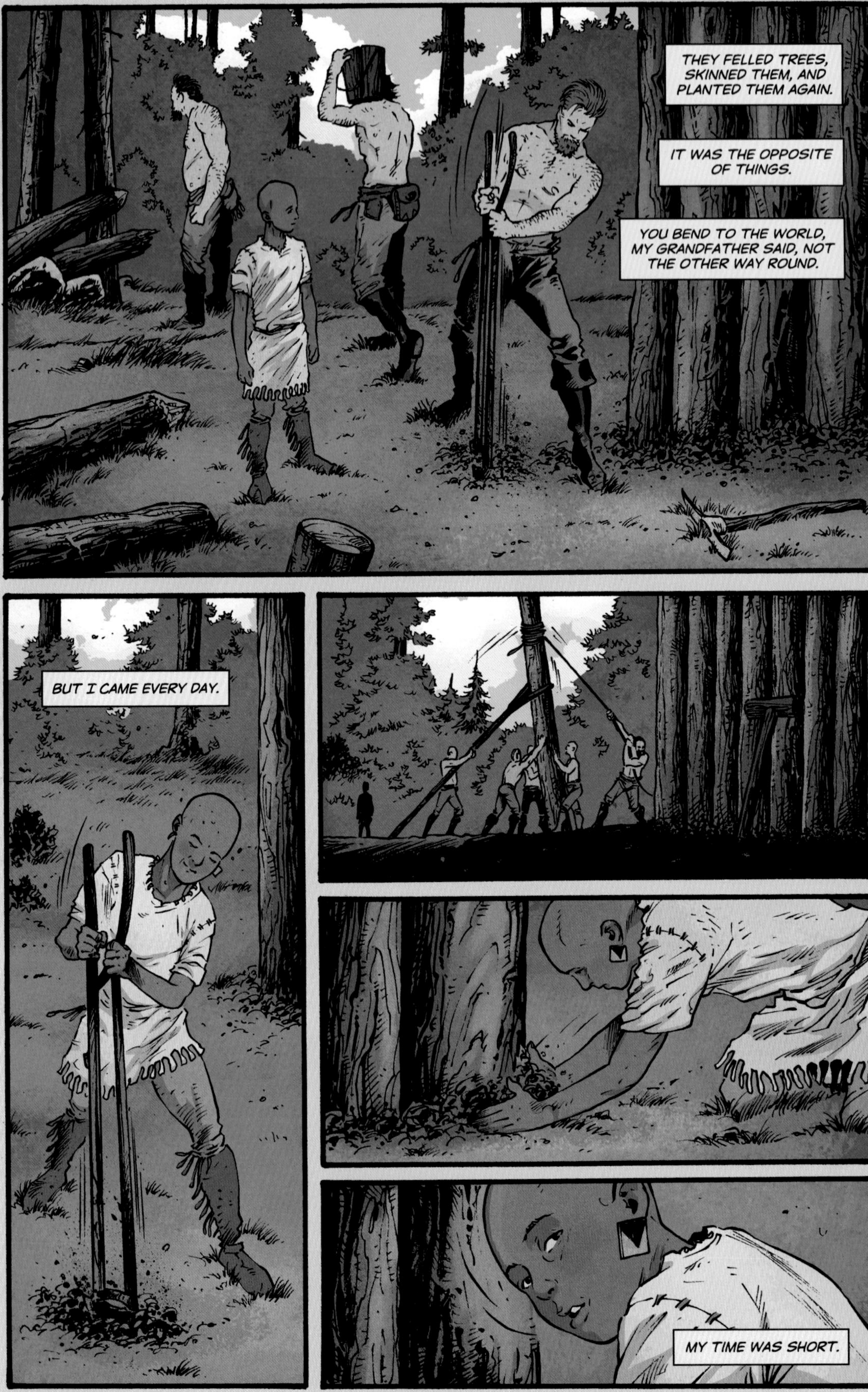
THEY FELLED TREES, SKINNED THEM, AND PLANTED THEM AGAIN.
IT WAS THE OPPOSITE OF THINGS.
YOU BEND TO THE WORLD, MY GRANDFATHER SAID, NOT THE OTHER WAY ROUND.
BUT I CAME EVERY DAY.
MY TIME WAS SHORT.

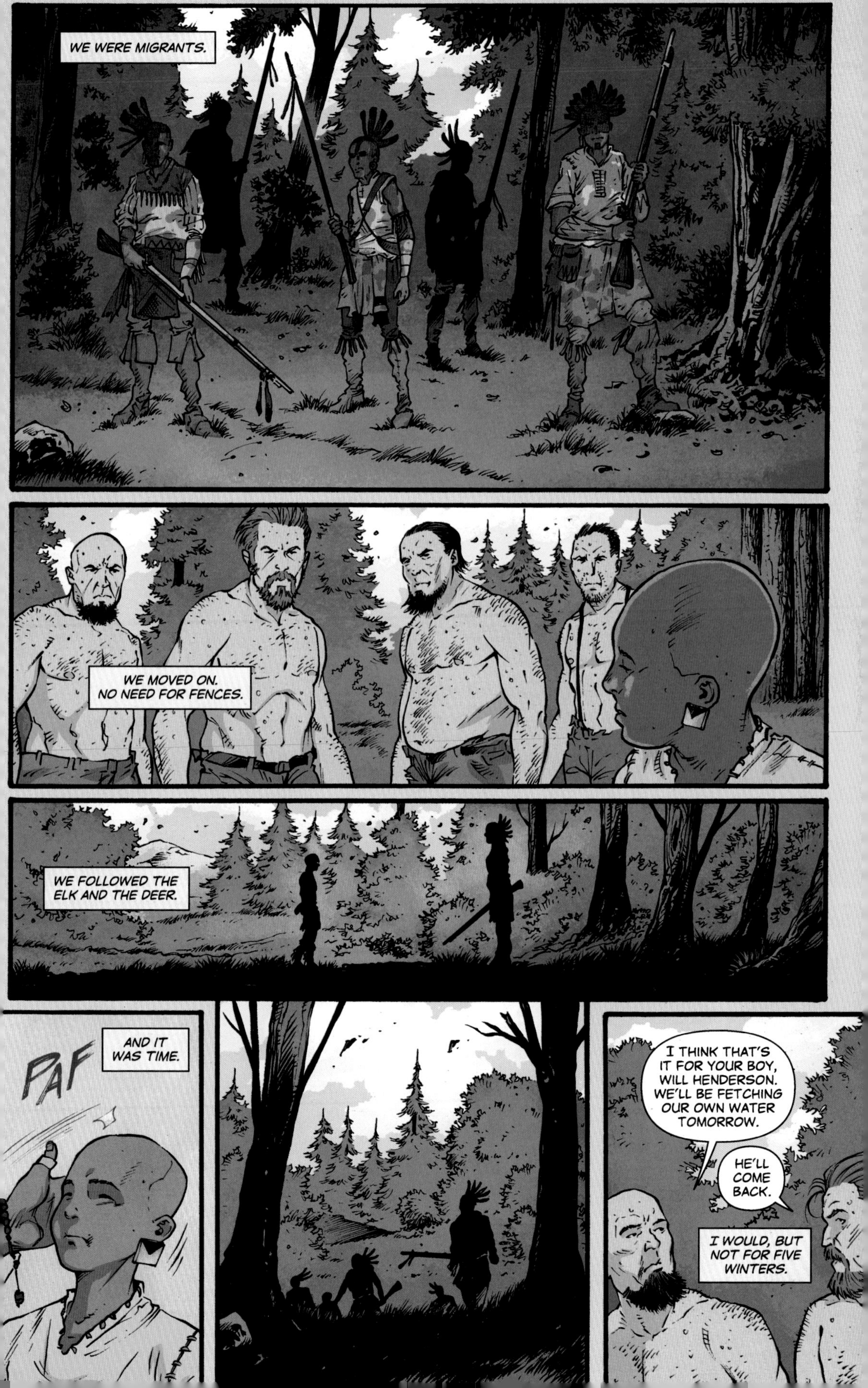
WE WERE MIGRANTS.
WE MOVED ON. NO NEED FOR FENCES.
WE FOLLOWED THE ELK AND THE DEER.
AND IT WAS TIME.
PAF
I THINK THAT'S IT FOR YOUR BOY, WILL HENDERSON. WE'LL BE FETCHING OUR OWN WATER TOMORROW.
HE'LL COME BACK.
I WOULD, BUT NOT FOR FIVE WINTERS.

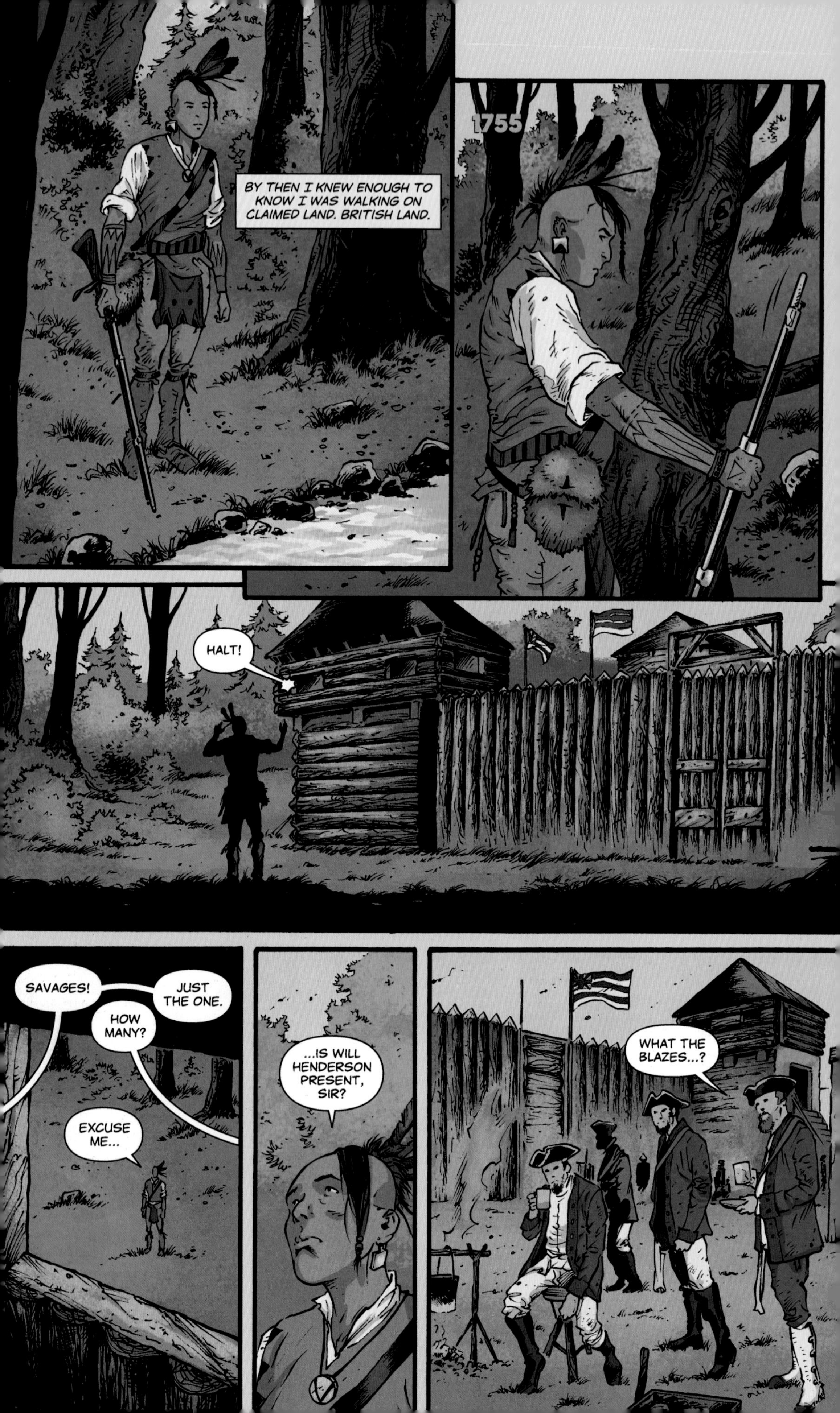
BY THEN I KNEW ENOUGH TO KNOW I WAS WALKING ON CLAIMED LAND. BRITISH LAND.
1755
HALT!
SAVAGES!
HOW MANY?
JUST THE ONE.
EXCUSE ME...
...IS WILL HENDERSON PRESENT, SIR?
WHAT THE BLAZES...?

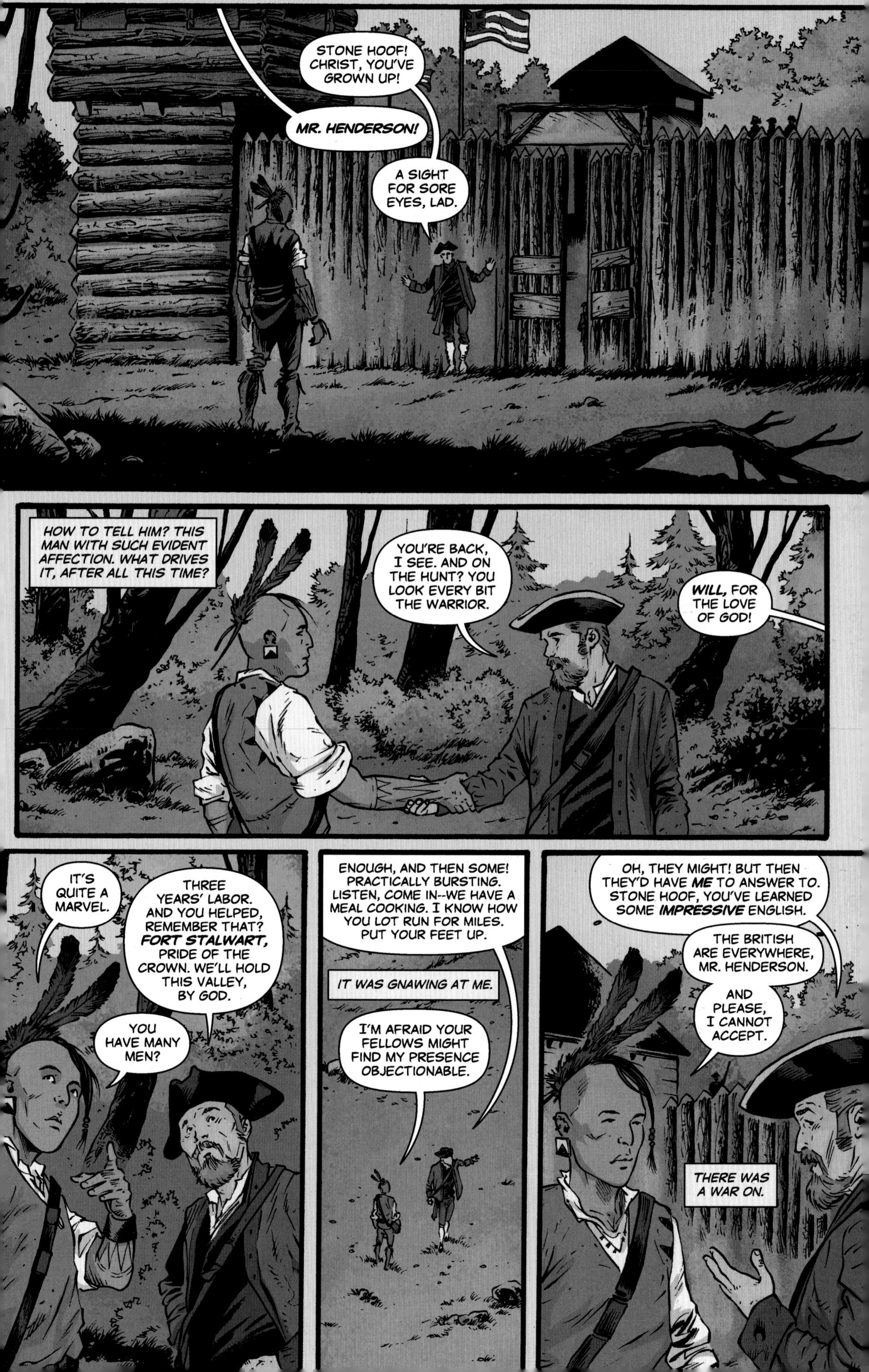
MR. HENDERSON!
STONE HOOF! CHRIST, YOU'VE GROWN UP!
A SIGHT FOR SORE EYES, LAD.
HOW TO TELL HIM? THIS MAN WITH SUCH EVIDENT AFFECTION. WHAT DRIVES IT, AFTER ALL THIS TIME?
YOU'RE BACK, I SEE. AND ON THE HUNT? YOU LOOK EVERY BIT THE WARRIOR.
WILL, FOR THE LOVE OF GOD!
IT'S QUITE A MARVEL.
THREE YEARS' LABOR. AND YOU HELPED, REMEMBER THAT? FORT STALWART, PRIDE OF THE CROWN. WE'LL HOLD THIS VALLEY, BY GOD.
YOU HAVE MANY MEN?
ENOUGH, AND THEN SOME! PRACTICALLY BURSTING. LISTEN, COME IN--WE HAVE A MEAL COOKING. I KNOW HOW YOU LOT RUN FOR MILES. PUT YOUR FEET UP.
IT WAS GNAWING AT ME.
I'M AFRAID YOUR FELLOWS MIGHT FIND MY PRESENCE OBJECTIONABLE.
OH, THEY MIGHT! BUT THEN THEY'D HAVE ME TO ANSWER TO. STONE HOOF, YOU'VE LEARNED SOME IMPRESSIVE ENGLISH.
THE BRITISH ARE EVERYWHERE, MR. HENDERSON.
AND PLEASE, I CANNOT ACCEPT.
THERE WAS A WAR ON.

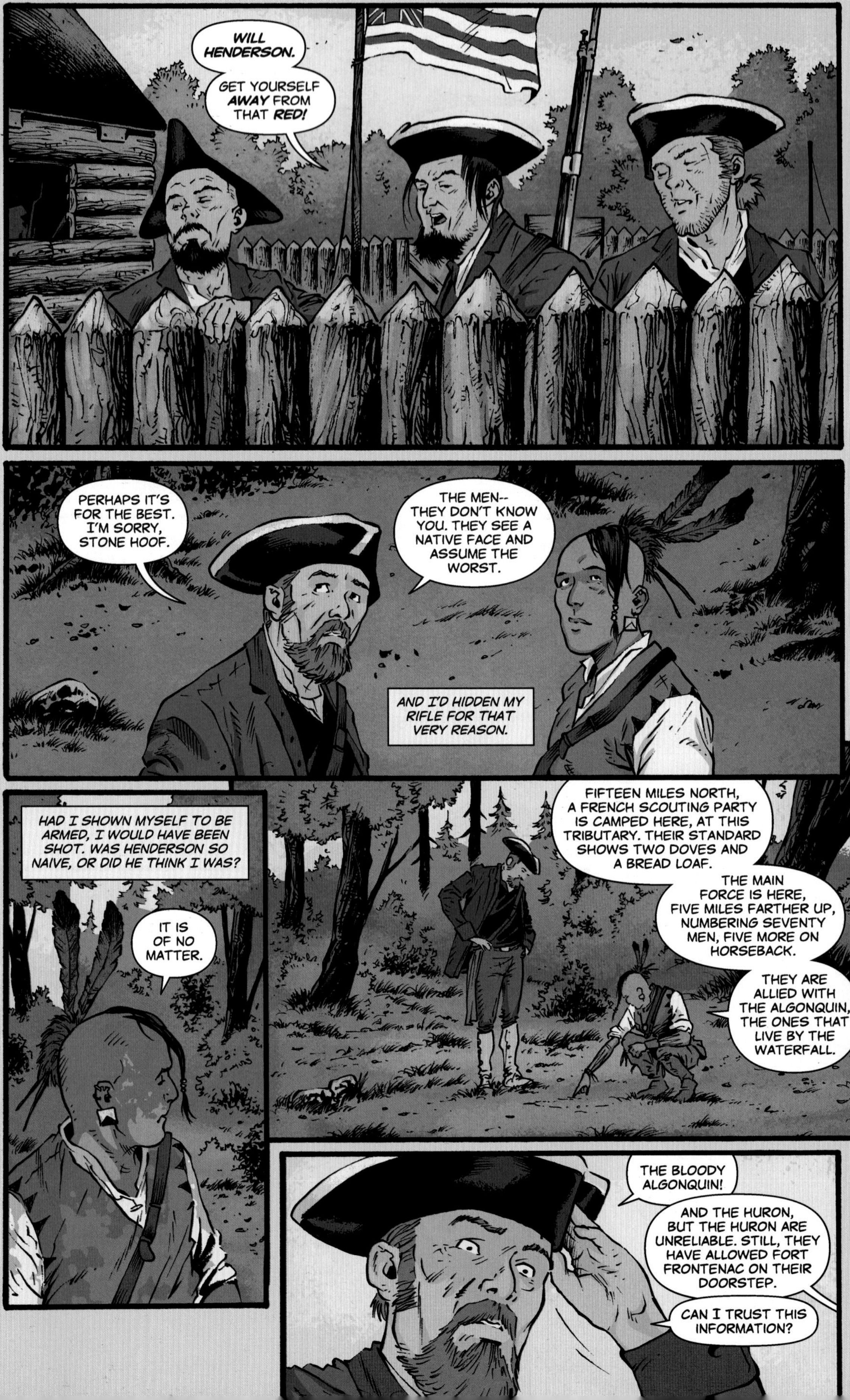
WILL HENDERSON.
GET YOURSELF AWAY FROM THAT RED!
PERHAPS IT'S FOR THE BEST. I'M SORRY, STONE HOOF.
THE MEN-- THEY DON'T KNOW YOU. THEY SEE A NATIVE FACE AND ASSUME THE WORST.
AND I'D HIDDEN MY RIFLE FOR THAT VERY REASON.
HAD I SHOWN MYSELF TO BE ARMED, I WOULD HAVE BEEN SHOT. WAS HENDERSON SO NAIVE, OR DID HE THINK I WAS?
IT IS OF NO MATTER.
FIFTEEN MILES NORTH, A FRENCH SCOUTING PARTY IS CAMPED HERE, AT THIS TRIBUTARY. THEIR STANDARD SHOWS TWO DOVES AND A BREAD LOAF.
THE MAIN FORCE IS HERE, FIVE MILES FARTHER UP, NUMBERING SEVENTY MEN, FIVE MORE ON HORSEBACK.
THEY ARE ALLIED WITH THE ALGONQUIN, THE ONES THAT LIVE BY THE WATERFALL.
THE BLOODY ALGONQUIN!
AND THE HURON, BUT THE HURON ARE UNRELIABLE. STILL, THEY HAVE ALLOWED FORT FRONTENAC ON THEIR DOORSTEP.
CAN I TRUST THIS INFORMATION?

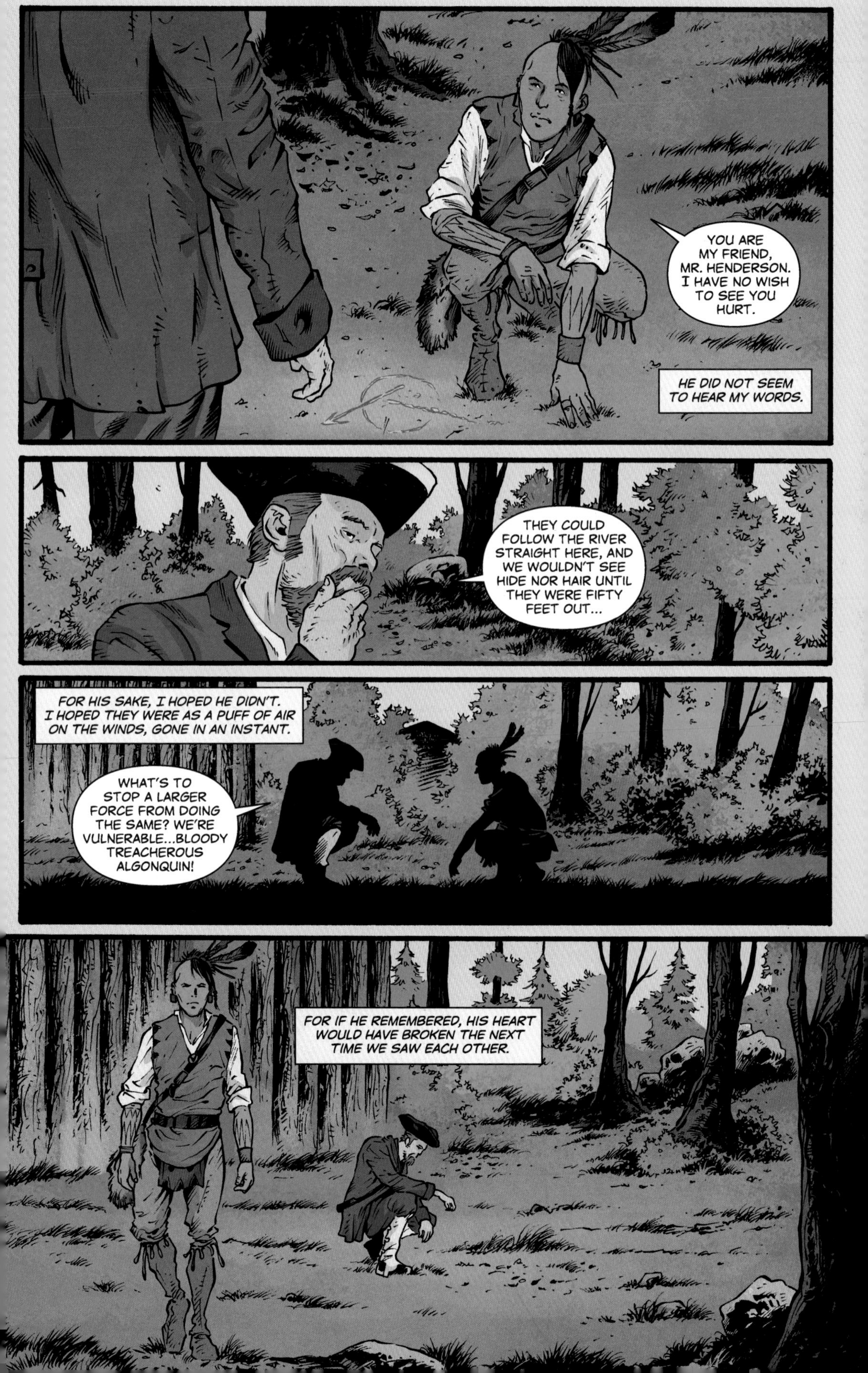
YOU ARE MY FRIEND, MR. HENDERSON. I HAVE NO WISH TO SEE YOU HURT.
HE DID NOT SEEM TO HEAR MY WORDS.
THEY COULD FOLLOW THE RIVER STRAIGHT HERE, AND WE WOULDN'T SEE HIDE NOR HAIR UNTIL THEY WERE FIFTY FEET OUT...
FOR HIS SAKE, I HOPED HE DIDN'T. I HOPED THEY WERE AS A PUFF OF AIR ON THE WINDS, GONE IN AN INSTANT.
WHAT'S TO STOP A LARGER FORCE FROM DOING THE SAME? WE'RE VULNERABLE...BLOODY TREACHEROUS ALGONQUIN!
FOR IF HE REMEMBERED, HIS HEART WOULD HAVE BROKEN THE NEXT TIME WE SAW EACH OTHER.

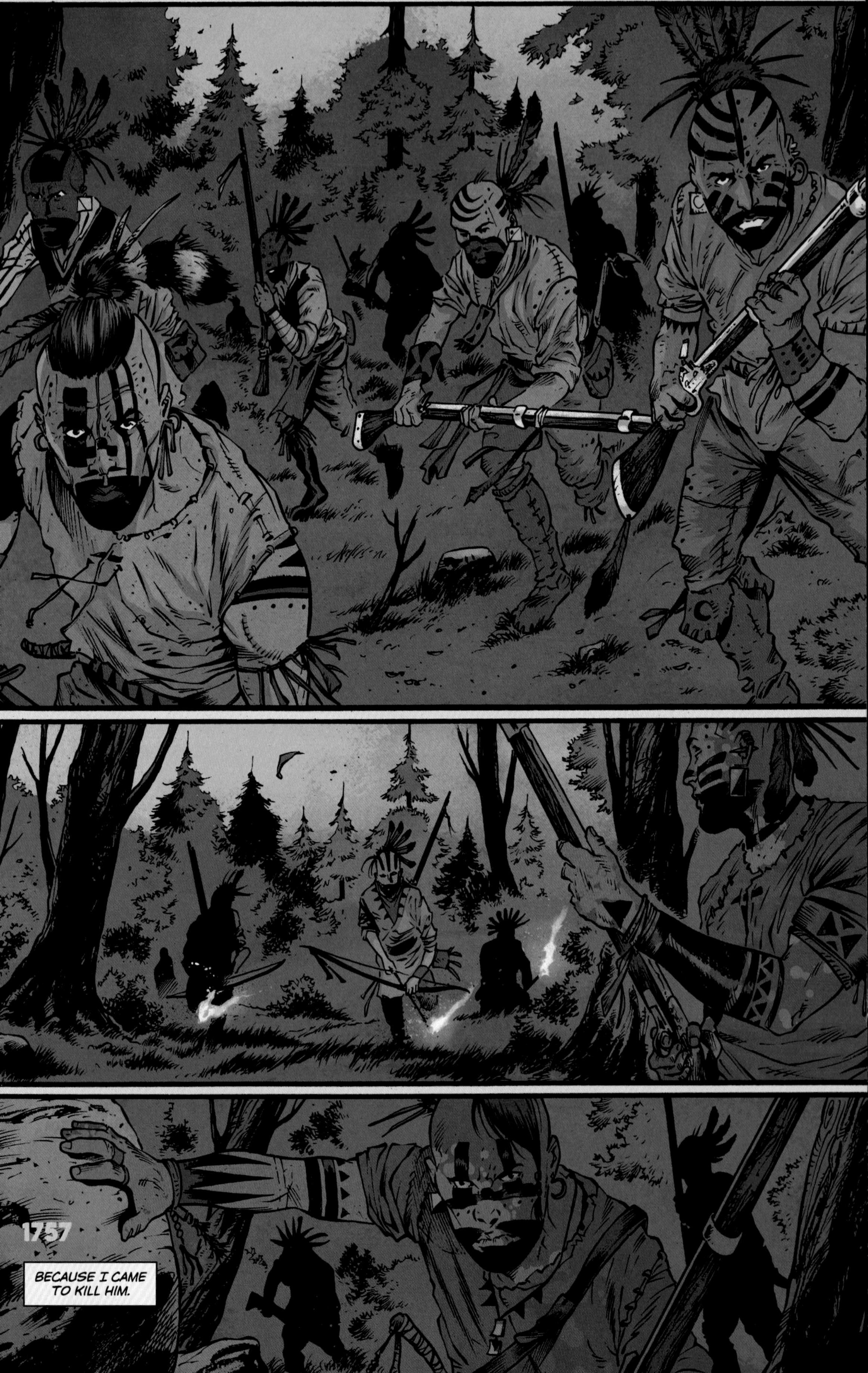
1757
BECAUSE I CAME TO KILL HIM.

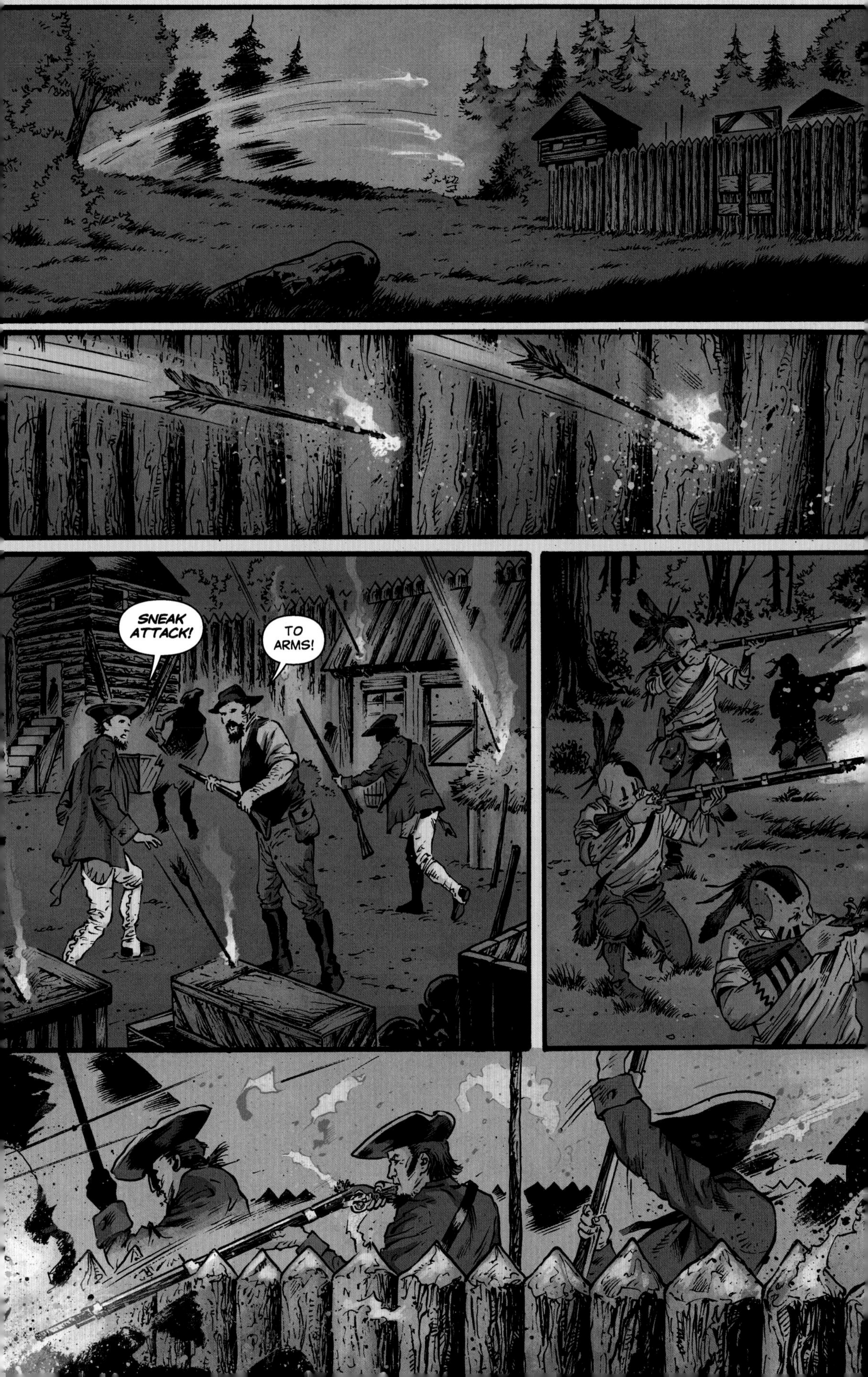
SNEAK ATTACK!
TO ARMS!

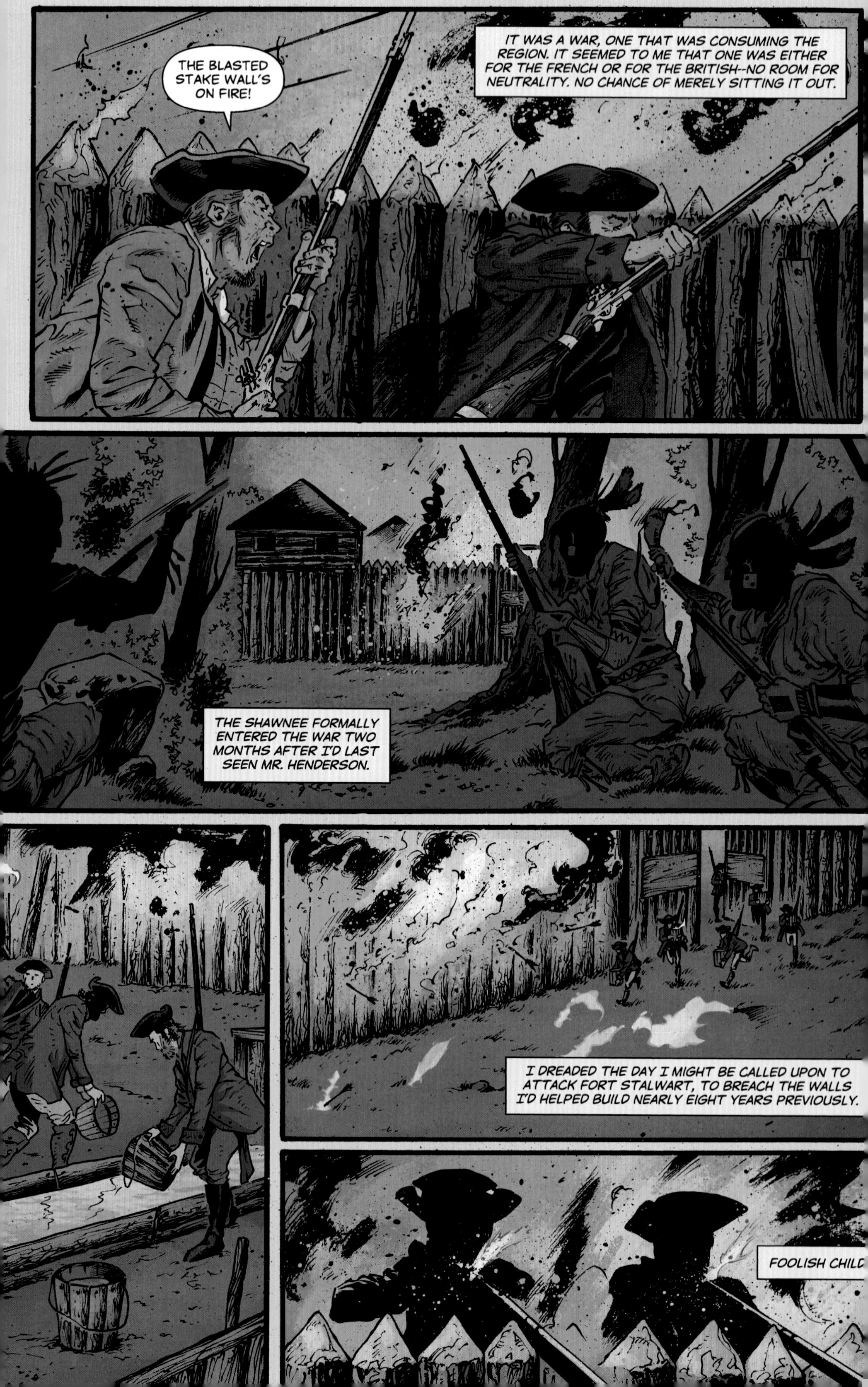
THE BLASTED STAKE WALL'S ON FIRE!
IT WAS A WAR, ONE THAT WAS CONSUMING THE REGION. IT SEEMED TO ME THAT ONE WAS EITHER FOR THE FRENCH OR FOR THE BRITISH--NO ROOM FOR NEUTRALITY. NO CHANCE OF MERELY SITTING IT OUT.
THE SHAWNEE FORMALLY ENTERED THE WAR TWO MONTHS AFTER I'D LAST SEEN MR. HENDERSON.
I DREADED THE DAY I MIGHT BE CALLED UPON TO ATTACK FORT STALWART, TO BREACH THE WALLS I'D HELPED BUILD NEARLY EIGHT YEARS PREVIOUSLY.
FOOLISH CHILD

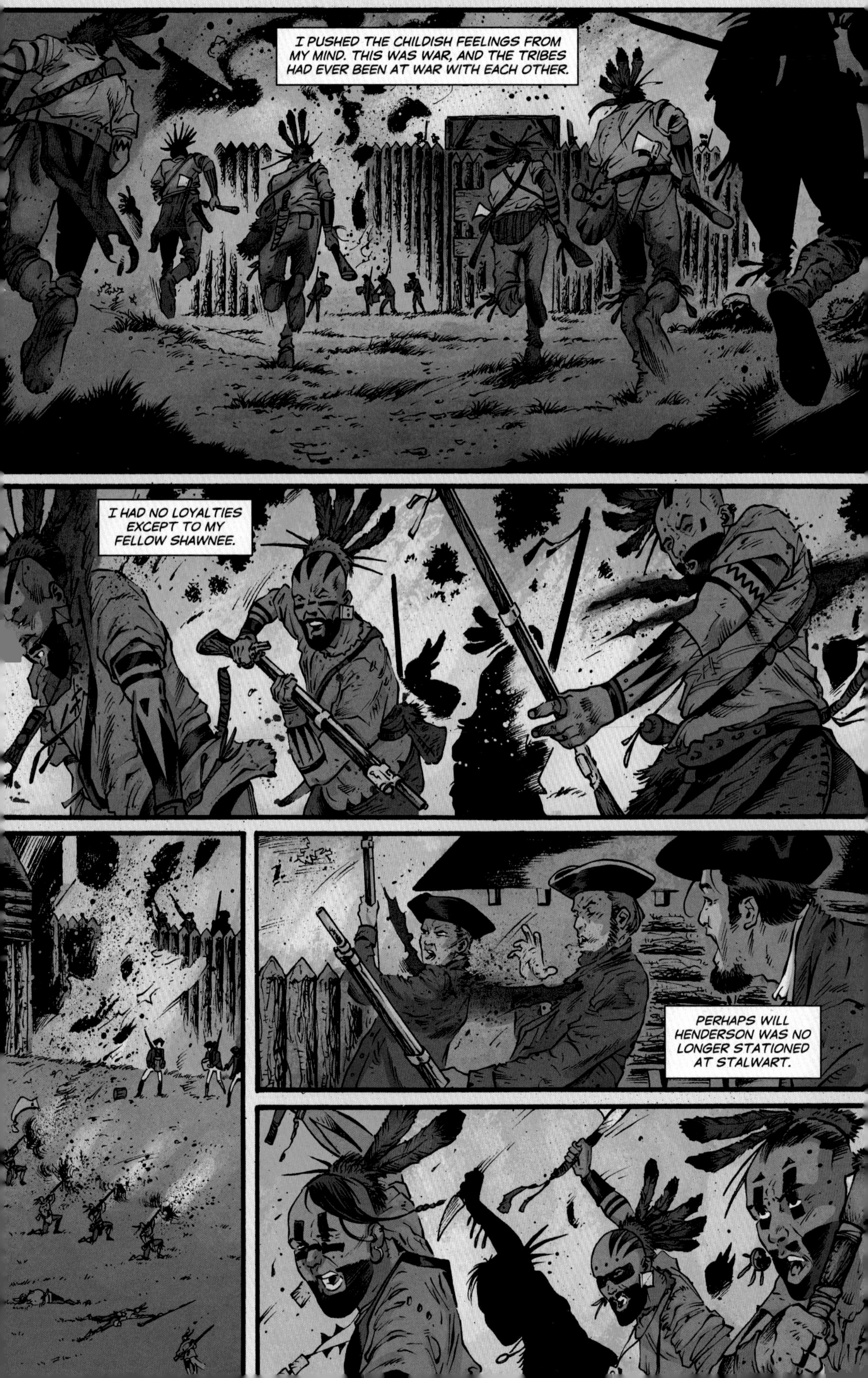
I PUSHED THE CHILDISH FEELINGS FROM MY MIND. THIS WAS WAR, AND THE TRIBES HAD EVER BEEN AT WAR WITH EACH OTHER.
I HAD NO LOYALTIES EXCEPT TO MY FELLOW SHAWNEE.
PERHAPS WILL HENDERSON WAS NO LONGER STATIONED AT STALWART.

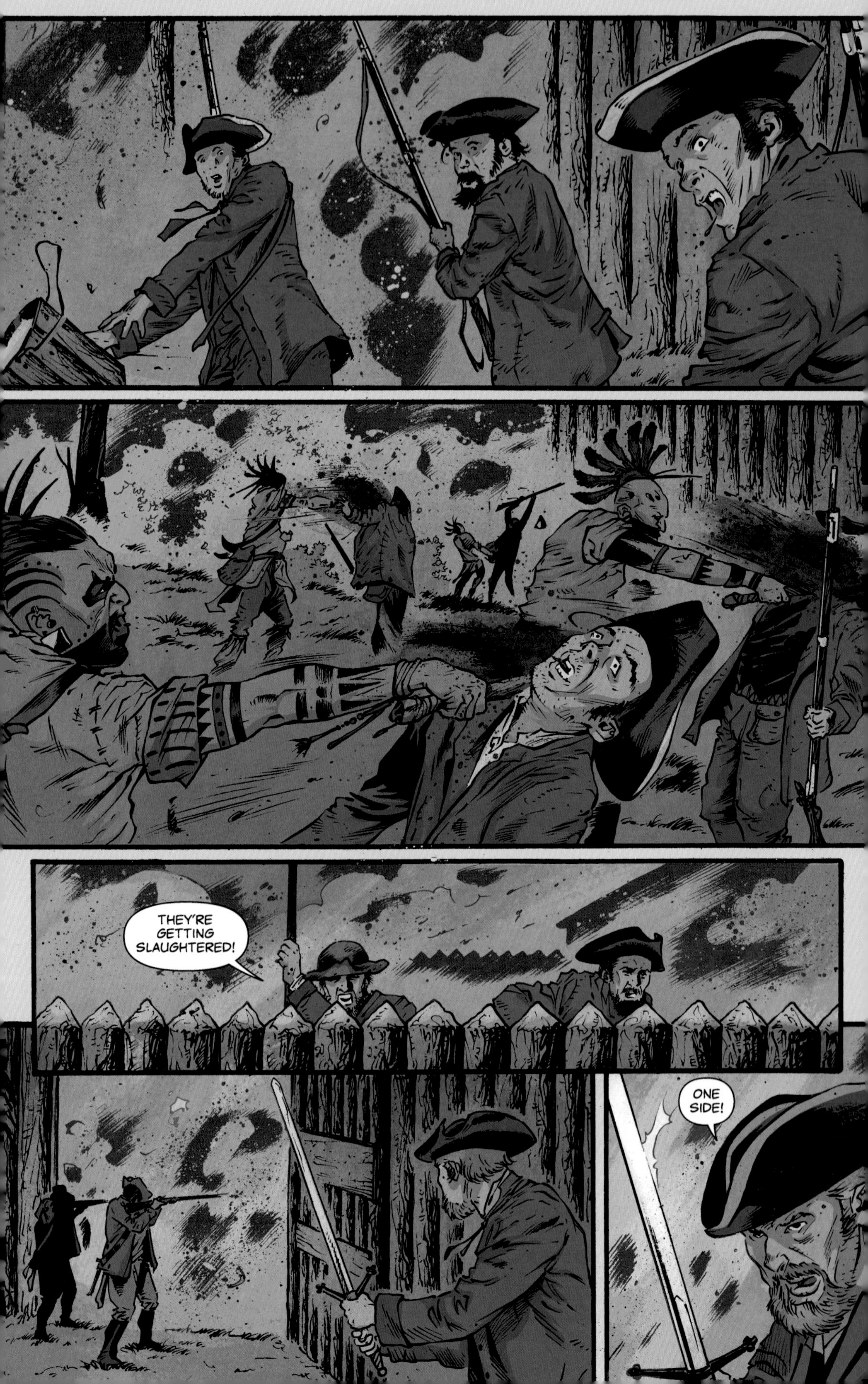
THEY'RE GETTING SLAUGHTERED!
ONE SIDE!

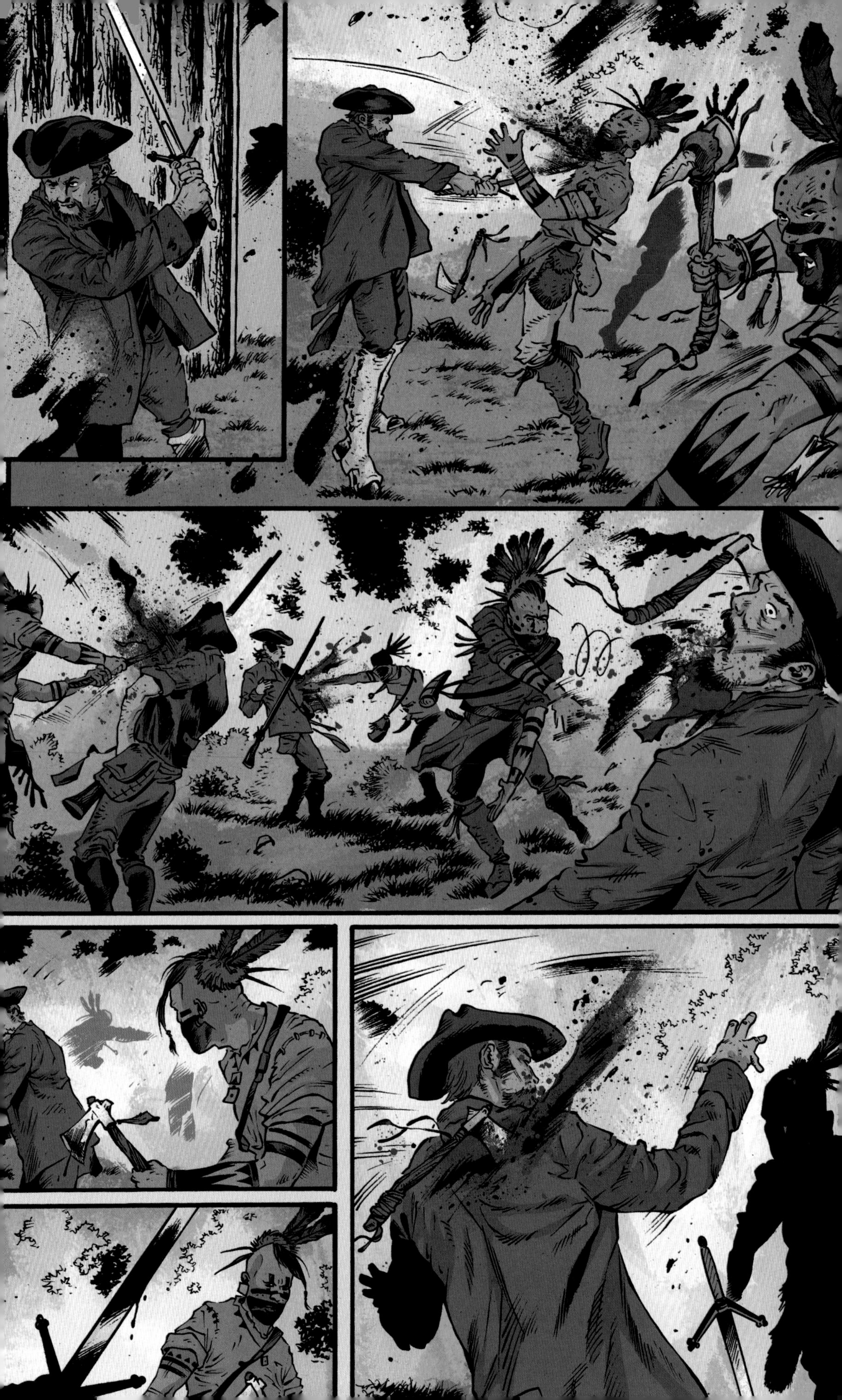

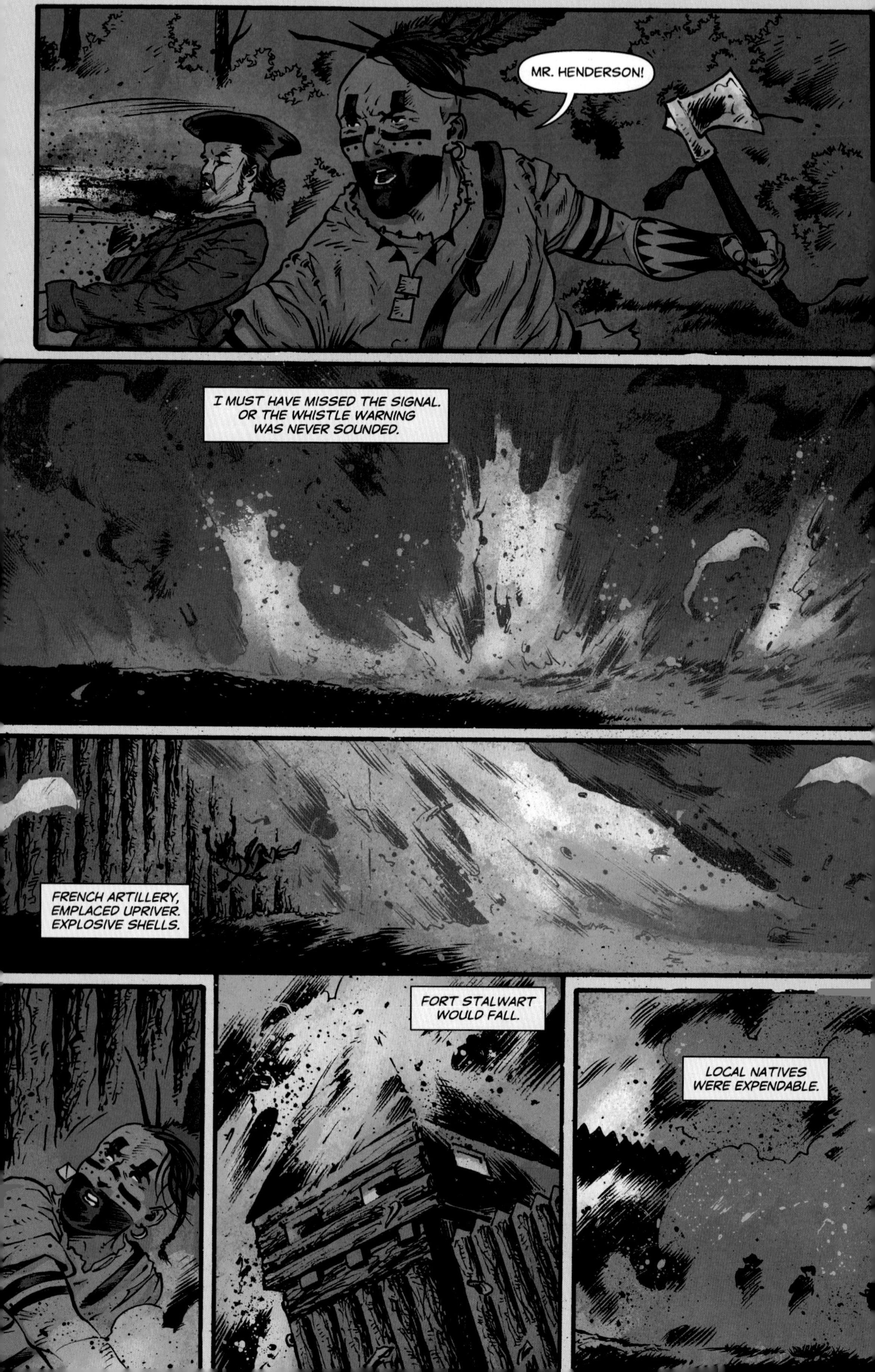
MR. HENDERSON!
I MUST HAVE MISSED THE SIGNAL. OR THE WHISTLE WARNING WAS NEVER SOUNDED.
FRENCH ARTILLERY, EMPLACED UPRIVER. EXPLOSIVE SHELLS.
FORT STALWART WOULD FALL.
LOCAL NATIVES WERE EXPENDABLE.

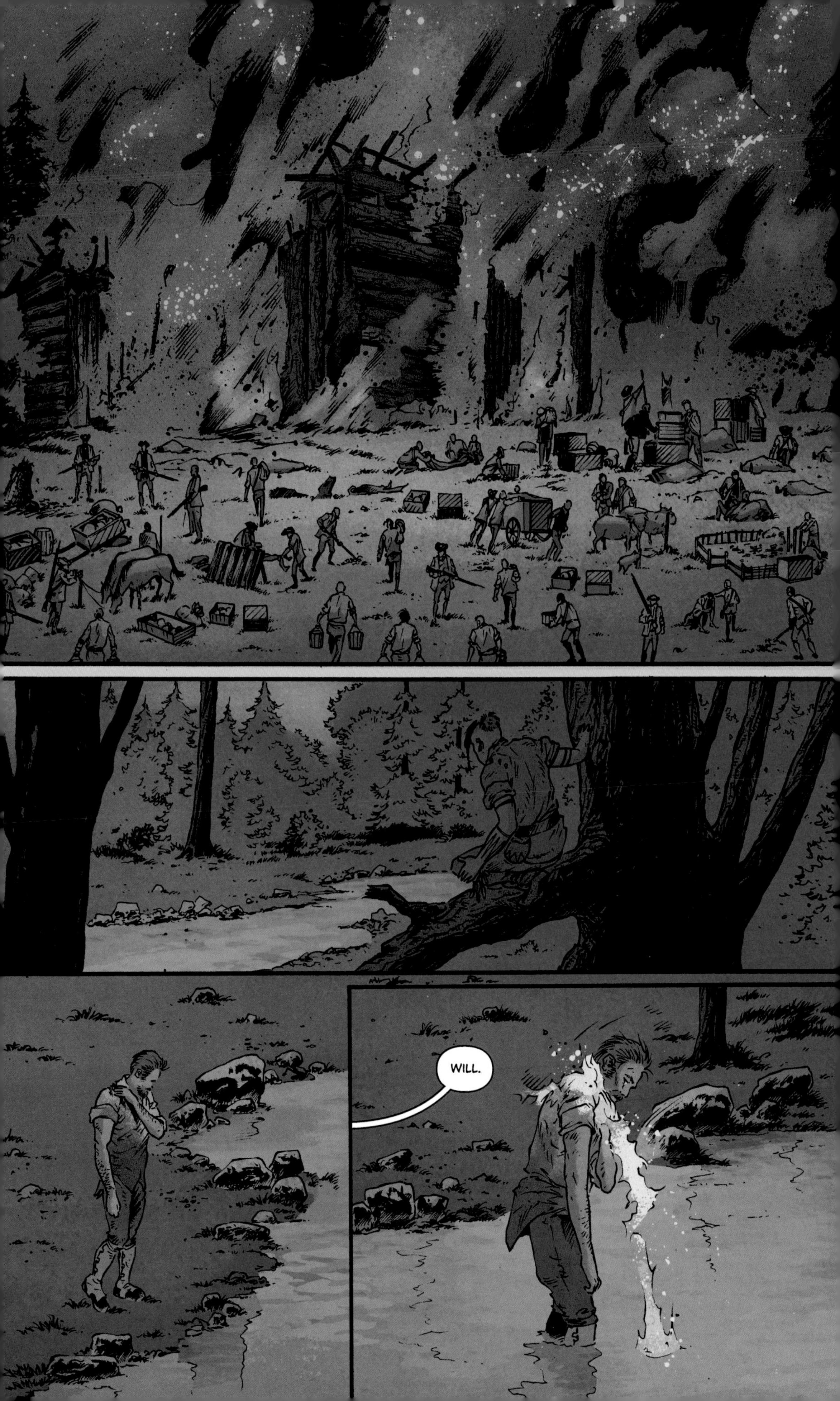
WILL.

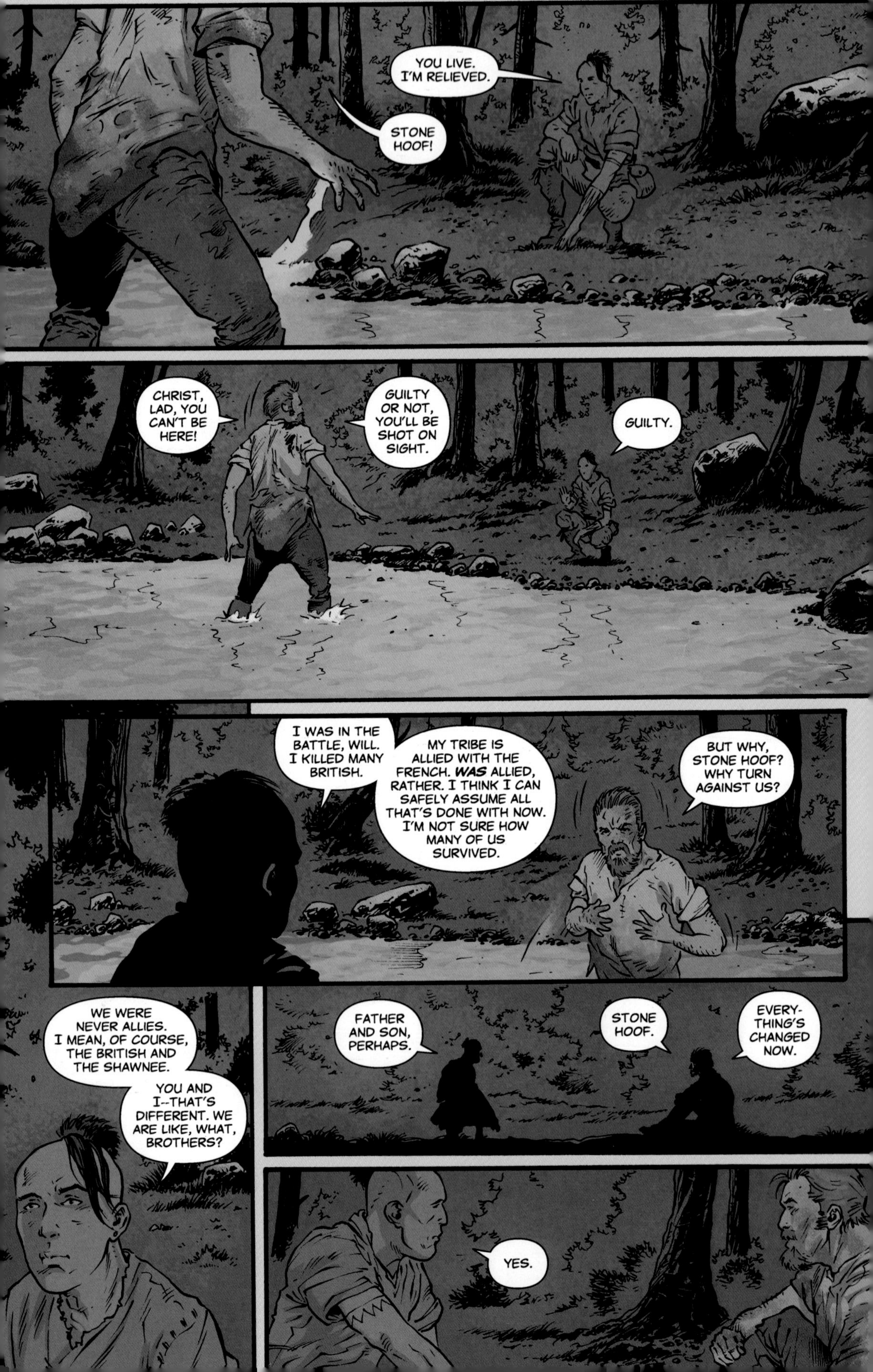
STONE HOOF!
YOU LIVE. I'M RELIEVED.
CHRIST, LAD, YOU CAN'T BE HERE!
GUILTY OR NOT, YOU'LL BE SHOT ON SIGHT.
GUILTY.
I WAS IN THE BATTLE, WILL. I KILLED MANY BRITISH.
MY TRIBE IS ALLIED WITH THE FRENCH. WAS ALLIED, RATHER. I THINK I CAN SAFELY ASSUME ALL THAT'S DONE WITH NOW. I'M NOT SURE HOW MANY OF US SURVIVED.
BUT WHY, STONE HOOF? WHY TURN AGAINST US?
WE WERE NEVER ALLIES. I MEAN, OF COURSE, THE BRITISH AND THE SHAWNEE.
YOU AND I--THAT'S DIFFERENT. WE ARE LIKE, WHAT, BROTHERS?
FATHER AND SON, PERHAPS.
STONE HOOF.
EVERY-THING'S CHANGED NOW.
YES.

IT TOOK ME A LONG TIME TO UNDERSTAND THE EUROPEAN'S OBSESSION WITH LAND OWNERSHIP. YOU WILL FIGHT TOOTH AND NAIL OVER A SCRAP OF LAND. YOU'LL DIE FOR IT.

SECURITY, RESOURCES, AGRICULTURE. ALL MEN HAVE THESE SAME NEEDS.

SO WHAT IS THE DIFFERENCE BETWEEN YOUR LOT AND MINE, IN THIS RESPECT?

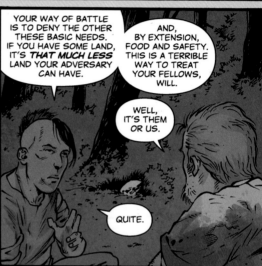

YOUR WAY OF BATTLE IS TO DENY THE OTHER THESE BASIC NEEDS. IF YOU HAVE SOME LAND, IT'S *THAT MUCH LESS* LAND YOUR ADVERSARY CAN HAVE.

AND, BY EXTENSION, FOOD AND SAFETY. THIS IS A TERRIBLE WAY TO TREAT YOUR FELLOWS, WILL.

WELL, IT'S THEM OR US.

QUITE.

AND SOON THIS WHOLE CONTINENT WILL BE CONSUMED, WITH ALL INVOLVED IN A CONSTANT STATE OF FEAR.

BIT DRAMATIC.

THE LAND HERE IS ENDLESS.

YOU USE HYPERBOLE. THE ONLY THING THAT IS ENDLESS IS YOUR CAPACITY TO FEEL FEAR AND ENVY.

I LIKED YOU BETTER AS A BARELY LITERATE CHILD, STONE HOOF. FETCHING MY GOD DAMNED WATER.

THE HELL WITH THIS.

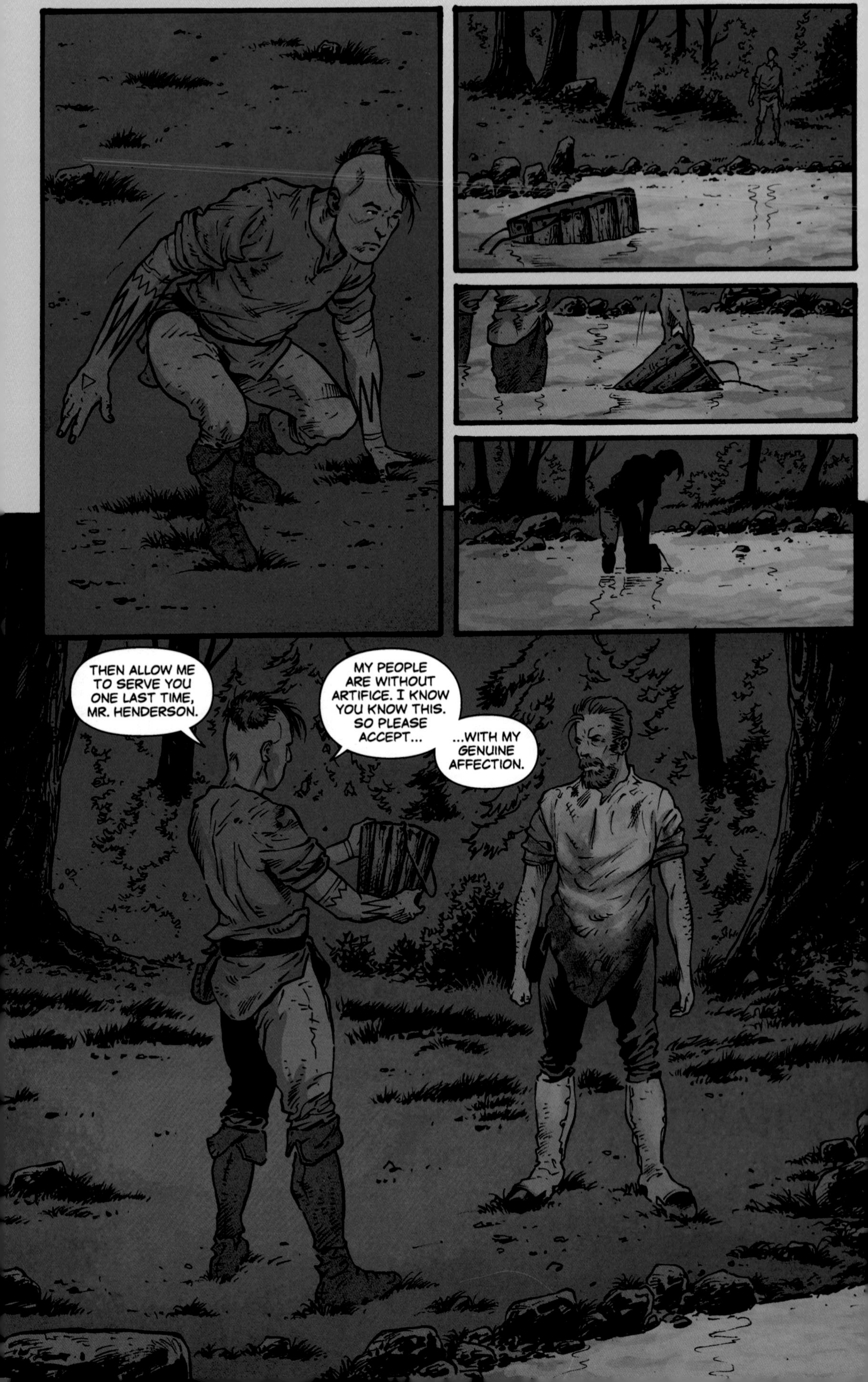

THEN ALLOW ME TO SERVE YOU ONE LAST TIME, MR. HENDERSON.
MY PEOPLE ARE WITHOUT ARTIFICE. I KNOW YOU KNOW THIS. SO PLEASE ACCEPT...
...WITH MY GENUINE AFFECTION.

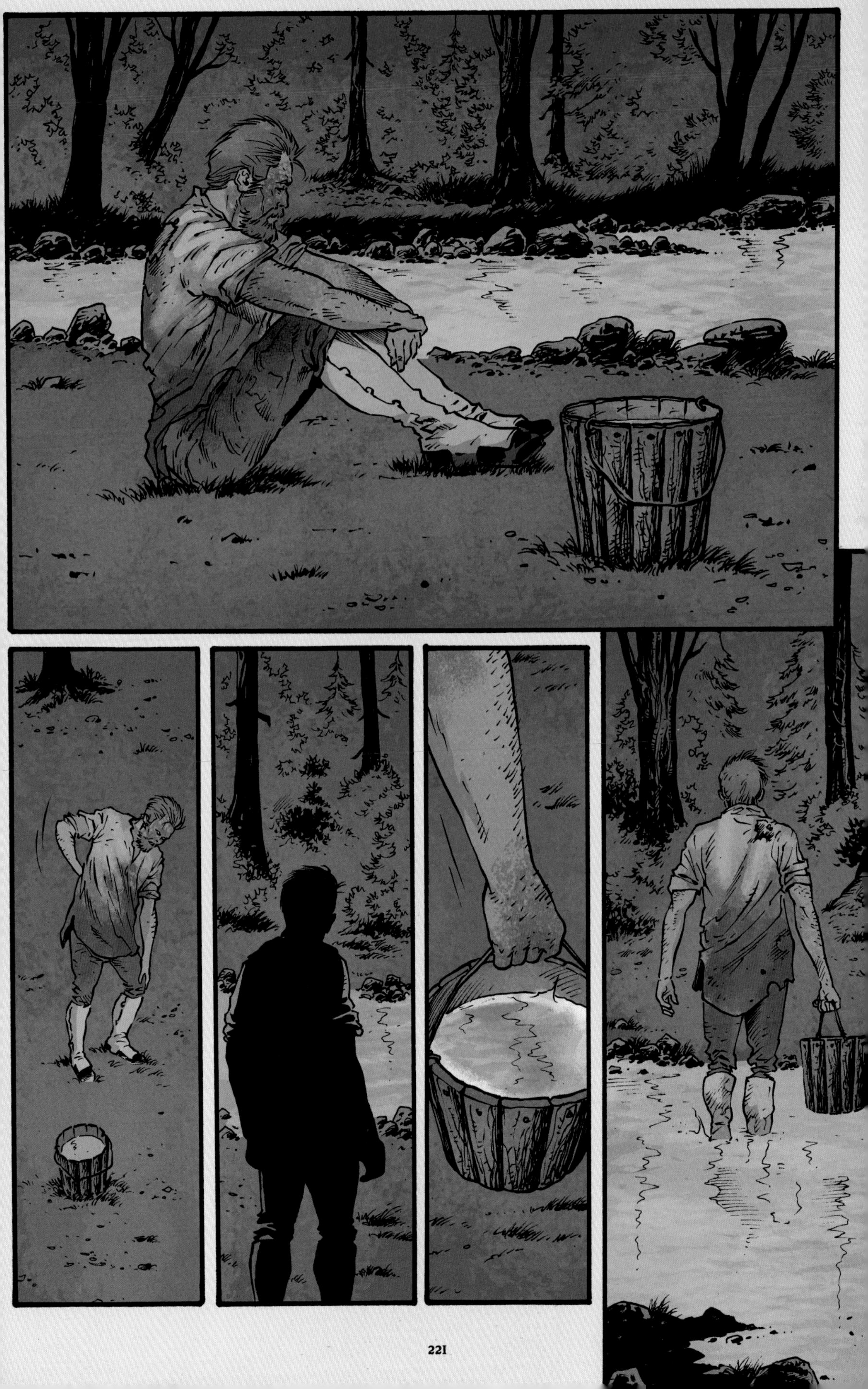

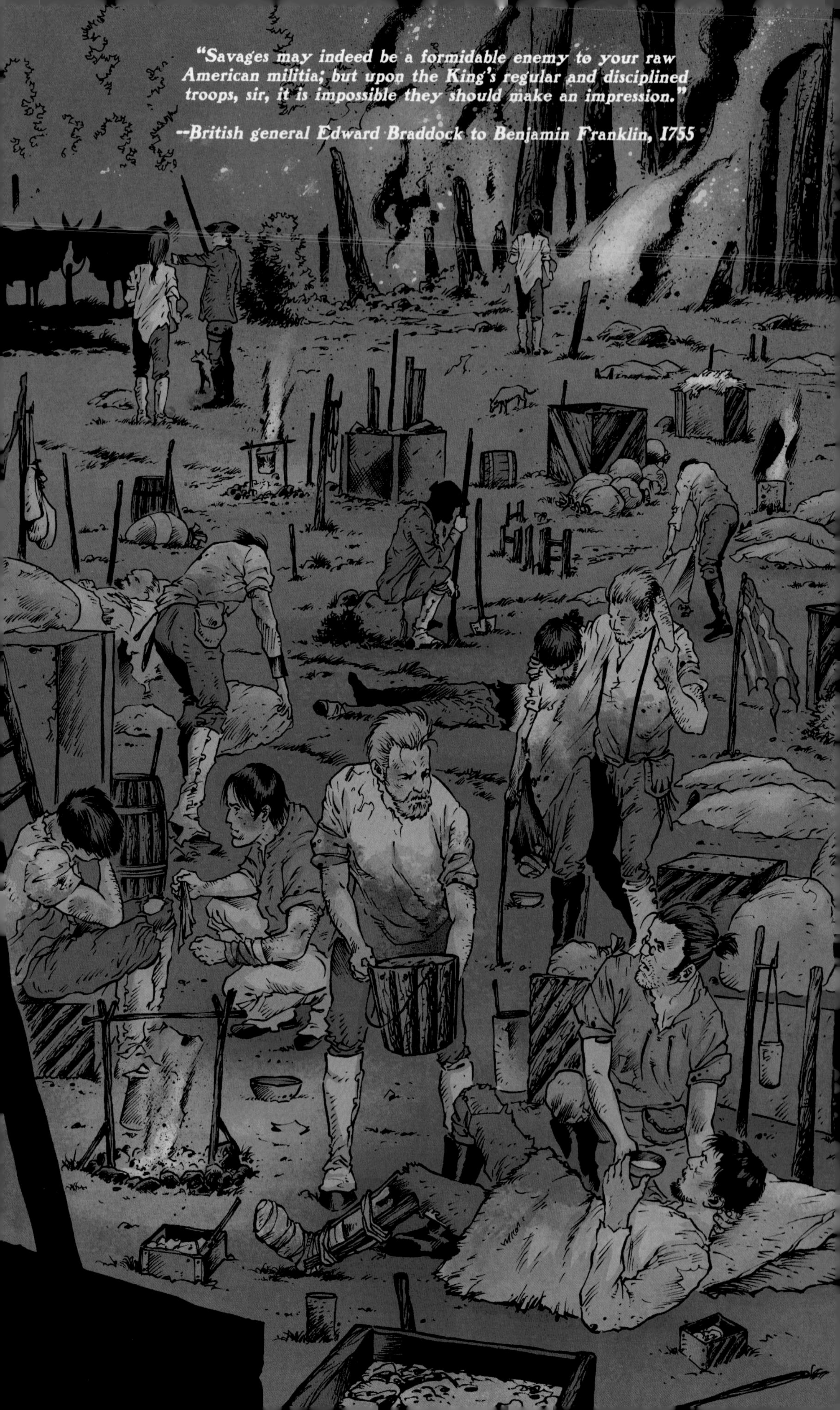
"Savages may indeed be a formidable enemy to your raw American militia; but upon the King's regular and disciplined troops, sir, it is impossible they should make an impression."
--British general Edward Braddock to Benjamin Franklin, 1755

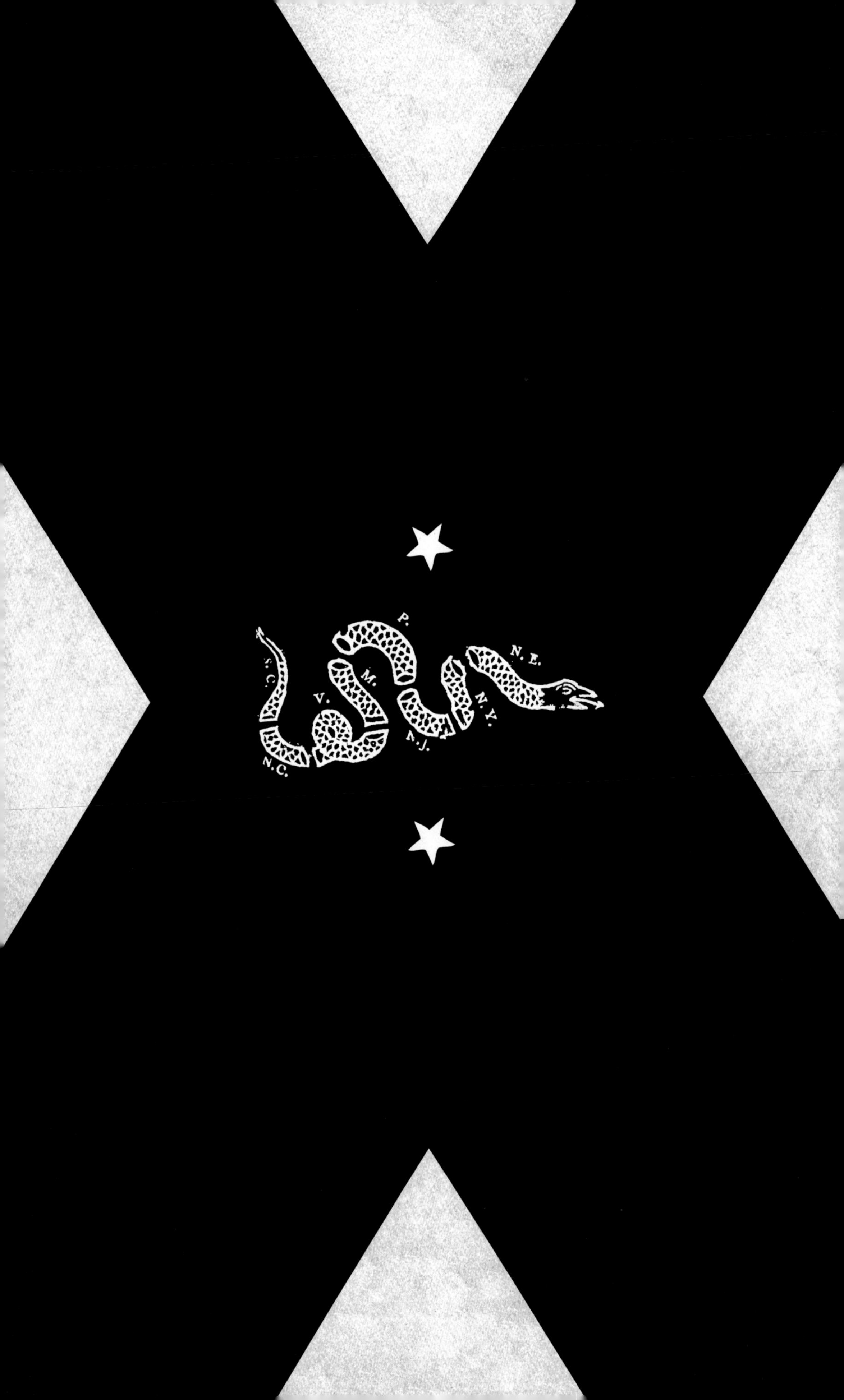
S.C.
N.C.
V.
M.
P.
N.J.
N.Y.
N.E.

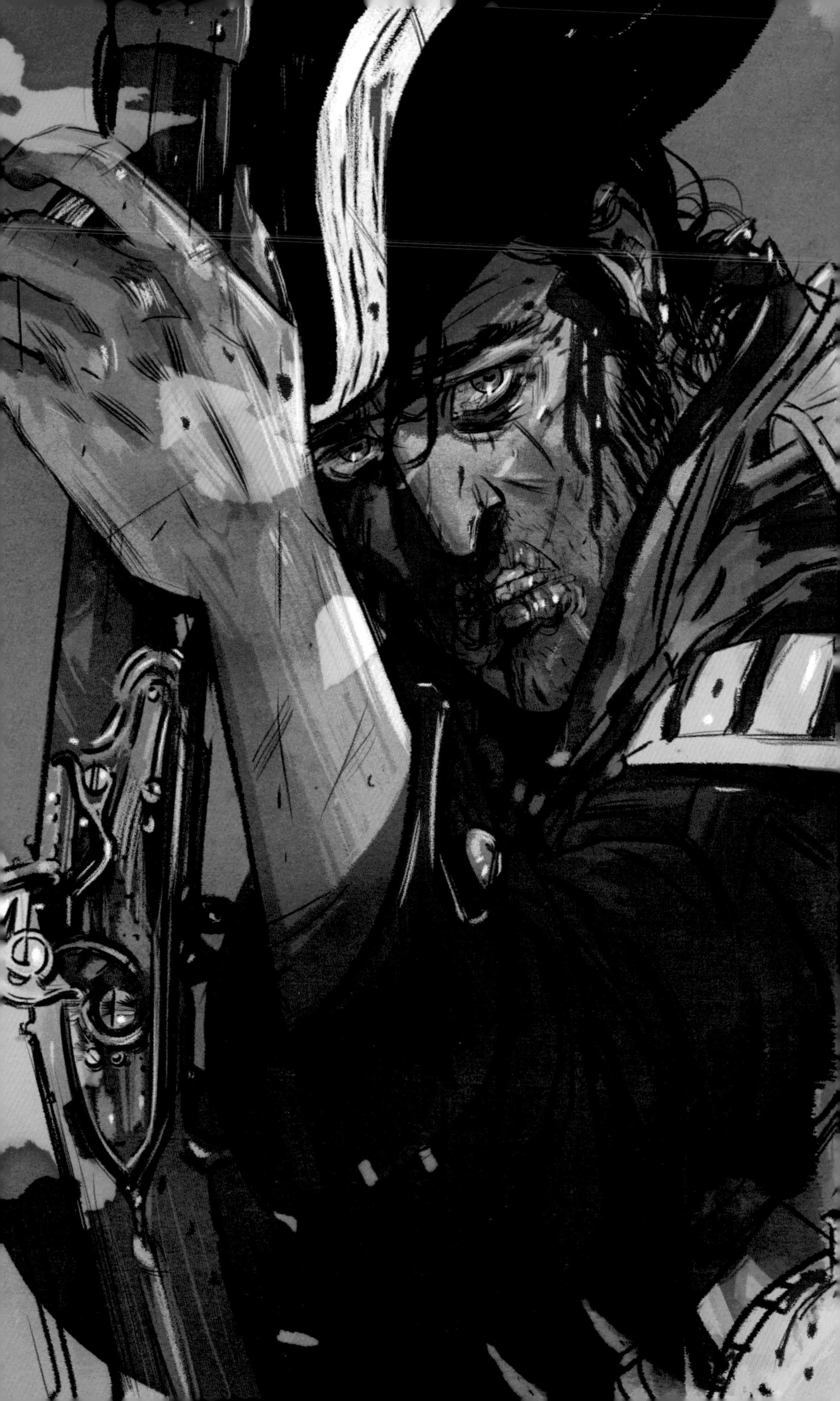

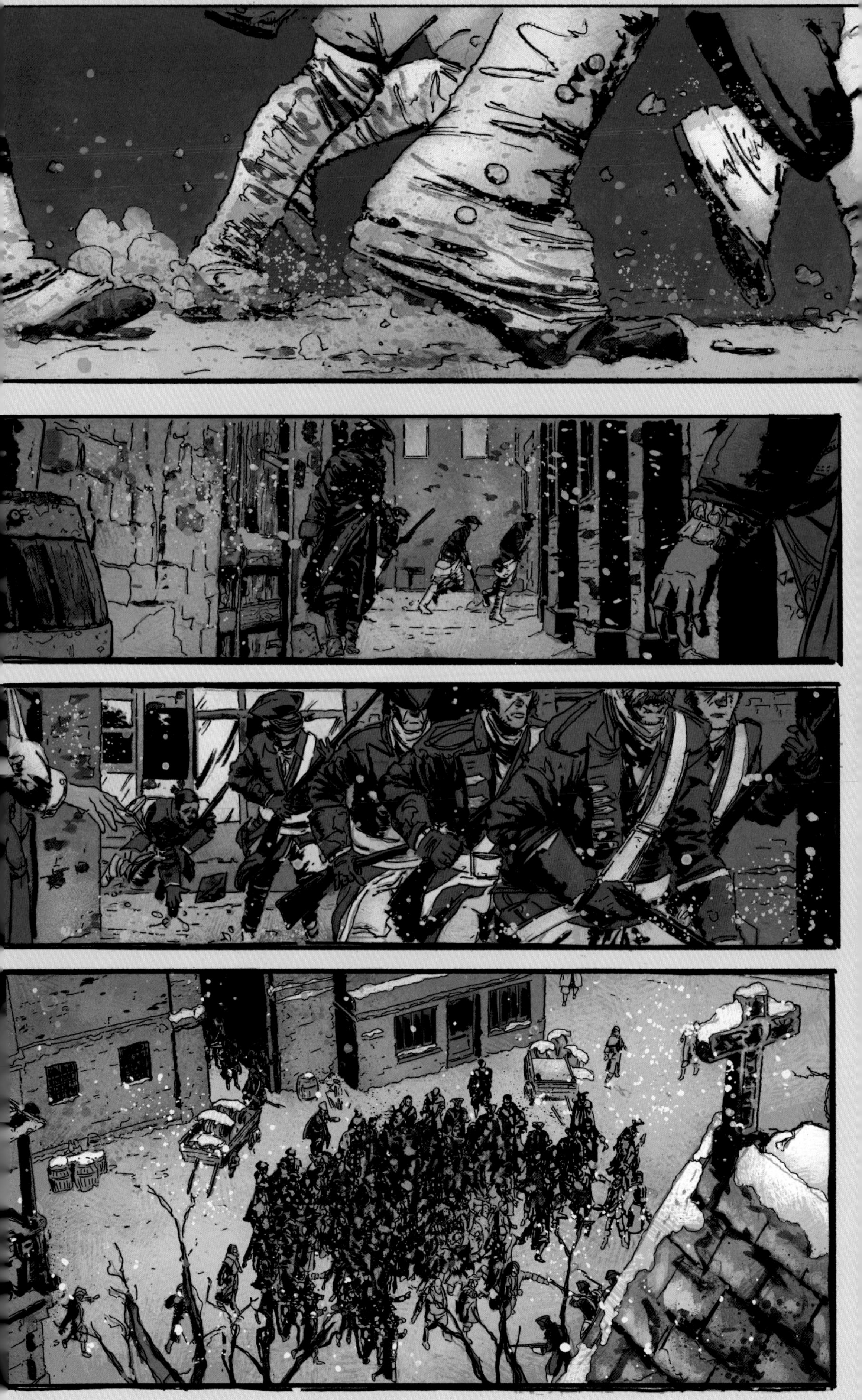

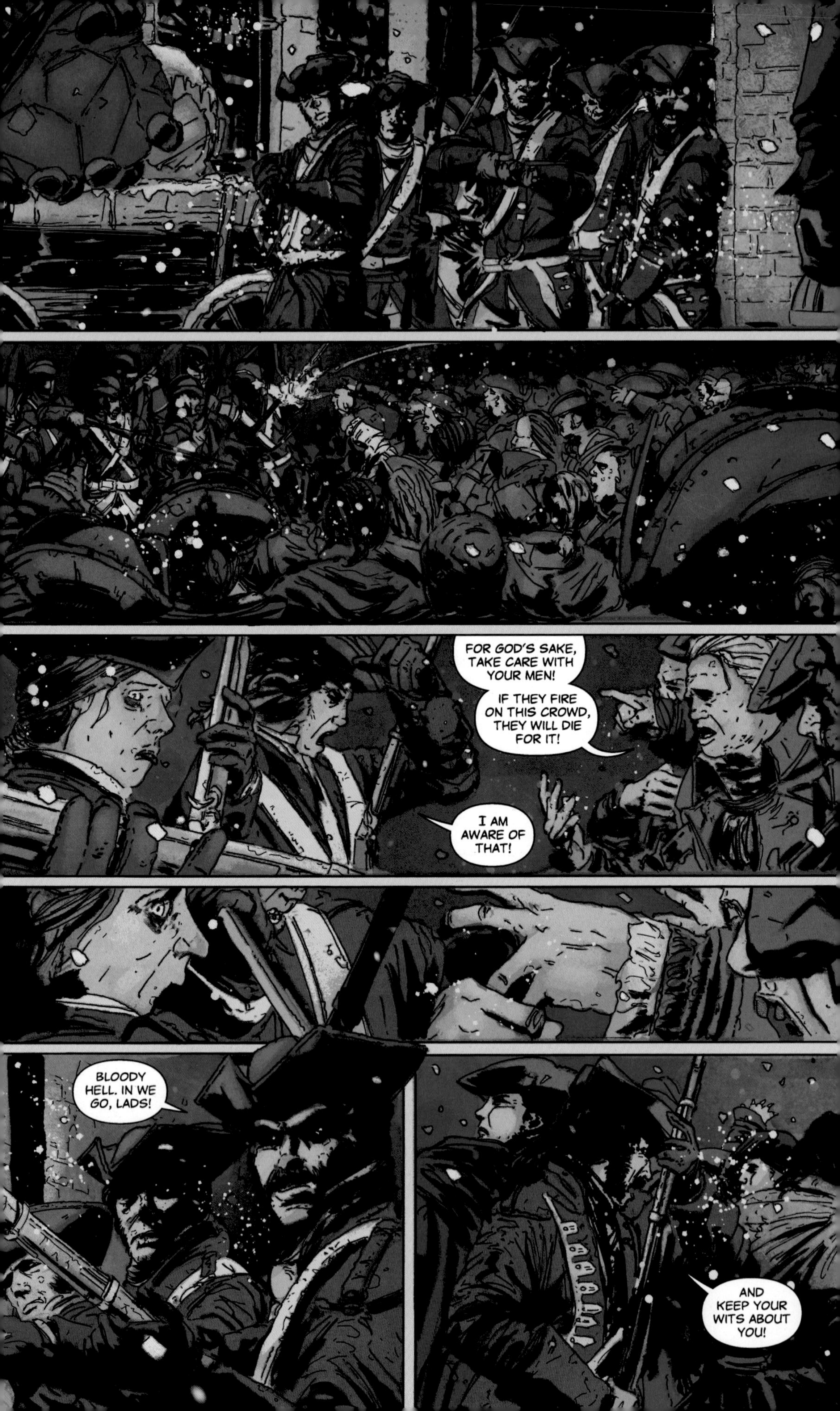
FOR GOD'S SAKE, TAKE CARE WITH YOUR MEN!
IF THEY FIRE ON THIS CROWD, THEY WILL DIE FOR IT!
I AM AWARE OF THAT!
BLOODY HELL. IN WE GO, LADS!
AND KEEP YOUR WITS ABOUT YOU!

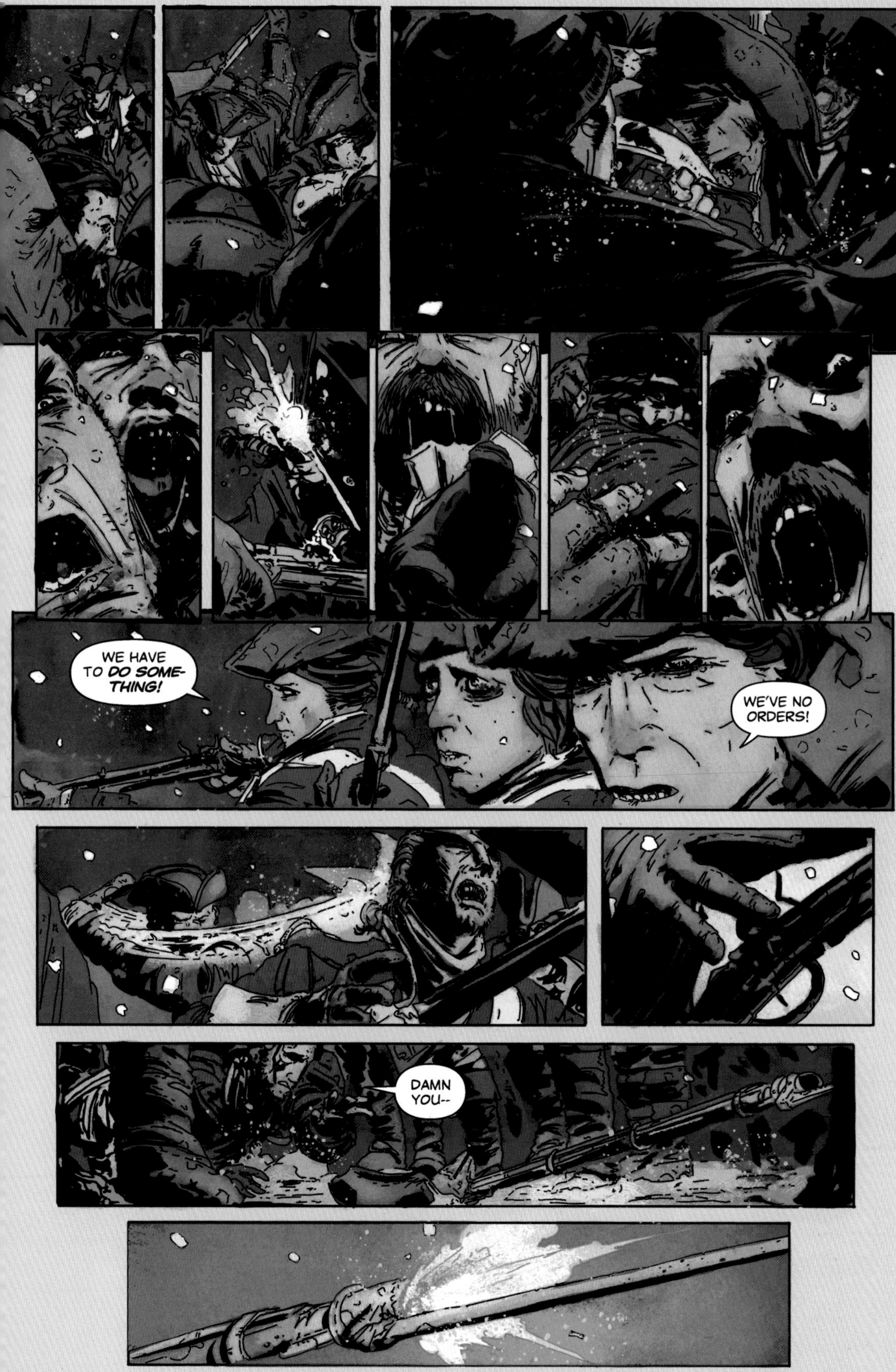
WE HAVE TO DO SOME-THING!
WE'VE NO ORDERS!
DAMN YOU--

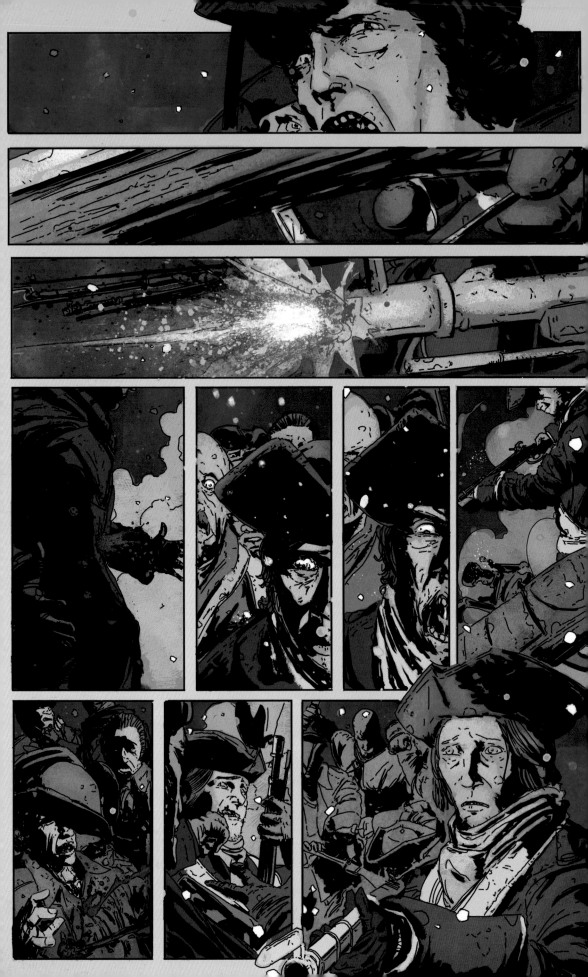

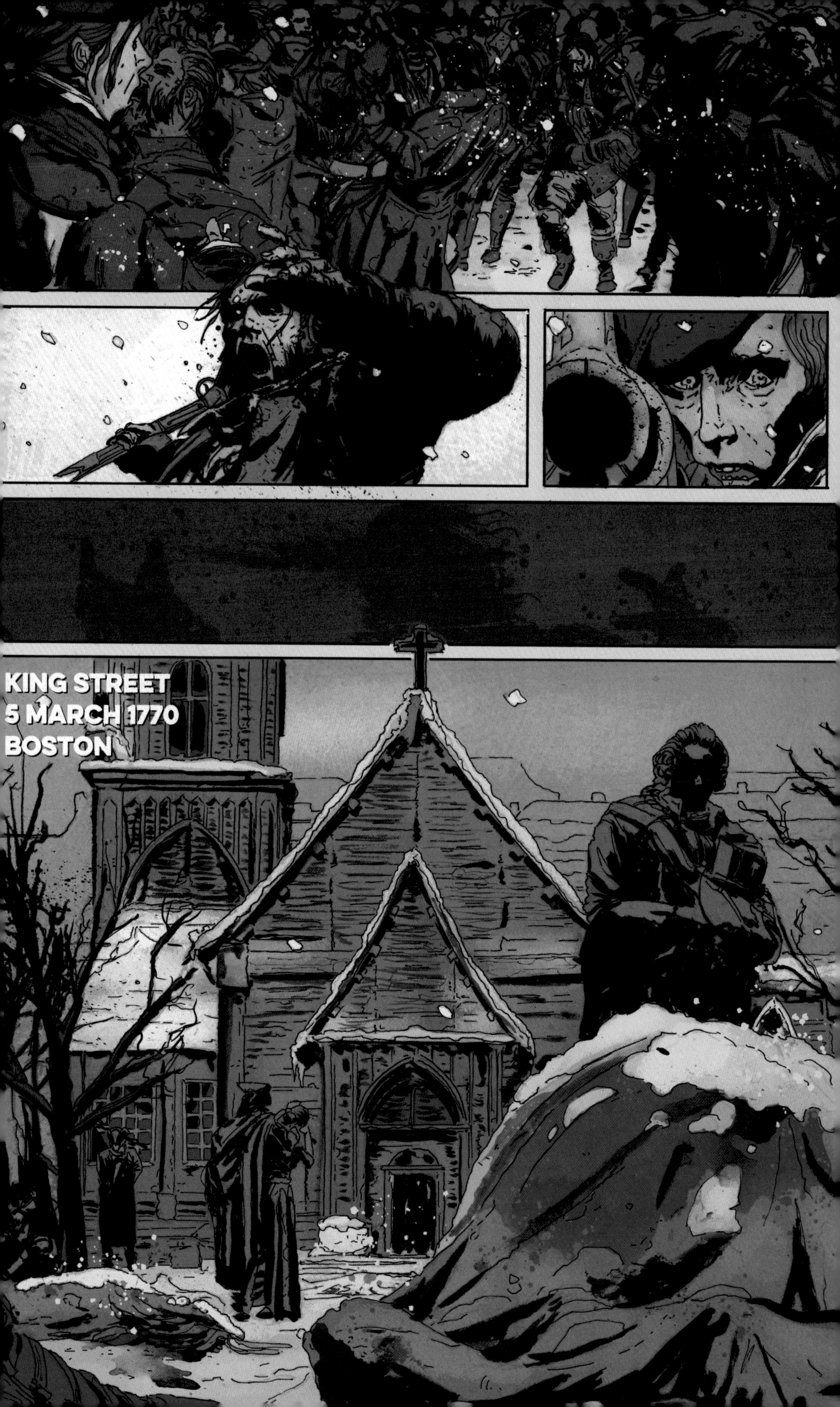
KING STREET
5 MARCH 1770
BOSTON

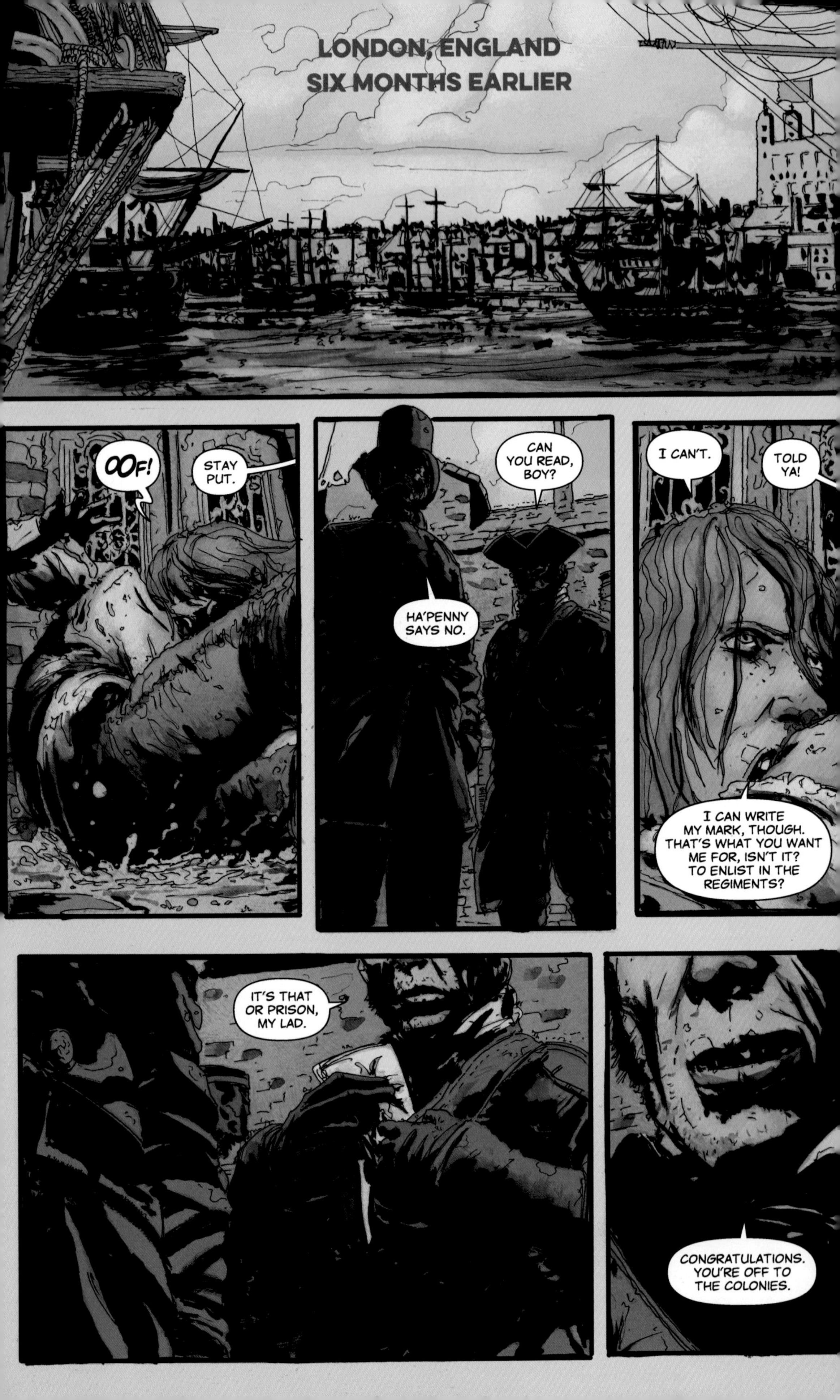
LONDON, ENGLAND
SIX MONTHS EARLIER
OOF!
STAY PUT.
CAN YOU READ, BOY?
HA'PENNY SAYS NO.
I CAN'T.
TOLD YA!
I CAN WRITE MY MARK, THOUGH. THAT'S WHAT YOU WANT ME FOR, ISN'T IT? TO ENLIST IN THE REGIMENTS?
IT'S THAT OR PRISON, MY LAD.
CONGRATULATIONS. YOU'RE OFF TO THE COLONIES.

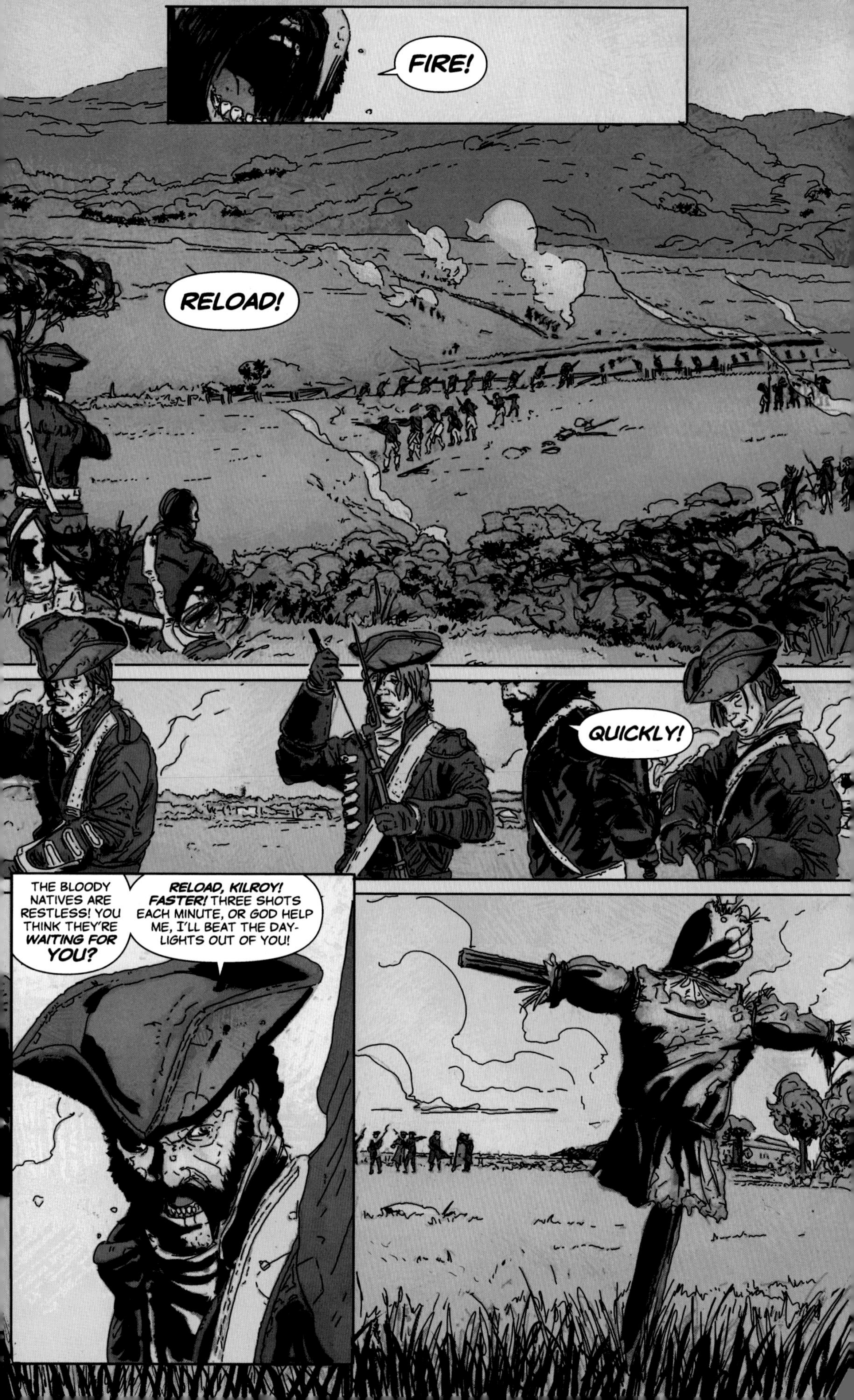
FIRE!
RELOAD!
QUICKLY!
THE BLOODY NATIVES ARE RESTLESS! YOU THINK THEY'RE WAITING FOR YOU?
RELOAD, KILROY! FASTER! THREE SHOTS EACH MINUTE, OR GOD HELP ME, I'LL BEAT THE DAYLIGHTS OUT OF YOU!

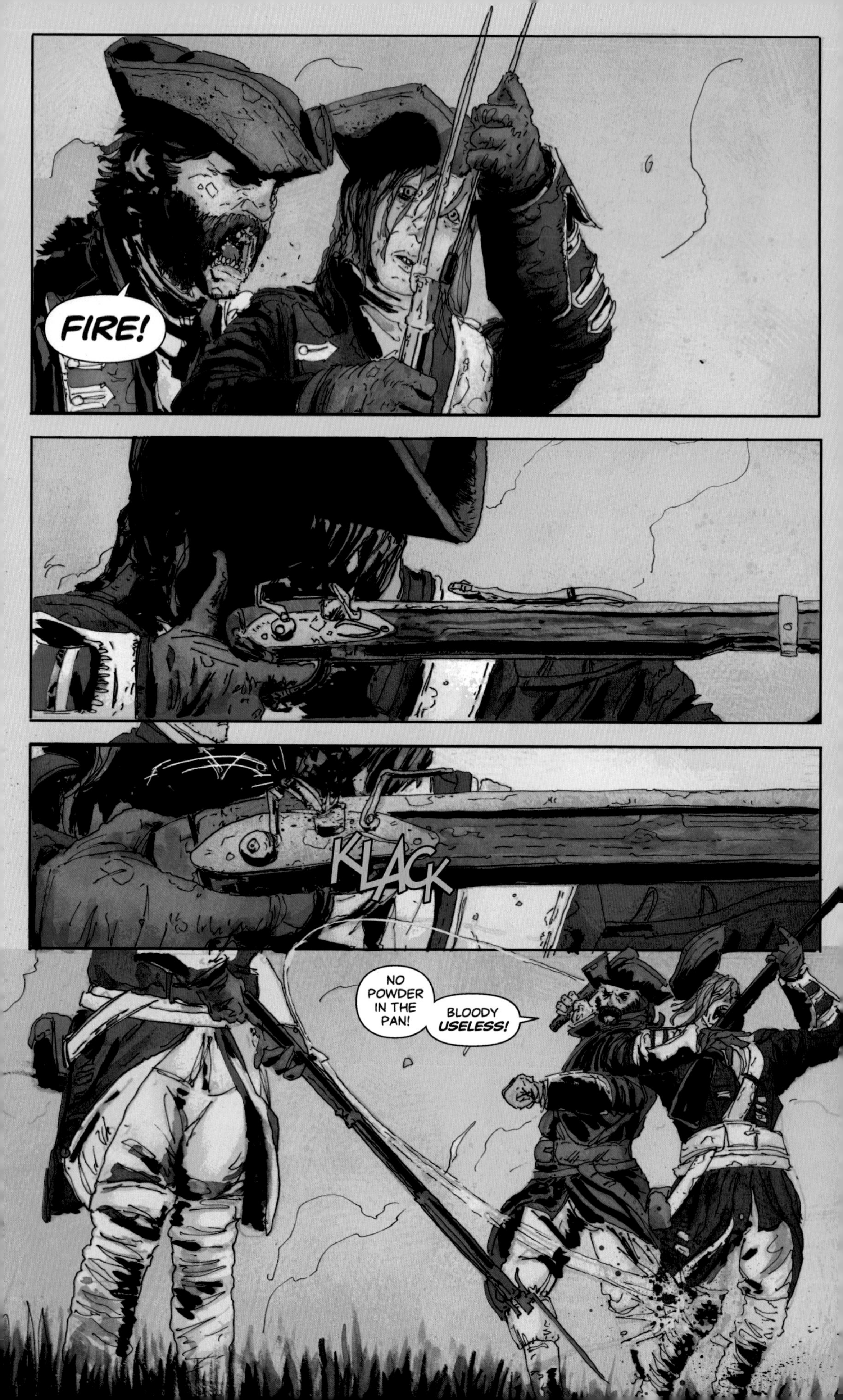
FIRE!
KLACK
NO POWDER IN THE PAN!
BLOODY USELESS!

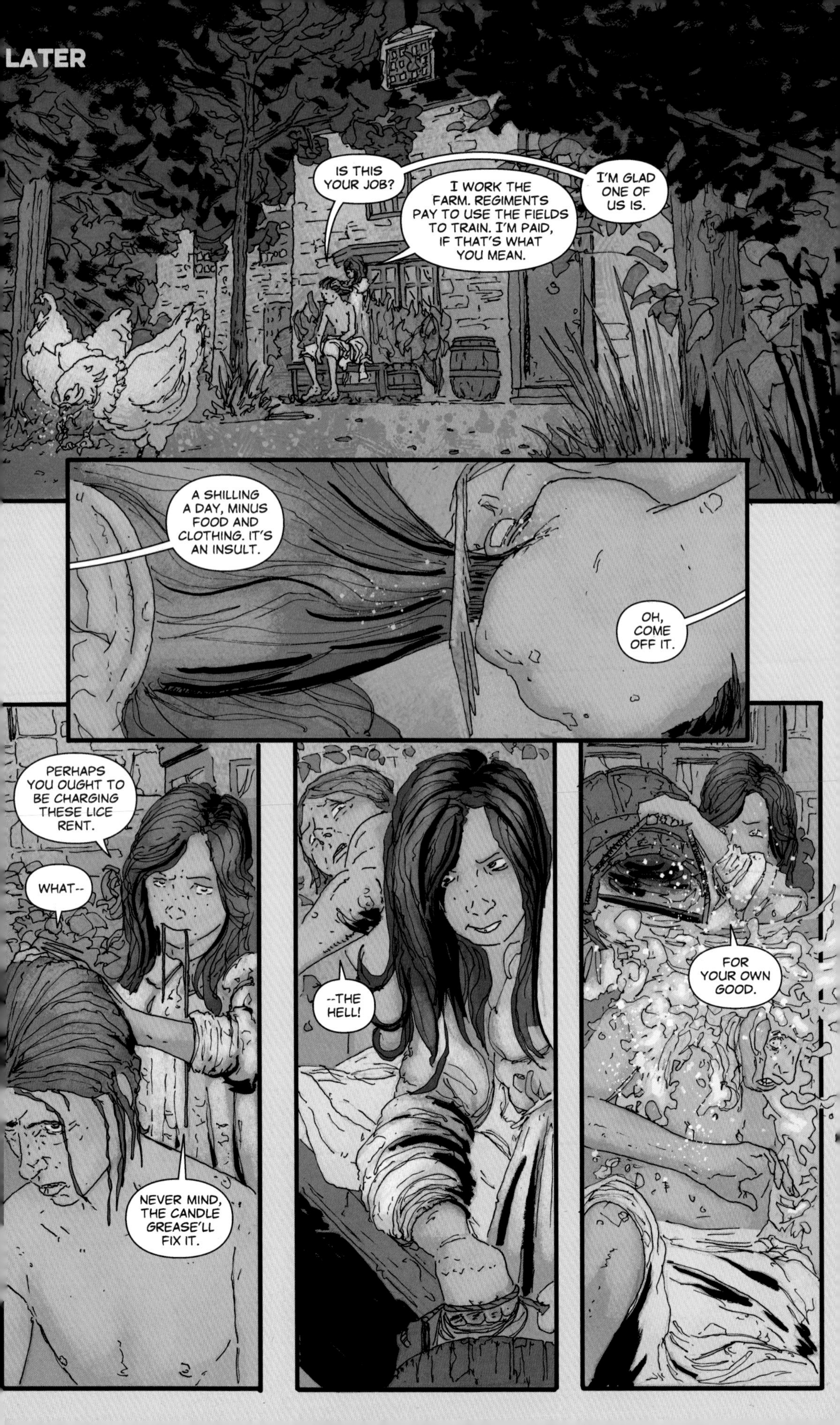
LATER
IS THIS YOUR JOB?
I WORK THE FARM. REGIMENTS PAY TO USE THE FIELDS TO TRAIN. I'M PAID, IF THAT'S WHAT YOU MEAN.
I'M GLAD ONE OF US IS.
A SHILLING A DAY, MINUS FOOD AND CLOTHING. IT'S AN INSULT.
OH, COME OFF IT.
PERHAPS YOU OUGHT TO BE CHARGING THESE LICE RENT.
WHAT--
NEVER MIND, THE CANDLE GREASE'LL FIX IT.
--THE HELL!
FOR YOUR OWN GOOD.

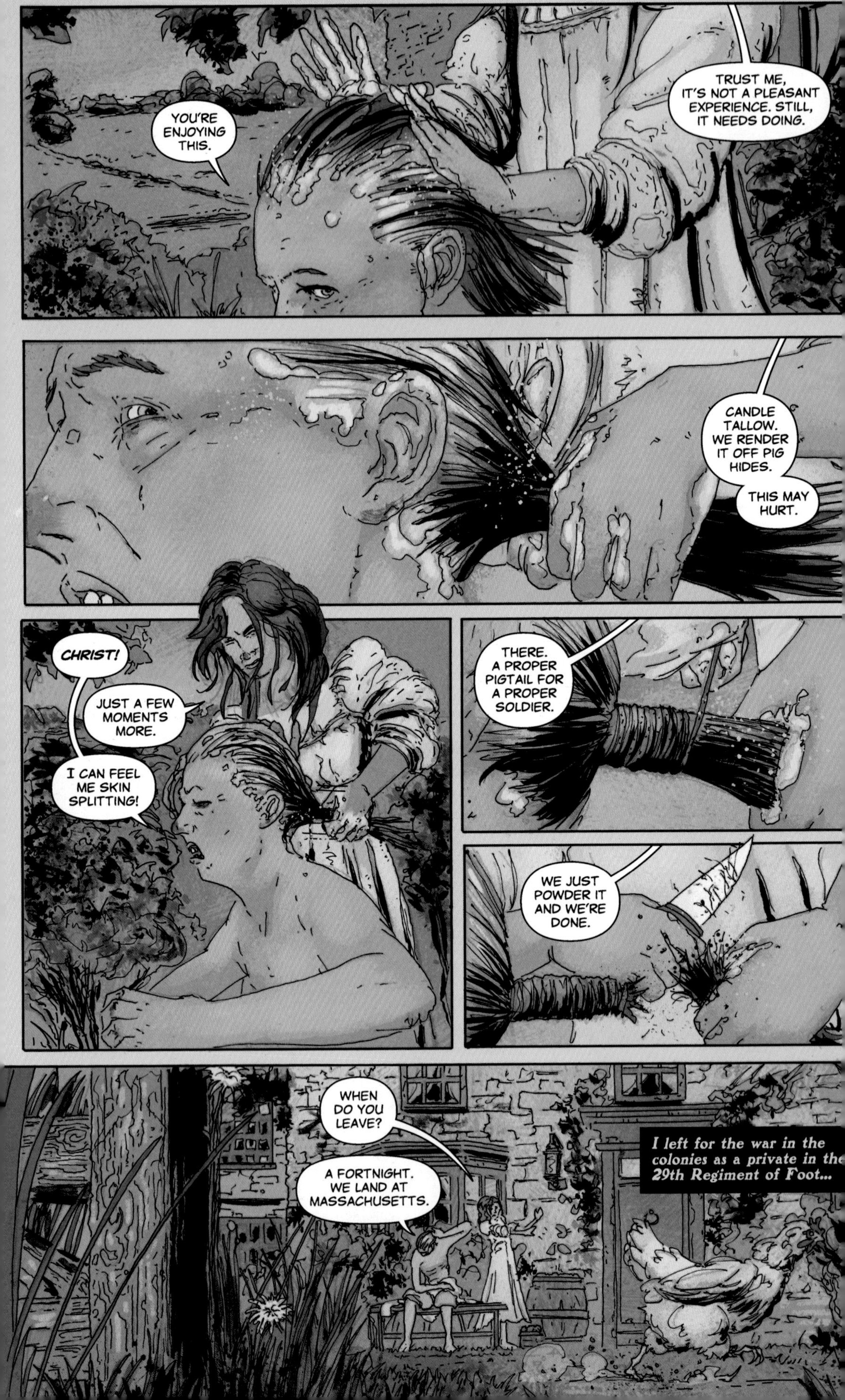
YOU'RE ENJOYING THIS.
TRUST ME, IT'S NOT A PLEASANT EXPERIENCE. STILL, IT NEEDS DOING.
CANDLE TALLOW. WE RENDER IT OFF PIG HIDES.
THIS MAY HURT.
CHRIST!
JUST A FEW MOMENTS MORE.
I CAN FEEL ME SKIN SPLITTING!
THERE. A PROPER PIGTAIL FOR A PROPER SOLDIER.
WE JUST POWDER IT AND WE'RE DONE.
WHEN DO YOU LEAVE?
A FORTNIGHT. WE LAND AT MASSACHUSETTS.
I left for the war in the colonies as a private in the 29th Regiment of Foot...

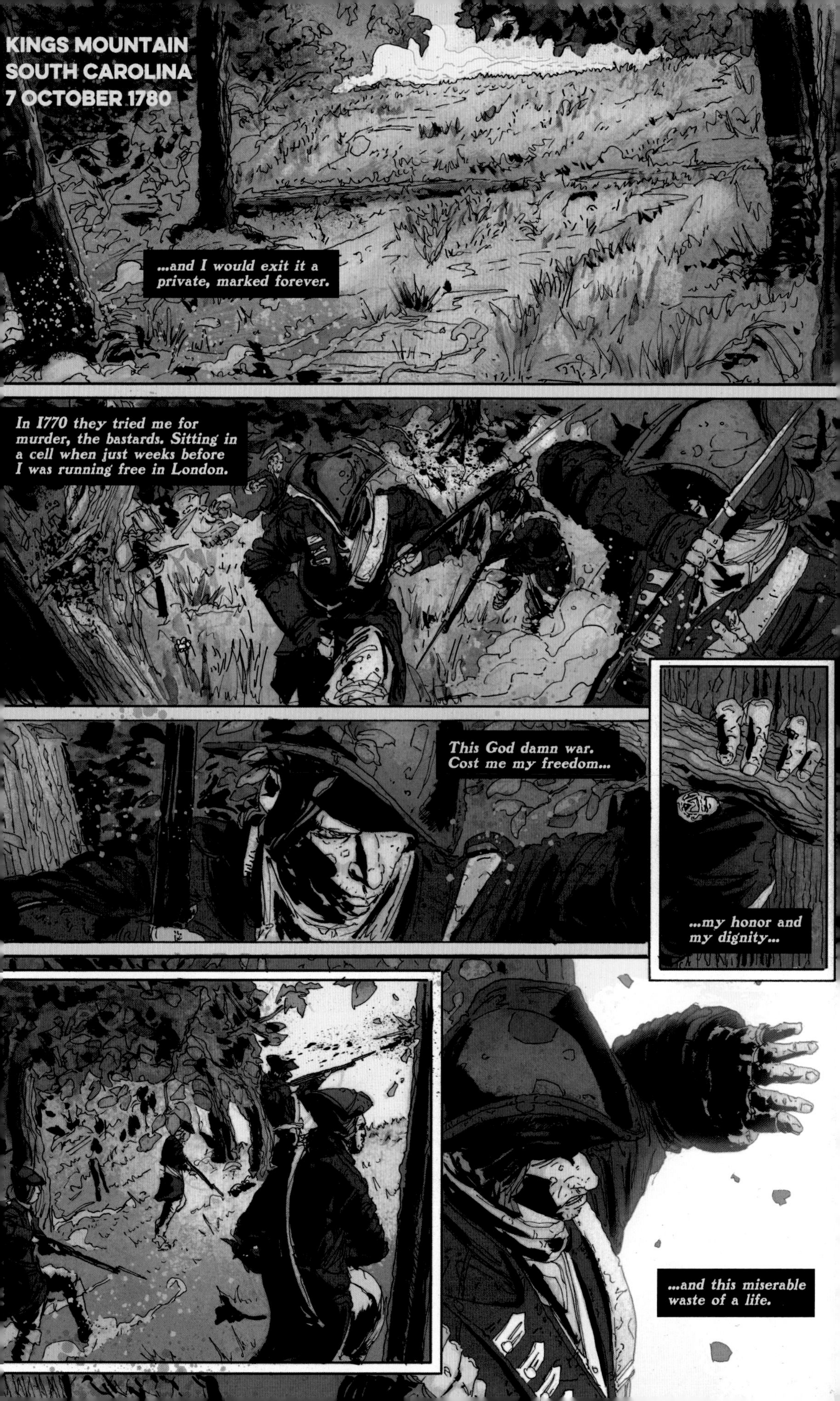
KINGS MOUNTAIN
SOUTH CAROLINA
7 OCTOBER 1780
...and I would exit it a private, marked forever.
In 1770 they tried me for murder, the bastards. Sitting in a cell when just weeks before I was running free in London.
This God damn war. Cost me my freedom...
...my honor and my dignity...
...and this miserable waste of a life.

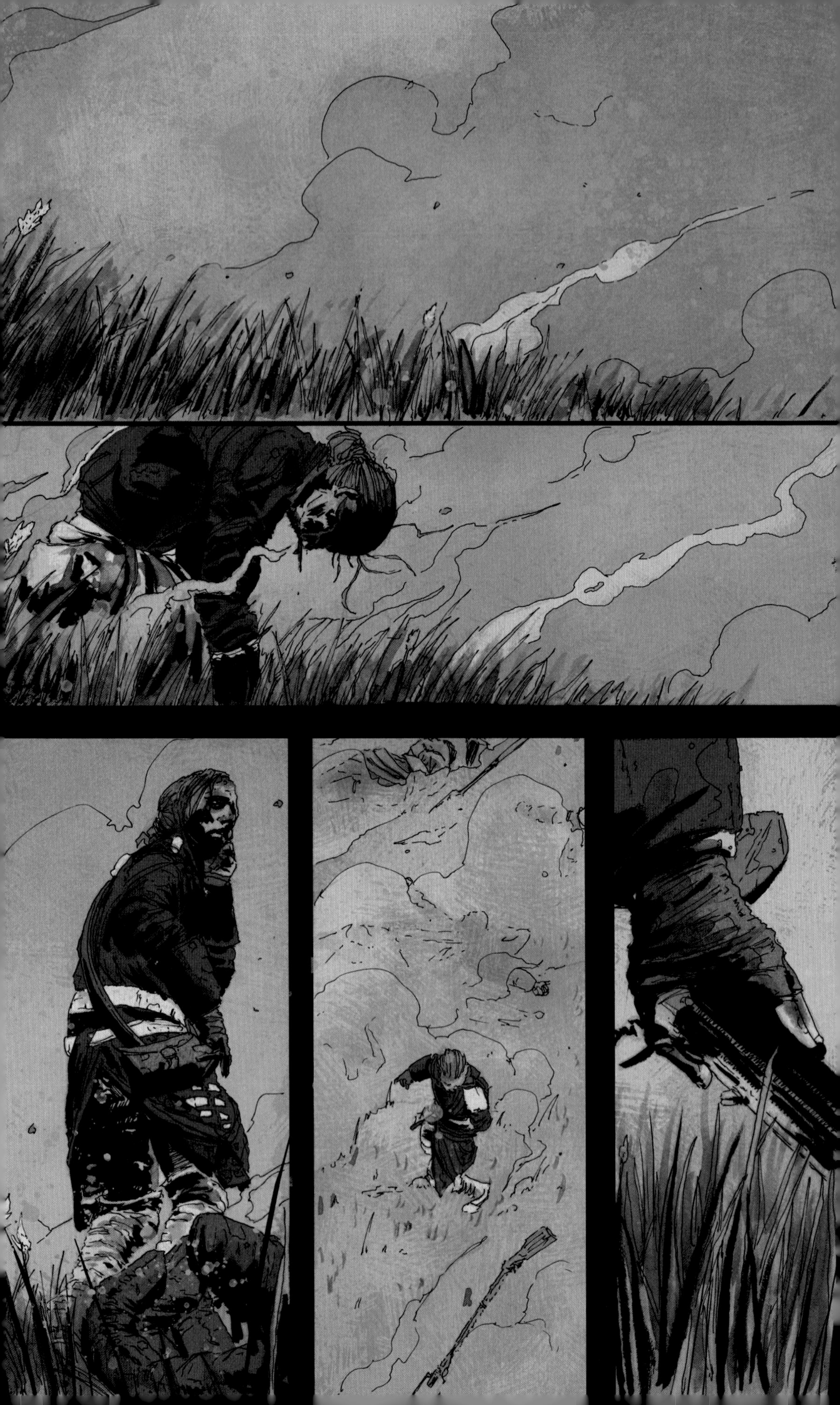

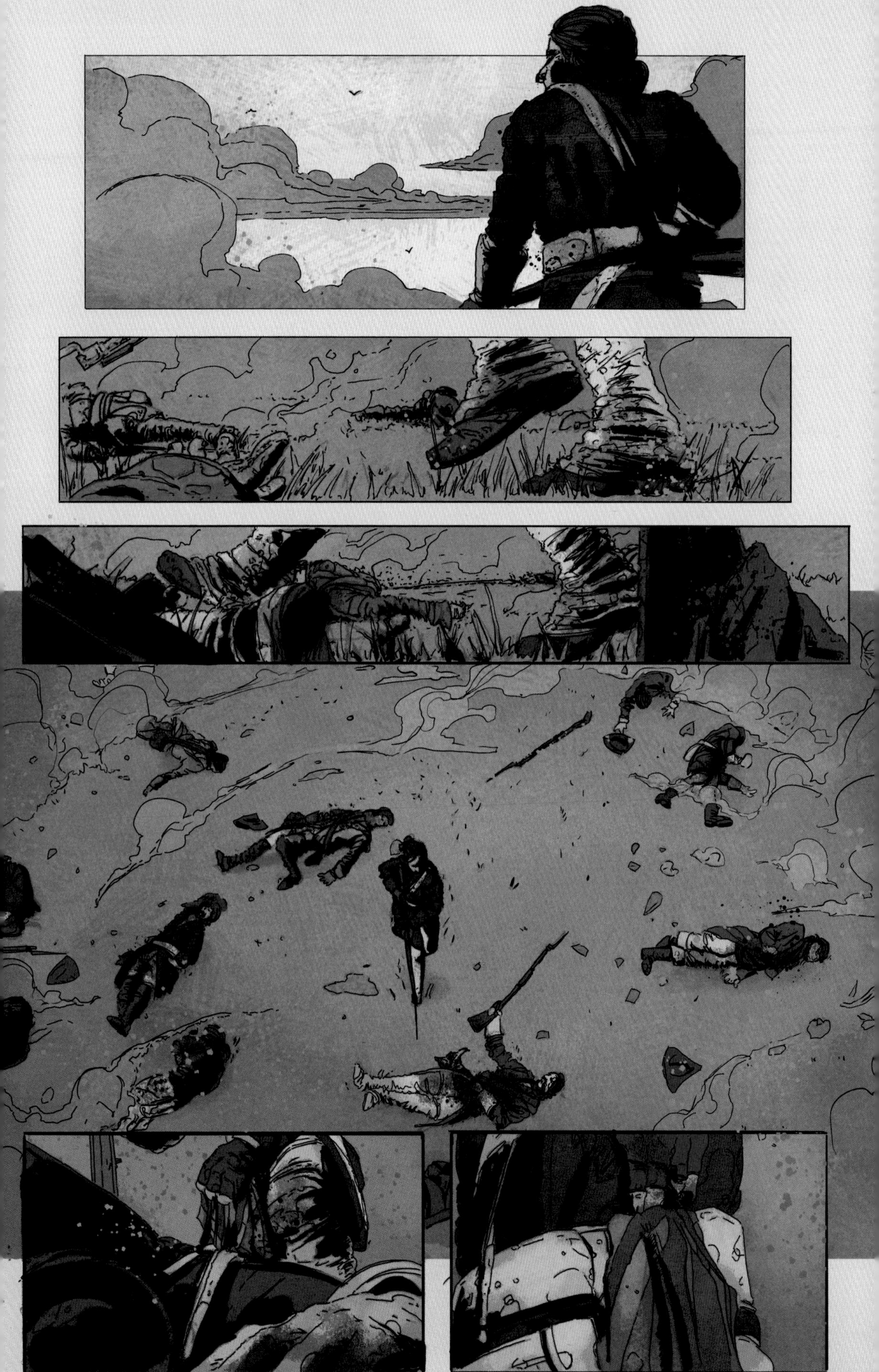

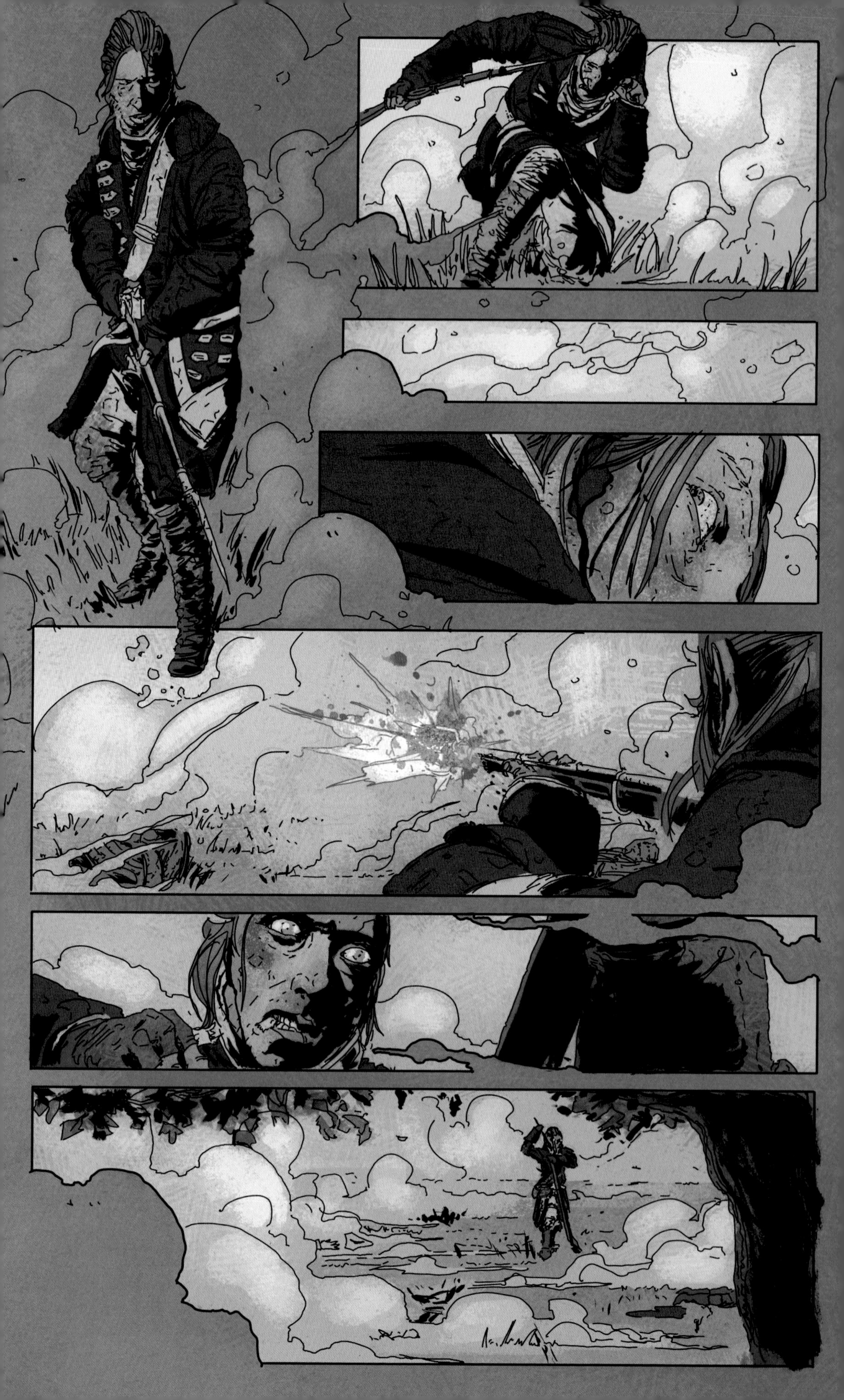

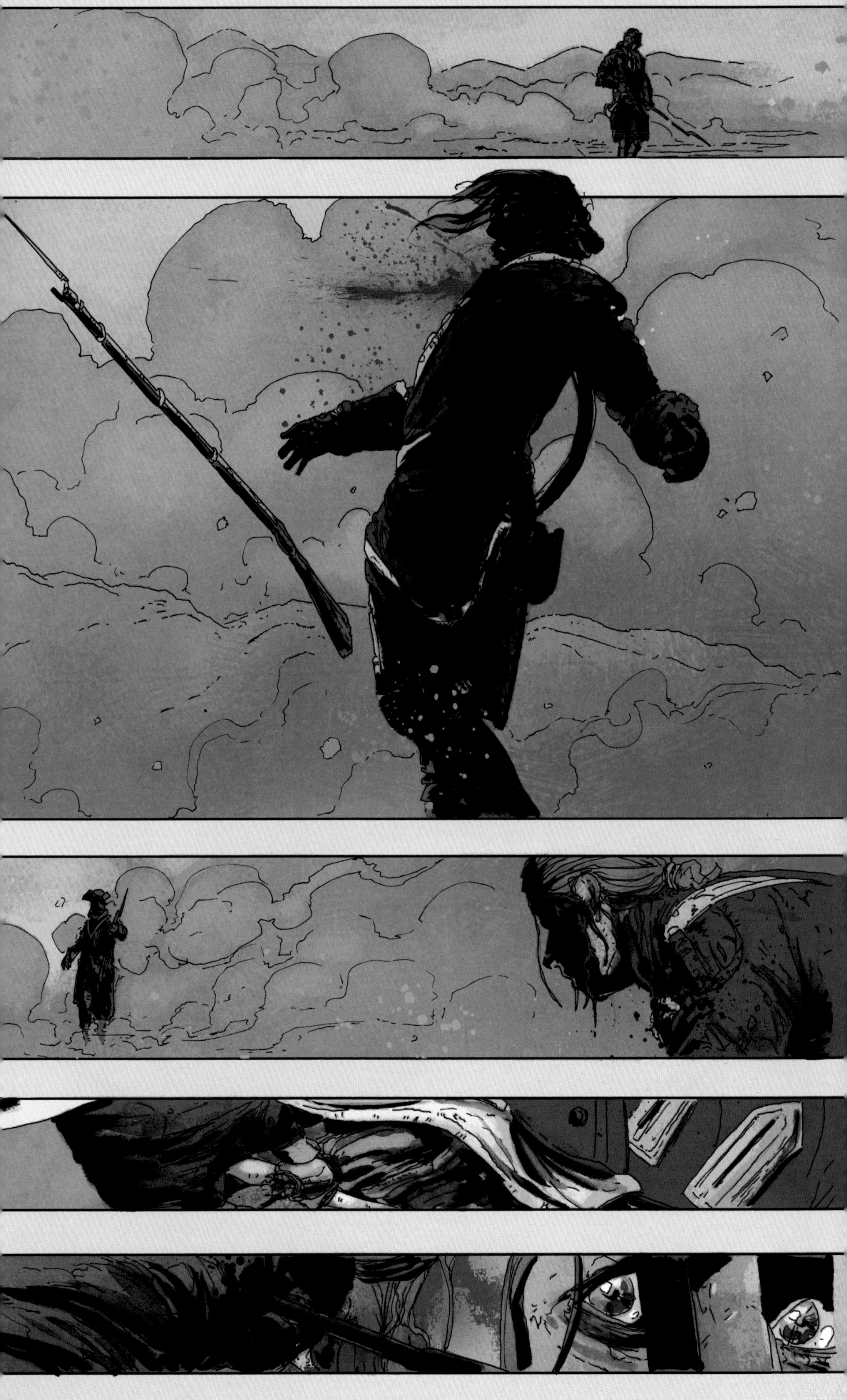

Rule, Britannia.
Britannia, rule the waves.

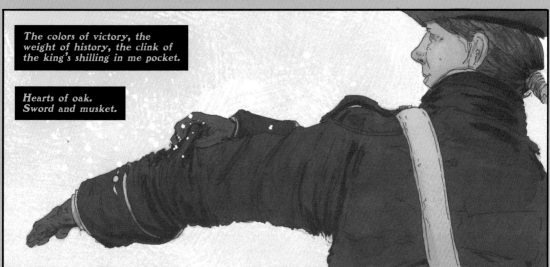

The colors of victory, the weight of history, the clink of the king's shilling in me pocket.

Hearts of oak.
Sword and musket.

I felt terrible proud.

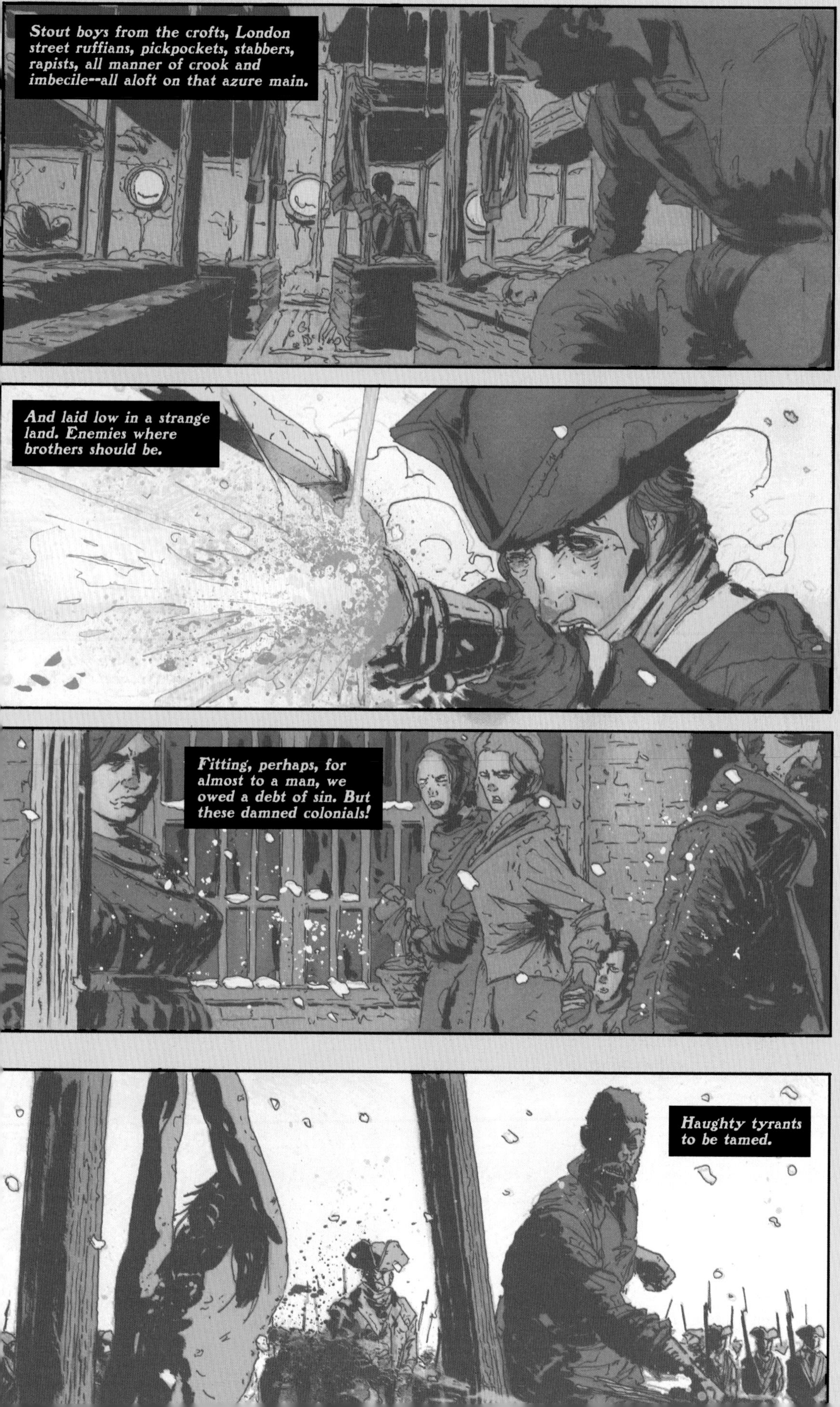
Stout boys from the crofts, London street ruffians, pickpockets, stabbers, rapists, all manner of crook and imbecile--all aloft on that azure main.
And laid low in a strange land. Enemies where brothers should be.
Fitting, perhaps, for almost to a man, we owed a debt of sin. But these damned colonials!
Haughty tyrants to be tamed.

Victory. History.
The same damn shilling.
Rule, Britannia.

Such a fine land, fertile and warm,
the envy of all empires. A limitless
land. I should know--I marched it.

Britons never
will be slaves.

Rule, Britannia.

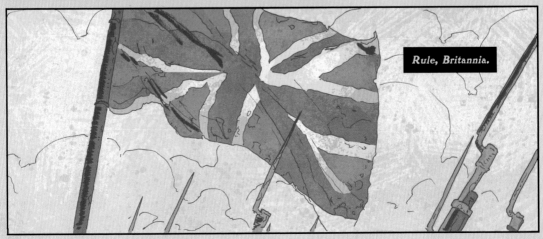

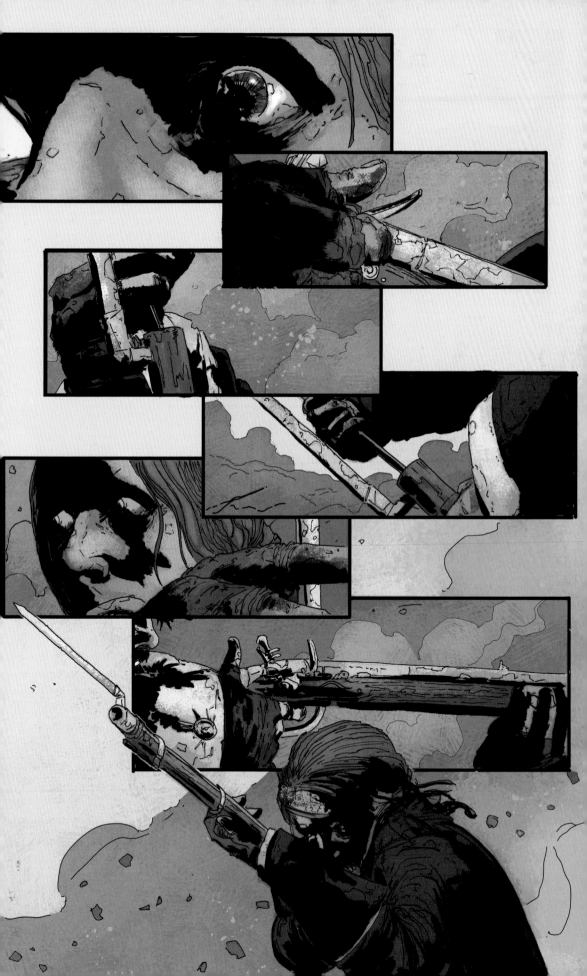

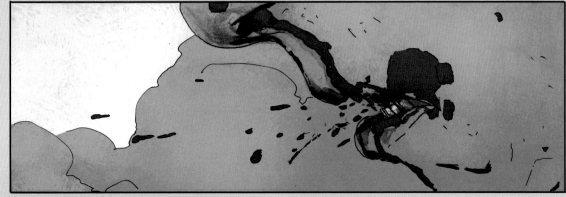

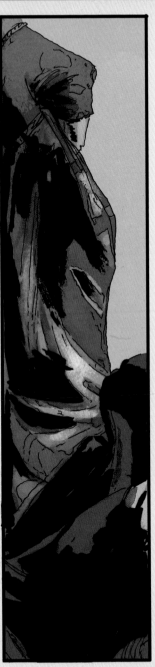

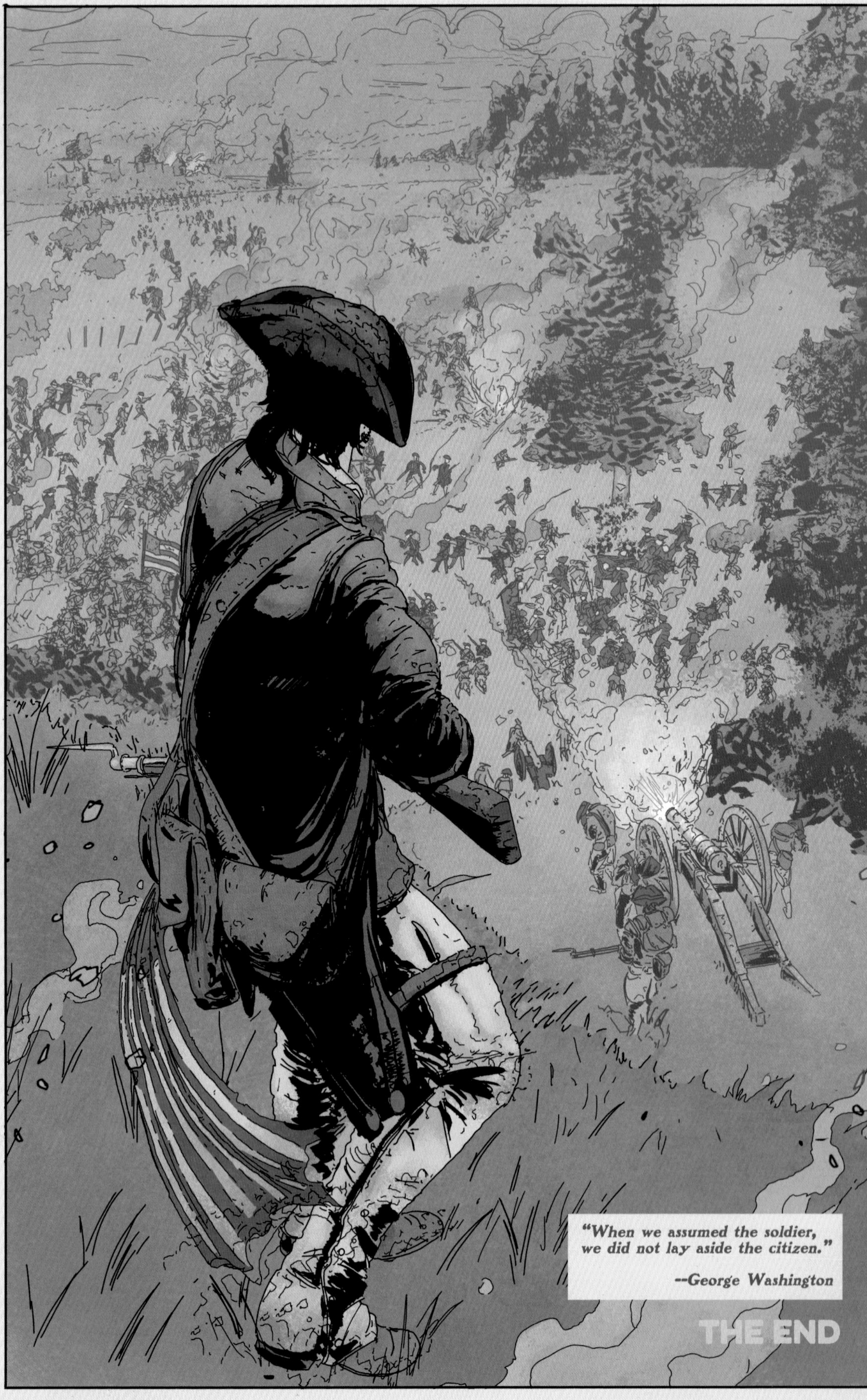
"When we assumed the soldier,
we did not lay aside the citizen."
--George Washington
THE END

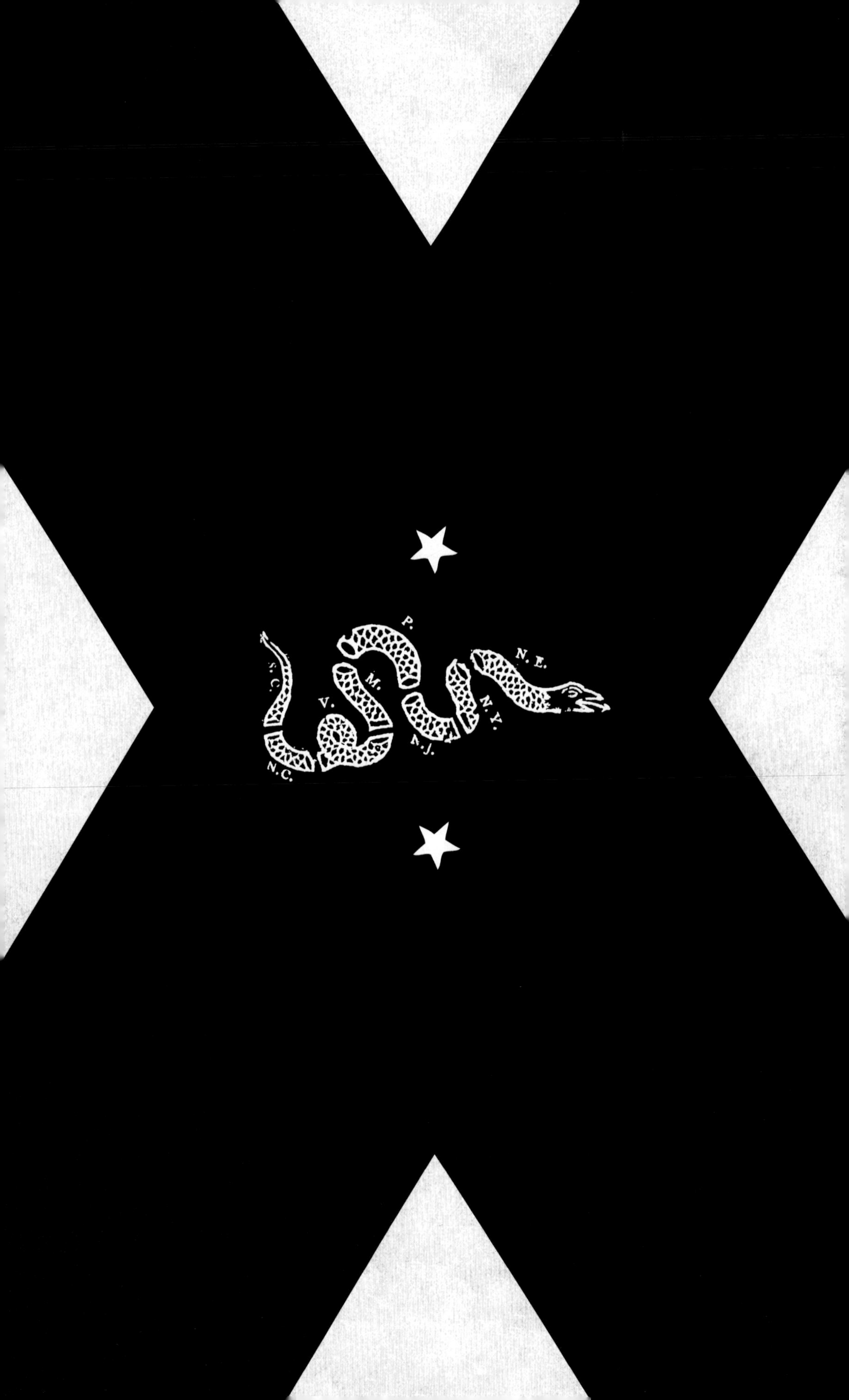
S.C.
N.C.
V.
M.
P.
N.J.
N.Y.
N.E.

THE MAKING OF REBELS

BY BRIAN WOOD

I describe myself as a patriot, and whenever I do I can sense raised eyebrows and skeptical looks, which I totally understand. I'm pretty open about being a lefty politically, even an outright socialist when it comes to certain human issues. I'm also the guy that created and wrote *DMZ*, a scathing seventy-two-issue takedown of modern American war and media. I suspect when I announced *Rebels*, a big chunk of my potential audience believed it was going to be some sort of hatchet job on our beloved shared history and identity. Not just *suspect*—I know this was the case, because I started getting e-mails about it. But nothing could be further from the truth.

Since 9/11, and I think to a lesser degree the Reagan years, there's been an association that comes with words like *patriotism* and some of the uglier policies our culture has brought forth. I know I developed a reflex after this war on terror started, an instinctual rejection of anything that smacked of "pro-America," the whole "with us or against us" mentality. It made being a proud American an extreme partisan position. It meant lining yourself up with horrible people and abusive ideas. And it's that ugly side of American culture that *DMZ* took a blowtorch to.

But I knew that didn't have to be the case, and it bothered me. It made me angry. Because I love this country's history; I love the mythology, the folktales, the heroes and the language and the imagery. I love the idea of a country founded on the concept of laws. Not royal lineage, or military might, or racial identity, or religious ideology. Okay, sure, there were some bum laws in there, like the Three-Fifths Compromise, but we fixed them. We, as Americans, improved ourselves in that respect, and still strive to improve, to live up to the promise this country was founded on. That's something to be proud of, and I was angry that I felt robbed of the ability to openly express that and still be me, thanks to the post-9/11 climate.

Rebels is, in part, my reclaiming of this aspect of my identity, for me and for anyone else like me. It doesn't matter that politicians on all sides use this history and twist it around to sell what they're selling, to demonize the other, to justify all sorts of lies and bullshit and anger and bigotry. I'm writing *Rebels* with honesty and pride and

I can metaphorically (and even literally) wave the flag and celebrate our history and believe in common-sense gun ownership and support my veteran friends and buy American whenever possible and still be the guy who wrote *DMZ* and *Channel Zero* and vote Green if I want and believe in universal health care and wear my Bernie Sanders pin (a Vermonter!) and not be a hypocrite but rather a run-of-the-mill, complex human being with opinions and beliefs, like anyone else.

I'm really resisting wrapping up this essay with some clichéd line like "and that's what makes America great!" because in all honesty, America as it is today isn't all great. It's got a lot of flaws, and I think that's part of the reason the history of our independence and the whole Spirit of '76 thing has such mass appeal—it reminds us of that promise I just mentioned. Of that ideal to keep striving to reach, and the terrible struggle men, women, and even children endured to create a brand-new kind of nation where such a thing was possible.

Some literal flag-waving at Washington's HQ, Valley Forge.

SKETCHBOOK

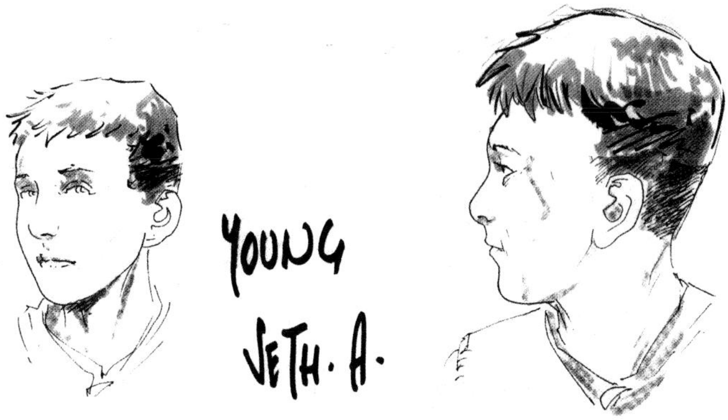
YOUNG
SETH. A.

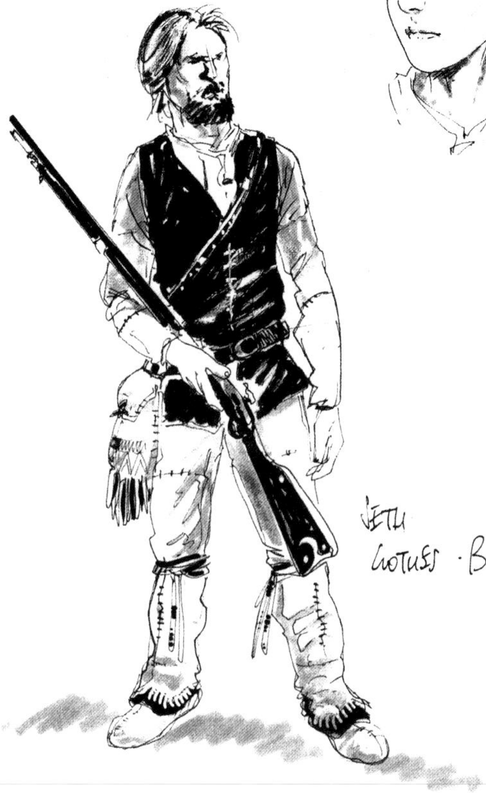
SETH
CLOTHES .B.

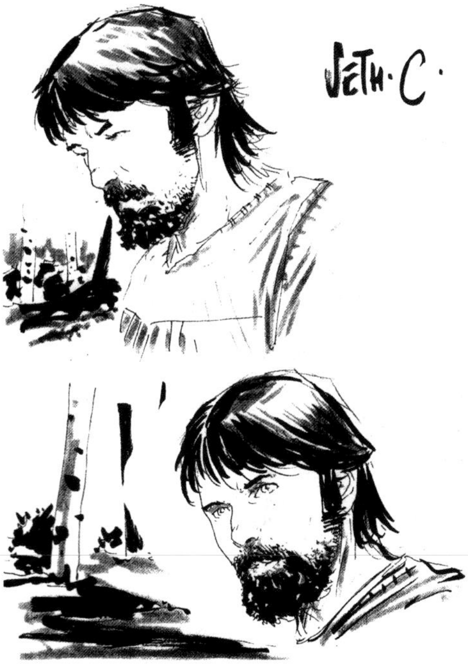
SETH. C.

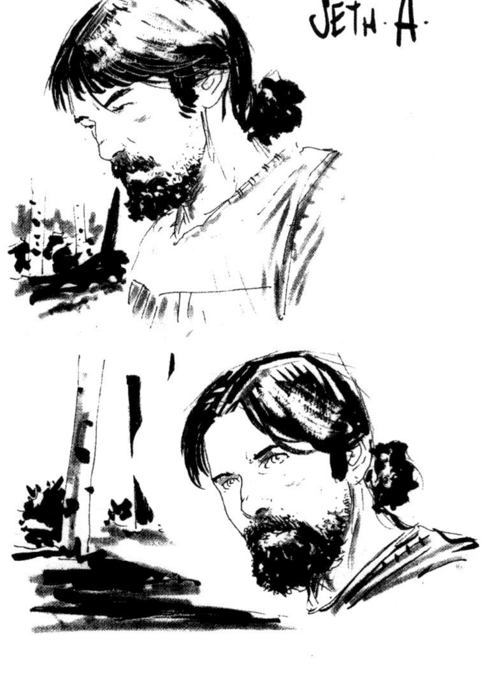
SETH. A.

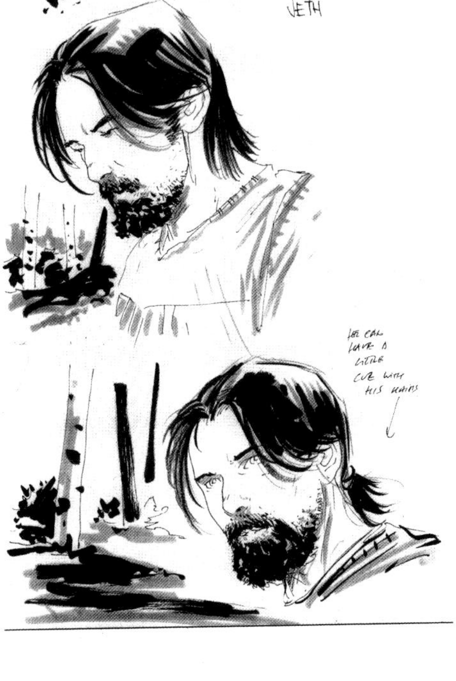
SETH
HE CAN HAVE A LITTLE CUE WITH HIS HAIRS

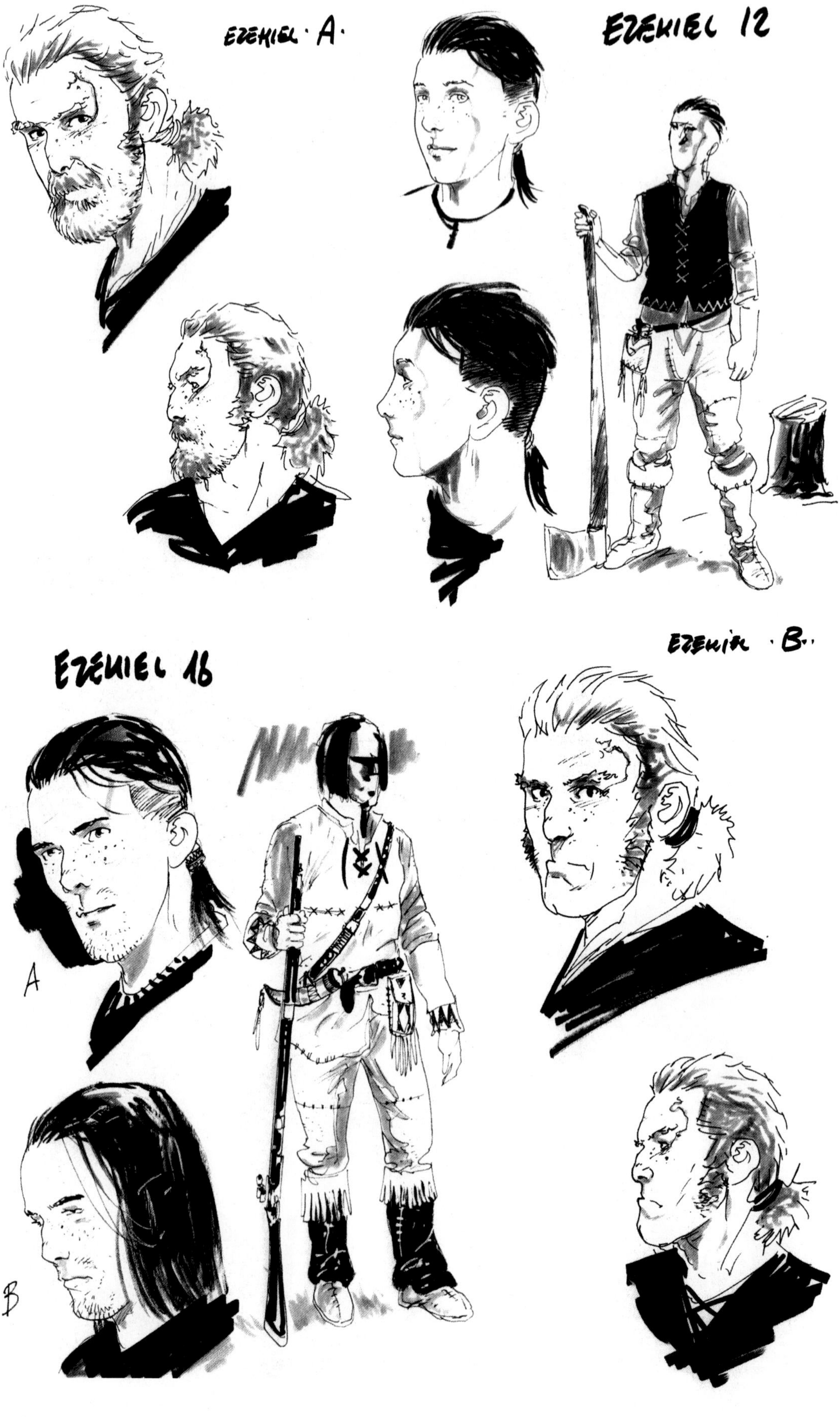
EZEKIEL ·A·
EZEKIEL 12
EZEKIEL ·B·
EZEKIEL 16
A
B

MERCY

JETU'S
FATHER

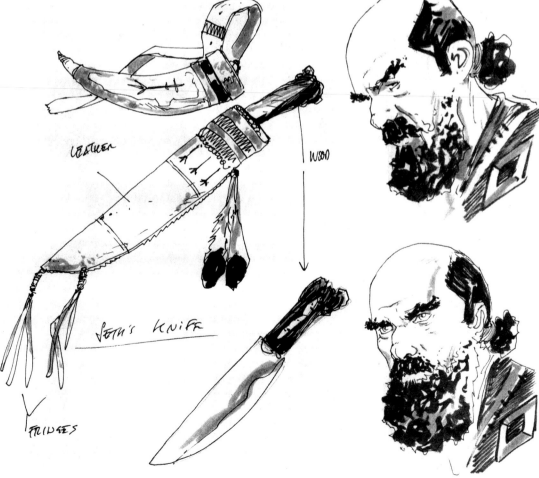

LEATHER

WOOD

SETH'S KNIFE

FRINGES

THE PROCESS BEHIND *REBELS*

BY ANDREA MUTTI

Shelburne Longboat Society
www.shelburnelongboats.com
Delaney Images, Shelburne

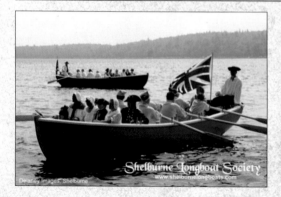

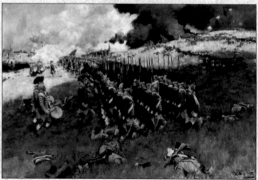

Rebels is a serial about freedom and the War of Independence, and issue #4's battle against the redcoats is a climactic chapter.

When I read each script my first thought is figuring out how to show the dirt and violence of the war. I want to drag the readers through the battlefields—the smoke and blood, the dust and gunpowder. I try to convey the noise and the smell of all that.

At the same time, I want to show the desperation, the fear, and the panic of the soldiers. One of the best moments for me in issue #4 is when the redcoats jump out of the boats and march up the hill with their muskets in hand, accompanied by the music of drums and fife. They're ready to die for the cause.

The Green Mountain Boys are ready to fight. They are less prepared but, as we know, preparation is nothing, and will is everything.

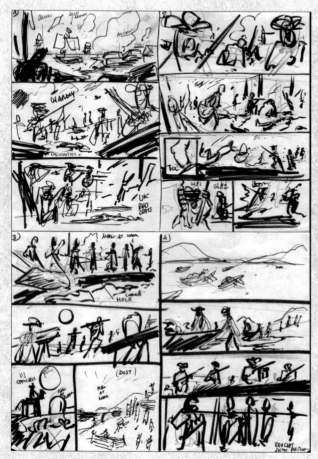

The first step is to make quick rough layouts of where in each panel I must put the figures, the background details, and of course, the dialogue balloons. The text is really important, even when we have an action scene. It's like the soundtrack to everything!

The roughs can be changed in the clean pencils version, but it is very important to get the story idea across. And working with a creative team like Brian, Spencer, Sierra, and Dave, I know they are always ready to suggest solutions to storytelling obstacles I did not see in the first pass. Very important!

The second step is the clean pencils. During this process, I must have good reference for everything. I receive several images from Brian in the script, and I look for reference for everything else I need on the Internet or in books I have at home. It's always the adventure *inside* the adventure, a story *inside* another one. It's fantastic and exciting. This is the kind of work that teaches you new details about history. There are lots of great paintings of various battles and characters that inspire me, such as the one above. Wow!

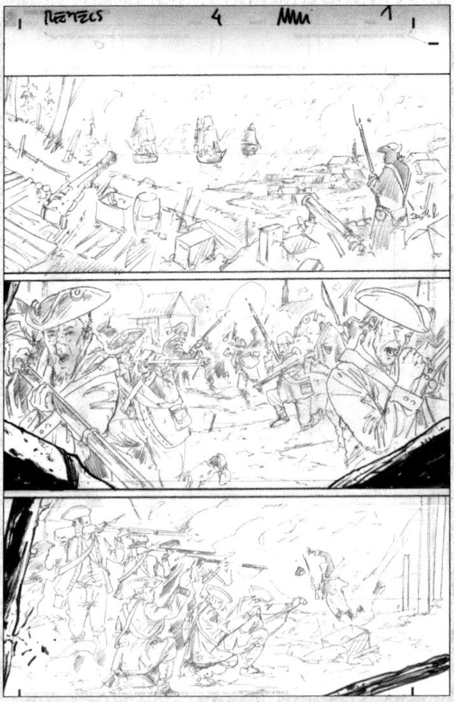

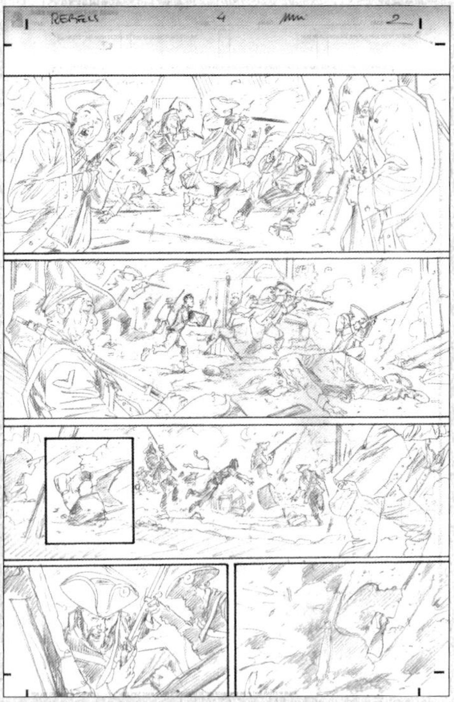

The pencils are pretty detailed. I use two different sizes of pencils. I use a micro 0.3 mm for the details, and a classic 0.5 for the rest. I sometimes use a 0.7 if I need heavier lines on some details, like the wood or the barricades. The wood grain may not seem like heavy detail. The 0.7 is a pretty soft pencil, and it helps me prepare for the inking process. That is the last step!

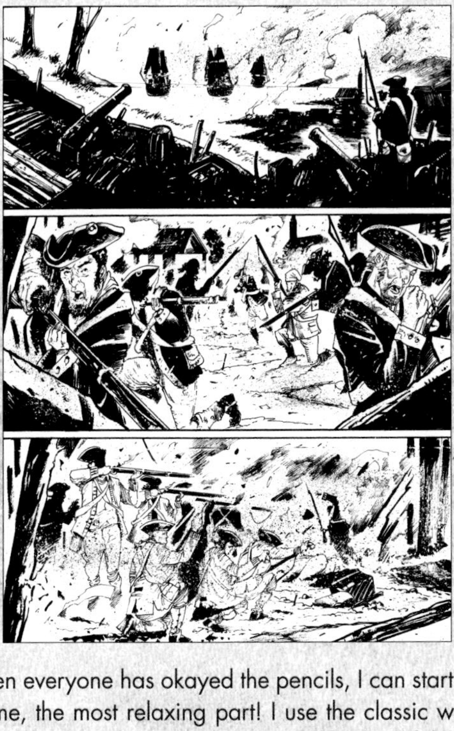

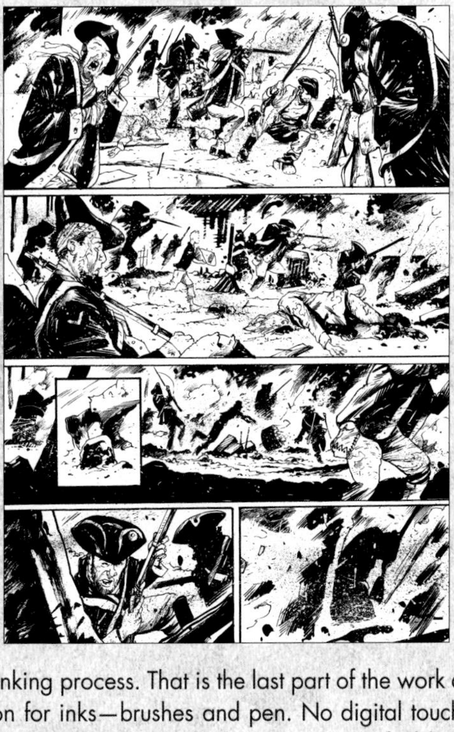

When everyone has okayed the pencils, I can start the inking process. That is the last part of the work and, for me, the most relaxing part! I use the classic weapon for inks—brushes and pen. No digital touchups like other artists might use. I'm not a big fan of that, and I think for this kind of story, we must *feel* the real world around the characters. I hope that the readers feel the "natural and realistic" approach I've taken. I've added a lot of extra effects here, like the dust, the smoke, and the powder all around the characters. But everything has been made with brushes or with dry sponges and dry ink. I think I can obtain a pretty realistic approach . . . not too far from what war might look like, I guess.

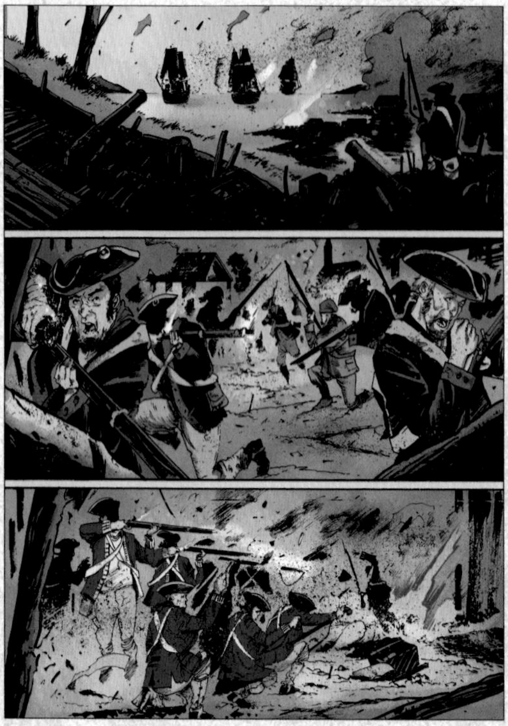

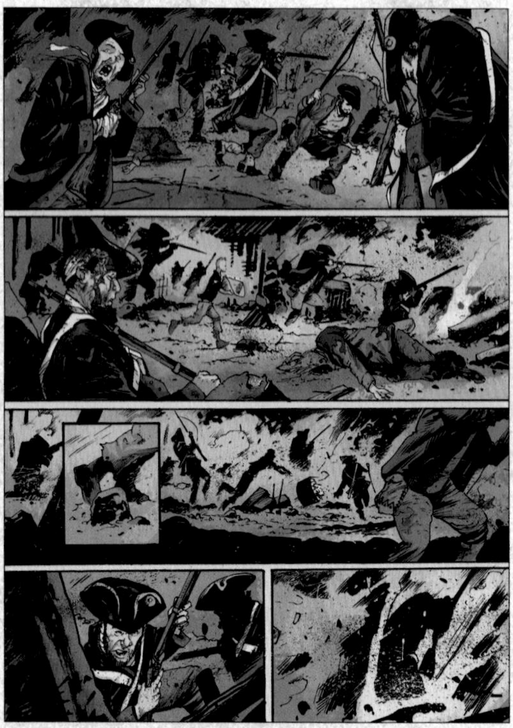

And then of course there are Jordie's beautiful colors! Wow, the last master touch! What can I say? They're so great and a perfect fit with the style. Jordie nails the emotion of the scenes. We'll let the pages speak for themselves!

★

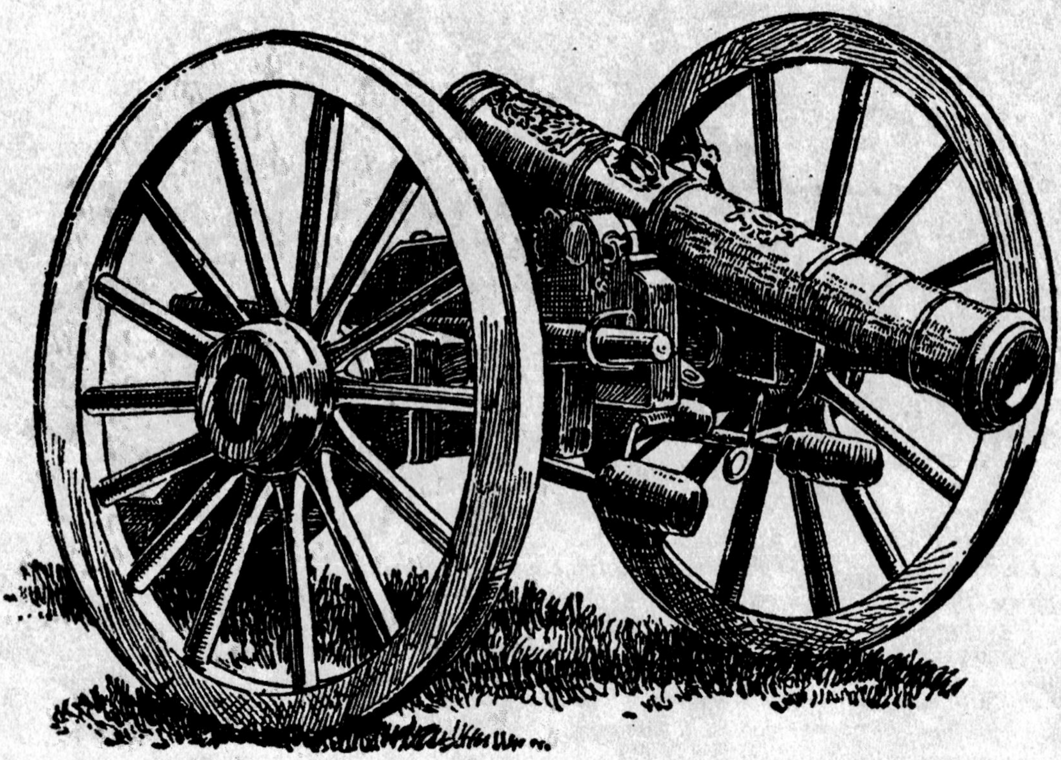

AMERICAN MYTHOLOGY

BY BRIAN WOOD

I have a file on my desktop that contains all the dream comics projects I want to get to someday. These are not likely candidates for acceptance somewhere, but rather the really weird, totally uncommercial projects that I guess I'm saving for the time when my ship comes in and I can just do whatever I want, and to hell with having to worry about income. In it is an idea to do a collection of short stories based on North American folk heroes like Paul Bunyan, John Henry, Calamity Jane, Mike Fink, and Captain Stormalong. On that list is Molly Pitcher, but I can cross her off because I wrote her story in "Goodwife, Follower, Patriot, Republican."

Not exactly, but close enough. There is no real Molly Pitcher; in a sense, that name is collectively applied to the class of women who stepped into combat roles during the early American wars. The "pitcher" part references the idea of them carrying water to the thirsty male soldiers, but there is also an undeniable, well-documented record of countless women engaging in actual combat.

I wanted to touch on multiple aspects of the story of the camp followers, the women and children and servants who, for lack of any other place to be, followed the army as it marched around and waged war. They would cook, clean, haul, and forage. And sure, they would carry water. This was Sarah Hull's role until her husband was wounded and she stepped into his place on the cannon.

That was the first part of the history I wanted to write: the retelling of a classic American folktale. The second half of the story is no less close to my heart and an example of why I love writing historical comics. I love finding interesting ways to connect history to modern times. The history is

rich all on its own, but there is an added benefit in drawing these parallels. Here it's the idea of the wounded soldier not compensated or cared for as he (or she) should be. What I love so much about how Matthew Woodson depicted the final scene in chapter 2 is the ramrod-straight back, the icy manners, the complete unwillingness on Sarah's part to make it easy on the officers. She knows what she did, and she knows what's right in terms of compensation, but she also knows there's no way in hell these men will set the precedent by giving it to her. They give me goose bumps, those panels. This is exactly the type of story I cocreated *Rebels* to tell.

Chapter 3 is set before the war in occupied Boston and deals with early resistance to the presence of the soldiers. Chapter 4 touches, too briefly, on the seemingly backward situation of freed slaves putting on red uniforms to fight on the side of the Crown. Andrea Mutti returns in full force for chapter 5, which introduces one of my new favorite characters: Stone Hoof, a Shawnee warrior who gets tangled up with some colonists during the French and Indian War. Chapter 6 contains art by Tristan Jones and is told from the point of view of a redcoat soldier who slogs through the war, from the Boston Massacre to Kings Mountain, with only blind idealism and loyalty to see him through.

This history is our shared American mythology. We're a young country, so this is all we've got, but it's potent, muscular, idealistic, and universal. As I wrote in my pitch for this series, the longer this book runs, the richer it gets. Each of these little stories fills in a tiny bit of the overall picture, and I feel I am only doing my job properly if I paint the most complete image of these times I can.

THE COVER PROCESS

BY TULA LOTAY

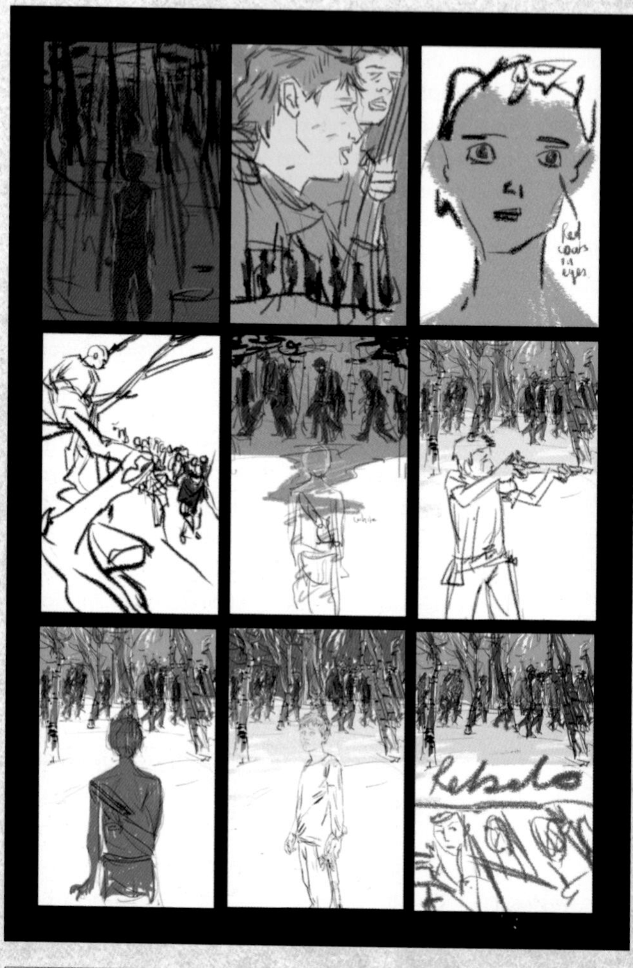
Red colours in eyes.

1

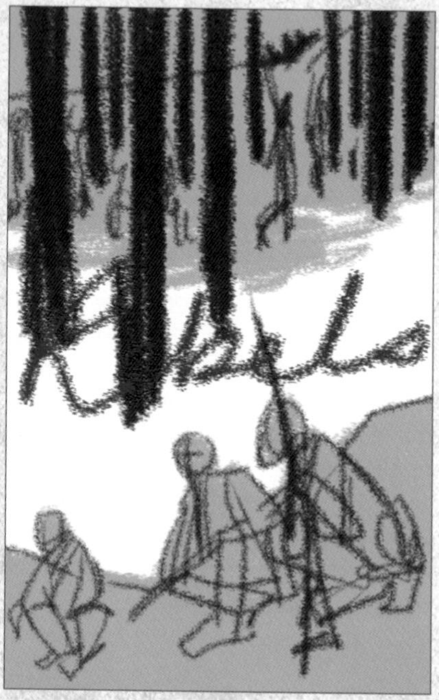

2

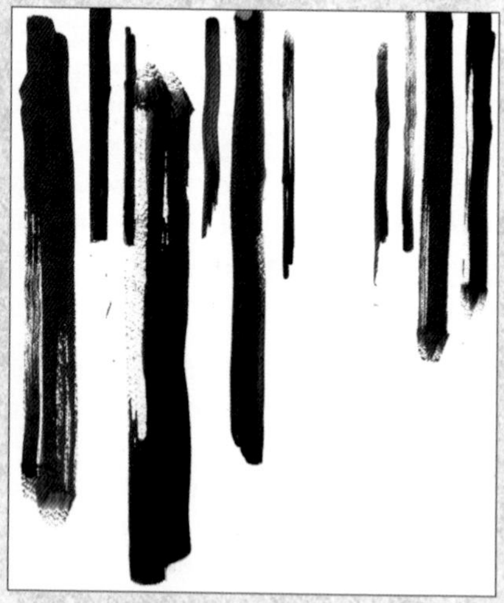

5

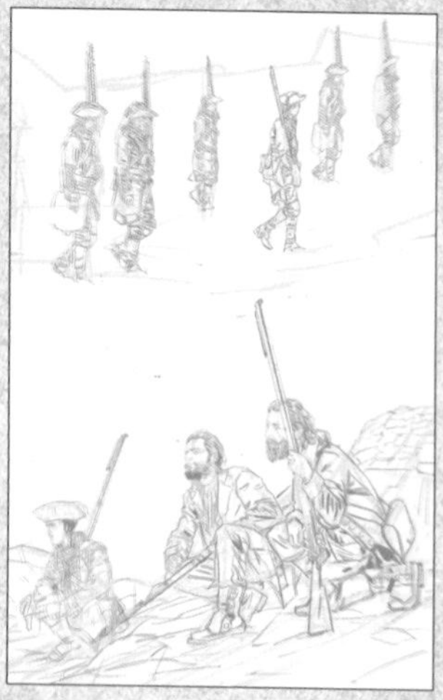

3

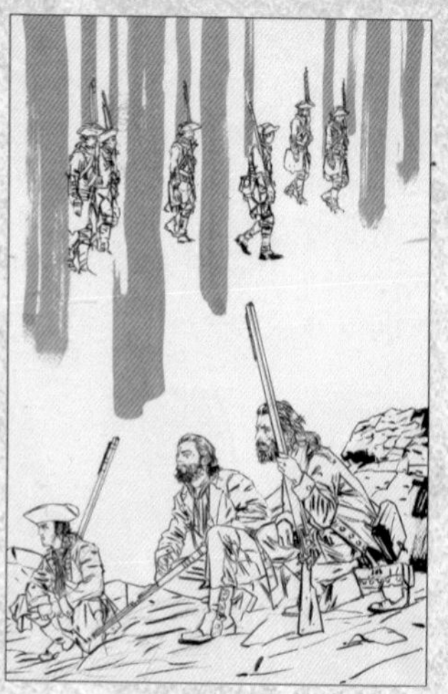

4

1. Thumbnail sketches.
2. Main thumbnail selected.
3. Digital blue-line sketch to print for inks.
4. Main inks.
5. Tree watercolor washes, created separately so they have a freer feel and can be moved around within the image once scanned.

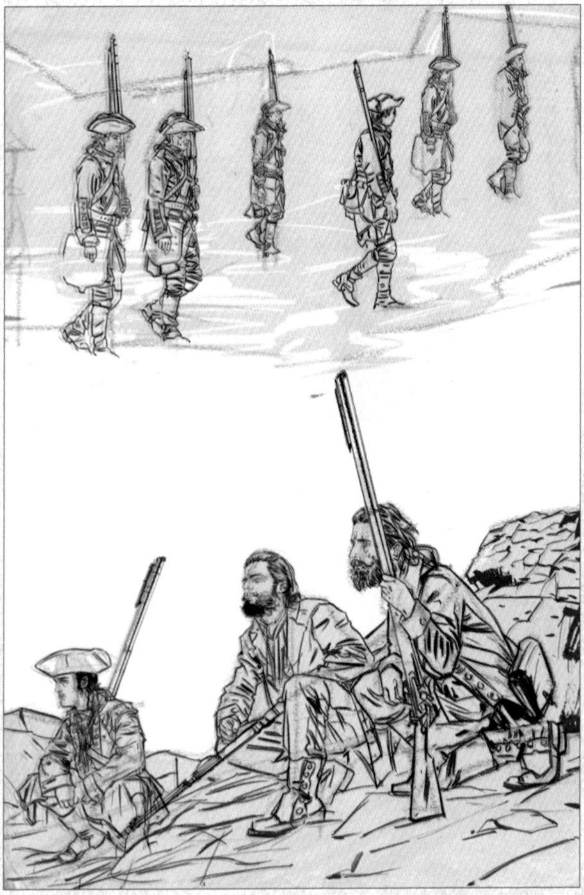

6

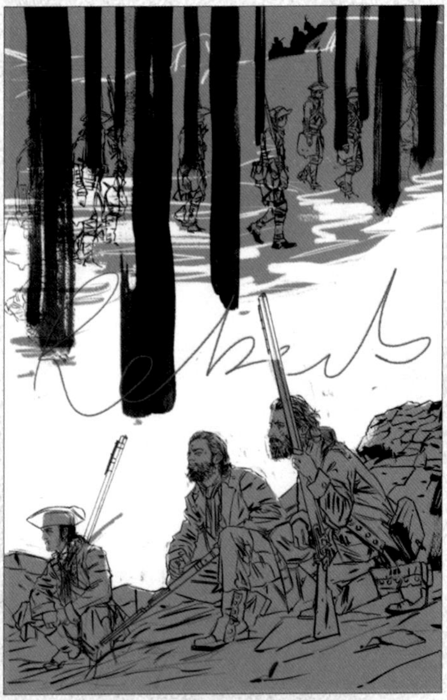

7

6. I drop in background textures as a starting point. I always leave my rough lines there, because sometimes they can add an extra dimension to an image, make it a bit more interesting.

7. I bring the darker blue back to define the white, check that the composition of the white is right, and make sure that the image flows correctly from top to bottom.

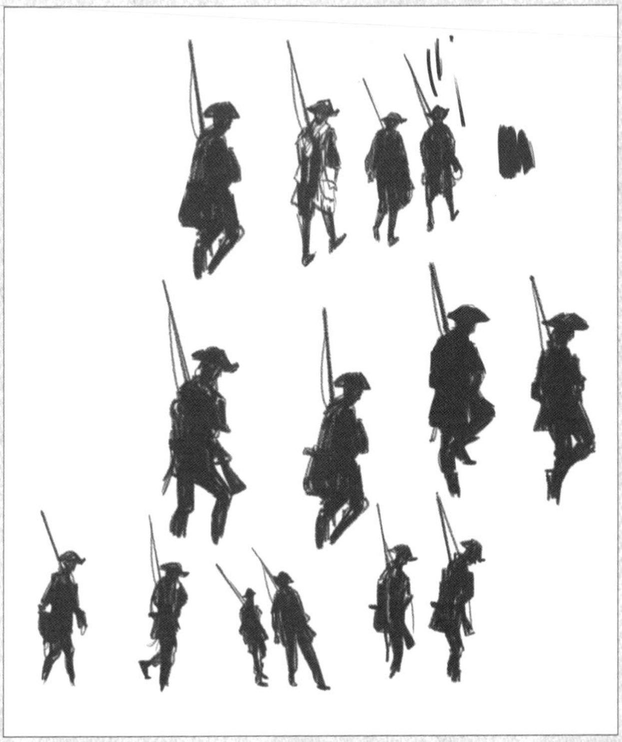

8

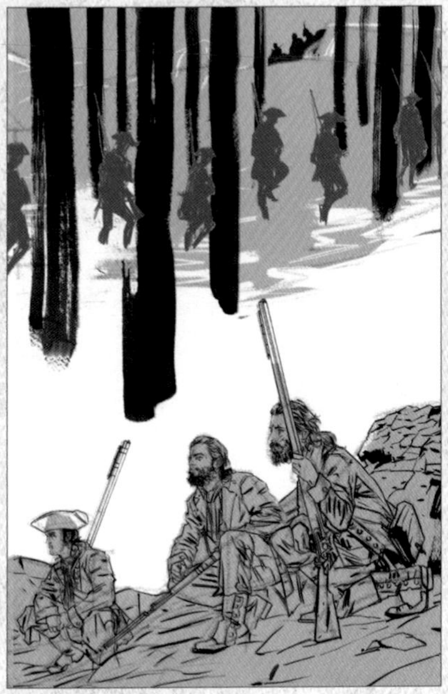

9

9. The soldiers still don't feel right, and I really want to bring the red out for the redcoats.

8. I don't like the way the original redcoat soldiers at the top look. Too static and too detailed. So I experiment with new versions. I try to simplify. I practice drawing them really loose, similar to some of the *Saturday Evening Post* illustrations of the fifties and sixties. Parts of those illustrations are super detailed, and other parts are very loose and sketchy.

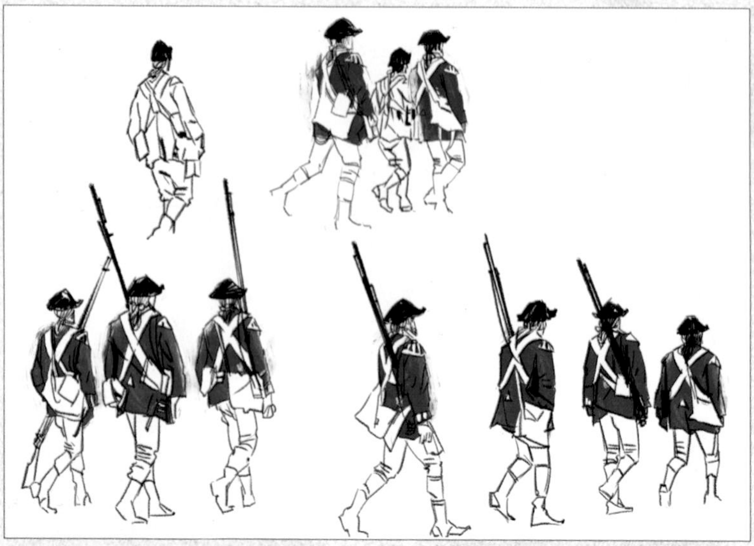

10

10. I try again with the redcoat illustrations, keeping them loose but incorporating the color too.

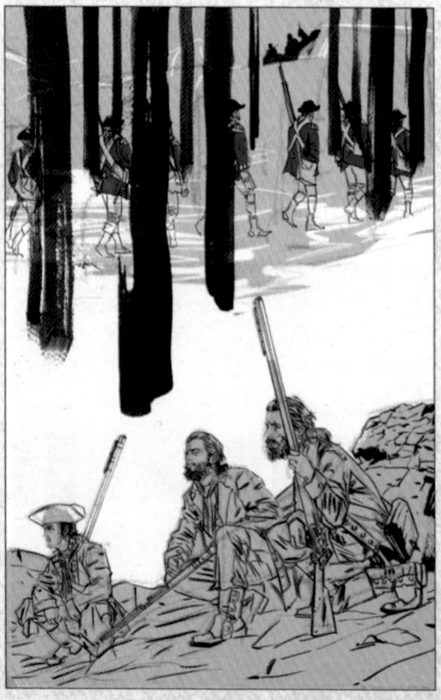

11

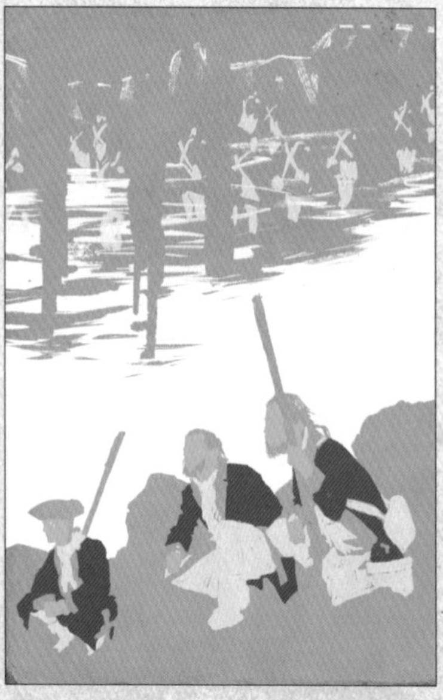

12

11. I'm happy with these now. I just want to make a few more tweaks.

12. Here I start to paint in color flats.

13. Base color for the Mountain Boys. I usually paint this on another layer under the line work.

14. I add more redcoats, change the line color, and work on them a bit more.

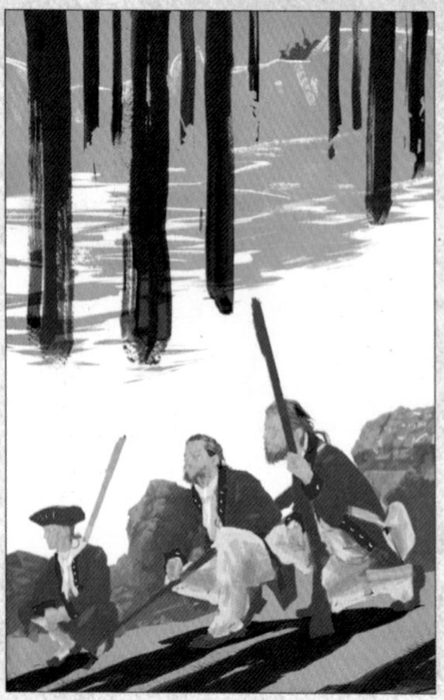

13

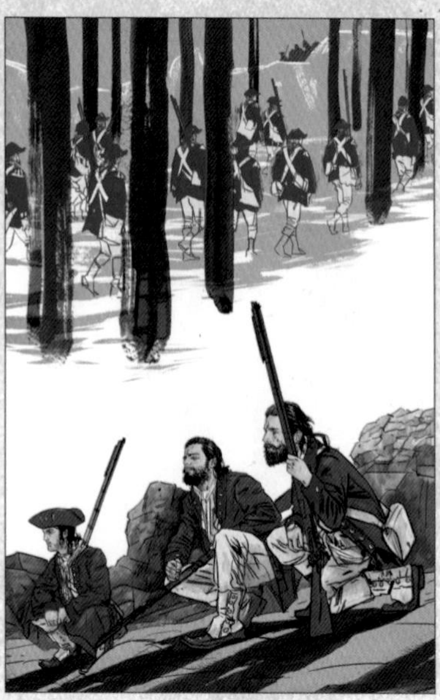

14

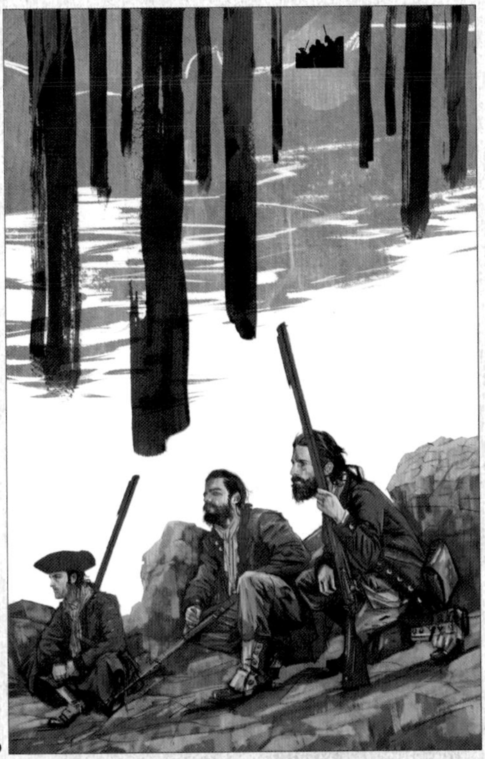

15

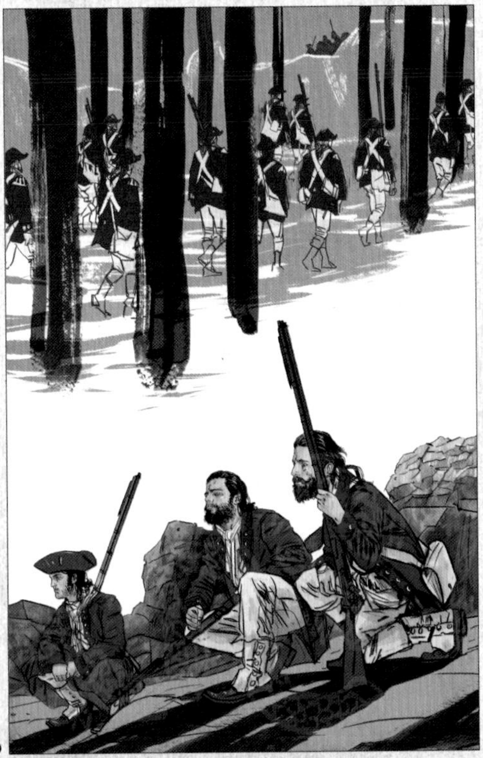

16

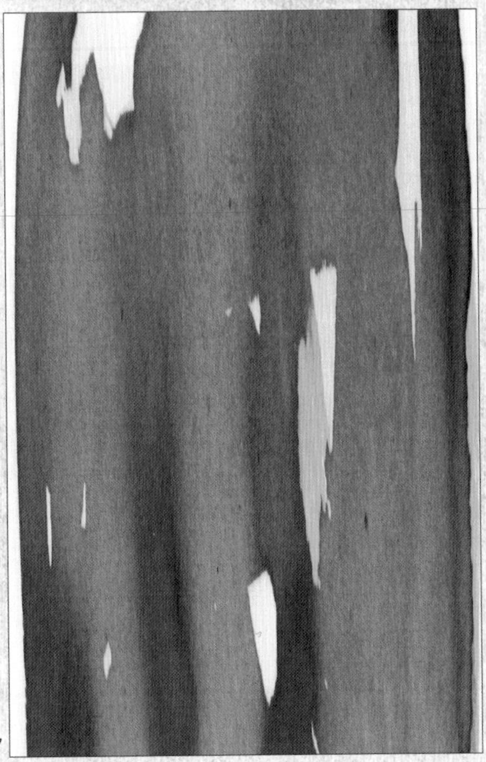

17

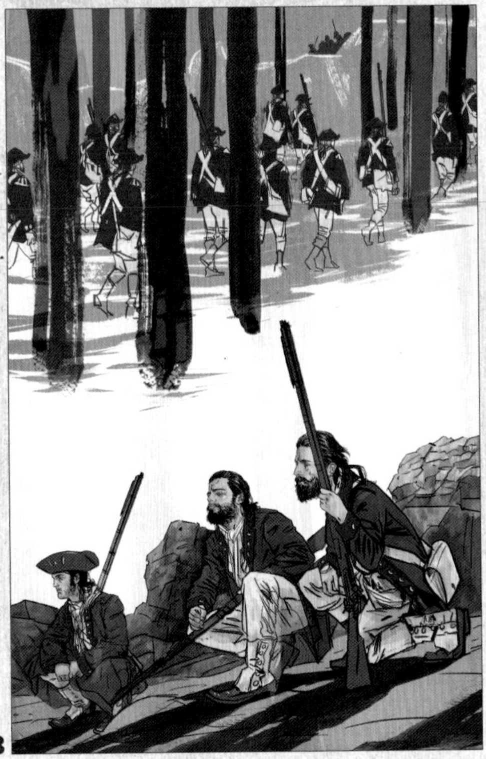

18

15. Now the line art and color are ready. I start to overlay watercolor textures to see if any bring the image out more. Sometimes there are some really nice surprises at this stage; other times it's too much. I like the pink here, but it doesn't work for the feel of the book.

16. Another idea: laying the "Join or Die" flag design over the Mountain Boys at the bottom. It's too much though.

17. Coffee and orange juice texture scanned and laid over the final image on the Hard Light setting in Photoshop.

18. Final image.

A GREEN MOUNTAIN BOY

BY BRIAN WOOD

So I grew up in Vermont, big surprise. It explains the focus on Vermont (then called the New Hampshire Grants) in this first *Rebels* story, and it's a common question in every interview I do: why this specific history? Why the Green Mountain Boys? Because I lived there.

I feel blessed for the childhood I had. Not that it's unique in any way, or charmed. I'm not sure what you would call it now, but to my recollection it seems like it was pretty solidly lower middle class. I lived in a small village, and our street butted right up against the woods. Not a patch of trees or a woodsy park, but the WOODS woods, an expanse of forest that went for miles. We played in the woods, we walked on paths through the woods to get to school, and that was normal. We built forts and caught critters and waded in brooks.

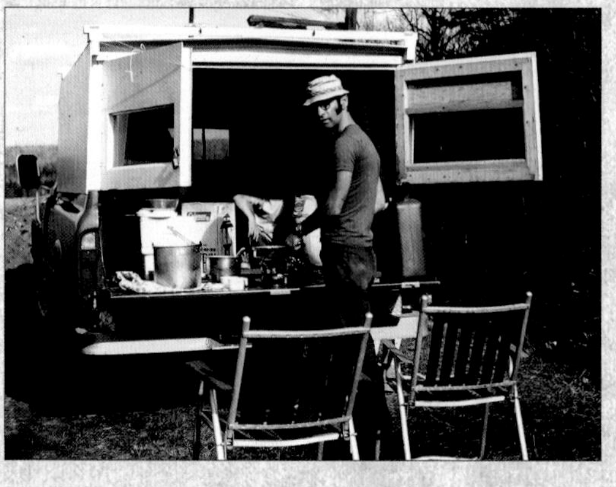

My father was like Seth Abbott's father in the sense that he was an outdoorsman. We hunted for food, and we chopped trees for firewood. One of the best days of the fall was when the truckloads of wood were dumped in our yard, and it was all hands on deck to transfer several cords from the lawn into the basement. After my parents were divorced, my dad moved to a rural area, literally the last house at the end of a road on top of a mountain. There was a pond, steep hills to climb, a vegetable garden to dork around in, and chickens to fight with over eggs in the mornings.

We shot guns. As the youngest child, I was spared a lot of the gun stuff that my older siblings did. As far as I can recall I never shot a deer, although plenty of deer were shot. I remember going along for squirrel and duck hunting, and I remember, in the autumn, shooting away at rotting leftover vegetables in the garden for target practice. My parents were skeet-shooting champions. I remember getting the same advice from my dad that Seth got from his at the start of *Rebels*, about training the eye for horizontal shapes in the mostly vertical forest. Truth? I could never figure it out. It never seemed to work for me the way it worked for Seth.

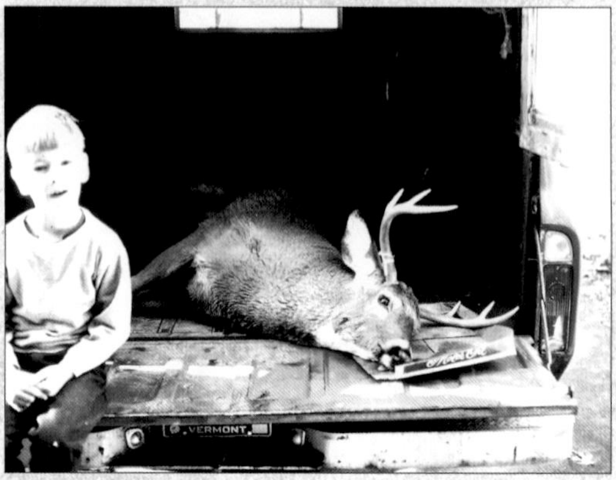
VERMONT

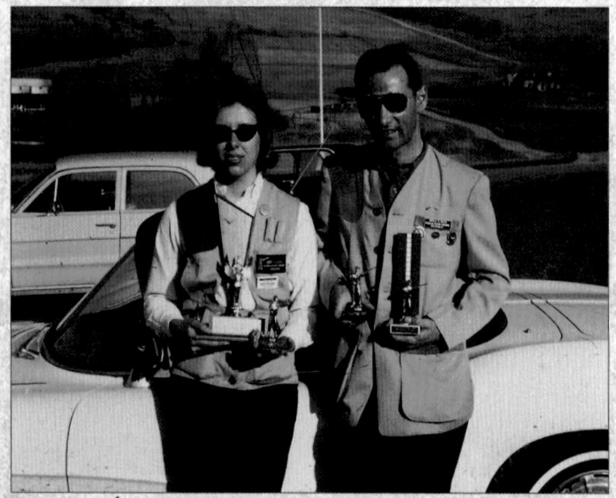

In the winter we ice-fished on Lake Champlain. It seems crazy to me now, driving the truck all the way out onto a lake that, these days, rarely

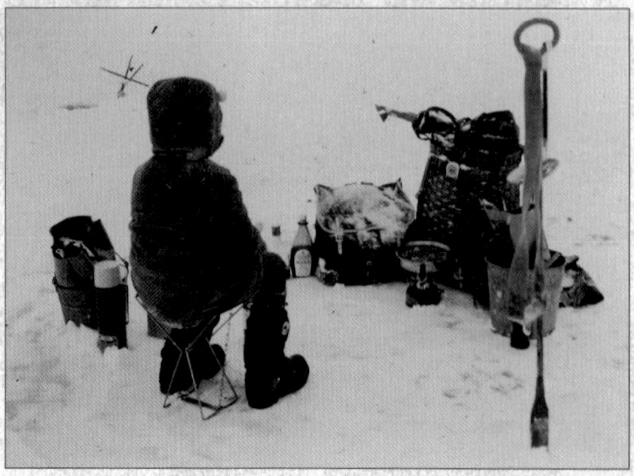

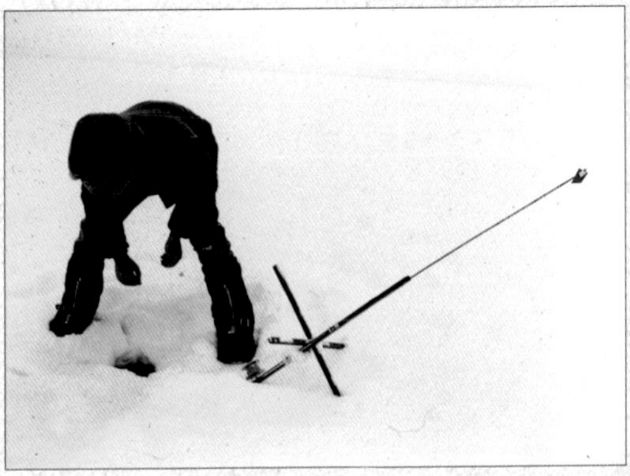

freezes over. We had our shanty on the truck and would deploy that onto the ice, bore the holes, freeze in our Sorels and snowsuits, and eat reheated beans, and come home with dozens and dozens of perch caught with the ice-fishing rods my dad hand carved at home. The most "Vermont" thing he would do was keep the fish bait—often the eyeballs from last week's catch—in his mouth to stay warm and soft before baiting his hook with them.

I liked to eat the fried perch fins. With salt, they tasted like potato chips.

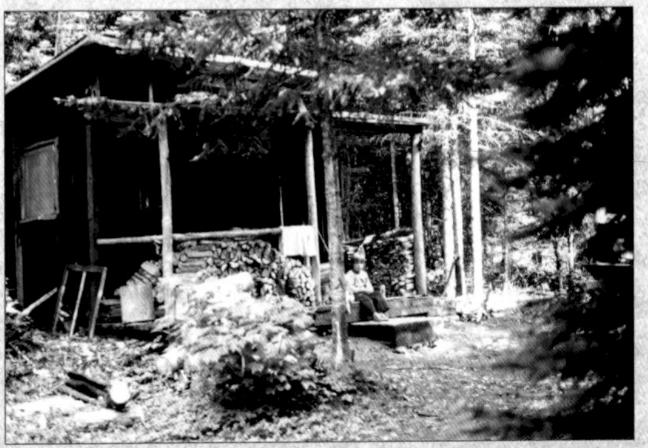

In the summertime, we'd spend a few weeks at this hunting cabin in Maine, a one-room shack that lacked electricity, running water, and a bathroom. We sunk food to the bottom of a creek to keep it cool, and shat in a pretty dicey outhouse. The lake would invariably give us leeches (to be burned off with a match). It was great (said only slightly ironically).

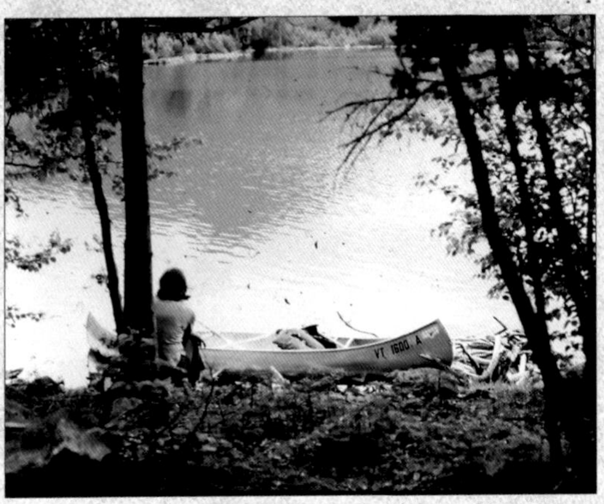

All this may sound idealized. And it is. I'm in my midforties, and everything I just described happened before my father's death when I was eight years old. So while I can vouch for the accuracy of the basic details, I'm sure it was far from happy and rarely *that* much fun. But I still feel blessed.

It's important for me in *Rebels* to capture both the fantasy and the reality of frontier living—the swimming-hole fun and the backbreaking manual labor. I can look back and see how my mother probably *hated* a lot of this stuff (I'm thinking about the summer cabin—she spent at least one stinky, sweaty summer there pregnant with me), and I'm trying to apply that to how I write Mercy Abbott.

Colonial times were not easy on the women, and as romantic and sweet as Ma Ingalls's life read, I didn't want that sort of depiction for Mercy. Seth was off fighting a war, and her struggle was just as hard, lonely, sorrowful, and dangerous. Perhaps more so, as she was tethered to the house—there were no safe places to run to or comrades in arms to protect her. She ate what she could pull out of the ground and stayed alive in winter only if she adequately prepared in advance. Not a great time, neither charmed nor ideal. If you asked her, I wonder if she would say she felt blessed.

Photos by Merle Wood

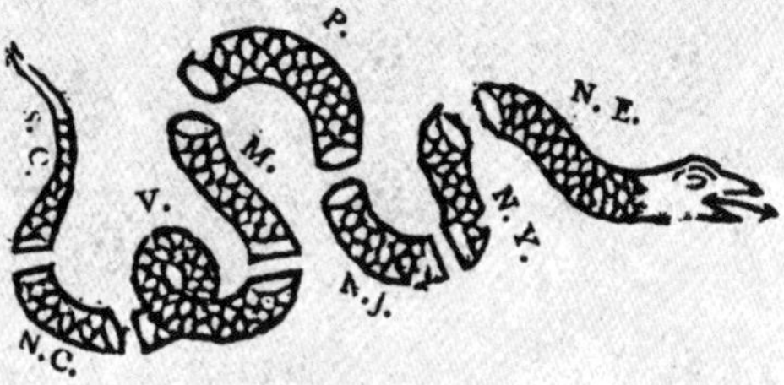
S.C.
N.C.
V.
M.
P.
N.J.
N.Y.
N.E.

MORE FROM *NEW YORK TIMES* BEST-SELLING AUTHOR

BRIAN WOOD

"Someone remembered what comics are for. Meet Brian Wood."
—Warren Ellis

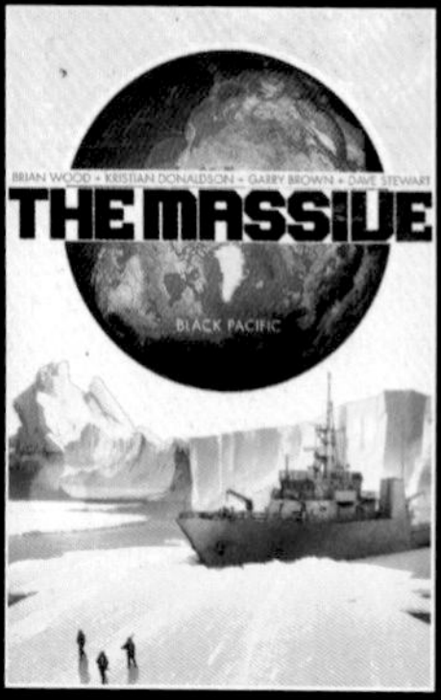
THE MASSIVE
BLACK PACIFIC

REBELS VOLUME 1: A WELL-REGULATED MILITIA

Written by Brian Wood, Art by Andrea Mutti and Jordie Bellaire

This is 1775, and the War for Independence plays out across the colonies. *Rebels* details the epic story of the colonists who, in a few short, turbulent years, created the nation of America.

ISBN 978-1-61655-908-3 | $24.99

THE MASSIVE

Written by Brian Wood, Art by Kristian Donaldson and Garry Brown

In a post-war, post-Crash, post-disaster world, the environmental-action trawler *Kapital* scours the oceans for its mysteriously missing sister ship, *The Massive*.

Volume 1: Black Pacific
ISBN 978-1-61655-132-2 | $19.99

Volume 2: Subcontinental
ISBN 978-1-61655-316-6 | $19.99

Volume 3: Longship
ISBN 978-1-61655-446-0 | $19.99

Volume 4: Sahara
ISBN 978-1-61655-508-5 | $19.99

Volume 5: Ragnarok
ISBN 978-1-61655-652-5 | $19.99

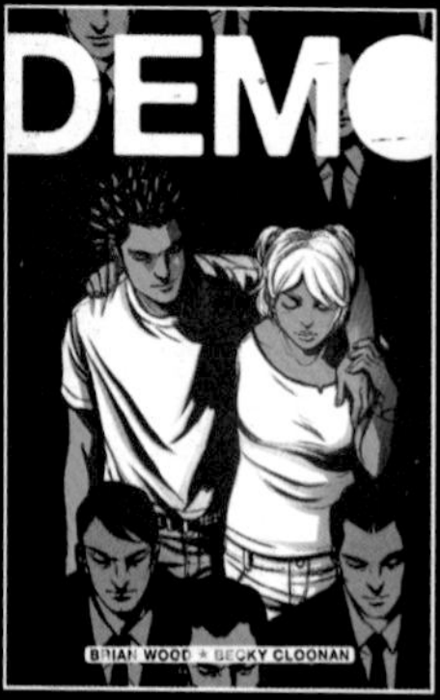
DEM
BRIAN WOOD + BECKY CLOONAN

DEMO

Written by Brian Wood, Art by Becky Cloonan

It's hard enough being a teenager. Now try being a teenager with *powers*. *Demo* chronicles the lives of young people who are on their separate journeys to self-discovery in a world—just like our own—where being different is feared.

ISBN 978-1-61655-682-2 | $24.99

THE NEW YORK FOUR

Written by Brian Wood, Art by Ryan Kelly

Worlds collide when four young women begin college at the prestigious New York University. But that freedom comes at a price: roommate drama, mysterious love interests, school troubles, and family conflicts. Welcome to adulthood!

ISBN 978-1-61655-605-1 | $19.99

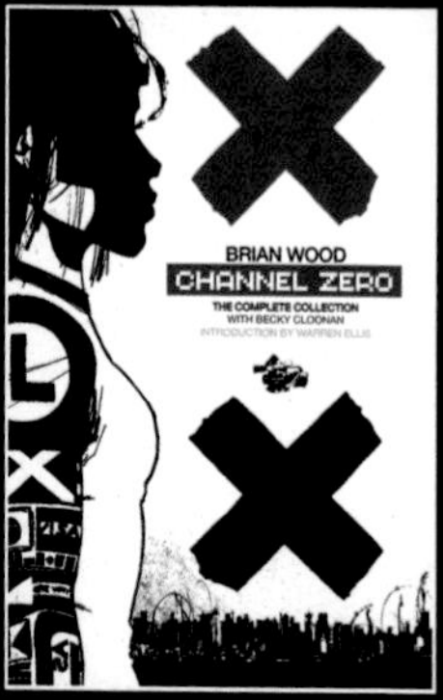
BRIAN WOOD
CHANNEL ZERO
THE COMPLETE COLLECTION WITH BECKY CLOONAN

CHANNEL ZERO

Written by Brian Wood, Art by Becky Cloonan

A blistering take on media control in a repressive future America! *DMZ* and *The Massive* creator Brian Wood launched an all-out assault on the comics medium in 1997 with *Channel Zero*, an influential, forward-thinking series that combined art, politics, and graphic design in a unique way.

ISBN 978-1-59582-936-8 | $19.99

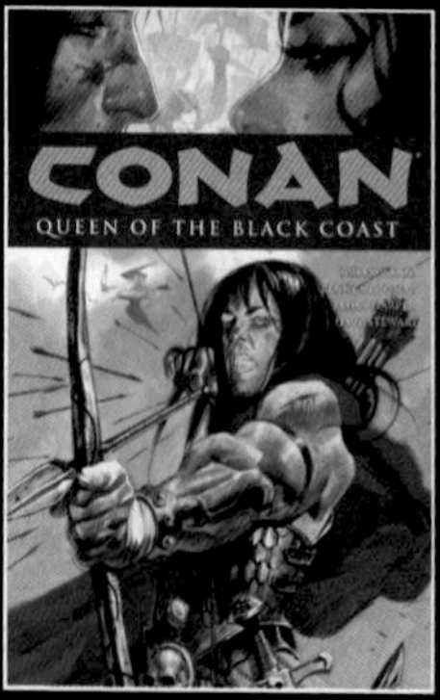
CONAN
QUEEN OF THE BLACK COAST

CONAN VOLUME 13: QUEEN OF THE BLACK COAST

Written by Brian Wood, Art by Becky Cloonan and James Harren

TPB: ISBN 978-1-61655-043-1 | $19.99
HC: ISBN 978-1-61655-042-4 | $24.99

CONAN VOLUME 14: THE DEATH

Written by Brian Wood, Art by Becky Cloonan, Vasilis Lolos, and Declan Shalvey

TPB: ISBN 978-1-61655-123-0 | $19.99
HC: ISBN 978-1-61655-122-3 | $24.99

CONAN VOLUME 15: THE NIGHTMARE OF THE SHALLOWS

Written by Brian Wood, Art by Andrea Mutti, Davide Gianfelice, and Mirko Colak

TPB: ISBN 978-1-61655-385-2 | $19.99
HC: ISBN 978-1-61655-233-6 | $24.99

CONAN VOLUME 16: THE SONG OF BÊLIT

Written by Brian Wood, Art by Paul Azaceta and Riccardo Burchielli

TPB: ISBN 978-1-61655-524-5 | $19.99
HC: ISBN 978-1-61655-430-9 | $24.99

AVAILABLE AT YOUR LOCAL COMICS SHOP OR BOOKSTORE! • To find a comics shop in your area, call 1-888-266-4226.
For more information or to order direct visit DarkHorse.com or call 1-800-862-0052 Mon.–Fri. 9 AM. to 5 PM. Pacific Time. Prices and availability subject to change without notice.

CREATIVE GIANTS!

GET YOUR FIX OF DARK HORSE BOOKS FROM THESE INSPIRED CREATORS!

MESMO DELIVERY SECOND EDITION - Rafael Grampá

Eisner Award–winning artist Rafael Grampá (*5*, *Hellblazer*) makes his full-length comics debut with the critically acclaimed graphic novel *Mesmo Delivery*—a kinetic, bloody romp starring Rufo, an ex-boxer; Sangrecco, an Elvis impersonator; and a ragtag crew of overly confident drunks who pick the wrong delivery men to mess with.

ISBN 978-1-61655-457-6 | $14.99

SIN TITULO - Cameron Stewart

Following the death of his grandfather, Alex Mackay discovers a mysterious photograph in the old man's belongings that sets him on an adventure like no other—where dreams and reality merge, family secrets are laid bare, and lives are irrevocably altered.

ISBN 978-1-61655-248-0 | $19.99

DE:TALES - Fábio Moon and Gabriel Bá

Brazilian twins Fábio Moon and Gabriel Bá's (*Daytripper*, *Pixu*) most personal work to date. Brimming with all the details of human life, their charming tales move from the urban reality of their home in São Paulo to the magical realism of their Latin American background.

ISBN 978-1-59582-557-5 | $19.99

THE TRUE LIVES OF THE FABULOUS KILLJOYS - Gerard Way, Shaun Simon, and Becky Cloonan

Years ago, the Killjoys fought against the tyrannical megacorporation Better Living Industries. Today, the followers of the original Killjoys languish in the desert and the fight for freedom fades. It's left to the Girl to take down BLI!

ISBN 978-1-59582-462-2 | $19.99

DEMO - Brian Wood and Becky Cloonan

It's hard enough being a teenager. Now try being a teenager with *powers*. A chronicle of the lives of young people on separate journeys to self-discovery in a world—just like our own—where being different is feared.

ISBN 978-1-61655-682-2 | $24.99

SABERTOOTH SWORDSMAN - Damon Gentry and Aaron Conley

When his village is enslaved and his wife kidnapped by the malevolent Mastodon Mathematician, a simple farmer must find his inner warrior—the Sabertooth Swordsman!

ISBN 978-1-61655-176-6 | $17.99

JAYBIRD - Jaakko and Lauri Ahonen

Disney meets Kafka in this beautiful, intense, original tale! A very small, very scared little bird lives an isolated life in a great big house with his infirm mother. He's never been outside the house, and he never will if his mother has anything to say about it.

ISBN 978-1-61655-469-9 | $19.99

MONSTERS! & OTHER STORIES - Gustavo Duarte

Newcomer Gustavo Duarte spins wordless tales inspired by Godzilla, King Kong, and Pixar, brimming with humor, charm, and delightfully twisted horror!

ISBN 978-1-61655-309-8 | $12.99

SACRIFICE - Sam Humphries and Dalton Rose

What happens when a troubled youth is plucked from modern society and thrust though time and space into the heart of the Aztec civilization—one of the most blood-thirsty times in human history?

ISBN 978-1-59582-985-6 | $19.99

GABRIEL BÁ AND FÁBIO MOON!